Worth Series in Outstanding Contributions

International Economics

Worth Series in Outstanding Contributions

ORLEY ASHENFELTER, SERIES EDITOR

PUBLISHED TITLES

LABOR ECONOMICS   *Orley Ashenfelter*

PUBLIC FINANCE   *Alan Auerbach*

INTERNATIONAL ECONOMICS   *Edward Leamer*

FORTHCOMING TITLES

INDUSTRIAL ORGANIZATION   *Robert H. Porter*

MACROECONOMICS   *John Taylor*

Worth Series in Outstanding Contributions

International Economics

EDITED BY

Edward Leamer

UNIVERSITY OF CALIFORNIA, LOS ANGELES

WORTH PUBLISHERS

International Economics

Copyright © 2001 by Worth Publishers

All rights reserved

Manufactured in the United States of America

Library of Congress Catalog Card Number: 00-110476

ISBN: 1-57259-820-4

Printing: 1 2 3 4 5 04 03 02 01

Executive Editor: Alan McClare

Production Editor: Margaret Comaskey

Production Manager: Barbara Anne Seixas

Art Director: Barbara Reingold

Composition: Progressive Information Technologies

Printing and Binding: R. R. Donnelley & Sons Company

Worth Publishers
41 Madison Avenue
New York, NY 10010
http://www.worthpublishers.com

CONTENTS

SERIES PREFACE   VII

PREFACE   IX

THE RICARDO-VINER MODEL (SPECIFIC FACTORS)

SHORT-RUN CAPITAL SPECIFICITY AND THE PURE THEORY OF
INTERNATIONAL TRADE   3
    J. Peter Neary

HECKSCHER-OHLIN MODEL OF INTERNATIONAL COMPETITION

INTERNATIONAL FACTOR-PRICE EQUALISATION ONCE AGAIN   19
    Paul A. Samuelson

THE STRUCTURE OF SIMPLE GENERAL EQUILIBRIUM MODELS   34
    Ronald W. Jones

THE GENERAL VALIDITY OF THE LAW OF COMPARATIVE ADVANTAGE   55
    Alan V. Deardorff

DOES EUROPEAN UNEMPLOYMENT PROP UP AMERICAN WAGES?
NATIONAL LABOR MARKETS AND GLOBAL TRADE   72
    Donald R. Davis

THE GENERALIZED THEORY OF DISTORTIONS AND WELFARE   96
    Jagdish N. Bhagwati

MULTICOUNTRY, MULTIFACTOR TESTS OF THE FACTOR ABUNDANCE THEORY   113
    Harry P. Bowen, Edward E. Leamer, and Leo Sveikauskas

THE LEONTIEF PARADOX, RECONSIDERED   142
    Edward E. Leamer

THE CASE OF THE MISSING TRADE AND OTHER MYSTERIES   151
    Daniel Trefler

INTERNATIONAL TRADE AND AMERICAN WAGES IN THE 1980s:
GIANT SUCKING SOUND OR SMALL HICCUP? (EXCERPTS)   177
    Robert Z. Lawrence and Matthew J. Slaughter

IN SEARCH OF STOLPER-SAMUELSON LINKAGES BETWEEN
INTERNATIONAL TRADE AND LOWER WAGES (EXCERPTS)   204
   Edward E. Leamer

GRAVITY MODEL

HOW WIDE IS THE BORDER?   233
   Charles Engel and John H. Rogers

CHAMBERLINIAN MODEL (ECONOMIES OF SCALE, IMPERFECT COMPETITION, AND STRATEGIC INTERACTIONS)

INCREASING RETURNS, MONOPOLISTIC COMPETITION,
AND INTERNATIONAL TRADE   255
   Paul R. Krugman

A 'RECIPROCAL DUMPING' MODEL OF INTERNATIONAL TRADE   267
   James Brander and Paul Krugman

NATIONAL AND INTERNATIONAL RETURNS TO SCALE IN THE MODERN
THEORY OF INTERNATIONAL TRADE   278
   Wilfred J. Ethier

INCREASING RETURNS AND ECONOMIC GEOGRAPHY   301
   Paul Krugman

OPTIMAL TRADE AND INDUSTRIAL POLICY UNDER OLIGOPOLY   317
   Jonathan Eaton and Gene M. Grossman

MONOPOLISTIC COMPETITION AND INTERNATIONAL TRADE:
RECONSIDERING THE EVIDENCE (EXCERPTS)   339
   David Hummels and James Levinsohn

NONTRADITIONAL PRODUCTION FUNCTIONS

MULTINATIONALS, MULTI-PLANT ECONOMIES, AND THE GAINS FROM TRADE   361
   James R. Markusen

THE O-RING THEORY OF ECONOMIC DEVELOPMENT   383
   Michael Kremer

POLITICAL ECONOMY OF PROTECTION

PROTECTION FOR SALE   407
   Gene M. Grossman and Elhanan Helpman

Series Preface

In the fall of 1997 Worth Publishers approached me with a question: "What can we at Worth do to offer a useful product to assist with the graduate training of academic economists? There is only one catch, we would like this book or books to begin to appear within the next year."

I responded with a proposal that I felt certain no publisher would agree to: "Create a beautifully typeset and designed set of readings for graduate courses in economics where up-to-date textbooks do not exist; make sure the readings are selected because they are the articles most widely used in graduate courses; and, most important, put a low enough price on the book so graduate students might actually want to buy it!"

My proposal was a reaction to my own experience in graduate teaching and advising. First, since the scale of operation is so small, graduate-level textbooks in most fields simply do not exist. Even in the larger fields, where texts do exist, it is usually necessary to supplement them with additional readings. Second, although there are many books of collected essays or articles, they are rarely designed to represent the revealed preferences of graduate instructors. The essays are often selected by topic or author, rather than by the demand for them as supplementary reading in a graduate course. Finally, the pricing of textbooks and collections of essays, at both the graduate and undergraduate level, has reached such dizzying heights that many students simply refuse to purchase them.

The set of books in this series is a direct response to these concerns and to Worth's original question. The editors have tried to create volumes that will be useful to a wide range of economists, and especially useful for graduate instruction. In return, Worth Publishers has prepared attractive books that should be affordable for virtually anyone.

An additional benefit of typesetting these articles rather than replicating them is that many authors have taken the opportunity to correct typesetting errors in the original publications and to update references. In this sense, the reprinted articles in these volumes are actually superior to the originals. It is my hope that this series of books will continue to grow and provide a valuable service to the economics profession.

Orley Ashenfelter
Princeton University
1998

Preface

EDWARD E. LEAMER[1]

Anderson Gradute School of Management at UCLA

This book is a recording of the collective research conversation in international economics over the last half century. Here you can listen to the voices of Paul Samuelson in the 1950s, of Ron Jones in the 1960s, of Jagdish Bhagwati in the 1970s, of Paul Krugman in the 1980s, and a chorus of voices in the 1990s.

The research papers reprinted in this book can form the core of a graduate course in international economics. These articles, together with a large number of other references, are displayed in Table 1 as a suggested reading list. In addition to the papers reprinted in this volume, the table lists essential articles that for reasons of space could not be included. The reading list also includes important review articles, monographs, and textbooks.

READ THESE PAPERS TO "MASTER" THE FIELD

A mastery of the references on this reading list is enough to certify you as an authority in the field of international microeconomics. This list includes some classic articles that are known and appreciated by all experts in this field. This list includes some of the "hottest" articles that are currently being studied in many graduate courses around the world. This list includes also some recent articles on the research frontier that may emerge as the "hot" articles of the future. These are the ones you might want to look at carefully if you are thinking of doing research in the field. But be careful. Academic enterprise is a fast moving business. By the time you get your research done, we will have all moved on to more interesting topics.

The articles and books in Table 1 cover adequately most of the principal intellectual subcategories of international economics. But the field of international economics is very broad and very deep, and students will need to pursue more fully some of these topics or to explore topics not covered here at all. This is where instructors are very important since classrooms desperately need some intellectual excitement and some special intellectual direction. For this, an instructor's distinctive knowledge and personal enthusiasm for a topic are essential and can be infectious. Instructors thus need to add to the suggested reading list the articles and books they really enjoy and can get excited over. More often than not, that means the instructor's own articles or the instructor's instructor's articles. (Acorns do not fall very far from the mighty oaks.)

---

[1] With the assistance of Peter Schott and with the advice and wisdom but not necessarily the approval of Peter Neary, Gene Grossman, and Don Davis.

TABLE 1

Suggested Reading List[a]

Author(s)	Title	Year	No. of Lists	Score	Source
Textbooks					
Bhagwati, Panagariya, and Srinivasan	Lectures on International Trade	98	7	1.0	Book
Wong	International Goods Trade and Factor Mobility	95	4	0.5	MIT
Bowen, Hollander, and Viaene	Applied International Trade Analysis	98	0	0.0	
Survey Books					
Jones and Kenen	Handbook of International Economics, Vol. 1	84	15	1.3	Elsevier
Bhagwati	International Trade: Selected Readings	87	13	1.2	MIT
Grossman	Imperfect Competition and International Trade	92	12	1.5	MIT
Grossman and Rogoff	Handbook of International Economics, Vol. 3	95	10	1.3	Elsevier
Greenaway and Winters	Surveys of International Trade	94	5	0.6	Basil Blackwell
I. Ricardian Theory (Labor Inputs Only)					
Dornbusch, Fischer, and Samuelson	Comparative Advantage, Trade and Payments in a Ricardian Model with a Continuum of Goods	77	15	1.5	AER
II. The Ricardo-Viner Model (Specific Factors)					
* Neary	Short-Run Capital Specificity and the Pure Theory of International Trade	78	16	1.4	EJ
III. Heckscher-Ohlin Model of International Competition					
HO Theory: Positive					
Stolper and Samuelson	Protection and Real Wages	41	6	12.0	REStud
* Samuelson	International Factor-Price Equalization Once Again	49	8	4.7	EJ
* Jones	The Structure of Simple General Equilibrium Models	65	15	2.8	JPE
Jones	A Three Factor Model in Theory, Trade, and History	71	10	1.9	Bhagwati (1982)
Mundell	International Trade and Factor Mobility	57	8	1.6	AER

TABLE 1 (CONTINUED)

Author(s)	Title	Year	No. of Lists	Score	Source
Samuelson	The Gains From International Trade Once Again	62	7	1.5	EJ
Rybczynski	Factor Endowments and Relative Commodity Prices	55	6	1.3	Ec
Findlay and Grubert	Factor Intensities, Technological Progress and the Terms of Trade	59	6	1.2	OEP
Ethier	Higher Dimensional Issues in Trade Theory	84	14	1.2	JK
Mussa	The Two-Sector Model in Terms of its Dual: A Geometric Exposition	79	13	1.1	JIE
Bhagwati	Immizerizing Growth: A Geometric Note	56	5	1.0	REStud
* Deardorff	The General Validity of the Law of Comparative Advantage	80	12	1.0	JPE
Vanek	The Factor Proportions Theory: The N-Factor Case	68	5	0.9	Kyklos
Deardorff	The General Validity of the Heckscher-Ohlin Theorem	82	10	0.9	AER
Leamer	Sources of International Comparative Advantage, Chapter 1	84	10	0.9	MIT
Deardorff	Weak Links in the Chain of Comparative Advantage	79	10	0.8	JIE
Jones and Neary	The Positive Theory of International Trade	84	8	0.7	JK
Ethier and Svensson	The Theorems of International Trade with Factor Mobility	86	6	0.5	JIE
Davis	Intraindustry Trade: A Heckscher-Ohlin-Ricardo Approach	95	4	0.5	JIE
Jones and Scheinkman	The Relevance of the Two-Sector Production Model in Trade Theory	77	5	0.5	JPE
* Davis	Does European Unemployment Prop Up American Wages? National Labor Markets and Global Trade	98	0	0.0	AER
Leamer	Paths of Development in the Three-Factor n-Good General Equilibrium Model	87	0	0.0	JPE

(*continued*)

TABLE 1 (CONTINUED)

Author(s)	Title	Year	No. of Lists	Score	Source
Leamer	The Heckscher-Ohlin Model in Theory and Practice	95	0	0.0	Princeton
Leamer	Effort, Wages and the International Division of Labor	99	0	0.0	JPE
HO Policy: Normative					
Lerner	The Symmetry Between Import and Export Taxes	36	4	8.0	Ec
* Bhagwati	The Generalized Theory of Distortions and Welfare	71	12	2.2	Bhagwati et al. (1982)
Mussa	Tariffs and the Distribution of Income: The Importance of Factor Specificity, Substitutability, and Intensity in the Short and Long Run	74	8	1.3	JPE
Bhagwati	On the Equivalence of Tariffs and Quotas	65	7	1.3	Baldwin (1988)
Johnson	Optimal Trade Intervention in the Presence of Domestic Distortions	65	7	1.3	Caves, Johnson, and Kenan (1965)
Dixit	Taxation in an Open Economy	86	8	0.7	Auerbach and Feldstein (1986)
Regionalism					
Lipsey	The Theory of Custom Unions: A General Survey	60	8	1.7	EJ
Baldwin and Venables	Regional Economic Integration	95	6	0.8	GR
Sources of Comparative Advantage					
MacDougall	British and American Exports: A Study Suggested by the Theory of Comparative Costs, Part I	51	5	1.7	EJ
Baldwin	Determinants of the Commodity Structure of US Trade	71	8	1.5	AER
Leamer and Levinsohn	International Trade Theory: The Evidence	94	12	1.4	GR
Leamer	Sources of International Comparative Advantage	84	10	0.9	MIT
Deardorff	Testing Trade Theory and Predicting Trade Flows	84	10	0.9	JK
Hufbauer	The Impact of National Characteristics and Technology on the Commodity Composition of Trade in Manufacturing Goods	70	3	0.6	Vernon (1970)

TABLE 1 (CONTINUED)

Author(s)	Title	Year	No. of Lists	Score	Source
Stern and Maskus	Determinants of the Commodity Structure in US Trade	71	3	0.6	AER
Harrigan	Technology, Factor Supplies and International Specialization: Estimating the Neoclassical Model	97	3	0.4	AER
Hunter and Markusen	Per-Capita Income as a Determinant of Trade	88	4	0.4	Feenstra (1988)
Hunter	The Contribution of Non-Homothetic Preferences to Trade	91	3	0.4	JIE
Davis and Weinstein	An Account of Global Factor Trade	0	0		AER, forthcoming
Misc. HO Data Analysis					
Feenstra	Empirical Methods for International Trade	88	6	0.6	MIT
Feenstra	How Costly Is Protectionism	92	4	0.5	JEP
Leontief Paradox Factor Contents					
* Trefler	The Case of the Missing Trade and Other HOV Mysteries	95	12	1.5	AER
Trefler	International Factor Price Differences: Leontief Was Right!	93	13	1.5	JPE
* Bowen, Leamer, and Sveikauskas	Multicountry, Multifactor Tests of the Factor Abundance Theory	87	15	1.4	AER
Leontief	Domestic Production and Foreign Trade: The American Capital Postion Re-examined	54	5	1.1	Econ. Inter-nazionale
* Leamer	The Leontief Paradox Reconsidered	80	10	0.8	JPE
Trade and Wages					
Sachs and Shatz	Trade and Jobs in US Manufacturing	94	5	0.6	Brookings
* Lawrence and Slaughter	Trade and US Wages: Great Sucking Sound or Small Hiccup? (excerpts)	93	4	0.5	Brookings
* Leamer	In Search of Stolper Samuelson Effects on US Wages (excerpts)	95	3	0.4	Collins (1997)

(*continued*)

TABLE 1 (CONTINUED)

Author(s)	Title	Year	No. of Lists	Score	Source
Feenstra and Hansen	Foreign Investment Outsourcing, and Relative Wages	96	0	0.0	Feenstra et al., eds. (1996)
Deardorff and Hakura	Trade and Wages—What are the Questions	85	3	0.3	Bhagwati and Kosters (1995)
Baldwin and Cain	Shifts in U.S. Relative Wages: The Role of Trade, Technology and Factor Endowments	97	0	0.0	NBER

IV. Gravity Model

Author(s)	Title	Year	No. of Lists	Score	Source
* Engel and Rogers	How Wide Is the Border?	96	0	0.0	AER
Frankel, Stein, and Wei	Trading Blocs: The Natural, the Unnatural and the Supernatural	95	0	0.0	JDE 47:61-96

V. Chamberlinian Model (Economies of Scale and Imperfect Competition)

Chamberlinian Theory: Positive

Author(s)	Title	Year	No. of Lists	Score	Source
Helpman and Krugman	Market Structure and Foreign Trade	85	17	1.5	MIT
Grossman	Imperfect Competition and International Trade	92	12	1.5	MIT
* Krugman	Increasing Returns, Monopolistic Competition, and International Trade	79	14	1.2	JIE
* Brander and Krugman	A Reciprocal Dumping Model of International Trade	83	13	1.1	JIE
* Ethier	National and International Returns to Scale in the Modern Theory of International Trade	82	10	0.9	AER
* Krugman	Increasing Returns and Economic Geography	91	7	0.9	JPE
Krugman	Scale Economies, Product Differentiation and the Pattern of Trade	80	10	0.8	AER
Ethier	Decreasing Costs in International Trade and Frank Graham's Argument for Protection	82	9	0.8	Econometrica
Helpman	International Trade in the Presence of Product Differentiation, Economies of Scale and Monopolistic Competition: A Chamberlin-Heckscher-Ohlin Approach	81	9	0.8	JIE
Krugman	Geography and Trade	92	6	0.7	MIT
Markusen	Trade and the Gains from Trade with Imperfect Competition	81	8	0.7	JIE

TABLE 1 (CONTINUED)

Author(s)	Title	Year	No. of Lists	Score	Source
Krugman	Increasing Returns, Imperfect Competition and the Positive Theory of International Trade	95	5	0.6	GR
Helpman	Increasing Returns, Imperfect Markets and Trade Theory	84	7	0.6	GR
Krugman	Intra-Industry Specialization and the Gains from Trade	81	7	0.6	JPE
Ethier	Internationally Decreasing Costs and World Trade	79	5	0.4	JTE
Lancaster	Intra-Industry Trade Under Perfect Monopolistic Competition	80	5	0.4	JIE
Multinational Corporations					
Helpman	A Simple Theory of International Trade with Multinational Corporations	84	9	0.8	JPE
Markusen	The Boundaries of Multinational Enterprises and the Theory of International Trade	95	5	0.6	JEP
* Markusen	The Multinationals, Multi-Plant Economies, and the Gains from Trade	84	7	0.6	JIE
Ethier	The Multinational Firm	86	6	0.5	QJE
Dynamic Scale Economies and Other Production Functions					
Grossman and Helpman	Innovation and Growth in the Global Economy	91	13	1.6	MIT
Vernon	International Investment and International Trade in the Product Cycle	66	7	1.4	QJE
Young	Learning by Doing and the Dynamic Effects of International Trade	91	5	0.6	QJE
Rivera-Batiz and Romer	Economic Integration and Endogenous Growth	91	5	0.6	QJE
Krugman	A Model of Innovation, Technology Transfer, and the World Distribution of Income	79	7	0.6	JPE
* Kremer	The O-Ring Theory of Economic Development	93	0	0.0	QJE
Matsuyama	Agricultural Productivity, Comparative Advantage, and Economic Growth	91	0	0.0	JET

(continued)

TABLE 1 (CONTINUED)

Author(s)	Title	Year	No. of Lists	Score	Source
Strategic Policy: Normative					
* Eaton and Grossman	Optimal Trade and Industrial Policy under Oligopoly	86	15	1.3	QJE
Brander	Strategic Trade Policy	95	10	1.3	GR
Krishna	Trade Restrictions as Facilitating Practices	89	10	1.1	JIE
Helpman and Krugman	Trade Policy and Market Structure	89	10	1.1	MIT
Johnson	Optimal Tariffs and Retaliation	53	4	1.0	REStud
Markusen and Venables	Trade Policy with Increasing Returns and Imperfect Competition	88	7	0.7	JIE
Brander and Spencer	Tariff Protection and Imperfect Competition	84	9	0.8	Kierzkowski (1984)
Dixit	International Trade Policy for Oligopolistic Industries	84	9	0.8	EJ
Grossman and Helpman	Trade Wars and Trade Talks	95	5	0.6	JPE
Maggi	Strategic Trade Policies with Endogenous Modes of Competition	96	4	0.6	AER
Brander and Spencer	Export Subsidies and International Market Share Rivalry	85	7	0.6	JIE
Krugman	Import Protection as Export Promotion: International Competition in the Presence of Oligopoly and Economy of Scales	84	7	0.6	Kierzkowski (1984)
Chamberlinian Data Analysis					
* Hummels and Levinsohn	Monopolistic Competition and International Trade: Reconsidering the Evidence	95	10	1.3	QJE
Helpman	Imperfect Competition and International Trade: Evidence From Fouteen Industrialized Countries	87	10	0.9	Journal of Japanese and International Economies
Baldwin and Krugman	Market Access and International Competition: A Simulation Study of 16K Random Access Memories	88	6	0.6	Feenstra (1988)
Dixit	Optimal Trade and Industrial Policies for the U.S. Automobile Industry	88	6	0.6	Feenstra (1988)

TABLE 1 (CONTINUED)

Author(s)	Title	Year	No. of Lists	Score	Source
Berry, Levinsohn, and Pakes	Voluntary Export Restraints on Automobiles: Evaluating a Strategic Trade Policy	99	4	0.6	AER
Grubel and Lloyd	Intra-Industry Trade	75	3	0.4	book
VI. Uncertainty					
VII. Political Economy					
Theory of Political Economy					
Krueger	The Political Economy of the Rent-Seeking Society	74	10	1.7	AER
* Grossman and Helpman	Protection for Sale	94	10	1.2	AER
Hillman	The Political Economy of Protection	89	6	0.7	book
Rodrik	Political Economy of Trade Policy	95	5	0.6	GR
Mayer	Endogenous Tariff Formation	84	5	0.4	AER
Political Economy Data Analysis					
Trefler	Trade Liberalization and the Theory of Endogenous Protection	93	4	0.5	JPE
Goldberg and Maggi	Protection for Sale: An Empircal Investigation	96	3	0.4	AER

[a] Reprinted articles designated with an *.

HOW WAS THIS LIST COMPILED?

The selection of the articles reprinted in this book is based on their frequency of appearance on the 19 recent graduate reading lists identified in Table 2. These aren't all the fish in the sea, by a long shot, but these were all that my extensive trolling could pull in. Included are reading lists from Harvard, M.I.T. and Princeton, and also a mixed group of lists from the United States and Europe, and even as far away as UCLA.

THESE LISTS ARE VERY, VERY DIFFERENT

"Idiosyncratic" is the adjective that most accurately summarizes these 19 reading lists. Although there are several dozen articles that occur on many lists, there are many, many articles that appear on only one list. Figure 1 depicts the frequency of occurrence of the 791 references that show up on one or more of the 19 reading lists. Notice that over 500

TABLE 2

READING LISTS CONSIDERED

Contributor	Affiliation	Year
Anderson	Boston College	1998
Davis	Harvard	1997
Deardorff	Michigan	1997
Ethier	Pennsylvania	1997
Fairburn/Smith	Sussex	1997
Flam	Stockholm	1997
Grossman	Princeton	1998
Hanson	Austin	1997
Harrigan	Pittsburgh	1995
Helpman	Harvard	1997
Krishna	Penn State	1998
Krueger	Stanford	1998
Krugman	MIT	1988
Leamer	UCLA	1998
Lovely	Syracuse	1990
Markusen	Colorado	1997
Rauch	UCSD	1998
Srinivasan	Yale	1995
Staiger	Wisconsin	1998

of these 791 references occur on only one list. Less than 2% of the articles occur on 10 or more of the lists. In other words, what students read in school X is very different from what they read in school Y.

WHAT ARE THE MOST FREQUENT ARTICLES AND BOOKS?

Tables 3 and 4 report the top 22 articles and top 17 books and review articles based on frequency of occurrence on the 19 reading lists. The two most frequent references are books: a general textbook by Dixit and Norman and a more specialized text by Helpman and Krugman. These books are found, respectively, on 18 and 17 of the 19 lists. Students of international economics will surely want to examine these two books. I have chosen not to include Dixit and Norman (1980) on my suggested reading list, however. It has been 20 years since its publication but, more importantly, it emphasizes a dual approach

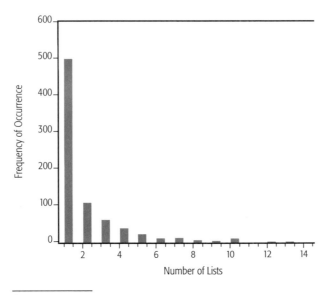

Figure 1

to the GDP maximization problem that underlies international economics. As for me, I am a primal kind of guy.

The most frequently included article is Peter Neary's "Short-Run Capital Specificity and the Pure Theory of International Trade," which was selected by 16 of the 19 instructors. That is a very good reason to include it in this volume, but I reserve the right to make my own selections, for a variety of reasons that are now discussed.

WHY NOT INCLUDE JUST THE MOST POPULAR ARTICLES?

I could have turned the choice of articles over completely to the 19 instructors simply by pasting together the most frequently cited articles in Table 3. I have chosen not to do this for a variety of reasons. A list with only the most popular articles is intellectually unbalanced; it over-represents articles that are reprinted in existing volumes of readings.[2] It is likely to be taken over by a fad that won't be relevant in a year or two. It over-represents articles that were published about 15 years ago—long enough to make it onto the lists but not so long that the instructors who put it on their lists have gone off to the intellectual tundra. Each of these effects should somehow be controlled for.

---

[2] Books of readings edited by Bhagwati and Grossman contaminate the frequency data with the editor's choices. Table 3 indicates that 17 of the top 32 articles are reprinted in either Bhagwati (1987) or Grossman(1992).

TABLE 3

Top 22 Most Frequently Listed Articles

Rank	Reference Author(s)	Title	Lists	Year	In[a]	Source
1*	Neary	Short-Run Capital Specificity and the Pure Theory of International Trade	16	78	B, N	EJ
2*	Bowen, Leamer, and Sveikauskas	Multicountry, Multifactor Tests of the Factor Abundance Theory	15	87	N	AER
2	Dornbusch, Fischer, and Samuelson	Comparative Advantage, Trade and Payments in a Ricardian Model with a Continuum of Goods	15	77	N	AER
2*	Eaton and Grossman	Optimal Trade and Industrial Policy under Oligopoly	15	86	B,G, N	QJE
2*	Jones	The Structure of Simple General Equilibrium Models	15	65	N	JPE
6*	Krugman	Increasing Returns, Monopolistic Competition, and International Trade	14	79	B	JIE
7*	Brander and Krugman	A Reciprocal Dumping Model of International Trade	13	83	G	JIE
7	Mussa	The Two-Sector Model in Terms of its Dual: A Geometric Exposition	13	79	B	JIE
7	Trefler	International Factor Price Differences: Leontief Was Right!	13	93		JPE
10*	Deardorff	The General Validity of the Law of Comparative Advantage	12	80	N	JPE

10*	Trefler	The Case of the Missing Trade and Other HOV Mysteries	12	95		AER
12	Deardorff	Weak Links in the Chain of Comparative Advantage	10	79	B	JIE
12	Deardorff	The General Validity of the Heckscher-Ohlin Theorem	10	82		AER
12*	Ethier	National and International Returns to Scale in the Modern Theory of International Trade	10	82	G	AER
12*	Grossman and Helpman	Protection for Sale	10	94		AER
12	Helpman	Imperfect Competition and International Trade: Evidence From Fourteen Industrialized Countries	10	87	N	JIE
12*	Hummels and Levinsohn	Monopolistic Competition and International Trade: Reconsidering the Evidence	10	95		QJE
12	Jones	A Three Factor Model in Theory, Trade, and History	10	71		Bhagwati (1982)
12	Krishna	Trade Restrictions as Facilitating Practices	10	89	G	JIE
12	Krueger	The Political Economy of the Rent-Seeking Society	10	74	B, N	AER
12	Krugman	Scale Economies, Product Differentiation and the Pattern of Trade	10	80	G, N	AER
12*	Leamer	The Leontief Paradox Reconsidered	10	80	B, N	JPE

aCodes for Volumes of Readings:
B Bhagwati International Trade: Selected Readings 1987
G Grossman (1992) Imperfect Competition and International Trade 1982
N Neary (1995) International Trade, Volumes I and II 1995

TABLE 4

Top 17 Books and Review Articles

Rank	Reference Author(s)	Title	Source	Year	Lists
1	Dixit and Norman	Theory of International Trade	Cambridge	80	18
2	Helpman and Krugman	Market Structure and Foreign Trade	MIT	85	17
3	Jones and Kenen	Handbook of International Economics, Vol. 1	Elsevier	84	15
4	Ethier	Higher Dimensional Issues in Trade Theory	Jones and Kenen (1984)	84	14
5	Grossman and Helpman	Innovation and Growth in the Global Economy	MIT	91	13
5	Bhagwati	International Trade: Selected Readings	MIT	87	13
7	Grossman	Imperfect Competition and International Trade	MIT	82	12
7	Leamer and Levinsohn	International Trade Theory: The Evidence	Grossman and Rogoff (1995)	94	12
7	Bhagwati	The Generalized Theory of Distortions and Welfare	Bhagwati et al. (1971)	71	12
10	Grossman and Rogoff	Handbook of International Economics, Vol. 3	Elsevier	95	10
10	Krugman and Helpman	Trade Policy and Market Structure	MIT	89	10
10	Leamer	Sources of International Comparative Advantage	MIT	84	10
10	Brander	Strategic Trade Policy	Grossman and Rogoff (1995)	95	10
10	Deardorff	Testing Trade Theory and Predicting Trade Flows	Jones and Kenen (1984)	84	10
15	Jones and Neary	The Positive Theory of International Trade	Jones and Kenen (1984)	84	8
15	Lipsey	The Theory of Custom Unions: A General Survey	EJ	60	8
15	Dixit	Taxation in an Open Economy	Auerbach and Feldstein (1986)	86	8

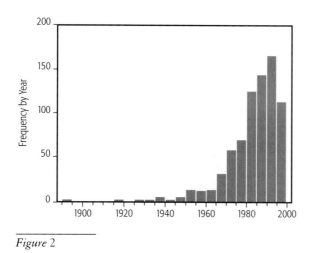

Figure 2

VINTAGE EFFECTS: WHERE HAVE YOU GONE, HARRY JOHNSON?

There is a sobering fact that sinks in when one peruses these reading lists. The fantasy of intellectual immortality that drives some of us has very little chance of becoming a reality. Harry Johnson was one of the most prolific authors of his generation and the reading lists of 1970 were stuffed full of his articles. He must have been the most frequently cited author. But he has sunk to number 28 on the authors list discussed below. He is destined to fall further when he no longer is held up by Bhagwati's endorsement.

The disappearance of Harry Johnson raises a problem: vintage effects. The reading lists of the 19 respondents have articles with publication years concentrated in the early 1980s. Figure 2 is a histogram of year of publication of these 783 articles. The mean publication date is 1983 with a standard error of 12 years. If we passively selected only the most frequently cited articles we would have most 1980s publications.

I have two approaches to solving this vintage problem. One is to correct the frequency data for the vintage effect. The second is to compile the "Hit-Parade" of articles by 5-year intervals, and to assure that some articles from each 5-year interval are represented here.[3]

The classics listed in Table 5 are the articles that have the highest citation frequencies after vintage correction by Score = Number of lists/Vintage index. As is to be expected, the coverage over decades in Table 5 is much more constant than the unadjusted scores suggest—all those 1980s articles disappear since none of them stands out.

---

[3]The vintage correction is computed using a nonparametric smoother to form a "typical" citation count by year of publication, with some adjustments for the end-points where data are very scarce. This index is flat at 1/2 list before 1950. (It is remarkable for such an old article to show up at all.) The index is around 5 in the 1950s and 1960s and jumps to 12 in the early 1980s but falls back to under 8 by 1997.

TABLE 5

The Classics: Based on Number of Lists Divided by Vintage Index

Rank	Reference Author(s)	Title	Lists	Score[a]	Year	Source
1	Stolper and Samuelson	Protection and Real Wages	6	12.00	41	REStud
2	Lerner	The Symmetry Between Import and Export Taxes	4	8.00	36	Ec
3*	Samuelson	International Factor-Price Equalization Once Again	8	6.67	49	EJ
4*	Jones	The Structure of Simple General Equilibrium Models	15	2.80	65	JPE
5	Samuelson	International Trade and Equalization of Factor Prices	3	2.50	48	EJ
6*	Bhagwati	The Generalized Theory of Distortions and Welfare	12	2.24	71	Bhagwati et al. (1971)
7	Jones	A Three Factor Model in Theory, Trade, and History	10	1.87	71	Bhagwati (1982)
8	MacDougall	British and American Exports: A Study Suggested by the Theory of Comparative Costs, Part I	5	1.72	51	EJ
9	Lipsey	The Theory of Custom Unions: A General Survey	8	1.69	60	EJ
10	Krueger	The Political Economy of the Rent-Seeking Society	10	1.66	74	AER
11	Mundell	International Trade and Factor Mobility	8	1.61	57	AER
12*	Trefler	The Case of the Missing Trade and Other HOV Mysteries	12	1.51	95	AER
13	Baldwin	Determinants of the Commodity Structure of US Trade	8	1.49	71	AER
14	Trefler	International Factor Price Differences: Leontief Was Right!	13	1.48	93	JPE
15	Dornbusch, Fischer, and Samuelson	Comparative Advantage, Trade and Payments in a Ricardian Model with a Continuum of Goods	15	1.48	77	AER
16	Samuelson	The Gains From International Trade Once Again	7	1.46	62	EJ
17*	Neary	Short-Run Capital Specificity and the Pure Theory of International Trade	16	1.40	78	EJ
18*	Bowen, Leamer, and Sveikauskas	Multicountry, Multifactor Tests of the Factor Abundance Theory	15	1.38	87	AER
19	Vernon	International Investment and International Trade in the Product Cycle	7	1.36	66	QJE
20	Mussa	Tariffs and the Distribution of Income: The Importance of Factor Specificity, Substitutability, and Intensity in the Short and Long Run	8	1.32	74	JPE

[a]Score = Number of Lists/Vintage Index.

Another way to correct for vintage is to select the most cited articles in each time period. Table 6 is the hit-parade of original articles, the top five in each 5-year interval. I think that my book of readings should contain at least one article from each of these periods.

INTELLECTUAL COVERAGE

A book of readings needs to have some sensible intellectual coverage. If we allow the frequencies to dictate the list, we may get a very unbalanced book. My proposed reading list reported in Table 1 is organized by intellectual topic, and this book of readings is designed to cover adequately the full range of topics.

There is an interesting interaction between topic and vintage—articles on particular topics tend to be highly clustered in time. Table 7 reports the number of articles in each major subject together with three percentiles of the age distribution. The subjects are sorted by the 75th percentiles from oldest to most recent. By that measure Ricardian theory is the oldest literature, with 75% of the articles written before 1979, but there are only two such articles and the percentiles are not altogether meaningful. The big 1970s topic was the Heckscher-Ohlin theory, positive and normative. In the 1980s it was economies of scale and strategic interactions. In the 1990s it was the analysis of data and political economy.

The interquartile range from the 25th percentile to the 75th percentile that is reported in the last column of Table 7 is a measure of the lifespan of a topic. The empirical topic "sources of comparative advantage" has the longest life; indeed the interquartile range extends from the 1970s into the 1990s. The theory of the Heckscher-Ohlin model also has a long life. Of the subjects with a relatively large number of articles, strategic trade policy seems to have had the shortest life.

The subjects at the bottom of this table need to be represented in a book of readings for the twenty-first century. These are the research topics of the 1990s that students will be reading in the century. It is very interesting that these topics are all empirical, with the exception of the theory of political economy.

Most of these topics are represented in this volume of readings but there is one glaring omission. I have reprinted nothing empirical on sources of comparative advantage—I just couldn't find the right article to crowd out any others. I also don't have anything on "endogenous growth," a subject that might more accurately be called dynamic scale economies. The central message of this diverse and important literature, it seems to me, is that we need to think more carefully about the nature of the production function.[4]

---

[4] Kremer's (1993) O-ring paper on complexity merits special attention in that regard, along with mine on effort, "Effort, Wages and the International Division of Labor," *Journal of Political Economy*, Vol. 107, Number 6, part 1, Dec. 1999, 1127–1163.

TABLE 6

THE HIT-PARADE BY FIVE-YEAR INTERVAL

Period	Reference Author(s)	Title	Source	Year	Lists
1995	* Trefler	The Case of the Missing Trade and Other HOV Mysteries	AER	95	12
	* Hummels and Levinsohn	Monopolistic Competition and International Trade: Reconsidering the Evidence	QJE	95	10
	Davis, Weinstein, and Shimpo	Using International and Japanese Regional Data to Determine When the Factor Abundance Theory of Trade Works	AER	97	5
	Grossman and Helpman	Trade Wars and Trade Talks	JPE	95	5
	Berry, Levinsohn, and Pakes	Voluntary Export Restraints on Automobiles: Evaluating a Trade Policy	AER	99	4
	Maggi	Strategic Trade Policies with Endogenous Modes of Competition	AER	96	4
1990	Trefler	International Factor Price Differences: Leontiff Was Right!	JPE	93	13
	* Grossman and Helpman	Protection for Sale	AER	94	10
	* Krugman	Increasing Returns and Economic Geography	JPE	91	7
1985	* Bowen, Leamer, and Sveikauskas	Multicountry, Multifactor Tests of the Factor Abundance Theory	AER	87	15
	* Eaton and Grossman	Optimal Trade and Industrial Policy under Oligopoly	QJE	86	15
	Krishna	Trade Restrictions as Facilitating Practices	JIE	89	10
	Helpman	Imperfect Competition and International Trade: Evidence From Fourteen Industrialized Countries	Journal of Japanese and International Economies	87	10
	Markusen and Venables	Trade Policy with Increasing Returns and Imperfect Competition	JIE	88	7
	Brander and Spencer	Export Subsidies and International Market Share Rivalry	JIE	85	7
1980	* Brander and Krugman	A Reciprocal Dumping Model of International Trade	JIE	83	13

TABLE 6 (CONTINUED)

Period	Reference Author(s)	Title	Source	Year	Lists
1980	* Deardorff	The General Validity of the Law of Comparative Advantage	JPE	80	12
	Deardorff	The General Validity of the Heckscher-Ohlin Theorem	AER	82	10
	* Ethier	National and International Returns to Scale in the Modern Theory of International Trade	AER	82	10
	Krugman	Scale Economies, Product Differentiation and the Pattern of Trade	AER	80	10
	* Leamer	The Leontief Paradox Reconsidered	JPE	80	10
1975*	Neary	Short-Run Capital Specificity and the Pure Theory of International Trade	EJ	78	16
	Dornbusch, Fischer, and Samuelson	Comparative Advantage, Trade and Payments in a Ricardian Model with a Continuum of Goods	AER	77	15
	* Krugman	Increasing Returns, Monopolistic Competition, and International Trade	JIE	79	14
	Mussa	The Two-Sector Model in Terms of its Dual: A Geometric Exposition	JIE	79	13
	Deardorff	Weak Links in the Chain of Comparative Advantage	JIE	79	10
1970	* Bhagwati	The Generalized Theory of Distortions and Welfare	Bhagwati et al. (1971)	71	12
	Krueger	The Political Economy of the Rent-Seeking Society	AER	74	10
	Jones	A Three Factor Model in Theory, Trade, and History	Bhagwati (1982)	71	10
	Mussa	Tariffs and the Distribution of Income: The Importance of Factor Specificity, Substitutability, and Intensity in the Long and Short Run	JPE	74	8
	Baldwin	Determinants of the Commodity Structure of US Trade	AER	71	8
1960	* Jones	The Structure of Simple General Equilibrium Models	JPE	65	15

(continued)

TABLE 6 (CONTINUED)

Period	Reference Author(s)	Title	Source	Year	Lists
1960	Vernon	International Investment and International Trade in the Product Cycle	QJE	66	7
	Bhagwati	On the Equivalence of Tariffs and Quotas	Baldwin (1988)	65	7
	Johnson	Optimal Trade Intervention in the Presence of Domestic Distortions	Caves, Johnson, and Kenan (1965)	65	7
	Samuelson	The Gains From International Trade Once Again	EJ	62	7
1950	Mundell	International Trade and Factor Mobility	AER	57	8
	* Samuelson	International Factor-Price Equalization Once Again	EJ	49	8
	Findlay and Grubert	Factor Intensities, Technological Progress and the Terms of Trade	OEP	59	6
	Rybczynski	Factor Endowments and Relative Commodity Prices	Ec	55	6
	Stolper and Samuelson	Protection and Real Wages	REStud	41	6

PEOPLE COVERAGE

Research is a collective conversation, not a soliloquy. An accurate recording of this conversation includes the softer voices as well as the louder ones. I have leaned very far, therefore, to include as many different authors as possible. Of course I wanted more Grossman, Helpman, and Krugman. But each time I put in another article by the three "men" of international economics, it drove out one by someone else. I chose, as you can see, to maximize the author coverage, even at the expense of distorting the recording somewhat.

TAKE-AWAYS

Last but not least of my criteria is a clear take-away. What really is the point of this article? Too many articles are published that are only elaborate and complicated ways of restating the obvious. One of the exercises in my class is to write down a one-sentence statement of the take-away for every article we read. You'd be surprised how hard a task that turns out to be.

TABLE 7

WHEN WERE THESE SUBJECTS DISCUSSED AND HOW INTENSELY?

Subject	Number of Articles	Percentiles of Age Distribution			Interquartile Range
		5%	25%	75%	
Ricardian Theory	2	1977	1978	1979	2
Ricardo-Viner Theory	4	1975	1977	1980	3
HO Theory: Positive	41	1948	1965	1984	19
HO Policy: Normative	26	1954	1970	1984	15
Chamberlinian Theory: Positive	28	1979	1981	1988	7
Strategic Policy: Normative	19	1978	1985	1989	4
Uncertainty	6	1985	1986	1989	4
Regionalism	6	1964	1978	1989	11
Multinational Corporations	7	1983	1984	1990	6
Dynamic Scale Economies	8	1971	1986	1991	5
Sources of Comparative Advantage	12	1952	1971	1992	21
Misc. HO Data Analysis	8	1985	1988	1992	4
Trade and Wages	4	1986	1991	1994	3
Theory of Political Economy	7	1977	1987	1995	8
Leontief Paradox: Factor Contents	9	1964	1982	1995	13
Chamberlinian Data	9	1980	1988	1995	7
Political Economy Data Analysis	2	1993	1994	1995	2

A message has a sender and a receiver, of course, and when I tell you that I don't think there is a take-away in the frequently cited Dornbusch, Fisher, and Samuelson (1977), I admit that may be my problem and not theirs. But perhaps by my decision to exclude it, and your objection, we will stimulate a closer examination of all the other articles on our reading lists. I recommend instead Feenstra and Hanson (1996), which uses the same mathematical tools but applies them to the interesting and modern question: why is income inequality rising in both developed and developing countries?

MIRROR, MIRROR ON THE WALL

And now for the really important news. Authors, you want to know your score, don't you? Students, you are wondering if anyone else in the world is reading all those articles

TABLE 8

OUR FAVORITE AUTHORS[a]

Rank	Author	Total	Self Cites	Net	Rank	Author	Total	Self Cites	Net
1	Krugman	159	11	148	38	Brainard	13		13
2	Helpman	138	32	106	39	Corden	13		13
3	Grossman	94	12	82	40	Kemp	13		13
4	Leamer	71	16	55	41	Svensson	13		13
5	Bhagwati	66		66	42	Rodrik	12		12
6	Ethier	61	2	59	43	Romer	12		12
7	Markusen	60	15	45	44	Smith	12	4	8
8	Deardorff	56	16	40	45	Vernon	12		12
9	Samuelson	51		51	46	Weinstein	12		12
10	Jones	50		50	47	Young	12		12
11	Dixit	49		49	48	Hummels	11		11
12	Brander	46		46	49	Lawrence	11		11
13	Levinsohn	35		35	50	Mundell	11		11
14	Neary	34		34	51	Rauch	11	8	3
15	Krishna	30	2	28	52	Razin	11		11
16	Trefler	30		30	53	Lipsey	10		10
17	Venables	30		30	54	Maggi	10		10
18	Mussa	29		29	55	Rivera-Batiz	10		10
19	Baldwin, Bob	28		28	56	Bagwell	9		9
20	Spencer	26		26	57	Caves	9		9
21	Eaton	24		24	58	Harris	9		9
22	Feenstra	24		24	59	Melvin	9		9
23	Bowen	21		21	60	Norman	9		9
24	Davis	21	6	15	61	Horn	8		8
25	Staiger	20	8	12	62	Lancaster	8		8
26	Brecher	19		19	63	Leontief	8		8
27	Stern	19		19	64	MacDougall	8		8
28	Johnson	18		18	65	Taylor	8		8
29	Dornbusch	17		17	66	Hanson	7	3	4
30	Findlay	17		17	67	Harkness	7		7
31	Mayer	17		17	68	Harrigan	7	4	3
32	Srinivasan	17	12	5	69	Hillman	7		7
33	Sveikauskas	17		17	70	Horstmann	7		7
34	Baldwin, Dick	16		16	71	Hunter	7		7
35	Fischer	16		16	72	Magee	7		7
36	Krueger	16	2	14	73	Maskus	7		7
37	Anderson	13	2	11	74	Stiglitz	7		7

[a]Number of times an author's name appears on the 19 lists, excluding textbooks and surveys.

by your instructor, aren't you? Table 8 has the frequency of occurrence of the authors' names on my 19 reading lists, with self-citations and surveys removed. You can see from this list that I have managed to include quite a few of the players on the scorecard.

Incidentally, don't be upset if your name isn't as high on this list as you expected. I know how smart you really are. I completely agree with your mother on that. There must be a vicious plot against you. On the other hand, if you find your name on this list, don't start gloating. You aren't going to last long.

ANSWERS TO THE QUESTIONS

Finally, I bring your attention to the pictures and self-statements that most of the authors have provided. I have not imposed any hard and fast constraints for their self-statements but I have posed to each of them a set of questions about themselves and their papers to which many have responded.

Worth Series in Outstanding Contributions

International Economics

The Ricardo-Viner Model
(Specific Factors)

J. Peter Neary

Short-Run Capital Specificity and the Pure Theory of International Trade

J. PETER NEARY

Among its many abstractions from reality, the pure theory of international trade, associated with the names of Heckscher, Ohlin, and Samuelson, assumes that both capital and labour are costlessly and instantaneously transferable between sectors. More recently, however, beginning with articles by Jones (1971b) and Samuelson (1971a, b), a number of writers have returned to an older tradition, traceable in the works of Marshall, Ohlin himself, and Harrod, which assumes that, in the short run at least, capital goods are sector-specific. In the light of this tradition, the Heckscher-Ohlin-Samuelson model is seen as describing positions of long-run equilibrium only. In the short run any disturbance will lead to a reallocation of the labour force between sectors. But capital in each sector is a fixed factor, and so differences emerge between the rentals in the two sectors. Over a longer time-horizon capital will flow between sectors in response to these rental differentials, tending eventually (unless another disturbance intervenes) to a new long-run equilibrium with all capital goods earning the same rental.

This view of the adjustment process, which I propose to call the "short-run capital specificity" hypothesis, is hardly novel; apart from the earlier writers already cited, it is implicit, for example, in Harberger (1962) and Kemp and Jones (1962). However, as formalised in recent work, especially by Mayer (1974) and Mussa (1974), it provides a plausible hypothesis about the economy's response to exogenous disturbances. Moreover these writers have shown that it may be used to explain why there is no necessary contradiction between the somewhat counterintuitive predictions of traditional international trade theory, and the more "commonsensical" views of politicians, businessmen, and trade-union leaders.

The aim of this paper is threefold. First, it presents a new diagrammatic technique to illustrate the short-run capital specificity adjustment process in a small open economy. This technique is used in sections 1 through 3 to demonstrate the process of adjustment towards long-run equilibrium, following changes in commodity prices, population, and the level of factor market distortions. Sections 1 and 2 expound the findings of Mussa and Mayer on the effects of changes in the terms of trade and in total factor supplies, noting some extensions of these writers' analyses. Section 3 then applies the technique to the consideration of changes in the level of factor market distortions. It is shown that conflicts between long-run and short-run interests may arise in this case: for example, workers in a labour-intensive sector may have an incentive to press for higher wages, despite the fact that in the long run their action will lower wages in both sectors.

Second, the implications of the short-run capital specificity adjustment process are examined in the context of an open economy with preexisting factor market distortions. Much of the recent literature in this area (see especially Jones 1971a and Magee 1976) has been concerned with the elucidation of a number of paradoxes which can arise in the presence of such factor market distortions, of which two of the more notable are a perverse price-output response and a perverse distortion-output response. Section 4 begins by giving a new diagrammatic exposition of these paradoxes, and then shows that, if the economy is assumed to adjust according to the short-run capital specificity hypothesis, then *these paradoxes will never be observed*, because they correspond to *dynamically unstable* long-run equilibria. For devotees of the Heckscher-Ohlin-Samuelson model, this is an encouraging conclusion, since it implies that the long-run predictions of that model in the presence of factor market distortions are much more consistent with simple economic intuition than had been thought. The analysis of this section complements that of a companion paper, Neary (1978b), where the same conclusions are shown to hold under a wider class of disequilibrium adjustment mechanisms.

The third aim of the paper is to point out the central role of the assumption of intersectoral capital mobility in traditional international trade theory. Section 5 surveys a number of cases, additional to those in sections 1 through 3, where this assumption is responsible for "paradoxical" or counterintuitive conclusions. It is argued in section 6 that both common sense and the implications of observed self-interested behaviour on the part of market participants make this assumption inappropriate in the short run, and that the peculiar nature of the primary factor capital which it assumes—a fixed stock of homogeneous, infinitely long-lived, and perfectly mobile machines—makes it suspect in the long run.

1. SHORT-RUN AND LONG-RUN RESPONSES TO CHANGES IN THE TERMS OF TRADE

We begin by introducing the diagrammatic technique to be used in this paper. Essentially this combines two diagrams: the Edgeworth-Bowley production box, introduced to international trade theory by Stolper and Samuelson (1941), and the sector-specific capital diagram, familiar in writings on economic development and used by Jones (1971b) and Mussa (1974). As shown in figure 1, measuring the economy's labour force on the horizontal axis of the Edgeworth-Bowley box enables us to place the two diagrams vertically above one another, and thus to examine simultaneously the short-run and long-run consequences of any exogenous change.

The usual assumptions of the two-sector model of international trade are built into figure 1, where the initial equilibrium is indicated by the points A_0 and B_0 in the upper and lower parts of the figure, respectively. The economy produces two goods, X and Y, under perfectly competitive conditions in both commodity and factor markets, using fixed supplies of the two factors, labour and capital, and subject to constant returns to scale. In the long run both factors are completely mobile between sectors. In the short run, however, there are diminishing returns to labour in each sector because of the fixity of capital goods. Hence entrepreneurs in each sector maximise profits by increasing employment until the value marginal product of labour equals the wage. Assuming that

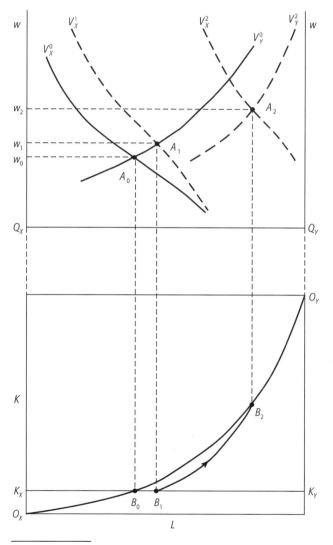

Figure 1

Short-run and long-run adjustments to an increase in the relative price of the labour-intensive good X

the wage rate adjusts to ensure full employment at all times, the initial wage rate and labour force allocation is therefore determined by the intersection of the two value marginal product of labour schedules, V_X^0 and V_Y^0, at A_0 in the upper part of figure 1. The location of these schedules depends on the initial commodity prices and on the initial allocation of capital to each sector, with the latter represented by the distances $O_X K_X$ and $O_Y K_Y$ in the lower part of the figure. Finally, the fact that the initial position is one of long-run as well as of short-run equilibrium is shown by the fact that B_0, the point in the lower part of the diagram which corresponds to A_0, lies on the contract curve of the Edgeworth-Bowley box. This contract curve lies below the diagonal of the box, reflecting our last assumption, that X is the relatively labour-intensive sector.

Consider now the effect of a displacement of this initial equilibrium by a once-and-for-all change in the terms of trade, involving an increase in the relative price of X. With capital sector-specific in the short run, we may begin by examining the upper part of figure 1. Choosing good Y as numeraire, the value marginal product of labour in Y schedule, V_Y^0, is unaffected, whereas the corresponding schedule for the X sector shifts upwards, from V_X^0 to V_X^1, by the same proportional amount as the price increase. Therefore the new short-run equilibrium will be that represented by the points A_1 and B_1. (The latter point satisfies the restrictions that it lies vertically below A_1, and on the same capital allocation line, $K_X K_Y$, as B_0.) Labour has moved out of Y into X, and since the amount of capital in X is unchanged, the output of X has increased: thus even in the short run the economy responds to the rise in the relative price of X by expanding its output, to an extent determined by the slopes of the two value marginal product of labour schedules.

The short-run reactions of factor prices to this change have been considered in detail by Mussa (1974). The wage rate increases in terms of Y but falls in terms of X (this may be seen from the fact that the capital-labour ratio rises in sector Y but falls in sector X), so that the effect on the real income of wage earners is not independent of their consumption pattern. As for the rentals on capital, that in the X sector increases in terms of both goods, whereas that in the Y sector falls in terms of both. However, while all of these changes are of interest from the point of view of income distribution, the crucial fact from the point of view of resource allocation is that the capital rental in X has increased relative to that in Y. This may also be seen from the lower part of the diagram: since B_1 lies below the efficiency locus, it follows that the rental wage ratio is relatively higher in X, and since the same wage prevails in each sector this means that the rental must be higher in X than in Y. Given our assumed adjustment process therefore, competitive pressures will lead in the "medium run" to a reallocation of capital from the low to the high rental sector.[1] In the lower part of the diagram, this has the effect of causing the capital allocation line to shift upwards; in the upper part, both the V_X^1 and V_Y^0 schedules shift to the right, since an increase (decrease) in the quantity of capital in a sector must lead the marginal product of labour to rise (fall) at all levels of employment.

To establish the effects of this capital reallocation on factor rewards and on factor usage in each sector, we note first that the transfer of a given amount of capital from Y to X leads the former sector to seek to shed labour and the latter to try to acquire labour.[2] Since X

is the relatively labour-intensive sector, the quantity of labour it wishes to acquire will, at the initial factor prices, exceed that which the Y sector is willing to give up. Excess demand for labour in the economy as a whole therefore develops, and so the wage rate is bid up. With both commodity prices constant, the increase in the wage must reduce the rental in each sector. This follows from the fact that the proportional change in the price of each good is a weighted average of the changes in factor prices in each sector, the weights being the share of each factor in the value of output of that sector:

$$\hat{p}_X = \theta_{LX}\hat{w} + \theta_{KX}\hat{r}_X, \tag{1}$$

$$\hat{p}_Y = \theta_{LY}\hat{w} + \theta_{KY}\hat{r}_Y. \tag{2}$$

Since the wage rental ratio rises in each sector as capital reallocates, both capital-labour ratios must also rise. The economy therefore moves away from B_1 in a northeasterly direction, along the path shown by a heavy line, which satisfies the properties that at every point along it the slope of the path is greater than the slope of the ray from O_X to that point, and less than the slope of the ray from O_Y to that point. This path may be called a *"labour-market equilibrium locus,"* because although it is characterised throughout by disequilibrium in the capital market, the labour market is in equilibrium at all points along it (in the sense that full employment of labour and a uniform wage rate prevail).

Finally, what happens to the intersectoral rental differential as the economy moves along this locus? The fact that X is the relatively labour-intensive sector means that the distributive share of labour is greater in X than in Y; hence to keep relative commodity prices constant, it is necessary for the rental in X to fall by more than that in Y. This may be seen by setting the proportional changes in price in equations (1) and (2) equal to zero, and manipulating the equations to obtain:

$$\hat{r}_X - \hat{r}_Y = -\frac{\theta}{\theta_{KX}\theta_{KY}}\hat{w}, \tag{3}$$

where θ is the determinant of the matrix of sectoral shares, which is positive in this case, because X is relatively labour intensive.[3] Equation (3) shows that as a result of the transfer of capital between sectors and the consequent increase in the wage, the gap between the rentals in the two sectors has been partially closed. This process of capital reallocation continues until the gap is fully closed; at which time a new long-run equilibrium, corresponding to the points A_2 and B_2, is attained. This new equilibrium is exactly that predicted by Stolper and Samuelson (1941), at which, relative to the initial equilibrium at A_0 and B_0, the wage has risen and the rental common to both sectors has fallen in terms of each good. Thus the short-run effect of the price change in increasing the rental on capital in the X sector is eroded, and eventually reversed, in the course of the adjustment process, as capital flows into the X sector in response to the higher return obtainable there.

Having examined the case where X is relatively labour-intensive, the case where it is relatively capital intensive is straightforward. It is illustrated in figure 2. Perhaps the most important feature is that the initial reaction to the increase in the relative price of X is qualitatively identical to that in figure 1: as before, the wage rises initially in terms of Y, while the rentals on capital in X and Y rise and fall respectively in terms of both goods. It is only in the course of the adjustment process that relative factor intensities play a role, as the verbal description above will have made clear. In this case, the movement of capital into the relatively capital-intensive sector reduces the demand for labour in the economy; hence the rental in both sectors rises, and the common wage rate falls, throughout the adjustment process. The capital-labour ratio in each sector therefore falls

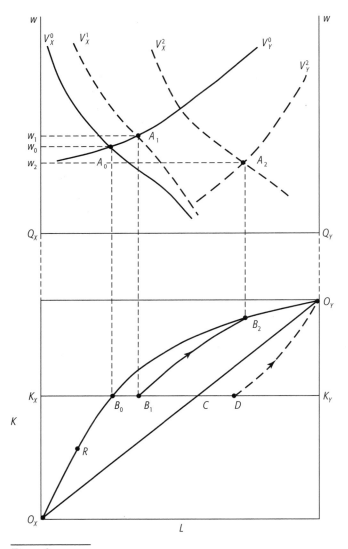

Figure 2

Short-run and long-run adjustments to an increase in the relative price of the capital-intensive good X

as capital reallocates, and so the path of adjustment from B_1 to B_2 is less steeply sloped at any point than the ray from O_X to that point, and more steeply sloped than the corresponding ray from O_Y. At the new long-run equilibrium (represented by A_2 and B_2) the wage will be lower than its initial value of w_0. But, despite this, it is possible for labour actually to favour the change on completely rational grounds, if its consumption pattern is sufficiently biased towards Y, and if either the speed of capital reallocation is sufficiently slow, or the rate at which labour discounts its future consumption to the present is sufficiently high.

The only additional qualification which must be made to the case where X is initially relatively capital intensive, is that a sufficiently large price increase could cause the new short-run equilibrium point to lie to the right of C in the Edgeworth-Bowley box, thus reversing the initial factor intensity ranking of the two sectors. This possibility was pointed out by Mussa (1974, p. 1200, n. 10), who claimed that such a factor intensity reversal would only be temporary, and that the factor allocation point in the Edgeworth-Bowley box would eventually recross the diagonal. However, this is incorrect: if the new short-run equilibrium occurs at a point such as D, to the right of C in figure 2, the factor allocation point will *not* recross the diagonal but will move instead towards O_Y along the labour-market equilibrium locus indicated by the dashed line. The Y industry will eventually be completely eliminated, and the economy will specialise in the production of X. This follows from the fact (already established above) that as capital reallocates, the expansion of the now labour-intensive sector X increases the wage rental ratio in both sectors. Hence the capital-labour ratio in sector Y cannot fall during the adjustment process, as it would have to if the labour-market equilibrium locus were to cross the diagonal.

In summary, this section has illustrated the conclusions of Mayer and Mussa that an increase in the relative price of X under the short-run capital specificity adjustment process will always imply a conflict between the short-run and long-run interests of at least one group of factor income recipients: when X is relatively labour-intensive, this is true of the owners of sector X capital, and when X is relatively capital intensive, it is true of both wage-earners and owners of sector Y capital. In addition it has been shown that contrary to the suggestion of Mussa, a change in the terms of trade can never lead to a temporary reversal of the relative factor intensities of the two sectors, since the price change required to induce a short-run factor intensity reversal is more than sufficient to induce complete specialisation in the long run.

2. SHORT-RUN AND LONG-RUN RESPONSES TO CHANGES IN FACTOR ENDOWMENTS

The next case to be considered is that of a once-and-for-all increase in population, as examined by Mayer (1974). In figure 3 the initial equilibrium is at A_0 and B_0, with X the relatively capital-intensive sector. Suppose now that the labour force (assumed to be identical to the population) increases by an amount equal to the distance $Q_Y^0 Q_Y^1$. With unchanged capital allocations, the V_Y^0 schedule is shifted to the right by the full extent of the population increase, leading to a new short-run equilibrium at A_1, corresponding to the point B_1 in the production box.[4] It is clear from the diagram that the wage falls, and hence at constant (absolute and relative) commodity prices, the rental in each sector must rise. Moreover, from equation (3) it follows that the rental must increase by a greater proportional amount in the relatively labour-intensive sector. Hence, in the "medium run," capital moves along the labour-market equilibrium locus B_1B_2 from the capital-intensive sector X into the labour-intensive sector Y, causing the wage rate to

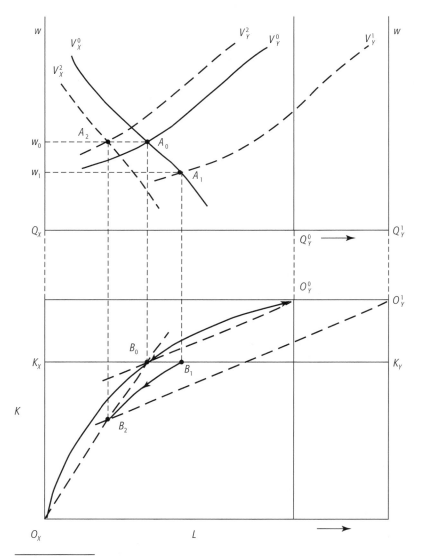

Figure 3

Short-run and long-run adjustments to population growth

increase steadily, and the rental to fall in each sector, with the gap between the two rentals narrowing and finally being eliminated.

From the Rybczynski theorem (Rybczynski 1955) we know that the final long-run equilibrium must be at B_2 in the production box: with unchanged commodity prices and rentals equalised between sectors, relative factor prices, and hence factor proportions in each sector must be identical to those which prevailed before the population increase. This may also be seen from the upper part of the diagram: the V_X and V_Y schedules have both shifted to the left to intersect at A_2, restoring the original wage w_0. Despite this long-run independence of the wage from the size of population, however, if workers have any positive discount rate, they will, for example, oppose immigration in a small open economy on perfectly rational grounds. Furthermore the strong Rybczynski prediction, that at constant relative commodity prices the output of the capital-intensive sector must fall, is shown to be a long-run result only: with sector-specific capital in the short run, the increased employment in X represented by the move from A_0 to A_1 means that the output of X will initially *rise* as a result of the population growth.

The case where X is relatively labour-intensive may be examined in the same way. As in section 1, this makes no qualitative difference to the new short-run equilibrium, but from equation (3) the intersectoral differential in capital rentals will be the opposite to the case just considered, leading to the familiar Rybczynski result of a fall in the output of Y in the long (though not in the short) run. Finally, the same diagrammatic technique may also be applied to the case of capital accumulation. Assuming the new capital is initially usable in one sector only, say X, it will displace the value marginal product of labour schedule of that sector to the right. Thus in the short run the wage rate will increase, and so from equation (3) the rental in the relatively capital-intensive sector will increase by more than that in the other sector. Hence, assuming that both the initial and the new capital goods become mobile in the long run, capital will move into the relatively capital-intensive sector, until a new long-run equilibrium is attained where the original factor prices are restored. If X is the relatively capital-intensive sector, its output will increase both in the short and the long run. But if it is relatively labour intensive, its output must fall in the long run. Indeed, in the latter case, not only the proportional, but the absolute amount of capital in use in X will be less in the final long-run equilibrium than that quantity which it used before the initial capital accumulation.

3. SHORT-RUN AND LONG-RUN ADJUSTMENTS TO CHANGES IN FACTOR MARKET DISTORTIONS[5]

In this section we apply the same framework of analysis to an examination of the process of adjustment to a change in the level of a factor market distortion, such as a trade-union imposed wage differential or a sector-specific factor tax. We continue to assume that the economy has no influence over its terms of trade. Moreover we assume that the factor market distortion is introduced in a situation where factor markets are initially distortion free. This assumption, of no preexisting distortions, is a crucial one, and the consequences of relaxing it are examined in section 4.

We consider first the case of a wage differential, where the high-wage sector is relatively labour-intensive. In figure 4 the initial equilibrium is at A_0 and B_0, with the same wage rate prevailing in each sector.[6] Suppose now that workers in Y become unionised, and succeed in obtaining a wage which exceeds that in the X sector by a proportionate amount measured by the distortion parameter α:

$$w_Y = \alpha w_X \quad (\alpha > 1). \tag{4}$$

This change has no immediate effect on the V_X^0 and V_Y^0 schedules in the top half of figure 4: with an unchanged capital allocation they continue to represent the value marginal product of labour in each sector. However, the effect of the union action is to drive a wedge between the value marginal products which can prevail in equilibrium in each sector. Faced with the obligation to pay higher wages, entrepreneurs in the Y sector will shed labour, and so a new short-run equilibrium will be established where the ratio between the value marginal product of labour in the two sectors — that is, the ratio between the distance DE and CE — equals the distortion parameter, α. Clearly, the initial impact of the differential is, in qualitative terms, independent of the relative factor intensities of the two sectors: the wage in the unionised sector rises and that in the X sector falls, and each of these changes is less, proportionately, than the change in the differential.

Turning to the lower part of figure 4, one effect of the introduction of the wage differential is to shift the contract curve downwards as shown, since in long-run equilibrium the X sector now faces a lower effective wage rental ratio than the Y sector. The new distorted contract curve must therefore cut the initial capital allocation line, $K_X K_Y$, to the right of B_0. However, it cannot cut it at or to the right of the new short-run equilibrium point B_1, because the short-run fall in the X sector wage rate combined with the rise in the Y sector wage rate must at constant output prices lead to an intersectoral rental differential in favour of sector X; hence B_1 must lie below the distorted contract curve. From a similar reasoning to that in section 2, it follows that in the medium run capital will reallocate from the unionised sector Y into the X sector, moving the economy upwards and to the right along the labour market equilibrium locus through B_1; and as capital reallocates into the relatively capital-intensive sector the wage rate is reduced in both sectors, and the intersectoral rental differential is narrowed.

Where will the new long-run equilibrium occur? Evidently it must be at B_2, the intersection of the labour-market equilibrium locus and the distorted contract curve to the northeast of B_1, where the intersectoral rental differential is finally eliminated.[7] (The intersection to the southwest, at J, will be considered in the next section.) Moreover, as Magee (1971) has shown (and as will be demonstrated in the next section), the capital-labour ratio must fall in both sectors between the old and the new long-run equilibria; hence B_2 must lie above the ray $O_Y B_0$. It follows that the long-run effect of unionisation in the labour-intensive sector is to increase the rental and lower the wage in both sectors (implying that nonunion wages must fall by more than the proportional wage differential).[8] This of course is the well-known result, derived in various ways by Harberger (1962), Johnson and Mieszkowski (1970), Jones (1971a), and Magee (1971), that an increase in the differential paid to a factor in the sector which uses it intensively may—and, when commodity prices are constant, must—reduce the factor's reward in

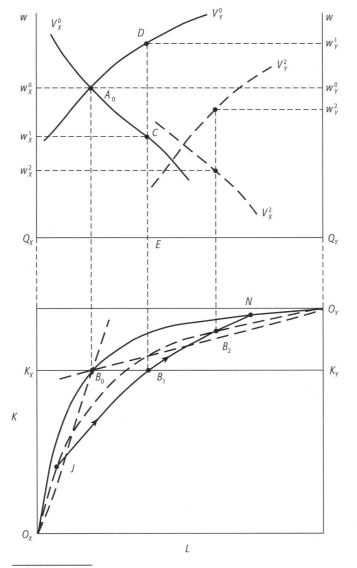

Figure 4

Short-run and long-run adjustments to the introduction of a wage differential in favour of the labour-intensive sector Y

both sectors. However, we have shown that this result is a long-run one only, for the short-run effect of the union action was to increase the wage in the Y sector. Hence, contrary to the implication of the result just mentioned, it may be perfectly rational for a union in a relatively labour-intensive sector to press for higher wages, if its discount rate is high enough, and the process of capital reallocation sufficiently slow. Similar results may be derived for the case where the unionised sector is relatively capital intensive: in the long run, labour in both sectors must gain, but once again a conflict between short-run and long-run interests arises, this time in the case of labour in X.

Finally, what can be said of distortions in the capital market, such as a corporate income tax of the kind studied by Harberger (1962)? The imposition of such a tax has no effect on resource allocation in the short run: since capital in the taxed sector is a fixed factor, its income amounts to a Marshallian quasi rent, the taxation of which will have no immediate impact on behaviour.[9] However, the resulting differential between the net rentals in the two sectors will lead eventually to a reallocation of capital away from the taxed sector. This shows an important difference between the short-run consequences of a capital and a labour tax, which follows from our assumption about the relative adjustment speeds of the two factors: the imposition of a capital market distortion has no immediate effect on resource allocation, whereas that of a labour market distortion leads to an immediate contraction of the sector obliged to pay the higher wage. In the long run, on the other hand, there is a basic symmetry between the two types of distortion, at fixed commodity prices, in the sense that qualitatively the same effects will follow the imposition of a tax (or a trade union differential) on labour in sector Y as will follow the granting of a *subsidy* to capital in the other sector.

NOTES

1. The timing and speed of this reallocation will depend on a variety of considerations including reallocation costs and entrepreneurial wage and price expectations. For a study which examines these aspects in greater detail, see Mussa (1975).

2. I am very grateful to Alasdair Smith, whose comments suggested a major simplification of the remainder of this section.

3. That is

$$\theta = \begin{vmatrix} \theta_{LX} & \theta_{LY} \\ \theta_{KX} & \theta_{KY} \end{vmatrix} = \begin{vmatrix} \theta_{LX} & \theta_{LY} \\ 1 - \theta_{LX} & 1 - \theta_{LY} \end{vmatrix} = \theta_{LX} - \theta_{LY}.$$

4. The point B_1 is above the new contract curve (not drawn) of the enlarged production box, since at B_1 the wage rental ratio in X exceeds that in Y.

5. Since this section was written, I have found a somewhat similar analysis in Hu (1973).

6. I am very grateful to Dermot McAleese, who pointed out a serious error in an earlier version of this diagram.

7. If the initial move from B_0 to B_1 had been caused by an increase in the relative price of X, the new long-run equilibrium would lie on the original efficiency locus at N. Thus, comparing a price change and a wage differential change, each of which has the same short-run effect, the long-run effect of the

price change is greater than that of the wage differential change. This is intuitively plausible, since wage costs are a smaller percentage of variable costs in the long run than in the short run.

8. This is another example of what Jones (1965) has called the "magnification effect" in the two-sector model with intersectoral capital mobility, which does not arise when capital is sector-specific.

9. As is well known, this statement is crucially dependent on the validity of the assumption of profit maximisation.

REFERENCES

Amano, A. 1977. Specific factors, comparative advantage, and international investment. *Economica* 44, 131–144.

Bhagwati, J. N. 1958. Immiserizing growth: A geometrical note. *Review of Economic Studies* 25, 201–205.

Bhagwati, J. N. 1973. The theory of immiserizing growth: Further applications. In *International Trade and Money*, M. Connolly and A. K. Swobada eds., pp. 45–54. London: Allen and Unwin.

Bhagwati, J. N., and Srinivasan, T. N. 1971. The theory of wage differentials: Production response and factor price equalization. *Journal of International Economics* 1, 19–35.

Brecher, R. A. 1974. Minimum wage rates and the pure theory of international trade. *Quarterly Journal of Economics* 88, 98–116.

Caves, R. E. 1971. International corporations: the industrial economics of foreign investment. *Economica* 38, 1–27.

Corden, W. M., and Findlay, R. 1975. Urban unemployment, intersectoral capital mobility and development policy. *Economica* 42, 59–78.

Ethier, W. 1974. Some of the theorems of international trade with many goods and factors. *Journal of International Economics* 4, 199–206.

Findlay, R., and Grubert, H. 1959. Factor intensities, technological progress and the terms of trade. *Oxford Economic Papers* 11, 111–121.

Hahn, F. H. 1965. On two sector growth models. *Review of Economic Studies* 32, 339–346.

Harberger, A. C. 1962. The incidence of the corporation income tax. *Journal of Political Economy* 70, 215–240.

Harris, J. R., and Todaro, M. P. 1970. Migration, unemployment and development: A two-sector analysis. *American Economic Review* 60, 126–142.

Helpman, E. 1976. Macroeconomic policy in a model of international trade with a wage restriction. *International Economic Review* 17, 262–277.

Hicks, J. R. 1953. An inaugural lecture: 2. The long-run dollar problem. *Oxford Economic Papers* 5, 121–135.

Hu, S. C. 1973. Capital mobility and the effects of unionization. *Southern Economic Journal* 39, 526–534.

Johnson, H. G. 1959. International trade, income distribution and the offer curve. *Manchester School of Economic and Social Studies* 27, 241–260.

Johnson, H. G. 1970. The efficiency and welfare implications of the international corporation. In *The International Corporation: A Symposium* C. P. Kindleberger ed. Cambridge: MIT Press.

Johnson, H. G., and Mieszkowski, P. M. 1970. The effects of unionization on the distribution of income: A general equilibrium approach. *Quarterly Journal of Economics* 84, 539–561.

Jones, R. W. 1965. The structure of simple general equilibrium models. *Journal of Political Economy* 73, 557–572.

Jones, R. W. 1971a. Distortions in factor markets and the general equilibrium model of production. *Journal of Political Economy* 79, 437–459.

Jones, R. W. 1971b. A three-factor model in theory, trade and history. In *Trade, Balance of Payments and Growth: Essays in Honor of C. P. Kindleberger*, ed. J. N. Bhagwati et al. Amsterdam: North Holland.

Jones, R. W. 1975. Income distribution and effective protection in a multi-commodity trade model. *Journal of Economic Theory* 11, 1–15.

Jones, R. W., and Corden, W. M. 1976. Devaluation, non-flexible prices, and the trade balance for a small country. *Canadian Journal of Economics* 9, 150–161.

Kemp, M. C., and Jones, R. W. 1962. Variable labour supply and the theory of international trade. *Journal of Political Economy* 70, 30–36.

Magee, S. P. 1971. Factor market distortions, production, distribution, and the pure theory of international trade. *Quarterly Journal of Economics* 86, 623–643.

Magee, S. P. 1976. *International Trade and Distortions in Factor Markets*. New York: Marcel Dekker.

Magee, S. P. 1977. Three simple tests of the Stolper-Samuelson theorem. The University of Texas at Austin, Graduate School of Business. Working Paper 77–28, February.

Martin, J. P. 1976. Variable factor supplies and the Heckscher-Ohlin-Samuelson model. *Economic Journal* 86, 820–831.

Mayer, W. 1974. Short-run and long-run equilibrium for a small open economy. *Journal of Political Economy* 82, 955–968.

McCulloch, R. 1976. Technology, trade and the interests of labor: A short run analysis of the development and international dissemination of new technology. Harvard Institute of Economic Research, Discussion Paper No. 489, June.

Mussa, M. 1974. Tariffs and the distribution of income: The importance of factor specificity, substitutability, and intensity in the short and long run. *Journal of Political Economy* 82, 1191–1204.

Mussa, M. 1975. Dynamic adjustment to relative price changes in the Heckscher-Ohlin-Samuelson model. University of Rochester, Department of Economics. Discussion Paper No. 75–6, May. *Journal of Political Economy* 86 (1978), 775–791.

Neary, J. P. 1977. On the Harris-Todaro model with intersectoral capital mobility. Nuffield College, Oxford. Mimeo, July. *Economica* 48 (1981), 219–234.

Neary, J. P. 1978a. Capital subsidies and employment in an open economy. *Oxford Economic Papers* 30, 334–356.

Neary, J. P. 1978b. Dynamic stability and the theory of factor market distortions. *American Economic Review* 69, 671–682.

Rybczynski, T. N. 1955. Factor endowments and relative commodity prices, *Economica* 22, 336–341.

Samuelson, P. A. 1971a. An exact Hume-Ricardo-Marshall model of international trade. *Journal of International Economics* 1, 1–18.

Samuelson, P. A. 1971b. Ohlin was right. *Swedish Journal of Economics* 73, 365–384.

Stolper, W. F., and Samuelson, P. A. 1941. Protection and real wages. *Review of Economic Studies* 9, 58–73.

Woodland, A. D. 1977. A dual approach to equilibrium in the production sector in international trade theory. *Canadian Journal of Economics* 10, 50–68.

ABOUT THE AUTHOR

J. Peter Neary

Born 1950 in Drogheda, Ireland; educated at University College Dublin and Oxford University; Professor of Political Economy at University College Dublin since 1980. I have written many (though not enough) papers on international trade and served on many (too many) professional committees and editorial boards. I have paid extended visits to quite a few universities in the United States, Canada, and Europe, but for personal reasons have always preferred to live in Ireland. Perhaps there are professional gains too; as Saul Bellow said of Chicago, it is far from the beaten track and, by the time new ideas reach there, they are old and their holes are easily seen through!

Editor's Queries

What are the major unresolved questions of international economics? What are likely to be the hot topics of the next decade?   Although we have made a lot of progress, I still feel we do not know nearly enough about the effects of trade on efficiency and about the interaction between trade and growth, especially non-steady-state growth. As for future hot topics, I suspect that the current vogue for empirical work will continue unabated (though it may degenerate into fad for empirical embellishments of theoretical papers); and that both real-world trends and the internal logic of the subject will prompt further work on globalization, fragmentation of production, and agglomeration.

What advice do you have to offer graduate students in the field of international economics?   This is hard to answer without sounding like Polonius's advice to his son ("Neither a borrower nor a lender be") or the instruction to exam candidates in *1066 and All That* ("Do not write on both sides of the paper at once"). Seriously though, let me make a few suggestions. Read the literature, but think about the world; learn as much technique as you can, but use as little as you need to prove your results; never forget that trade theory is just a branch of microeconomics, but keep in mind that it is a distinct branch (so, for example, merely translating a general micro paper to a trade context rarely makes a lasting contribution); above all, write as clearly as possible: there is no surer way of increasing your readership and maybe even improving your own thought processes.

International Economics

HECKSCHER-OHLIN MODEL
OF INTERNATIONAL COMPETITION

Paul A. Samuelson

Ronald W. Jones

Alan V. Deardorff

Donald R. Davis

Jagdish N. Bhagwati

Harry P. Bowen, Edward E. Leamer, and Leo Sveikauskas

Edward E. Leamer

Daniel Trefler

Robert Z. Lawrence and Matthew J. Slaughter

Edward E. Leamer

International Economics

International Factor-Price Equalisation Once Again

PAUL A. SAMUELSON

1. INTRODUCTION

My recent paper attempting to show that free commodity trade will, under certain speci-fied conditions, inevitably lead to complete factor-price equalisation appears to be in need of further amplification.[1] I propose therefore (1) to restate the principal theorem, (2) to expand upon its intuitive demonstration, (3) to settle the matter definitively by a brief but rigorous mathematical demonstration, (4) to make a few extensions to the case of many commodities and factors, and finally (5) to comment briefly upon some realistic qualifications to its simplified assumptions.

I cannot pretend to present a balanced appraisal of the bearing of this analysis upon interpreting the actual world, because my own mind is not made up on this question: on the one hand, I think it would be folly to come to any startling conclusions on the basis of so simplified a model and such abstract reasoning; but on the other hand, strong simple cases often point the way to an element of truth present in a complex situation. Still, at the least, we ought to be clear in our deductive reasoning; and the elucidation of this side of the problem plus the qualifying discussion may contribute towards an ultimate appraisal of the theorem's realism and relevance.

2. STATEMENT OF THE THEOREM

My hypotheses are as follows:

1. There are but two countries, America and Europe.

2. They produce but two commodities, food and clothing.

3. Each commodity is produced with two factors of production, land and labour. The production functions of each commodity show "constant returns to scale," in the sense that changing all inputs in the same proportion changes output in that same proportion, leaving all "productivities" essentially unchanged. In short, all production functions are mathemati-cally "homogeneous of the first order" and subject to Euler's theorem.

4. The law of diminishing marginal productivity holds: as any one input is increased rel-ative to other inputs, its marginal productivity diminishes.

Reprinted with permission from Paul A. Samuelson, "International Factor-Price Equalisation Once Again," *The Economic Journal:* (1949), vol. 59, pp. 181–197. © 1949 by Blackwell Publishers.

5. The commodities differ in their "labour and land intensities." Thus, food is relatively "land using" or "land intensive," while clothing is relatively "labour intensive." This means that whatever the prevailing ratio of wages to rents, the optimal proportion of labour to land is greater in clothing than in food.

6. Land and labour are assumed to be qualitatively identical inputs in the two countries, and the technological production functions are assumed to be the same in the two countries.

7. All commodities move perfectly freely in international trade, without encountering tariffs or transport costs, and with competition effectively equalising the market price-ratio of food and clothing. No factors of production can move between the countries.

8. Something is being produced in both countries of both commodities with both factors of production. Each country may have moved in the direction of specialising on the commodity for which it has a comparative advantage, but it has not moved so far as to be specialising completely on one commodity.[2]

All of this constitutes the hypothesis of the theorem. The conclusion states:

> Under these conditions, real factor prices must be exactly the same in both countries (and indeed the proportion of inputs used in food production in America must equal that in Europe, and similarly for clothing production).

Our problem is from now on a purely logical one. Is "If H, then inevitably C" a correct statement? The issue is not whether C (factor-price equalisation) will actually hold; nor even whether H (the hypothesis) is a valid empirical generalisation. It is whether C can fail to be true when H is assumed true. Being a logical question, it admits of only one answer: either the theorem is true or it is false.

One may wonder why such a definite problem could have given rise to misunderstanding. The answer perhaps lies in the fact that even so simple a setup as this one involves more than a dozen economic variables: at least four inputs for each country, four marginal productivities for each country (marginal productivity of American labour in food, of American land in food ...), two outputs for each country, the prices of the two commodities, the price in each country of the two inputs, the proportions of the inputs in different lines of production, and so forth. It is not always easy for the intellect to move purposefully in a hyperspace of many dimensions.

And the problem is made worse by the fact, insufficiently realised, that constant returns to scale is a very serious limitation on the production functions. A soon as one knows a single "curve" on such a surface, all other magnitudes are frozen into exact quantitative shapes and cannot be chosen at will. Thus, if one knows the returns of total product to labour working on one acre of land, then one already knows everything: the marginal productivity schedule of land, all the iso-product curves, the marginal-rate-of-substitution schedules, and so forth. This means one must use a carefully graduated ruler in drawing the different economic functions, making sure that they are numerically consistent in addition to their having plausible qualitative shapes.

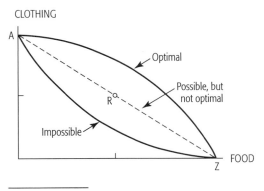

CLOTHING

Optimal

Possible, but
not optimal

Impossible

FOOD

Figure 3.1

3. Intuitive Proof

In each country there is assumed to be given totals of labour and land. If all resources are devoted to clothing, we get a certain maximum amount of clothing. If all are devoted to food production, we get a certain maximum amount of food. But what will happen if we are willing to devote only part of all land and part of total labour to the production of food, the rest being used in clothing production? Obviously, then we are in effect sacrificing some food in order to get some clothing. The iron law of scarcity tells us that we cannot have all we want of both goods but must ultimately give up something of one good in getting some of another.

In short there is a best "production possibility," or "transformation" curve showing us the maximum obtainable amount of one commodity for each amount of the other [figure 3.1]. Such a production possibility schedule was drawn up for each country in figure 1.1 of my earlier article. And in each case it was made to be a curve *convex* from above, so that the more you want of any good the greater is the cost, at the margin, in terms of the other good. This convexity property is very important and is related to the law of diminishing marginal productivity. Few readers had any qualms about accepting convexity, but perhaps some did not realise its far-reaching implications in showing why the factor-price equalisation theorem had to be true. I propose, therefore, to show why the production possibility curve must obviously be convex (looked at from above).[3]

To show that convexity—or increasing relative marginal costs must hold—it is sufficient for the present purpose to show that concavity, or decreasing marginal costs, involves an impossible contradiction. Now at the very worst, it is easily shown we can move along a straight-line opportunity cost line between the two axes. For suppose we agree to give up half of the maximum obtainable amount of food. How much clothing can we be sure of getting? If we send out the crudest type of order that "half of all labour and half of all land is to be shifted to clothing production," we will (because of the assumption of constant returns to scale) *exactly halve* food production; and we will acquire *exactly half* of the maximum amount of clothing producible with all resources. Therefore, we end up at a point R, exactly half-way between the limiting points A and Z. Similarly, if we decide to give up 10, 20, 30, or 90 percent of the maximum amount of food producible, we can give out crude orders to transfer exactly 10, 20, 30, or 90 percent of *both* inputs from food to clothing. Because of constant returns to scale, it follows that we can be sure of getting 90, 80, 70, or 10 percent of maximum clothing.

In short, by giving such crude down-the-line orders that transfer both resources *always in the same proportion*, we can at worst travel along a straight line between the two limiting intercepts. Any concave curve would necessarily lie inside such a constant-cost straight line and can therefore be ruled out: hence decreasing (marginal, opportunity) costs are incompatible with the assumption of constant returns to scale.

But of course we can usually do even better than the straight-line case. A neophyte bureaucrat might be satisifed to give crude down-the-line orders, but there exist more efficient ways of giving up food for clothing. This is where social-economist (or "welfare economist") can supplement the talents of the mere technician who knows how best to use inputs in the production of any one good and nothing else. There are an infinity of ways of giving up, say, 50 percent of good: we may simply give up labour land, constant percentages of labour and land, or still other proportions. But there will be only one best way to do so, only one best combination of labour and land that is to be transferred. Best in what sense? Best in the sense of getting for us the maximum obtainable amount of clothing, compatible with our preassigned decision to sacrifice a given amount of food.

Intuition tells us that, qualitatively, we should transfer a larger proportion of labour than of land to clothing production. This is because clothing is the labour-intensive commodity by our original hypothesis. This means that the proportion of labour to land is actually declining in the food line as its production declines. What about the proportion of labour to land in clothing production? At first we were able to be generous in sparing labour, which after all was not "too well adapted" for food production. But now, when we come to give up still more food, there is less labour left in food production relative to land; hence, we cannot contrive to be quite so generous in transferring further labour to clothing production. As we expand clothing production further, the proportion of labour to land must also be falling in that line; but the labour-land ratio never falls to as low as the level appropriate for food, the land-intensive commodity.[4]

Intuition tells us that by following an optimal pattern which recognises the difference in factor intensities of the two goods, we can end up on a production possibility curve that is bloated out beyond a constant-cost straight line: in short, on a production possibility curve that is convex, obeying the law of increasing marginal costs of one good as it is expanded at the expense of the other good. Or, to put the same thing in the language of the marketplace, as the production of clothing expands, upward pressure is put on the price of the factor it uses most intensively — on wages relative to land rent. An increase in the ratio of wages to rent must in a competitive market press up the price of the labour-intensive commodity relative to the land-intensive commodity.

This one-directional relationship between relative factor prices and relative commodity prices is an absolute necessity, and it is vital for the recognition of the truth in the main theorem. Let me elaborate therefore upon the market mechanism bringing it about. Under perfect competition everywhere within a domestic market there will be set up a uniform ratio of wages to rents. In the food industry there will be one, and only one, optimal proportion of labour to land; any attempt to combine productive factors in proportions that deviate from the optimum will be penalised by losses, and there will be set up a process of corrective adaptation. The same competitive forces will force an adaptation of the input proportion in clothing production, with equilibrium being attained only when the input proportions are such as to equate exactly the ratio of the physical marginal productivities of the factors (the "marginal rate of substitution" of labour for land in clothing production) to the ratio of factor prices prevailing in the market. The price mechanism has an unconscious wisdom. As if led by an invisible hand, it causes the economic system to move out to the optimal production possibility curve. Through the intermediary of a common market factor-price ratio, the marginal rates of substitution of the factors become the same in both industries. And it is this marginal condition which intuition (as well as geometry and mathematics) tells us prescribes the optimal allocation of resources so as to yield maximum output. Not only does expanding clothing production result in the earlier described qualitative pattern of dilution of the ratio of labour to land in both occupations; more than that, a price system is one way of achieving the exactly optimal quantitative degree of change in proportions.

I have established unequivocally the following facts:

> Within any country: (a) an increase in the ratio of wages to rents will cause a definite decrease in the proportion of labour to land in both industries; (b) to each determinate state of factor proportion in the two industries there will correspond one, and only one, commodity price ratio and a unique configuration of wages and rent; and (c) the change in factor proportions incident to an increase in wages/rents must be followed by a one-directional increase in clothing prices relative to food prices.

An acute reader may try to run ahead of the argument and may be tempted to assert: "But all this holds for one country, as of a given total factor endowment. Your established chain of causation is only from factor prices (and factor proportions) to commodity prices. Are you entitled to reverse the causation and to argue that the same commodity-price ratio must—even in countries of quite different total factor endowments—lead back to a common unique factor-price ratio, a common unique way of combining the inputs in the food and clothing industries, and a common set of absolute factor prices and marginal productivities?"

My answer is yes. This line of reasoning is absolutely rigorous. It is only proportions that matter, not scale. In such a perfectly competitive market each small association of factors (or firms, if one prefers that word) feels free to hire as many or as few extra factors as it likes. It neither knows nor cares anything about the totals for society. It is like a group of molecules in a perfect gas which is everywhere in thermal equilibrium. The

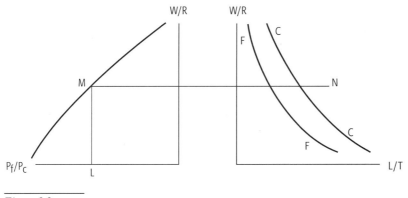

Figure 3.2

molecules in any one small region behave in the same way regardless of the size of the room around them. A sample observed in the middle of a huge spherical room would act in the same way as a similar sample observed within a small rectangular room. Similarly, if we observe the behaviour of a representative firm in one country it will be exactly the same in all essentials as a representative firm taken from some other country—regardless of the difference in total factor amounts and relative industrial concentration—provided only that factor-price ratios are really the same in the two markets.[5]

All this follows from the italicised conclusion reached just above, especially from (3) taken in conjunction with (1) and (2).

This really completes the intuitive demonstration of the theorem. The same international commodity price ratio, must—so long as both commodities are being produced and priced at marginal costs—enable us to infer backwards a unique factor-price ratio, a unique set of factor proportions, and even a unique set of absolute wages and rents.

All this is summarised in the chart [figure 3.2]. On the right-hand side I have simply duplicated figure 1.2 of my earlier paper. On the left-hand side I have added a chart showing the one-directional relation of commodity prices to factor prices.[6] As wages fall relative to rents the price of food is shown to rise relative to clothing in a monotonic fashion. The accompanying chart applies to either country and—so long as neither country is specialising completely—its validity is independent of their differing factor endowments. It follows that when we specify a common price ratio (say at L), we can move backward unambiguously (from M to N, etc.) to a common factor-price ratio and to a common factor proportion setup in the two countries.

4. MATHEMATICAL PROOF

Now that the theorem has been demonstrated by commonsense reasoning, let me confirm it by more rigorous mathematical proof. The condition of equilibrium can be written in a variety of ways, and can be framed so as to involve more than a dozen equations. For example, let me call America's four marginal physical productivities—of labour in food, of land in food, of labour in clothing, of land in clothing—a, b, c, and d. I use Greek letters—α, β, γ, δ—to designate the corresponding marginal productivities in Europe. Then we can end up with a number of equilibrium expressions of the form

$$\frac{a}{b} = \frac{c}{d}, \quad \frac{\alpha}{\beta} = \frac{\gamma}{\delta}, \quad \frac{a}{c} = \frac{\alpha}{\gamma}, \dots, \text{etc.}$$

A number of economists have tortured themselves trying to manipulate these expressions so as to result in $a = \alpha$, etc., or at least in $a/b = \alpha/\beta$, etc. No proof of this kind is possible. The essential thing is that these numerous marginal productivities are by no means independent. Because proportions rather than scale are important, knowledge of the behaviour of the marginal productivity of labour tells us exactly what to expect of the marginal-productivity schedule of land. This is because increasing the amount of labour with land held constant is equivalent to reducing land with labour held constant.[7]

Mathematically, instead of writing food production, F, as any joint function of labour devoted to it, L_f, and of land, T_f, we can write it as

$$F = F(L_f, T_f) = T_f f\left(\frac{L_f}{T_f}\right), \tag{1}$$

where the function f can be thought of as the returns of food on one unit of land, and where the number of units of land enters as a scale factor. The form of this function is the same for both countries, and there is, of course, a similar type of function holding for cloth production, C, in terms of L_c and T_c namely

$$C = C(L_c, T_c) = T_c c\left(\frac{L_c}{T_c}\right). \tag{2}$$

It is easy to show mathematically, by simple partial differentiation of (1), the following relations among marginal physical productivities:

$$\text{MPP labour in food} = \frac{\partial F}{\partial L_f} = f'\left(\frac{L_f}{T_f}\right),$$

where f' represents the derivative of f and depicts the schedule of marginal product of labour (working on one unit of land). This must be a declining schedule according to our hypothesis of diminishing returns, so that we must have

$$f''\left(\frac{L_f}{T_f}\right) < 0.$$

By direct differentiation of (1), or by use of Euler's theorem, or by use of the fact the marginal product of land can also be identified as a rent residual, we easily find that

$$\text{MPP land in food} = \frac{\partial F}{\partial T_f} = f\left(\frac{L_f}{T_f}\right) - \frac{L_f}{T_f} f'\left(\frac{L_f}{T_f}\right) = g\left(\frac{L_f}{T_f}\right),$$

where g is the name for the rent residual. It is easy to show that

$$g'\left(\frac{L_f}{T_f}\right) = -\frac{L_f}{T_f} f''\left(\frac{L_f}{T_f}\right)$$

By similar reasoning, we may write the marginal productivity of land in clothing production in its proper relation to that of labour:

$$\text{MPP labour in clothing} = \frac{\partial C}{\partial L_c} = c'\left(\frac{L_c}{T_c}\right)$$

$$\text{MPP land in clothing} = \frac{\partial C}{\partial T_c} = c\left(\frac{L_c}{T_c}\right) - \frac{L_c}{T_c} c'\left(\frac{L_c}{T_c}\right) = h\left(\frac{L_c}{T_c}\right)$$

$$h'\left(\frac{L_c}{T_c}\right) = -\frac{L_c}{T_c} c''\left(\frac{L_c}{T_c}\right)$$

The art of analysis in these problems is to select out the essential variables so as to reduce our equilibrium equations to the simplest form. Without specifying which country we are talking about, we certainly can infer from the fact that something of both goods is being produced with both factors the following conditions:

Real wages (or labour marginal "value" productivities) must be the same in food and clothing production when expressed in terms of a common *measure,* such as clothing; the same is true of real rents (or land marginal "value" productivities). Or

$$\left(P_f\right)\binom{\text{MPP labour}}{\text{in food}} = \left(P_c\right)\binom{\text{MPP labour}}{\text{in clothing}}$$

$$\left(P_f\right)\binom{\text{MPP land}}{\text{in food}} = \left(P_c\right)\binom{\text{MPP land}}{\text{in clothing}},$$

which can be written in terms of previous notation as

$$\left(\frac{P_f}{P_c}\right) f'\left(\frac{L_f}{T_f}\right) - c'\left(\frac{L_c}{T_c}\right) = 0$$

$$\left(\frac{P_f}{P_c}\right)\left[f\left(\frac{L_f}{T_f}\right) - \frac{L_f}{T_f} f'\left(\frac{L_f}{T_f}\right)\right] - \left[c\left(\frac{L_c}{T_c}\right) - \frac{L_c}{T_c} c'\left(\frac{L_c}{T_c}\right)\right] = 0.^8$$

Now these are two equations in the three variables L_f/T_f, L_c/T_c, and P_f/P_c. If we take the latter price ratio as given to us by international-demand conditions, we are left with *two* equations to determine the *two* unknown factor proportions. This is a solvent situation, and we should normally expect the result to be determinate.

But a purist might still have doubts: "How do you know that these two equations or schedules might not twist around and intersect in multiple equilibria?" Fortunately, the answer is simple and definite. On our hypothesis, any equilibrium configuration turns out to be absolutely unique. We may leave to a technical footnote the detailed mathematical proof of this fact.[9]

5. MULTIPLE COMMODITIES AND FACTORS

Adding a third or further commodities does not alter our analysis much. If anything, it increases the likelihood of complete factor-price equalisation. For all that we require is that at least *two* commodities are simultaneously being produced in both countries and then our previous conclusion follows. If we add a third commodity which is very much like either of our present commodities, we are not changing the situation materially. But if we add new commodities which are more extreme in their labour-land intensities, then we greatly increase the chance that two regions with very different factor endowments can still come into complete factor-price equalisation. A "queer" region is not penalised for being queer if there is queer work that needs doing.

I do not wish at this time to go into the technical mathematics of the n commodity, and r factor case. But it can be said that (1) so long as the two regions are sufficiently close together in factor proportions, (2) so long as the goods differ in factor intensities, and (3) so long as the number of goods, n, is greater than the number of factors, r, we can hope to experience complete factor-price equalisation. On the other hand, if complete specialisation takes place it will do so for a whole collection of goods, the dividing line between exports and imports being a variable one depending upon reciprocal international demand (acting on factor prices) as in the classical theory of comparative advantage with multiple commodities.[10]

When we add a third productive factor and retain but two commodities, then the whole presumption towards factor-price equalisation disappears. Suppose American labour and American land have more capital to work with than does European labour and land. It is then quite possible that the marginal physical productivities of labour and land might be double that of Europe in both commodities. Obviously, commodity-price *ratios* would still be equal, production of both commodities will be taking place, but nonetheless absolute factor prices (or relative for that matter) need not be moved towards equality. This is our general expectation wherever the number of factors exceeds the number of commodities.

6. THE CONDITIONS OF COMPLETE SPECIALISATION

If complete specialisation takes place in one country, then our hypothesis is not fulfilled, and the conclusion does not follow. How important is this empirically, and when can we expect complete specialisation to take place? As discussed earlier, the answer depends upon how disparate are the initial factor endowments of the two regions—how disparate in comparison with the differences in factor intensities of the two commodities.[11]

Unless the two commodities differ extraordinarily in factor intensities, the production possibility curve will be by no means so convex as it is usually drawn in the neoclassical literature of international trade, where it usually resembles a quarter circle whose slope ranges the spectrum from zero to infinity. It should rather have the crescentlike shape of the new moon. Opportunity costs tend to be more nearly constant than I had previously realised. This is a step in the direction of the older classical theory of comparative advantage. But with this important difference: the same causes that tend to produce *constant* costs also tend to produce *uniform* cost ratios between nations, which is not at all in the spirit of classical theory. (Undoubtedly much of the specialisation observed in the real world is due to something different from all this, namely decreasing-cost indivisibilities, tempered and counteracted by the existence of localised resources specifically adapted to particular lines of production.)

A parable may serve the double purpose of showing the range of factor endowment incompatible with complete specialisation and of removing any lingering element of paradox surrounding the view that commodity mobility may be a perfect substitute for factor mobility.

Let us suppose that in the beginning all factors were perfectly mobile, and nationalism had not yet reared its ugly head. Spatial transport costs being of no importance, there would be one world price of food and clothing, one real wage, one real rent, and the world's land and labour would be divided between food and clothing production in a determinate way, with uniform proportions of labour to land being used everywhere in clothing production, and with a much smaller—but uniform—proportion of labour to land being used in production of food.

Now suppose that an angel came down from heaven and notified some fraction of all the labour and land units producing clothing that they were to be called Americans, the rest to be called Europeans; and some different fraction of the food industry that henceforth they were to carry American passports. Obviously, just giving people and areas national labels does not alter anything: it does not change commodity or factor prices or production patterns.

But now turn a recording geographer loose, and what will he report? Two countries with quite different factor proportions, but with identical real wages and rents and identical modes of commodity production (though with different relative importances of food and clothing industries). Depending upon whether the angel makes up America by concentrating primarily on clothing units or on food units, the geographer will report a very high or a very low ratio of labour to land in the newly synthesised "country." But this he will never find: that the ratio of labour to land should ever exceed the proportions characteristic of the most labour-intensive industry (clothing) or ever fall short of the proportions of the least labour-intensive industry. Both countries *must* have factor proportions intermediate between the proportions in the two industries.

The angel can create a country with proportions *not* intermediate between the factor intensities of food and clothing. But he cannot do so by following the above-described procedure, which was calculated to leave prices and production unchanged. If he wrests some labour in food production away from the land it has been working with, "sending" this labour to Europe and keeping it from working with the American land, then a substantive change in production and prices will have been introduced. Unless there are abnormal repercussions on the pattern of effective demand, we can expect one or both of the countries to specialise completely and real wages to fall in Europe relative to America in one or both commodities, with European real rents behaving in an opposite fashion. The extension of this parable to the many-commodities case may be left to the interested reader.

7. SOME QUALIFICATIONS

A number of qualifications to this theoretical argument are in order. In the first place, goods do not move without transport costs; and to the extent that commodity prices are not equalised, it of course follows that factor prices will not tend to be fully equalised. Also, as I indicated in my earlier article, there are many reasons to doubt the usefulness of assuming identical production functions and categories of inputs in the two countries; and consequently, it is dangerous to draw sweeping practical conclusions concerning factor-price equalisation.

What about the propriety of assuming constant returns to scale? In justice to Ohlin, it should be pointed out that he, more than almost any other writer, has followed up the lead of Adam Smith and made *increasing returns* an important cause for trade. It is true that increasing returns *may* at the same time create difficulties for the survival of perfect competition, difficulties which cannot always be sidestepped by pretending that the increasing returns are due primarily to *external* rather than internal economies. But these difficulties do not give us the right to deny or neglect the importance of scale factors.[12] Where scale is important it is obviously possible for real wages to differ greatly between large free-trade areas and small ones, even with the same relative endowments of productive factors. And while it may have been rash of me to draw a moral concerning the worth of emigration from Europe out of an abstract simplified model, I must still record the view that the more realistic deviations from constant returns to scale and the actual production functions encountered in practice are likely to reinforce rather than oppose the view that high standards of life are possible in densely populated areas such as the island of Manhattan or the United Kingdom.

There is no ironclad a priori necessity for the law of diminishing marginal productivity to be valid for either or both commodities.[13] In such cases the usual marginal conditions of equilibrium are replaced by inequalities, and we have a boundary maximum in which we go the limit and use zero of one of the inputs in one industry. If it still could be shown that one commodity is always more labour intensive than the other, then the main theorem would probably still be true. But it is precisely in these pathological cases that factor intensities may become alike or reverse themselves, giving rise to the difficulties discussed in note 6.

In conclusion, some of these qualifications help us to reconcile results of abstract analysis with the obvious facts of life concerning the extreme diversity of productivity and factor prices in different regions of the world. Men receive lower wages in some countries than in others for a variety of reasons: because they are different by birth or training; because their effective know-how is limited and the manner of their being combined with other productive factors is not optimal; because they are confined to areas too small to develop the full economies of scale; because some goods and materials cannot be brought to them freely from other parts of the world, as a result of natural or man-made obstacles; and finally because the technological diversity of commodities with respect to factor intensities is not so great in comparison with the diversity of regional factor endowments to emancipate labourers from the penalty of being confined to regions lacking in natural resources. In the face of these hard facts it would be rash to consider the existing distribution of population to be optimal in any sense, or to regard free trade as a panacea for the present geographical inequalities.

NOTES

1. International trade and the equalisation of factor prices, *Economic Journal* 58 (June 1948), pp. 163–184. I learn from Professor Lionel Robbins that A. P. Lerner, while a student at LSE, dealt with this problem. I have had a chance to look over Lerner's mimeographed report, dated December 1933, and it is a masterly, definitive treatment of the question, difficulties and all.

2. Actually we may admit the limiting case of "incipient specialisation," where nothing is being produced of one of the commodities, but where it is a matter of indifference whether an infinitesimal amount is or is not being produced, so that price and marginal costs are equal.

3. I am indebted for this line of reasoning to my colleague at MIT, Professor Robert L. Bishop, who for some years has been using it on beginning students in economics, with no noticeable disastrous effects. This proof is suggestive only, but it could easily be made rigorous.

4. Some readers may find it paradoxical that — with a fixed ratio of total labour to total land — we nevertheless lower the ratio of labour to land *in both industries* as a result of producing more of the labour-intensive good and less of the other. Such readers find it hard to believe that men's wages and women's wages can both go up at the same time that average wages are going down. They forget that there is an inevitable shift in the industries' weights used to compute the average-factor ratio. Really to understand all this, the reader must be referred to the Edgeworth box-diagram depicted in W. F. Stolper and P. A. Samuelson, Protection and real wages, *Review of Economic Studies* 9 (1941): 58–73.

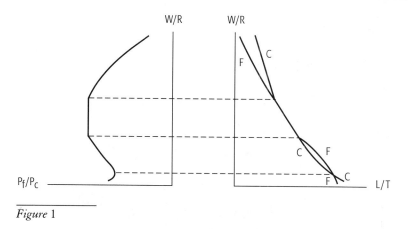

Figure 1

5. The representative firm concept is in the case of homogeneous production functions not subject to the usual difficulties associated with the Marshallian concept; in this case, it should be added, the "scale" of the firm is indeterminate and, fortunately, irrelevant.

6. The left-hand curve is drawn in a qualitatively correct fashion. Actually its exact quantitative shape is determined by the two right-hand curves; but the chart is *not* exact in its quantitative details.

We may easily illustrate the importance of point 5 of our hypothesis, which insists on differences in factor intensities. Consider the depicted pathological case which does not meet the requirements of our hypothesis, and in which factor intensities are for a range identical, and in still other regions food becomes the labour-intensive good [figure 1, above]. The resulting pattern of commodity prices does *not* necessarily result in factor-price equalisation. Compare figure 1.3 of my earlier article.

7. J. B. Clark recognised in his *Distribution of Wealth* that the "upper triangle" of his labour-marginal-pro-ductivity diagram must correspond to the "rectangle" of his other-factors diagram. But his draughtsman did *not* draw the curve accordingly! This is a mistake that Philip Wicksteed in his *Co-ordination of the Laws of Distribution* (London School of Economics Reprint) could not have made. Clark, a believer in Providence, was unaware of the blessing—in the form of Euler's theorem on homogeneous functions—that made his theory possible. Wicksteed, a man of the cloth, appreciated and interpreted the generosity of Nature. Compare also F. H. Knight, *Risk, Uncertainty and Profit*, chap. 4, for a partial treatment of these reciprocal relations. G. J. Stigler, *Production and Distribution Theories: The Formative Period*, gives a valuable treatment of Wicksteed's theory as exposited by Flux and others.

8. In terms of our earlier $a, b, ..., \alpha, \beta, ...,$ these equations are of the form

$$\frac{P_f}{P_c} a = c, \qquad \frac{P_f}{P_c} b = d, \qquad \text{etc.}$$

9. The Implicit Function Theorem tells us that two suitably continuous equations of the form $W_1(y_1, y_2) = 0 = W_2(y_1, y_2)$, possessing a solution (y_1^0, y_2^0), cannot have any other solution provided

$$\Delta = \begin{vmatrix} \dfrac{\partial W_1}{\partial y_1} & \dfrac{\partial W_1}{\partial y_2} \\ \dfrac{\partial W_2}{\partial y_1} & \dfrac{\partial W_2}{\partial y_2} \end{vmatrix} \neq 0.$$

In this case, where $y_1 = L_f/T_f$, etc., it is easy to show that

$$
\Delta = \begin{vmatrix} \dfrac{P_f}{P_c} f'' & -c'' \\[2ex] -\dfrac{P_f}{P_c} \dfrac{L_f}{T_f} f'' & +\dfrac{L_c}{T_c} c'' \end{vmatrix} = \dfrac{P_f}{P_c} f'' c'' \left[\dfrac{L_c}{T_c} - \dfrac{L_f}{T_f} \right].
$$

By hypothesis of diminishing returns, f'' and c'' are negative, and the term in brackets (representing the respective labour intensities in food and clothing) cannot be equal to zero. Hence, the equilibrium is unique. As developed earlier, if the factor intensities become equal, or reverse themselves, the one-to-one relation between commodity and factor prices *must* be ruptured.

10. The real wage of every resource must be the same in every place that it is used, when expressed in a common denominator. This gives us $r(n - 1)$ independent equations involving the $(n - 1)$ commodity-price ratios and the $n(r - 1)$ factor proportions. If $n = r$, we have a determinate system once the goods-price ratios are given. If $n > r$, we have the same result, but now the international price ratios cannot be presented arbitrarily as there are constant-cost paths on the production possibility locus, with one blade of Marshall's scissors doing most of the cutting, so to speak. If $n < r$, it is quite possible for free commodity trade to exist alongside continuing factor-price differentials. It is never enough simply to count equations and unknowns. In addition we must make sure that there are not multiple solutions: that factor intensities in the different commodities and the laws of returns are such as to lead to a one-to-one relationship between commodity prices and factor prices.

11. The reader may be referred to the earlier paper's discussion of figures 1 and 2, with respect to "step-like formations" and overlap.

12. Statical increasing returns is related to, but analytically distinct from, these irreversible cost economies induced by expansion and experimentation and which provide the justification for "infant industry" protection. Statical increasing returns might justify permanent judicious protection but not protection all around, since our purpose in bringing about large-scale production is to achieve profitable trade and consumption.

    One other point needs stressing. For very small outputs, increasing returns to scale may take place without affecting the above analysis, provided that total demand is large enough to carry production into the realm of constant returns to scale. Increasing the "extent of the market" not only increases specialisation, it also increases the possibility of viable pure competition.

13. A "Pythagorean" production function of the form $F = \sqrt{L^2 + T^2}$ is an example of such a homogeneous function with increasing marginal productivity. So long as neither factor is to have a negative marginal productivity, *average* product must not be rising; but this is quite another thing. Surprisingly enough, the production possibility curve may still be convex with increasing marginal productivity. I have been asked whether any essential difference would be introduced by the assumption that one of the commodities, such as clothing, uses no land at all, or negligible land. Diminishing returns would still affect food as more of the transferable factor is added to the now specific factor of land, but no essential modifications in our conclusions are introduced.

ABOUT THE AUTHOR

Paul A. Samuelson

Paul A. Samuelson won the Nobel Prize in economics in 1970. He has been on the faculty of the Massachusetts Institute of Technology since 1941. As adviser to Presidents Kennedy and Johnson, he helped shape the tax legislation and antipoverty efforts of the 1960s. A supporter of Keynesian economics, he is well known for his book *Economics* (1948; 12th edition, 1985), a widely used textbook for many years.

The Structure of Simple General Equilibrium Models

University of Rochester

I. INTRODUCTION

It is difficult to find any major branch of applied economics that has not made some use of the simple general equilibrium model of production. For years this model has served as the work horse for most of the developments in the pure theory of international trade. It has been used to study the effects of taxation on the distribution of income and the impact of technological change on the composition of outputs and the structure of prices. Perhaps the most prominent of its recent uses is to be found in the neoclassical theory of economic growth.

Such intensive use of the simple two-sector model of production suggests that a few properties are being retranslated in such diverse areas as public finance, international trade, and economic growth. The unity provided by a common theoretical structure is further emphasized by the dual relationship that exists between sets of variables in the model itself. Traditional formulations of the model tend to obscure this feature. My purpose in this article is to analyze the structure of the simple competitive model of production in a manner designed to highlight both the dual relationship and the similarity that exists among a number of traditional problems in comparative statics and economic growth.

The model is described in Sections II and III. In Section IV I discuss the dual nature of two theorems in the theory of international trade associated with the names of Stolper and Samuelson on the one hand and Rybczynski on the other. A simple demand relationship is added in Section V, and a problem in public finance is analyzed—the effect of excise subsidies or taxes on relative commodity and factor prices. The static model of production is then reinterpreted as a neoclassical model of economic growth by letting

I am indebted to the National Science Foundation for support of this research in 1962–64. I have benefited from discussions with Hugh Rose, Robert Fogel, Rudolph Penner, and Emmanuel Drandakis. My greatest debt is to Akihiro Amano, whose dissertation, *Neo-Classical Models of International Trade and Economic Growth* (Rochester, N.Y.: University of Rochester, 1963), was a stimulus to my own work.

one of the outputs serve as the capital good. The dual of the "incidence" problem in public finance in the static model is shown to have direct relevance to the problem of the stability of the balanced growth path in the neoclassical growth model. In the concluding section of the paper I show how these results can be applied to the analysis of technological progress. Any improvement in technology or in the quality of factors of production can be simply viewed as a composite of two effects, which I shall term the "differential industry" effect and the "differential factor" effect. Each effect has its counterpart in the dual problems discussed in the earlier part of the paper.

II. THE MODEL

Assume a perfectly competitive economy in which firms (indefinite in number) maximize profits, which are driven to the zero level in equilibrium. Consistent with this, technology in each of two sectors exhibits constant returns to scale. Two primary factors, labor (L) and land (T), are used in producing two distinct commodities, manufactured goods (M) and food (F). Wages (w) and rents (r) denote the returns earned by the factors for use of services, whereas p_M and p_F denote the competitive market prices of the two commodities.

If technology is given and factor endowments and commodity prices are treated as parameters, the model serves to determine eight unknowns: the level of commodity outputs (two), the factor allocations to each industry (four), and factor prices (two). The equations of the model could be given by the production functions (two), the requirement that each factor receive the value of its marginal product (four), and that each factor be fully employed (two). This is the format most frequently used in the theory of international trade and the neoclassical theory of growth.[1] I consider, instead, the formulation of the model suggested by activity analysis.

The technology is described by the columns of the A matrix,

$$A = \begin{pmatrix} a_{LM} \, a_{LF} \\ a_{TM} \, a_{TF} \end{pmatrix},$$

where a_{ij} denotes the quantity of factor i required to produce a unit of commodity j. With constant returns to scale total factor demands are given by the product of the a's and the levels of output. The requirement that both factors be fully employed is thus given by equations (1) and (2). Similarly, unit costs of production in each industry are given by the columns of A multiplied by the factor prices. In a competitive equilibrium with both goods being produced, these unit costs must reflect market prices, as in equations (3)

[1] As an example in each field see Murray C. Kemp, *The Pure Theory of International Trade* (Englewood Cliffs, N. J.: Prentice-Hall, Inc., 1964), pp. 10–11; and J. E. Meade, *A Neo-Classical Theory of Economic Growth* (London: Allen & Unwin, 1961), pp. 84–86.

and (4).[2] This formulation serves to emphasize the dual relationship between factor endowments and commodity outputs on the one hand (equations [1] and [2]) and commodity prices and factor prices on the other (equations [3] and [4]).

$$a_{LM}M + a_{LF}F = L, \tag{1}$$

$$a_{TM}M + a_{TF}F = T, \tag{2}$$

$$a_{LM}w + a_{TM}r = p_M, \tag{3}$$

$$a_{LF}w + a_{TF}r = p_F, \tag{4}$$

In the general case of variable coefficients the relationships shown in equations (1)–(4) must be supplemented by four additional relationships determining the input coefficients. These are provided by the requirement that in a competitive equilibrium each a_{ij} depends solely upon the ratio of factor prices.

III. THE EQUATIONS OF CHANGE

The comparative statics properties of the model described in Section II are developed by considering the effect of a change in the parameters on the unknowns of the problem. With unchanged technology the parameters are the factor endowments (L and T) and the commodity prices (p_M and p_F), the right-hand side of equations (1)–(4).

Let an asterisk indicate the relative change in a variable or parameter. Thus p_F^* denotes dp_F/p_F and L^* denotes dL/L.[3] The four equations in the rates of change are shown in (1.1) through (4.1):

$$\lambda_{LM}M^* + \lambda_{LF}F^* = L^* - [\lambda_{LM}a_{LM}^* + \lambda_{LF}a_{LF}^*], \tag{1.1}$$

$$\lambda_{TM}M^* + \lambda_{TF}F^* = T^* - [\lambda_{TM}a_{TM}^* + \lambda_{TF}a_{TF}^*], \tag{2.1}$$

$$\theta_{LM}w^* + \theta_{TM}r^* = p_M^* - [\theta_{LM}a_{LM}^* + \theta_{TM}a_{TM}^*], \tag{3.1}$$

$$\theta_{LF}w^* + \theta_{TF}r^* = p_F^* - [\theta_{LF}a_{LF}^* + \theta_{TF}a_{TF}^*]. \tag{4.1}$$

The λ's and θ's are the transforms of the a's that appear when relative changes are shown. A fraction of the labor force is used in manufacturing (λ_{LM}), and this plus the fraction of the labor force used in food production (λ_{LF}) must add to unity by the full-employment

---

[2] These basic relationships are usually presented as inequalities to allow for the existence of resource(s) in excess supply even at a zero price or for the possibility that losses would be incurred in certain industries if production were positive. I assume throughout that resources are fully employed, and production at zero profits with positive factor and commodity prices is possible. For a discussion of the inequalities, see, for example, R. Dorfman, Paul A. Samuelson, and Robert M. Solow, *Linear Programming and Economic Analysis* (New York: McGraw-Hill Book Co., 1958), chap. xiii; or J. R. Hicks, "Linear Theory," *Economic Journal*, December, 1960.

[3] This is the procedure used by Meade, *op. cit.* The λ and θ notation has been used by Amano, *op. cit.* Expressing small changes in relative or percentage terms is a natural procedure when technology exhibits constant returns to scale.

assumption (shown by equation [1]). Similarly for λ_{TM} and λ_{TF}. The θ's, by contrast, refer to the factor shares in each industry. Thus θ_{LM}, labor's share in manufacturing, is given by $a_{LM}w/p_M$. By the zero profit conditions, θ_{Lj} and θ_{Tj} must add to unity.

In this section I assume that manufacturing is labor-intensive. It follows that labor's share in manufacturing must be greater than labor's share in food, and that the percentage of the labor force used in manufacturing must exceed the percentage of total land that is used in manufacturing. Let λ and θ be the notations for the matrices of coefficients shown in ([1.1], [2.1]) and ([3.1], [4.1]).

$$\lambda = \begin{pmatrix} \lambda_{LM} & \lambda_{LF} \\ \lambda_{TM} & \lambda_{TF} \end{pmatrix}, \qquad \theta = \begin{pmatrix} \theta_{LM} & \theta_{TM} \\ \theta_{LF} & \theta_{TF} \end{pmatrix}.$$

Since each row sum in λ and θ is unity, the determinants $|\lambda|$ and $|\theta|$ are given by

$$|\lambda| = \lambda_{LM} - \lambda_{TM},$$
$$|\theta| = \theta_{LM} - \theta_{LF},$$

and both $|\lambda|$ and $|\theta|$ are positive by the factor-intensity assumption.[4]

If coefficients of production are fixed, equations (1.1)–(4.1) are greatly simplified as every a_{ij}^* and, therefore, the λ and θ weighted sums of the a_{ij}^*'s reduce to zero. In the case of variable coefficients, sufficient extra conditions to determine the a^*'s are easily derived. Consider, first, the maximizing role of the typical competitive entrepreneur. For any given level of output he attempts to minimize costs; that is he minimizes unit costs. In the manufacturing industry these are given by $(a_{LM}w + a_{TM}r)$. The entrepreneur treats factor prices as fixed, and varies the a's so as to set the derivative of costs equal to zero. Dividing by p_M and expressing changes in relative terms leads to equation (6). Equation (7) shows the corresponding relationship for the food industry.

$$\theta_{LM} a_{LM}^* + \theta_{TM} a_{TM}^* = 0, \tag{6}$$
$$\theta_{LF} a_{LF}^* + \theta_{TF} a_{TF}^* = 0. \tag{7}$$

With no technological change, alterations in factor proportions must balance out such that the θ-weighted average of the changes in input coefficients in each industry is zero.

---

[4]Let P and W represent the diagonal matrices,

$$\begin{pmatrix} p_M & 0 \\ 0 & p_F \end{pmatrix} \quad \text{and} \quad \begin{pmatrix} w & 0 \\ 0 & r \end{pmatrix},$$

respectively, and E and X represent the diagonal matrices of factor endowments and commodity outputs. Then $\lambda = E^{-1}AX$ and $\theta = P^{-1}A'W$. Since $|A| > 0$ and the determinants of the four diagonal matrices are all positive, $|\lambda|$ and $|\theta|$ must be positive. This relation among the signs of $|\lambda|, |\theta|$, and $|A|$ is proved by Amano, *op. cit.*, and Akira Takayama, "On a Two-Sector Model of Economic Growth: A Comparative Statics Analysis," *Review of Economic Studies*, June, 1963.

This implies directly that the relationship between changes in factor prices and changes in commodity prices is *identical* in the variable and fixed coefficients cases, an example of the Wong-Viner envelope theorem. With costs per unit of output being minimized, the change in costs resulting from a small change in factor prices is the same whether or not factor proportions are altered. The saving in cost from such alterations is a second-order small.[5]

A similar kind of argument definitely does *not* apply to the λ-weighted average of the a^*'s for each factor that appears in the factor market-clearing relationships. For example, $(\lambda_{LM} a^*_{LM} + \lambda_{LF} a^*_{LF})$ shows the percentage change in the total quantity of labor required by the economy as a result of changing factor proportions in each industry at unchanged outputs. The crucial feature here is that if factor prices change, factor proportions alter in the same direction in both industries. The extent of this change obviously depends upon the elasticities of substitution between factors in each industry. In a competitive equilibrium (and with the internal tangencies implicit in earlier assumptions), the slope of the isoquant in each industry is equal to the ratio of factor prices. Therefore the elasticities of substitution can be defined as in (8) and (9):

$$\sigma_M = \frac{a^*_{TM} - a^*_{LM}}{w^* - r^*}, \tag{8}$$

$$\sigma_F = \frac{a^*_{TF} - a^*_{LF}}{w^* - r^*}. \tag{9}$$

Together with (6) and (7) a subset of four equations relating the a^*'s to the change in the relative factor prices is obtained. They can be solved in pairs; for example (6) and (8) yield solutions for the a^*'s of the M industry. In general,

$$a^*_{Lj} = -\theta_{Tj}\sigma_j(w^* - r^*); \qquad j = M, F.$$

$$a^*_{Tj} = \theta_{Lj}\sigma_j(w^* - r^*); \qquad j = M, F.$$

These solutions for the a^*'s can then be substituted into equations (1.1)–(4.1) to obtain

$$\lambda_{LM} M^* + \lambda_{LF} F^* = L^* + \delta_L(w^* - r^*), \tag{1.2}$$

$$\lambda_{TM} M^* + \lambda_{TF} F^* = T^* - \delta_T(w^* - r^*), \tag{2.2}$$

$$\theta_{LM} w^* + \theta_{TM} r^* = p^*_M, \tag{3.2}$$

$$\theta_{LF} w^* + \theta_{TF} r^* = p^*_F, \tag{4.2}$$

where

$$\delta_L = \lambda_{LM}\theta_{TM}\sigma_M + \lambda_{LF}\theta_{TF}\sigma_F,$$

$$\delta_T = \lambda_{TM}\theta_{LM}\sigma_M + \lambda_{TF}\theta_{LF}\sigma_F.$$

---

[5]For another example of the Wong-Viner theorem, for changes in real income along a transformation schedule, see Ronald W. Jones, "Stability Conditions in International Trade: A General Equilibrium Analysis," *International Economic Review*, May, 1961.

In the fixed-coefficients case, δ_L and δ_T are zero. In general, δ_L is the aggregate percentage saving in labor inputs at unchanged outputs associated with a 1 per cent rise in the relative wage rate, the saving resulting from the adjustment to less labor-intensive techniques in both industries as relative wages rise.

The structure of the production model with variable coefficients is exhibited in equations (1.2)–(4.2). The latter pair *states that factor prices are dependent only upon commodity prices, which is the factor-price equalization theorem.*[6] If commodity prices are unchanged, factor prices are constant and equations (1.2) and (2.2) state that changes in commodity outputs are linked to changes in factor endowments via the λ matrix in precisely the same way as θ links factor price changes to commodity price changes. This is the basic duality feature of the production model.[7]

IV. THE MAGNIFICATION EFFECT

The nature of the link provided by λ or θ is revealed by examining the solutions for M^* and F^* at constant commodity prices in (1.2) and (2.2) and for w^* and r^* in equations (3.2) and (4.2).[8] If both endowments expand at the same rate, both commodity outputs expand at identical rates. But if factor endowments expand at different rates, the commodity intensive in the use of the fastest growing factor expands at a greater rate than either factor, and the other commodity grows (if at all) at a slower rate than either factor. For example, suppose labor expands more rapidly than land. With M labor-intensive,

$$M^* > L^* > T^* > F^*.$$

This *magnification effect* of factor endowments on commodity outputs at unchanged commodity prices is also a feature of the dual link between commodity and factor prices. In the absence of technological change or excise taxes or subsidies, if the price of M grows more rapidly than the price of F,

$$w^* > p_M^* > p_F^* > r^*.$$

Turned the other way around, the source of the magnification effect is easy to detect. For example, since the relative change in the price of either commodity is a positive

---

[6] Factor endowments come into their own in influencing factor prices if complete specialization is allowed (or if the number of factors exceeds the number of commodities). See Samuelson, "Prices of Factors and Goods in General Equilibrium," *Review of Economic Studies*, Vol. XXI, No. 1 (1953–54), for a detailed discussion of this issue.

[7] The reciprocal relationship between the effect of a rise in the price of commodity i on the return to factor j and the effect of an increase in the endowment of factor j on the output of commodity i is discussed briefly by Samuelson, *ibid*.

[8] The solutions, of course, are given by the elements of λ^{-1} and θ^{-1}. If M is labor-intensive, the diagonal elements of λ^{-1} and θ^{-1} are positive and exceed unity, while off-diagonal elements are negative.

weighted average of factor price changes, it must be bounded by these changes. Similarly, if input coefficients are fixed (as a consequence of assuming constant factor and commodity prices), any disparity in the growth of outputs is reduced when considering the consequent changes in the economy's demand for factors. The reason, of course, is that each good requires both factors of production.

Two special cases have been especially significant in the theory of international trade. Suppose the endowment of only one factor (say labor) rises. With L^* positive and T^* zero, M^* exceeds L^* and F^* is negative. This is the Rybczynski theorem in the theory of international trade: At unchanged commodity prices an expansion in one factor results in an absolute decline in the commodity intensive in the use of the other factor.[9] Its dual underlies the Stolper-Samuelson tariff theorem.[10] Suppose p_F^* is zero (for example, F could be taken as numeraire). Then an increase in the price of M (brought about, say, by a tariff on imports of M) raises the return to the factor used intensively in M by an even greater relative amount (and lowers the return to the other factor). In the case illustrated, the *real* return to labor has unambiguously risen.

For some purposes it is convenient to consider a slight variation of the Stolper-Samuelson theorem. Let p_j stand for the *market* price of j as before, but introduce a set of domestic excise taxes or subsidies so that $s_j p_j$ represents the price received by producers in industry j; s_j is one plus the ad valorem rate of subsidy to the industry.[11] The effect of an imposition of subsidies on factor prices is given in equations (3.3) and (4.3):

$$\theta_{LM} w^* + \theta_{TM} r^* = p_M^* + s_M^*, \tag{3.3}$$

$$\theta_{LF} w^* + \theta_{TF} r^* = p_F^* + s_F^*. \tag{4.3}$$

At fixed commodity prices, what impact does a set of subsidies have on factor prices? The answer is that all the subsidies are "shifted backward" to affect returns to factors in a *magnified* fashion. Thus, if M is labor-intensive and if the M industry should be especially favored by the subsidy,

$$w^* > s_M^* > s_F^* > r^*.$$

[9]T. M. Rybczynski, "Factor Endowments and Relative Commodity Prices," *Economica*, November, 1955. See also Jones, "Factor Proportions and the Heckscher-Ohlin Theorem," *Review of Economic Studies*, October, 1956.

[10]W. F. Stolper and P. A. Samuelson, "Protection and Real Wages," *Review of Economic Studies*, November, 1941. A graphical analysis of the dual relationship between the Rybczynski theorem and the Stolper-Samuelson theorem is presented in Jones, "Duality in International Trade: A Geometrical Note," *Canadian Journal of Economics and Political Science*, August, 1965.

[11]I restrict the discussion to the case of excise subsidies because of the resemblance it bears to some aspects of technological change, which I discuss later. In the case of taxes, $s_j = 1/(1 + t_j)$ where t_j represents the ad valorem rate of excise tax.

The *magnification* effect in this problem and its dual reflects the basic structure of the model with fixed commodity prices. However, if a demand relationship is introduced, prices are determined within the model and can be expected to adjust to a change in factor endowments or, in the dual problem, to a change in excise subsidies (or taxes). In the next section I discuss the feedback effect of these induced price changes on the composition of output and relative factor prices. The crucial question to be considered concerns the extent to which commodity price changes can dampen the initial magnification effects that are produced at constant prices.

V. THE EXTENDED MODEL: DEMAND ENDOGENOUS

To close the production model I assume that community taste patterns are homothetic and ignore any differences between the taste patterns of laborers and landlords. Thus the ratio of the quantities consumed of M and F depends only upon the relative commodity price ratio, as in equation (5).

$$\frac{M}{F} = f\left(\frac{p_M}{p_F}\right). \tag{5}$$

In terms of the rates of change, (5.1) serves to define the elasticity of substitution between the two commodities on the demand side, σ_D.

$$(M^* - F^*) = -\sigma_D(p_M^* - p_F^*). \tag{5.1}$$

The effect of a change in factor endowments at constant commodity prices was considered in the previous section. With the model closed by the demand relationship, commodity prices adjust so as to clear the commodity markets. Equation (5.1) shows directly the change in the ratio of outputs consumed. Subtracting (2.2) from (1.2) yields the change in the ratio of outputs produced.

$$(M^* - F^*) = \frac{1}{|\lambda|}(L^* - T^*) + \frac{(\delta_L + \delta_T)}{|\lambda|}(w^* - r^*).$$

The change in the factor price ratio (with no subsidies or taxes) is given by

$$(w^* - r^*) = \frac{1}{|\theta|}(p_M^* - p_F^*),$$

so that, by substitution,

$$(M^* - F^*) = \frac{1}{|\lambda|}(L^* - T^*) + \sigma_S(p_M^* - p_F^*),$$

where

$$\sigma_S = \frac{1}{|\lambda||\theta|}(\delta_L + \delta_T).$$

σ_S represents the elasticity of substitution between commodities on the *supply* side (along the transformation schedule).[12] The change in the commodity price ratio is then given by the mutual interaction of demand and supply:

$$(p_M^* - p_F^*) = -\frac{1}{|\lambda|(\sigma_S + \sigma_D)} (L^* - T^*). \tag{10}$$

Therefore the resulting change in the ratio of commodities produced is

$$(M^* - F^*) = \frac{1}{|\lambda|} \cdot \frac{\sigma_D}{\sigma_S + \sigma_D} (L^* - T^*). \tag{11}$$

With commodity prices adjusting to the initial output changes brought about by the change in factor endowments, the composition of outputs may, in the end, not change by as much, relatively, as the factor endowments. This clearly depends upon whether the "elasticity" expression, $\sigma_D/(\sigma_S + \sigma_D)$, is smaller than the "factor-intensity" expression, $|\lambda|$. Although it is *large* values of σ_S (and the underlying elasticities of factor substitution in each industry, σ_M and σ_F) that serve to dampen the spread of outputs, it is *small* values of σ_D that accomplish the same end. This comparison between elasticities on the demand and supply side is familiar to students of public finance concerned with questions of tax (or subsidy) incidence and shifting. I turn now to this problem.

The relationship between the change in factor prices and subsidies is given by (3.3) and (4.3). Solving for the change in the ratio of factor prices,

$$(w^* - r^*) = \frac{1}{|\theta|} \{(p_M^* - p_F^*) + (s_M^* - s_F^*)\}. \tag{12}$$

Consider factor endowments to be fixed. Any change in factor prices will nonetheless induce a readjustment of commodity outputs. On the supply side,

$$(M^* - F^*) = \sigma_S \{(p_M^* - p_F^*) + (s_M^* - s_F^*)\}.$$

---

[12] I have bypassed the solution for M^* and F^* separately given from (1.2) and (2.2). After substituting for the factor price ratio in terms of the commodity price ratio the expression for M^* could be written as

$$M^* = \frac{1}{|\lambda|} [\lambda_{TF} L^* - \lambda_{LF} T^*] + e_M(p_M^* - p_F^*),$$

where, e_M, the shorthand expression for $1/|\lambda||\theta| (\lambda_{TF} \delta_L + \lambda_{LF} \delta_T)$, shows the percentage change in M that would be associated with a 1 per cent rise in M's relative price along a given transformation schedule. It is a "general equilibrium" elasticity of supply, as discussed in Jones, "Stability Conditions ...," *op. cit.* It is readily seen that $\sigma_S = e_M + e_F$. Furthermore, $\theta_M e_M = \theta_F e_F$, where θ_M and θ_F denote the share of each good in the national income.

The relative commodity price change that equates supply and demand is

$$(p_M^* - p_F^*) = -\frac{\sigma_S}{\sigma_S + \sigma_D}(s_M^* - s_F^*). \tag{13}$$

Substituting back into the expression for the change in the factor price ratio yields

$$(w^* - r^*) = \frac{1}{|\theta|} \cdot \frac{\sigma_D}{\sigma_S + \sigma_D}(s_M^* - s_F^*). \tag{14}$$

This is a familiar result. Suppose M is subsidized more heavily than F. Part of the subsidy is shifted backward, affecting relatively favorably the factor used intensively in the M-industry (labor). Whether labor's relative return expands by a greater proportion than the spread in subsidies depends upon how much of the subsidy has been passed forward to consumers in the form of a relatively lower price for M. And this, of course, depends upon the relative sizes of σ_S and σ_D.

Notice the similarity between expressions (11) and (14). Factors produce commodities, and a change in endowments must result in an altered composition of production, by a magnified amount at unchanged prices. By analogy, subsidies "produce" returns to factors, and a change in the pattern of subsidies alters the distribution of income. In each case, of course, the extent of readjustment required is eased if commodity prices change, by a factor depending upon the relative sizes of demand and supply elasticities of substitution.

VI. THE AGGREGATE ELASTICITY OF SUBSTITUTION

The analysis of a change in factor endowments leading up to equation (11) has a direct bearing on a recent issue in the neoclassical theory of economic growth. Before describing this issue it is useful to introduce yet another elasticity concept—that of an economy-wide elasticity of substitution between factors.[13] With no subsidies, the relationship between the change in the factor price ratio and the change in endowments can be derived from (10). Thus,

$$(w^* - r^*) = -\frac{1}{|\lambda||\theta|(\sigma_S + \sigma_D)}(L^* - T^*). \tag{15}$$

By analogy with the elasticity of substitution in a particular sector, define σ as the percentage rise in the land/labor endowment ratio required to raise the wage/rent ratio by

---

[13] For previous uses see Amano, "Determinants of Comparative Costs: A Theoretical Approach," *Oxford Economic Papers*, November, 1964; and E. Drandakis, "Factor Substitution in the Two-Sector Growth Model," *Review of Economic Studies*, October, 1963.

1 per cent. Directly from (15),

$$\sigma = |\lambda||\theta|(\sigma_S + \sigma_D).$$

But recall that σ_S is itself a composite of the two elasticities of substitution in each industry, σ_M and σ_F. Thus σ can be expressed in terms of the three *primary* elasticities of substitution in this model:

$$\sigma = Q_M\sigma_M + Q_F\sigma_F + Q_D\sigma_D,$$

where

$$Q_M = \theta_{LM}\lambda_{TM} + \theta_{TM}\lambda_{LM},$$
$$Q_F = \theta_{LF}\lambda_{TF} + \theta_{TF}\lambda_{LF},$$
$$Q_D = |\lambda|\cdot|\theta|.$$

Note that σ is not just a linear expression in σ_M, σ_F, and σ_D—it is a weighted average of these three elasticities as $\Sigma Q_i = 1$. Note also that σ can be positive even if the elasticity of substitution in each industry is zero, for it incorporates the effect of inter-commodity substitution by consumers as well as direct intracommodity substitution between factors.

Finally, introduce the concept, σ, into expression (11) for output changes:

$$(M^* - F^*) = \frac{|\theta|\sigma_D}{\sigma}(L^* - T^*), \tag{11$'$}$$

and into expression (14) for the change in factor prices in the subsidy case:

$$(w^* - r^*) = \frac{|\lambda|\sigma_D}{\sigma}(s_M^* - s_F^*). \tag{14$'$}$$

One consequence is immediately apparent: If the elasticity of substitution between commodities on the part of consumers is no greater than the over-all elasticity of substitution between factors, the *magnification* effects discussed in Section IV are more than compensated for by the damping effect of price changes.

VII. CONVERGENCE TO BALANCED GROWTH

The two-sector model of production described in Sections I–VI can be used to analyze the process of economic growth. Already I have spoken of increases in factor endowments and the consequent "growth" of outputs. But a more satisfactory growth model would allow for the growth of at least one factor of production to be determined by the system rather than given parametrically. Let the factor "capital" replace "land" as the second factor in the two-sector model (replace T by K). And let M stand for machines rather than manufacturing goods. To simplify, I assume capital does not depreciate. The new feedback element in the system is that the rate of increase of the capital stock, K^*, depends on the current output of machines, M. Thus $K^* = M/K$. The "demand" for M now represents savings.

Suppose the rate of growth of the labor force, L^*, is constant. At any moment of time the rate of capital accumulation, K^*, either exceeds, equals, or falls short of L^*. Of special interest in the neoclassical theory of growth (with no technological progress) is the case of balanced growth where $L^* = K^*$. Balance in the growth of factors will, as we have seen, result in balanced growth as between the two commodities (at the same rate). But if L^* and K^* are not equal, it becomes necessary to inquire whether they tend toward equality (balanced growth) asymptotically or tend to diverge even further.

If machines are produced by labor-intensive techniques, the rate of growth of machines exceeds that of capital if labor is growing faster than capital, or falls short of capital if capital is growing faster than labor. (This is the result in Section IV, which is dampened, but not reversed, by the price changes discussed in Section V.) Thus the rate of capital accumulation, if different from the rate of growth of the labor supply, falls or rises toward it. The economy tends toward the balanced-growth path.

The difficulty arises if machines are capital intensive. If there is no price change, the change in the composition of outputs must be a magnified reflection of the spread in the growth rates of factors. Thus if capital is growing more rapidly than labor, machine output will expand at a greater rate than either factor, and this only serves to widen the spread between the rates of growth of capital and labor even further.[14] Once account is taken of price changes, however, the change in the composition of outputs may be sufficiently dampened to allow convergence to balanced growth despite the fact that machines are capital intensive.

Re-examine equation (11′), replacing T^* by K^* and recognizing that $|\theta|$ is negative if machines are capital intensive. If σ exceeds $-|\theta|\sigma_D$, on balance a dampening of the ratio of outputs as compared to factor endowments takes place. This suggests the critical condition that must be satisfied by σ, as compared with σ_D and $|\theta|$, in order to insure stability. But this is not precisely the condition required. Rather, stability hinges upon the *sign* of $(M^* - K^*)$ being opposite to that of $(K^* - L^*)$. There is a presumption that when $(M^* - F^*)$ is smaller than $(K^* - L^*)$ (assuming both are positive) the output of the machine sector is growing less rapidly than is the capital stock. But the correspondence is not exact.

To derive the relationship between $(M^* - K^*)$ and $(M^* - F^*)$ consider the two ways of expressing changes in the national income (Y). It can be viewed as the sum of returns to factors or the sum of the values of output in the two sectors. Let θ_i refer to the share of

---

[14]See Y. Shinkai, "On Equilibrium Growth of Capital and Labor," *International Economic Review*, May, 1960, for a discussion of the fixed-coefficients case. At constant commodity prices the impact of endowment changes on the composition of output is the same regardless of elasticities of substitution in production. Thus a necessary and sufficient condition in Shinkai's case is the factor-intensity condition. For the variable coefficients case the factor-intensity condition was first discussed by Hirofumi Uzawa, "On a Two-Sector Model of Economic Growth," *Review of Economic Studies*, October, 1961.

factor i or commodity i in the national income. In terms of rates of change,

$$Y^* = \theta_L(w^* + L^*) + \theta_K(r^* + K^*) = \theta_M(p_M^* + M^*) + \theta_F(p_F^* + F^*).$$

But the share of a factor in the national income must be an average of its share in each sector, with the weights given by the share of that sector in the national income. This, and equations (3.2) and (4.2), guarantee that

$$\theta_L w^* + \theta_K r^* = \theta_M p_M^* + \theta_F p_F^*.$$

That is, the rates of change of the financial components in the two expressions for Y^* balance, leaving an equality between the physical terms:

$$\theta_L L^* + \theta_K K^* = \theta_M M^* + \theta_F F^*.$$

The desired relationship is obtained by observing that θ_K equals $(1 - \theta_L)$ and θ_M is $(1 - \theta_F)$. Thus

$$(M^* - K^*) = \theta_F(M^* - F^*) - \theta_L(K^* - L^*).$$

With this in hand it is easy to see that (from [11']) $(M^* - K^*)$ is given by

$$(M^* - K^*) = \frac{\theta_L}{\sigma} \times \left\{ -\frac{\theta_F |\theta|}{\theta_L} \sigma_D - \sigma \right\} (K^* - L^*). \tag{16}$$

It is not enough for σ to exceed $-|\theta|\sigma_D$, it must exceed $-(\theta_F/\theta_L)|\theta|\sigma_D$ for convergence to balanced growth.[15] It nonetheless remains the case that σ greater than σ_D is sufficient to insure that the expression in brackets in (16) is negative. For (16) can be rewritten as (16'):

$$(M^* - K^*) = -\frac{\theta_L}{\sigma} \times \left\{ \sigma - \left[1 - \frac{\theta_{LM}}{\theta_L} \right] \sigma_D \right\} (K^* - L^*). \tag{16'}$$

Thus it is overly strong to require that σ exceed σ_D.[16]

VIII. SAVINGS BEHAVIOR

A popular assumption about savings behavior in the literature on growth theory is that aggregate savings form a constant percentage of the national income.[17] This, of course, implies that σ_D is unity. In this case it becomes legitimate to inquire as to the values of σ

---

[15]The two requirements are equivalent if $\theta_F = \theta_L$, that is, if total consumption ($p_F F$) is matched exactly by the total wages (wL). This equality is made a basic assumption as to savings behavior in some models, where laborers consume all and capitalists save all. For example, see Uzawa, *ibid.*

[16]A condition similar to (16'), with the assumption that $\sigma_D = 1$, is presented by Amano, "A Two-Sector Model of Economic Growth Involving Technical Progress" (unpublished).

[17]For example, see Solow, "A Contribution to the Theory of Economic Growth," *Quarterly Journal of Economics*, February, 1956.

or σ_M and σ_F as compared with unity. For example, if each sector's production function is Cobb-Douglas (σ_M and σ_F each unity), stability is guaranteed. But the value "unity" that has a crucial role in this comparison only serves as a proxy for σ_D. With high σ_D even greater values for σ_M and σ_F (and σ) would be required.

If σ_D is unity when the savings ratio is constant, is its value higher or lower than unity when the savings ratio depends positively on the rate of profit? It turns out that this depends upon the technology in such a way as to encourage convergence to balanced growth precisely in those cases where factor intensities are such as to leave it in doubt.

The capital goods, machines, are demanded not for the utility they yield directly, but for the stream of additional future consumption they allow. This is represented by the rate of return (or profit), which is linked by the technology to the relative price of machines according to the magnification effects implicit in the Stolper-Samuelson theorem. The assumption that the savings ratio (the fraction of income devoted to new machines) rises as the rate of profit rises implies that the savings ratio rises as the relative price of machines rises (and thus that σ_D is less than unity) if and only if machines are capital intensive. Of course the savings assumption also implies that σ_D exceeds unity (that is, that the savings ratio falls as the relative price of machines rises) if machines are labor intensive, but convergence to balanced growth is already assured in this case.[18]

IX. THE ANALYSIS OF TECHNOLOGICAL CHANGE

The preceding sections have dealt with the structure of the two-sector model of production with a given technology. They nonetheless contain the ingredients necessary for an analysis of the effects of technological progress. In this concluding section I examine this problem and simplify by assuming that factor endowments remain unchanged and subsidies are zero. I concentrate on the impact of a change in production conditions on relative prices. The effect on outputs is considered implicitly in deriving the price changes.

Consider a typical input coefficient, a_{ij}, as depending both upon relative factor prices and the state of technology:

$$a_{ij} = a_{ij}\left(\frac{w}{r}, t\right).$$

In terms of the relative rates of change, a_{ij}^* may be decomposed as

$$a_{ij}^* = c_{ij}^* - b_{ij}^*.$$

---

[18] For a more complete discussion of savings behavior as related to the rate of profit, see Uzawa, "On a Two-Sector Model of Economic Growth: II," *Review of Economic Studies*, June, 1963; and Kenichi Inada, "On Neoclassical Models of Economic Growth," *Review of Economic Studies*, April, 1965.

c_{ij}^* denotes the relative change in the input-output coefficient that is called forth by a change in factor prices as of a given technology. The b_{ij}^* is a measure of technological change that shows the alteration in a_{ij} that would take place at constant factor prices. Since technological progress usually involves a *reduction* in the input requirements, I define b_{ij}^* as $-1/a_{ij} \cdot \partial a_{ij}/\partial t$.

The b_{ij}^* are the basic expressions of technological change. After Section III's discussion, it is not surprising that it is the λ and θ weighted averages of the b_{ij}^* that turn out to be important. These are defined by the following set of π's:

$$\pi_j = \theta_{Lj} b_{Lj}^* + \theta_{Tj} b_{Tj}^* \qquad (j = M, F),$$

$$\pi_i = \lambda_{iM} b_{iM}^* + \lambda_{iF} b_{iF}^* \qquad (i = L, T).$$

If a B^* matrix is defined in a manner similar to the original A matrix, π_M and π_F are the sums of the elements in each column weighted by the relative factor shares, and π_L and π_T are sums of the elements in each row of B^* weighted by the fractions of the total factor supplies used in each industry. Thus π_M, assumed non-negative, is a measure of the rate of technological advance in the M-industry and π_L, also assumed non-negative, reflects the over-all labor-saving feature of technological change.

Turn now to the equations of change. The c_{ij}^* are precisely the a_{ij}^* used in equations (6)–(9) of the model without technological change. This subset can be solved, just as before, for the response of input coefficients to factor price changes. After substitution, the first four equations of change (equations [1.1]–[4.1]) become

$$\lambda_{LM} M^* + \lambda_{LF} F^* = \pi_L + \delta_L (w^* - r^*), \qquad (1.4)$$

$$\lambda_{TM} M^* + \lambda_{TF} F^* = \pi_T - \delta_T (w^* - r^*), \qquad (2.4)$$

$$\theta_{LM} w^* + \theta_{TM} r^* = p_M^* + \pi_M, \qquad (3.4)$$

$$\theta_{LM} w^* + \theta_{TF} r^* = p_F^* + \pi_F. \qquad (4.4)$$

The parameters of technological change appear only in the first four relationships and enter there in a particularly simple form. In the first two equations it is readily seen that, in part, technological change, through its impact in reducing input coefficients, has precisely the same effects on the system as would a change in factor endowments. π_L and π_T replace L^* and T^* respectively. In the second pair of equations the improvements in industry outputs attributable to technological progress enter the model precisely as do industry subsidies in equations (3.3) and (4.3) of Section IV. Any general change in technology or in the quality of factors (that gets translated into a change in input coefficiencies) has an impact on prices and outputs that can be decomposed into the two kinds of parametric changes analyzed in the preceding sections.

Consider the effect of progress upon relative commodity and factor prices. The relationship between the changes in the two sets of prices is the same as in the subsidy case (see equation [12]):

$$(w^* - r^*) = \frac{1}{|\theta|}\{(p_M^* - p_F^*) + (\pi_M - \pi_F)\}. \tag{17}$$

Solving separately for each relative price change,

$$(p_M^* - p_F^*) = -\frac{|\theta|}{\sigma}\{(\pi_L - \pi_T) + |\lambda|\sigma_S(\pi_M - \pi_F)\}, \tag{18}$$

$$(w^* - r^*) = -\frac{1}{\sigma}\{(\pi_L - \pi_T) - |\lambda|\sigma_D(\pi_M - \pi_F)\}. \tag{19}$$

For convenience I refer to $(\pi_L - \pi_T)$ as the "differential factor effect" and $(\pi_M - \pi_F)$ as the "differential industry effect."[19]

Define a change in technology as "regular" if the differential factor and industry effects have the same sign.[20] For example, a change in technology that is relatively "labor-saving" for the economy as a whole ($[\pi_L - \pi_T]$ positive) is considered "regular" if it also reflects a relatively greater improvement in productivity in the labor-intensive industry. Suppose this to be the case. Both effects tend to depress the relative price of commodity M: The "labor-saving" feature of the change works exactly as would a relative increase in the labor endowment to reduce the relative price of the labor-intensive commodity (M). And part of the differential industry effect, like a relative subsidy to M, is shifted forward in a lower price for M.

Whereas the two components of "regular" technological change reinforce each other in their effect on the commodity price ratio, they pull the factor price ratio in opposite directions. The differential factor effect in the above case serves to depress the wage/rent ratio. But part of the relatively greater improvement in the labor-intensive M industry is shifted backward to increase, relatively, the return to labor. This "backward" shift is more pronounced the greater is the elasticity of substitution on the demand side. There will be some "critical" value of σ_D, above which relative wages will rise despite the downward

---

[19]The suggestion that a change in technology in a particular industry has both "factor-saving" and "cost-reducing" aspects has been made before. See, for example, J. Bhagwati and H. Johnson, "Notes on Some Controversies in the Theory of International Trade," *Economic Journal*, March, 1960; and G. M. Meier, *International Trade and Development* (New York: Harper & Row, 1963), chap. i. Contrary to what is usually implied, I point out that a Hicksian "neutral" technological change in one or more industries has, nonetheless, a "factor-saving" or "differential factor" effect. The problem of technological change has been analyzed in numerous articles; perhaps those by H. Johnson, "Economic Expansion and International Trade," *Manchester School of Economic and Social Studies*, May, 1955; and R. Findlay and H. Grubert, "Factor Intensities, Technological Progress and the Terms of Trade," *Oxford Economic Papers*, February, 1959, should especially be mentioned.

[20]Strictly speaking, I want to allow for the possibility that one or both effects are zero. Thus technological change is "regular" if and only if $(\pi_L - \pi_T)(\pi_M - \pi_F) \geqq 0$.

pull of the differential factor effect:

$$(w^* - r^*) > 0 \text{ if and only if } \sigma_D > \frac{(\pi_L - \pi_T)}{|\lambda|(\pi_M - \pi_F)}.$$

If technological progress is not "regular," these conclusions are reversed. Suppose $(\pi_L - \pi_T) > 0$, but nonetheless $(\pi_M - \pi_F) < 0$. This might be the result, say, of technological change where the primary impact is to reduce labor requirements in food production. Labor is now affected relatively adversely on both counts, the differential factor effect serving to depress wages as before, and the differential industry effect working to the relative advantage of the factor used intensively in food production, land. On the other hand, the change in relative commodity prices is now less predictable. The differential factor effect, in tending to reduce M's relative price, is working counter to the differential industry effect, whereby the F industry is experiencing more rapid technological advance. The differential industry effect will, in this case, dominate if the elasticity of substitution between goods on the supply side is high enough.

$$(p_M^* - p_F^*) > 0 \text{ if and only if } \sigma_S > -\frac{(\pi_L - \pi_T)}{|\lambda|(\pi_M - \pi_F)}.$$

The differential factor and industry effects are not independent of each other. Some insight into the nature of the relationship between the two can be obtained by considering two special cases of "neutrality."

Suppose, first, that technological change is "Hicksian neutral" in each industry, implying that, at unchanged factor prices, factor proportions used in that industry do not change.[21] In terms of the B^* matrix, the rows are identical $b_{Lj}^* = b_{Tj}^*$. As can easily be verified from the definition of the π's, in this case

$$(\pi_L - \pi_T) = |\lambda|(\pi_M - \pi_F),$$

and technological change must be "regular." If, over-all, technological change is "labor-saving" (and note that this can happen even if it is Hicksian neutral in each industry), the price of the relatively labor-intensive commodity must fall. Relative wages will, nonetheless, rise if σ_D exceeds the critical value shown earlier, which in this case reduces to unity.

The symmetrical nature of this approach to technological change suggests an alternative definition of neutrality, in which the columns of the B^* matrix are equal. This type of neutrality indicates that input requirements for any factor, i, have been reduced by the same relative amount in every industry. The relationship between the differential factor and industry effects is given by

$$(\pi_M - \pi_F) = |\theta|(\pi_L - \pi_T).$$

---

[21] See Hicks, *The Theory of Wages* (New York: Macmillan Co., 1932).

Again, technological change must be "regular." If the reduction in labor coefficients in each industry exceeds the reduction in land coefficients, this must filter through (in dampened form unless each industry uses just one factor) to affect relatively favorably the labor-intensive industry. The remarks made in the case of Hicksian neutrality carry over to this case, except for the fact that the critical value which σ_D must exceed in order for the differential industry effect to outweigh the factor effect on relative wages now becomes higher. Specifically, σ_D must exceed $1/|\lambda||\theta|$, which may be considerably greater than unity. This reflects the fact that in the case of Hicksian neutrality $(\pi_L - \pi_T)$ is smaller than $(\pi_M - \pi_F)$, whereas the reverse is true in the present case.

With Hicksian neutrality the paramount feature is the difference between rates of technological advance in each industry. This spills over into a differential factor effect only because the industries require the two factors in differing proportions. With the other kind of neutrality the basic change is that the input requirements of one factor are cut more than for the other factor. As we have just seen, this is transformed into a differential industry effect only in dampened form.

These cases of neutrality are special cases of "regular" technological progress. The general relationship between the differential factor and industry effects can be derived from the definitions to yield

$$(\pi_L - \pi_T) = Q_M\beta_M + Q_F\beta_F + |\lambda|(\pi_M - \pi_F), \tag{20}$$

and

$$(\pi_M - \pi_F) = Q_L\beta_L + Q_T\beta_T + |\theta|(\pi_L - \pi_T). \tag{21}$$

In the first equation the differential factor effect is broken down into three components: the labor-saving bias of technical change in each industry (β_j is defined as $b^*_{Lj} - b^*_{Tj}$) and the differential industry effect.[22] In the second expression the differential industry effect is shown as a combination of the relatively greater saving in each factor in the M industry (β_L, for example, is $b^*_{LM} - b^*_{LF}$) and the differential factor effect.[23] With these relationships at hand it is easy to see how it is the possible asymmetry between the row elements and/or the column elements of the B* matrix that could disrupt the "regularity" feature of technical progress.[24]

---

[22] Note that Q_M and Q_F are the same weights as those defined in Section VI. The analogy between the composition of σ and that of $(\pi_L - \pi_T)$ becomes more apparent if $|\lambda|(\pi_M - \pi_F)$ is rewritten as $Q_D \cdot \{(\pi_M - \pi_F)/|\theta|\}$. The differential factor effect is a weighted average of the Hicksian factor biases in each industry and a magnified $(1/|\theta|)$ differential industry effect.

[23] Q_L equals $(\lambda_{LF}\theta_{LM} + \lambda_{LM}\theta_{LF})$, and Q_T is $(\lambda_{TF}\theta_{TM} + \lambda_{TM}\theta_{TF})$. Note that $Q_L + Q_T$ equals $Q_M + Q_F$.

[24] These relationships involve the *difference* between π_L and π_T, on the one hand, and π_M and π_F on the other. Another relationship involving *sums* of these terms is suggested by the national income relationship, as discussed in Section VII. With technical progress. $\theta_M\pi_M + \theta_F\pi_F$ equals $\theta_L\pi_L + \theta_T\pi_T$.

For some purposes it is useful to make the substitution from either (20) or (21) into the expressions for the changes in relative factor and commodity prices shown by (17)–(19). For example, if technological change is "neutral" in the sense described earlier, where the reduction in the input coefficient is the same in each industry (although different for each factor), β_L and β_T are zero in (21) and the relationship in (17) can be rewritten as

$$(w^* - r^*) = \frac{1}{|\theta|}(p_M^* - p_F^*) + (\pi_L - \pi_T).$$

To make things simple, suppose π_T is zero. The uniform reduction in labor input coefficients across industries might reflect, say, an improvement in labor quality attributable to education. Aside from the effect of any change in commodity prices on factor prices (of the Stolper-Samuelson variety), relative wages are directly increased by the improvement in labor quality.

Alternatively, consider substituting (20) into (19), to yield (19'):

$$(w^* - r^*) = -\frac{1}{\sigma}\left\{ Q_M\beta_M + Q_F\beta_F + Q_D(1 - \sigma_D)\frac{(\pi_M - \pi_F)}{|\theta|}\right\}. \tag{19'}$$

Will technological change that is Hicks neutral in every industry leave the factor price ratio unaltered at a given ratio of factor endowments? Equation (19') suggests a negative answer to this query unless progress is at the same rate in the two industries ($\pi_M = \pi_F$) or unless σ_D is unity.[25]

There exists an extensive literature in the theory of international trade concerned with (a) the effects of differences in production functions on pre-trade factor and commodity price ratios (and thus on positions of comparative advantage), and (b) the impact of growth (in factor supplies) or changes in technological knowledge in one or more countries on the world terms of trade.[26] The analysis of this paper is well suited to the

---

[25]Recalling n. 22, consider the following question: If the elasticity of substitution between factors is unity in every sector, will a change in the ratio of factor endowments result in an equal percentage change in the factor price ratio? From Section VI it is seen that this result can be expected only if σ_D is unity.

[26]See H. Johnson, "Economic Development and International Trade," *Money, Trade, and Economic Growth* (London: George Allen & Unwin, 1962), chap. iv, and the extensive bibliography there listed. The most complete treatment of the effects of various differences in production conditions on positions of comparative advantage is given by Amano, "Determinants of Comparative Costs ...," *op. cit.*, who also discusses special cases of Harrod neutrality. For a recent analysis of the impact of endowment and technology changes on the terms of trade see Takayama, "Economic Growth and International Trade," *Review of Economic Studies*, June, 1964.

discussion of these problems. The connection between (a) and expressions (17)–(19) is obvious. For (b) it is helpful to observe that the impact of any of these changes on world terms of trade depends upon the effect in each country separately of these changes on production and consumption at constant commodity prices. The production effects can be derived from the four equations of change for the production sector (equations [1.1]–[4.1] or later versions) and the consumption changes from equation (5.1).[27] The purpose of this paper is not to reproduce the results in detail but rather to expose those features of the model which bear upon all of these questions.

---

[27] Account must be taken, however, of the fact that with trade the quantities of M and F produced differ from the amounts consumed by the quantity of exports and imports.

ABOUT THE AUTHOR

Ronald W. Jones

Ronald W. Jones is the Xerox Professor of International Economics at the University of Rochester, where he has taught since 1958. He has also held visiting positions at the University of California at Berkeley, Columbia University, Simon Fraser University, and the Institute for International Economic Studies in Stockholm. He specializes in the theory of international trade and is the author of dozens of articles on this and related areas.

The General Validity of the Law of Comparative Advantage

ALAN V. DEARDORFF

Institute for International Economic Studies, University of Stockholm, and University of Michigan

It is well known that the law of comparative advantage breaks down when applied to individual commodities or pairs of commodities in a many-commodity world. This paper shows that the law is nonetheless valid if restated in terms of averages across all commodities. Specifically, a theorem and several corollaries are derived which establish correlations between vectors of trade and vectors containing relative-autarky-price measures of comparative advantage. These results are proven in a general many-commodity model that allows for tariffs, transport costs, and other impediments to trade.

The purpose of this paper is to demonstrate, in a general model, the validity of a weak form of the Law of Comparative Advantage, that is, that the *pattern of international trade is determined by comparative advantage*. This is surely the oldest proposition in the pure theory of international trade and is common both to the Ricardian comparative-costs theory and the Heckscher-Ohlin factor-proportions theory, so long as comparative advantage is measured by relative autarky prices. As such, one might think that the proposition requires no further comment except in the basic textbooks whose job it is to explain important truths in simple terms.

Yet this proposition, like other more recent theorems of trade theory, has proven somewhat difficult to extend beyond the simple models in which it was first formulated. Three examples should suffice to illustrate this difficulty. First, when Jones (1961) extended the doctrine of comparative advantage to a classical model with many goods and countries, he was forced to restate the concept of comparative costs in a form that lacked most of the simplicity and intuitive appeal of the original. Second, in the context of the Heckscher-Ohlin model, Melvin (1968) showed that if there are more goods than primary factors of production then the indeterminacy of the structure of production,

I would like to thank Ted Bergstrom, Paul Courant, Ronald Jones, Robert Stern, Lars Svensson, and Hal Varian for their helpful comments on an earlier draft of this paper, originally titled "Comparative Advantage and Natural Trade in General Equilibrium."

Reprinted with permission from Alan V. Deardorff, "The General Validity of the Law of Comparative Advantage," *Journal of Political Economy:* (1980), vol. 88, no. 5, pp. 941–957. © 1980 by The University of Chicago.

that had been noted previously by Samuelson (1953), implies that any good may be exported by any country. This, it would seem, destroys altogether any determinate relationship between the pattern of trade and anything else. And third, Travis (1964, 1972) has argued that the introduction of impediments to trade, and particularly of tariffs, can alter the pattern of trade, causing goods that would have been exported to be imported and vice versa. Thus, it appears that if the two-commodity, two-country, free-trade model is extended or modified in plausible ways, it then ceases to be possible to explain the pattern of trade by simple comparisons of autarky prices. Most recently, this impossibility has been shown by Drabicki and Takayama (1979).

I will show in this paper, however, that a version of the comparative-advantage proposition *does* hold in a general model that allows for all of the complications just mentioned. This is not to say that the authors cited in the last paragraph were wrong. Instead, what is needed is to relax somewhat the rigidity of the proposition itself and require only that it hold in the sense of an appropriate average rather than for each commodity individually. While several forms of the proposition will be proved below, all may be summarized by the following statement: There must exist a negative correlation between any country's relative autarky prices and its pattern of net exports. Thus, on average, high autarky prices are associated with imports and low autarky prices are associated with exports.

This proposition will be demonstrated in a model that includes a variety of impediments to trade, as well as free trade, as special cases. I allow in a general way for transport costs, and I allow domestic and world prices to differ by additional amounts to reflect such artificial trade impediments as tariffs and quantitative restrictions. Unlimited interference with trade is not allowed, however, since it is clear that sufficient use of trade *subsidies* could lead to any pattern of trade and thus invalidate the law of comparative advantage. For ease of reference, and to distinguish it from the more restrictive case of free trade, I will refer to this combination of assumptions as defining "natural trade." Thus a natural trade equilibrium is one in which there are no trade subsidies or other artificial stimulants to trade, but in which trade impediments of any sort may or may not be present. Free trade is then a special case of natural trade.[1]

My treatment of transport costs is somewhat unusual and should therefore also be mentioned in this introduction. Rather than postulate an explicit form for transport costs, I will distinguish goods on the basis of where they are delivered and incorporate transportation technology into a more general specification of the technology of production. For each country, a single production possibility set will define the constraints on its ability to produce for delivery at home and for delivery abroad. Thus any resources used up in transportation will be taken into account when the competitive

---

[1] Natural trade also includes autarky as another special case, though my results are, of course, of interest only in situations in which some trade actually does take place.

producers and traders of the economy maximize the value of net delivered output. In the body of the paper I will simplify notation somewhat by assuming that all world trade passes through a single international port, though in an Appendix I show that most of my results carry over to a world of any number of such ports.

With this introduction the analysis can proceed. In Section I, I will state and discuss the assumptions of the model, which are broad enough to encompass a wide variety of models that have appeared in the literature. In Section II, I will first prove a basic theorem, which uses autarky prices to value the vector of goods that a country trades in a natural trade equilibrium. This result then leads readily to four corollaries which provide alternative statements of the law of comparative advantage in the average sense discussed above. In Section III, I discuss several ways that these results can be strengthened or modified. Finally, I return in Section IV to the particular issues raised above and show how my results contribute to an understanding of the various phenomena noted by other authors.

I. THE MODEL

Consider a world of m countries, $i = 1, ..., m$, and n goods, $j = 1, ..., n$. The list of goods includes all final goods, intermediate goods, and services of primary factors of production. Each good may be delivered either on the country's home market or at the international port. Let Q^i be an n-vector of net supplies to country i's home market and T^i be an n-vector of net supplies by country i to the international port. Thus positive elements of Q^i represent goods available for consumption in country i, while negative elements represent net use of goods or factor services by production processes in country i. Similarly, the elements of the vector T^i represent the country's trade in each of the n goods: exports if positive and imports if negative. The country's total production, net of goods and resources used up in production and transport, is then $X^i = Q^i + T^i$.

Each country has its own net production possibility set, F^i, defined as the set of all feasible pairs of n-vectors, Q^i and T^i, given its technology and any constraints it may face on endowments of primary factors. Of the sets, F^i, I assume whatever is necessary to permit existence of the equilibria I will be studying. Thus, they must be closed, convex, and, in some weak sense, bounded from above.[2] In addition, I make the following assumption that says essentially that transport costs are nonnegative: If

$$(Q^i, T^i) \in F^i,$$

then   (1)

$$(Q^i + T^i, 0) \in F^i,$$

---

[2] It would be sufficient, though not necessary, to assume the existence of a vector $\overline{X}^i$ such that $Q + T \leq \overline{X}^i$ for all $(Q, T) \in F^i$.

where 0 here represents an n-vector of zeros. This says that any total net output vector that is feasible with trade is also feasible without, since resources can only be used up, but never created, by transporting goods between the domestic market and the international port. Thus if it is feasible to produce a good and deliver it abroad, $T_j^i > 0$, then it is also feasible to produce it and deliver it at home. Likewise, if it is feasible to import a good, $T_j^i < 0$, then it is also feasible not to import it and to reduce deliveries on the home market by the same amount.[3]

To represent demand in each country, stronger assumptions will be used. I assume that preferences in each country can be represented by a family of n-dimensional community indifference curves, which it will be convenient to represent by a community utility function, U^i. These utility functions are assumed to have the property of local nonsatiation: For any Q^{i^0} there exists a Q^{i^1} arbitrarily close to Q^{i^0} such that

$$U(Q^{i^1}) > U(Q^{i^0}). \tag{2}$$

This assumption will be used to rule out "thick" indifference curves.

Both producers and consumers are assumed to behave competitively, so that they maximize, respectively, the value of net output and the utility of consumption, subject to the prices that they face in each country.[4] In autarky equilibrium, production is for the domestic market only, while with trade, producers maximize the sum of the value of output delivered at home and the value of output delivered abroad, the prices of which will in general be different due to transportation costs. The price of output delivered abroad will also in general be different from the world price, due to impediments to trade such as tariffs. Equilibrium in the home market requires that the vector of net supplies to the home market be consumed. Equilibrium in international trade requires in addition that the sum of all countries' net supplies to the international port be zero and that each country's trade be balanced at world prices.

I begin by characterizing autarky equilibrium. Let Q^{a^i} be a vector of net outputs both supplied and demanded on the domestic market of country i under autarky, and let p^{a^i} be a corresponding vector of autarky prices. Then the following three assumptions require

---

[3] Note that this assumption includes, as a special case, the more explicit assumption made by Samuelson (1954), who specified that some fraction, α_j, of each good be used up in transport. If I let G be a more conventional production possibility set in which location of delivery is not specified, then my $F = \{(Q, T)$ such that $\overline{X} \in G$ where $\overline{X}_j = Q_j + T_j + \alpha_j |T_j|\}$. Assumption (1) then follows immediately.

[4] In order for producers to maximize the value of net output, I make the standard assumptions that domestic economies are competitive and that there are no externalities, production taxes, or other domestic distortions. Increasing returns to scale must also be ruled out.

that Q^{a^i} be feasible, maximal, and preferred, given the prices p^{a^i}:

$$(Q^{a^i}, 0) \in F^i, \tag{3}$$

$$p^{a^i} Q^{a^i} \geq p^{a^i} Q \text{ for all } (Q, 0) \in F^i, \tag{4}$$

$$U^i(Q^{a^i}) \geq U^i(Q) \text{ for all } Q \text{ such that } p^{a^i} Q \leq p^{a^i} Q^{a^i}. \tag{5}$$

Here, and throughout the paper, all products of vectors represent inner products.

To characterize a natural trade equilibrium, more notation is needed. Let Q^{n^i} and T^{n^i} be vectors of net supply by country i to domestic and foreign markets in a natural trade equilibrium. Let p^{q^i} and p^{t^i} be corresponding vectors of prices facing domestic producers, consumers, and traders in these markets, defined in terms of a single international numeraire. Thus the elements of p^{q^i} are simply the domestic prices in country i, while those of p^{t^i} are the prices paid or received by domestic traders at the international port and will be referred to as traders' prices. In particular, p^{t^i} includes any tariffs that must be paid on domestic imports and is net of any export taxes paid on exports. The two vectors of prices will have to differ by enough to cover transport costs if trade is to take place, but this will be assured by the maximization assumption below. Assumptions analogous to those above require that production, trade, and consumption be feasible, maximal, and preferred given these prices:

$$(Q^{n^i}, T^{n^i}) \in F^i, \tag{6}$$

$$p^{q^i} Q^{n^i} + p^{t^i} T^{n^i} \geq p^{a^i} Q + p^{t^i} T \text{ for all } (Q, T) \in F^i, \tag{7}$$

$$U^i(Q^{n^i}) \geq U^i(Q) \text{ for all } Q \text{ such that } p^{q^i} Q \leq p^{q^i} Q^{n^i}. \tag{8}$$

Within the international port, there is also a vector of world prices, p^w, also measured in terms of the international numeraire. It represents the price at which international exchange actually takes place and may differ from the national traders' prices, p^{t^i}, to the extent that countries levy tariffs or export taxes. Each country's trade is assumed to be balanced at these world prices:

$$p^w T^{n^i} = 0. \tag{9}$$

The relationship between world prices and national traders' prices can in general be complicated, depending both on the precise nature of trade impediments and on the direction of trade itself. However, all I need to characterize natural trade is to rule out trade subsidies, and this is done by the following simple assumption:

$$(p_j^w - p_j^{t^i}) T_j^{n^i} \geq 0 \text{ for } \quad j = 1, ..., n. \tag{10}$$

What this says is that if a good is exported, $T_j^{n^i} > 0$, then the world price must be at least as large as the price the exporter receives, any differences between the two representing an export tax levied by country i. And if a good is imported, $T_j^{n^i} < 0$, then the world price must be no greater than the price the importer pays, any difference representing a tariff. Of course, if there were no policies interfering with trade, then (10) would be an equality.

Finally, I require that the world market for each good clear:

$$\sum_{i=1}^{m} T^{n^i} = 0.$$
(11)

Assumptions (1) through (11) are sufficient for most of my results. However, later in the paper I will have occasion to make comparisons among autarky and world prices. For that purpose it will be convenient to normalize world prices and each country's autarky prices to lie on the unit simplex:

$$\sum_{j=1}^{n} p_j^w = \sum_{j=1}^{n} p_j^{a^i} = 1 \qquad i = 1, ..., m.$$
(12)

This is equivalent to taking, as numeraire, a bundle containing one unit of each good.

It may be well to note, before I proceed, that my list of assumptions does *not* include a number that are often made in trade theory. The utility functions have not been assumed to be differentiable and neither have the boundaries of the production possibility sets. The latter have not been assumed to be convex, nor the former to be homothetic. And neither have been assumed to be in any sense identical across countries. Thus the countries can differ arbitrarily in tastes, technologies, and factor endowments. None of this should be too surprising, however, since, while some of these assumptions may make certain modes of analysis more convenient, they are not really needed for establishing the role of comparative advantage.

More surprising, perhaps, is the limited amount I have had to say about the role of, and availability of, factor endowments in the model. Since the assumption of natural trade permits any of the "goods" to be nontraded, one can as well include the services of any or all factors of production as elements in the vector of n goods and even allow them to be in variable supply. One could even allow some or all of them to be traded internationally, so that the concept of comparative advantage is then extended to trade in the services of factors of production. Or, at the other extreme, one could identify as separate factors those which are employed in different industries and thus allow for various degrees of interindustry factor immobility. Finally, with some care one can allow for dynamic factor accumulation by interpreting the sets F as constraints on steady-state net output per capita.[5]

The point is that, while the list of assumptions earlier in this section was a long one, the assumptions themselves are much less restrictive than one often meets in models of international trade. With some care and ingenuity in interpreting the model, the results I

---

[5]Care is needed here in assuring that a competitive economy will still, in a dynamic context, maximize the steady-state value of net output per capita. If technology permits inputs and outputs at different times, then it is the discounted value of the input-output stream that is maximized by a competitive economy. This can be resolved for one's purposes either by assuming that the interest rate equals the natural rate of growth or, more generally, by making a distinction between rental markets for the services of stocks of goods and the markets for their flow as final sales.

am about to derive can shed light on the mechanism of international trade in quite a variety of contexts.

II. A THEOREM AND ITS COROLLARIES

Now consider any one of the countries described in Section I. I will show first that if one uses autarky prices to evaluate its net trade vector in a natural trade equilibrium then that value must be less than or equal to zero. That is, the value of what a country gives up in trade is no greater, at autarky prices, than the value of what it acquires. While this may not seem to be a very surprising property, its proof uses most of the assumptions that were introduced in Section I. And once it is established, it leads fairly easily to a variety of results concerning comparative advantage.

The meaning of the theorem can be illustrated with the simple offer-curve diagram of Figure 1. For a country which trades only two goods, the curve *COC'* shows the various possibilities for exports and imports of both goods with free trade. My theorem says that any trade which takes place will have a negative value when valued at autarky prices. But since autarky prices are given by the slope of the line tangent to the offer curve at the origin, *POP'*, this means merely that *COC'* lies wholly to one side of this line. Well-behaved offer curves will have this property, and the reader may recognize a number of my assumptions as necessary to prevent the offer curve from "bending backward." Of course my model is far more general than Figure 1, since it allows an arbitrary number of goods and does not require free trade. Still, one can interpret the theorem as saying that autarky prices provide a supporting hyperplane for the set of all possible trades.

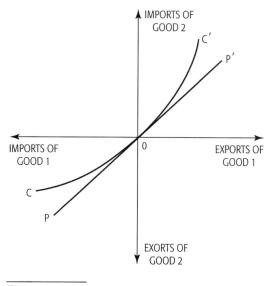

Figure 1

THEOREM: *If prices and quantities in autarky and trade satisfy assumptions (1) – (10) for a particular country, i, then*

$$p^{a^i} T^{n^i} \leq 0. \tag{13}$$

Proof: Since I am dealing with only a single country, I will omit the country superscript in what follows. I begin by adding up the inequalities in (10) to get

$$p^w T^n - p^t T^n \geq 0, \tag{14}$$

from which, using (9),

$$p^t T^n \leq p^w T^n = 0. \tag{15}$$

From (3) and (7) it then follows that

$$p^q Q^a \leq p^q Q^n + p^t T^n \leq p^q Q^n, \tag{16}$$

and this, from (8), implies

$$U(Q^n) \geq U(Q^n). \tag{17}$$

Thus the vector of goods consumed in natural trade is at least as preferred as that consumed in autarky. It follows from (2) and (5) that

$$p^a Q^n \geq p^a Q^a, \tag{18}$$

for if this were not the case, (2) would permit one to find another vector, $\overline{Q}$, in the neighborhood of Q^n, that would also cost less at autarky prices than Q^a but would be strictly preferred, violating (5).

Now (6) and (1) imply that $(Q^n + T^n, 0) \in F$, so that (4) implies

$$p^a Q^a \geq p^a (Q^n + T^n). \tag{19}$$

Rearranging and using (18) one gets the desired result:

$$p^a T^n \leq p^a Q^a - p^a Q^n \leq 0. \tag{20}$$

Q.E.D.

The theorem has been stated in the form of a weak inequality. Still it should be clear, from the chain of reasoning used in its proof, that there are many ways that the inequality can be strengthened. Some of these will be mentioned in Section III.

Consider, now, the issue of comparative advantage. My theorem is already very suggestive in this regard: For the autarky-price value of trade to be negative, it would have to be true that the autarky prices of exports are low compared with those of imports, and thus the country is exporting those goods with relatively low autarky prices as the principle of comparative advantage would suggest. To make this relationship more precise, I will now examine several correlations between particular vectors of relative autarky prices and net exports. By showing these correlations to be less than or equal to zero, I establish a *tendency* for high-autarky-priced items to be imported and for low-autarky-priced items to be exported. I do not attempt to say anything about the pattern of trade in any particular commodity, or pair of commodities, for it is known from the work of others that such statements are likely to be invalid in a model as general as mine. Still, if I can show a negative correlation such as just described, I will have demonstrated that comparative advantage is nonetheless valid as at least a partial determinant of the pattern of trade overall.

The sign of a correlation between two vectors is, of course, the same as the sign of their covariance. For any two *n*-vectors, x^1 and x^2, by definition

$$\text{cor}\,(x^1, x^2) = \frac{\text{cov}\,(x^1, x^2)}{\sqrt{\text{var}\,(x^1)\,\text{var}\,(x^2)}} \tag{21}$$

where

$$\text{cov}\,(x^1, x^2) = \sum_{j=1}^{n} (x_j^i - \bar{x}^i)(x_j^2 - \bar{x}^2), \tag{22}$$

$$\text{var}\,(x^i) = \sum_{j=1}^{n} (x_j^i - \bar{x}^i)^2 \quad \text{for } i = 1, 2, \tag{23}$$

and

$$\bar{x}^i = \frac{1}{n} \sum_{j=1}^{n} x_j^i \quad \text{for } i = 1, 2. \tag{24}$$

Since the denominator of (21) is nonnegative (and nonzero if the correlation is defined), the correlation and covariance must have the same sign.[6] Furthermore, the covariance can be rewritten as follows:

$$\text{cov}\,(x^1, x^2) = x^1 x^2 - n\bar{x}^1 \bar{x}^2. \tag{25}$$

Thus if either of the vectors sums to zero, so that it has zero mean, then the sign of their correlation is just the sign of their inner product. Since I will use this property several times, I state it formally for ease of reference: If

$$\sum_{j=1}^{n} x_j^i = 0 \quad \text{for } i = 1 \quad \text{or} \quad i = 2, \tag{26}$$

---

[6]I ignore, in what follows, the possibility of either vector having a zero variance so that the correlation is undefined. When that happens, as it will when there is no trade or when relative autarky prices are all identical, my conclusions about correlations can be restated as conclusions about the corresponding covariances only.

then

$$\mathrm{cor}\,(x^1, x^2) \gtreqless 0 \quad \text{as } x^1 x^2 \gtreqless 0.$$

In stating the role of comparative advantage, my first problem is to decide what is meant by "relative autarky prices." With many countries, there is no single set of foreign autarky prices with respect to which one country's can be compared. I will resolve this problem first by using world prices with trade as the basis for comparison. This gives corollaries 1 and 2 below. Then I show in corollary 3 that if in fact there are only two countries, so that a single vector of foreign autarky prices can be identified, then a comparison of the two vectors of autarky prices also yields the appropriate correlation with the vector of trade. Finally, in corollary 4 I establish a correlation between trade and autarky prices for a world of many countries without reference to world prices.

COROLLARY 1: *For any country let ρ be the vector of ratios of its autarky prices to the world prices that prevail with trade,*

$$\rho_j = p_j^a \big| p_j^w \quad j = 1, ..., n, \tag{27}$$

and let e be the vector of the country's net exports, valued at world prices,

$$e_j = p_j^w T_j^n \quad j = 1, ..., n. \tag{28}$$

Then if assumptions (1)–(10) are satisfied for that country, it must be true that

$$\mathrm{cor}\,(\rho, e) \leq 0. \tag{29}$$

Proof: From balanced trade (9),

$$\sum_{j=1}^n e_j = p^w T^n = 0 \tag{30}$$

so that (26) permits one to consider only the inner product, ρe. But

$$\rho e = \sum_{j=1}^n \frac{p_j^a}{p_j^w} p_j^w T_j^n = \sum_{j=1}^n p_j^a T_j^a = p^a T^n \leq 0 \tag{31}$$

by the theorem.   Q.E.D.

Here I have used ratios of autarky to world prices as the basis for comparison of industries. A slightly different comparison is also possible using the difference between autarky and world prices. For this difference to be meaningful, I assume that both price vectors are normalized to lie on the unit simplex, as stated in assumption (12).

COROLLARY 2: *If assumptions (1)–(10) are satisfied for any country and if prices are normalized as in (12), then*

$$\mathrm{cor}\,(p^a - p^w, T^n) \leq 0. \tag{32}$$

Proof: For the inner product I have

$$(p^a - p^w)T^n = p^a T^n - p^w T^n = p^a T^n \leq 0 \tag{33}$$

by (9) and the theorem. Since, by (12),

$$\sum_{j=1}^{n} (p_j^a - p_j^w) = \sum_{j=1}^{n} p_j^a - \sum_{j=1}^{n} p_j^w = 0, \tag{34}$$

(26) permits one to deduce (32) from (33).   Q.E.D.

Notice that both of these results obtain for any particular country without any assumptions whatever about behavior in the rest of the world. Also, no use has been made of the requirement that world markets clear, assumption (11). This, of course, is because I have not yet tried to make comparisons across countries. I now make such a comparison for a two-country world.

COROLLARY 3: *If the world contains only two countries, i = 1, 2, both satisfying (1)–(10), and if (11) is also satisfied, then*

$$\operatorname{cor}(p^{a^1} - p^{a^2}, T^{n^1}) \leq 0, \tag{35}$$

where p^{a^1} and p^{a^2} are both normalized to the unit simplex (12).

Proof: From (11) with $m = 2$ note that

$$T^{n^1} = -T^{n^2}. \tag{36}$$

Thus

$$(p^{a^1} - p^{a^2})T^{n^1} = p^{a^1} T^{n^1} + p^{a^2} T^{n^2}, \tag{37}$$

which is seen to be nonpositive by applying the theorem to each of the two terms on the right-hand side separately. The normalization (12), together with (26), then implies (35). Q.E.D.

This result, though derived only for a two-country world, has the advantage of placing a clear restriction on the possible pattern of natural trade. Given the two vectors of autarky prices, it says that, of all the conceivable patterns of trade that might emerge, only those which yield the indicated nonpositive correlation will be observed. Corollaries 1 and 2, on the other hand, do not embody such a clear restriction on the pattern of trade, since they contain the world-price vector which must be determined simultaneously with the pattern of trade.

To obtain a similar restriction for a many-country world I now prove a final corollary which deals with all countries and industries simultaneously. Let P^a be a vector of length mn containing the autarky prices of all countries and all industries, and let E be a vector of the same length containing the net exports of all countries and all industries, arranged in the same order as in P^a.

COROLLARY 4: *If the world contains m countries, all satisfying assumptions (1)–(10), and if (11) is also satisfied, then*

$$\operatorname{cor}(p^a, E) \le 0. \tag{38}$$

Proof: From the construction of E, it is clear that

$$\sum_{k=1}^{mn} E_k = \sum_{j=1}^{n} \left(\sum_{i=1}^{m} T_j^{n^i} \right) = 0 \tag{39}$$

by (11). Thus (26) allows one to look only at the inner product of P^a and E. But

$$p^a E = \sum_{k=1}^{mn} p_k^a E_k = \sum_{i=1}^{m} \left(\sum_{j=1}^{n} p_j^{a^i} T_j^{n^i} \right)$$

$$= \sum_{i=1}^{m} p^{a^i} T^{n^i}. \tag{40}$$

From the theorem, each term in this summation is nonpositive, implying (38).   Q.E.D.

To summarize, the first two corollaries provide alternative explanations of a single country's trade, one in value terms, the other in terms of quantities, with comparative advantage measured by comparisons of autarky prices with world prices. The third corollary provides the general analogue to the traditional comparative-advantage proposition for two countries in terms of a good-by-good comparison of the two countries' autarky prices. Finally, the fourth and last corollary provides the most general statement of comparative advantage for the world as a whole.

III. REFINEMENTS

In this section I point out two ways that the proofs above can be modified, either to strengthen the results or to alter the assumptions needed for their validity.

STRONG INEQUALITIES

The theorem and its corollaries are stated in terms of weak inequalities. These can be strengthened by any of several additional assumptions which serve to contribute a strict inequality somewhere in the chain of reasoning used to prove the theorem. I leave it to the reader to verify that any of the following assumptions would serve this purpose. (1) Transport costs are strictly positive for nonzero trade. (2) Tariff or export tax revenues are strictly positive in the natural trade equilibrium. (3) The optimal consumption bundle given any positive price vector is unique and different in natural trade and autarky. (4) The production possibility set is strictly convex, and trade and autarky prices differ.

While the first of these assumptions, especially, is realistic, I have chosen not to use any of them throughout the paper since they would exclude one of the best-known models and results of trade theory. That is the classical Ricardian constant-costs model with two countries of different size. In that model a trade equilibrium can arise in which the world prices equal the autarky prices of the large country, which then alters production, but not consumption, when it moves from autarky to trade. In that case the value of its trade at its own autarky prices is of course zero, as are the correlations of corollaries 1 and 2 for the large country. However, aside from this and perhaps other equally special cases, one can expect strictly negative correlations to be the normal result.

RELATION TO THE GAINS FROM TRADE

The reader will already have noted that part of the proof of the theorem bears a marked similarity to the proof of the gains from trade (Samuelson 1939). I showed first that natural trade would be preferred to autarky (inequality [17]) and then that this implies the theorem. An alternative proof could have begun, then, with the assumption that trade is beneficial.

While this would not really be an improvement over the present analysis, since it would leave unanswered the question of whether there would indeed be gains from trade, this modification does suggest an alternative proof that does not rely on the fiction of community preferences.[7] Suppose that each country contains many individuals, each with his own preferences, and that a move from autarky to trade is accompanied by suitable redistribution of income so as to leave all individuals better off. Then an inequality like (18) can be obtained for each consumer individually, and (18) itself can be obtained by adding these up. The rest of the proof then follows.

IV. DISCUSSION

At the beginning of the paper I noted that familiar simple statements about the role of comparative advantage become difficult or impossible when models are complicated in a variety of realistic ways. I have now developed an alternative way of representing the relationship between autarky prices and trade by looking at correlations between the two. This has enabled me to state a variety of simple propositions regarding comparative advantage, and I have proved these propositions in a very general model. I will now compare these results with others that have appeared in the literature.

Consider first the classical model of constant costs. Here it must be admitted that my contribution is limited, for the role of comparative advantage is already well understood in the classical model. The familiar proposition for a two-country world, that goods can be ranked in terms of comparative advantage with one end of the chain being exportable and the other importable, is considerably stronger than my own corollary 3 for the same case.[8] I note only what has sometimes been doubted: that while the classical theory

---

[7] This alternative proof was suggested by Ted Bergstrom.

[8] The explanation of trade in terms of a chain of comparative advantage was apparently first demonstrated by Haberler (1936).

predicts only the direction and not the magnitude of trade, it nonetheless permits one to infer a negative correlation between relative costs and net exports.[9]

With both many countries and many goods, the classical model has been examined in detail by Jones (1961). His results, again, allow a much more precise determination of the pattern of international specialization than does, say, my corollary 4. Still, my results do show that a straightforward comparison of costs does have something to say about the pattern of trade without going all the way to the solution of a mathematical programming problem as is done by Jones.[10]

Turning now to generalizations of the factor-proportions theory of trade, one sees that my model is consistent with the 3-good, 2-factor model in which Melvin (1968) found the pattern of trade to be indeterminate. But this indeterminacy has not prevented me from obtaining meaningful correlations. What I have done, in a sense, is to exploit those limitations that Melvin *was* able to place, implicitly, on the pattern of trade, as he did in his elegant figure 8, and to show that these limitations are enough to assure that the pattern of trade still, in a general sense, follows the dictates of comparative advantage. In his figure, Melvin showed that trade could be represented by any of an infinite number of lines, connecting two other parallel lines and passing through a single point representing demand. The clue to the validity of my correlations is that the two parallel lines must lie on opposite sides of the demand point in a manner that is prescribed by relative autarky prices. Thus in Melvin's model, and in more general multicommodity, multifactor models, the law of comparative advantage is weakened but not destroyed by the indeterminacy of the pattern of production.

Finally, a great advantage of my model is that it allows for a considerable amount of interference with the free flow of trade by such impediments to trade as transport costs and tariffs. It is true, as Travis (1964, 1972) has suggested, that such impediments can cause particular goods to be exported that would have been imported and vice versa.[11] But while this is possible for particular goods, my analysis shows that it cannot be true of so many goods as to reverse the average relationship that must hold between comparative

---

[9]Doubt that this should be true has been expressed, e.g., by Bhagwati (1964, p. 11) in criticizing empirical tests of the comparative-costs theory. Similar doubts in the context of the factor-proportions theory also led Harkness and Kyle (1975) to employ logit analysis, rather than least-squares regression, to test that theory. While my results do not deal directly with factor endowments or factor intensities, they nonetheless suggest that tests for simple correlations may not, after all, be inappropriate.

[10]In a further discussion of his results, Jones (1977) remarks that "alternative and equivalent criteria in two-by-two cases may not prove equivalent in more general settings. But knowledge of the general case can aid in recasting criteria in the simple model so that it can generalize." My results provide another example of this phenomenon, for my correlations, when applied to the two-by-two case, are equivalent to alternative statements of the comparative advantage criterion.

[11]An example of this is given in Deardorff (1979) and requires the presence of intermediate goods, as well as tariffs or transport costs, in a multicommodity model.

advantage and trade. Only by subsidies could this average relationship be made not to hold—subsidies either of production, which would violate my assumptions (4) and (7), or of trade, which could violate my assumption (10).

APPENDIX

Instead of the single international port assumed in the body of the paper, let there now be an arbitrary number of ports, l, indexed $h = 1, ..., l$. While it is not necessary, these could now be identified with the countries of the model, in which case one would have $l = m$. Instead of a single trade vector for each country, I must now distinguish trade vectors for each of the l destinations. Let $^h t^i$ represent country i's vector of net supplies to port h. Then the total trade vector, $T^i = \Sigma_{h=1}^l {}^h t^i$. In addition I must now distinguish separate world-price vectors at each port, $^h p^w$, and separate vectors of traders' prices facing country i's traders at each port, $^h p^{t^i}$. A country's production possibilities set, F^i, now contains all feasible collections of the $l + 1$ vectors (Q^i, $^1 t^i$, ..., $^l t^i$).

The following assumptions now replace those in Section I:

$$\text{If } (Q^i, {}^1t^i, ..., {}^lt^i) \in F^i, \quad \text{then} \quad \left(Q^i + \sum_{h=1}^l {}^h t^i, 0, ..., 0 \right) \in F^i, \tag{A1}$$

$$(Q^{a^i}, 0, ..., 0) \in F^i, \tag{A3}$$

$$p^{a^i} Q^{a^i} \geq p^{a^i} Q \quad \text{for all } (Q, 0, ..., 0) \in F^i, \tag{A4}$$

$$(Q^{n^i}, {}^1t^{n^i}, ..., {}^lt^{n^i}) \in F^i, \tag{A6}$$

$$p^{q^i} Q^{n^i} + \sum_{h=1}^l {}^h p^{t^i}\, {}^h t^{n^i} \geq p^{q^i} Q + \sum_{h=1}^l {}^h p^{t^i}\, {}^h t \quad \text{for all } (Q, {}^1l, ..., {}^1t) \in F^i, \tag{A7}$$

$$\sum_{h=1}^l {}^h p^{nh}\, {}^h t^{n^i} = 0, \tag{A9}$$

$$({}^h p_j^w - {}^h p_j^{t^i})\, {}^h t_j^{n^i} \geq 0 \quad \text{for } j = 1, ..., n; h = 1, ..., l, \tag{A10}$$

$$\sum_{i=1}^m {}^h t^{n^i} = 0 \quad \text{for } h = 1, ..., l, \tag{A11}$$

$$\sum_{j=1}^n p_j^{a^i} = 1 \quad i = 1, ..., m. \tag{A12}$$

The remaining assumptions are unchanged.

The statement of the theorem is unchanged, but its proof must be modified. Inequality (14) is obtained for each port individually, and thus from (A9), I get

$$^h p^i\, {}^h t^n \leq 0 \quad \text{for } h = 1, ..., l. \tag{A15}$$

Inequality (16) then follows from (A7) as before; (17) and (18) are unchanged, while (19) follows from (A1), (A6), and (A4) as before; (20) follows, and the theorem is proved.

Corollaries 1 and 2 no longer make sense, as there are now many vectors of world prices. However, corollaries 3 and 4 can still be proved by using the theorem and (A11).

Thus most of the results of the paper continue to be valid in a world of many ports, and the fiction of a single port was needed only to simplify notation.

REFERENCES

Bhagwati, Jagdish N. "The Pure Theory of International Trade: A Survey." *Econ. J.* 74 (March 1964): 1–84.

Deardorff, Alan V. "Weak Links in the Chain of Comparative Advantage." *J. Internat. Econ.* 9 (May 1979): 197–209.

Drabicki, John Z., and Takayama, Akira. "An Antinomy in the Theory of Comparative Advantage." *J. Internat. Econ.* 9 (May 1979): 211–23.

Haberler, Gottfried von. *The Theory of International Trade, with Its Applications to Commercial Policy.* London: Hodge, 1936.

Harkness, Jon, and Kyle, John F. "Factors Influencing United States Comparative Advantage." *J. Internat. Econ.* 5 (May 1975): 153–65.

Jones, Ronald W. "Comparative Advantage and the Theory of Tariffs: A Multi-Country, Multi-Commodity Model." *Rev. Econ. Studies* 28 (June 1961): 161–75.

——— "'Two-ness' in Trade Theory: Costs and Benefits." Special Papers in International Economics no. 12, Princeton Univ., Internat. Finance Sec., April 1977.

Melvin, James R. "Production and Trade with Two Factors and Three Goods." *A.E.R.* 58 (December 1968): 1249–68.

Samuelson, Paul A. "The Gains from International Trade." *Canadian J. Econ. and Polit. Sci.* 5 (May 1939): 195–205.

——— "Prices of Factors and Goods in General Equilibrium." *Rev. Econ. Studies* 21 (February 1953): 1–20.

——— "The Transfer Problem and Transport Costs, II: Analysis of Effects of Trade Impediments." *Econ. J.* 64 (June 1954): 264–89.

Travis, William P. *The Theory of Trade and Protection.* Cambridge, Mass.: Harvard Univ. Press, 1964.

——— "Production, Trade, and Protection When There Are Many Commodities and Two Factors." *A.E.R.* 62 (March 1972): 87–106.

ABOUT THE AUTHOR

Alan V. Deardorff

Alan V. Deardorff is the John W. Sweetland Professor of International Economics, as well as Professor of Economics and Public Policy, at the University of Michigan. He received his Ph.D. from Cornell University. He has served as a consultant to many governmental and international agencies, including the Departments of State, Treasury, and Labor, as well as the World Bank and the OECD. He is on the editorial boards of the *Journal of International Economics*, the *International Trade Journal*, and *The World Economy*. He is co-author, with Robert M. Stern, of the *Michigan Model of World Production and Trade and Measurement of Nontariff Barriers*.

Editor's Queries:

Which article authored by you but not reprinted in this volume would you most highly recommend to graduate students in international economics? I should probably recommend my 1982 paper on Heckscher-Ohlin. But for just the fun of trade theory, let me suggest instead my much more obscure paper "The Directions of Developing Country Trade: Examples from Pure Theory," in a 1987 World Bank volume edited by Ole Havrylyshyn. Two of its models come straight out of science fiction novels.

What are the major unresolved questions of international economics? What are likely to be the hot topics of the next decade? Questions: Why don't countries trade more than they do? How can we (and should we?) persuade the public that trade is good for them? Why do some major economics departments think they can get along without international economists? (Or the related question: If we are as scarce as we seem, why aren't we paid more?) Hot topics are whatever Grossman, Krugman, and Helpman work on next. Or perhaps "effects of a stock-market crash on trade flows."

What advice do you have to offer graduate students in the field of international economics? Listen to people who know something about the world. Then try to make sense of it. And have fun.

Does European Unemployment Prop Up American Wages? National Labor Markets and Global Trade

Donald R. Davis

I consider trade between a flexible-wage America and a rigid-wage Europe. In a benchmark case, a move from autarky to free trade doubles European unemployment. American wages rise to the European level. Entry of the unskilled "South" to world markets raises European unemployment. Europe's commitment to the high wage wholly insulates America from the shock. Immigration to America raises American income, but lowers European income dollar for dollar, while European unemployment rises. Absent South–North migration of the unskilled from 1970–1990, Europe could have maintained the same wage with from one-eighth to one-fourth less unemployment. (JEL F11, J31, E24)

I. A GLOBAL APPROACH

In recent years, factor market developments in the United States and United Kingdom have contrasted sharply with those in continental Europe. In the United States and United Kingdom, the relative wage of the unskilled has declined significantly. In the span of a decade (1979–1989) the wage of a U.S. worker in the 90th percentile relative to that of one in the 10th percentile rose by over 20 percent (Richard B. Freeman and Lawrence F. Katz, 1995). This rising wage inequality was much less evident in continental Europe. However, unemployment has risen sharply in Europe. The early postwar decades are now thought of as a "Golden Age" for Europe, with unemployment rates of 2 to 3 percent. Beginning in the 1970's these rates have climbed dramatically, reaching double digits in many of these countries (Center for Economic Policy Research [CEPR], 1995).

Department of Economics, Harvard University, Cambridge, MA 02138, and National Bureau of Economic Research. I would like to acknowledge, without implication, the helpful comments of Richard Brecher, Carolyn Evans, John Leahy, Howard Shatz, David Weinstein, and Jeff Williamson. I am also grateful for the support for this project from the Harvard Institute for International Development (HIID).

An extensive empirical literature has considered the provenance of these factor market developments. The studies are of two principal types (Freeman and Katz, 1995). The individual country studies provide a rich account of local developments in institutions, factor supplies, and demand conditions. The comparative (cross-country) studies abstract from local idiosyncrasies to search for common themes. However, even the comparative studies suffer from an important drawback: they remain a collection of individual stories. They do not pretend to provide a common framework—and the consistency this enforces—to provide a unified account.

This suggests the value of a third approach, which may be termed "global." It is, in the first instance, a general equilibrium story. Consistency is enforced by the fact that there is a simultaneous determination of equilibrium in all of the factor markets. Naturally, tractability limits the degree of local institutional detail that may be considered. Considering some important differences in factor market institutions will nonetheless be an important feature of such an approach.

However, a global approach is more than just general equilibrium. It aims at a *unified* explanation of very divergent experience. There are two reasons for seeking such a unified account. First, many of the shocks hitting the industrial "North" are common—for example, the entry to the integrated world economy of important new trading partners from the newly industrializing "South."[1] If we are to believe such accounts, we need to see how these shocks interact with a variety of local institutions. A more subtle—but by this more important—reason for considering a global approach is that the consequences even of purely local institutions and shocks often depend crucially on the links to the global market.

The paper joins two elements that have figured prominently in these discussions, but whose implications have not previously been worked out in a consistent manner. The first is the stylized characterization of America as a flexible-wage economy, and Europe as an economy in which a variety of institutions—unions, explicit minimum wages, etc.—make wages more rigid.[2] The second is the Heckscher-Ohlin model, widely acknowledged to be the appropriate framework for examining movements in relative wages (Paul R. Krugman, 1996).

---

[1] Another source of common shocks—those due to global technological change—is analyzed in Davis (1998).

[2] There are alternative approaches to introducing unemployment into general equilibrium trade models. For example, Steven J. Matusz (1996) develops an elegant model merging elements of efficiency-wage unemployment with monopolistic competition to show how the increased market size due to trade can raise real wages, so reduce equilibrium unemployment in both countries. This provides insight for questions such as European integration. The simpler model that is developed here, though, captures the essential elements of relative demand shifts that have been seen as the heart of recent developments in both Europe and America. See, e.g., Kevin M. Murphy (1995).

Thus, we will build a model of world trade between a flexible-wage America and a minimum-wage Europe. In doing so, we build on the classic work of Richard A. Brecher (1974a, b). The America versus Europe dichotomy has been featured in a variety of recent work.[3] The distinctive feature of the present work is the explicit focus on factor markets in *both* countries, and particularly on their interaction owing to their link via trade in goods.

This paper confirms that national factor market institutions matter. They profoundly affect global patterns of output, employment, and wages. Surprisingly, though, in the present context they have no power in accounting for cross-country differences in the evolution of relative wages. Often forgotten in this context is that even countries with distinctive factor market institutions are linked by world commodity prices and producers' zero profit conditions. Hence an account of the observed wage trends must move beyond an appeal to local institutional differences.

This paper is comprised of seven parts. Section II examines the consequences of differing labor-market institutions for countries linked by world commodity trade in homogeneous goods. Section III examines the contrasting impacts on the stylized America and Europe posed by the appearance of newly industrializing countries. Section IV examines the effects of factor accumulation in the two countries on wages and unemployment. Section V considers the implications of South–North migration for unemployment in Europe. Section VI returns to the issue of divergent wage experience between America and Europe. Section VII concludes.

II. NATIONAL LABOR MARKETS AND GLOBAL TRADE

A. UNEMPLOYMENT IN THE GLOBAL EQUILIBRIUM

The aim of this paper is to develop a model of trade between two countries, one of which has flexible wages, while the other imposes a binding minimum wage on unskilled labor. It is convenient to develop this in three stages. The first considers a conventional two-sector general equilibrium model of a closed economy and establishes some relations that are key to later analysis. The second introduces a binding minimum wage within the

---

[3] This includes Giuseppe Bertola and Andrea Ichino (1995), Freeman and Katz (1995), Krugman (1994, 1995), and Adrian Wood (1994). Bertola and Ichino develop an insightful approach that identifies rising volatility of idiosyncratic shocks as a potential account of the growing wage dispersion in the United States and rising unemployment in Europe. Their focus on homogeneous labor suggests a story of growing within-group dispersion. The remaining papers are closer to the approach of the present paper, focusing on heterogeneous labor. Here I provide a consistent general equilibrium model integrating the flexible/rigid dichotomy in the context of heterogeneous labor.

closed economy. Finally, I show the isomorphism between this economy and the two-country trading world of interest.[4]

Consider a closed flexible-wage economy. There are two factors of production: skill and labor (also termed the unskilled). They are available in fixed supply given respectively by H^W and L^W (shortly these will be the world endowments of a two-country world). These are used to produce two goods under constant returns to scale. Assume that at any common factor prices, good X is skill intensive relative to Y. Assume that preferences are homothetic, and that both goods are necessary in consumption. Let w be the return to labor, r the return to skill, and P the relative price of X in terms of Y. Then the competitive cost conditions insure that for each sector price equals unit cost:

$$c_X(w, r) = P \qquad c_Y(w, r) = 1. \tag{1}$$

Assume that marginal products are always strictly positive. Then flexible wages insure full employment. Factor market clearing requires that employment in the two sectors equal the world endowment:

$$H_X + H_Y = H^W \qquad L_X + L_Y = L^W. \tag{2}$$

By Walras' law, goods market clearing is insured by equality of demand and supply of good X.

Three relations are key to our analysis. The first is a relation between the price P in a closed economy and the endowment ratio, $h^W \equiv H^W/L^W$, of that economy. The Heckscher-Ohlin theorem insures that a rise in skill abundance reduces the relative price of the skill-intensive good. This relation can be expressed as:

$$P = \lambda(h), \text{ where } \lambda'(h) < 0. \tag{3}$$

The second is the Stolper-Samuelson relation between goods prices and factor prices. Given the assumption that X is always the skill-intensive sector, this defines a monotonic relation, of which I focus on only a part. By Stolper-Samuelson:

$$w = \psi(P), \text{ where } \psi'(P) < 0. \tag{4}$$

Thus given the endowment ratio of the closed economy, h^W, one can determine directly the equilibrium goods price in the flexible-wage case, $P^F = \lambda(h^W)$. Likewise, one can derive the resulting flexible wage, $w^F = \psi(P^F) = \psi(\lambda(h^W))$, as well as the associated skilled wage. These suffice to establish the basic characteristics of the world equilibrium.

I now introduce within the closed economy a binding minimum wage for labor at rate $w^* > w^F$. This will be consistent with an equilibrium featuring diversified production if and only if the relative goods price is $P^* = \psi^{-1}(w^*) < P^F$. However, these will be the

---

[4]Two additional papers have independently considered two-country models with unemployment. N. Boccard et al. (1996) develop a political economy model focused on redistribution and "social dumping." Paul Oslington (1996) considers trade patterns and "false" comparative advantage in a factor price equalization (FPE) setting, suggesting that transport costs may resolve indeterminacies in the cross-country distribution of unemployment.

equilibrium goods and factor prices if and only if *employed* factors are in the ratio $h^* = \lambda^{-1}(\psi^{-1}(w^*)) > h^W$. The flexible rental for skill insures that it will always be fully employed. However with a binding minimum wage, this need not be true for labor. Thus the manner in which relative employed factors rise to h^* is for the denominator to fall via unemployed labor. With w^* given, h^* is determined, and H^W and L^W are the fixed world endowments. Let N be the level of labor actually employed. Then simple algebra shows that unemployment in this economy, $U = L^W - N$, is given by the third key relation (Brecher):

$$U^* = L^w - H^w/h^*$$
$$\equiv \beta(h^*; H^w, L^w), \text{ where } \beta'(h^*) > 0. \tag{5}$$

These three key relations characterizing the minimum-wage economy can be considered in Figure 1. The Heckscher-Ohlin relation, $P = \lambda(h)$, appears in quadrant one. The Stolper-Samuelson relation, $w = \psi(P)$, appears in quadrant two. Finally, the link between endowments, the employment ratio, and the level of unemployment is depicted in quadrant four. In the flexible-wage case, the employment ratio equals the endowment ratio h^W. This determines wages, prices, and unemployment as w^F, P^F, and zero, respectively. In the minimum-wage case, the path of determination is different. The given minimum wage $w^* > w^F$ directly determines the goods price, the employment ratio, and the unemployment level as P^*, h^*, and U^*, respectively.

The basic link between the minimum wage and the appearance of unemployment in this economy is very simple. For competitive firms to pay the high wage w^*, this must be supported by an appropriate goods price P^*. When the minimum wage binds, the appropriate goods price will be attained only if the relative scarcity of the labor-intensive

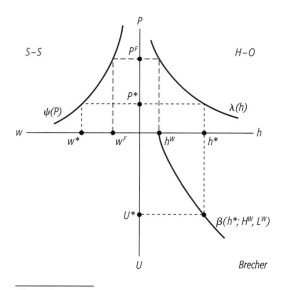

Figure 1

Unemployment in General Equilibrium

good rises relative to the flexible-wage equilibrium. And this will occur only if a sufficient amount of labor is unemployed.

I now establish an isomorphism between the closed economy with a minimum wage and a trading world in which one economy imposes a minimum wage while the other maintains a flexible wage. This relies on a concept introduced by Avinash K. Dixit and Victor F. Norman (1980) known as the integrated equilibrium. This establishes conditions under which trade in goods alone suffices to establish the same world equilibrium as occurs in the closed economy with both goods and factor mobility.

Consider, then, a world of two countries with free trade and zero transport costs. One country—America—has flexible wages. The other country—Europe—has imposed a minimum wage at the level w^*. The technologies and preferences in the two countries are identical to those in the closed economy. The technologies are constant returns to scale, while the preferences are identical and homothetic. Let a bar over a variable represent the level of that variable in the integrated equilibrium. Let i index goods and j index countries. The set of divisions of world endowments among the two countries consistent with replicating the integrated equilibrium can then be described. This is called the FPE set, and is described as:

$$
\text{FPE} = \left\{
\begin{array}{l}
[(H^A, L^A), (H^E, L^E)] \,\big|\, \exists \lambda_{ij} \geq 0 \text{ such that } \sum_j \lambda_{ij} = 1, \\[2mm]
(H^E, L^E) = \sum_i \lambda_{i,E}(\overline{H}(i), \overline{L}(i)) + (0, U^*) \\[2mm]
(H^A, L^A) = \sum_i \lambda_{i,A}(\overline{H}(i), \overline{L}(i)) \qquad i = X, Y \quad j = A, E
\end{array}
\right\}
$$

These conditions are very intuitive. If the integrated equilibrium is to be replicated, then world unemployment must be at the same level as in the integrated economy. But unemployment cannot arise in the flexible-wage America. Hence Europe must endure the entire integrated equilibrium level of unemployment, U^*, to maintain the wage w^*. Beyond this, we need only satisfy the conventional restrictions in terms of *employed* factors. These require that both countries use the integrated equilibrium techniques (with the skill intensities $h_X^* = H_X^*/L_X^*$ and $h_Y^* = H_Y^*/L_Y^*$, that the integrated equilibrium output in both sectors be divided among the countries, and that this exactly exhaust employed factors in the two countries (which exist in the ratio h^*).[5] The FPE set is depicted as the bold parallelogram in Figure 2. The level of world (hence European) unemployment is indicated by the line segment $O^E U$.

This allows me to state a key result: Under the conditions noted above, international trade equalizes factor prices between the flexible-wage and the minimum-wage economies. The proof is simply that under free and costless trade, competitive producers in the two countries face the same goods prices, have the same technologies, and are (at

---

[5]Since preferences are assumed to be identical and homothetic, the level of spending by the unemployed does not matter for the pattern of world spending. Implicitly, though, it is assumed that any spending by the unemployed is financed via lump-sum transfers.

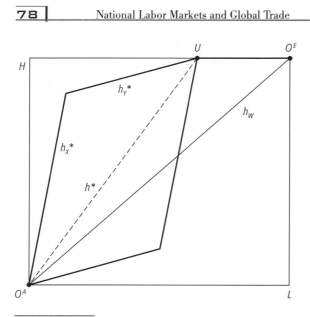

Figure 2

Unemployment in the Integrated World Economy

least weakly) diversified. The equality of factor prices then follows directly from the common competitive cost conditions.

This is an important result. Even in the face of sharply divergent factor market institutions, free commodity trade in a global market fully equalized factor prices. As will be considered more fully below, this will sharply restrict the nature of shocks that can be appealed to in explaining divergent wage trends between Europe and America.[6]

[6]For analytic simplicity, I developed this within a conventional Heckscher-Ohlin framework. One feature of this model—that American and European goods are perfectly homogeneous— may appear crucial to the results on FPE and consequent international spillovers to European unemployment. However, such an impression would be incorrect, at least in the longer run with which this model is concerned. It would be straightforward, although not as clean, to consider a model in which the homogeneous goods X and Y were replaced by two monopolistically competitive industries, {X} and {Y}, each with many varieties (see Elhanan Helpman and Krugman, 1985). In this case, all goods, wherever produced, are imperfect substitutes for all others. Yet under the same institutional assumptions, one could still apply precisely the same integrated equilibrium approach to again demonstrate factor price equalization with unemployment in Europe alone. What is crucial for the strong result is that European and American labor of the various categories are effectively homogeneous. In such a case, a disturbance may in the short run introduce a divergence from unity in the relative price of European and American varieties. This could give rise to cross-country factor price inequalities. However in the long run, this will induce entry, exit, and other adjustments that return us to the integrated equilibrium and restore full factor price equalization. Thus, to depart from this paper's results in the long run, it does not suffice to observe that American and European goods are imperfect substitutes. One must believe that on a deep level, American and European labor of the various classes are different factors.

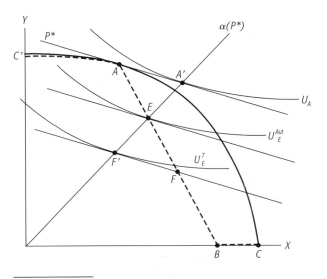

Figure 3

Benchmark: Free Trade Doubles European Unemployment

B. TRADE AND UNEMPLOYMENT

I have shown how to construct a model of trade between a flexible-wage economy and one with a minimum-wage. But I have not yet examined what impact trade has on these economies relative to autarky. It is convenient to start with a highly stylized example that establishes a benchmark. Further insight into the workings of this model will be provided by the many comparative statics in later sections.

Take as a benchmark a world in which Europe and America are alike in every respect — endowments, technologies, and preferences. The one exception is that America has a flexible wage, while Europe has a minimum wage at level w^*, assumed to bind in autarky. As before, technologies are constant returns to scale. For simplicity, assume that preferences of the representative consumer are homothetic.

Figure 3 depicts the salient aspects of the equilibrium.[7] The technological production frontier, CC', is common to America and Europe. In Europe, to support the wage w^*, the equilibrium price must be P^*. The consumption ratio of Y to X at P^* is given by $\alpha(P^*)$. Thus under full employment, production at prices P^* in Europe would be at A, and demand at A'. This implies an incipient excess demand for X, tending to raise P and lower w below w^*. The incipient fall in the wage is instead stanched via a decline in unskilled employment in Europe. With goods prices fixed at P^*, this is just the Rybczynski theorem in reverse, shifting output along a minimum wage-constrained

---

[7]This builds on a diagram of Brecher (1974a); see also Krugman (1995).

production possibility frontier (PPF) indicated by *AB*. Autarky equilibrium in Europe is at *E*, at which the constrained supply exactly matches the demand at prices *P**. The shift of production in Europe from *A* to *E* reflects the contraction of employment just necessary to eliminate the excess demand indicated by *AA′*. By contrast, in America, the autarky equilibrium features a price $P > P^*$ and so an unskilled wage $w < w^*$ (not depicted). There is no unemployment in America.

Now consider the equilibrium when America and Europe trade freely. In order to support the minimum wage *w**, Europe still needs to maintain the price *P** in equilibrium. At prices *P**, the American net trade offer is indicated by *AA′*. Thus world equilibrium at these prices requires that Europe be willing to make this trade at prices *P**. This requires that European production be at point *F*, and absorption at *F′*. As demand is homothetic, and production linear at all points along *AB*, the loss of employment in moving from *E* to *F* matches the preexisting unemployment indexed by *AE*.[8]

This implies a striking contrast between Europe and America in the labor market. Europe's commitment to a high wage gave rise to unemployment in autarky. In this stylized example the opening of Europe to trade with America *doubles* European unemployment, as it is forced to absorb the full integrated equilibrium level of unemployment to sustain *w** for both. In America, the absence of unemployment in autarky came at the cost to workers of a lower real wage. However once trade commenced, American workers came to share the high European wage even as they suffered none of the unemployment that sustains that wage. The fact that they suffer no unemployment is a consequence of the flexible wage in America. The fact that they nonetheless share the European high wage under trade follows from the fact that trade links goods prices, that both countries remain diversified, and that producers still must meet price-equals-unit-cost conditions. In effect, trade has forced European workers to bear the burden of high unemployment to maintain not only their own high wage, but that in America as well.

How robust is this result? This is most easily illustrated by placing the same information in a framework of export supply and import demand. As we have seen, the minimum-wage constraint makes European export supply at price *P** multivalued, corresponding to various levels of unemployment. Graphically, this implies that the constrained export supply curve has a horizontal segment that corresponds to the Rybczynski segment of the constrained PPF. In Figure 4 this is depicted along with the American import demand curve for the case in which the countries are otherwise identical.

Now consider perturbations in the position of the American import demand curve, and consider their implications for unemployment and wages. So long as the American

---

[8]An alternative way of seeing this is to note that $\beta(h^*; H^W, L^W)$ is linear homogeneous in H^W and L^W for a fixed h^*, and that opening to America is the same as doubling the world endowments (since Europe absorbs all of the unemployment).

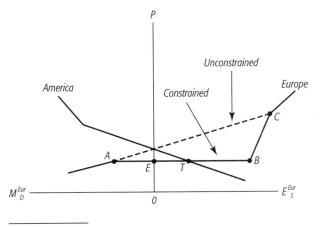

Figure 4

American Import Demand Determines European Unemployment

import demand curve cuts the export supply curve of Europe between *A* and *B*, the equilibrium price will be *P**, so the wage will be *w**. In all such cases, were Europe to abandon the minimum-wage policy, both European and American wages would fall in the free trade equilibrium. The effect of trade with America on European unemployment depends on whether the American import demand curve cuts the European export supply curve in the region *TB*, *ET*, or *AE*. If the equilibrium is in the region *TB*, then European unemployment will more than double, reaching its maximum at *B*. If in the region *ET*, European unemployment will be higher than in autarky, although at less than the double rate. If, instead, the equilibrium is in the region *AE*, then trade with America actually lowers European unemployment. It continues to be true in all three cases, though, that under free trade high American wages depend on the European minimum-wage policy fully as much as European wages do.[9]

III. SHOCKS FROM THE SOUTH: IMPLICATIONS FOR EUROPE AND AMERICA

The impact of growing trade with developing countries on labor markets in developed countries has been a source of great concern. It was at the heart of the vigorous opposition of the AFL-CIO to the North American Free Trade Agreement, and has figured

---

[9]When contemplating the recent unemployment experience of Europe, one should not read from this that it was *caused* by increasing integration with America. Rather this is designed to provide a simple window on the trade-offs a country may face between a wage target and unemployment in an open economy. In the benchmark case, the unemployment cost of any given wage target is higher by a factor of two.

prominently in the presidential campaigns of Ross Perot and Patrick Buchanan. Correlate concerns have been raised over rapid integration of Eastern Europe into the markets of the European Union.

The evidence for the growing trade, particularly in manufactures, is indisputable. In the period 1970-1990, the less-developed countries (LDC) share in manufactured imports of the United States and Europe more than doubled—rising to more than a third for the United States (Freeman, 1995). Correspondingly, the share of manufactures in total non-fuel exports from LDCs rose from less than one-fourth in 1970 to nearly three-fourths by 1989 (Wood, 1994).

However, what role—if any—this played in the factor market developments in Europe and America is still in contest. Wood (1994) has been the strongest proponent of the view that trade with the LDCs has mattered. Qualified support for this view has come from Edward E. Leamer (1995). By contrast, Krugman and Robert Z. Lawrence (1993) have argued forcefully that the volume of trade is insufficient to account for relative wage movements in the United States. Similarly, Franco Modigliani (1995, p. 7) insists that the argument that increased trade with developing countries raised unemployment in Europe is "nonsense, reflecting economic illiteracy."

Krugman (1995) examined the impact of a trade shock on a minimum-wage Europe and a flexible-wage America, concluding that it would raise unemployment in the former and reduce wages in the latter. However his study, on a theoretical plane, belongs to the category earlier identified as "comparative." That is, he examines this one country at a time. As we will see, the results change importantly when we turn to a global approach, in which Europe and America exist within the same world economy.[10]

I begin again with a flexible-wage America, and a minimum-wage Europe. For simplicity, and without loss of generality, I shift the base case to consider that in which P^* is the American autarky price. This is also the European autarky price with the minimum wage in place. And so when free trade is allowed between America and Europe, P^* remains the equilibrium price, with no actual trade taking place. Europe has the same level of unemployment as in autarky, and both have the same wages in autarky as under free trade.

I now consider the introduction of a previously isolated region, which will be called the NICs, to the American and European free trade system. Assume that the NICs have a

---

[10]This comparative theoretical approach is at work as well in an argument by the Center for Economic Policy Research (1995, p. 53). It is argued there that evidence, as in Lawrence and Matthew J. Slaughter (1993), exculpating Stolper-Samuelson in America, likewise refutes claims that trade with the newly industrialized countries (NICs) may have raised unemployment in Europe. However, as the discussion here makes clear, one reason that increased trade with the NICs may not account for falling wages in America is precisely that it *does* raise unemployment in Europe.

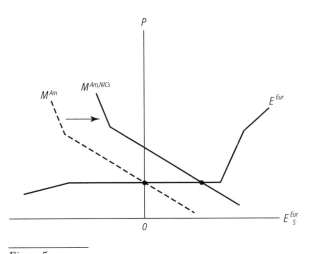

Figure 5

A NICs Shock Raises European Unemployment, Leaves America Unaffected

strictly downward-sloping import demand curve, and at prices P^* are importers of the good X. My concern will be to trace through the implications of this for Europe and America. In the diagram, this can be represented as a rightward shift of the joint American-NIC import demand curve. However, so long as Europe is not completely driven out of the Y industry, and given Europe's commitment to its minimum wage, the world price P^* does not change (see Figure 5).

At an unchanged world price, the American import demand is unchanged. So the United States absorbs none of the imports from the NICs. American wages continue to be protected by the European commitment to a high-wage policy. In Europe, by contrast, there will be a surge of imports from the NICs.[11] The impact of this is similar to that analyzed above. Given the European commitment to a high-wage policy, this will not show up in reduced wages, but rather in higher unemployment.

This integrated global economy presents an important contrast with the results of Krugman (1995). There he treated the American and European cases as though they were part of different global economies. However, as is seen here, the links via goods trade are crucial for understanding the broader story. So long as Europe maintains a commitment to both free trade and a high-wage policy, America is fully insulated from the NIC shock.

---

[11] The actual pattern of trade—whether NICs deliveries are to America or Europe—is inconsequential. The important point is that the price P^* defines the world net offer to Europe. Europe must absorb this net offer to maintain the price P^*, and so accept the employment consequences.

IV. GLOBAL LABOR SUPPLIES, EUROPEAN UNEMPLOYMENT

A. DISCUSSION

Leading labor economists have identified cross-country differences in the evolution of the labor force as an important explanatory factor in the divergent evolution of wages between continental Europe and the United States and United Kingdom (Katz and Murphy, 1992; Katz et al., 1995). As insightful as this line of research has been, it would be more satisfying to consider this in a theoretical framework in which the cross-country structure of labor demand is endogenous. It might seem obvious that cross-country differences in the levels and growth rates of relative factor supplies should help to explain differences in relative wages. However, this need not be true when countries are linked by commodity trade. In fact, the absence of such a relation is the central message of Paul A. Samuelson's factor price equalization theorem (1949). Under the conditions in which that theorem is valid, the structure of relative wages depends on the evolution of the global labor force.[12] However cross-country differences in the composition or growth rates of the labor force will contribute nothing to an understanding of divergent wage trends. Given that it has been seen that the model with unemployment likewise yields factor price equalization, it can likewise be concluded that differential labor-force growth will not help to account for divergent wage patterns.

Although changes in relative factor supplies will not play a role in accounting for cross-country differences in relative wages, they will be essential for understanding the evolution of unemployment in Europe. There will be a correlate to the factor price equalization theorem: The *level* of European unemployment depends on global—not local—factor supplies. One consequence of this is that dramatic changes in American factor accumulation—the shifts due to baby booms and busts—may leave their most profound mark not on American but on European labor markets. By contrast, the unemployment *rate* in Europe will depend importantly on *where* factor accumulation occurs. The conditions under which European unemployment falls are less stringent when factor accumulation is in Europe than in America.

The model also features an important asymmetry. The fixed European minimum wage insulates America from all shocks caused by factor accumulation in Europe. But the reverse is not true. Factor accumulation in America has very profound effects on Europe.

In the conventional Heckscher-Ohlin framework, the central theorem dealing with endowment changes is that of Rybczynski. It says that at fixed goods prices, an increase

---

[12] In fact, this extends to a more general setting. It is straightforward to write down a model in which only a subset of the world enjoys factor price equalization (Davis et al., 1997). Subject to the general restrictions underlying FPE (see Dixit and Norman, 1980), the site of endowment changes among those sharing FPE matters neither for comparative nor absolute wages.

in the endowment of a factor leads to a more-than-proportional increase in output in the sector that uses that factor intensively, and a contraction in the other sector. At the initial equilibrium price this would be expected to create an excess supply of the good that uses that factor intensively, lowering its equilibrium relative price, and by Stolper-Samuelson reducing the return to that factor. In the conventional setting, at fixed prices, changes in the endowment of one country have no effect on output supplies in the other.

B. Derivation of Principal Results

I now turn to a systematic evaluation of the impact of factor accumulation in the present model. I begin by considering the implications for the global economy, and then turn to examine how these effects are distributed according to where the accumulation takes place. It is assumed throughout that Europe's minimum wage at w^* remains binding and that both economies are diversified.

Several observations will make the derivation of the results more transparent. Europe's commitment to maintain the high wage w^* is likewise a commitment to maintain a domestic relative price P^*, as given by the zero profit conditions for the two goods. With free trade, this will also be the world relative price. We saw above that the common goods prices yield factor price equalization. Cost-minimizing firms with identical technologies will then pick the same factor intensities in both countries, denoted h_X^* and h_Y^*. With P^* fixed in all equilibria that are considered, these factor intensities will also be fixed. Because of identical and homothetic demand, P^* also fixes the ratio in which X and Y will be consumed. This implies directly that world output at equilibrium must be supplied in the same proportion. This absorbs factors in the proportion $h^*[=\lambda^{-1}(P^*)]$. This represents both the minimum skill intensity that the world economy needs to yield the wage w^* in a flexible-wage world, and the actual skill abundance of total *employed* factors in the world with at least one economy with a minimum wage at w^*. Unemployment will arise when the actual world endowment, h^W, is such that $h^W < h^*$. The Rybczynski theorem is usually stated for a fixed exogenous price. Here we consider the case in which the price is held fixed by the commitment of Europe to maintain the minimum wage. Finally, recall that unemployment can be written as $U^* = L^W - H^W/h^*$.

Although my principal interest is in the effects of factor accumulation, it is convenient to begin with a version of the Heckscher-Ohlin theorem for trade between a flexible-wage economy and a minimum-wage economy. Let h^A denote the skill-to-labor ratio in flexible-wage America. Given a minimum wage w^* that binds where applied, and that both economies are diversified, the world employment ratio of skill to labor is fixed at h^*. The flexible-wage America will be an exporter of the skill intensive good if and only if $h^A > h^*$. The minimum-wage Europe will have a complementary trade pattern. The easiest way to see how the Heckscher-Ohlin theorem works here is simply to delete Europe's unemployed from Figure 2. They do not contribute income, so consume only from transfers that they will spend in the same pattern as those employed. Having done this, the diagram just becomes the conventional Heckscher-Ohlin model, although now in terms of *employed* factors.

I now turn to the results concerning accumulation of factors. A rise in the world endowment of skill raises employment of labor so as to maintain employed factors in the ratio h^*. As a result, output of both goods rises proportionally. If the skill accumulation occurs in flexible-wage America, it will have conventional Rybczynski effects, raising the output of X more than proportionally and decreasing the local output of Y. However this also affects Europe, which has a rise in employment. Recalling that $U^* = L^W - H^W/h^*$, it follows that $\Delta U^* = -\Delta H^W/h^*$. Thus it has Rybczynski effects skewed the other direction, with output of Y rising more than proportionally, and output of X declining. The net impact of the output changes in the two countries must, as noted, raise output of X and Y in proportion to the initial world output.

If instead the skill accumulation occurs in minimum-wage Europe, we have a very different picture. In Europe we fail to have conventional Rybczynski effects. Incipient excess supply of X threatens to raise the wage above w^* at the initial level of employment. This allows employment to rise by $\Delta N = \Delta H^W/h^*$. That is, total employment of factors in Europe has risen in exact proportion to total initial employment in the world as a whole, h^*. Thus, output in Europe expands proportional to initial world output. America is entirely unaffected, as its net trade vector is fully determined by the constant price ratio P^*.

Now consider the effect of accumulation of labor. At the global level, unemployment rises by the full increment to the labor force, so $\Delta U^* = \Delta L^W > 0$. There is no effect on global output. If the accumulation occurs in minimum-wage Europe, unemployment rises directly with no effect on output in either country. However, if accumulation of labor happens in America, there are very dramatic shifts. America continues to have conventional Rybczynski effects, raising the output of Y more than proportionally, and reducing the output of X. Income in America rises linearly, so $\Delta I^A = w^*\Delta L^A$. Europe is also strongly affected. In fact, European unemployment rises one for one with accumulation of labor in America. And European income falls dollar for dollar with the rise in American income. Its shift in output exactly offsets that of America, so that global output is unchanged.

V. SOUTH–NORTH MIGRATION AND UNEMPLOYMENT

A. MIGRATION IN A MODEL OF ADJUSTED FACTOR PRICE EQUALIZATION

In this section I develop a model of endogenous South–North migration that builds on Daniel Trefler (1993, 1996), and use this to consider the consequences for European unemployment. Think of a North composed of Europe and America. They are just as before, with Europe imposing a minimum wage and America having a flexible wage. Following Trefler (1993), it is assumed that factor price equalization between North and South holds, but only when labor is measured in efficiency (rather than natural) units. For simplicity I neglect the possibility that there are efficiency differences across countries in skill. Let L_E^W and N_E^W be the world labor force and employment when measured in efficiency units, and let $h_E \equiv H^W/N_E^W$. Then it is a straightforward application of our previous model to show that when Europe imposes a minimum wage at the level w^*, unemployment of labor is given as

$$U^* = L_E^W - H^W/h_E^*. \tag{6}$$

Consideration of the incentives for migration forces us to consider an issue familiar from the standard Ricardian trade model, namely the reason for variation in efficiency units per natural unit of labor. Cross-country variation that reflects only *individual characteristics* of the workers would provide no motive for migration, so are neglected.[13] If instead this also reflects cross-country *technological differences*, then labor will have a reason for migration—access to the superior Northern technology.[14] Let ϕ^N and ϕ^S reflect labor-augmenting productivity differences specific to the location of production. By choice of units, let $\phi^N = 1$. Assuming that labor productivity is higher in the North restricts $\phi^S \in (0, 1)$.

Let the efficiency equivalent labor force for the North and South be L_E^N and L_E^S respectively, where $L_E^N + L_E^S = L_E^W$. Let L^S be the number of nationals of the South, some of whom in the latter period move to the North. Let L^N be the number of nationals of the North (all of whom remain there). Then prior to migration, the world labor force measured in efficiency units is $L_E^W = L^N + \phi^S L^S$. When migration of size M occurs from South to North, this changes to $L_E^{W'} = L^N + \phi^S(L^S - M) + M$. As labor was already in excess supply, and noting that H^W and h_E^* are unaltered by the migration, the change in the world labor force measured in efficiency units is equivalent to the rise in European unemployment. This is given as:

$$\Delta U^* = \Delta L_E^W = (1 - \phi^S)M. \tag{7}$$

Thus two parameters, ϕ^S and M, identify the contribution of South–North migration to European unemployment. In this world with FPE in efficiency units, technologically based differences in productivity (ϕ^S) will be identified by the increment in wages to

---

[13] Moreover this would be reflected in a native-immigrant wage gap. Since empirical estimates suggest that such gaps are small (on the order of 10 percent) for workers with similar backgrounds, these can safely be ignored for present purposes.

[14] This also implies that "outsourcing" to the South may have the same implications as developed here for migration. The key element is the matching of Northern technology and Southern workers, which increases the effective world supply of unskilled labor, rather than the locale in which this matching occurs.

those who migrate from South to North. M is the amount of migration from developing countries to the OECD.

B. Migration Induced by Large Endowment Differences

I now consider an alternative way to model the impact of migration on unemployment in rigid-wage Europe. The most plausible alternative yields conclusions which are qualitatively similar, though quantitatively more dramatic. Consider the case in which the motive for migration is a failure of FPE because of large differences across countries in factor composition. Let there be three goods, X, Y, and Z, in decreasing order of skill intensity. As before, the minimum wage in the North is set in terms of the numeraire, Y. For simplicity, assume the technologies are Leontief. Skill-abundant countries of the North produce the relatively skill-intensive goods X and Y, while the skill-scarce South produces Y and Z. As in the conventional two-factor, multiple production cone Heckscher-Ohlin model, the labor-scarce North enjoys higher wages, motivating immigration from the South. Consider the impact of the migration of a single worker from South to North. By the Rybczynski theorem, the migrant leads to an expansion in Y production in the North, and a contraction in X output at the initial prices. Moreover, the loss of an unskilled worker in the South leads to an expansion of Y in the South (since this is its relatively skilled industry), and a contraction of Z output. Thus output movements in both countries are putting downward pressure on the relative price of Y (upward pressure on prices of both X and Z). This suggests the conventional result that migration places pressure for wages to rise in the source country and fall in the destination country. By how much would unemployment have to rise in the North to relieve this pressure? A full answer would require a more complete specification. Note, though, what would happen if unemployment in the North were to rise exactly one for one with immigration at the initial prices. Then the immigration would have left unskilled employment, so output in the North of X and Y, unchanged. However, there would still have been the effect on output in the South, raising output of Y and reducing that of Z. This suggests residual pressure for both the prices of X and Z to rise relative to Y to move toward equilibrium. If in fact the price of X did rise, this would push the Northern unskilled wage below the minimum. And this suggests that to meet the minimum wage, unemployment in the North would have to rise by a factor of *more* than one for one relative to migration from the South.

C. An Empirical Application

An extensive literature has considered the impact of immigration on labor-market outcomes of natives. Rachel M. Friedberg and Jennifer Hunt (1995) provide a valuable survey. The analytic approach pursued here is closest to that of George J. Borjas et al. (1992). I consider a simple counterfactual based on the theoretical models developed above: How would European unemployment have differed if unskilled immigration to the North (America and Europe) from 1970–1990 had been constrained to zero? The parsimonious specification of the two theoretical models above imply that two parameters suffice to answer this question: (1) the number of unskilled migrants from South to North; and (2) the wage gain for those who migrate. For the former, I will take a conservative definition, using the estimate of the 1970–1990 flows of unskilled migrants from the South who entered the labor force in the United States, a figure calculated as approximately 4.4 million (see the Appendix). For the latter I note that Trefler (1993), using International Labour Organization data that fit his FPE model well, calculated U.S. wages for aggregate labor relative to those of various other countries, for example coming up with figures ranging from a U.S. advantage of 20 to 1 relative to Bangladesh, 5 to 1 relative to Yugoslavia, and 3.3 to 1 relative to Colombia. No doubt an important element in this is differences in skill composition. However, direct evidence on the wage gains of individual migrants suggests that the gains that motivated the migration may be substantial. For the purposes of the calculations for Model A, I will assume conservatively that the wage gain relative to that earned premigration ranges between a factor of 2 and 3. Thus, under the hypothesis of the adjusted-FPE Model A, as reflected in equation (7), the counterfactual yields incremental European unemployment of between 2.2 million and 2.9 million. Under the hypothesis of Model B, the multicone approach, the corresponding incremental unemployment would be something greater than 4.4 million. If it is noted that in 1993 there were 17 million unemployed in Europe, the ceteris paribus figures suggest that absent this unskilled immigration, the same wage in Europe could have been targeted with a reduction of between one-eighth and one-quarter of this unemployment.

These figures are meant only to suggest an order of magnitude—that these effects could matter empirically. The data underlying these calculations is rough, while the model to which they are applied is sharp. Moreover, it would be inappropriate here, as in any ceteris paribus experiment, to infer from this that unskilled immigration "caused" the rise in European unemployment. Nevertheless, the possibility that unskilled immigration to the North could matter for European employment, given a commitment to a specific wage, is not implausible. This was in fact the point of the very restrictive immigration policies of Europe post-1973. Yet while the front door may have been shut, the open door provided for unskilled immigration to the United States implied incipient downward pressure on wages on both sides of the Atlantic. Europe's commitment to high wages forced it to adjust to these pressures via higher unemployment.

VI. DIVERGENT WAGE EXPERIENCE

This paper began with the observation that American and European factor market experience has diverged in two respects: rising unemployment in Europe, but not in America, and a growing skilled-unskilled wage gap in America, but not in Europe. A great deal has been said about the former, and so the latter will be addressed here.

The conjunction of relative factor demand shocks and institutional differences has been an important theme in explanations of the divergent relative wage experience of America and Europe. Thus the demonstration that this wage divergence does not in fact arise in the standard model is an important analytic contribution of this paper. However, the divergent experience still needs to be understood.

From an analytic perspective the crucial insight is that shocks that move us from one integrated equilibrium to another will not explain the wage divergence. Thus endowment changes, demand shocks, and global technology shocks are all consistent with maintaining FPE across the countries, in spite of the institutional differences.

This leaves a variety of amendments to the baseline model that could potentially explain the divergent experience. One class concerns divergent evolution of policies or technological shocks. The factor price link comes through producers' zero profit conditions. For FPE we need free trade, zero internal taxes, common technologies, and diversified production, in addition to the conventional assumptions. Thus differences in the evolution of trade and fiscal policy, idiosyncratic technology shocks (e.g. convergence), or specialization can lead FPE to break down, so offer paths for interpreting the divergent wage experience. The role of technical change in understanding these factor market developments is considered at length in Davis (1998).

However one need not rely on divergent policies or technological shocks to explain the divergent wage experience. If one adds a little more structure to the basic framework, alternative accounts are possible. For example, Davis and Trevor A. Reeve (1997) develop a model of endogenous human capital accumulation in a framework that is otherwise identical to that developed here. In their model, the threat of unemployment has feedback effects on individuals' decisions to accumulate human capital. Since unemployment is prevalent in Europe but not in America, even common shocks can lead to divergent accumulation decisions, hence wage outcomes.

Thus the basic framework that has been developed is consistent with a variety of accounts of the divergent wage experience between America and Europe. Importantly, the principal insights that have been developed in this paper are robust to consideration of any of these variations.

VII. Conclusion

This paper has one overarching message. Even when factor markets are strictly national, with idiosyncratic institutional features, they cannot be considered in isolation when goods markets are global. This strongly suggests the importance of a unified "global" approach to explaining recent factor market developments in Europe and America. This will be an important complement to existing studies, which are either of individual countries or comparative.

A striking example of the importance of the global perspective emerges in the contrasting effects of trade on a flexible-wage America and a minimum-wage Europe. In the central example, a move from autarky to free trade doubles the European unemployment rate while leading American wages to converge to the high European level.[15]

Moreover, commodity trade leads local institutional features to have important spillover effects on other countries. These go far beyond the simple general equilibrium fact that they will affect the level of wages and the composition of production. They may fundamentally alter the nature of a country's relation with the international environment. For example, if Europe and America are both flexible-wage economies, then the entry of the NICs to world markets may depress wages in each. However, we saw that when Europe imposed a minimum wage, it absorbed the full impact of the NIC shock and wholly insulated America from its effects. That is, a local European institutional feature has sharply altered America's relation to the trading world.

The local institutional features may likewise introduce important asymmetries in the relations between the countries. As noted, America is wholly insulated from external shocks, including factor-supply shocks in Europe. By contrast, factor-supply shocks in America have very powerful effects in Europe. A striking example occurs with an increase in the supply of labor in America. This raises American income, yet lowers European income dollar for dollar, while raising European unemployment one for one.

The importance of considering the links via commodity trade is particularly important when thinking about the evolution of wages. In spite of important differences in factor market institutions, which in a closed economy would induce differences in factor prices, goods trade here insures full factor price equalization. Thus insofar as policy makers in a country see a trade-off between the two, the willingness of one to bear high unemployment spills over to raise wages in both.

The major analytics of this paper have been derived in a framework in which America and Europe replicate an integrated equilibrium with factor price equalization. This contributes greatly to the transparency of the results. As well, it has emphasized the important point that Europe's commitment to a minimum wage cushions the impact of a variety of shocks on America. However it also suggests an important respect in which additional inquiry is indicated. A key stylized fact we want to understand is the divergent relative wage experience of America and Europe. Insofar as the shocks considered here move the world economy between equilibria featuring factor price equalization, they will not account for this fact. I have indicated a variety of directions in which the framework may be amended to account for this fact. This suggests the value of extensions that may help to identify which of these may matter most empirically.

---

[15] Why was European unemployment lower than that in America pre-1973, yet higher thereafter? One account would be to think of there being two components of unemployment—one frictional and the other due to rigidities. For a variety of reasons, America may have a higher base frictional rate than Europe. If in one period the rigidities are nonbinding in Europe, it may be found that total unemployment is relatively low. If in another period those rigidities do bind, it may instead be found that unemployment there is relatively high.

This paper has derived these results in a stylized model. Care should be taken in reading these results too readily into actual historical experience. Nonetheless the issue that it raises of the powerful interaction between local factor market institutions and global goods markets is no doubt very important. And the results are sufficiently provocative to warrant closer examination.

APPENDIX: AUTHOR'S CALCULATION OF THE CONTRIBUTION OF SOUTH–NORTH MIGRATION TO THE WORLD EFFECTIVE STOCK OF UNSKILLED LABOR

As discussed in the text, over the last two decades Europe has pursued a restrictive immigration policy, while America has had strong growth in immigration, particularly among the unskilled. The stock of foreign population in Europe grew by 2.9 million from 1981–1991 (John Salt et al., 1994). However, much of this growth is from the end of the period, and naturally the growth of the unskilled labor force would be less than this. Since I want to be conservative, and since Europe's policy was overtly restrictive, for the purposes of my calculations I will assume that there was zero Southern unskilled immigration to Europe.

The calculations for America (here just the United States) must of necessity be imprecise. The desired category of immigrants is not readily available, so must be calculated. Here I detail those calculations, first for legal immigrants. The stock of foreign-born persons 18 years of age or older in the United States in 1990 was 17.7 million (U.S. Department of Commerce; Bureau of the Census [1990], Table 3: Social Characteristics of Selected Ancestry Groups by Nativity, Citizenship and Year of Entry: 1990). Of these, 6.9 million entered between 1980–1990 (U.S. Department of Commerce, Bureau of the Census, 1990). The 1970's saw approximately 4.5 million immigrants to the United States (Borjas, 1990, p. 6). Of these, close to 4 million would have been aged 18 or over (Borjas, 1990, p. 41). Summing, the 1970–1990 immigration of those aged 18 and over would have been approximately 10.9 million. The labor-force participation rate for male immigrants is approximately 90 percent (Borjas, 1990, p. 41), while that for women is lower, which I will estimate by the native female participation rate of circa 50 percent. Thus the average labor-force participation rate will be taken as 70 percent. This implies that of the 10.9 million immigrants aged 18 and over, approximately 7.6 million would be in the labor force. Of the 1990 stock, approximately 60 percent of those aged 18 or over had a high-school education or less (U.S. Department of Commerce, Bureau of the Census, 1990). Thus of these 7.6 million in the labor force, a little over 4.5 million would fall into the category of the unskilled. Not all of these, though, come from the South. If we define the South operationally as Asia (except Japan), Africa, and the Americas (except Canada), approximately three-fourths of immigrants in the 1970's came from the South (Borjas, 1990, p. 230). If it is conservatively assumed that the unskilled were no more likely to come from the South than from the North, this would imply that the contribution of legal immigration from the South to the unskilled labor force in the North is approximately 3.4 million.

To this must be added the contribution to the labor force by illegal immigration. While newspaper reports of illegal immigration are often huge, the work of Borjas et al. (1991) suggests that in 1980 the stock of Mexican illegal immigrants to the United States was 1.8 million. I do not have data that provide similarly careful estimates for illegal flows for 1970–1990, or that incorporate the full complement of countries of the South. Realizing that this leaves out flows from the 1980's from Mexico, as well as all flows from other countries of the South, while it includes some who arrived prior to 1970, I will (with a great dollop of optimism) take the figure of 1.8 million as the relevant measure of inflows from 1970–1990. If it is assumed, as above, that approximately 90 percent of these are aged 18 and above, this reduces the figure to approximately

1.6 million. Assuming that the labor-force participation rate again is 70 percent, this implies that approximately 1.1 million are in the labor force. It is known that educational attainment of typical Mexican immigrants is very low, with over three-fourths having less than a high-school education (Borjas et al., 1992). If those with a high-school education are included among the unskilled, then this will provide a figure of approximately 1 million additional unskilled workers. If this is summed to the contribution of legal immigration, a figure is arrived at which indicates that South–North migration to the United States from 1970–1990 raised the labor force of the unskilled by approximately 4.4 million workers. This estimate should be considered very rough.

REFERENCES

Bertola, Giuseppe and Ichino, Andrea. "Wage Inequality and Unemployment: United States vs. Europe." *NBER macroeconomics annual*, Vol. 10. Cambridge, MA: MIT Press, 1995, pp. 13–54.

Boccard, Nicolas.; van Ypersele, Tanguy and Wunsch, P. "Comparative Advantage, Redistribution and the Political Process: A Perspective on Social Dumping." Center for Operations Research and Econometrics (CORE) Discussion Paper No. 9651, Louvain-la-Neuve, Belgium, 1996.

Borjas, George J. *Friends or strangers: The impact of immigrants on the U.S. economy.* New York: Basic Books, 1990.

Borjas, George J.; Freeman, Richard B. and Katz, Lawrence F. "On the Labor Market Effects of Immigration and Trade," in George J. Borjas and Richard B. Freeman, eds., *Immigration and the work force.* Chicago: University of Chicago Press, 1992, pp. 213–44.

Borjas, George J.; Freeman, Richard B. and Lang, Kevin. "On the Labor Market Effects of Immigration and Trade," in John Abowd and Richard B. Freeman, eds., *Immigration, trade, and the labor market.* Chicago: University of Chicago Press, 1991, pp. 77–100.

Brecher, Richard A. "Minimum Wage Rates and the Pure Theory of International Trade." *Quarterly Journal of Economics*, February 1974a, *88*(1), pp. 98–116.

————. "Optimal Commercial Policy for a Minimum-Wage Economy." *Journal of International Economics*, May 1974b, *4*(2), pp. 139–49.

Center for Economic Policy Research (CEPR). *Unemployment: Choices for Europe.* London: CEPR, 1995.

Davis, Donald R. "Technology, Relative Wages, and Unemployment in a Global Economy." *European Economic Review*, 1998 (forthcoming).

Davis, Donald R. and Reeve, Trevor. "Human Capital, Unemployment, and Trade." Harvard Institute for Economic Research Working Paper No.1804, Harvard University, August 1997.

Davis, Donald R.; Weinstein, David E.; Bradford, Scott C. and Shimpo, Kazushige. "Using International and Japanese Regional Data to Determine When the Factor Abundance Theory of Trade Works." *American Economic Review*, June 1997, 87(3), pp. 421–46.

Dixit, Avinash K. and Norman, Victor F. *Theory of international trade.* Cambridge: Cambridge University Press, 1980.

Freeman, Richard B. "Are Your Wages Set in Beijing?" *Journal of Economic Perspectives*, Summer 1995, *9*(3), pp. 15–32.

Freeman, Richard B. and Katz, Lawrence F., eds. *Differences and changes in wage structures.* Chicago: University of Chicago Press, 1995.

Friedberg, Rachel M. and Hunt, Jennifer. "The Impact of Immigrants on Host Country Wages, Employment and Growth." *Journal of Economic Perspectives*, Spring 1995, *9*(2), pp. 23–44.

Helpman, Elhanan and Krugman, Paul R. *Market structure and foreign trade*. Cambridge, MA: MIT Press, 1985.

Katz, Lawrence F.; Loveman, Gary and Blanchflower, David. "A Comparison of Changes in the Structure of Wages in Four OECD Countries," in Richard B. Freeman and Lawrence F. Katz, eds., *Differences and changes in wage structures*. Chicago: University of Chicago Press, 1995, pp. 25–65.

Katz, Lawrence F. and Murphy, Kevin M. "Changes in Relative Wages, 1963–1987: Supply and Demand Factors." *Quarterly Journal of Economics*, February 1992, *107*(1), pp. 35–78.

Krugman, Paul R. "Europe Jobless, America Penniless?" *Foreign Policy*, Summer 1994, No. 95, pp. 19–34.

―――. "Growing World Trade: Causes and Consequences." Mimeo, Stanford University, April 6–7, 1995.

―――. "But For, As If, and So What? Thought Experiments on Trade and Factor Prices." Mimeo, Massachusetts Institute of Technology, November 1996.

Krugman, Paul R. and Lawrence, Robert Z. "Trade, Jobs, and Wages." National Bureau of Economic Research (Cambridge, MA) Working Paper No. 4478, September 1993.

Lawrence, Robert Z. and Slaughter, Matthew J. "International Trade and American Wages in the 1980s: Giant Sucking Sound or Small Hiccup?" *Brookings Papers on Economic Activity*, 1993, (1), pp. 161–210.

Leamer, Edward E. "In Search of Stolper-Samuelson Effects Between Trade and U.S. Wages." Mimeo, Yale University and University of California, Los Angeles, 1995.

Matusz, Steven J. "International Trade, the Division of Labor, and Unemployment." *International Economic Review*, February 1996, *37*(1), pp. 71–84.

Modigliani, Franco. "The Shameful Rate of Unemployment in the EMS: Causes and Cures." Mimeo, Massachusetts Institute of Technology, 1995.

Murphy, Kevin M. "Comment—Wage Inequality and Unemployment: United States vs. Europe." *NBER macroeconomics annual*. Cambridge, MA: MIT Press, 1995, pp. 54–59.

Oslington, Paul. "Factor Price Equalization and Trade Patterns with Unemployment." Macquarie Economics Research Papers 2/96, Macquarie University, Australia, June 1996.

Salt, John; Singleton, Ann and Hogarth, Jennifer. *Europe's international migrants*. Lanham, MD: Bernan Associates, 1994.

Samuelson, Paul A. "International Factor-Price Equalisation Once Again." *Economic Journal*, June 1949, *59*(234), pp. 181–97.

Trefler, Daniel. "International Factor Price Differences: Leontief Was Right!" *Journal of Political Economy*, December 1993, *101*(6), pp. 961–87.

―――. "Immigrants and Natives in General Equilibrium Trade Models." Mimeo, National Academy of Sciences, September 12, 1996.

U.S. Department of Commerce, Bureau of the Census. *Statistical abstract of the United States*. Washington, DC: U.S. Government Printing Office, various issues.

Wood, Adrian. *North-South trade, employment, and inequality*. New York: Oxford University Press, 1994.

ABOUT THE AUTHOR

Donald R. Davis

Donald Davis is a professor of economics at Columbia University. He has also served on the faculty of Harvard University. He received his B.A. from the University of California at Berkeley, and his Ph.D. from Columbia University.

Editor's Queries

What are the major unresolved questions of international economics? What are likely to be the hot topics of the next decade? The central unresolved question in international trade is what determines the cross-national pattern of production and trade. Answering this central positive question is essential to determine which of the competing policy and normative frameworks are relevant for the world in which we actually live.

What advice do you have to offer graduate students in the field of international economics? By the time a graduate student reads these words it will be time for her to stop thinking like a student and start thinking like a researcher. The primary attitude of the researcher is to appreciate the existing literature, to learn from it, but never to be reverent toward it. The most important advances come from critiques of existing literature. Even the most insightful papers fail to capture features of reality that may matter quite a lot. Thinking about the parts of reality left out of the existing work is an important step toward novel research. There are also a number of practical points in research. The literature in any field is vast, and while you need to master the core papers that form the language of the field, the advantage in research does not always go to the best-read economist. A practical suggestion is to start at the frontier and read backward only as necessary. In the third and succeeding years of your graduate program, you should be taking courses only if there is a truly compelling reason. Attend the department seminar in your field. Where possible, reduce your teaching: Your job is to produce exciting research. Identify the dozen or so leaders of the intellectual community that you aim to join. Check their web sites for working papers on the problems they are grappling with now, rather than looking in journals to find out what they were wondering about some years ago. Become a part of that community by contributing to it. Stop reading and start writing. Present your work as often as you have the chance.

The Generalized Theory
of Distortions and Welfare

Jagdish N. Bhagwati

The theory of trade and welfare has recently developed independently in seven areas that have apparently little analytical relationship among themselves:

1. The Suboptimality of Laissez-Faire under Market Imperfections   It has been shown that, when market imperfections exist, laissez-faire (otherwise described as "a policy of unified exchange rates" [5]) will not be the optimal policy. Among the market imperfections for which the suboptimality of laissez-faire has been demonstrated are four key types: (i) factor market imperfection, a wage differential between sectors;[1] (ii) product market imperfection, a production externality;[2] (iii) consumption imperfection, a consumption externality;[3] and (iv) trade imperfection, monopoly power in trade.[4]

2. Immiserizing Growth   Examples have been produced where a country, after growth (in factor supplies and/or technological know-how), becomes worse off, phenomena described as *immiserizing growth*. I produced an example of such a phenomenon in 1958 [1] (as also did Harry Johnson independently at the time) where growth led to such a deterioration in the country's terms of trade that the loss from the worsened terms of trade outweighted the primary gain from growth. Subsequently, Johnson [19] produced another example of immiserization, in which the country had no ability to influence her terms of trade but there was a tariff (which is necessarily welfare reducing in view of the assumed absence of monopoly power in trade) in both the pregrowth and the postgrowth situations, and growth impoverished the country in certain cases. I later produced yet other examples of immiserizing growth [6], one in which there was a wage differential in the factor market, and another in which the country had monopoly power in trade (as in my original 1958 example), but the country had an optimum tariff (before growth) which became suboptimal after growth.

> This paper is the result of thinking and research over a period of many years, originating in my 1958 paper on immiserizing growth [1] and developing considerably since my joint paper with the late V. K. Ramaswami in 1963 [2] on domestic distortions. Since 1965, T. N. Srinivasan and I have collaborated on research in related matters, pertaining to the theory of optimal policy intervention when noneconomic objectives are present [7], a subject pioneered by Max Corden's brilliant work [12]. In many ways, therefore, this paper has grown out of the ferment of ideas in Delhi during 1963–1968, when Srinivasan, Ramaswami, and I happened to work together and independently on the diverse subjects which are brought together in this paper. The work of others, particularly Murray Kemp [23], [24] and Harry Johnson [18], has also contributed to the development of my thinking.

Reprinted with permission from Jagdish N. Bhagwati, Ronald W. Jones, Robert A. Mundell, Jaroslav Vanek, editors. *Trade, Balance of Payments, and Growth: Papers in International Economics in Honor of Charles P. Kindleberger,* North-Holland Publishing Company, 1971.

3. Ranking of Alternative Policies under Market Imperfections For the four major imperfections described earlier, the optimal policy intervention has been analyzed by several economists. Hagen [16] has argued that the optimal policy for the case of the wage differential would be a factor tax-cum-subsidy. For the production externality, Bhagwati and Ramaswami [2] have shown that the optimal policy intervention is a production tax-cum-subsidy. For the consumption externality case, it follows from the general arguments in Bhagwati and Ramaswami [2] that a consumption tax-cum-subsidy ought to be used. Finally, for the case of monopoly power in trade, it has been known since the time of Mill and has been demonstrated rigorously by (among others) Graaff [14] and Johnson [17] that a tariff is the optimal policy. Recent work of Bhagwati, Ramaswami, and Srinivasan [8] has then extended the analysis, for each market imperfection, to the ranking of *all* alternative policies: the tariff (trade subsidy) policy, the production tax-cum-subsidy policy, the consumption tax-cum-subsidy policy, and the factor tax-cum-subsidy policy.[5]

4. Ranking of Tariffs Yet another area of research in trade and welfare has raised the question of ranking policies that constitute impediments themselves to the attainment of optimality. Thus, for example, Kemp [22] has analysed, for a country without monopoly power in trade (and no other imperfections), the question as to whether a higher tariff is worse than a lower tariff. Similarly, Bhagwati and Kemp [10] have analysed the problem for tariffs around the optimal tariff for a country *with* monopoly power in trade.

5. Ranking of Free Trade and Autarky A number of trade theorists have compared free trade with autarky, when there were market imperfections such as wage differentials (Hagen [16]) and production externality (Haberler [15]), to deduce that free trade was no longer necessarily superior to self-sufficiency. Melvin [26] and Kemp [23] have recently considered the comparison between free trade and autarky when there are commodity taxes.

6. Ranking of Restricted Trade and Autarky Aside from the case in which trade is tariff restricted (wherein the comparison between restricted trade and autarky becomes the comparison of tariffs discussed in item 4) Bhagwati [4] has considered the ranking of other policies (e.g., production tax-cum-subsidies) that restrict trade and autarky.

7. Noneconomic Objectives and Ranking of Policies Finally, a number of economists have addressed themselves to the question of optimal policy intervention when the values of different variables are constrained, as noneconomic objectives, so that full optimality is unattainable. Four key types of noneconomic objectives have been analyzed. Corden [12] has shown that a production tax-cum-subsidy is optimal where the constrained variable is production (for reasons such as defense production). Johnson [18] has shown a tariff to be optimal when imports are constrained instead (in the interest of "self-sufficiency"). Bhagwati and Srinivasan [7] have demonstrated that a factor tax-cum-subsidy is optimal when the constrained variable is employment of a factor in an activity (i.e., in the interest of "national character") and a consumption tax-cum-subsidy when the constrained variable is domestic availability of consumption (i.e., to restrict "luxury consumption"). Bhagwati and Srinivasan have also extended the analysis to the ranking of *all* policy instruments for a number of these noneconomic objectives.

This paper is aimed at putting these diverse analyses into a common analytical framework. This results in the logical unification of a number of interesting and important results, leading in turn to fresh insights while also enabling us to derive remarkable "duality" relationships between the analysis of policy rankings under market imperfections and policy rankings to achieve noneconomic objectives.

ALTERNATIVE TYPES OF DISTORTIONS

It can be readily shown, in fact, that the diverse results reviewed so far belong to what might aptly be described as the theory of distortions and welfare.

The theory of distortions is built around the central theorem of trade and welfare: that laissez-faire is Pareto optimal for a perfectly competitive system with no monopoly power in trade.[6] Ruling out the phenomenon of diminishing cost of transformation between any pair of commodities (i.e., the concavity of the production possibility set in the familiar, two-commodity system),[7] the Pareto optimality of the laissez-faire policy follows quite simply from the fact that the economic system will operate with technical efficiency (i.e., on the "best" production possibility curve, if we think again of two commodities for simplicity). The economic system will also satisfy further the (first-order) conditions for an economic maximum: DRT = FRT = DRS (where DRT represents the marginal rate of transformation in domestic production, FRT represents marginal foreign rate of transformation, and DRS represents the marginal rate of substitution in consumption).[8]

The theory of distortions is then concerned with the following four pathologies which may characterize, singly or in combination, the economic system:

Distortion 1: FRT $\neq$ DRT = DRS

Distortion 2: DRT $\neq$ DRS = FRT

Distortion 3: DRS $\neq$ DRT = FRT

Distortion 4: Nonoperation on the efficient production possibility curve.

"ENDOGENOUS" DISTORTIONS

These distortions (implying departures from full optimality) may arise when the economy is characterised by *market imperfections* under a policy of laissez-faire. Thus, the presence of national monopoly power in trade will lead to Distortion 1, because foreign prices will not equal FRT. The case of the Meade type of production externality[9] leads to Distortion 2. Distortion 3 will follow when sellers of the importable commodity, for example, charge a uniform premium on imported as well as home-produced supplies. Distortion 4 follows when there is a factor market imperfection resulting from a wage differential, for a factor, between the different activities.[10] In these cases, therefore, the resulting distortions (arising from the market imperfections) are appropriately described as "endogenous" distortions.

"POLICY-IMPOSED" DISTORTIONS

On the other hand, the four varieties of distortions listed earlier may be result of economic policies, as distinct from endogenous phenomena such as market imperfections.

Thus, Distortion 1 will arise for a country with no monopoly power in trade if the country has a tariff; it will also arise for a country with monopoly power in trade if the tariff is less or greater than the optimal tariff. Distortion 2 will follow if the government imposes a production tax-cum-subsidy. Distortion 3 will be the consequence similarly of a consumption tax-cum-subsidy policy. Finally, the adoption of a factor tax-cum-subsidy policy will result in Distortion 4.[11] These are instances therefore of "policy-imposed" distortions.

But as soon as we probe the reasons for the existence of such policy-imposed distortions, two alternative interpretations are possible. Either we can consider these policies as *autonomous* (i.e., a tariff, which leads to Distortion 1, may for example be a historic accident), or we may consider these policies as *instrumental* (a tariff, leading to Distortion 1, may be the policy instrument used in order to reduce imports)—as in the case of the theory of noneconomic objectives when Distortion 1 is created through the deployment of a tariff when the objective is to reduce imports in the interest of "self-sufficiency."

We thus have altogether three sets of "causes" for the four varieties of distortions that can be distinguished: *endogenous; autonomous, policy-imposed*; and *instrumental, policy-imposed*. The entire literature that I reviewed earlier can then be given its logical coherence and unity around these alternative classes and causes of distortions.

Before formulating the general theory of distortions and generalizing the theorems discussed in the introduction into other areas, it would be useful to underline the precise manner in which these theorems relate to the different varieties of distortions that we have distinguished so far.

1. The theorems on the suboptimality of different market imperfections clearly relate to the theory of endogenous distortions. Within a static welfare context, they demonstrate that these market imperfections result in the different types of Distortions 1–4, thus resulting in the breakdown of the Pareto optimality of laissez-faire in these cases.

2. The theorems on immiserizing growth, on the other hand, relate to the comparative statics of welfare when distortions are present. The theorems developed in this literature involve cases in which growth takes place under given distortions, either endogenous or policy imposed, and the primary improvement in welfare (which would have accrued if fully optimal policies were followed both before and after growth) is outweighed by the accentuation of the loss from the distortion in the postgrowth situation [6].

Thus, in the original Bhagwati example of immiserizing growth, the assumed free trade and hence failure to impose an optimum tariff (to exploit the monopoly power in trade) in both the pregrowth and the postgrowth situations involves welfare-reducing "distortionary" policies in both situations. Immiserization occurs therefore because the gain, which would necessarily accrue from growth if the optimal tariff were imposed in both situations, is smaller than the incremental loss arising from the accentuation (if any) in the postgrowth situation of the welfare loss resulting from the "distortionary" free-trade policy (implying an endogenous Distortion 1 in this instance) in both situations.

Harry Johnson's example of immiserization where the country has no monopoly power in trade but a tariff (which thus constitutes an autonomous policy-imposed Distortion 1) in both the pregrowth and the postgrowth situations, is to be explained in terms of the same logic. In the absence of monopoly power in trade, the tariff is necessarily "distortionary" and, compared with the fully optimal free-trade policy, causes a loss of welfare in each situation. If the growth were to occur with free trade, there would necessarily be an increment in welfare. However, since growth occurs under a tariff, there arises the possibility that the loss from the tariff may be accentuated after growth, and that this incremental loss may outweigh the gain (that would occur under the optimal, free-trade policy), thus resulting in immiserization. Thus, the policy-imposed distortion (i.e., the tariff) generates the possibility of immiserizing growth.

3. The theorems that rank alternative policies under market imperfections are addressed to a different range of questions. They relate to endogenous distortions, of each of the four varieties we have distinguished, and then seek to rank the different, available policy instruments (extending to the full complement: production, consumption, trade, and factor tax-cum-subsidies) in relation to one another and vis-à-vis laissez-faire itself. The problem has been posed in this fashion by Bhagwati, Ramaswami, and Srinivasan [8] in their recent work.

4. The theorems of Kemp [22] and Bhagwati and Kemp [10], which rank tariffs in relation to one another, however, belong to a yet different genre. They relate to policy-imposed distortions, autonomous in the sense defined in this paper, and aim at ranking different levels at which policy may impose the specified distortion (e.g., Distortion 1 in the cases in which tariffs are ranked).

5. The ranking of free trade and autarky under situations involving market imperfections or taxes involves, on the other hand, a comparison of essentially two levels (the zero tariff level and the prohibitive tariff level) at which a policy-imposed distortion (the tariff) is used, in a situation which is itself characterized by another distortion (either endogenous, such as the wage differential in Hagen [16], or policy-imposed, such as a tax on consumption of a commodity).

6. The ranking of a situation with trade restricted by a nontariff policy with a situation of autarky (with therefore an implicit, prohibitive tariff) involves an altogether different type of comparison: of one distortion with another, both autonomous policy-imposed in Bhagwati's analysis [4].

7. The theory of noneconomic objectives [7], on the other hand, relates to the optimal nature of intervention and the ranking of alternative policies, when certain variables are precluded from specified ranges of values in the interest of "noneconomic" objectives. It is therefore, from an analytical point of view, a theory of how optimally (i.e., at minimum cost) to *introduce* distortions in the economic system, when the attainment of the full optimum is precluded by the noneconomic-objective constraints and also of what the relative costs of alternative policies or methods of introducing such distortions, in pursuit of the noneconomic

objectives, are. It is thus a theory pertaining to the ranking of instrumental, policy-imposed distortions, with each distortion being defined under a common set of economic and non-economic constraints.

It is clear, therefore, that these diverse theorems relate to different types of distortions and raise a number of diverse questions relating thereto. But as soon as we grasp this central fact, it is possible to unify and extend the entire body of this literature and thus to develop a general theory of distortions and welfare.

DISTORTIONS AND WELFARE: GENERAL THEORY

This generalized theory of distortions and welfare can be developed in terms of seven central propositions.

PROPOSITION 1. There are four principal types of distortions:

1. FRT $\neq$ DRT = DRS;

2. DRT $\neq$ DRS = FRT;

3. DRS $\neq$ DRT = FRT; and

4. Nonoperation on the efficient production possibility curve.

These, in turn, can be caused by factors that are

1. Endogenous;

2. Autonomous, policy-imposed; and

3. Instrumental, policy-imposed.

This proposition is merely a recapitulation of the concepts and analysis developed in the preceding section and requires no further comment. Note merely, by way of reemphasis, that in each of the $(4 \times 3 = 12)$ distortionary situations, the economic system departs from full Pareto optimality.

PROPOSITION 2

i. Optimal policy intervention, in the presence of distortions, involves a tax-cum-subsidy policy addressed directly to offsetting the source of the distortions, when the causes are endogenous or autonomous, policy-imposed. Dual to (i) is the theorem that:

ii. When distortions have to be introduced into the economy, because the values of certain variables (e.g., production or employment of a factor in an activity) have to be constrained, the optimal (or least-cost) method of doing this is to choose that policy intervention that creates the distortion affecting directly the constrained variable.

These two propositions, which constitute a remarkable duality of theorems, extend between themselves to all the classes of Distortions 1 to 4 and their three possible causes, endogenous, autonomous policy-imposed, and instrumental policy-imposed. Furthermore, each proposition is readily derived from the theorems on market imperfections and on noneconomic objectives.

Proposition 2(i) was formulated, in essentially similar form, by Bhagwati and Ramaswami [2] and later by Johnson [18], for the case of endogenous distortions. For Distortion 1, resulting from monopoly power in trade under laissez-faire, it is well known that the optimal policy intervention is a tariff. For Distortion 2, Bhagwati and Ramaswami showed that the optimal policy was a production tax-cum-subsidy. For Distortion 3, correspondingly, the optimal policy is a consumption tax-cum-subsidy. Finally, when a wage differential causes Distortion 4, Hagen [16] showed that the optimal intervention was through a factor tax-cum-subsidy. In each instance, therefore, the policy required is one that directly attacks the source of the distortion.

It follows equally, and trivially, that if these distortions are autonomous policy-imposed, the optimal intervention is to eliminate the policy itself: hence, again the optimal policy intervention is addressed to the source of the distortion itself. Thus, with a suboptimal tariff leading to Distortion 1, the optimal policy is to change the tariff to an optimal level (equal to zero, if there is no monopoly power in trade). Similarly, if a consumption tax-cum-subsidy causes Distortion 3, the optimal policy is to offset it with an equivalent consumption tax-cum-subsidy (which leaves zero net consumption tax-cum-subsidy and thus restores full optimality).

But the extension of these results, via the "dual" Proposition 2(ii), to the class of instrumental, policy-imposed distortions, is far from trivial. And the duality is remarkable. Corden [12] has shown that the optimal policy, if the binding noneconomic constraint relates to production, is a *production* tax-cum-subsidy. Johnson [18] has demonstrated that the optimal policy, if the binding noneconomic constraint relates to import (export) level, is a *tariff or trade subsidy*. Bhagwati and Srinivasan [7] have extended the analysis to show that, if the binding noneconomic constraint relates to the level of employment of a factor of production in a sector, the optimal policy is to use a *factor* tax-cum-subsidy that directly taxes (subsidises) the employment of the factor in the sector where its employment level must be lowered (raised) to the constrained level.[12] They have also demonstrated that the optimal policy for raising (lowering) consumption to a constrained level is a *consumption* tax-cum-subsidy policy.

To put it somewhat differently, a trade-level noneconomic objective is achieved at least cost by introducing a policy-imposed Distortion 1 via a trade tariff or subsidy; a production noneconomic objective by introducing a policy-imposed Distortion 2 via a production tax-cum-subsidy; a consumption noneconomic objective by introducing a policy-imposed Distortion 3 via a consumption tax-cum-subsidy; and a factor-employment (in a sector) noneconomic objective by introducing a policy-imposed Distortion 4 via a factor tax-cum-subsidy.

PROPOSITION 3

i. For each distortion, whether endogenous or autonomous, policy-imposed, in origin, it is possible to analyse the welfare ranking of all alternative policies, from the (first best) optimal to the second best and so on.

ii. a. When distortions have to be introduced into the economy, because the values of certain variables have to be constrained (e.g., production or employment of a factor in an activity), the policy interventions that do this may similarly be welfare ranked. b. The ranking of these policies is further completely symmetrical with that under the "corresponding" class of endogenous or autonomous policy-imposed distortions (e.g., the ranking of policies for production externality, an endogenous Distortion 2, is identical with the ranking of policies when production is constrained as a noneconomic objective).

Since there are four different types of policies (factor, production, consumption, and trade tax-cum-subsidies), the propositions listed here are aimed at ranking *all* of them for each of the (twelve) varieties of distortions and establishing "duality" relations of the kind we discovered for optimal policies alone in Proposition 2(ii).

Bhagwati, Ramaswami, and Srinivasan [8] have recently analyzed the welfare ranking of all policies for endogenous distortions and established the following rankings:[13]

Distortion 1: FRT $\neq$ DRT = DRS

This is the case of monopoly power in trade. The ranking of policies then is

  i. First best: tariff;

  ii. Second best: either production or consumption or factor tax-cum-subsidy (all policies are superior to laissez-faire but cannot be ranked uniquely vis-à-vis one another).[14]

Distortion 2: DRT $\neq$ DRS = FRT

This is the case of a pure production externality. The ranking of policies then is

  i. First best: production tax-cum-subsidy;

  ii. Second best: either tariff (trade subsidy) or factor tax-cum-subsidy (both policies are superior to laissez-faire but cannot be ranked uniquely vis-à-vis each other);

  iii. Consumption tax-cum-subsidy will not help.[15]

Distortion 3: DRS $\neq$ DRT = FRT

This is the case in which, for example, the sellers of a commodity uniform premium to buyers over the cost of supplies, whether imported or domestically produced. The ranking of policies then is

  i. First best: consumption tax-cum-subsidy;

  ii. Second best: tariff;

  iii. Production or factor tax-cum-subsidy will not help.[16]

Distortion 4: Nonoperation on the efficient production possibility curve

This is the case in which there is a wage differential, a factor market imperfection. In this case, the ranking of policies is

  i. First best: factor tax-cum-subsidy;

  ii. Second best: production tax-cum-subsidy;

iii. Third best: tariff (trade subsidy);

iv. Consumption tax-cum-subsidy will not help.[17]

It is clear that the extension of these rankings to the corresponding cases where the distortions are autonomous policy-imposed (e.g., Distortion 2 resulting from the autonomous levy of a governmental tax, or Distortion 4 resulting from the grant of a governmental subsidy on employment of a factor in one activity) is total and trivial. It is interesting and remarkable, however, that these rankings carry over also to the class of instrumental, policy-imposed distortions.

Thus, for the case of noneconomic objectives, Bhagwati and Srinivasan [7] have provided the basis for analyzing the rankings of different policies, which I now proceed to develop fully:

Trade-level as a Constraint: The ranking of policies in this case is

  i. First best: tariff;

  ii. Second best: either production tax-cum-subsidy or factor tax-cum-subsidy or consumption tax-cum-subsidy (these policies cannot be ranked vis-à-vis one another).[18]

Note the complete symmetry with the rankings under Distortion I earlier.

Production level as a Constraint: The ranking of policies in this case is

  i. First best: production tax-cum-subsidy;

  ii. Second best: either tariff (trade subsidy) or factor tax-cum-subsidy (these policies cannot be ranked vis-à-vis each other);

  iii. Consumption tax-cum-subsidy will not help.[19]

Note again the complete symmetry with the rankings under Distortion 2.

Consumption level as a Constraint: The ranking of policies in this case is

  i. First best: consumption tax-cum-subsidy;

  ii. Second best: tariff;

  iii. Production or factor tax-cum-subsidy, when it helps meet the consumption constraint, will be third-best.[20]

Again, the symmetry with the ranking under Distortion 3 is total.

Factor Employment (in a Sector) as a Constraint: The ranking of policies in this case is

  i. First best: factor tax-cum-subsidy;

  ii. Second best: production tax-cum-subsidy;

  iii. Third best: tariff (trade subsidy);

  iv. Consumption tax-cum-subsidy will not help.[21]

In this final case as well, the symmetry with the corresponding Distortion 4 is complete.

Thus, the duality of the policy rankings, for endogenous and autonomous policy-imposed distortions on the one hand and instrumental policy-imposed distortions on the other hand, is altogether complete and remarkable.

PROPOSITION 4. For each kind of distortion, growth may be immiserizing.

For endogenous and autonomous policy-imposed distortions, belonging to each of the varieties 1 to 4 that we have distinguished, this proposition has already been demonstrated by Bhagwati [6].

Thus, for example, where Distortion 1 obtains endogenously under laissez-faire because of monopoly power in trade, Bhagwati's 1958 analysis [1] demonstrates the possibility of immiserization. Where Distortions 2 and 4 obtain simultaneously as a result of an endogenous wage differential, the same possibility has again been demonstrated by Bhagwati [6]. Johnson's demonstration [19] of immiserization when a country has no monopoly power in trade but a tariff, illustrates Proposition 2 for the case of an autonomous policy-imposed Distortion 1.

Note again that the underlying reason for immiserizing growth is that the growth takes place in the presence of a distortion. This distortion produces a loss of welfare from the fully optimal welfare level. Thus, if there is an accentuation in this loss of welfare, when growth has occurred and the distortion has continued, this incremental loss could outweigh the gain that would have accrued if fully optimal policies had been followed in the pregrowth and postgrowth situations [6]. It also follows that such immiserizing growth would be impossible if fully optimal policies were followed in each situation, i.e., if the distortions resulting from the endogenous and policy-imposed cause were offset by optimal policy intervention, as discussed under Proposition 2(i) earlier.[22]

But so far we have discussed only distortions resulting from the endogenous and policy-imposed, autonomous factors. However, Proposition 4 applies equally, and can be generalized, to *instrumental* policy-imposed distortions as well.

In complete symmetry with the endogenous and autonomous policy-imposed distortions, the phenomenon of immiserizing growth will be precluded when the constrained variable (e.g., production in the case of a production objective) is attained (in the pregrowth and the postgrowth situations) by optimal policy. On the other hand, immiserization becomes possible as soon as any of the second-best (or third best) policies is adopted to constrain the variable (to a preassigned value in both the pregrowth and postgrowth situations).

This generalization of the theory of immiserizing growth is readily illustrated with reference to production as the constrained variable. Remember that a production tax-cum-subsidy is the optimal policy in this case and a tariff a second best policy. Figure 1a then illustrates how it is impossible, after growth, to become "worse off" if the production level of a commodity is constrained to the required level by a suitable production tax-cum-subsidy policy. The y production is constrained to level $\bar{y}$; the production possibility curve shifts out from AP to $A'B'$. With a suitable production tax-cum-subsidy used in both the

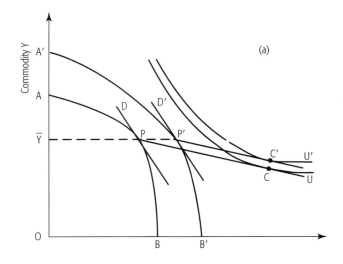

Figure 1a

AB is the pregrowth production possibility curve; *A'B'* the postgrowth production possibility curve. The international price ratio is given at *PC = P'C'*. Production of *y* is constrained to level *ȳ*. A suitable production tax-cum-subsidy takes production, before growth, to *P* at domestic, producer price ratio *DP*. After growth, a suitable production tax-cum-subsidy takes producer price ratio to *D'P'* and production to *P'*. Welfare level has increased, after growth, to *U'*(>*U*).

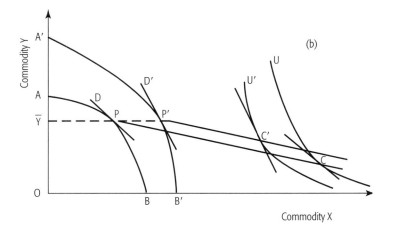

Commodity X

Figure 1b

The production possibility curve shifts, after growth, from *AB* to *A'B'*. In each case, the production of *y* is constrained to *ȳ* by a tariff. In the pregrowth case, this tariff leads to production at *P* (with domestic price ratio *DP*, consumption at *C*, and welfare at *U*. After growth, production is at *P'*, consumption at *C'*, and welfare has reduced to *U'* (<*U*), implying immiserizing growth.

pregrowth and the postgrowth situations, to constrain *y* production to *ȳ*, it is clear that it is impossible to worsen welfare after growth. Figure 1b illustrates, however, the possibility of immiserizing growth when the suboptimal tariff policy is followed instead in each case to constrain *y* output to level *ȳ*. Note that this demonstration, where the welfare level reduces after growth to U' from U, does not require the assumption of inferior goods.

Similar illustrations could be provided for the other three cases, where consumption, factor employment in a sector, and trade-level are constrained. In each case, only the pursuit of a suboptimal policy to achieve the specified noneconomic objective could lead to immiserization.

PROPOSITION 5. Reductions in the "degree" of an only distortion are successively welfare increasing until the distortion is fully eliminated.

This theorem holds whether we take endogenous or policy-imposed distortions. However, it needs to be qualified, so as to exclude inferior goods for all cases except where a *consumption* tax-cum-subsidy is relevant.

For autonomous, policy-imposed Distortion 1, the Kemp [22] and Bhagwati-Kemp [10] theorems are special cases of Proposition 5: Each further requires the exclusion of inferior goods and attendant multiple equilibria if the possibility of the competitive system "choosing" an inferior-welfare equilibrium under the lower degree of distortion is to be ruled out.[23] In point of fact, identical propositions could be derived for alternative forms of autonomus policy-imposed distortions, factor tax-cum-subsidy, production tax-cum-subsidy, and consumption tax-cum-subsidy.[24]

Similarly, we can argue that reduction in the degree of each market imperfection, insofar as it reduces the degree of its consequent distortion, will raise welfare. Thus, for example, a reduction in the degree of production externality will reduce the degree of Distortion 2 and increase the level of welfare.[25]

Finally, identical conclusions apply if we reduce the degree of "required" distortion, of the instrumental policy-imposed type, by relaxing the binding constraint on the "noneconomic"-objective variable. Thus, marginally relaxing the constraint on production will suffice to improve welfare. As is clear from figure 2a, the relaxation of the constraint on y production, from $\bar{y}$ to $\bar{y}_n$, will necessarily improve welfare by shifting the "availability line" outwards—if, in each case, the policy adopted is a production tax-cum-subsidy policy.

If, however, as figure 2b illustrates, a (suboptimal) tariff policy is followed instead, to constrain y-production to the required level, the result of a relaxation in the constraint is identical; the only qualification is relating to that arising from inferior goods. Further, an identical conclusion holds, as in the case of a production tax-cum-subsidy, for the case of a factor tax-cum-subsidy instead.

Thus, Proposition 5 applies in the case of instrumental policy-imposed distortions, no matter *which* policy is considered (in other words, no matter which distortion is introduced in pursuit of the specific noneconomic objective).

PROPOSITION 6. Reductions in the "degree" of a distortion will not necessarily be welfare increasing if there is another distortion in the system.

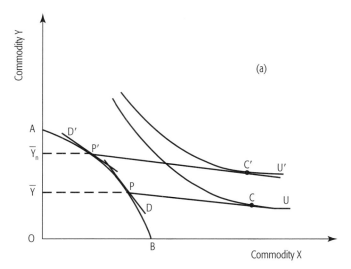

Figure 2a

With AB as the production possibility curve, $\bar{y}$ and $\bar{y}_n$ are the successive noneconomic constraints on y production, which are met by use of a suitable production subsidy policy in each case. For $\bar{y}$, production then is at P, consumption at C, and welfare level at U. For $\bar{y}_n$, a relaxation in the constraint, production shifts to P' (with producer price ratio at $D'P'$ now), consumption to C', and welfare has increased to U' ($>U$).

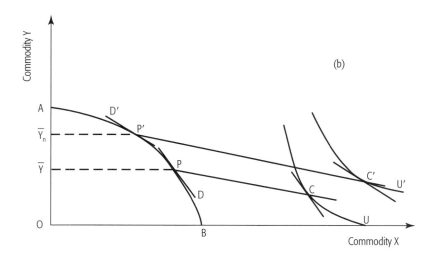

Figure 2b

With production of y-commodity constrained successively at $\bar{y}$ and $\bar{y}_n$, a tariff used for that purpose, and production possibility curve AB, the production for $\bar{y}$ constraint is at P, consumption at C, and welfare at U'. Relaxation in the constraint to $\bar{y}_n$ leads to production at P' and consumption at C' (at price $D'P'$) and welfare increases to U' ($>U$).

This proposition is readily established for endogenous or autonomous policy-imposed distortions.

Let us first consider a case in which reductions in one distortion *do* lead to improvement in welfare despite the presence of another distortion in the system. Thus, consider the case in which a production externality, an endogenous Distortion 2 where DRT $\neq$ DRS = FRT, is combined with a consumption tax-cum-subsidy, an autonomous policy-imposed Distortion 3 where DRS $\neq$ FRT = DRT, but there is no monopoly power in trade. Assume further that the two distortions combine so as to yield altogether the initial situation where DRT $\neq$ DRS $\neq$ FRT (so that they are not mutually offsetting as far as one inequality is concerned). In this case, successive reductions in the consumption tax-cum-subsidy will necessarily be welfare increasing, given the production externality; and successive reductions in the production externality will improve welfare (except for the complication introduced by inferior goods).[26]

Next, however, consider the case where there is a production externality (endogenous, DRT $\neq$ DRS = FRT) combined with a tariff without monopoly power in trade (autonomous policy-imposed FRT $\neq$ DRS = DRT) and assume that the resulting initial situation is characterized by FRT $\neq$ DRT $\neq$ DRS. In this case, successive reductions in the tariff will not necessarily improve welfare steadily, if at all, and the gains may turn into losses.[27] The theorems on the possible inferiority of free trade (i.e., zero tariff) to no trade (i.e., prohibitive tariff) when there is a production externality [15] or a wage differential [2], [16] are only special cases of this general theorem that illustrates Proposition 6.

It is interesting to note further that this theorem can with equal insight be analyzed in terms of Proposition 4 if we recognize that, if optimal policies are followed in *both* the autarkic and the trading "situations", the trade situation must necessarily enable the economy to be "better off" — as is obvious to trade theorists familiar with the Baldwin-envelope technique. If then there is a distortion common to both situations, as with an endogenous wage differential or production externality or with an autonomous policy-imposed production tax-cum-subsidy, the transition to the (free) trading situation may well be immiserizing (i.e., therefore, free trade inferior to autarky) if the loss from this distortion is accentuated and outweighs the primary gain from the shift to (free) trade itself.

PROPOSITION 7. Distortions cannot be ranked (uniquely) vis-à-vis one another.

This is a readily apparent proposition and applies clearly to all the classes of distortions we have discussed.

Bhagwati's demonstration [4] that Kemp's theorem [22] of the superiority of tariff-restricted trade over no trade will not extend to cases where the trade is restricted instead by policies such as consumption and production tax-cum-subsidies becomes intuitively obvious as soon as it is seen that it falls into the class of theorems belonging to Proposition 7. For, in this instance, two distortions are being compared: (i) a consumption tax-cum-subsidy leading to Distortion 3, DRS $\neq$ DRT = FRT, with a situation of autarky and hence implicit prohibitive tariff, thus involving Distortion 1, FRT ≠ DRT = DRS; and (ii) a production tax-cum-subsidy leading to Distortion 2, DRT = DRS = FRT, with autarky involving Distortion 1, FRT ≠ DRT = DRS. In principle, of course, the demonstration of impossibility of unique ranking between autarky and restricted trade could be carried equally into the case where trade-restriction occurs via use of a factor tax-cum-subsidy involving Distortion 4 along with 2.

CONCLUDING REMARKS

We have thus succeeded in unifying a considerable body of literature on the welfare economics of trade into a series of major propositions that consitute a generalized theory of distortions and welfare. Aside from the intrinsic elegance of such unification, this has resulted in a number of insights into, and extensions of, the theorems to date in this significant area of economic policy.

REFERENCES

1. Bhagwati, J. "Immiserizing Growth: A Geometrical Note." *Review of Economic Studies*, 25 (June 1958).

2. Bhagwati, J., and Ramaswami, V. K. "Domestic Distortions, Tariffs and the Theory of Optimum Subsidy." *Journal of Political Economy*, 71 (February 1963).

3. Bhagwati, J. "Non-Economic Objectives and the Efficiency Properties of Trade." *Journal of Political Economy*, 76 (October 1968).

4. Bhagwati, J. "Gains from Trade Once Again." *Oxford Economic Papers*, 20 (July 1968).

5. Bhagwati, J. *The Theory and Practice of Commercial Policy*. Frank Graham Memorial Lecture (1967), Special Papers in International Economics No. 8, Princeton University, 1968.

6. Bhagwati, J. "Distortions and Immiserizing Growth: A Generalization," *Review of Economic Studies*, 35 (November 1968).

7. Bhagwati, J. and Srinivasan, T. N. "Optimal Intervention to Achieve Non-Economic Objectives." *Review of Economic Studies*, 36 (January 1969).

8. Bhagwati, J., Ramaswami, V. K. and Srinivasan, T. N. "Domestic Distortions, Tariffs and the Theory of Optimum Subsidy: Some Further Results." *Journal of Political Economy*, 77 (November/December 1969).

9. Bhagwati, J., "Optimal Policies and Immiserizing Growth." *American Economic Review*, 59 (December 1969).

10. Bhagwati, J. and Kemp, M. C. "Ranking of Tariffs under Monopoly Power in Trade." *Quarterly Journal of Economics*, 83 (May 1969).

11. Bhagwati, J. and Srinivasan, T. N. "The Theory of Wage Differentials: Production Response and Factor Price Equalisation," *Journal of International Economics*, 1 (February 1971).

12. Corden, W. M. "Tariffs, Subsidies and the Terms of Trade." *Economica*, 24 (August 1957).

13. Fishlow, A. and David, P. "Optimal Resource Allocation in an Imperfect Market Setting." *Journal of Political Economy*, 69 (December 1961).

14. Graaff, J. "On Optimum Tariff Structures." *Review of Economic Studies*, 17 (1949–1950).

15. Haberler, G. "Some Problems in the Pure Theory of International Trade," *Economic Journal*, 30 (June 1950).

16. Hagen, E. "An Economic Justification of Protectionism," *Quarterly Journal of Economics*, 72 (November 1958).

17. Johnson, H. G. *International Trade and Economic Growth*, London: George Allen and Unwin Ltd, 1958.

18. Johnson, H. G. "Optimal Trade Intervention in the Presence of Domestic Distortions." in R. E. Caves, H. G. Johnson and P. B. Kenen (eds.), *Trade, Growth and the Balance of Payments*, Amsterdam: North-Holland Publishing Company, 1965.

19. Johnson, H. G. "The Possibility of Income Losses from Increased Efficiency or Factor Accumulation in the Presence of Tariffs." *Economic Journal*, 77 (March 1967).

20. Johnson, H. G. "Factor Market Distortions and the Shape of the Transformation Curve." *Econometrica*, 34 (July 1966).

21. Kemp, M. C. *The Pure Theory of International Trade*. Englewood Cliffs, N. J.: Prentice-Hall, 1964.

22. Kemp, M. C. "The Gain from International Trade." *Economic Journal*, 72 (December 1962).

23. Kemp, M. C. "Some Issues in the Analysis of Trade Gains." *Oxford Economic Papers*, 20 (July 1968).

24. Kemp, M. C. and Negishi, T. "Domestic Distortions, Tariffs and the Theory of Optimum Subsidy," *Journal of Political Economy*, 77 (November/December 1969).

25. Melvin, J. "Demand Conditions and Immiserizing Growth." *American Economic Review*, 59 (September 1969).

26. Melvin, J. "Commodity Taxation as a Determinant of Trade." University of Western Ontario, *mimeographed*, 1968.

27. Matthews R. C. O. "Reciprocal Demand and Increasing Returns." *Review of Economic Studies*, 17 (1949–1950).

28. Samuelson, P. A. "The Gains from International Trade." *Canadian Journal of Economics and Political Science*, 5 (May 1939).

29. Samuelson, P. A. "The Gains from International Trade Once Again." *Economic Journal*, 72 (December 1962).

30. Tinbergen, J. *International Economic Cooperation, Amsterdam*: North-Holland Publishing Company, 1946.

ABOUT THE AUTHOR

Jagdish N. Bhagwati

Jagdish Bhagwati is Arthur Lehman Professor of Economics and Professor of Political Science at Columbia University. He is the winner of the Bernhard Harms Prize, the Mahalanobis Memorial Medal, the Kenan Enterprise Award, and the Freedom Prize. He was Ford International Professor of Economics at the Massachusetts Institute of Technology. He served as the Economic Policy Adviser to the Director General of GATT from 1991 to 1993. Among his many books are *Protectionism* (1988), an international bestseller, and *A Stream of Windows: Unsettling Reflections on Trade, Immigration and Democracy* (1998), both from MIT Press. He is married to Padma Desai, who is a professor of economics at Columbia and an expert on the Russian economy. They have one daughter, Anuradha Kristina.

Multicountry, Multifactor Tests
of the Factor Abundance Theory

HARRY P. BOWEN

Graduate School of Business, New York University

EDWARD E. LEAMER

National Bureau of Economic Research, University of California-Los Angeles

LEO SVEIKAUSKAS

Bureau of Labor Statistics, Washington, D.C.

The Heckscher-Ohlin-Vanek model predicts relationships among industry input requirements, country resource supplies, and international trade in commodities. These relationships are tested using data on twelve resources, and the trade of twenty-seven countries in 1967. The Heckscher-Ohlin propositions that trade reveals gross and relative factor abundance are not supported by these data. The Heckscher-Ohlin-Vanek equations are also rejected in favor of weaker models that allow technological differences and measurement errors.

The Heckscher-Ohlin (H-O) hypothesis is most widely understood in its two-good, two-factor form: a country exports the commodity which uses intensively its relatively abundant resource. Tests of this hypothesis have been inconclusive for two reasons. First, the three pairwise comparisons required by this two × two model cannot be made unambiguously in a multifactor, multicommodity world. Most previous papers that claim to present tests of the hypothesis have used intuitive but inappropriate generalizations of the two × two model to deal with a multidimensional reality. Second, the H-O hypothesis is a relation among three separately observable phenomena: trade, factor

Bowen's work on this paper was completed while on leave as an Olin Fellow at the NBER. Sveikauskas expresses his appreciation to Rensselaer Polytechnic Institute where he conducted most of his work on this paper while on a one-year leave. The work presented here does not necessarily represent the views of the U.S. Department of Labor. This paper benefited from the comments of two referees and the participants at seminars at Harvard, MIT, and New York University. The original version of this paper was presented at the 1982 meeting of the Western Economic Association.

input requirements, and factor endowments. A proper test of the hypothesis requires measurements of all three of these variables. Much prior work that claims to have tested the hypothesis has used data on only two of the three hypotheticals.

This paper reports conceptually correct tests of the H-O hypothesis as suggested by Edward Leamer (1980) and Leamer and Harry Bowen (1981). We use a valid multi-dimensional extension of the two X two model known as the Heckscher-Ohlin-Vanek (H-O-V) theorem, which equates the factors embodied in a country's net exports to the country's excess supplies of factor endowments. And we use separately measured data on trade, factor input requirements, and factor endowments to conduct the first systematic and complete evaluation of the relationships implied by the H-O-V hypothesis among these three sets of variables.

Our methods contrast sharply with traditional approaches to testing the H-O hypothesis. The classic test of the H-O hypothesis is Wassily Leontief's (1953), which compares the capital per man embodied in a million dollars worth of exports with the capital per man embodied in a million dollars worth of imports. Leamer (1980) shows this comparison does not reveal the relative abundance of capital and labor in a multifactor world. Moreover, Leontief's study uses data on trade and factor input requirements but not factor endowments and, in addition, his data are only for a single country.

A second type of purported test uses a regression of trade of many commodities on their factor input requirements for a single country (for example, Robert Baldwin, 1971; William Branson and Nicholas Monoyios, 1977; Jon Harkness, 1978, 1983; Robert Stern and Keith Maskus, 1981). If the estimated coefficient of some factor is positive, the country is inferred to be abundant in that resource. Leamer and Bowen (1981) show this also is an inappropriate inference in a multifactor world since there is no guarantee that the signs of the regression coefficients will reveal the abundance of a resource. Moreover, these studies do not use factor endowment data.[1]

A third approach used to study the sources of comparative advantage involves regression of net exports of a single commodity for many countries on measures of national factor supplies (Bowen, 1983; Hollis Chenery and Moses Syrquin, 1975; and Leamer, 1974, 1984). These papers use no measures of factor input requirements and they study the weakened hypothesis that the structure of trade can be explained by the availability of resources. This contrasts with the stricter H-O-V hypothesis studied here that factor supplies, factor input requirements, and trade fit together in a special way.

---

[1] An exception is Jon Harkness (1978, 1983), who tests the H-O-V sign and rank propositions (see below) by comparing measured factor contents with excess factor supplies that are inferred from coefficients estimated by regressing factor contents on input requirements. This analysis is sus-pect, however, since the estimated coefficients need not correspond either in sign or rank to a country's true excess factor supplies. See Leamer and Bowen (1981).

The present study computes the amount of each of twelve factors embodied in the net exports of 27 countries in 1967, using the U.S. matrix of total input requirements for 1967. The factors embodied in trade are then compared with direct measures of factor endowments to determine the extent to which the data conform to the predictions of the H-O-V theory.

We first test the traditional interpretation of the H-O hypothesis that trade reveals relative factor abundance.[2] This analysis is analogous to Leontief's attempt to determine the relative abundance of capital and labor in the United States using U.S. data alone. Our empirical results offer little support for this facet of the H-O-V model. Several types of measurement error could account for these results. Moreover, the H-O-V model implies a set of equalities, not inequalities, among the variables. We therefore extend the analysis of the H-O-V model to a regression context, and conduct a second set of tests which examine these equalities while allowing different hypotheses about consumer's preferences, technological differences, and various forms of measurement error.

Overall, our results do not support the H-O-V hypothesis of an exact relationship between factor contents and factor supplies. Support is found for the H-O-V assumption of homothetic preferences, but estimates of the parameters linking factor contents and factor supplies are found to differ significantly from their theoretical values. The data suggest that the poor performance of the H-O-V hypothesis is importantly related to measurement error in both trade and national factor supplies across countries, and the data favor a model that allows neutral differences in factor input matrices across countries.

I. THEORETICAL FRAMEWORK

Derivation of the relationships studied here starts with the equilibrium identity expressing a country's net factor exports as the difference between factors absorbed in production and factors absorbed in consumption.

$$\mathbf{A}_i\mathbf{T}_i = \mathbf{A}_i\mathbf{Q}_i - \mathbf{A}_i\mathbf{C}_i, \tag{1}$$

where $\mathbf{A}_i = K \times N$ matrix of factor input requirements which indicate the total (direct plus indirect) amount of each of K factors needed to produce one unit of output in each of N industries,

$\mathbf{T}_i = N \times 1$ vector of net trade flows of country i,

$\mathbf{Q}_i = N \times 1$ vector of country i's final outputs,

$\mathbf{C}_i = N \times 1$ vector of country i's final consumption.

---

[2]Maskus (1985) reports conceptually correct tests of this interpretation of the H-O-V theorem for the United States using 1958 and 1972 data.

Full employment implies $\mathbf{A}_i\mathbf{Q}_i = \mathbf{E}_i$, where $\mathbf{E}_i$ is the $K \times 1$ vector of country i's factor supplies. Thus, the vector of factors embodied in net trade is

$$\mathbf{A}_i\mathbf{T}_i = \mathbf{E}_i - \mathbf{A}_i\mathbf{C}_i. \tag{2}$$

This identity is transformed into a testable hypothesis by making one or more of the following three assumptions:

(A1) ASSUMPTION 1: All individuals face the same commodity prices.

(A2) ASSUMPTION 2: Individuals have identical and homothetic tastes.

(A3) ASSUMPTION 3: All countries have the same factor input matrix, $\mathbf{A}_i = \mathbf{A}$.

Ordinarily, the assumption of identical input matrices (A3) would be replaced by the assumption of factor price equalization and internationally identical technologies. The alternative to factor price equalization permitted here is that input requirements are technologically fixed and identical across countries, but countries have different factor prices and therefore produce different subsets of commodities.

Assumptions (A1) and (A2) imply that the consumption vector of country i is proportional to the world output vector $(\mathbf{Q}_w)$, $\mathbf{C}_i = s_i\mathbf{Q}_w$, where s_i is country i's consumption share. The consumption share can be derived by premultiplying the net trade identity $(\mathbf{T}_i = \mathbf{Q}_i - s_i\mathbf{Q}_w)$ by the vector of common goods prices

$$s_i = (Y_i - B_i)/Y_w, \tag{3}$$

where Y_i is GNP and B_i is the trade balance. If trade is balanced, then s_i equals country i's share of world GNP.[3]

If, in addition, the factor input matrices are identical, we can write $\mathbf{A}_i\mathbf{C}_i = s_i\mathbf{A}\mathbf{Q}_w = s_i\mathbf{E}_w$, where $\mathbf{E}_w = \Sigma_i\mathbf{E}_i$ is the $K \times 1$ vector of world factor supplies. Then, (2) can be written as

$$\mathbf{A}\mathbf{T}_i = \mathbf{E}_i - \mathbf{E}_w(Y_i - B_i)/Y_w. \tag{4}$$

Equation (4) specifies an exact relationship between factor contents and factor endowments. This relationship can be tested by measuring the net export vector $\mathbf{T}_i$, the factor input matrix $\mathbf{A}$, and the excess factor supplies $\mathbf{E}_i - s_i\mathbf{E}_w$, and computing the extent to which these data violate the equality given by (4). Such analysis requires some sensible way of measuring the distance between two matrices: the matrix with columns equal to the factor contents of trade for each country, and the matrix with columns equal to the excess factor supplies for each country. In Section II we first examine the extent to which row and column

---

[3]If factor prices are equalized, s_i can also be derived by premultiplying (2) by the vector of factor prices. If factor prices are unequal, (2) can still be premultiplied by the vector of factor prices prevailing in country i to obtain an expression analogous to (3), but with both internal and external factor earnings evaluated only in terms of country i's factor prices.

elements of these matrices conform in sign and rank without reference to any specific alternative hypotheses. In Section III we then report tests against alternatives involving nonproportional consumption, measurement errors, and differences in input matrices.

Our analysis uses data on the 367-order U.S. input-output table for 1967, and the 1967 trade and the 1966 supply of twelve resources for 27 countries.[4] The countries are those for which both occupational data and detailed trade data were available. The twelve resources are net capital stock, total labor, professional/technical workers, managerial workers, clerical workers, sales workers, service workers, agricultural workers, production workers, arable land, pastureland, and forestland.

Net capital stocks were computed as the sum of discounted real investment flows in domestic currency and converted to U.S. dollars using 1966 nominal exchange rates. Industry capital requirements (plant, equipment, and inventories) were constructed from data on U.S. industry capital stocks.

The seven labor categories are those defined at the one-digit level of International Standard Classification of Occupations. Total labor is a country's economically active population. Input requirements for each type of labor were constructed using occupational data from the 1971 *U.S. Survey of Occupational Employment* and the 1970 *U.S. Census of Population*. Labor data are measured in numbers of people.

The three land types conform to the definitions used by the Food and Agricultural Organization. Industry land requirements were based on the U.S. input-output table; I/O sector 1 was used for pastureland, I/O sector 2 was used for arable land, and I/O sector 3 (forest and fisheries) was used for forestland. Land is measured in hectares.

Finally, data on each country's trade in 1967 were obtained at the four- and five-digit level of the Standard International Trade Classification (SITC) and concorded to input-output sectors to perform the required vector multiplications.

II. Tests of Qualitative Hypotheses

The traditional implication of the H-O theory is that factor abundance determines which commodities are exported and which are imported, in other words, the sign of net exports. In this section we report tests of the analogous qualitative implications of the H-O-V equations concerning the sign and ordering of the factor content data.

A typical kth element of (4) can be written as

$$(F_{ki}^A/E_{kw})/(Y_i/Y_w) = [(E_{ki}/E_{kw})/(Y_i/Y_w)] - 1, \tag{5}$$

where F_{ki} is the kth element of the factor content vector $\mathbf{F}_i = \mathbf{A}\mathbf{T}_i$, and $F_{ki}^A = (F_{ki} - E_{kw}B_i/Y_w)$ is the factor content if trade were balanced. The quantity on the right-hand side of (5) is a measure of the relative abundance of resource k. If this equation is accurate, the factor content of trade can be used as an indirect measure of factor abundance. We study

---

[4]The Data Appendix provides detailed discussion of the data.

here two qualitative implications of (5); first, that trade reveals the abundance of resources compared with an average of all resources, and second, that trade reveals the relative abundance of resources.

The income share in (5) is an average of the resource shares weighted by world earnings: $(Y_i/Y_w) = \sum_k [w_k E_{ki}/\sum_k w_k E_{kw}] = \sum_k [(w_k E_{kw})(E_{ki}/E_{kw})/\sum_k w_k E_{kw}]$, where w_k is the world price of factor k. If equation (5) is accurate, then the sign of the net trade in factor services, corrected for the trade imbalance, will reveal the abundance of a resource, compared with other resources on the average.[5] This sign proposition is tested for each factor (country) by computing the proportion of sign matches between corresponding elements in each row (column) of the matrix of adjusted factor contents and the matrix of factor abundance ratios. In addition, Fisher's Exact Test (one-tail) is used to test the hypothesis of independence between the sign of the factor contents and of the excess factor shares against the alternative of a positive association.

Equation (5) also implies that trade reveals the relative abundance of resources when considered two at a time. If equation (5) is accurate, the adjusted net exports of country i of factor k exceed the adjusted net exports by country i of factor k', $(F^A_{ki}/E_{kw})/(Y_i/Y_w) > (F^A_{k'i}/E_{k'w})/(Y_i/Y_w)$, if and only if factor k is more abundant than factor k', $(E_{ki}/E_{kw})/(Y_i/Y_w) > (E_{k'i}/E_{k'w})/(Y_i/Y_w)$; and the adjusted net exports by country i of factor k exceeds the adjusted net exports by country i' of factor k, $(F^A_{ki}/E_{kw})/(Y_i/Y_w) > (F^A_{ki}/E_{kw})/(Y_{i'}/Y_w)$, if and only if country i is more abundant in factor k than country i', $(E_{ki}/E_{kw})/(Y_i/Y_w) > (E_{ki'}/E_{kw})/(Y_{i'}/Y_w)$. More generally, for each country and factor, the ranking of adjusted net factor exports F^A_{ki}/E_{kw} should conform to the ranking of factors by their abundance. This rank proposition is tested for each country (factor) by computing the Kendall rank correlation between corresponding columns (rows) of the matrix of adjusted factor content and the matrix of factor abundance ratios. In addition, we compute the proportion of correct rankings when the corresponding elements of the columns (rows) of the two matrices are compared two at a time.[6]

---

[5] Other definitions of factor abundance are possible. In an earlier version of this paper, we wrote (5) without adjusting the left-hand side for the trade imbalance as $F_{ki}/s_i E_{kw} = (E_{ki}/E_{kw}) - s_i$, where s_i is the consumption share $(Y_i - B_i)/Y_w$. In this form the theory can be said to imply that the sign of the net trade in factor services reveals the abundance of a factor compared with the consumption share. Equivalently, the right-hand side of this equation takes the sign of the difference between world output per factor input and the domestic consumption per factor input. This form of comparison is made by Richard Brecher and Ehasan Choudhri (1982) who point out that Leontief's findings of a positive net trade in labor services is inconsistent with the relatively high consumption per worker of the United States. Though this comparison is appropriate, we have opted here for the comparison suggested by equation (5), because it is based on a more appealing notion of factor abundance. See Kohler (1987) for a related discussion.

[6] Subsequent tests of the rank and sign propositions based on the proportion of "successes" do not refer to any specific alternative hypothesis and thus leaves unclear the choice of significance level. Without knowing the proportion of successes expected under a specific alternative hypothesis, judging the relative performance of the H-O-V model is largely impressionistic. The absence of alternative hypotheses when testing the sign and rank propositions is, in large part, the motivation for our subsequent tests of the H-O-V equations in a regression framework.

Table 1 summarizes the factor content data by listing for each country the ratio of adjusted net exports of each factor in 1967 to the endowment of the corresponding factor in 1966, $100 \times F_{ki}^A / E_{ki}$. According to these data, the United States exports .08 percent of the services of its capital stock, .23 percent of the services of its professional/technical workers but imports labor services amounting to .25 percent of the services of its labor force. Thus, among these resources, U.S. trade reveals the United States to be most abundant in professional and technical workers, capital, and then labor. Among all resources, however, the United States is revealed most abundant in arable land, followed by agricultural workers.

Leamer (1980) computed these factor content ratios using Leontief's 1947 data and found that U.S. trade revealed the United States to be abundant in capital compared to labor, thus reversing Leontief's paradoxical finding. Likewise, no "Leontief paradox" is evident in Table 1 since the United States exports capital services but imports labor services, and this ordering conforms to the ordering of the U.S. shares of world capital (41 percent) and world labor (22 percent). This result, and others like it, would lead us to accept the H-O theorem on the basis of a rank test.

Although a rank test supports the two-factor version of the H-O theorem for the United States, a contrary finding is that while the United States is a net exporter of capital services, the U.S. share of world income (47 percent) exceeds its share of world capital, which implies that there is a measured scarcity of capital in the United States. This result, and others like it, would lead us to reject the H-O theorem using a sign test.

Some obvious anomalies in Table 1 are that, after adjusting for trade imbalances, Denmark, Finland, Korea, the Netherlands, and Norway export more than 100 percent of the services of their pastureland. These anomalies probably reflect difficulties in applying U.S. input-output coefficients to other countries. For example, Denmark is a substantial exporter of agricultural products and U.S. input coefficients apparently overstate the amount of pastureland used per unit of output in Denmark. The analysis conducted in Section III will formally test the assumption of identical input coefficients, but it is clear from the anomalies in Table 1 that assumption (A3) is not entirely accurate.[7]

Formal tests of the conformity of the adjusted net factor export data (F_{ki}^A / E_{kw}) with the factor abundance data $[(E_{ki}/E_{kw})/(Y_i/Y_w) - 1]$ are reported in Tables 2 and 3. The first column of Table 2 lists the proportion of sign matches between adjusted net factor exports and the abundance ratios for each factor. The first column of Table 3 lists comparable percentages for each country. For example, the sign of adjusted net capital exports and of excess capital shares matched in 52 percent of the countries.

---

[7]These anomalous data values may also reflect errors of measurement in either the factor contents or endowments. In particular, Denmark and Norway probably export more than 100 percent of their forestland because these countries export fish and fish products, and fisheries are included in the input-output coefficients for forestland.

TABLE 1

RATIO OF ADJUSTED NET TRADE IN FACTOR TO NATIONAL ENDOWMENT

Country	Capital	Labor	Prof/Tech	Manager	Clerical	Sales	Service	Agriculture	Production	Arable	Forest	Pasture
Argentina	1.32	−0.30	−1.64	−2.60	−1.07	−0.62	−0.83	4.30	−1.46	21.24	−6.94	2.40
Australia	−3.77	−0.41	−2.95	−1.79	−1.68	0.21	−0.11	18.10	−3.65	17.15	−13.68	0.80
Austria	−2.03	3.01	2.74	5.64	2.91	3.81	3.20	3.12	2.59	−80.74	13.52	24.35
Bene-Lux	−2.36	1.81	0.88	1.82	1.90	1.36	2.39	−4.26	2.76	−364.25	−922.53	53.27
Brazil	−5.54	−0.27	−0.85	−0.49	−0.82	−0.32	−0.23	−0.04	−0.61	2.10	−0.04	20.02
Canada	1.82	−3.49	−3.40	−2.23	−4.00	−2.73	−1.88	4.00	−6.84	12.13	6.16	2.84
Denmark	−4.89	5.82	2.37	8.70	4.25	5.08	4.51	24.56	1.21	33.57	803.73	1763.42
Finland	4.69	2.14	0.49	4.22	1.78	1.94	1.89	1.26	3.21	−24.44	30.48	434.70
France	−4.07	0.82	0.70	1.17	1.02	0.90	1.06	0.16	1.04	−21.33	−198.68	1.79
Germany	−1.05	−0.43	1.01	1.34	0.51	−1.08	−1.05	−11.86	2.07	−323.61	−377.64	2124.77
Greece	−5.50	2.93	4.48	14.95	5.37	4.49	4.68	2.20	2.02	46.92	−61.16	1.08
Hong Kong	−46.06	4.52	5.24	3.68	8.10	3.48	3.03	−14.19	6.46	−21568	−30532	−91627216
Ireland	−1.93	6.73	4.49	13.84	7.19	6.10	8.07	10.59	2.67	17.31	−129.98	72.68
Italy	−7.03	0.74	1.25	4.67	1.42	0.39	1.27	−1.73	1.87	−39.91	−431.67	−131.90
Japan	−5.47	0.10	0.44	0.48	0.33	−0.05	−0.03	−1.54	1.18	−341.42	−268.58	−1998.58
Korea	−30.51	0.61	1.53	2.85	1.81	0.76	1.73	0.27	0.85	−42.34	−29.42	1206.60
Mexico	−0.78	0.57	0.19	0.47	0.51	0.80	0.70	0.87	−0.21	12.40	5.69	0.97
Netherlands	−4.56	4.61	3.49	6.36	3.65	4.72	5.53	22.78	1.41	82.74	−719.88	330.86
Norway	−5.54	5.57	3.75	6.15	7.98	10.22	10.58	14.59	−0.06	−125.48	105.96	660.35
Philippines	−13.94	−0.10	−0.59	−0.36	−0.81	0.03	0.06	0.14	−0.81	10.47	28.43	−17.03
Portugal	−10.31	1.92	3.92	10.85	3.75	2.83	2.72	0.63	2.49	−28.46	24.79	12.03
Spain	−6.19	3.04	4.56	13.88	4.36	4.13	3.89	2.45	2.23	−2.74	−12.00	4.92
Sweden	0.79	1.36	0.59	2.26	1.05	1.09	1.44	−0.66	2.18	−67.23	30.93	48.00
Switzerland	−5.72	3.42	4.46	11.57	3.52	5.42	4.13	−0.79	3.04	−862.95	−352.36	−12.18
UK	−12.86	0.63	1.77	2.04	1.37	1.30	1.32	−18.57	1.11	−313.42	−2573.99	−91.89
US	0.08	−0.25	0.23	−0.11	−0.19	−1.10	−0.68	1.54	−0.34	19.45	−23.82	−1.63
Yugoslavia	−3.15	0.68	0.39	1.59	1.12	2.05	1.15	0.46	0.76	−0.08	2.81	14.24

Note: Numbers in percent. Factor content data are for 1967; endowment data are for 1966.

TABLE 2

SIGN AND RANK TESTS, FACTOR BY FACTOR

Factor	Sign Test[a]	Rank Tests[b]	
Capital	.52	0.140	.45
Labor	.67	0.185	.46
Prof/Tech	.78	0.123	.33
Managerial	.22	− 0.254	.34
Clerical	.59	0.134	.48
Sales	.67	0.225	.47
Service	.67	0.282[c]	.44
Agricultural	.63	0.202	.47
Production	.70	0.345[c]	.48
Arable	.70	0.561[c]	.73
Pasture	.52	0.197	.61
Forest	.70	0.356[c]	.65

[a] Proportion of 27 countries for which the sign of net trade in factor matched the sign of the corresponding factor abundance.
[b] The first column is the Kendall rank correlation among 27 countries; the second column is the proportion of correct rankings out
of 351 possible pairwise comparisons.
[c] Statistically significant at 5 percent level.

In general, the proposition of conformity in sign between factor contents and excess factor shares receives relatively little support when tested for each factor (Table 2). Although the proportion of sign matches exceeds 50 percent for eleven resources, the proportion of sign matches is 70 percent or greater for only four of the twelve factors with the highest proportion of sign matches for professional and technical workers (78 percent). Moreover, using Fisher's Exact Test, the hypothesis of independence between the sign of the factor contents and of the excess factor shares can be rejected (results not shown) at the 95 percent level for only one resource – arable land.

Similar results are obtained when the sign proposition is tested for each country (Table 3). The proportion of sign matches exceeds 50 percent for 18 countries, and exceeds 90 percent for five countries (Greece, Hong Kong, Ireland, Mexico, and the UK). However, the proportion of sign matches is below 70 percent for 19 of the 27 countries. In addition, the hypothesis of independence between the classification of signs is rejected (95 percent level) for only four countries: Greece, Ireland, Hong Kong, and the United Kingdom.[8] Finally, for the entire sample, the proportion of sign matches out of a possible 324 is only 61 percent.

---

[8] No variation was observed in the sign of factor abundance for Yugoslavia (each was positive).

TABLE 3

SIGN AND RANK TESTS, COUNTRY BY COUNTRY

Country	Sign Tests[a]	Rank Tests[b]	
Argentina	.33	0.164	.58
Australia	.33	− 0.127	.44
Austria	.67	0.091	.56
Belgium-Luxembourg	.50	0.273	.64
Brazil	.17	0.673[c]	.86
Canada	.75	0.236	.64
Denmark	.42	− 0.418	.29
Finland	.67	0.164	.60
France	.25	0.418	.71
Germany	.67	0.527[c]	.76
Greece	.92	0.564[c]	.80
Hong Kong	1.00	0.745[c]	.89
Ireland	.92	0.491[c]	.76
Italy	.58	0.345	.69
Japan	.67	0.382	.71
Korea	.75	0.345	.69
Mexico	.92	0.673[c]	.86
Netherlands	.58	− 0.236	.38
Norway	.25	− 0.236	.38
Philippines	.50	0.527[c]	.78
Portugal	.67	0.091	.56
Spain	.67	0.200	.62
Sweden	.42	0.200	.62
Switzerland	.67	0.382	.69
United Kingdom	.92	0.527[c]	.78
United States	.58	0.309	.67
Yugoslavia	.83	2 0.055	.49

[a]Proportion of 12 factors for which the sign of net trade in factor matched the sign of the corresponding excess supply of factor.
[b]The first column is the Kendall rank correlation among 11 factors (total labor excluded); the second column is the proportion of correct rankings out of 55 possible pairwise comparisons.
[c]Statistically significant at the 5 percent level.

The sign proposition deals with the abundance of a resource compared with a value-weighted average of other resources (that is, Y_i/Y_w), but we can also compare resources two at a time. For example, the data in Table 1 indicate the United States is more abundant in capital than labor while the U.S. resource share data (not shown) also indicate an abundance in capital compared to labor. The many possible pairwise comparisons are summarized by the rank proposition, which states that the order of adjusted factor contents and the order of the resource abundance ratios conform.

Two formal measures of the conformity between the factor content and factor abundance rankings are shown in Tables 2 and 3. The second column in these tables shows the Kendall rank correlation between the rankings while the third column shows the proportion of correct orderings when the comparisons are made two at a time.[9] For example, the results for capital in Table 2 indicate that we cannot reject (5 percent level) the hypothesis of a zero-rank correlation and that the proportion of correct orderings when the ranking between the net exports of capital services and the capital abundance ratios is compared for all pairs of countries is 45 percent.

In general, the rank proposition receives little support when tested for each factor (Table 2). The hypothesis of a zero-rank correlation is rejected (95 percent level) for only four resources (service workers, production workers, arable land, and forestland) and one of the correlations (managerial workers) is of the wrong sign. Little support is also found for the rank proposition when the comparisons are made among all possible pairs of countries. Specifically, the proportion of correct orderings exceeds 50 percent only for the three land variables.

The rank proposition also receives little support when tested country by country (Table 3). The hypothesis of a zero-rank correlation is rejected for only eight of the 27 correlations (95 percent level) and five of the correlations are of the wrong sign. Somewhat greater support is found for the rank proposition when pairwise comparisons are considered: for 22 of the 27 countries, the proportion of correct orderings exceeds 50 percent. That the rank proposition receives relatively more support when tested country by country suggests that something is affecting all the data similarly, since adding a number that is constant within a country would not affect the country rank test results but would alter the other three tests. A possible source of this kind of problem would be differences in factor input matrices across countries.

Overall, the results for the sign and rank propositions offer little support for the H-O-V model. However, the tests of these propositions do not refer to specific alternative hypotheses and may cast doubt on the H-O-V hypothesis for a variety of reasons, including nonproportional consumption, various kinds of measurement error, and

---

[9]These proportions are interpreted as the probability, for a given factor (country), that the ranking of factor contents will match the ranking of factor abundance for a randomly selected pair of countries (factors).

differences in factor input matrices. These alternatives can be studied by regressions of factor contents on endowments as described below.

III. TESTS OF THE H-O-V EQUATIONS

The tradition since Leontief's study has been to examine only propositions concerning factor rankings. But as shown in Section I, the H-O-V model actually implies an equality between factor contents and resource supplies. A study of this system of equations has the advantage that it allows explicit consideration of alternative hypotheses—a practice that has generally been absent in empirical tests of trade theory. Here we consider three reasons why the H-O-V equations may be inexact: nonproportional consumption, measurement errors, and technological differences.

A. ALTERNATIVE HYPOTHESES

We first consider an alternative to the assumption of proportional consumption (A2). The general hypothesis of nonidentical, nonhomothetic tastes cannot be allowed since then trade, which is the difference between production and consumption, would be completely indeterminate.[10] Instead, we study a specific alternative to assumption A2:

(Ã2) All individuals have identical preferences with linear Engel curves; within each country, income is equally distributed.

The modification of (4) implied by (Ã2) is derived by noting that (Ã2) implies that per capita consumption is a linear function of per capita income. Therefore, we can write country i's total consumption of commodity j (C_{ij}) as a linear function of its population L_i and its total expenditure $(Y_i - B_i)$:[11]

$$C_{ij} = \lambda_j L_i + \psi_j((Y_i - B_i) - L_i y^0), \tag{7}$$

where λ_j = per capita "autonomous" consumption of commodity j,

ψ_j = marginal budget shares, $\Sigma_j \psi_j = 1$,

$y_0 = \Sigma_j \lambda_j$.

Summing (7) over i gives the marginal budget shares ψ_j:

$$\psi_j = (Q_{wj} - \lambda_j L_w)/(Y_w - L_w y^0), \tag{8}$$

where L_w is world population. Inserting (8) into (7) and premultiplying by the kth row of $A(a_k)$, the amount of factor k absorbed in consumption $a_k C_i$ is

$$a_k C_i = (\varphi_k - \beta_k y^0)L_i + \beta_k Y_i, \tag{9}$$

---

[10]In the sense that complete information on each country's preferences would be required to determine trade.

[11]Equation (7) is based on the Linear Expenditure System.

where

$$\varphi_k = \sum_j a_{kj} \lambda_j,$$

$$\beta_k = \left(\sum_j a_{kj} Q_{wj} - \sum_j a_{kj} \lambda_j L_w \right) \Big/ (Y_w - L_w y^0),$$

$$\beta_k = (E_{kw} - \varphi_k L_w)/(Y_w - L_w y^0).$$

Equation (9) implies that equation (4) can be written

$$\mathbf{F}_i = \mathbf{E}_i - \theta L_i - \beta(Y_i - B_i), \tag{10}$$

where θ and β are $K \times 1$ vectors with elements $\theta_k = (\varphi_k - \beta_k y^0)$ and β_k, respectively. Given (10), assumption (A2) amounts to restricting $\theta = 0$ and $\beta_k = E_{kw}/Y_w$.

Next we allow for measurement errors. We assume measurement of net trade differs from its true value by a constant plus a random error

$$\mathbf{T}_i^m = \omega + \mathbf{T}_i + \mathbf{T}_i^e, \tag{$\tilde{\text{M}}$1}$$

where the vector $\mathbf{T}_i^m$ is the measured value of the vector $\mathbf{T}_i$, ω is an $N \times 1$ vector of constants, and $\mathbf{T}_i^e$ is the error vector. The null hypothesis is that there is no measurement error bias

$$\omega = 0. \tag{M1}$$

Assumption ($\tilde{\text{M}}$1) implies the factor content vector is also measured with error:

$$\mathbf{F}_i^m = \mathbf{A}\mathbf{T}_i^m = \mathbf{A}\omega + \mathbf{A}\mathbf{T}_i + \mathbf{A}\mathbf{T}_i^e$$
$$= \alpha + \mathbf{F}_i + \mathbf{F}_i^e, \tag{11}$$

where $\mathbf{F}_i^m$ is the measured value of $\mathbf{F}_i$, $\alpha = \mathbf{A}\omega$ is a $K \times 1$ vector of unknown constants, and $\mathbf{F}_i^e$ is the error vector with covariance matrix that is assumed diagonal for convenience.

The measurements of the endowments are also assumed to be imperfect but in a different way:

$$E_{ki} = \gamma_k E_{ki}^m, \tag{$\tilde{\text{M}}$2}$$

where E_{ki}^m is the measured value, E_{ki} the true value, and γ_k is a positive error multiplier. The null hypothesis of no measurement errors is

$$\gamma_k = 1 \text{ for all } k. \tag{M2}$$

The form of the measurement error contained in ($\tilde{\text{M}}$2) is also chosen for convenience since random-measurement errors in more than one variable would force us into consideration of an "errors-in-variables" model, which entails regressions in more than one direction. With our assumptions, factor contents are always the dependent variable.

A third source of measurement error we consider is the incomplete coverage of countries. World endowments and world GNP are estimated here by summing across the sample of countries. The resulting underestimates of the world totals would not affect our analysis if excluded countries had total endowments proportional to the sample totals. As an alternative to this assumption, we can assume that the calculated totals contain no information about world totals. This latter assumption can be stated formally as

$$E_{kw} = \sigma_{kS} E_{kS}. \tag{M̃3}$$

$$Y_w = \phi_S Y_S.$$

The subscript S refers to the subset of countries in the sample; σ_s is a set of unknown positive elements; and ϕ_s is an unknown positive scalar. The null hypothesis is

$$\sigma_{kS} = 1 \quad \text{for all } k \text{ and } \phi_S = 1. \tag{M3}$$

Combining the assumption of nonproportional consumption (Ã2) with the measurement error assumptions M̃1–M̃3, the expression for country i's net trade in factor k becomes

$$F_{ki} = \alpha_k + \gamma_k E_{ki} - \theta_k L_i - \beta_k(Y_i - B_i) + F_{ik}^e, \tag{12}$$

where the superscript "m" is suppressed for notational convenience.

The third source of alternative hypotheses is technological differences. The alternative to the assumption of identical input matrices (A3) that we consider is the assumption that input matrices differ by a proportional constant. This amounts to assuming neutral differences in technology across countries.[12] Since we calculate factor contents using the U.S. input matrix, the proportional difference in input matrices is measured relative to the U.S. input matrix. This assumption can be written

$$\mathbf{A}_{us} = \delta_i \mathbf{A}_i, \tag{Ã3}$$

where $\delta_i > 0$ and $\delta_{us} = 1$.

Assumption (Ã3) implies that the parameters θ_k and β_k, and the values F_{ki}, are now $\theta_k/\delta_i, \beta_k/\delta_i$ and F_{ki}^{us}/δ_i, respectively, where F_{ki}^{us} is country i's net trade in factor k computed using the U.S. input matrix. Substituting these new values into (12) gives

$$F_{ki}^{us}/\delta_i = (\alpha_k/\delta_i) + \gamma_k E_{ki} - (\theta_k/\delta_i)L_i - (\beta_k/\delta_i)(Y_i - B_i) + F_{ki}^e/\delta_i. \tag{13}$$

The γ_k are not scaled by δ_i since the endowments are measured independent of the input matrix. Multiplication of (13) by δ_i yields the bilinear form

$$F_{ki}^{us} = \alpha_k + (\delta_i \gamma_k)E_{ki} - \theta_k L_i - \beta_k(Y_i - B_i) + F_{ki}^e. \tag{14}$$

---

[12]The specification of neutral technological differences was chosen because of its tractability in estimation. Data limitations prevented us from considering more general specifications, such as allowing input requirements to differ across industries and countries.

TABLE 4

ALTERNATIVE ASSUMPTIONS AND PARAMETER RESTRICTIONS

Hypothesis	Assumptions[a]						Parameter Restrictions				
	A1	A2	A3	M1	M2	M3	θ_k	δ_i	α_k	γ_k	β_k
HG	*										
H1	*	*	*			*	0	1			E_{ks}/Y_s
H2	*	*		*	*	*	0		0	1	E_{ks}/Y_s
H3	*	*				*	0				E_{ks}/Y_s
H4	*	*	*	*	*		0	1	0	1	
H5	*	*	*				0	1			
H6	*	*		*	*		0		0	1	
H7	*	*					0				
H8	*		*	*	*			1	0	1	
H9	*		*					1			
H10	*			*	*				0	1	

[a] Absence of an asterisk indicates selection of the alternative $\tilde{A}_i$ or $\tilde{M}_i$. Each parameter restriction is listed in the same order as the corresponding assumptions A2–M3.

 Definitions: A1 = identical commodity prices; A2 = identical and homothetic tastes; A3 = identical input intensities; M1 = unbiased measurement of factor contents; M2 = perfect measurement of endowments; and M3 = complete coverage of countries.

Equation (14) identifies our most general model,[13] which we estimate using an iterative maximum likelihood procedure discussed below.

In addition to the general hypothesis contained in (14) (hereafter denoted HG), we consider ten alternative hypotheses H1–H10 selected from the set of possibilities corresponding to different choices from the list of assumptions about the theory and the nature of measurement errors. Table 4 states each alternative in terms of the restrictions it imposes on the parameters of (14).

Hypotheses HG–H10 each maintain the assumption of common goods prices (A1). Hypotheses H1–H7 further maintain the assumption of proportional consumption while allowing tests of the assumptions of identical input matrices (A3), measurement error in trade and the endowments, and incomplete coverage of countries. The hypotheses of special interest are: H4, which leaves only β_k unrestricted and corresponds to the H-O-V

---

[13] This specification was selected after testing it against the more general specification

$$F_{ki} = \pi_k + \delta_i[\alpha_k + \gamma_k E_{ki}] - \theta_k L_i - \beta_k(Y_i - B_i) + F_{ki}^\epsilon.$$

where π_k is an unknown constant.

hypothesis that the parameter-linking factor contents and national factor supplies is unity; H3, which maintains the assumptions of proportional consumption (A2) and complete coverage of countries (M3); H9, which maintains only the assumption of identical technologies (A3); and H10, which maintains the hypothesis that both trade and the endowments are measured without error (M1 and M2).

B. MEASURING PERFORMANCE AND ESTIMATION ISSUES

Given estimates of the unrestricted parameters in (14) under each hypothesis, a method is required to determine the overall performance of each alternative. One possibility is to form indexes based on the maximized value of the likelihood function associated with (14)

$$L = (\text{ESS})^{-(NK/2)}, \tag{15}$$

where ESS is the error sum-of-squares (summed over countries and factors) and NK is the total number of observations. Values of L, like an R^2, necessarily increase as the number of parameters increases and some form of degrees of freedom correction is required. We adopt the asymptotic Bayes' formula proposed in the context of regression by Leamer (1978, p. 113) and more generally by G. Schwarz (1978):

$$L^* = L(NK)^{-(p/2)}, \tag{16}$$

where p is the number of parameters estimated under a given hypothesis. Given an alternative hypothesis j and a null hypothesis i, we form the ratio

$$\Lambda = \mathbf{L}_j^*/\mathbf{L}_i^* = (\text{ESS}_i/\text{ESS}_j)^{(NK/2)}(NK)^{(p_i - p_j)/2}. \tag{17}$$

The evidence is then said to favor the alternative if $\Lambda > 1$. If the parameter values associated with each hypothesis are considered equally likely a priori, then Λ is interpreted as the posterior odds in favor of the alternative.

The variances of the residuals in equation (14) are assumed to be different for different factors. Processing of the data would be relatively easy if these variances were all equal. For example, if the endowments were measured without error ($\gamma_k = 1$), then equation (14) could be estimated by ordinary least squares with dummy variables. But the assumption of equal variances makes little sense unless the data are scaled in comparable units. To achieve comparability, we scale all the data by the sample "world" endowment levels E_{ks}. Furthermore, to eliminate heteroscedasticity associated with country size, we also divide by the adjusted GNP: $Y_i - B_i$. After these adjustments, equation (14) becomes

$$F_{ki}^{us}S_{ki} = \alpha_k S_{ki} + \gamma_k \delta_i(E_{ki}S_{ki}) - \theta_k(L_i S_{ki}) - \beta_k E_{kS}^{-1} + F_{ki}^{e*}, \tag{18}$$

where $S_{ki} = [(Y_i - B_i)E_{ks}]^{-1}$. The errors F_{ki}^{e*} are assumed to be normally distributed with mean zero and variance σ^2.

Given observations on factor contents, resource supplies, and population, the parameters in (18) are estimated using an iterative procedure, which solves the set of first-order conditions for maximizing the likelihood function (15). Given estimates δ_i^0 ($= 1$ initially), estimates α_k^0, γ_k^0, θ_k^0, and β_k^0 are obtained from a regression equation for each factor as

$$F_{ki}^{us}S_{ki} = \alpha_k S_{ki} + \gamma_k(\delta_i^0 E_{ki}S_{ki}) - \theta_k(L_i S_{ki}) - \beta_k E_{kS} + F_{ki}^{e*}, \tag{19}$$

The estimates α_k^0, γ_k^0, θ_k^0, and β_k^0 are then used to obtain new estimates δ_k^0 from a regression equation for each country as

$$W_{ki} = \delta_i(\gamma_k E_{ki}/E_{kS}), \tag{20}$$

where $W_{ki} = F_{ki}^{us}S_{ki} - \alpha_k^0 S_{ki} - \theta_k^0(L_i S_{ki}) - \beta_k^0 E_{ks}^{-1}$. Prior to using the new estimates of δ_i obtained from (20) to re-estimate (19), each estimate of δ_i is divided by the estimated value for the United States to maintain the restriction that $\delta_{us} = 1$. The process of iteratively estimating (19) and (20) continues until the value of (15) converges.

The above two-step procedure is used to estimate the parameters in (18) under hypotheses HG, H3, and H7 since each involves the specification that $\gamma_k \neq 1$ and $\delta_i \neq 1$. Estimates of the unrestricted parameters under hypotheses H1, H5, and H9 are estimated using OLS while the parameters under hypotheses H2, H4, H6, H8, and H10, which restrict $\gamma_k = 1$, are estimated using a dummy variables model applied to the data set pooled across countries and factors, and imposing the restriction $\delta_{us} = 1$.

C. ANALYSIS

Table 5 reports information on the performance of each hypothesis. The second column of Table 5 indicates the value of the error sum-of-squares (ESS) for each hypothesis. The ESS is of course smallest for the least-restricted model (HG), although hypotheses H3 and H7 do almost as well. The corresponding log-likelihood values are reported in the next column.

Conventional hypothesis testing would compare the difference between these log-likelihood values with χ^2 values at arbitrarily selected levels of significance. For example, the χ^2 statistic for testing H3 against the unrestricted hypothesis is 58.6 ($= 2[-41.1 -(-70.4)]$), which would be compared against a number like 33.92, the upper 5 percent of a χ^2 random variable with 22 degrees of freedom (the number of restrictions). The suggested conclusion is then that the restrictions embodied in hypothesis H3 can be rejected in comparison with the unrestricted model HG. But this kind of treatment inadequately deals with the power of the test, which is inappropriately allowed to grow with the sample size while the significance level is held fixed. This emphasis on power leads to tests that avoid type II errors merely by rejecting the alternative hypothesis and it creates a serious tendency to reject restrictions as the sample size grows. This problem is alleviated here through the use of the asymptotic Bayes' factor (17), which has a certain arbitrariness in construction, but nonetheless has the effect of lowering the significance level as the sample size grows and thus maintaining some reasonable relationship between the significance level and the power.

TABLE 5

PERFORMANCE STATISTICS FOR ALTERNATIVE HYPOTHESES

Hypothesis	ESS[a]	ln(L)	Number of Parameters	Adjusted[b] ln(L)	Odds of Hypothesis[c] Relative to H3
HG	1.32	−41.1	71	808.1	3.15E-15
H1	6.63	−280.9	22	707.8	nil
H2	14.56	−397.7	27	576.8	nil
H3	1.61	−70.4	49	841.5	1.0
H4	961.80	−1020.0	11	0.0	nil
H5	6.35	−274.6	33	682.8	nil
H6	11.85	−367.2	38	576.0	nil
H7	1.51	−60.9	60	819.6	32.20E-10
H8	492.39	−920.6	22	68.1	nil
H9	6.25	−272.1	44	653.9	nil
H10	11.58	−363.7	49	548.1	nil

[a] In millions.
[b] Adjusted $\ln(L) = \ln(L) - (p/2)\ln(297) + 1051$, where p = number of parameters and 1051 is the value of equation (16) under hypothesis H4.
[c] Odds = $\exp[\text{adjusted } \ln(L) - 841.5]$. "Nil" entries indicate a value less than 10^{-50}.

The fifth column of Table 5 reports the log-likelihood values adjusted for the dimensionality of the parameter space according to (16). A constant has been added to these numbers so that they are all nonnegative. The corresponding Bayes' factors (or odds ratios) are reported in the last column. The clear winner is hypothesis H3, which allows neutral differences in factor input matrices, biased measurements of factor contents, and multiplicative errors in the endowments,[14] but maintains the assumptions of identical homothetic tastes and complete coverage of countries. Second best (though far behind) is hypothesis H7, which weakens H3 by allowing for incomplete coverage of countries. The third-best hypothesis is HG, the unrestricted model. The other hypotheses

---

[14] To examine the potential extent of measurement error in the endowments, we compared measured U.S. endowments with the amount of each factor absorbed directly and indirectly in producing the 1967 vector of U.S. final demand in both manufacturing and services (a total of 354 sectors). The ratio of the amount absorbed in production to the endowment for each factor was: capital 2.1; total labor, .88; prof/tech, .62; managerial, .45; clerical, .92; sales, 1.41; service, .68; agricultural, .98; production, .99. The discrepancy for capital likely occurs because the depreciation rates used in computing industry capital stocks were typically lower than the rate used to compute national capital stocks. The discrepancy for managerial workers likely reflects the exclusion of government employees in calculating industry input requirements.

are essentially "impossible," given the data evidence. Such extreme values for the Bayes' factors are not uncommon, and should probably be viewed with suspicion since they depend on a number of assumptions, normality being a potentially important example.

Although hypothesis H3 is favored, it does not lead to sensible estimates of many of the parameters. Table 6 reports estimates of the technological differences δ_i. The hypothesis that the technology is the same as that of the United States, $\delta_i = 1$, can be rejected for all but three countries (Australia, Canada, and Mexico),[15] but most of the estimates are wildly different from one, and eight take on implausible negative values. Furthermore, 15 countries have estimated δ's in excess of one, indicating that their factors are more productive than those of the United States.

It is possible that these peculiar estimates are due to one or more "rogue" observations. Table 1 indicates that eight countries with negative estimates all have large imports of the services of one or more of the land factors: arable land, forestland, and pastureland, and accounting for these extreme values may require a dramatic alteration of the H-O-V model. However, contrary to the suggested importance of these observations, reestimation of the model for each hypothesis with the land variables excluded produced few changes in the estimated parameters (results not shown). Hypothesis H3 remained most favored, followed by hypothesis H7 and then HG. Under hypothesis H3, seventeen of the estimated technological differences δ_i exceeded unity and the number of countries with negative values of the technological difference parameter increased from eight to ten.[16] We thus remain confused about the exact source of the peculiar estimates.

The estimates reported in Table 7 are also cause for concern. The predicted values of the factor supplies can be found by inserting the observed values into these estimated equations. A negative value of γ_k indicates that the observed endowment and the "corrected" endowment are negatively correlated. This happens for four of the labor endowments, although three of these coefficients have large enough standard errors that the sign remains in doubt. This leaves production workers as the anomaly: the number of production workers embodied in trade is negatively related to the measured number of production workers.[17]

---

[15] The Bayes' criterion in equation (17) implies a critical t-value of 2.19. The critical value is computed as $[(T - k)(T^{1/T} - 1)]^{1/2}$, where T is the number of observations (297) and k is the number of parameters (49). See Leamer (1978, p. 114) for discussion.

[16] The estimate for Belgium-Luxembourg switched from negative to positive, while the estimates for the Netherlands, Norway, and Spain switched from positive to negative.

[17] Parameter estimates for the unrestricted model HG were very similar to those reported for hypothesis H3. In particular, of the eight countries with negative values of δ_i in Table 6, only the value for France was positive. In addition, the signs and levels of significance of the parameters γ_k paralleled those shown in Table 7.

TABLE 6

H-O-V Regressions and Country Coefficients under
Hypothesis H3

Country	δ_i^a	Standard Error	t-Statistics[b]
Argentina	1.5769	0.0941	6.129
Australia	1.1315	0.0751	1.751
Austria	3.9479	0.8720	3.380
Belgium-Luxembourg	−7.1774	2.7668	−2.955
Brazil	0.1327	0.0474	−18.281
Canada	0.9431	0.1225	−0.463
Denmark	7.2536	0.6196	10.092
Finland	4.4885	0.2966	11.758
France	−0.7803	0.7591	−2.345
Germany	−16.9248	2.0573	−8.712
Greece	6.1582	0.2809	18.357
Hong Kong	−174.4016	24.7673	−7.081
Ireland	13.4523	0.4147	30.024
Italy	2 1.5930	0.7419	−3.494
Japan	−21.3424	2.2211	−10.059
Korea	3.0928	0.2646	7.906
Mexico	1.1999	0.1121	1.782
Netherlands	18.5644	3.2888	5.340
Norway	13.0655	0.8802	13.706
Philippines	2.2965	0.1057	12.258
Portugal	1.9940	0.1640	6.060
Spain	0.3709	0.2131	2 2.950
Sweden	2.9687	0.7193	2.736
Switzerland	−16.2249	5.0798	2 3.390
United Kingdom	−17.4481	2.0614	2 8.949
United States	1.0000	NA	NA
Yugoslavia	1.7798	0.1524	5.115

Note: Number of observations = 297.
[a]Values are divided by U.S. estimates ($\delta_{us} = 1.0012$).
[b]Asymptotic t-values for testing δ_i is unity. The critical t-value based on equation (17) is 2.19.

TABLE 7

H-O-V Regressions and Factor Coefficients under Hypothesis H3

	Parameters	
Resource	$\alpha_k{}^a$	$\gamma_k{}^b$
Capital	−990620794	13.431
	(−6.665)	(2.142)
Labor		
Agricultural	−7853	13.631
	(−1.376)	(2.721)
Clerical	−4628	−1.111
	(−1.426)	(−0.386)
Prof/Tech	−4376	2 0.360
	(−1.866)	(−0.128)
Managerial	−1815	−0.528
	(−1.587)	(−0.370)
Production	−19608	−2.671
	(−1.997)	(−2.152)
Sales	−1214	0.216
	(−0.515)	(0.175)
Service	−1302	0.053
	(−0.498)	(0.052)
Land		
Arable	−2570651	1718.648
	(−62.891)	(52.545)
Forest	−2454843	833.206
	(−21.263)	(20.427)
Pasture	−202638	199.930
	(−2.275)	(9.163)

[a] Asymptotic t-values in parentheses. The critical t-value based on equation (17) is 2.19.
[b] Values of γ_k scaled by 10^3.

Overall, our results cast doubt on the hypothesis that the H-O-V equations are exact in favor of a model that allows neutral differences in factor input matrices and measurement errors in both trade and national resource supplies. This finding suggests that technological differences and measurement errors are also significant reasons for the relatively poor performance of the sharp hypotheses contained in the rank and sign propositions considered previously. However, our results do support the assumptions of proportional consumption[18] and complete coverage of countries. However, these conclusions are rendered suspect by the peculiar point estimates that are produced by the favored hypothesis.

---

[18] This contrast with Yutaka Horiba's (1979) test of the proportional consumption assumption using data on U.S. regional trade. Using a specification similar to ours, he rejected the assumption in terms of the value of β_k but not its sign.

IV. CONCLUDING REMARKS

This paper has reported conceptually correct tests of the Heckscher-Ohlin proposition that trade in commodities can be explained in terms of an interaction between factor input requirements and factor endowments. An exact specification of this interaction in a multicountry, multicommodity, multifactor world was derived in the form of the Heckscher-Ohlin-Vanek (H-O-V) theorem, which equates the factors embodied in net trade to excess factor supplies. The H-O-V theorem was weakened to allow nonproportional consumption and technological differences and was supplemented with various assumptions about measurement errors. Using 1967 trade and input requirements, we tested the null hypothesis that the H-O-V equations are exact against several of these weaker alternatives. In addition, we examined sign and rank corollaries of the H-O-V theorem analogous to those implicitly studied by Leontief.

The Leontief-type sign and rank propositions, whether examined across countries or across factors, were generally not supported. The sign of net factor exports infrequently predicted the sign of excess factor supplies and therefore does not reliably reveal factor abundance. The ranking of factor contents infrequently conforms to the ranking of factor abundance ratios, as examined through either rank correlations or pairwise rankings.

The hypothesis that the H-O-V equations are exact was also not supported. The data suggest errors in measurement in both trade and national factor supplies, and favor the hypothesis of neutral technological differences across countries. However, the form of the technological differences favored by the data involves a number of implausible estimates, including some in which factors yield strictly negative outputs.[19] Thus, to a considerable extent, the conclusions that come from a study of the sign and rank propositions apply to the more promising regression study: The Heckscher-Ohlin model does poorly, but we do not have anything that does better. It is easy to find hypotheses that do as well or better in a statistical sense, but these alternatives yield economically unsatisfying parameter estimates.

These generally negative conclusions concerning the empirical validity of the H-O-V model appear to contrast sharply with Leamer's (1984) conclusion that "the main currents of international trade are well understood in terms of the abundance of a remarkably limited list of resources. In that sense the Heckscher-Ohlin theory comes out looking rather well." However, the present paper tests a different set of hypotheses. Leamer (1984) studies the weakened hypothesis that the structure of trade can be

---

[19]Although the assumption of factor price equalization is not explicit in our analysis, the performance of hypothesis H3 together with the results shown in Table 6 could be taken as evidence against the assumption of factor price equalization. Factor price differences might help explain the variability in the estimates of δ_i since such differences would imply nonneutral differences in factor input matrices. We intend to examine the possibility of nonneutral technological differences in later research.

explained by the availability of resources. This paper examines the stricter H-O-V hypothesis that factor supplies, factor input requirements, and trade interact in a particular way. In addition, the present results suggest that there are important differences in selected input intensities between the United States and the other countries. Leamer's (1984) study may come to a more optimistic conclusion because he makes no commitment to the U.S. input intensities.[20]

DATA APPENDIX

Data on 1966 factor and 1967 trade endowments were collected for 27 countries. The twelve resources are capital, total labor, professional/technical workers, managerial workers, clerical workers, sales workers, service workers, agricultural workers, production workers, arable land, pastureland, and forestland. In accordance with this *Review's* policy of ensuring clear documentation of data, Table A1 lists the data on countries' population, GNP, and trade balance, as well as their trade and endowment of each factor. The following provides a concise discussion of data sources and methods, and includes citation to previously published work which contains further information on these data.

Factor endowment data were obtained from Bowen (1980, 1983). Net capital stocks for each country were computed by summing annual real gross domestic investment flows starting in 1949 with annual depreciation assumed to be 13.33 percent. The underlying investment data were derived from the World Bank's Economic and Social Data Bank tape and appear in the World Bank publication *World Tables*. Detailed discussion of the methods used to construct net capital stocks appears in Bowen (1982).

Labor endowments were derived from issues of the International Labour Office (ILO) publication *Yearbook of Labor Statistics*. The labor categories are those defined at the one-digit level of the ILO's International Standard Classification of Occupations (ISCO). Total labor is defined as a country's total economically active population. For each country, the number of workers in each ISCO category was computed by multiplying the share of a country's total labor belonging to a category times its total labor. Since occupational data are not regularly collected, the share of each labor type in each country in 1966 was derived from a time-series regression of the available share data against time. Bowen (1982) provides discussion of this method and presents the years for which occupational data were available for each country.

Land endowments were taken from issues of the Food and Agricultural Organization (FAO) publication *Production Yearbook*. The definitions of arable land, pastureland, and forestland are those used by the FAO.

The total content (direct plus indirect) of each factor embodied in net trade was calculated by premultiplying each country's net trade vector by a matrix of total factor input requirements. Total factor input requirements were calculated from data on direct and indirect factor input requirements for each industry according to the 367-order U.S. input-output table for 1967. Data on each country's trade in 1967 were obtained from the U.N. Trade Data Tapes at the four- and five-digit level of the SITC and concorded to the input-output sectors to perform the required vector multiplications. The concordances are available from the authors upon request.

On the production side, capital (plant, equipment, and inventories) input requirements were constructed from data prepared by the Bureau of Labor Statistics Economic Growth Project, which provided industry capital stock figures measured in 1958 dollars. Industry occupation requirements, measured in number of

---

[20] See also Anderson's (1987) review of Leamer (1984).

TABLE A1

DATA BASE

(1)	(2)	(3)	Country		(4)	(5)	(6)	(7)
22.0	2.17431E10	4.68938E8	Argentina	E	2.40180E10	8496000	1342368	953251
				T	8.67853E8	77647	79417	1701
11.6	2.27360E10	−1.16039E8	Australia	E	3.50530E10	4727000	461828	702905
				T	−1.45799E9	−44830	78226	−14787
7.3	1.01688E10	−6.44060E8	Austria	E	1.56530E10	3363000	605340	393135
				T	−1.07484E9	−40112	−10955	−4982
9.8	1.89645E10	−3.45010E8	Bene-Lux	E	2.25630E10	3764000	236379	477652
				T	−9.38096E8	−7454	−26037	293
83.9	2.90170E10	2.45233E8	Brazil	E	3.04760E10	26463000	12696947	1267578
				T	−1.39899E9	−18704	6813	−4128
20.0	5.68412E10	4.24574E8	Canada	E	7.65370E10	7232000	690656	984998
				T	1.88821E9	2158932	47260	−28570
4.8	1.11664E10	−5.88141E8	Denmark	E	1.30180E10	2230000	304618	249760
				T	−1.32815E9	805	47564	−4358
4.6	8.64730E9	−2.20552E8	Finland	E	1.39290E10	2176000	574029	173862
				T	3.94420E8	−1796	−3009	−2530
49.2	1.08118E11	−9.53400E8	France	E	1.46052E11	21233000	3709405	2299534
				T	−7.06224E8	−34336	−38160	−736
59.7	1.22675E11	2.11160E9	Germany	E	1.81079E11	26576000	2854262	4217611
				T	5.72919E7	349286	−240808	75288
8.6	6.72160E9	−8.16871E8	Greece	E	7.22300E9	4314000	2065975	250212
				T	−1.35709E9	−52749	7616	−7373
3.6	1.97080E9	−4.43437E8	Hong Kong	E	2.08700E9	1525000	78842	104462
				T	−1.48229E9	−28429	−31726	−2834
2.9	2.93960E9	−3.84555E8	Ireland	E	3.37000E9	1109000	346895	90273
				T	−5.16958E8	−9731	18912	−3303

Note: See notes at end of table for column definitions.

Country		(8)	(9)	(10)	(11)	(12)	(13)	(14)	(15)
Argentina	E	588773	161424	2948112	927763	956650	30248000	60130000	145802000
	T	2998	−12	−6990	2886	1645	6561280	−3745350	3835996
Australia	E	443865	300164	2018429	369651	355470	39614000	35151000	447208000
	T	−15213	−6415	−82554	−1348	−2767	6762249	−4913655	3498840
Austria	E	260969	68941	1362688	261978	357487	1686000	3203000	2249000
	T	−4728	−1852	−14008	−1885	−1710	−1546894	−156822	87684
Bene-Lux	E	426461	145290	1778490	409900	275148	981000	687000	818000
	T	−2621	−436	22601	−805	−451	−3672691	−6653807	189337
Brazil	E	1098214	727732	5440793	1595719	2344622	31910000	522600000	141400000
	T	−4805	−1407	−14172	−646	−363	741997	15142	152291
Canada	E	868563	625568	2438630	496115	770208	43404000	322271000	20957000
	T	−21686	−10161	−134350	−5712	−5798	5389052	20253445	899259
Denmark	E	231474	35680	861226	224784	247530	2701000	472000	326000
	T	−5349	−2138	−34661	570	−824	737315	3254944	5328684
Finland	E	224998	32640	797286	165811	207590	2753000	21930000	110000
	T	−2960	2587	8710	−846	−579	−736283	6481551	320649
France	E	2344123	626373	7905046	1751722	1783572	20214000	12714000	13632000
	T	−1197	−1145	9304	−1872	−527	−4585442	−26133156	−437494
Germany	E	2479541	728182	11153947	2320085	2551296	8228000	7184000	5802000
	T	64071	28574	392143	13849	16244	−26018409	−25195922	−5730951
Greece	E	198444	29335	1134582	289901	309314	3851000	2608000	5239000
	T	−6174	−2893	−39697	−2046	−2187	1571541	−2343192	−526643
Hong Kong	E	77927	76097	755180	180102	247660	13000	10000	1
	T	−4095	−1153	14839	−1916	−1547	−2931651	−3459434	−1232976
Ireland	E	87278	14417	370739	109569	87611	1199000	208000	3554000
	T	−3175	−1431	−19559	−407	−769	96740	−622571	2308561

(1)	(2)	(3)	Country		(4)	(5)	(6)	(7)
52.0	7.96580E10	−5.39406E8	Italy	E	9.04360E10	19998000	4527547	1763824
				T	−6.98937E9	28922	−103119	11262
98.9	1.10388E11	2.53711E8	Japan	E	1.65976E11	49419000	11905037	6478831
				T	−8.78167E9	107388	−172142	27674
29.1	4.13000E9	−4.87021E8	Korea	E	3.02500E9	9440000	4936176	370048
				T	−1.49530E9	−49392	−9346	−5712
44.1	2.21625E10	−5.61792E8	Mexico	E	2.16390E10	12844000	5878699	910640
				T	−8.28121E8	−50163	25306	−9625
12.5	2.08090E10	−1.26535E9	Netherlands	E	2.99410E10	4699000	388607	657390
				T	−2.85259E9	−60964	29917	−8221
3.8	7.65510E9	−8.39611E8	Norway	E	1.28830E10	1464000	223699	125758
				T	−1.70045E9	−102657	−6254	−11350
32.7	6.18600E9	−1.04685E8	Philippines	E	6.59700E9	12470000	6660227	379088
				T	−1.04236E9	−35637	4721	−5728
9.3	4.26650E9	−4.03294E8	Portugal	E	3.75700E9	3381000	1166445	196436
				T	−8.61326E8	−23677	−11321	22897
32.0	2.82285E10	−2.31879E9	Spain	E	3.47920E10	11849000	3673190	940811
				T	−4.87847E9	−148941	−17365	−17993
7.8	2.35715E10	−3.01150E8	Sweden	E	3.15550E10	3450000	368805	375705
				T	−1.03381E8	−19339	−16365	−3741
6.0	1.50576E10	−6.65988E8	Switzerland	E	2.33150E10	2843000	263546	457723
				T	−2.11706E9	−48845	−32919	2870
54.7	1.06534E11	−2.55290E9	United Kingdom	E	1.10717E11	25396000	891400	3512267
				T	−1.72415E10	−400012	−283790	−16862
196.5	7.62700E11	4.34870E9	United States	E	7.85933E11	76595000	3707198	2515623
				T	5.76114E9	764413	258625	87377
19.7	8.60700E9	−3.55350E8	Yugoslavia	E	1.40230E10	8837000	4539567	451571
				T	−8.59292E8	−17986	4413	−4003

Country		(8)	(9)	(10)	(11)	(12)	(13)	(14)	(15)
Italy	E	1181882	185981	8233177	2225777	897910	15258000	6099000	5147000
	T	4838	3877	112909	−1250	435	−62445355	−26821582	−7174026
Japan	E	2826767	1433151	16940833	5757313	3553226	5839000	25400000	157000
	T	16998	9108	220165	1543	4057	−19862383	−67987781	−2956563
Korea	E	244496	75520	1666160	927008	465392	2293000	6656000	18000
	T	−5232	−2186	−23143	−1903	−1873	−1111149	−2404532	−130644
Mexico	E	624218	245320	2766598	1075043	1344767	26000000	78000000	72100000
	T	−9184	−3865	−48936	−1760	−2103	3061733	3920090	297403
Netherlands	E	535686	123114	1823682	467550	429019	946000	292000	1299000
	T	−4618	−3443	−71238	−1260	22084	417979	−3260982	3394099
Norway	E	158551	50508	653676	122390	129271	841000	730000	158000
	T	−9529	−4377	−64732	−2976	−3447	−1297301	6966388	443706
Philippines	E	448920	342925	2035104	746953	872900	8330000	14100000	830000
	T	−4561	−2158	−24600	−1722	−1595	842059	−1283864	−216082
Portugal	E	109206	24005	1103220	225513	273185	4070000	3400000	530000
	T	−3159	−990	−3460	−1060	−791	−1274623	473446	−224250
Spain	E	596005	98347	4397164	893415	1071150	20156000	13600000	12000000
	T	−15604	−7010	−79483	−5828	−5650	−1221046	−3755719	−1066016
Sweden	E	566835	77625	1390350	317745	334305	3158000	22794000	525000
	T	−2183	−926	7287	−2105	−1317	−2210020	6774374	36931
Switzerland	E	307613	48900	1205432	209245	307897	401000	981000	1778000
	T	1446	−278	−14405	−948	−876	−3652367	−4066582	−692250
United Kingdom	E	2450714	789816	12027546	2460872	3088154	7480000	1829000	12107000
	T	−3730	−6651	−62500	−15201	−11232	−24179333	−49416509	−12948250
United States	E	9911393	7284184	28799720	5108886	9275654	177550000	306850000	258000000
	T	102628	30444	235781	24053	25598	35789032	−69100970	−1108796
Yugoslavia	E	609753	98974	2212785	269528	534638	8266000	8812000	6450000
	T	−4187	−1595	−10469	−1032	−1117	−108893	−78267	664739

Notes: E = 1966 endowment. T = 1967 net trade in factor. Units of T are those of the corresponding endowment. Columns are: 1) Population (mil.); 2) GNP (1966; $US); 3) Trade Balance (1966, $US); 4) Capital (1966, $US); Labor; 5) Total; 6) Agricultural; 7) Clerical; 8) Professional/Technical; 9) Managerial; 10) Production; 11) Sales; 12) Services; Land (hectares); 13) Arable; 14) Forest; 15) Pasture.

persons, were based upon the 1971 Survey of Occupational Employment and the 1970 Census of Population. These data were reclassified, to the extent possible, to be consistent with the one-digit occupational categories defined by ISCO. (It was often not feasible to translate industry skill requirements into the ILO definitions; white-collar employment in certain nontraded sectors was a particular difficulty.) Sveikauskas (1983, Appendix) and especially Sveikauskas (1984) provide a complete description of the factor requirements data and a detailed table listing the input requirements data that can be made available.

Land inputs were constructed from information contained in the U.S. input-output table. Arable land is defined as proportional to total purchases from I/O sector 2; pastureland as proportional to total purchases from I/O sector 1 and forestland as proportional to total purchases from I/O sector 3 (which includes fisheries). This method of measuring land (natural resource) inputs corresponds to a rent definition of quantity and has been used by Baldwin (1971) and Harkness (1978), among others.

Land input coefficients are measured in dollars, whereas land endowments are measured in hectares. To adjust for this difference in units of measurement, the net trade in each land type was deflated using an inputed price. The prices were derived by dividing the total value of each type of land input absorbed in producing total U.S. output in 1967 by the corresponding U.S. endowment of each type of land in 1966. The prices, in 1967 dollars, are: arable land, \$142.767 per hectare; pastureland, \$108.942 per hectare; forestland, \$5.688 per hectare.

REFERENCES

Anderson, James E., "Review of *Sources of International Comparative Advantage: Theory and Evidence*, by Edward E. Leamer," *Journal of Economic Literature*, March 1987, 25, 146–47.

Baldwin, Robert E., "Determinants of the Commodity Structure of U.S. Trade," *American Economic Review*, March 1971, 61, 126–46.

Bowen, Harry P., *Resources, Technology and Dynamic Comparative Advantage: A Cross-Country Test of the Product Cycle Theory of International Trade*, unpublished doctoral dissertation, UCLA, 1980.

———, "Statistical Appendix to *Sources of International Comparative Advantage*," published, in part, as Appendix B of *Sources of International Comparative Advantage*, by Edward E. Leamer, Cambridge: MIT Press, 1982.

———, "Changes in the International Distribution of Resources and Their Impact on U.S. Comparative Advantage," *Review of Economics and Statistics*, August 1983, 65, 402–14.

Branson, William and Monoyios, Nicholas, "Factor Inputs in U.S. Trade," *Journal of International Economics*, May 1977, 7, 111–31.

Brecher, Richard and Choudhri, Ehsan, "The Leontief Paradox, Continued," *Journal of Political Economy*, August 1982, 90, 820–23.

Chenery, Hollis and Syrquin, Moses, *Patterns of Development*, 1950–1970, New York and London: Oxford University Press for World Bank, 1975.

Harkness, Jon, "Factor Abundance and Comparative Advantage," *American Economic Review*, December 1978, 68, 784–800.

———, "The Factor-Proportions Model with Many Nations, Goods and Factors: Theory and Evidence," *Review of Economics and Statistics*, May 1983, 65, 298–305.

Horiba, Yutaka, "Testing the Demand Side of Comparative Advantage Models," *American Economic Review*, September 1979, 69, 650–61.

Kohler, Wilhelm K., "A Note on the Meaning of Leontief-Type Paradoxa," unpublished paper, 1987.

Leamer, Edward E., *Sources of International Comparative Advantage: Theory and Evidence*, Cambridge: MIT Press, 1984.

————, "The Leontief Paradox Reconsidered," *Journal of Political Economy*, June 1980, *88*, 495–503.

————, *Specification Searches*, New York: Wiley & Sons, 1978.

————, "The Commodity Composition of International Trade in Manufactures: An Empirical Analysis," *Oxford Economic Papers*, November 1974, *26*, 350–74.

———— and Bowen, Harry P., "Cross-Section Tests of the Heckscher-Ohlin Theorem: Comment," *American Economic Review*, December 1981, *71*, 1040–43.

Leontief, Wassily, "Domestic Production and Foreign Trade: The American Capital Position Re-Examined," *Proceedings of the American Philosophical Society*, 1953, *97*, 332–49.

Maskus, Keith V., "A Test of the Heckscher-Ohlin-Vanek Theorem: The Leontief Commonplace," *Journal of International Economics*, November 1985, *9*, 201–12.

Schwarz, G., "Estimating the Dimension of a Model," *Annals of Statistics*, 1978, *6*, 461–64.

Stern, Robert M. and Maskus, Keith V., "Determinants of the Structure of U.S. Foreign Trade, 1958–76," *Journal of International Economics*, May 1981, *11*, 207–24.

Summers, Robert, Kravis, Irving and Heston, Alan, "International Comparisons of Real Product and Its Composition: 1950–1977," *The Review of Income and Wealth*, March 1980, *26*, 19–66.

Sveikauskas, Leo, "Science and Technology in United States Foreign Trade," *Economic Journal*, September 1983, *93*, 542–54.

————, "Science and Technology in Many Different Industries: Data for the Analysis of International Trade," *Review of Public Data Use*, June 1984, 133–56.

Vanek, Jaroslav, "The Factor Proportions Theory: The N-Factor Case," *Kyklos*, October 1968, *21*, 749–55.

International Labour Office, *Yearbook of Labor Statistics*, Geneva: International Labour Office, various years.

U.S. Department of Labor, Bureau of Labor Statistics (1974), *Survey of Occupational Employment*, Series of Reports 430, Occupational Employment in Manufacturing, 1971, Washington, D.C.

U.S. Bureau of the Census, U.S. Department of Commerce, *1970 Census of Population*, Occupation by Industry. PC(2)-7C, Washington: USGPO, 1972.

World Bank, *World Tables*, Baltimore: Johns Hopkins University Press for the World Bank, various years.

ABOUT THE AUTHORS

Harry P. Bowen

Dr. Bowen is Professor of Economics and International Business at the Vlerick-Leuven-Gent (VLG) Management School in Belgium. He was Visiting Associate Professor of Economics at the University of California at Irvine. He also served on the faculty of the Stern School of Business at New York University. He was Staff Economist in the Office of Foreign Economic Research, U.S. Department of Labor.

Editor's Queries:

Which article not authored by you would you most highly recommend to graduate students in international economics? Paul Samuelson's "Prices of Factors and Goods in General Equilibrium" (1953, *Review of Economics and Statistics*). The paper gives a very clear statement of the competitive workhorse model of traditional trade theory. Here is where we find, among other things, the reciprocity relations. It is always a treat to go the fountainhead.

What are the major unresolved questions of international economics? What are likely to be the hot topics of the next decade? Despite a number of insights in recent years, we still do not know the relative importance of technological versus factor cost differences in determining trade patterns. A related issue is the relative importance (empirically) of trade patterns in altering factor prices. Lastly, the role of trade in fostering factor accumulation and economic development is still an area of limited understanding.

What advice do you have to offer graduate students in the field of international economics? Learn the theory and don't ignore, or be afraid of, data. The field of international trade has many sub-areas where both theory and empirical work are lacking, so there is something for everyone.

Edward E. Leamer

Edward Leamer is the Chauncey J. Medberry Professor of Management, Professor of Economics, Professor of Statistics, and Director of the Business Forecast Project at the University of California at Los Angeles (UCLA). He received a B.A. in mathematics from Princeton, a Ph.D. in economics and an M.A. in mathematics from the University of Michigan. After serving as assistant and associate professor at Harvard University, he joined UCLA in 1975 as professor of economics and served as chair from 1983 to 1987. Professor Leamer is a fellow of the American Academy of Arts and Sciences, and a fellow of the Econometric Society.

Editor's Queries

What advice do you have to offer graduate students in the field of international economics?　Find your passion and pursue it. The Epicureans tell us "pleasure, not truth, is the end aim of life," to which I would add "truth is pleasure." If things go well, you will be asked to edit a volume of readings and you can stuff it full of your own works.

Leo Sviekauskus

Leo Sveikauskus is an economist at the Bureau of Labor Statistics and a specialist in productivity and the role of technology in economic growth.

Editor's Queries

What are the major unresolved questions of international economics?　I see as the main future issue the further understanding of the process through which advanced countries generate new innovations and the new industries which grow up to produce and implement these new ideas. Equally important, it is necessary to understand the barriers and limitations which make it difficult for poorer countries to gain access to these new perspectives. Given this viewpoint, it's not surprising that my favorite article in the literature is Paul Krugman's 1979 *JPE* article "A Model of Innovation, Technology Transfer, and the World Distribution of Income," which presents this process with stark clarity.

The Leontief Paradox, Reconsidered

EDWARD E. LEAMER

University of California, Los Angeles

Using the Heckscher-Ohlin-Vanek model of trade, it is shown that a country is revealed to be relatively well endowed in capital compared with labor if and only if one of the following three conditions holds, where $K_x, K_m, L_x, L_m, K_c, L_c$ are capital and labor embodied in exports, imports, and consumption: (a) $K_x - K_m > 0, L_x - L_m < 0$; (b) $K_x - K_m > 0, L_x - L_m > 0, (K_x - K_m)/(L_x - L_m) > K_c/L_c$; (c) $K_x - K_m < 0, L_x - L_m < 0, (K_x - K_m)/(L_x - L_m) < K_c/L_c$. Leontief's data for the United States in 1947 satisfy b, and the United States is actually revealed by trade to be capital abundant. The comparison by Leontief of K_x/L_x with K_m/L_m is shown to be theoretically inappropriate.

The Leontief paradox (1954) rests on a simple conceptual misunderstanding. It makes use of the intuitively appealing but nonetheless false proposition that if the capital per man embodied in exports is less than the capital per man embodied in imports, the country is revealed to be poorly endowed in capital relative to labor. This is a true proposition if the net export of labor services is of the opposite sign of the net export of capital services, but when both are positive, as in Leontief's data, the proper comparison is between the capital per man embodied in *net* exports and the capital per man embodied in consumption. Leontief's figures, which produced the so-called paradoxical result that U.S. exports are less capital intensive than U.S. competing imports, can also be used to show that U.S. net exports are more capital intensive than U.S. consumption, which in fact implies that capital is abundant relative to labor. There is no paradox if the conceptually correct calculations are made.

The first section of this paper shows that a country is revealed to be relatively well endowed in capital compared with labor if and only if one of the following three conditions holds, where $K_x, K_m, L_x, L_m, K_c, L_c$ are capital and labor embodied in exports,

Written with the assistance of Harry P. Bowen and with the support of Ford Foundation grant 775-0692. Comments from Larry Kotlikoff and a referee are also gratefully acknowledged.

imports, and consumption:

(a) $K_x - K_m > 0, L_x - L_m < 0.$

(b) $K_x - K_m > 0, L_x - L_m > 0, (K_x - K_m)/(L_x - L_m) > K_c/L_c.$

(c) $K_x - K_m < 0, L_x - L_m < 0, (K_x - K_m)/(L_x - L_m) < K_c/L_c.$

Although Leontief found that $K_x/L_x < K_m/L_m$, his data are shown in Section II to satisfy b, and therefore the United States is revealed to be capital abundant. In a largely overlooked article, Williams (1970) makes a related point.

I. TRADE-REVEALED FACTOR ABUNDANCE

This reconsideration of the Leontief paradox rests on the Heckscher-Ohlin-Vanek (HOV) theorem (Vanek 1968).

THE HECKSCHER-OHLIN-VANEK THEOREM

Given: (a) There are n commodities which are freely mobile internationally. (b) There are n factors which are perfectly immobile internationally. (c) All individuals have identical homothetic preferences. (d) Production functions are the same in all countries and exhibit constant returns to scale. (e) There is perfect competition in the goods and factors markets. (f) Factor prices are equalized across countries.

Then: There exists a set of positive scalars $\alpha_i, i = 1, ..., I$, such that the vector of net exports of country i, T_i, the vector of factor endowments of country i, E_i, and the $n \times n$ matrix of total factor requirements A, bear the following relationship to each other:

$$AT_i = E_i - E_w\alpha_i, \qquad i = 1, ..., I, \tag{1}$$

where E_w is the world's endowment vector, $E_w = \Sigma_i E_i$.

Proof: The proof of this result is straightforward. The equalization of factor prices and constant-returns-to-scale production functions imply the matrix of total factor inputs A, where A_{jk} is the amount of factor j used to produce one unit of commodity k. If Q_i is the vector of outputs of country i, then equilibrium in the factor markets requires factor demand equal to factor supply $AQ_i = E_i$. The summation of this equation over all countries produces $AQ_w = E_w$. Then, identical homothetic tastes imply that the consumption vectors C_i of each country are proportional to each other and also proportional to world output Q_w: $C_i = Q_w\alpha_i$. Country i's trade is $T_i = Q_i - C_i$, and the factors embodied in trade are $AT_i = A(Q_i - C_i) = E_i - AQ_w\alpha_i = E_i - E_w\alpha_i$.

The set of equations (1) serves as a logically sound foundation for a study of trade-revealed factor abundance. Two of these equations describe the relationship between capital and labor endowments and the implicit trade in capital and labor services:

$$K_T = K_i - \alpha_i K_w, \tag{2a}$$

$$L_T = L_i - \alpha_i L_w, \tag{2b}$$

where (K_T, L_T) are capital and labor embodied in net exports, (K_i, L_i) are the factor endowments of country i, and (K_w, L_w) are the world's factor endowments.

We take the following definition of factor abundance.

Definition: Capital in country i is said to be abundant in comparison with labor if and only if the share of the world's capital stock located in i exceeds the share of the world's labor force: $K_i/K_w > L_i/L_w$.

Factor abundance is revealed by trade through a comparison of the vector of factors used to produce various vectors of commodities. These vectors may be defined as follows.

Definition: The vector of factors embodied in the vector of commodities z is Az, where A is the matrix of total factor requirements.

The following result establishes necessary and sufficient conditions for trade to reveal an abundance of capital.

COROLLARY 1: Capital is revealed by trade to be abundant relative to labor if and only if

$$K_i/(K_i - K_T) > L_i/(L_i - L_T). \tag{3}$$

Proof: Equations (2a) and (2b) can be rewritten as

$$K_w = (K_i - K_T)/\alpha_i,$$
$$L_w = (L_i - L_T)/\alpha_i.$$

Thus

$$K_i/K_w = \alpha_i K_i/(K_i - K_T),$$
$$L_i/L_w = \alpha_i L_i/(L_i - L_T),$$

from which (3) is a consequence.

There are three useful ways of rewriting (3). If K_c is the amount of capital embodied in the commodities used in country i, then $K_i - K_T = K_c$ and, similarly, $L_i - L_T = L_c$. Then (3) is equivalent to

$$K_i/L_i > K_c/L_c, \tag{3a}$$

which means that a country is revealed to be capital abundant if its production is more capital intensive than its consumption.

Another way to rewrite (3) is $K_i(L_i - L_T) > L_i(K_i - K_T)$, or

$$- K_i L_T > -L_i K_T. \tag{3b}$$

If L_T is positive, then this inequality becomes $K_T/L_T > K_i/L_i$, or $K_T/K_i > L_T/L_i$. Thus a country which is an exporter of both labor services and capital services is revealed by trade to be relatively capital abundant if trade is more capital intensive than production or, equivalently, if the share of capital exported exceeds the share of labor exported.

Similarly, if L_T is negative the inequalities are reversed, and a country which is an importer of both labor services and capital services is revealed by trade to be relatively capital abundant if trade is less capital intensive than production or, equivalently, if the share of capital imported is less than the share of labor imported.

Yet another possibility is to rewrite (3b) as $-(K_c + K_T)L_T > -(L_c + L_T)K_T$, or

$$-K_c L_T > -L_c K_T. \tag{3c}$$

Thus a country which is an exporter of both labor services and capital services is revealed by trade to be relatively capital abundant if the capital intensity of net exports exceeds the capital intensity of consumption, $K_T/L_T > K_c/L_c$, and a country which is an importer of both capital and labor services is revealed by trade to be capital abundant if the capital intensity of net exports is less than the capital intensity of consumption, $K_T/L_T < K_c/L_c$.[1]

Inequalities (3a), (3b), and (3c) identify three equivalent ways of computing trade-revealed factor abundance. Trade even more directly reveals relative capital abundance if the services of one factor are exported and the services of the other are imported, since inequality (3b) is satisfied if $K_T > 0$ and $L_T < 0$ and is violated if $K_T < 0$ and $L_T > 0$. For reference, this will be stated as a corollary.

COROLLARY 2: If the net export of capital services and the net export of labor services are opposite in sign, then the factor with positive net exports is revealed to be the relatively abundant factor.

Corollaries 1 and 2 imply that one should be examining the factor content of net exports, but the tradition beginning with Leontief is to distinguish exports from imports. In some cases, this is an equivalent procedure.

COROLLARY 3: Given that the net export of capital services and the net export of labor services are opposite in sign, then the capital per man embodied in exports (K_x/L_x) exceeds the capital per man embodied in imports (K_m/L_m) if and only if the country is relatively abundant in capital, $K_i/K_w > L_i/L_w$.

Proof: Suppose first that $K_T > 0$ and $L_T < 0$; then by corollary 2, $K_i/K_w > L_i/L_w$. But $0 < K_T = K_x - K_m$ implies $K_x/K_m > 1$, and $0 > L_T = L_x - L_m$ implies $1 > L_x/L_m$. Thus $K_x/K_m > L_x/L_m$, and $K_x/L_x > K_m/L_m$. Similarly $K_T < 0$ and $L_T > 0$ imply both $K_i/K_w < L_i/L_w$ and $K_x/L_x < K_m/L_m$.

---

[1]It may be observed that Williams (1970) uses (2) to form his equation (23): $(K_w - K_i)/K_i = (1/\alpha_i) - [(K_T + \alpha_i K_i)/\alpha_i K_i]$, which he calls the "plentifulness ratio." This formula suggests erroneously that the consumption share α_i is necessary to infer the relative abundance of capital. Moreover, Williams (1970, p. 121) reports that "the percentage of United States net capital, labour and natural resources exported as 7.14, 4.24, and 3.55, respectively. Intuition would suggest that, under these circumstances the United States must be implicitly plentiful in capital." Actually, this is enough (see his eq. 36) to establish the capital abundance of the United States, given $K_T > 0, L_T > 0$. This is discussed further below.

A substantial practical defect of corollary 3 is that it assumes that K_T and L_T are opposite in sign. In fact, using Leontief's 1947 data, K_T and L_T are both positive: The United States exported both capital services and labor services. In that event, the ordering $K_x/L_x < K_m/L_m$ reveals nothing about the relative magnitudes of K_i/K_w and L_i/L_w.

COROLLARY 4: If there are more than two commodities, the ordering of exports and imports by factor intensity, say $K_x/L_x > K_m/L_m$, is compatible with either order of factor abundance, $K_i/K_w < L_i/L_w$ or $K_i/K_w > L_i/L_w$.

Proof: An example of the "paradoxical" case $K_x/L_x < K_m/L_m$ and $K_i/K_w > L_i/L_w$ will suffice. Let the factor requirements matrix be given as

$$A = \begin{bmatrix} 4 & 1 & 1 \\ 3 & 2 & .5 \\ 1 & 0 & 3 \end{bmatrix}$$

where the first row corresponds to capital inputs, the second row to labor inputs, and the third to land inputs. Suppose that the output vectors are given by

$$Q_i = (8, 16, 5)'$$

and

$$Q_w = (12, 68, 52)'.$$

The endowment vectors are then

$$AQ_i = E_i = (53, 58.5, 23)'$$

and

$$AQ_w = E_w = (168, 198, 168)'.$$

If the prices of the commodities are all one, then trade balance, $0 = 1'T_i$, implies

$$\alpha_i = \frac{1'Q_i}{1'Q_w} = \frac{29}{132} = .22.$$

Using this, and the endowment vectors, we can compute the excess factor supplies

$$(E_i - \alpha_i E_w)' = (53, 58.5, 23) - .22(168, 198, 168)$$
$$= (16.04, 14.94, - 13.96).$$

Therefore, country i, on net, exports the services of both capital and labor and imports the services of land. The commodity trade vector implied by the above system is

$$T_i = (5.36, 1.04, - 6.44)'.$$

Partitioning this into two vectors, exports (X_i) and imports (M_i), we obtain

$$X_i = (5.36, 1.04, 0)'$$

and

$$M_i = (0, 0, 6.44)'.$$

Computing the factor content of exports and imports separately we have

$$AX_i = (22.48, 18.16, 5.36)'$$

and

$$AM_i = (6.44, 3.22, 19.32)'.$$

Thus, for example, country i exports 22.64 units of capital and imports 6.44 units. Computing the capital-labor content ratio we obtain

$$\lambda = \frac{(K_x/L_x)}{(K_m/L_m)} = \frac{1.24}{2} = .62,$$

which is less than one. From this we might, as does Leontief, erroneously conclude that capital is scarce relative to labor in this country. However, the true ordering of factor abundance is given by the ratio of country i's endowment to the world's endowment. Computing these ratios for each factor we obtain

$$\frac{K_i}{K_w} = .315,$$

$$\frac{L_i}{L_w} = .295.$$

This ranking indicates that contrary to the inference based on λ, the country is *abundant* in capital relative to labor.

Corollary 4 indicates that Leontief's method of computing trade-revealed factor abundance orderings is erroneous. However, in the unlikely world of two commodities, it is a correct method.

COROLLARY 5: If there are only two commodities, and if one is exported and the other is imported, the ordering of exports and imports by capital intensity is the same as the ordering of factor abundance; that is, $K_x/L_x \geq K_m/L_m$ if and only if $K_i/K_w \geq L_i/L_w$.

Proof: It is necessary to show that a capital-abundant country exports the capital-intensive good, assuming one good is exported and the other is imported. If X and M are the quantity of exports and imports, then equation (1) can be written as

$$A_{Kx}X - A_{Km}M = K_i - \alpha_i K_w,$$

$$A_{Lx}X - A_{Lm}M = L_i - \alpha_i L_w.$$

The ordering $K_i/K_w \geq L_i/L_w$ is equivalent to $(A_{Kx}X - A_{Km}M)/K_w \geq (A_{Lx}X - A_{Lm}M)/L_w$, which can be rewritten as

$$X\left(\frac{A_{Kx}}{A_{Lx}} - \frac{K_w}{L_w}\right) \geq M\left(\frac{A_{Km}}{A_{Lm}} - \frac{K_w}{L_w}\right)\left(\frac{A_{Lm}}{A_{Lx}}\right).$$

The world's capital-labor ratio K_w/L_w must be between the industry intensity ratios A_{Kx}/A_{Lx} and A_{Km}/A_{Lm}, which implies that the left or right sides of the inequality above are opposite in sign, which is compatible only with $A_{Kx}/A_{Lx} > A_{Km}/A_{Lm}$. Thus $K_i/K_w \geq L_i/L_w$ is equivalent to $A_{Kx}/A_{Lx} > A_{Km}/A_{Lm}$.

II. LEONTIEF'S DATA REEXAMINED

Tables 1, 2, and 3 contain information extracted from Leontief (1954) and from Travis (1964). Table 1 is Leontief's basic summary table, which reveals that $K_x/L_x < K_m/L_m$. But Table 2 indicates that the United States in 1947 was a net exporter of both capital services and labor services. For this reason, the information contained in Table 1 does not reveal the relative factor abundance of capital and labor (see corollary 4). The appropriate comparison, as described in corollary 1, is reported in Table 3. Since net exports are much more capital intensive than consumption, the United States is revealed by its trade to be relatively well endowed in capital compared with labor.[2]

Finally, it is necessary to comment on why the United States had such a large trade surplus according to the data in Table 2. This is partly due to the fact that "noncompeting" imports, such as coffee, tea, and jute, have been eliminated from the vector of imports. It is

TABLE 1

DOMESTIC CAPITAL AND LABOR REQUIREMENTS PER MILLION DOLLARS OF UNITED STATES EXPORTS AND OF COMPETITIVENESS IMPORT REPLACEMENTS (OF AVERAGE 1947 COMPOSITION)

	Exports	Imports
Capital ($, 1947 prices)	2,550,780	3,091,339
Labor (man-years)	182.313	170.004

Source: Leontief (1954, sec. VI).

TABLE 2

ADDITIONAL INFORMATION ON TRADE AND ENDOWMENTS

Trade or factor	Value
Exports	$16,678.4 million
Imports (competitive)	$ 6,175.7 million
Net exports of capital services (K_T)	$23,450 million
Net exports of labor services (L_T)	1.990 million man-years
Capital-labor intensity of trade (K_T/L_T)	$11,783 /man-year

Source: Leontief (1954, table 2, n.).

TABLE 3

CAPITAL INTENSITY OF CONSUMPTION, PRODUCTION, AND TRADE

	Production	Net Exports	Consumption*
Capital	$328.519 million	$23,450 million	$305,069 million
Labor	47.273 million man-years	1.99 million man-years	45.28 million man-years
Capital/labor	$6,949/man-year	$11,783/man-year	$6,737/man-year

Source: For production figures, Travis (1964).
*Uses the identity, Consumption = Production − Net Exports.

difficult to find a theoretically sound justification for this procedure. The HOV theorem uses the factor-price-equalization theorem, which requires incomplete specialization. It is necessary, therefore, to imagine that the United States in fact produces at least small amounts of coffee, tea, and jute, and so forth. It is natural to suppose that the production of these commodities uses capital, labor, and "tropical land" which is very scarce in the United States. But any capital and labor embodied in the imports of "noncompeting" goods should be included in the above calculations. May we suppose that these products are labor intensive, which works also to explain the Leontief paradox?

REFERENCES

Baldwin, Robert E. "Determinants of the Commodity Structure of U.S. Trade." *A.E.R.* 61 (March 1971): 126–46.

Leontief, Wassily. "Domestic Production and Foreign Trade: The American Capital Position Reexamined." *Econ. Internazionale* 7 (February 1954): 3–32. Reprinted in Readings *in International Economics*, edited by Richard E. Caves and Harry G. Johnson. Homewood, Ill.: Irwin, 1968.

Travis, William P. *The Theory of Trade and Protection.* Cambridge, Mass.: Harvard Univ. Press, 1964.

Vanek, Jaroslav. "The Factor Proportions Theory: The N-Factor Case." *Kyklos* 21 (October 1968): 749–54.

Williams, James R. "The Resource Content in International Trade." *Canadian J. Econ.* 3 (February 1970): 111–22.

[2]Baldwin's (1971) finding that the Leontief paradox holds also for 1962 data cannot be explained away so easily. Baldwin reports capital in 1958 dollars embodied in a million (1958) dollars of imports and exports to be $2,132,000 and $1,876,000, respectively. The corresponding man-year figures are 119 and 131. Merchandise exports in millions of 1962 dollars were 20,781 and merchandise imports were 16,260. As in 1947 the United States was a net exporter of both capital services and labor services, $K_T > 0, L_T > 0$, but the ratio had fallen to $K_T/L_T = \$5,579$ in 1958 dollars per man year. This number falls below Travis's estimate of the 1947 capital per man equal to $6,949/man year and is likely to fall below any estimates for 1962 as well.

ABOUT THE AUTHOR

Edward E. Leamer

Edward Leamer is the Chauncey J. Medberry Professor of Management, Professor of Economics, Professor of Statistics, and Director of the Business Forecast Project at the University of California at Los Angeles (UCLA). He received a B.A. in mathematics from Princeton, a Ph.D. in economics and an M.A. in mathematics from the University of Michigan. After serving as assistant and associate professor at Harvard University, he joined UCLA in 1975 as professor of economics and served as chair from 1983 to 1987. Professor Leamer is a fellow of the American Academy of Arts and Sciences, and a fellow of the Econometric Society.

Editor's Queries
What advice do you have to offer graduate students in the field of international economics? Find your passion and pursue it. The Epicureans tell us "pleasure, not truth, is the end aim of life," to which I would add "truth is pleasure." If things go well, you will be asked to edit a volume of readings and you can stuff it full of your own works.

The Case of the Missing Trade and Other Mysteries

DANIEL TREFLER

Harris Graduate School of Public Policy Studies, University of Chicago,
Department of Economics, University of Toronto

The Heckscher-Ohlin-Vanek (HOV) theorem, which predicts that
countries will export products that are made from factors in great supply,
performs poorly. However, deviations from HOV follow pronounced
patterns. Trade is missing relative to its HOV prediction. Also, rich
countries appear scarce in most factors and poor countries appear
abundant in all factors, a fact that squares poorly with the HOV
prediction that abundant factors are exported. As suggested by the
patterns, HOV is rejected empirically in favor of a modification that
allows for home bias in consumption and international technology
differences. (JEL F11, F14)

What is known about international trade in factor services? Theoretically, the Heckscher-Ohlin theorem states that a capital-abundant country exports the capital-intensive good. Its generalization, the Heckscher-Ohlin-Vanek (HOV) theorem, states that a capital-abundant country exports capital services (see Eli F. Heckscher, 1919; Bertil G. Ohlin, 1933; Paul A. Samuelson, 1948; James R. Melvin, 1968; Jaroslav Vanek, 1968; Edward E. Leamer, 1980). Empirically, the HOV theorem has been repeatedly rejected over the years and rightfully so: it performs horribly. Factor endowments correctly predict the direction of factor service trade about 50 percent of the time, a success rate that is matched by a coin toss. Since the HOV theorem extends to a variety of models displaying increasing returns to scale and imperfect competition (Elhanan Helpman and Paul R. Krugman, 1985), this poor performance has distressing implications for these

I am indebted to Werner Antweiler, Jr. for jointly pursuing the empirical work in an earlier version
of this paper. Harry Bowen, Edward Leamer, and Leo Sveikauskas encouraged and helped in my
critique of their work. I am grateful to the anonymous referees for suggesting substantive improvements. I benefited from seminar presentations at the NBER, the University of British Columbia,
the University of Chicago, the University of Minnesota, MIT, the University of Pennsylvania, and
the University of Wisconsin, especially from the comments of Robert Staiger. Research was supported by the Social Sciences and Humanities Research Council (SSHRC) of Canada.

trade theories as well. In other fields of economics, the poor performance of a major theory leads to more careful consideration of the data and to new theories that can accommodate the anomalies. Yet years of research into why the HOV theorem performs poorly has only produced conjectures. It has not provided a deeper understanding of factor service trade, nor has it identified an alternative hypothesis that performs better. These two failings are the subject of this paper.

First, almost nothing is known about the features of factor service trade that are inconsistent with the HOV theorem. An exception is the Leontief paradox. However, it deals with only two of many factors in only one of many countries; that is, the United States exports too much labor and too little capital. Also, it is not a paradox (Leamer, 1980), and it disappeared from the data at least 20 years ago (Robert M. Stern and Keith E. Maskus, 1981). Thus, with the exception of a few laconic and outdated references, nothing is known. A goal of this paper is to demonstrate that the HOV theorem is rejected because factor service trade departs from its endowments-based prediction in *systematic* and informative ways.

Understanding trade in factor services rather than trade in goods is not simply an academic exercise; it is central to the conduct of trade policy. For example, the number of cars the United States imports from Japan is uninteresting in and of itself. It takes on importance because of its factor-market consequences: the U.S. jobs displaced and the effect on wages, the supplanted investment, and the effect on rates of return to capital. These are concerns about factor service trade.

Second, is there a general equilibrium model of factor service trade that is known to perform better than the HOV theorem? The answer is no. The HOV theorem has frequently been rejected in favor of statistical hypotheses such as a zero correlation (e.g., Maskus, 1985; Richard A. Brecher and Ehsan U. Choudhri, 1988; Robert W. Staiger, 1988). This is valuable for showing how poorly the HOV theorem performs but cannot be used to identify economically meaningful models that perform better than the theorem. Harry P. Bowen et al. (1987) pioneered a method for testing the HOV hypothesis against economic alternatives, only to arrive at a negative conclusion: "The Heckscher-Ohlin model does poorly, but we do not have anything that does better. It is easy to find hypotheses that do as well or better in a statistical sense, but these alternatives yield economically unsatisfying parameter estimates" (p. 805). A second goal of this paper is to identify economic hypotheses that perform better than the HOV theorem. Adopting the Bowen et al. method, I consider a large number of hypotheses, including ones with capital accumulation, nontradables, trade in services, and linear expenditure demand. The model that clearly dominates the HOV theorem allows for home bias in consumption (Paul S. Armington, 1969) and international differences in technology. The systematic departures from the HOV theorem noted above are used to explain why some hypotheses perform well and others do not. Along the way I explain Staiger's (1988) result that HOV model is misspecified and overturn the Bowen et al. (1987) result that no simple modification of the HOV theorem performs well.

A number of citations serve to demarcate the area of study. First, this paper provides a logically complete test of the HOV theorem in the Leamer and Bowen (1981) sense that it uses data on technology, trade, and endowments. Much of the literature relating to the theorem only used two of these three (e.g., Wassily W. Leontief, 1953; Leamer, 1984). Second, this paper is related to a previous work of mine (Trefler, 1993) dealing with international factor-price differences. In that work I considered a variant of the HOV model that allows for international productivity differences. The variant necessarily fits the trade and endowments data perfectly, thus ruling out hypothesis-testing. In contrast, hypothesis-testing is central to what follows. Also, in what follows I cover a wide range of alternative hypotheses and use the systematic patterns in the deviations from the HOV theorem to identify many models that perform poorly and two models that perform well. In contrast, my previous work only examined one model.

I. TESTING THE HOV THEOREM AGAINST STATISTICAL ALTERNATIVES

Let $c = 1, ..., C$ index countries and $f = 1, ..., F$ index factors. Let V_{fc} be the endowment of factor f in country c and let $V_{fw} = \Sigma_c V_{fc}$ be world factor endowments. Let F_{fc} be the factor content of net exports, that is, the amount of factor f needed to produce the net exports of country c. Let $s_c = (Y_c - B_c)/Y_w$ be the consumption share of country c where B_c is the trade balance, Y_c is gross national product (GNP), and $Y_w = \Sigma_c Y_c$. The following "HOV equation" is implied by the usual HOV assumptions (see, for example, Leamer [1980] or the proof below of a more general result):

$$F_{fc} = V_{fc} - s_c V_{fw} \qquad f = 1, ..., F \qquad c = 1, ..., C. \tag{1}$$

It states that if country c is abundant in factor $f(V_{fc}/V_{fw} > s_c)$, then it exports the services of factor f $(F_{fc} > 0)$.

The following data will be used to investigate this HOV equation. All data are from 1983 unless indicated otherwise. There are 33 countries in the sample which together account for 76 percent of world exports and 79 percent of world GNP. The choice of countries was largely dictated by the availability of trade data at a detailed industry level. There are nine factors: capital, cropland, pasture, and six categories of labor. The labor categories are professional and technical workers, clerical workers, sales workers, service workers, agriculture workers, and production, transport, and unskilled workers.[1] Under the usual HOV assumptions the factor content of trade is $(F_{1c}, ..., F_{Fc})' = \mathbf{A}\mathbf{T}_c$ where $\mathbf{T}_c$ is the vector of net commodity exports and $\mathbf{A}$ is the "technology

---

[1] Administrative and managerial workers, forests, oil, coal, and minerals have been used in other studies but were not included in this study. The results are similar when all these factors are included in the analysis, except as noted in part 7 of the Appendix. Nevertheless, they were omitted either on theoretical grounds or because of concerns about data quality.

matrix" giving the amount of each factor needed to produce one unit of each commodity. A was built using the 1983 U.S. input–output total-requirements table and data on factor usage by industry from various 1982 U.S. industry censuses and the 1983 Annual Survey of Manufactures. The usual caveat about using U.S. technology to evaluate the factor content of non-U.S. trade applies here, albeit with less force since below the technology matrix will be modified in a country-specific fashion. The relevant data are detailed in Trefler (1993).

Factors must be expressed in comparable units in order to satisfy the statistical hypothesis of homoscedasticity. To this end let ε_{fc} be the deviations from the HOV theorem:

$$\varepsilon_{fc} = F_{fc} - (V_{fc} - s_c V_{fw}). \tag{2}$$

Fix f and let σ_f be the standard error of the ε_{fc}: $\sigma_f^2 = \Sigma_c (\varepsilon_{fc} - \bar{\varepsilon}_f)^2/(C - 1)$ where $\bar{\varepsilon}_f = \Sigma_c \varepsilon_{fc}/C$. I scale all data relating to factor f by σ_f so that factors are expressed in statistically comparable units. In addition, to control for country size I scale by $s_c^{1/2}$. Hence, throughout this paper observation (f, c) is scaled by $\sigma_f s_c^{1/2}$. (See part 8 of the Appendix for additional discussion of scaling.)

From equation (1), the simple correlation between F_{fc} and $V_{fc} - s_c V_{fw}$ provides a test of the HOV equation against a statistical alternative. With nine factors and 33 countries there are 297 observations. The resulting correlation is 0.28, which is statistically significant but hardly impressive. An alternative statistic follows from a weaker statement of the HOV theorem: country c exports the services of its abundant factors and imports the services of its scarce factors. That is, $F_{fc} > 0$ if and only if $V_{fc} - s_c V_{fw} > 0$. I call this "sign HOV." Bowen et al. (1987) reported the percentage of observations for which F_{fc} and $V_{fc} - s_c V_{fw}$ have the same sign. Under the sign-HOV hypothesis, the statistic equals 100 percent. In fact, it equals 49.8 percent (148/297), which means that the HOV prediction is about as good as a coin toss. The sign statistic treats all observations equally. An alternative is to attach more weight to observations with large net factor contents of trade, that is, to weight the sign statistic by

$$|F_{fc}| \Big/ \sum_{f,c} |F_{fc}|.$$

The weighted statistic equals 71 percent. That is, the sign-HOV hypothesis is more accurate when net factor service trade flows are large. Nevertheless, the statistic of 71 percent is far from the HOV null of 100 percent and uncomfortably close to the coin-toss alternative of 50 percent. In short, the HOV theorem performs poorly.

II. A View Through the HOV Window

In order to investigate the failure of the HOV theorem, consider its deviations, $\varepsilon_{fc} = F_{fc} - (V_{fc} - s_c V_{fw})$. Surprisingly, plots of factor service trade against endowments have never been reported. Figure 1 plots ε_{fc} against $V_{fc} - s_c V_{fw}$. Points to the right of the

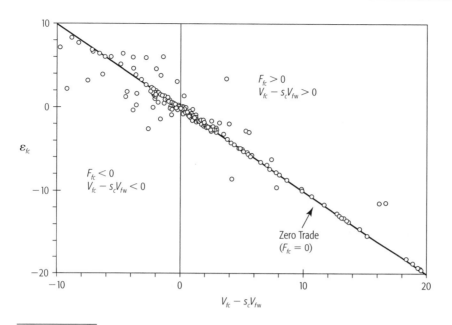

Figure 1

Plot of $\varepsilon_{fc} = F_{fc} - (V_{fc} - s_c V_{fw})$ against $V_{fc} - s_c V_{fw}$

vertical line $V_{fc} - s_c V_{fw} = 0$ correspond to abundant factors. The diagonal line is $\varepsilon_{fc} = -(V_{fc} - s_c V_{fw})$ or $F_{fc} = 0$ so that points above it correspond to $F_{fc} > 0$. The sign-HOV theorem predicts that all observations will lie in two of the four demarcated areas, either where $F_{fc} > 0$ and $V_{fc} - s_c V_{fw} > 0$ or where $F_{fc} < 0$ and $V_{fc} - s_c V_{fw} < 0$. Only half of the observations lie in these areas. Under the HOV equation (1), $F_{fc} = V_{fc} - s_c V_{fw}$ or $\varepsilon_{fc} = 0$; that is, all the observations lie on a horizontal line at zero. Nothing like this pattern emerges.

The main feature of Figure 1 is that all the observations lie close to the $F_{fc} = 0$ line (12 observations far from the origin were truncated, but all of these lie close to the $F_{fc} = 0$ line). In absolute values, factor service trade is much smaller than its factor-endowments prediction. I call this phenomenon "the case of the missing trade." A similar phenomenon appears in the Bowen et al. (1987) data for 1966–1967.

Further patterns in the deviations from HOV appear when the data are examined by country. The left panel of Figure 2 displays the number of negative deviations ($\varepsilon_{fc} < 0$) per country. With nine factors this number lies between 0 and 9. Countries are sorted by purchasing-power-parity (PPP) adjusted per capita GDP from the Penn World Tables. Poor countries tend to have negative deviations, and rich countries tend to have positive deviations. The correlation of the number of negative deviations per country with per capita GDP is 0.87. Since F_{fc} is typically "small," results about $\varepsilon_{fc} = F_{fc} - (V_{fc} - s_c V_{fw})$ are

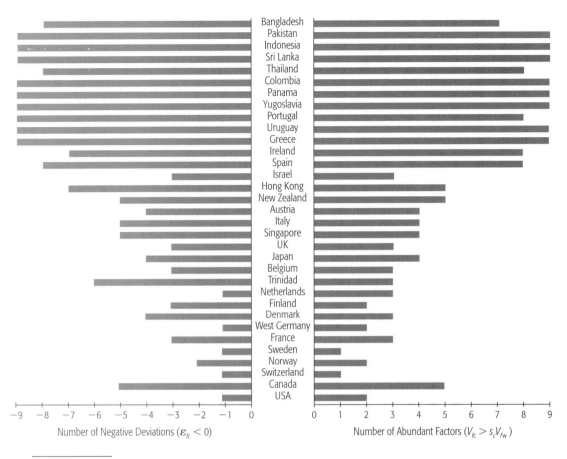

Figure 2

Deviations from HOV and Factor Abundance

likely to be reflected in $V_{fc} - s_c V_{fw}$. The right panel of Figure 2 displays the number of abundant factors per country. Rich countries tend to be scarce in most factors, and poor countries tend to be abundant in all factors. The correlation with per capita GDP is -0.89. I call this phenomenon "the endowments paradox." It appears in the Leontief (1953) data for 1947 (recall that Leamer [1980] showed the United States to be scarce in both labor and capital), in the Bowen et al. (1987) data for 1966–1967, in the Leamer (1984) data for 1958 and 1975, and in the Maskus (1991) data for 1984. It may also underpin Staiger's (1988) observation that country-specific deviations from the HOV theorem are correlated with country-specific data on endowments and size.

Ranking factors in order of abundance for country c, the HOV theorem may be illustrated as in Figure 3. Note that s_c puts a break in the Vanek chain that distinguishes scarce imported factors from abundant exported factors. Figure 2 shows that s_c often lies

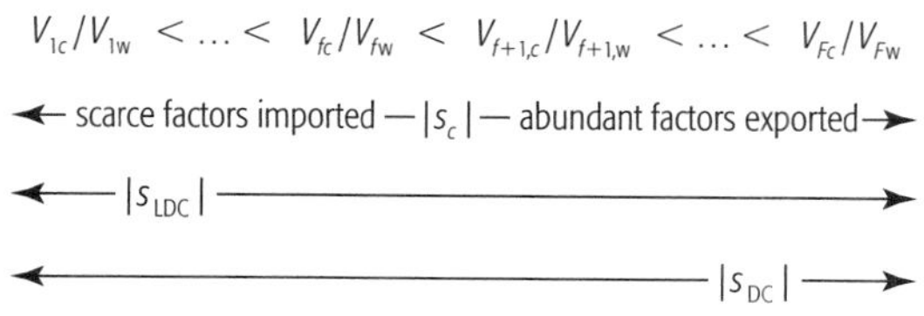

$$V_{1c}/V_{1w} < ... < V_{fc}/V_{fw} < V_{f+1,c}/V_{f+1,w} < ... < V_{Fc}/V_{Fw}$$

← scarce factors imported — $|s_c|$ — abundant factors exported →

← $|s_{LDC}|$ →

← $|s_{DC}|$ →

Figure 3

Factor Abundance and Scarcity

either to the extreme right or extreme left of this ranking, thus undermining the HOV theorem. This is illustrated in Figure 3 where LDC and DC denote poor and rich countries, respectively. There are two explanations for this: trade imbalances and omitted factors. This follows from the relationship $\Sigma_f w_{fc}(V_{fc} - s_c V_{fw}) = B_c$ where w_{fc} is the price of factor f in country c. Hence, if there were no omitted factors and $B_c = 0$, then country c could not be abundant or scarce in all factors. The pattern of Figure 2 would occur if rich countries ran trade deficits ($B_c < 0$) and poor countries ran trade surpluses ($B_c > 0$). If anything, the opposite is true: the rank correlation of B_c with per capita GDP is 0.14. Thus, unless there are omitted factors that are scarce in poor countries, the pattern in the right panel of Figure 2 is inconsistent with the spirit and the letter of a theory whose cornerstone is factor abundance.

III. ECONOMICALLY MEANINGFUL ALTERNATIVE HYPOTHESES: TECHNOLOGY

It remains to search for economically meaningful alternatives to the HOV theorem that can account for the case of the missing trade and the endowments paradox. In this section I consider alternatives that modify the technology assumptions of the HOV theorem; in the next I consider alternatives that modify the consumption assumptions.

A. THEORY

Let f_{ic} be the production function for good i in country c. Let $\mathbf{a}_{ic}$ be a typical $F \times 1$ column of the technology matrix $\mathbf{A}_c$ giving the amounts of each factor needed to produce one unit of good i. By definition, $f_{ic}(\mathbf{a}_{ic}) = 1$. I assume that international technology differences (the c subscript in f_{ic}) are factor-augmenting. That is, $f_{ic}(\mathbf{a}_{ic}) = f_i(\mathbf{\Pi}_c \mathbf{a}_{ic})$ for some internationally common production functions f_i and diagonal matrices $\mathbf{\Pi}_c = \text{diag}(\pi_{1c}, ..., \pi_{Fc})$. Since $f_i(\mathbf{\Pi}_c \mathbf{a}_{ic}) = 1$, the larger an element of $\mathbf{\Pi}_c$, the smaller is the corresponding element of $\mathbf{a}_{ic}$. In other words, larger $\mathbf{\Pi}_c$'s correspond to fewer inputs per unit of output or greater productivity. Without loss of generality $\mathbf{\Pi}_{US}$ is taken to be the identity matrix so that π_{fc} is the productivity of factor f in country c relative to U.S. productivity.

Let w_{fc} be the price of factor f in country c and $\mathbf{w}_c = (w_{1c}, ..., w_{Fc})'$, where a prime denotes matrix transposition. If U.K. labor were half as productive as U.S. labor ($\pi_{L,UK} = \frac{1}{2}$), then one would expect U.K. wages to be half of U.S. wages: $w_{L,UK} = \pi_{L,UK} w_{L,US}$. More generally, assume $w_{fc} = \pi_{fc} w_{fUS}$ or, in matrix notation, $\mathbf{w}_c = \Pi_c \mathbf{w}_{US}$. Support for this variant of factor price equalization is the main result in Trefler (1993).

Assuming that all goods are produced in all countries, that product prices are the same internationally, and that profits are zero, it follows that unit costs are the same internationally: $c_{iUS}(\mathbf{w}_{US}) = c_{ic}(\mathbf{w}_c)$. Differentiating with respect to $\mathbf{w}_{US}$ yields $A_{US}(\mathbf{w}_{US}) = \Pi_c A_c(\mathbf{w}_c)$.[2] Thus, given knowledge of Π_c and U.S. data, one can infer $A_c(\mathbf{w}_c) = \Pi_c^{-1} A_{US}(\mathbf{w}_{US})$ even if neither A_c nor $\mathbf{w}_c$ is observed. This fact allows me to place the discussion of factor prices in the background and to simply assume $A_{US} = \Pi_c A_c$.

Under this assumption the HOV equation (1) is replaced by

$$F_{fc}^{US} = \pi_{fc} V_{fc} - s_c \sum_j \pi_{fj} V_{fj} \qquad (3)$$

where $\mathbf{F}_c^{US} = (F_{1c}^{US}, ..., F_{Fc}^{US})' = A_{US} \mathbf{T}_c$ is the factor content of country c's net exports when calculated using U.S. technology.[3] F_{fc}^{US}/π_{fc} answers the important policy question about the quantity of domestic factors embodied in trade had imports been produced domestically.

A problem with equation (3) is that it has as many parameters as observations (FC) and so necessarily fits the data perfectly (i.e., it cannot be tested against the HOV equation). One approach to overfitting restricts the way the π_{fc} vary across factors: $\pi_{fc} = \delta_c$ for all f and c. The δ_c are Hicks-neutral factor-augmenting productivity measures. This yields

$$F_{fc}^{US} = \delta_c V_{fc} - s_c \sum_j \delta_j V_{fj} \qquad (4)$$

where $\delta_{US} = 1$.

A second approach restricts the way the π_{fc} vary across countries. The extreme restriction that $\pi_{fc} = \phi_f$ for all f and c (except $\pi_{fUS} = 1$) performs poorly empirically. An alternative is to divide the countries in the sample into two groups: poor countries that share one set of nonneutrality parameters and rich countries that share a different set of nonneutrality parameters. For example, this allows the French capital–labor ratio in agriculture to be similar to the corresponding German ratio and different from the

---

[2] To see this, note that $\partial c_{ic}(\mathbf{w}_c)/\partial \mathbf{w}_c = \mathbf{a}'_{ic}(\mathbf{w}_c)$ where a prime denotes matrix transposition. Differentiating $c_{iUS}(\mathbf{w}_{US}) = c_{ic}(\mathbf{w}_c)$ with respect to the vector w_{US} yields $\mathbf{a}'_{iUS}(\mathbf{w}_{US}) = \mathbf{a}'_{ic}(\mathbf{w}_c)\partial \mathbf{w}_c/\partial \mathbf{w}_{US} = \mathbf{a}'_{ic}(\mathbf{w}_c)\Pi_c$. Transposing, $\mathbf{a}_{iUS}(\mathbf{w}_{US}) = \Pi_c \mathbf{a}_{ic}(\mathbf{w}_c)$. Since $\mathbf{a}_{ic}$ is a column of A_c, $A_{US}(\mathbf{w}_{US}) = \Pi_c A_c(\mathbf{w}_c)$, as required.

[3] The proof of equation (3) is as follows. Let $\mathbf{Q}_c$ and $\mathbf{C}_c$ be vectors of production and consumption, respectively; let $\mathbf{V}_c = (V_{1c}, ..., V_{Fc})'$, and define $\mathbf{Q}_w = \Sigma_c \mathbf{Q}_c$, $\mathbf{C}_w = \Sigma_c \mathbf{C}_c$, and $\mathbf{V}_w = \Sigma_c \mathbf{V}_c$. By definition, $\mathbf{T}_c = \mathbf{Q}_c - \mathbf{C}_c$ so that $\mathbf{F}_c^{US} = A_{US}(\mathbf{Q}_c - \mathbf{C}_c)$. From preference homotheticity and world goods-market equilibrium $\mathbf{C}_c = s_c \mathbf{C}_w = s_c \mathbf{Q}_w$ so that $\mathbf{F}_c^{US} = A_{US}(\mathbf{Q}_c - s_c \mathbf{Q}_w)$. $A_c = \Pi^{-1} A_{US}$ and factor-market clearing, $A_c \mathbf{Q}_c = \mathbf{V}_c$ imply $A_{US} \mathbf{Q}_c = \Pi_c \mathbf{V}_c$ and $A_{US} \mathbf{Q}_w = \Sigma_j \Pi_j \mathbf{V}_j$ so that $\mathbf{F}_c^{US} = \Pi_c \mathbf{V}_c - s_c \Sigma_j \Pi_j \mathbf{V}_j$. This last is the matrix counterpart of equation (3).

Bangladeshi ratio. Let C_{DC} be the set of rich countries. This includes the United States with its $\pi_{f\text{US}} = 1$ so that $\pi_{fc} = 1$ for $c \in C_{\text{DC}}$. Let C_{LDC} be the set of poor countries: they share a common π_{fc} so that $\pi_{fc} = \phi_f$ for $c \in C_{\text{LDC}}$.

A third approach combines the neutral (δ_c) and nonneutral (ϕ_f) technology differences: $\pi_{fc} = \delta_c \phi_f$ for $c \in C_{\text{LDC}}$, $\pi_{fc} = \delta_c$ for $c \in C_{\text{DC}}$ and $\delta_{\text{US}} = 1$. To distinguish between average or neutral effects (δ_c) and nonneutral effects (ϕ_f) impose the identifying restriction $\Sigma_f \phi_f / F = 1$.[4] Then equation (3) becomes

$$F_{fc}^{\text{US}} = \begin{cases} \delta_c \phi_f V_{fc} - s_c \displaystyle\sum_{j \in C_{\text{LDC}}} \delta_j \phi_f V_{fj} - s_c \displaystyle\sum_{j \in C_{\text{DC}}} \delta_j V_{fj} & c \in C_{\text{LDC}} \\[2em] \delta_c V_{fc} - s_c \displaystyle\sum_{j \in C_{\text{LDC}}} \delta_j \phi_f V_{fj} - s_c \displaystyle\sum_{j \in C_{\text{DC}}} \delta_j V_{fj} & c \in C_{\text{DC}}. \end{cases} \tag{5}$$

To operationalize C_{LDC} fix a constant κ, let y_c be per capita GDP, and let country c be a member of $C_{\text{LDC}}(\kappa)$ if $y_c < \kappa$. Then κ will be estimated along with the δ_c and ϕ_f parameters. In principle there can be as many groupings of countries as is desired, and the groupings need not be along development lines. For example, it is a priori plausible to have three groups: the United States, other rich countries, and poor countries. However, distinguishing the United States from the other rich countries is statistically rejected by the data. Thus, equation (5) is sensible as judged by parsimony, the importance of the technology gap between developed and developing countries, and the correlation of deviations from HOV with per capita GDP.

B. RESULTS

Even if equation (5) held exactly, errors in measuring observables (F_{fc}^{US}, V_{fc}, s_c) would obscure this fact and lead one to estimate "best" values for unobservables (δ_c, ϕ_f). There are five potential sources of error: each of F_{fc}^{US}, V_{fc}, and s_c mismeasured, omitted factors, and omitted countries. In parts 1–4 of the Appendix, I show that results are remarkably similar across the five specifications of error. Thus, in this section I simply assume that only F_{fc}^{US} is mismeasured: $F_{fc}^m = F_{fc}^{\text{US}} + \mu_{fc}$ where F_{fc}^m is the measure and μ_{fc} is measurement error. Then equation (5) becomes

$$F_{fc}^m = \begin{cases} \delta_c \phi_f V_{fc} - s_c \displaystyle\sum_{j \in C_{\text{LDC}}} \delta_j \phi_f V_{fj} - s_c \displaystyle\sum_{j \in C_{\text{DC}}} \delta_j V_{fj} + \mu_{fc} & c \in C_{\text{LDC}} \\[2em] \delta_c V_{fc} - s_c \displaystyle\sum_{j \in C_{\text{LDC}}} \delta_j \phi_f V_{fj} - s_c \displaystyle\sum_{j \in C_{\text{DC}}} \delta_j V_{fj} + \mu_{fc} & c \in C_{\text{DC}} \end{cases} \tag{6}$$

---

[4]If one prefers a normalization other than $\Sigma \phi_f / F = 1$, say, $\Sigma \omega_f \phi_f = 1$ for some reader-chosen weights ω_f that measure the relative importance of factors, then divided each of the estimated ϕ_f in Table 3 by $\Sigma \omega_f \phi_f$ and multiply each of the estimated δ_c ($c \in C_{\text{LDC}}$) in Table 2 by $\Sigma \omega_f \phi_f$.

where $\delta_{US} = 1$ and $\Sigma_f\, \phi_f/F = 1$. I assume that the μ_{fc} are independently and identically distributed normal with mean zero. Adding an intercept ($E\mu_{fc} \neq 0$) makes little difference to the results. Common variance follows from scaling observation (f, c) by $\sigma_f s_c^{1/2}$ (see above).

Table 1 reports statistics for three hypotheses nested within equation (6). The null hypothesis (H_0) is the HOV equation (1). The number of parameters (k_i) is zero. T_1 is the neutral technology-differences model. With 33 countries and $\delta_{US} = 1$, there are 32 parameters. T_2 is the neutral and nonneutral technology-differences model of equation (6). With nine factors and the restriction $\Sigma_f\phi_f/F = 1$, there are eight ϕ_f's as well as κ for a total of 41 parameters. Appropriately parameterized, T_1 is a linear model and I use ordinary least squares (OLS) to estimate it subject to the linear restriction that $\delta_{US} = 1$. T_2 is nonlinear, and I use maximum-likelihood estimation.[5] From Table 1, the likelihood-ratio test rejects H_0 and T_1 in favor of the unrestricted model T_2. The test statistics are $X^2_{[41]} = 974$ and $X^2_{[9]} = 40$, respectively.[6]

The favored model, T_2, is heavily parameterized. A model-selection criterion that penalizes models with many parameters is the Schwarz criterion, here stated as $\ln(L_i) - k_i \ln(FC)/2$ where L_i is the maximized value of the likelihood function under hypothesis i and $FC = 9 \times 33 = 297$ is the number of observations. The Schwarz criterion favors hypotheses with large (close to zero) values of the criterion, namely, T_1.

Table 2 presents the estimates of δ_c from equation (6) for the unrestricted model T_2 and the neutral technology-differences model T_1. Countries are ordered by per capita GDP, y_c; y_c/y_{US} appears in column (i). The estimate of κ (relevant only for hypothesis T_2) implies that the top 10 countries in the table are included in C_{LDC} and that the remaining countries are included in C_{DC}. The δ_c under the two hypotheses are similar, so that attention is restricted to T_1. I offer three criteria for evaluating the reasonableness of the δ_c's.

First, they must be nonnegative; otherwise, factor inputs yield negative outputs. All of the estimated δ_c's are positive.

Second, the United States is among the most productive countries in the world so that δ_c should be less than unity for most countries, as is the case. Arguably, the δ_c's for countries such as Japan and West Germany are too low. Note though that for the

---

[5]Note that κ is equivalent to an integer indicating how many countries will be in C_{LDC}. This integer nature of κ and the implied nondifferentiability of the likelihood function have implications for the asymptotic standard errors of δ_c and ϕ_f, but I have not explored these. Having found the maximum-likelihood estimate of $(\kappa, \delta_c, \phi_f)$, I treated the optimal κ as a fixed constant and calculated the standard errors of (δ_c, ϕ_f) from the second derivative of the log-likelihood function with respect to (δ_c, ϕ_f).

[6]The model with only nonneutral effects (ϕ_f unrestricted and $\delta_c = 1$) is rejected by the data: the likelihood value is -870.

TABLE 1

HYPOTHESIS TESTING AND MODEL SELECTION

Hypothesis	Description		Likelihood		Mysteries		Goodness-of-fit	
	Parameters (k_i)	Equation	$\ln(L_i)$	Schwarz criterion	Endowment paradox	Missing trade	Weighted sign	$\rho(F, \hat{F})$
Endowment differences								
H_0: unmodified HOV theorem	(0)	(1)	$-1{,}007$	$-1{,}007$	-0.89	0.032	0.71	0.28
Technology differences								
T_1: neutral	δ_c (32)	(4)	-540	-632	-0.17	0.486	0.78	0.59
T_2: neutral and nonneutral	$\phi_f, \hat{\delta}_c, \kappa$ (41)	(6)	-520	-637	-0.22	0.506	0.76	0.63
Consumption differences								
C_1: investment/services/nontrade	β_c (32)	(7)	-915	$-1{,}006$	-0.63	0.052	0.73	0.35
C_2: Armington	α_c^* (24)	(11)	-439	-507	-0.42	3.057	0.87	0.55
Technology and consumption								
TC_1: $\delta_c = y_c/y_{US}$	(0)	(4)	-593	-593	-0.10	0.330	0.83	0.59
TC_2: $\delta_c = y_c/y_{US}$ and Armington	α_c^* (24)	(12)	-404	-473	0.18	2.226	0.93	0.67

Notes: Here k_i is the number of estimated parameters under hypothesis i. For "likelihood," $\ln(L_i)$ is the maximized value of the log-likelihood function, and the Schwarz-model selection criterion is $\ln(L_i) - k_i \ln(297)/2$. Let $\hat{F}_{fc}$ be the predicted value of F_{fc}. The "endowment paradox" is the correlation between per capita GDP, y_c, and the number of times $\hat{F}_{fc}$ is positive for country c (see Figure 2). "Missing trade" is the variance of F_{fc} divided by the variance of $\hat{F}_{fc}$ (see Figure 1). "Weighted sign" is the weighted proportion of observations for which F_{fc} and $\hat{F}_{fc}$ have the same sign. Finally, $\rho(F, \hat{F})$ is the correlation between F_{fc} and $\hat{F}_{fc}$. See Section V for further discussion.

TABLE 2

ESTIMATES OF δ_c FOR 1983

Country	y_c/y_{US} (i)	T_1 δ_c (ii)	t (iii)	T_2 δ_c (iv)	t (v)
Bangladesh	0.04	0.03	47.71	0.04	42.28
Pakistan	0.08	0.09	32.10	0.09	34.93
Indonesia	0.11	0.10	39.51	0.13	38.21
Sri Lanka	0.12	0.09	14.85	0.07	20.13
Thailand	0.16	0.17	23.80	0.21	20.17
Colombia	0.21	0.16	18.41	0.29	11.14
Panama	0.23	0.28	3.24	0.24	4.44
Yugoslavia	0.30	0.29	11.35	0.19	18.83
Portugal	0.30	0.14	9.63	0.10	14.78
Uruguay	0.31	0.11	19.46	<u>0.22</u>	9.40
Greece	0.35	0.45	4.63	0.46	4.88
Ireland	0.39	0.55	2.91	0.56	3.08
Spain	0.41	0.42	9.40	0.43	9.88
Israel	0.60	0.49	2.91	0.50	3.03
Hong Kong	0.61	0.40	4.12	0.41	4.35
New Zealand	0.62	0.38	7.89	0.38	8.42
Austria	0.65	0.60	3.03	0.62	3.13
Singapore	0.66	0.48	2.11	0.49	2.20
Italy	0.66	0.60	7.16	0.62	7.38
United Kingdom	0.66	0.58	8.04	0.60	8.30
Japan	0.66	0.70	7.15	0.71	7.25
Belgium	0.67	0.65	2.73	0.66	2.79
Trinidad	0.69	0.47	1.25	0.48	1.30
Netherlands	0.69	0.72	2.66	0.73	2.69
Finland	0.70	0.65	2.17	0.67	2.22
Denmark	0.72	0.73	1.92	0.74	1.94
West Germany	0.73	0.78	3.80	0.80	3.74
France	0.73	0.74	4.84	0.75	4.85
Sweden	0.75	0.57	4.09	0.58	4.25
Norway	0.82	0.69	1.80	0.70	1.83
Switzerland	0.91	0.79	1.41	0.81	1.37
Canada	0.95	0.55	9.82	0.56	10.29
United States	1.00	1.00	—	1.00	—
$\rho(\delta_c, y_c)$:		0.91		0.90	

Notes: Here, t is the asymptotic t statistic for the null hypothesis that $\delta_c = 1$. T_1 and T_2 indicate the restricted ($\phi_f = 1$) and unrestricted estimates, respectively, of equation (6): y_c is per capita GDP; $\rho(\delta_c, y_c)$ is the correlation of δ_c with y_c. The line in column (iv) separates $c \in C_{\text{LDC}}$ from $c \in C_{\text{DC}}$.

TABLE 3

NONNEUTRALITY PARAMETERS ϕ_f UNDER T_2

	T_2	
Factor	ϕ_f	t
Capital	1.89	-2.29
Labor		
Professional and technical	1.47	-1.71
Clerical	1.82	-2.45
Sales	0.37	2.41
Service	0.91	0.36
Agriculture	0.05	4.63
Production and transport	0.74	0.88
Land		
Cropland	1.36	-1.48
Pasture	0.38	4.01

Notes: Here, t is the asymptotic t statistic for the hypothesis $\phi_f = 1$. T_2 indicates the unrestricted estimates of equation (6). It allows for neutral (δ_c) and nonneutral (ϕ_f) technology differences.

countries with the largest δ_c (Switzerland, 0.79; West Germany, 0.78; France, 0.74; Denmark, 0.73; Netherlands, 0.72; Japan, 0.70), the δ_c's are similar, and the hypothesis that they are the same cannot be rejected. This suggests that it is the United States that has the unusual value of δ_c.

Third, international productivity differences should be reflected in international per capita income differences. For example, if West Germany is only 78 percent as productive as the United States ($\delta_{GER} = 0.78$) then one expects West German per capita GDP to be 78 percent of U.S. per capita GDP ($y_{GER}/y_{US} = 0.78$). As expected, the δ_c's are highly correlated with y_c, a remarkable 0.91. A related observation is used by Trefler (1993) in discussing international wage differences.

Table 3 reports the estimated ϕ_f's under hypothesis T_2. They are reasonable in three senses. First, all are positive as required by the theory. Second, let a_{fic} be the amount of factor f needed to produce one unit of good i in country c. Then, for example, a_{Kic}/a_{Lic} is the capital labor ratio in industry i. One expects rich countries to use relatively capital-intensive techniques, that is,

$$a_{Ki,DC}/a_{fi,DC} > a_{Ki,LDC}/a_{fi,LDC}$$

for all i and $f(f \neq K)$. Under hypothesis T_2, this reduces to $\phi_K > \phi_f$ for all $f(f \neq K)$.[7] As indicated in Table 3, the estimated ϕ_f's satisfy this condition. Third, one expects rich

[7]The assumption that $\mathbf{A}_{US} = \Pi_c \mathbf{A}_c$ may be rewritten as $\Pi_{DC}\mathbf{A}_{DC} = \Pi_{LDC}\mathbf{A}_{LDC}$ or $\pi_{f,DC}a_{fi,DC} = \pi_{f,LDC}a_{fi,LDC}$. Under hypothesis T_2, this reduces to $\delta_{DC}a_{fi,DC} = \delta_{LDC}\phi_f a_{fi,LDC}$ so that $a_{Ki,DC}/a_{fi,DC} = (\phi_K/\phi_f)a_{Ki,LDC}/a_{fi,LDC}$.

countries to be more productive (use less factors per unit of output) than poor countries: $a_{fi,\text{DC}} < a_{fi,\text{LDC}}$ for all i and f. Under hypothesis T_2 this is equivalent to $\delta_{\text{DC}} > \delta_{\text{LDC}} \, \phi_f$ for all f. From Table 2 the largest value of δ_{LDC} is 0.29, and from Table 3 the largest value of ϕ_f is 1.89, so that the condition is $\delta_{\text{DC}} > 0.55$. The ϕ_f's are reasonable in that this condition is satisfied for the richest countries in the sample. Not all the ϕ_f are sensible. In particular, it is not clear why clerical labor and cropland have such large ϕ_f's.

The international-technology-differences model not only does well fitting the data for 1983, it also does well fitting the Bowen et al. (1987) data for 1966–1967. I estimated T_1 using exactly the same methodology as for 1983, except that the choice of countries was dictated by the Bowen et al. data. There are $9 \times 27 = 243$ observations. The results appear in column (ii) of Table 4. As in 1983, the δ_c all lie between zero and unity, and the correlation of δ_c with per capita GDP is a high 0.76.

Bowen et al. (1987) also investigated T_1 but found that it performed poorly. For a related hypothesis, their estimated values of δ_c were poor: only three were between 0 and 1, and the range was $(-174, 19)$. This led Bowen et al. to conclude that "The Heckscher-Ohlin model does poorly, but we do not have anything that does better" (p. 805). This contrasts sharply with my estimates and conclusions. The difference is primarily related to an implementation problem in Bowen et al.'s paper. They estimated variants of

$$ F_{fc}^m = \delta_c V_{fc} - s_c \Sigma_j V_{fj} + \mu_{fc} $$

when they should have estimated variants of

$$ F_{fc}^m = \delta_c V_{fc} - s_c \Sigma_j \delta_j V_{fj} + \mu_{fc} $$

[i.e., my equation (4)].[8]

IV. ECONOMICALLY MEANINGFUL ALTERNATIVE HYPOTHESES: CONSUMPTION

In this section, I consider three alternatives to the HOV consumption assumption, two of which are suggested by the missing trade and endowments paradox. Throughout, let $\mathbf{C}_c$ and $\mathbf{Q}_c$ be the vectors of consumption and production in country c, respectively, and define world values $\mathbf{C}_w = \Sigma_c \mathbf{C}_c$ and $\mathbf{Q}_w = \Sigma_c \mathbf{Q}_c$. The HOV homothetic-consumption assumption implies that $\mathbf{C}_c = s_c \mathbf{C}_w$.

---

[8] More precisely, Bowen et al.'s (1987) H2 corresponds to my T_1, and the problem can be seen by plugging in their parameter restrictions for H2 (from their Table 4) into their equation (14). The problem spills over only to H3, their preferred hypothesis, which underlies the above quotation and estimates of δ_c.

TABLE 4

ESTIMATES OF δ_c AND α_c^* FOR 1966–1967

Country	y_c/y_{US} (i)	T$_1$		TC$_2$	
		δ_c (ii)	t (iii)	α_c^* (iv)	t (v)
Korea	0.10	0.07	15.11	0.42	2.73
Philippines	0.11	0.11	17.70	0.20	4.10
Brazil	0.17	0.22	19.68	0.12	9.64
Portugal	0.19	0.22	5.75	0.11	3.33
Yugoslavia	0.20	0.21	12.04	0.18	4.60
Greece	0.24	0.41	4.58	0.15	3.64
Hong Kong	0.28	0.17	5.02	1.09	− 0.27
Mexico	0.30	0.33	11.95	0.23	6.38
Argentina	0.32	0.34	13.01	0.37	5.18
Ireland	0.35	0.54	1.92	0.19	1.67
Spain	0.40	0.43	8.14	0.05	6.47
Japan	0.41	0.41	17.95	0.17	16.28
Italy	0.48	0.67	5.56	0.06	14.00
Austria	0.49	0.48	4.49	− 0.05	2.10
Finland	0.52	0.55	3.51	0.60	0.53
Belgium	0.58	0.65	3.07	0.26	2.60
Norway	0.59	0.48	3.48	0.50	1.08
United Kingdom	0.59	0.57	8.67	0.18	15.95
France	0.61	0.61	8.33	0.21	5.13
Netherlands	0.61	0.54	4.93	− 0.43	4.64
West Germany	0.63	0.57	10.95	0.31	7.31
Denmark	0.70	0.68	2.16	− 1.10	3.37
Sweden	0.72	0.65	3.65	0.56	1.54
Australia	0.73	0.13	29.72	0.13	38.68
Canada	0.77	0.59	7.44	0.24	12.89
Switzerland	0.93	0.52	4.41	0.08	6.38
United States	1.00	1.00	—	0.13	33.41
$\rho(\delta_c, y_c)$:		0.76			

Notes: Here y_c is per capita GDP, and t is the t statistic for the null hypothesis that $\delta_c = 1$ or $\alpha_c^* = 1$. T$_1$ is the restricted ($\phi_f = 1$) version of equation (6). TC$_2$ refers to equations (12)–(13) with $\delta_c = y_c/y_{US}$. $\rho(\delta_c, y_c)$ is the correlation of δ_c with y_c.

A. INVESTMENT, SERVICES, AND NONTRADABLES

The endowments paradox states that poor countries are abundant in most factors and rich countries are scarce in most factors. Let s_{LDC} and S_{DC} be representative consumption shares for poor and rich countries, respectively. As illustrated in Figure 3, the endowments paradox states that s_{LDC} is far left on the Vanek chain and s_{DC} is far right. Let β_c denote the "true" consumption share and suppose it were different from the measured consumption share s_c. If $s_{\text{LDC}} < \beta_{\text{LDC}}$ and $\beta_{\text{DC}} < s_{\text{DC}}$ then the endowments paradox would disappear.

The most obvious source of miscalculated consumption shares is investment: rich countries consume less than is indicated by the income-based measure $s_c = (Y_c - B_c)/Y_w$ because they devote part of their income to investment. Instead of starting the derivation of the HOV equation from $\mathbf{T}_c = \mathbf{Q}_c - \mathbf{C}_c$ and s_c defined by $\mathbf{C}_c = s_c\mathbf{C}_w$, begin with $\mathbf{T}_c = \mathbf{Q}_c - \mathbf{C}_c - \mathbf{Z}_c$, where $\mathbf{Z}_c$ is a vector of investment goods, and define β_c by $\mathbf{C}_c = \beta_c\mathbf{C}_w$. Let $\mathbf{p}$ be the output price vector. Then it is straightforward to show the following. First, $\beta_c = (Y_c - B_c - \mathbf{p}'\mathbf{Z}_c)/(Y_w - \Sigma_j\mathbf{p}'\mathbf{Z}_j)$ so that heavily investing rich countries have $\beta_{\text{DC}} < s_{\text{DC}}$ as required. Second,

$$F_{fc} = V_{fc} - \beta_c V_{fw} + \mu_{fc} \quad \text{subject to} \sum_c \beta_c = 1 \tag{7}$$

where $(\mu_{1c}, ..., \mu_{Fc})' = \mathbf{A}(\mathbf{Z}_c - \beta_c\Sigma_j\mathbf{Z}_j)$. Since data on $\mathbf{Z}_c$ (investment levels by industry for country c) are not available for poor countries, equation (7) may be treated as a linear regression model with slopes β_c and errors μ_{fc}. It turns out that *exactly* the same analysis goes through with $\mathbf{Z}_c$ interpreted as services and $\mathbf{C}_c$ as merchandise goods. Then $\beta_{\text{DC}} < s_{\text{DC}}$ because, empirically, rich countries devote proportionately more of their income to services and less of their income to merchandise goods (i.e., income [s_{DC}] overstates merchandise goods consumption [β_{DC}]). A similar argument can be made for $\mathbf{Z}_c$ interpreted as nontradables.

Column (i) of Table 5 reports the OLS estimates of equation (7). For ease of interpretation, I report β_c/s_c and the t statistics for the hypothesis $\beta_c/s_c = 1$. I also sort countries by per capita GDP to highlight the negative correlation between β_c/s_c and per capita GDP (-0.77). As is apparent from the table, $s_{\text{LDC}} < \beta_{\text{LDC}}$ and $\beta_{\text{DC}} < s_{\text{DC}}$, exactly as required to eliminate the endowments paradox. Such good parameter estimates are satisfying, but surprisingly the model barely outperforms the HOV model. (The Schwarz criterion is $-1,006$, compared to $-1,007$ for the HOV theorem. See the row for $\mathbf{C}_1$ in Table 1.) It is thus clear that a large class of models—which include investment, services, and nontradables—offer only limited insights into the poor performance of the HOV theorem. This is surprising because the hypotheses were custom-tailored to explain the endowments paradox and because the parameter estimates were as expected.

B. ARMINGTON HOME BIAS

It has frequently been observed that consumers display a bias toward domestically produced goods. Whatever the sources of this Armington (1969) behavior, the implication is

TABLE 5

ESTIMATES OF CONSUMPTION PARAMETERS β_c AND α_c^*

	C_1		C_2		TC_2	
Country	β_c/s_c (i)	t (ii)	α_c^* (iii)	t (iv)	α_c^* (v)	t (vi)
Bangladesh	10.33	−9.07	0.10	66.35	0.42	1.94
Pakistan	5.62	−6.58	0.08	45.15	0.35	2.48
Indonesia	4.42	−7.94	0.00	54.19	0.30	5.32
Sri Lanka	7.24	−3.68	0.14	20.04	0.27	1.27
Thailand	3.25	−3.66	0.21	34.35	0.82	1.35
Colombia	2.57	−2.46	0.11	27.19	0.07	5.86
Panama	2.17	−0.65	0.38	3.42	0.51	0.39
Yugoslavia	2.31	−2.55	−0.01	15.24	−0.52	3.86
Portugal	2.74	−2.18	0.02	12.38	−0.53	3.62
Uruguay	4.62	−2.34	0.03	27.53	0.14	7.93
Greece	1.46	−0.75	0.24	4.54	0.20	1.55
Ireland	1.29	−0.30	0.37	3.79	0.40	1.38
Spain	1.40	−1.36	−0.20**	14.78	0.07	6.52
Israel	1.15	−0.20	0.27	3.11	0.29	1.78
Hong Kong	1.49	−0.70	0.44	3.73	0.56	2.11
New Zealand	1.17	−0.21	0.22	12.75	0.28	7.76
Austria	1.06	−0.12	0.23	2.71	−0.07	2.66
Singapore	1.13	−0.15	0.48	1.97	0.33	1.89
Italy	1.08	−0.40	0.06	10.12	0.50	3.92
United Kingdom	1.04	−0.24	0.16	20.20	0.48	8.39
Japan	0.86	1.30	0.05	47.27	0.30	17.28
Belgium	0.97	0.08	0.23	3.87	0.83	0.64
Trinidad	1.23	−0.15	0.70	0.36	1.07	−0.07
Netherlands	0.74	0.76	−0.41**	8.96	−0.43	7.22
Finland	0.95	0.09	0.29	2.24	0.67	0.79
Denmark	0.84	0.29	0.01	3.41	−0.20	3.11
West Germany	0.82	1.19	0.14	16.12	0.53	6.21
France	0.88	0.73	−0.31**	13.89	−0.02	7.05
Sweden	1.00	0.01	0.24	5.38	0.48	3.04
Norway	0.84	0.29	0.38	2.90	0.39	2.30
Switzerland	0.78	0.56	0.28	4.10	0.44	2.51
Canada	1.18	−0.81	0.34	15.24	0.34	15.95
United States	0.78	4.13	0.02	74.23	0.37	16.87

Notes: In this table, t is the t statistic for the null hypothesis that $\beta_c/s_c = 1$ or the null hypothesis that $\alpha_c^* = 1$. C_1 is the investment equation (7), C_2 indicates the Armington equations (10)–(11), below, and TC_2 indicates the Armington plus technology differences equations (12)–(13), below.

** Coefficient is statistically negative at the 1-percent significance level.

missing trade relative to the HOV prediction. Consider generalizing the HOV demand assumption $C_c = s_c C_w = s_c Q_w$ by retaining linearity but distinguishing between domestic goods Q_c and foreign goods $Q_w - Q_c$:

$$C_c = s_c[\alpha_c Q_c + \alpha_c^*(Q_w - Q_c)] \tag{8}$$

where $\alpha_c > 1$ and $\alpha_c^* < 1$ capture home bias.

Premultiplying equation (8) by $\mathbf{p}'$ to impose budget balance yields

$$\alpha_c(Y_c/Y_w) + \alpha_c^*(1 - Y_c/Y_w) = 1. \tag{9}$$

World market-clearing, $\Sigma_c C_c = \Sigma_c Q_c$, implies the following:[9]

$$\sum_c s_c \left[(1 - \alpha_c^*)\frac{Y_w}{Y_c} V_{fc} + \alpha_c^* V_{fw}\right] = V_{fw}. \tag{10}$$

Equation (10) imposes F restrictions on the α_c^*'s. Assuming measurement error $F_{fc}^m = F_{fc} + \mu_{fc}$, the variant of the HOV equation implied by the Armington assumption is

$$F_{fc} = V_{fc} - s_c\left[(1 - \alpha_c^*)\frac{Y_w}{Y_c} V_{fc} + \alpha_c^* V_{fw}\right] + \mu_{fc} \tag{11}$$

where the α_c^* satisfy equation (10). Equations (10)–(11) nest the HOV equation (1) for $\alpha_c^* = 1$.

I estimate the α_c^* in equation (11) using OLS subject to the linear restrictions on α_c^* given by equation (10). Column (iii) of Table 5 reports the estimates. Many of them are unexpectedly small. For example, the United States gives only the small weight of $\alpha_c^* = 0.02$ to foreign goods. Also, it is difficult to interpret the negative α_c^*. Nevertheless, all of the α_c^* are less than unity as suggested by Armington home bias. Further, from the row for C_2 in Table 1, the model outperforms the HOV theorem (H_0) when judged by likelihood and Schwarz values.[10]

The strength of the results argues for combining the Armington and technology-difference models. For tractability, consider the neutral technology-difference model T_1. The resulting variant of the HOV equation is

$$F_{fc}^m = \delta_c V_{fc} - s_c\left[(1 - \alpha_c^*)\frac{Y_w}{Y_c} \delta_c V_{fc} + \alpha_c^* \sum_j \delta_j V_{fj}\right] + \mu_{fc} \tag{12}$$

---

[9]To derive equation (10), solve for α_c using equation (9), plug the result into equation (8), sum across countries, premultiply by $\mathbf{A}$, and use $\mathbf{AQ}_c = \mathbf{V}_c$ and $\mathbf{A\Sigma_c C}_c = \mathbf{AC}_w = \mathbf{AQ}_w = \mathbf{V}_w$.

[10]A very different consumption model is the linear expenditure system here stated as $C_c = \theta^0 L_c + \theta' s_c$ where L_c is population. This assumption leads to the estimating equation $F_{fc}^m = V_{fc} - s_c V_{fw} - \theta_f(L_c - s_c L_w) + \mu_{fc}$. Estimating the nine θ_f parameters using OLS yields a likelihood value of -806 which, from Table 1, is statistically better than the HOV and investment hypothesis (H_0 and C_1), but worse than the Armington hypothesis (C_2).

where the α_c^* satisfy

$$\sum_c s_c \left[(1 - \alpha_c^*) \frac{Y_w}{Y_c} \delta_c V_{fc} + \alpha_c^* \sum_j \delta_j V_{fj} \right] = \sum_c \delta_c V_{fc}. \tag{13}$$

To reduce the large number of parameters (δ_c, α_c^*) from 56 to 24, I set δ_c equal to per capita GDP relative to U.S. per capita GDP, $\delta_c = y_c/y_{US}$. Statistics for the Armington model combined with $\delta_c = y_c/y_{US}$ appear in row TC$_2$ of Table 1. The restriction $\alpha_c^* = 1$ is rejected (from row TC$_1$ of Table 1, $X^2_{[24]} = 378$), indicating a complementarity between home bias and technology differences.[11] The restricted OLS estimates of the α_c^* are reported in column (v) of Table 5. There is an improvement in the estimates as judged by the disappearance of statistically significant negative α_c^*'s and by the many parameters that have increased in size, particularly α_{US}^*.

The exact interpretation of the α_c^*'s is not clear in that the sources of Armington home bias have not been identified. To investigate, consider a simple model implying consumption behavior as in equation (8). There is one good, and there are two countries. Each country produces one variety of the good. Letting an asterisk denote the foreign variety, D_c and D_c^* are the country-c demands for the two varieties, and p_c and p_c^* are the respective prices prevailing in country c. The representative consumer maximizes $\rho_c \ln D_c + (1 - \rho_c) \ln D_c^*$, subject to the budget constraint $p_c D_c + p_c^* D_c^* = Y_c - B_c$. Prices are the same internationally except for trade restrictions and transport-cost markups: $p_c^* = \tau_c p_b$ for some constant $\tau_c \geq 1$ and $p_b^* = \tau_b p_c$ for some constant $\tau_b \geq 1$. Since trade is observed for the good, but not for the variety, interest centers on $C_c = D_c + D_c^*$. Solving for the general equilibrium of this model yields equation (8) with the following condition:[12]

$$\alpha_c^* = \frac{1 - \rho_c}{(1 - \rho_c)s_c + \rho_b(1 - s_c)\tau_c}. \tag{14}$$

---

[11] The mix of $\delta_c = y_c/y_{US}$ with the linear expenditure system or C$_1$ leads to worse likelihood values of -584 and -547, respectively.

[12] The details are as follows. From utility maximization $D_c = (Y_c - B_c)\rho_c/p_c$ and $D_c^* = (Y_c - B_c)(1 - \rho_c)/p_c^*$. There are four prices $(p_b, p_b^*, p_c,$ and $p_c^*)$ in the two countries (b and c). The four equilibrium conditions are as follows:

(i) Supply of the country-c variety equals world demand: $Q_c = D_c + D_b^*$.

(ii) Likewise, $Q_b = D_b + D_c^*$.

(iii) $p_c^* = \tau_c p_b$.

(iv) $p_b^* = \tau_b p_c$.

To obtain equation (14), solve for prices, plug prices into D_c and D_c^*, and plug (D_c, D_c^*) into $C_c = D_c + D_c^*$. The implications of $\tau_b \neq 1$ and $\tau_c \neq 1$ for factor price equalization and s_c are discussed in Leamer (1988).

TABLE 6

DETERMINANTS OF ARMINGTON HOME BIAS IN CONSUMPTION α_{ct}^*

Dependent variable: $\hat{\alpha}_{ct}^*$	Income s_{ct}	c.i.f./f.o.b. τ_{ct}	Tariff τ_{ct}	Years	n	R^2
Random effects, GLS	0.29	−2.38	−0.24	1966, 1983	36	0.06
	(0.49)	(−1.33)	(−0.16)			
Simple correlation	0.12	−0.39	−0.29	1983	18	
	(0.37)	(0.89)	(0.76)			
OLS	0.34	−4.52	−2.14	1983	18	0.19
	(0.36)	(−1.32)	(−0.75)			

Notes: The table reports estimates of equation (15) using $\hat{\alpha}_{ct}^*$ from TC2. For the GLS and OLS rows, t statistics are in parentheses, and intercepts are not reported. For the GLS row, the year dummy coefficient is not reported. For the correlation row, p values are in parentheses.

Since $\partial \alpha_c^* / \partial \rho_c < 0$ and $\partial \alpha_c^* / \partial \tau_c < 0$, the home bias implied by the estimated α_c^* in Table 5 may reflect either primitive preference bias toward the home good or high tariffs and transport costs. Somewhat surprisingly, $\partial \alpha_c^* / \partial s_c$ cannot be signed even under strong assumptions about trade impediments and preference differences. This may explain the weak correlations in Table 5 between the estimated α_c^* and per capita GDP.

Equation (14) suggests a multivariate regression of α_c^* on ρ_c, s_c, and τ_c. While preferences ρ_c have no observable counterpart, my 1983 data together with the Bowen et al. 1966–1967 data form a panel that identifies the ρ_c under the assumption that preferences are stable over time. Letting t index time, s_{ct} is observed, τ_{ct} is measured by c.i.f./f.o.b. factors and average tariffs, and α_{ct}^* is measured by its estimate $\hat{\alpha}_{ct}^*$ under hypothesis TC$_2$. Since α_{ct}^* is measured with error, write $\hat{\alpha}_{ct}^* = \psi_t + \alpha_{ct}^* + \mu_{ct}$, where μ_{ct} is unsystematic measurement error and ψ_t captures systematic differences in the construction of the 1966–1967 and 1983 data sets. Linearizing equation (14) and substituting in $\hat{\alpha}_{ct}^*$ yields

$$\hat{\alpha}_{ct}^* = \psi_t + \psi_s s_{ct} + \psi_{\text{cif}}(\text{c.i.f./f.o.b.})_{ct} + \psi_{\text{tar}}(\text{tariff})_{ct} + (\rho_c + \mu_{ct}) \tag{15}$$

where, because of the short two-year panel, ρ_c is treated as a random effect.

There are 18 countries for which all the necessary data are available.[13] The estimated

---

[13] These are the 21 countries that appears in both the 1966–1967 and 1983 data sets less Japan, Hong Kong, and Portugal, for which tariff data are unavailable. The tariff data are from two sources: (i) *IFS Supplement on Government Finance,* 1986 series. "Taxes on International Trade and Transactions (A.6) as Percent of Total Revenue (S.2)" and "Total Revenue (S.2) as Percent of GDP" and (ii) IFS series "GDP (99b)" and "Imports (98c)." (For Bangladesh and Singapore, 71v replaces 98c.) The data do not always match the 1966–1967 and 1983 dates, most often because the tariff data start in the early 1970's. The c.i.f./f.o.b. factors are from the *IFS Supplement on Balance of Payments, 1984.*

α_{ct}^*'s for 1966–1967 under hypothesis TC_2 appear in column (iv) of Table 4 and contain no surprises. The first line of Table 6 reports the generalized least-squares (GLS) estimates of the random-effects model.[14] The model correctly predicts the signs on c.i.f./f.o.b. factors and average tariffs: higher trade barriers lead to "missing trade." The variance of the random effects ρ_c is twice the variance of μ_{ct}, indicating that international preference differences are important. The model makes no prediction about the coefficient sign on s_c; however, the estimated coefficient is positive, indicating that larger economies tend to be inward-oriented. The size and noisiness of the sample (note the statistical insignificance and low goodness-of-fit) argue for a simpler model. Table 6 also reports simple correlations and OLS estimates for the 1983 sample alone. The same sign pattern repeats itself, a fact that lends some confidence to the estimates.

These results point to the benefits of more research into the Armington sources of the case of the missing trade. For present purposes, I am not bothered by this: my main point is that the bias is important and must be confronted theoretically and empirically.

V. MODEL SELECTION: ECONOMIC CRITERIA

This section evaluates the performance of each model using the same criteria applied to reject the HOV theorem. The criteria are based on $\hat{F}_{fc}$, the prediction of F_{fc}. For example, under the HOV theorem, $\hat{F}_{fc} \equiv V_{fc} - s_c V_{fw}$; and under TC_2, $\hat{F}_{fc}$ is defined as the right-hand side of equation (12) with $\mu_{fc} = 0$.

1. *Correlation of F_{fc} with $\hat{F}_{fc}$.*—Under the HOV theorem the correlation between F_{fc} and $\hat{F}_{fc}$ is a weak 0.28 and is not visually apparent in Figure 1. The last column of Table 1 reports the correlation for each model. The correlation rises to 0.67 when the neutral technology and Armington models are combined.

2. *Sign-HOV.*—Under the HOV theorem, the sign of $\hat{F}_{fc}$ correctly predicts the sign of F_{fc} for only 148 of 297 observations or slightly worse than a coin-toss prediction. Weighting by the size of the factor content of trade, the statistic rises to 0.71. This appears in the "weighted sign" column of Table 1. The statistic rises to 0.93 when the neutral-technology and Armington models are combined. (The unweighted sign statistics for H_0, T_1, C_2, and TC_2 are 0.50, 0.62, 0.64, and 0.72, respectively, showing comparable improvement.)

3. *Endowments Paradox.*—In Figure 2, the number of times $\hat{F}_{fc}$ is positive for country c was seen to be negatively correlated with per capita GDP. The correlation of -0.89 is reported in the "endowment paradox" column of Table 1. When the neutral-technology and Armington models are combined, a sensible result obtains: there is a weak positive correlation of 0.18 between per capita GDP and abundance.

---

[14]Weighting by the covariance matrix of the $\hat{\alpha}_{ct}^*$ or using per capita GDP in place of s_c does not alter the conclusions.

4. *Case of the Missing Trade.* — Let σ^2 be the variance of F_{fc} and let $\hat{\sigma}^2$ be the variance of $\hat{F}_{fc}$. Under the HOV hypothesis, $F_{fc} = \hat{F}_{fc}$ so that $\sigma^2 = \hat{\sigma}^2$. From Figure 1, the case of the missing trade can be summarized by noting that $\sigma^2/\hat{\sigma}^2 = 0.032$ (i.e., the variance is off by a factor of 32). This is reported in Table 1 in the "missing trade" column. Under TC_2 the variance ratio is 2.2, so that the second moment is only off by a factor of 2.2. Thus, TC_2 represents a significant improvement over the HOV theorem in dealing with the case of the missing trade.

By all these criteria the HOV theorem is dominated by a model allowing for Armington home bias and neutral technology differences. However, as indicated by the correlations between F_{fc} and $\hat{F}_{fc}$, not all the sample variation is explained. In particular, none of the models does well predicting observations for which $\hat{F}_{fc}$ is small. This suggests a tension between the theory and evidence. $\hat{F}_{fc}$ small means that the endowment of country c is "similar" to the world endowment in a cone-of-diversification sense. Thus, while the theory predicts that the model will do best where endowments are similar ($\hat{F}_{fc}$ small), the model actually does best where endowments are dissimilar ($\hat{F}_{fc}$ large).

VI. CAVEATS AND CONCLUSIONS

The HOV theorem performs poorly and, by implication, so do increasing returns to scale and imperfect-competition models that yield the HOV theorem. Yet little is known about the features of national endowments and net factor service trade that lead to this negative result. The only known anomaly, namely, the Leontief "paradox," was reversed in the data at least 20 years ago (Stern and Maskus, 1981).

In other fields of economics, the poor performance of a major theory leads to more careful consideration of the data and to new theories that can accommodate the anomalies. Yet in international economics, such important facts as "the case of the missing trade" and "the endowments paradox" have gone unnoticed.

The first contribution of the present paper was an investigation into the features of the data that lead to the poor performance of the HOV theorem. I identified pronounced patterns in the deviations from the HOV theorem. In presenting them I offered an informative graphical display of the HOV theorem. I view this as the most important contribution of the paper: in place of the countless theoretical conjectures about why the HOV theorem performs poorly, there are now several data patterns around which theoretical analysis can coalesce.

The second contribution of the paper was an examination of alternative hypotheses that could potentially explain the patterns. Models that contributed little to the explanation included those with linear expenditure demand, capital accumulation, nontradables, and trade in services. The importance of the specific alternative models I have advanced is in indicating which models are consistent with the data patterns and which models are not. For example, both the investment model and the Armington model were custom-tailored to fit the data, yet the former was a failure while the latter was a success. The model that performed best combined Armington home bias with neutral international technology differences. The results contrast sharply with those of Bowen et al. (1987) and provide the first rejection of the HOV hypothesis in favor of a satisfying, economically meaningful alternative.

More remains to be done. I am dissatisfied that some alternative hypotheses were data-instigated, because it implies that the reported test statistics overstate the rejection of the HOV theorem. Also, work is needed to explain why endowment similarity is associated with poor predictions. Finally, more detailed data are needed to investigate further the sources of international productivity differences and Armington home bias.

APPENDIX: MEASUREMENT ERROR AND OTHER SENSITIVITY ANALYSIS

This appendix summarizes the impact of alternate specifications on estimates of the δ_c parameters for the neutral-technology-differences model T_1. This is a linear model, so that familiar techniques can be brought to bear.

1. V_{fc} *is mismeasured.*—Suppose measured endowments are related to actual endowments by $V_{fc}^m = V_{fc} + \mu_{fc}^1$, where the μ_{fc}^1's are independently and identically distributed. Then from equation (4)

$$F_{fc}^{US} = \delta_c V_{fc}^m - s_c \sum_j \delta_j V_{fj}^m + \mu_{fc}^2 \tag{A1}$$

where $\mu_{fc}^2 = -(\delta_c \mu_{fc}^1 - s_c \sum_j \delta_j \mu_{fj}^1)$. Since $E(\mu_{fc}^2 | V_{fc}^m) \neq 0$, instrumental-variables (IV) estimation is indicated; however, it seems impossible to imagine a valid set of instruments for a primitive such as endowments.

Alternatively, the V_{fc}^m can be brought to the left-hand side. The next two facts can be proved along the lines of Trefler (1993 [proof of proposition 1]). First, equation (A1) may be written as

$$Y_{fc} = \delta_c + \mu_{fc} \qquad c \neq US \tag{A2}$$

where Y_{fc} is a function of the observables ($F_{fc}^{US}, V_{fc}^m, s_c$) and μ_{fc} is a function of the observables and errors μ_{fc}^2. Hence, equation (A2) is a fixed-effects model with fixed effects δ_c. Second, the covariance of μ_{fc} is heteroscedastick block diagonal.

Under the null hypothesis of endowment mismeasurement the OLS estimator of the δ_c in equation (A2) is inefficient, but *not* biased. Although the estimated δ_c for the tiny land-scarce countries of Hong Kong and Singapore are peculiar, when land is omitted all the estimated δ_c's are as good as or better than those reported in the main text. For example, their correlation with per capita GDP rises to 0.95. Further, under the null hypothesis of no mismeasurement, the White test should reject heteroscedasticity (though I caution that the error structure is also block diagonal). In fact, the White test resoundingly rejects heteroscedasticity and hence mismeasurement ($X^2 = 3.2$, which is less than the 5-percent critical value of $\chi_{[31]}^2 = 45.0$).

2. *Mismeasurement of s_c.*—There are two measures of s_c: the one from the World Bank used in this study and the one from the Penn World Tables. The estimates of the δ_c in equation (4) are not sensitive to the choice of s_c, indicating that measurement error is not a problem.

3. *Omitted Factors.*— Suppose data on factor g are not available. Inspection of equation (4) reveals that data for factor g do not enter into the equation for factor $f (f \neq g)$. Thus, omitting a factor reduces sample size, but does not lead to omitted-variable bias.

4. *Omitted Countries.*— The World Bank data document 137 countries. I have complete data for countries $c = 1, ..., 33$, but only incomplete data for countries $c = 34, ..., 137$. Define $s'_c = (Y_c - B_c)/\Sigma_{j \leq 137} Y_j$ and $s_c = (Y_c - B_c)/\Sigma_{j \leq 33} Y_j$ and modify equation (4) to read $F^{US}_{fc} = \delta_c V_{fc} - s'_c \Sigma_{j \leq 137} \delta_j V_{fj}$. The World Bank GNP data show $s'_c = 0.79 s_c$ so that $s'_c \Sigma_{j \leq 137} \delta_j V_{fj} = s_c \Sigma_{j \leq 33} \delta_j V_{fj} + s_c \gamma_f$, where $\gamma_f = 0.79 \Sigma_{33 < j \leq 137} \delta_j V_{fj} - 0.21 \Sigma_{j \leq 33} \delta_j V_{fj}$. Hence, interest focuses on

$$F^{US}_{fc} = \delta_c V_{fc} - s_c \sum_{j \leq 33} \delta_j V_{fj} - s_c \gamma_f. \tag{A3}$$

This is not stochastic, so assume that F^{US}_{fc} is mismeasured and estimate (δ_c, γ_f) in equation (A3) using OLS. The estimates of the γ_f are jointly significant, indicating that omitted countries may be an issue. However, the estimated δ_c from equation (18) are *identical* to those presented in the main text because, given the choice of scaling by $\sigma_f s_c^{1/2}$, each γ_f regressor is orthogonal to each δ_c regressor.

5. *Influential Observations.* — The omission of any single observation does not lead to large changes or sign reversals in the estimated δ_c, nor does omission of any group of observations associated with a single factor. However, there are influential groups of observations associated with some of the poor countries. An interesting pattern presents itself. Order country indexes by per capita GDP so that $y_c < y_{c+1}$. When country c is omitted and it is poor, then it induces a large change in δ_{c+1}, but not in any of the other coefficients.

6. *Fixed Effects.* — Including country or factor fixed effects makes little difference to the performance of the model.

7. *Additional Factors.* — Working with the 14 factors listed in footnote 1 rather than the nine factors that I use does not change the estimates of the δ_c. The case of the missing trade is not present for the oil, coal, and mineral endowments, but this may be because I have mismeasured them as flows when they should be stocks.

8. *Scaling.* — I have scaled each observation (f, c) by $\sigma_f s_c^{1/2}$. Similar results obtain when scaling by V_{fw} and, in a regression setting, when using a GLS correction involving an ancillary log regression of the first-stage squared residuals on (i) V_{fw}, σ_f, or factor-specific components and (ii) s_c or country-specific components. Only the $\log(s_c)$ scaling leads to substantially different results, and this only when its coefficient is large (i.e., when the United States and Japan receive almost no weight).

REFERENCES

Armington, Paul S. "A Theory of Demand for Products Distinguished by Place of Production." *International Monetary Fund Staff Papers*, March 1969, *16*(1), pp. 159–78.

Bowen, Harry P.; Leamer, Edward E. and Sveikauskas, Leo. "Multicountry, Multifactor Tests of the Factor Abundance Theory." *American Economic Review*, December 1987, *77*(5), pp. 791–809.

Brecher, Richard A. and Choudhri, Ehsan U. "The Factor Content of Consumption in Canada and the United States: A Two-Country Test of the Heckscher-Ohlin-Vanek Model," in Robert C. Feenstra, ed., *Empirical methods for international trade*. Cambridge, MA: MIT Press, 1988, pp. 5–17.

Heckscher, Eli F. "The Effect of Foreign Trade on the Distribution of Income" [in Swedish]. *Ekonomisk Tidskrift*, 1919, *21*(2), pp. 1–32; reprinted in *Readings in the theory of international trade*. Homewood, IL: Irwin, 1950, pp. 272–300.

Helpman, Elhanan and Krugman, Paul R. *Market structure and foreign trade: Increasing returns, imperfect competition, and the international economy.* Cambridge, MA: MIT Press, 1985.

Leamer, Edward E. "The Leontief Paradox, Reconsidered." *Journal of Political Economy*, June 1980, *88*(3), pp. 495–503.

———. *Sources of international comparative advantage: Theory and evidence.* Cambridge, MA: MIT Press, 1984.

———. "Cross-Section Estimation of the Effects of Trade Barriers," in Robert C. Feenstra, ed., *Empirical methods for international trade.* Cambridge, MA: MIT Press, 1988, pp. 51–82.

Leamer, Edward E. and Bowen, Harry P. "Cross-Section Tests of the Heckscher-Ohlin Theorem: Comment," *American Economic Review*, December 1981, *71*(5), pp. 1040–43.

Leontief, Wassily W. "Domestic Production and Foreign Trade: The American Capital Position Re-Examined." *Proceedings of the American Philosophical Society*, September 1953, *97*(4), pp. 332–49.

Maskus, Keith E. "A Test of the Heckscher-Ohlin-Vanek Theorem: The Leontief Commonplace." *Journal of International Economics*, November 1985, *19*(3/4), pp. 201–12.

———. "Comparing International Trade Data and Product and National Characteristics Data for the Analysis of Trade Models," in Peter Hooper and J. David Richardson, eds., *International economic transactions: Issues in measurement and empirical research.* Chicago: University of Chicago Press, 1991.

Melvin, James R. "Production and Trade with Two Factors and Three Goods." *American Economic Review*, December 1968, *58*(5), pp. 1249–68.

Ohlin, Bertil G. *Interregional and international trade.* Cambridge, MA: Harvard University Press, 1933.

Samuelson, Paul A. "International Trade and the Equalisation of Factor Prices." *Economic Journal*, June 1948, *58*(230), pp. 163–84.

Staiger, Robert W. "A Specification Test of the Heckscher-Ohlin Theory." *Journal of International Economics*, August 1988, *25*(1/2), pp. 129–41.

Stern, Robert M. and Maskus, Keith E. "Determinants of the Structure of U.S. Foreign Trade, 1958–76." *Journal of International Economics*, May 1981, *11*(2), pp, 207–24.

Trefler, Daniel. "International Factor Price Differences: Leontief was Right!" *Journal of Political Economy*, December 1993, *101*(6), pp. 961–87.

Vanek, Jaroslav. "The Factor Proportions Theory: The *N*-Factor Case." *Kyklos*, October 1968, *21*(4), pp. 749–56.

ABOUT THE AUTHOR

Daniel Trefler

Daniel Trefler is a professor of economics at the University of Toronto.

Editor's Queries

What is this arcicle all about? The HOV model is right. I know this because I read it once on a Venice Beach t-shirt. The puzzle is that such an intellectually compelling model is so resoundingly rejected by the data. So I asked a very simple question: What features of the data lead to rejection of the model? Once the question is posed, the answer is obvious: missing trade and the endowments paradox. (There are probably some other patterns in the data that I missed. The data are readily available so why not go fishing in it yourself?) Interest in the article stems from the fact that we now have a set of facts around which to discuss both the failure of the HOV model and the set of theoretical modifications needed to resuscitate it.

Which article not authored by you would most highly recommend to graduate students in international economics? The articles that realy inspire me are too wide-ranging for the classroom. I love Krugman's "Age of Diminished Expectations" and his more recent "Pop" writings. Leamer's *American Economic Review* papers on econometrics are also wonderful (March 1983 and May 1993).

International Trade and American Wages in the 1980s: Giant Sucking Sound or Small Hiccup? (Excerpts)

ROBERT Z. LAWRENCE

Harvard University

MATTHEW J. SLAUGHTER

Massachusetts Institute of Technology

The American dream is that each generation should live twice as well as its predecessor. During the hundred years before 1973, real average hourly earnings rose by 1.9 percent a year.[1] At that rate earnings doubled every thirty-six years, and the dream was realized.

The dream no longer holds. Since 1973 the United States has failed to match its historic track record. In 1973 average real hourly earnings, measured in 1982 dollars by the consumer price index (CPI), were $8.55. By 1992 they had actually *declined* to $7.43—a level that had been achieved in the late 1960s. Had earnings increased at their pre-1973 pace, they would have risen by 40 percent to more than $12.00. Or consider average real hourly compensation. This is a more comprehensive measure of the payments to labor because it includes fringe benefits as well as earnings. Between 1973 and 1991, real hourly compensation rose by only 5 percent. However the growth of labor income is measured, it clearly has slumped since 1973.

A second ominous development in the American economy has accompanied this slump: a dramatic increase in the inequality of earnings. In particular, the earnings of skilled workers have risen sharply relative to those of their less qualified counterparts. Bound and Johnson have calculated this divergence based on education. They found that between 1979 and 1988, the ratio of the average wage of a college graduate to the

This paper reflects research on a Brookings Institution project. "First Among Equals," funded by the Ford Foundation. We are grateful to Martin Neil Baily, Lawrence Katz, Edward Leamer, and John Pencavel and participants at the Brookings Panel and the National Bureau of Economic Research Summer Institute for comments, Lael Brainard and Paul Krugman for helpful discussions, Scott Bradford for research assistance, and Wayne Gray for data.

---

[1] See Johnson and Stafford (1993, p. 1).

average wage of a high school graduate rose by 15 percent.[2] Steven Davis has calculated this divergence in terms of work experience.[3] He found that between 1979 and 1987, the ratio of weekly earnings of males in their forties to weekly earnings of males in their twenties rose by 25 percent. The Employment Cost Index (ECI) tells a similar story. Assembled by the Bureau of Labor Statistics (BLS), the ECI classifies workers by occupation, and it indicates that between December 1979 and December 1992, the growth of compensation and earnings of white-collar occupations exceeded those of blue-collar occupations by 7.9 and 10.9 percent, respectively. However the skilled are distinguished from the unskilled, the sharp rise in wage inequality between the two in the 1980s is clear.

These two developments—sluggish and unequal real wage growth—have coincided with three major changes in the nation's international economic relations.

The first is convergence: the change in the United States' comparative position from global economic preeminence to "first among equals." In the 1950s output per worker in the United States was twice that in Europe and six times that in Japan. Today, both Europe and Japan have closed most of the output gap.[4] In addition, since the 1950s foreign stocks of both human and physical capital have been growing more rapidly than in the United States. The result has been a convergence in wage rates. In 1975 a trade-weighted average of foreign compensation rates expressed in U.S. dollars was equal to 64 percent of U.S. levels. By 1980 this measure stood at 72 percent, and by 1990 at 93 percent.[5]

The second major change is globalization: the increased volumes of foreign trade and foreign direct investment in America. Between 1970 and 1990 U.S. exports and imports rose from 12.7 percent of gross national product (GNP) to 24.9 percent. During the 1980s the ratio of the stock of inward foreign direct investment to GNP, valued on a historic cost basis, grew from 3 percent to 8.1 percent. Since the first oil shock in 1973, Americans have been forced to adjust to foreigners as suppliers of raw materials, as competitors in manufactures (such as automobiles), and, finally, as bankers and bosses.

The third major change is spending: the shift in American spending patterns in the 1980s, which produced record trade deficits. The Reagan administration's combination

---

[2] Bound and Johnson (1992). The education differential has risen most sharply among inexperienced workers. Murphy (1992) found that in 1979 the hourly wage of a college graduate with fewer than five years of work experience was 30 percent more than that of a high school graduate with similar experience. In 1989 this premium had soared to 74 percent.

[3] Davis (1992).

[4] McKinsey Global Institute (1992).

[5] This measure includes twenty-four U.S. trading partners; it excludes Brazil, Mexico, and Israel. When these countries are included, the 1990 trade-weighted foreign manufacturing compensation measure equals 88 percent of America's. Data come from the Bureau of Labor Statistics (1991).

of expansionary fiscal policy and contractionary monetary policy helped cause an unprecedented appreciation of the U.S. dollar until 1985. This record strength of the dollar priced many American exporters out of the world market, and it made imports a bargain for American consumers. The result was record trade deficits, which increased from 0.5 percent of gross domestic product (GDP) in 1980 to nearly 3.5 percent of GDP in 1987.

Because the United States' changed international economic relations coincided with the slow and uneven wage growth, it is scarcely surprising that the former has frequently been advanced as a primary cause of the latter. This connection is often made in policy discussions—recall Ross Perot, for example. In the 1992 presidential debates he claimed that ratification of the North American Free Trade Agreement would generate "a giant sucking sound," with high wages and challenging jobs fleeing to Mexico. This claim struck a nerve with millions, and helped him win 19 percent of the popular vote.

Many academics have also linked international factors to wage developments. For example, Johnson and Stafford argue that the erosion of high returns from American technological leadership has been the principal source of the slow rise in American real wages since 1973. Similarly, Leamer claims that increased claims that increased capital formation abroad is leading inevitably to "factor price equalization," in which American wage rates converge with those in other countries. According to Leamer this convergence is harmful because it entails not simply a rise in foreign wage levels, but also a decline in American wage levels. Reich argues that global competition has bifurcated American workers—and thereby American society—into two groups: high-earning "symbolic analysts" whose talents are rewarded by globalization, and the mass of ordinary production workers whose earnings are depressed by it. Referring to growing wage disparity, Murphy and Welch conclude that "the evolving pattern of international trade is perhaps a primary cause of recent wage changes."[6]

Other academics, however, have argued that international factors have played only a small role in recent wage changes. Borjas, Freeman, and Katz maintain that trade flows explain, at most, 15 percent (that is, 1.9 percentage points) of the 12.4 percent increase between 1980 and 1988 in the earnings differential between college-educated workers and their high-school-educated counterparts. Moreover, because the manufacturing trade deficit declined from $106 billion in 1988 to $47 billion in 1991, their method would attribute to trade less than one percentage point of the disparity in relative wage growth that persists today. Davis finds that increased trade is associated with a convergence across several countries of relative-wage structures. But he concludes that this factor-price equalization effect has been more than offset by the growing divergence across countries of relative industry wage structures. Freeman and Needels find that the college–high school wage differential increased only slightly in Canada during the

---

[6]Johnson and Stafford (1993); Leamer (1992); Reich (1991); and Murphy and Welch (1991).

1980s. They conclude from this that the wage divergence in the United States was not the result of "an inexorable shift in the economic structure of advanced capitalist countries," but a reflection of "specific developments in the U.S. labor market." Berman, Bound, and Griliches do not find much role for trade, and Bound and Johnson find that trade played basically no role in America's wage changes in the 1980s. Instead, they ascribe these changes to technological change and changes in unmeasured labor quality.[7]

The effect of America's international economic relations on both its real and relative wages is thus a controversial topic. It also consumes an increasing part of the policy debate. Although trade intervention is rarely the ideal instrument for redistributing income, it is often a tempting one. Leamer, for example, argues that liberalizing trade with developing countries such as Mexico costs the United States an important mechanism for maintaining the wages of its least fortunate workers.

In this paper we try to advance the debate by presenting a data analysis that uses insights from theory to investigate the effect of international trade on America's recent wage performance. We first look at the sluggish growth of average real wages. As a first approximation we expect the performance of average real wages to mirror the performance of output per worker. Accordingly, we explore reasons for the divergence between real wages and labor productivity. Our main finding is that trade had nothing to do with the slow increase in average compensation. The sluggish rise in real compensation and the accompanying convergence of U.S. and foreign wages reflected slow productivity in the nontraded goods sectors of the American economy. Real *product* compensation increased almost as rapidly as output per worker. Growth of real *consumption* compensation lagged behind real product compensation because of a rise in the relative price of housing (which workers consume but do not produce) and a decline in the relative price of investment goods (which workers produce but do not consume).

We next consider the rise in the relative wages of nonproduction workers. Standard international trade theory, as laid out by Stolper and Samuelson, suggests that changes in the relative returns of factors will reflect changes in the prices of the goods that they produce.[8] Many studies of relative wage performance have ignored this process, however.[9] Instead, they focus on trade volumes and trade deficits. As Bhagwati has emphasized, trade deficits are not the most suitable measures of the effects of trade because they are not necessarily associated with relative wage behavior.[10] We focus instead on the price behavior of traded goods, and we find no evidence that the relative prices of goods that use production labor relatively intensively have declined. From this

---

[7]Borjas, Freeman, and Katz (1992); Davis (1992); Freeman and Needels (1991); Berman, Bound, and Griliches (1993); and Bound and Johnson (1992).

[8]Stolper and Samuelson (1941).

[9]Leamer (1992) is a noteworthy exception.

[10]Bhagwati (1991).

evidence, we conclude that relative U.S. wages have not been driven by Stolper-Samuelson effects. We do, however, find a positive association between the growth of total factor productivity and the intensive use of nonproduction labor. This points to technological change as an important source of changes in relative wages. Indeed, we argue that the pervasive decline in the ratio of production to nonproduction workers actually employed—despite the decline in the relative wages of production workers—points to a dominant role for technological change, which has augmented employment of nonproduction workers. This accords well with anecdotal evidence of the shift toward computer-controlled, flexible manufacturing systems.

We then consider and reject two more complex hypotheses about the effect of trade on wages. We analyze models that assume complete specialization and the hypothesis that trade has eroded union rents. We conclude with a summary of our major findings and some observations on the important role played by the productivity slowdown outside of manufacturing.

RELATIVE WAGE PERFORMANCE

We have calculated that in American manufacturing between 1979 and 1989, the ratio of mean annual wages of nonproduction workers to production workers rose by nearly 10 percent (Figure 1A).[11] This fact corroborates the evidence presented in the introduction on growing wage inequality, and it is worrisome for two reasons. First, the increased wage divergence sharply reverses the trend from 1945 until 1979 of wage convergence between production and nonproduction workers. Second, sluggish average real wages and diverging relative wages imply that unskilled workers actually suffered declines in real wages in the 1980s.

One obvious explanation for this divergence is relative labor supply. All other things held constant, the wage differential between skilled and unskilled labor should grow if the supply of unskilled labor grows more than the supply of skilled labor. Studies suggest that shifts in relative supplies of labor in the 1980s may explain some of the wage behavior, but they also suggest that most of the shift remains to be attributed to demand.[12] Indeed, in the 1980s college graduates and women, two groups experiencing

---

[11] In 1979 the mean wage of nonproduction workers in manufacturing was $19,517, and the mean wage for production workers was $12,829. In 1989 these wages were $34,866 and $21,112, respectively. Note that these wage measures do not include compensation such as health insurance. The previous section noted that total compensation rather than just wages is the appropriate measure of factor returns. Unfortunately, data on total compensation that distinguish between nonproduction and production workers were not readily available. Therefore, we use the wage data that we have in light of this caveat.

[12] See, for example, Borjas, Freeman, and Katz (1992) on the immigration of unskilled workers, and Katz and Murphy (1992) on the slowdown of the growth in well-educated entrants. See Murphy and Welch (1992) and Bound and Johnson (1992) for convincing arguments on demand as a major explanation for the shift in relative labor supplies.

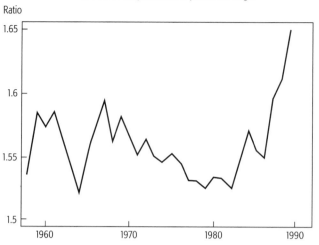

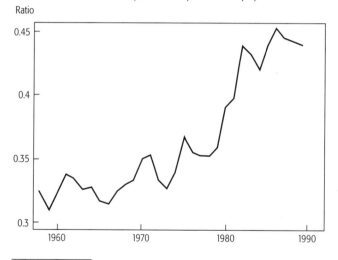

Figure 1

Evolution of Wages and Employment in Manufacturing

Source: Wage and employment data come from the NBER's Trade and Immigration Data Base. Wages are average wages; the ratio for labor employed is for all manufacturing industries taken together.

rising relative wages, also experienced rising relative supply. White-collar occupations constituted 67.2 percent of employment in 1983, and they represented 90 percent of the rise in employment between 1983 and 1990. Similarly, managerial and professional specialty occupations accounted for 24 percent of employment in 1983 and 45.7 percent of the growth between 1983 and 1990.[13]

If manufacturing shifts its demand away from production workers and toward nonproduction workers, the wage differential between the two groups should grow. A second stylized fact from the data supports this labor-demand story. Figure 1B shows the evolution of the ratio of nonproduction to production workers employed in manufacturing. The ratio rose 25 percent between 1979 and 1989, from 0.35 to 0.44. This rise was much sharper than the gentle upward trend of the earlier postwar decades.

Thus both the relative wages and the relative employment of nonproduction workers rose in American manufacturing in the 1980s. This combination indicates that the labor-demand mix must have shifted toward nonproduction labor.[14]

Several facts support this indication. Between 1983 (the earliest year for which consistent occupation data are available) and 1990, the rise in nonproduction workers in manufacturing was heavily concentrated in two occupational categories: managers and professional specialties. During these seven years, employment in these categories grew by 25 percent, while employment in total manufacturing grew by just 4.7 percent. Growth in these two categories constituted 91.5 percent of all employment growth in manufacturing during this period. This trend has continued despite the perception that middle-level managers in manufacturing are being laid off. Between March 1990 and March 1992, overall employment in manufacturing declined by 1.6 million workers, or 7.6 percent, but employment of managers and the professional specialties actually increased by 0.7 percent.

There is no doubt that the labor-demand mix shifted toward nonproduction labor. The question thus becomes why the demand for nonproduction workers in manufacturing has been so strong.

FRAMEWORK

To determine the relative contributions of trade and technology to shifts in labor demand, consider a general production function for industry j at time t.

$$Q_{jt} = \Theta_{jt} F^j(S_{jt}, U_{jt}, K_{jt}),\qquad(1)$$

---

[13] The mapping is quite tight between the nonproduction-production distinction and the white-collar–blue-collar distinction. We define as "white-collar" occupations such as managerial and professional specialty; technical, sales, and administrative support; and service occupations. See the BLS Handbook.

[14] A simple exercise of drawing relative-supply and relative-demand schedules shows that relative wages *and* relative employment can rise only if the relative-demand schedule shifts toward nonproduction labor, regardless of what happens to the relative-supply schedule.

where Q_{jt} is the output of industry j, $F^j(\cdot)$ is the time-invariant production function of industry j, and Θ_{jt} is the Hicks-neutral technology parameter for industry j at time t that boosts the productivity of any given combination of inputs. The factors of production employed at time t are capital (K_t), skilled (or nonproduction) labor (S_t), and unskilled (or production) labor (U_t). The demand schedule for each factor is the appropriate first-order condition of the profit-maximization problem. At time t, industry j demands factor i according to

$$w_{ijt} = P_{jt} \times \Theta_{jt} \times F^j_{it}(\cdot). \tag{2}$$

Here, w_{ijt} equals factor i's marginal revenue product in industry j at time t.[15] It is the amount that industry j is willing to pay factor i for a unit of its services. In equilibrium, this amount equals the actual wage set by the market. P_{jt} is the exogenously given price of output in industry j at time t, and $F^j_{it}(\cdot)$ is the partial derivative of $F^j(\cdot)$ with respect to factor i at time t.

To specify the labor market completely, one must add a supply schedule for factor i in industry j. The quantity of factor i supplied to industry j probably depends on at least the wage that factor i can receive both in industry j and elsewhere, that is, on w_{ij} and w_{i-j}. Quantity supplied probably does not depend on P_{jt} or Θ_{jt}, however. In this case shifts in P_{jt} and Θ_{jt} identify the supply schedule as shifts in the demand schedule trace it out.

In the following discussion we assume that the schedules are parameterized as described. We can therefore study shifts in the demand for labor by studying shifts in P_{jt} and Θ_{jt}. First, we analyze how international trade changes P_{jt}. Then we analyze how technological progress changes Θ_{jt}.

INTERNATIONAL TRADE THEORY AND RELATIVE WAGES

The classic Hecksher-Ohlin-Samuelson (HOS) trade theory assumes a world of constant returns to scale and perfect competition. One of the basic implications of this theory, typically set in a two-good world with trade, is the Stolper-Samuelson theorem. This theorem states that an increase in the price of a product raises the return to factors used relatively intensively in the production of that good and lowers the return to factors used relatively sparsely. International trade thus redistributes income by changing the terms of trade.

To understand the Stolper-Samuelson process, consider a small open economy that produces two products, software and textiles, with two factors, skilled and unskilled labor. "Open" means that this country freely trades both goods with the rest of the world. "Small" means that this country's production and consumption choices do not influence its terms of trade. Instead, these relative prices are determined in the rest of the world.

---

[15]This equation is derived, as was equation 1. Here, however, we distinguish between labor types and among industries. We also represent mpp_{ijt} as the product of Θ_{it} and $F^j_{it}(\cdot)$.

Furthermore, suppose that software uses skilled labor relatively intensively.[16] Initially, the country settles at some equilibrium output mix of software and textiles. To produce this mix, firms employ the country's skilled and unskilled labor. The labor market generates an equilibrium wage for each type of labor; at this wage the quantity of labor demanded by firms equals the total quantity supplied in the economy.

We can illustrate this equilibrium by choosing the production isoquants for software and textiles that correspond to their given relative price. In Figure 2A these are drawn as SS and TT, respectively. Note that SS lies above and to the left of TT. This indicates that software uses skilled labor relatively intensively. If both goods are produced, both isoquants must be tangent to the line that indicates the ratio of factor prices, (W_s/W_u). These tangency points indicate the ratio of skilled to unskilled labor $(S/U)_s$ and $(S/U)_t$, used to produce software and textiles, respectively.[17]

Now suppose that the international price of software rises. This is depicted in Figure 2B as an outward shift in the relevant textile isoquant to $T'T'$. The country will seek to make more software and fewer textiles. Output in textiles declines, releasing some of both factors. Output in software expands, requiring more of both factors. Because software employs skilled labor relatively intensively, the overall economy's relative demand shifts toward skilled labor and away from unskilled labor. If factor prices remained constant, however, the factor quantities released by textiles would not match those demanded by software because of the different factor intensities of the goods. The textile industry would release too much unskilled labor and too little skilled labor relative to the demands of the software industry.

Wages must therefore change. The wage for unskilled labor falls, and the wage for skilled labor rises. The new equilibrium ratio of the relative price of factors is $(W_s/W_u)' > (W_s/W_u)$. This higher ratio induces firms to substitute away from skilled labor and toward unskilled labor, and this substitution lowers the ratio of skilled to unskilled labor employed in each industry. (In Figure 2B, this substitution is represented as a flattening of each industry's (S/U) ray to $(S/U)'$.) Textiles thus releases less unskilled labor and more skilled labor relative to what it would have released without the wage change. Similarly, software demands more unskilled labor and less skilled labor relative to what it would have required without the wage change. Wages move just enough to reemploy all labor; at this point the economy attains its new equilibrium.

---

[16]This is an assumption about the technology of production. It means that for any given relative wages, the ratio of skilled to unskilled labor employed in making one unit of software exceeds the ratio of skilled to unskilled labor employed in making one unit of textiles. Because there are only two goods and two factors in this economy and because software uses skilled labor relatively intensively, it follows that textiles use unskilled labor relatively intensively.

[17]If technological capabilities are the same throughout the world, the unique relationship between the prices of goods and the prices of factors leads to FPE.

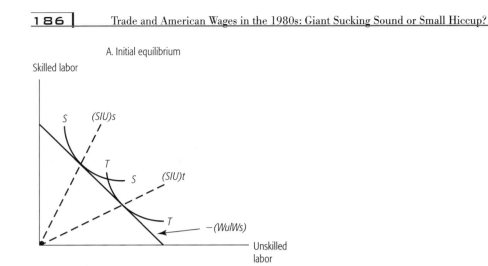

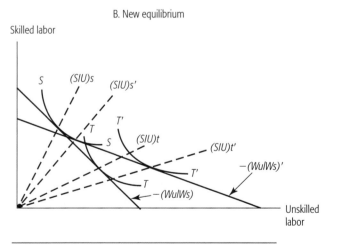

Figure 2A

The Stolper-Samuelson Process in a Small Open Economy

SS and *TT* are the initial production isoquants of software and textiles, respectively. $-(Wu/Ws)$ is the negative of the economy's initial relative-wage ratio. $(S/U)s$ and $(S/U)t$ are the initial ratios of skilled to unskilled labor employed in software and textiles, respectively.

Figure 2B

The Stolper-Samuelson Process in a Small Open Economy

The international price of software has risen. Software output increases, and textile output shrinks. This is represented as a shift in the textile isoquant to $T'T'$. $-(W_u/W_s)'$ is the negative of the economy's new relative-wage ratio: the wage of skilled labor has risen relative to unskilled labor. $(S/U)s'$ and $(S/U)t'$ are the new ratios of skilled to unskilled labor employed in software and textiles, respectively.

In the new equilibrium the economy makes more software and fewer textiles. This new output bundle implies a shift in the economy's relative factor demand toward skilled labor and away from unskilled labor. This shift has two important effects. It raises the wage for skilled labor and lowers the wage for unskilled labor. It also lowers the ratio of skilled to unskilled labor employed in both industries. Overall, changed terms of trade have translated into changed factor returns and changed factor-employment ratios by shifting the demand for these factors. With reference to equation 2, the w_{ijt}s change because both the P_{ji}s and the $F_{it}^{j}(\cdot)$s change (the latter because of the new relative employment levels in all industries). Thus, it is not trade volumes that matter in the Stolper-Samuelson process. It is the change in prices of traded goods.

We have presented the Stolper-Samuelson process in a very simple model. One might wonder whether the process still operates in more complicated—yet more realistic—models. The short answer is that it does. The model can be extended, for example, by allowing either or both of the industries to be imperfectly competitive thanks to increasing returns to scale. Helpman and Krugman lay out the basic imperfect-competition models, and they find that Stolper-Samuelson still operates.[18] The model can also be extended by increasing the number of factors of production and goods. Ethier studies how Stolper-Samuelson and other theorems generalize in a model with many factors and many goods.[19] He finds that Stolper-Samuelson still operates but differently, depending on the number of goods and factors. If the number of factors equals the number of goods, the model can identify, after a change in a good's price, the factor whose price rises in terms of every good and the factor whose price falls in terms of every good. If the number of factors does not equal the number of goods, the model cannot unambiguously identify these two factors. We acknowledge this qualification but assume in the work that follows that the simple Stolper-Samuelson story can be applied to the data. As a first approximation we think that this is a reasonable assumption.

EMPIRICAL EVIDENCE OF STOLPER-SAMUELSON

To explore the implications of the Stolper-Samuelson theorem, we examined the data for relationships consistent with the process's working. All other things equal in the Stolper-Samuelson framework, a rising relative wage of skilled labor should manifest itself in two relationships: first, a fall in all industries in the ratio of skilled to unskilled labor employed, and, second, an increase in the international price of skilled-labor-intensive products relative to those of unskilled-labor-intensive products. We consider each of these propositions in turn.

Our data set covers the U.S. manufacturing sector through 1989. Data on prices and quantities of inputs and outputs come from the Trade and Immigration Data Base of the

---

[18]Helpman and Krugman (1985).

[19]Ethier (1984).

National Bureau of Economic Research. Data on U.S. terms of trade come from the export and import price indexes produced by the BLS.[20] We have limited ourselves to manufacturing because very little data exist on trade in services. Because trade in manufactures constitutes nearly 70 percent of total U.S. trade, however, the Stolper-Samuelson process is unlikely to have a large role in overall trade without having a large role in manufacturing trade.[21]

First, we consider whether industries experienced a fall in the ratio of nonproduction to production labor employed. If the Stolper-Samuelson process alone had influenced American wages in the 1980s, rising relative wages of nonproduction labor would have compelled all industries to substitute toward production labor. Figure 3 checks whether industries did substitute in this way. It plots the percentage change between 1979 and 1989 of relative wages and relative employment in manufacturing industries disaggregated at the two-, three-, and four-digit SIC levels. Higher relative wages of nonproduction labor combined with a lower ratio of nonproduction to production labor employed would move industries into each of the upper-left quadrants of Figure 3.

Regardless of the level of disaggregation, however, only about 10 percent of all industries moved this way.[22] Indeed, one of the remarkable features of American manufacturing in the 1980s was a pervasive increase in the ratio of nonproduction to production workers employed—exactly the opposite of the HOS prediction. At every level of disaggregation, at least half of all industries (measured by share of total manufacturing employment) moved to a new equilibrium in the upper-right quadrant. This equilibrium entails both higher relative wages and higher relative employment of nonproduction labor. Thus, the majority of industries accompanied rising relative wages with rising, not falling, relative employment. So Figure 3 indicates that Stolper-Samuelson was not the predominant influence on relative labor demand in the 1980s.

Two points should be emphasized. First, we have conducted our analysis at several levels of disaggregation to eliminate the possibility that outsourcing was an important

---

[20] The export and import price indexes are generated from quarterly surveys of firms engaged in trade. The NBER data base draws primarily from the *Annual Survey of Manufactures*: see Abowd and Freeman (1991, introduction and summary) for a detailed description of this data base. Recall that in our data set "skilled labor" is defined as nonproduction labor and that "unskilled labor" is defined as production labor. See the appendix for more on this. In addition, all SIC classifications in this data set come from the revision #2 scheme. Revision #3 replaced #2 starting in 1988, and it redesignated about 25 percent of #2's industries. All data from 1988 and 1989 have been concorded back to revision #2.

[21] The United States has a comparative advantage in nonproduction-labor-intensive products. In 1979 the exports-weighted ratio of nonproduction to production labor employed in U.S. export industries was 0.501; the analogous ratio for imports was 0.384. In 1989 these ratios were 0.539 and 0.433, respectively.

[22] At the two-digit level, 8.2 percent; at the three-digit level, 9.8 percent; and at the four-digit level, 9.5 percent.

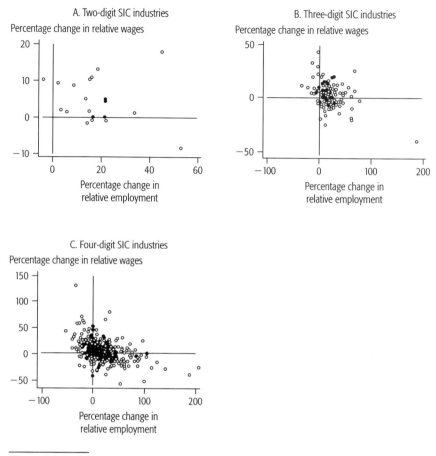

A. Two-digit SIC industries

B. Three-digit SIC industries

C. Four-digit SIC industries

Figure 3

Percentage Changes in the 1980s in the Relative Wages and Relative Employment of Nonproduction and Production Labor in Manufacturing

Source: Employment and wage data come from the NBER's Trade and Immigration Data Base.

reason for the shifts in relative labor use. By using industry data to explore the Stolper-Samuelson effects, we assume that we can identify each product with a unique industry and each industry with a unique production process. In practice, however, industries may make products using processes that differ in their factor intensity. For example, the production of semiconductors could involve both research and development (R&D), which uses skilled labor, and assembly, which uses unskilled labor. The availability of cheaper foreign labor might result not in the shrinking of entire industries, but rather in the international migration of particular production processes within an industry. This outsourcing could be confused with a change in production techniques if the data are analyzed at an aggregate level. The foreign outsourcing of assembly operations in semiconductors, for example, would raise skill intensity in the data for the industry as a whole because of the shrinking assembly activities, whereas separate data on R&D and assembly might indicate no shift in relative factor use.[23]

The fact that the rise in ratio of nonproduction to production workers is as pervasive at the four-digit level as it is at the two-digit level suggests that the rise does not reflect outsourcing. Berman, Bound, and Griliches corroborate this evidence against outsourcing.[24] They note that the *1987 Annual Survey of Manufactures* reported that foreign materials constituted only 8 percent of all materials purchased in manufacturing in 1987. Moreover, only a small fraction of materials purchased typically come from an establishment's own industry: 2 percent of materials originated in the same four-digit SIC category, 7 percent in the same three-digit category. They calculate that replacing all outsourcing with domestic activity would raise manufacturing employment of production workers by just 2.8 percent.

Second, all we can conclude from examining the relative employment ratios is that the Stolper-Samuelson effect was dominated by some larger effect. The sum of these effects was that most industries employed relatively more, not relatively less, nonproduction labor. We cannot yet say anything about the absolute size of the Stolper-Samuelson effect. Perhaps it was large; perhaps it was nonexistent.

To determine the absolute size of this effect, we examine international prices. Figures 4A and 4B graph percentage changes over the 1980s in industries' import prices against the ratio of nonproduction to production labor employed in these industries in 1980. In Figures 5A and 5B the import prices are replaced with export prices. In each pair of figures, the first classifies industries at the two-digit SIC level, and the second at the three-digit SIC level.[25]

Nonproduction-labor-intensive products are those that employ a high ratio of nonproduction to production labor.[26] If Stolper-Samuelson had any influence at all, then

---

[23] The BEA collects the most comprehensive data on the activity of multinationals. It does not release all these data by country at the three-digit SIC level of disaggregation, however, to avoid revealing the identity of individual corporations.

[24] Berman, Bound, and Griliches (1993).

[25] Unfortunately, the BLS does not report prices for all industries between 1979 and 1989. The import prices cover 93 percent of all manufacturing employment at the two-digit level and 50 percent at the three-digit level. The export prices cover 64 percent of all manufacturing employment at the two-digit level and 48 percent at the three-digit level. We assume that the price movements in these industries are reasonably representative. In addition, a minority of industries were not covered as far back as 1980. Almost all of these, however, were covered by 1982 and were therefore included in the diagrams.

[26] To ensure that no factor-intensity reversals occurred during the decade that could change the results, we also plotted changes in the terms of trade against employment ratios calculated for 1985 and 1989. These plots were very similar to Figures 4 and 5; they therefore have not been included.

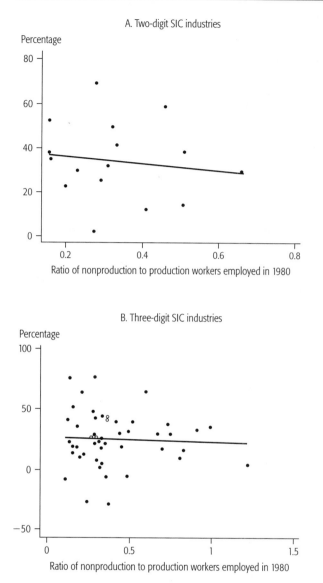

A. Two-digit SIC industries

Percentage

Ratio of nonproduction to production workers employed in 1980

B. Three-digit SIC industries

Percentage

Ratio of nonproduction to production workers employed in 1980

Figure 4

Percentage Changes in the 1980s of Import Prices by Industry Versus the Nonproduction-Worker Intensity of Industries

Source: Import and export prices come from the Bureau of Labor Statistics; employment data come from the NBER's Trade and Immigration Data Base.

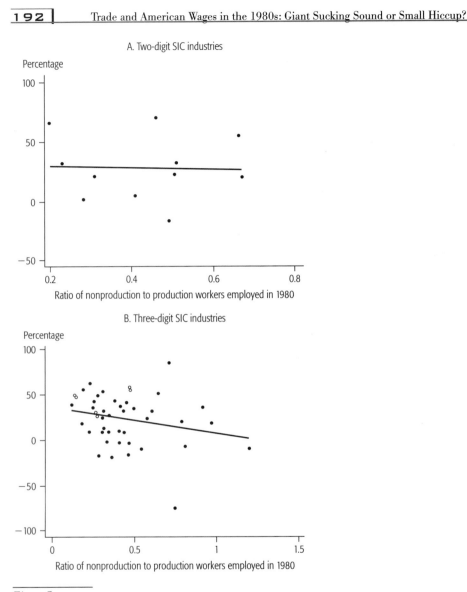

Figure 5

Percentage changes in the 1980s of Export Prices by Industry Versus the Nonproduction-Worker Intensity of Industries

Source: Import and export prices come from the Bureau of Labor Statistics; employment data come from the NBER's Trade and Immigration Data Base.

TABLE 1

EMPLOYMENT-WEIGHTED PERCENTAGE CHANGES IN INTERNATIONAL PRICES
AND HICKS-NEUTRAL PRODUCTIVITY, 1980–89

Industry	Percentage change, 1980–89		
	International prices	Hicks-neutral technology	Effective prices
Import-producing			
Nonproduction weights	26.0	20.5	46.5
Production weights	28.1	11.9	40.0
Difference	−2.1	8.6	6.5
Export-producing			
Nonproduction weights	26.3	18.6	44.9
Production weights	30.0	10.7	40.7
Difference	−3.7	7.9	4.2

Notes: Nonproduction weights weigh each industry's price and technology change by that industry's share of total manufacturing employment of nonproduction labor in 1980. Production weights weigh each industry's price and technology change by that industry's share of total manufacturing employment of production labor in 1980. All industries are defined at the three-digit SIC level.
Sources: International-price data come from the Bureau of Labor Statistics. Employment and technology (total-factor productivity) data come from the National Bureau of Economic Research's Trade and Immigration Data Base and Wayne Gray.

the international prices of these products should have risen relative to the international prices of production-labor-intensive products. But Figures 4 and 5 do not indicate a rise in the relative price of nonproduction-labor-intensive goods. Instead, the trend lines suggest that the relative price of nonproduction-labor-intensive products actually fell.[27]

Weighted-average price increases corroborate this suggestion. For both import and export prices at the three-digit level, we have constructed two price indexes. One weights each industry's price rise by the industry's share in 1980 employment of nonproduction workers, the other by the industry's share in 1980 employment of production workers.[28] As Table 1 shows, import prices weighted by shares of nonproduction labor rose by 26 percent in the 1980s. Weighted by shares of production labor, import prices rose by 28 percent. Similarly, export prices weighted by shares of nonproduction labor rose by 26 percent in the 1980s. Weighted by shares of production labor, they rose by 30 percent.

---

[27] These trend lines plot the estimated percentage price changes obtained from regressing actual percentage price changes on the ratio of skilled to unskilled labor employed and a constant. None of the four regressions estimated a coefficient on the ratio that was significantly negative at even the 10 percent level of significance.

[28] These price indexes were also calculated using 1989 employment shares as weights. The results were virtually identical, so only the results with 1980 employment shares as weights are presented.

Thus, the data suggest that the Stolper-Samuelson process did not have much influence on American relative wages in the 1980s. In fact, because the relative price of nonproduction-labor-intensive products fell slightly, the Stolper-Samuelson process actually nudged relative wages toward greater equality. No regression analysis is needed to reach this conclusion. Determining that the relative international prices of U.S. nonproduction-labor-intensive products actually fell during the 1980s is sufficient.[29]

TECHNOLOGICAL CHANGE AND RELATIVE WAGES

We have concluded that changes in the P_{jt}s prompted by international trade did not contribute to the growing U.S. wage dispersion in the 1980s. This leaves changes in the Hicks-neutral technology parameters, the Θ_{jt}s. The Θ_{jt}s, like the P_{jt}s, are indexed only by industry. Changes in Θ_{jt}s, therefore, shift the labor-demand equations, as do changes in the P_{jt}s. Industries with rising Θ_{jt}s attract producers and shift relative factor demands, as do industries with rising P_{jt}s. Thus, *under the assumption of given prices*, Hicks-neutral technological change occurring more rapidly in the nonproduction-labor-intensive industries should increase the relative wage of nonproduction labor.

We can therefore test for the influence of Hicks-neutral technical change on relative wages as we tested for the Stolper-Samuelson process. All other things equal, this change should manifest itself in two relationships similar to those analyzed for the Stolper-Samuelson process. First is a fall in all industries in the ratio of skilled to unskilled labor employed; second is greater Hicks-neutral technological progress for skilled-labor-intensive products relative to unskilled-labor-intensive products. Again, we examine each of these propositions in turn.

We measure growth of the Θ_{jt}s as the growth of total factor productivity (TFP) in each industry j. The TFP growth for an industry is calculated as the growth of real output minus the weighted average of the growth of the costs of five real inputs: nonproduction labor, production labor, capital, energy, and intermediate materials.[30] Transforming the annual changes into decade-long changes allows testing for their cumulative effect.

Figure 3 demonstrates that, as with international prices, Hicks-neutral technological change was not the predominant influence on relative labor demand in the 1980s. If it had been, industries would have moved into the upper-left quadrant as higher relative wages for nonproduction labor prompted lower ratios of nonproduction to production labor employed.

[29] If we had seen the relative international prices of nonproduction-labor-intensive U.S. products rise, regression analysis would have been appropriate to determine the contribution of Stolper-Samuelson to U.S. wage changes relative to other factors such as technological progress.

[30] Wayne Gray of Clark University in Massachusetts provided these TFP numbers. He assumed that cost shares sum to one and thereby calculated the cost share of capital as a residual. He also assumed that capacity utilization of capital remains constant. Real capital input is therefore a constant proportion of the real capital stock, and the rate of capital-input growth is simply the rate of capital-stock growth.

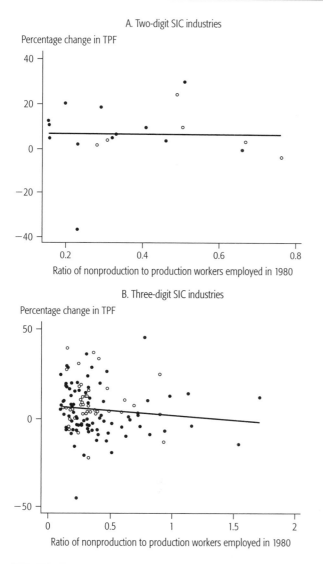

A. Two-digit SIC industries

B. Three-digit SIC industries

Figure 6

**Percentage Changes in the 1980s of Total Factor Productivity by Industry versus the
Nonproduction-Worker Intensity of Industries**

Source: TFP data come from Wayne Gray; employment data come from the NBER's Trade and Immigration Data Base.

To check the absolute size of the effect of Hicks-neutral technological progress, look at
Figures 6A and 6B. They graph percentage changes in industries' TFP during the 1980s
against the ratio of nonproduction to production labor employed in these industries
in 1980. Figure 16A classifies industries at the two-digit SIC level; Figure 6B at the

three-digit SIC level. If Hicks-neutral technological change raised the relative wage of nonproduction labor, it did so by raising TFP more in the nonproduction-labor-intensive products. Figures 6A and 6B do not display such a change.

When technology increases are weighted by shares of production and nonproduction labor, however, we do find that technological change has been concentrated in industries that use nonproduction labor intensively. As we did for import and export prices at the three-digit level, we calculated two different weighted-average TFP increases for both export and import industries.[31] Table 1 shows that in the import industries, TFP weighted by nonproduction-labor shares rose by 20.5 percent in the 1980s. Weighted by production-labor shares, however, TFP in the import industries rose by only 11.9 percent. Similarly, in the export industries, TFP weighted by nonproduction-labor shares rose by 18.6 percent in the 1980s. Weighted by production-labor shares, TFP in the export industries rose by only 10.7 percent.

Apparently, technological progress was concentrated in the skilled-labor-intensive industries. This helped raise the wages of skilled labor relative to unskilled labor. Indeed, it more than offset the effect on relative wages of the decline in the relative international price of nonproduction-labor-intensive products. To see this, define $(P_{jt} \times \Theta_{jt})$ as the "effective price" of good j at time t.[32] The percentage change over time in a good's effective price is simply the sum of the percentage change in its international price and the percentage change in its Hicks-neutral technology parameter. So adding the weighted-average increases in P_{jt} and Θ_{jt} in Table 1 yields the weighted-average increases in effective prices. The concentration of Hicks-neutral technological progress in nonproduction-labor-intensive industries offsets the concentration of international price increases in production-labor-intensive industries if and only if the nonproduction-weighted increase in effective prices exceeds the production-weighted increase.

Table 1 confirms that this was the case. For both exports and imports, the nonproduction-weighted increase in effective price was larger. This means that the combined effect of international prices and Hicks-neutral technology was to shift the labor-demand mix toward nonproduction labor. This shift helped raise the relative wage of nonproduction labor.

We can place this result in historical context by looking at the evolution of effective prices before 1980. Unfortunately, data on terms of trade go back only to 1980, so we use domestic price deflators instead.[33] Table 2 lists effective-price changes (weighted as

---

[31] As was done with prices, these TFP indexes were also calculated using 1989 employment shares as weights. The results were virtually identical, so only the results with 1980 employment shares as weights are presented.

[32] Because both P_{jt} and Θ_{jt} are indexed only by industry, we can call the product of the two an effective price. International trade theorists often use this construction to study simultaneously changes in the terms of trade and in technology.

TABLE 2

EMPLOYMENT-WEIGHTED PERCENTAGE CHANGES IN DOMESTIC PRICES AND
HICKS-NEUTRAL PRODUCTIVITY, 1960–89

All manufacturing industries	Percentage change		
	Domestic prices	Hicks-neutral technology	Effective prices
1960–69			
Nonproduction weights	13.3	12.6	25.9
Production weights	13.4	10.9	24.3
Difference	−0.1	1.7	1.6
1970–79			
Nonproduction weights	88.1	13.4	101.5
Production weights	93.3	6.5	99.8
Difference	−5.2	6.9	1.7
1980–89			
Nonproduction weights	33.1	11.5	44.6
Production weights	32.3	8.4	40.7
Difference	0.8	3.1	3.9

Notes: Nonproduction weights weigh each industry's price and technology change by that
industry's share of total manufacturing employment of nonproduction labor in 1980.
Production weights weigh each industry's price and technology change by that industry's
share of total manufacturing employment of production labor in 1980. All industries are
defined at the three-digit SIC level.
Sources: All data come from the National Bureau of Economic Research's Trade and
Immigration Data Base and Wayne Gray.

before) during three decades for all manufacturing industries at the three-digit SIC level.
Notice that the difference between growth in effective prices weighted by nonproduction
labor and growth weighted by production labor was 1.6 percent during the 1960s, 1.7
percent during the 1970s, and 4.1 percent during the 1980s. This sharp rise is consistent
with the increased wage dispersion of the 1980s. Notice, too, that in the 1970s the
concentration of technology growth in nonproduction-labor-intensive industries was
even larger than in the 1980s. This concentration in the 1970s was overshadowed by the
concentration of price increases in production-labor-intensive industries, however —
precisely what would have been expected in light of the declining U.S. terms of trade.

So the growth pattern of Hicks-neutral technology offset the growth pattern of
international prices. This helped shift the labor-demand mix toward nonproduction
labor and thereby helped raise the relative wage of nonproduction labor. We should
emphasize that because the relative supply of educated workers actually increased in the

---

[33] These calculations assume that changes in these domestic price deflators tracked changes in
international prices. This is a weaker assumption than the law of one price: it allows prices to
differ across countries by some fixed constant.

United States during the 1980s, the demand effects must have been particularly powerful. The Hicks-neutral technology growth was not the predominant influence on the labor-demand mix, however. As discussed earlier, Hicks-neutral technology growth that is concentrated in the nonproduction-labor-intensive industries should lead to a falling ratio of nonproduction to production labor employed in all industries. Figure 3 shows clearly, however, that, in reality, this ratio was rising in nearly all industries.

One possible explanation for this relative employment shift is that technological change was "biased" toward the use of nonproduction labor.[34] Indeed, Berman, Bound, and Griliches conclude that technological change that saves production labor is the most likely explanation for the shift in demand toward nonproduction workers. They support this conclusion with strong correlations between skill upgrading within industries and increased spending by firms on computers and research and development.[35] Kreuger corroborates the importance of biased technological progress with his estimate that from one- to two-thirds of the 1984–89 increase in the premium on education was related to the use of computers.[36] Bartel and Lichtenberg find that industries that use young technologies pay a premium wage.[37]

CONCLUSIONS

We have examined the pressures that stem from trade by emphasizing price rather than quantity behavior. We have found that trade has not been the major contributor to the performance of U.S. average and relative wages in the 1980s. The constancy of the U.S. terms of trade during the decade casts doubt on the argument that technological diffusion has robbed U.S. workers of their rents associated with technological leadership. Similarly, our finding that workers have, on average, been compensated for their product wages casts doubt on those who invoke a Stolper-Samuelson process as the source of poor average wage performance. In addition, we doubt that a Stolper-Samuelson mechanism has played an important role in placing pressure on production worker wages. Indeed, both import and export prices indicate that the relative price of production-labor-intensive products actually increased slightly during the decade. Both the traditional two-good and the more sophisticated three-good models with complete specialization forecast that the relative decline in the wage of U.S. production workers will be associated with an increase in the ratio of production to nonproduction labor. We

---

[34]In the framework presented earlier, biased technological progress can be represented by allowing $F^i(\cdot)$ to vary over time.

[35]Berman, Bound, and Griliches (1993).

[36]Kreuger (1993).

[37]Bartel and Lichtenberg (1991). It is unclear whether these workers justify their higher wages. Berndt and Morrison (1992), however, find a negative association between use of high-technology equipment and total factor productivity, although they also note that increases in high-tech equipment are labor using.

have found, however, a pervasive shift in U.S. manufacturing toward the increased use of nonproduction labor despite the rise in its relative wage.

This shift suggests that technological change has been the more important pressure on wages for production workers. Total factor productivity growth has been higher in manufacturing industries, which use nonproduction workers relatively intensively. Such a TFP change also implies an increase in the ratio of production to nonproduction labor, however. This means that in addition to TFP growth, technological progress was probably biased toward nonproduction labor. Finally, those who focus on real wage behavior without paying attention to productivity growth outside of manufacturing are writing *Hamlet* without the Prince. The major source of real wage convergence between the United States and other major industrial economies besides the United Kingdom lies in the disparate performance of services productivity. In addition, an important pressure on the relative wages of production workers may have been slow productivity growth in services.

REFERENCES

Abowd, John M., and Richard B. Freeman, eds. 1991. *Immigration, Trade, and the Labor Market.* Chicago: University of Chicago Press.

Baily, Martin Neil, and Robert J. Gordon, 1988. "The Productivity Slowdown, Measurement Issues, and the Explosion of Computer Power." *Brookings Papers on Economic Activity* 2:347–431.

Bartel Ann P., and Frank R. Lichtenberg, 1991. "The Age of Technology and Its Impact on Employee Wages." *Economic Innovation and New Technology* 1(2):215–31.

Berman, Eli, John Bound, and Zvi Griliches, 1993. "Changes in the Demand for Skilled Labor within U.S. Manufacturing Industries: Evidence from the Annual Survey of Manufacturing." Working Paper 4255. Cambridge, Mass.: National Bureau of Economic Research, January.

Berndt, Ernst R., and Catherine J. Morrison, 1992. *High-Tech Capital Formation and Economic Performance in U.S. Manufacturing Industries: An Exploratory Analysis.* Cambridge: Mass.: MIT Press.

Bhagwati, Jagdish, 1991. "Free Traders and Free Immigrationists: Strangers or Friends?" Working Paper 20. Russell Sage Foundation, New York, April.

Blackburn, Mckinley, David Bloom, and Richard Freeman, 1990. "The Declining Economic Position of Less Skilled American Males." In Burtless, Gary, ed. *A Future of Lousy Jobs?* Washington, D.C.: Brookings.

Borjas, George J., Richard Freeman, and Lawrence F. Katz, 1992. "On the Labor Market Effects of Immigration & Trade." In Borjas, George J. and Richard Freeman, eds. *Immigration and the Workforce.* Chicago: University of Chicago Press.

Bound, John, and George Johnson, 1992. "Changes in the Structure of Wages in the 1980s: An Evaluation of Alternative Explanations." *American Economic Review* 82 (June):371–92.

Bowen, H. P., E. Leamer, and L. Sveikauskas, 1987. "Multicountry, Multifactor Tests of the Factor Abundance Theory." *American Economic Review* 77 (December):791–809.

Bureau of Labor Statistics, U.S. Department of Labor, 1991. "International Comparisons of Hourly Compensation Costs for Production Workers in Manufacturing, 1975–90." Report 817, Washington, D.C.

Collins, Susan M. 1985. "Technical Progress in a Three-Country Ricardian Model with a Continuum of Goods." *Journal of International Economics* 19(August):171–79.

Cutler, David, and Lawrence Katz, 1991. "Macroeconomic Performance and the Disadvantaged." *Brookings Papers on Economic Activity* 2:1–74.

Davis, Steven J. 1992. "Cross-Country Patterns of Change in Relative Wages." In Blanchard, Olivier, and Stanley Fischer, eds. *1992 Macroeconomics Annual.* New York: National Bureau of Economic Research.

Davis, Steven J., and John Haltiwanger, 1991. "Wage Dispersion between and within U.S. Manufacturing Plants, 1963–1986." *Brookings Papers on Economic Activity: Microeconomics: 1991*:115–180.

Deardorff, Alan V., and Dalia Hakura, 1993. "Trade and Wages: What Are the Questions?" Paper delivered to a seminar on "The Influence of International Trade on Jobs and Wages." American Enterprise Institute, Washington, D.C. September.

Deardorff, Alan, and Robert Staiger, 1988. "An Interpretation of the Factor Content of Trade." *Journal of International Economics* 24 (February):93–107.

Dollar, David, 1986. "Technological Innovation, Capital Mobility, and the Product Cycle in North-South Trade." *American Economic Review* 76 (1, March):177–90.

Ethier, William, 1984. "Higher Dimension Trade Theory." In Jones, R. W., and P. B. Kenen, eds. *Handbook of International Economics.* Amsterdam: North-Holland.

Freeman, Richard B., and Lawrence Katz, 1991. "Industrial Wage and Employment Determination in an Open Economy." In Abowd and Freeman (1991).

Freeman, Richard B., and Karen Needels, 1991. "Skill Differentials in Canada in an Era of Rising Labor Market Inequality." Working Paper 3827. National Bureau of Economic Research, Cambridge, Mass, September.

Gullickson, William, 1992. "Multifactor Productivity in Manufacturing Industries." *Monthly Labor Review* 115 (October):20–32.

Hicks, John, 1953. "An Inaugural Lecture: The Long-Run Dollar Problem." *Oxford Economic Papers.* June.

Helpman, E., and K. Krugman, 1985. *Market Structure and Foreign Trade.* Cambridge, Mass.: MIT Press.

Johnson, George E., and Frank P. Stafford, 1993. "International Competition and Real Wages." Paper presented at American Economic Association Annual Meeting, January 5–7, 1993.

Katz, Lawrence F., and Kevin M. Murphy, 1992. "Changes in Relative Wages, 1963–1987: Supply and Demand Factors." *Quarterly Journal of Economics* 107 (February):35–78.

Katz, Lawrence F., and Lawrence H. Summers, 1989. "Industry Rents: Evidence and Implications." *Brookings Papers on Economic Activity: Micro-economics: 1989*:209–290.

Krueger, Alan B. 1993. "How Computers Have Changed the Wage Structure: Evidence from Microdata, 1984–1989." *Quarterly Journal of Economics* 108 (February):33–60.

Krugman, Paul, 1979. "A Model of Innovation, Technology Transfer, and the World Distribution of Income." *Journal of Political Economy* 87 (April):253–66.

———. 1992. "The Right, the Rich, and the Facts." *American Prospect* (11, Fall):19–31.

Lawrence, Robert Z. 1984. *Can America Compete?* Washington, D.C.: Brookings.

———. 1990. "U.S. Current Account Adjustment: An Appraisal." *Brookings Papers on Economic Activity* 2:343–92.

Leamer, Edward E. 1992. "Wage Effects of a U.S.-Mexican Free Trade Agreement." Working Paper 3991. National Bureau of Economic Research, Cambridge, Mass.

McKinsey Global Institute. 1992. *Service Sector Productivity*. Washington, D.C.

Murphy, Kevin M. 1992. "Changes in Wage Structures in the 1980s: How Can We Explain Them?" University of Chicago, February, Mimeo.

Murphy, Kevin M., and Finis Welch, 1991. "The Role of International Trade in Wage Differentials." In Kosters, Marvin, ed. *Workers and Their Wages*. Washington D.C.: American Enterprise Institute.

———. 1992. "The Structure of Wages." *Quarterly Journal of Economics* 107 (February):285–326.

Rangan, Subramanian, and Robert Z. Lawrence. Forthcoming. "The Responses of U.S. Firms to Exchange Rate Fluctuations: Piercing the Corporate Veil." *Brookings Papers on Economic Activity* 2.

Revenga, Ana L. 1992. "Exporting Jobs? The Impact of Import Competition on Employment and Wages in U.S. Manufacturing." *Quarterly Journal of Economics* 107 (February):255–82.

Reich, Robert B. 1991. *The Work of Nations: Preparing Ourselves for 21st Century Capitalism*. New York: Alfred A. Knopf.

Stolper, Wolfgang, and Paul A. Samuelson, 1941. "Protection and Real Wages." *Review of Economic Studies* (November):58–73.

UNCTC (United Nations Center on Transnational Corporations). 1991. *World Investment Report: 1991*. New York: United Nations.

Williamson, Jeffery, 1991. "Productivity and American Leadership: A Review Article." *Journal of Economic Literature* 29 (March):51–68.

ABOUT THE AUTHOR

Robert Z. Lawrence

Robert Z. Lawrence was a member of President Clinton's Council of Economic Advisers. Dr. Lawrence is currently on leave from Harvard University, where he is the Albert L. Williams Professor of Trade and Investment at the John F. Kennedy School of Government. He also held the New Century Chair at the Brookings Institution and founded and edited the Brooking Trade Forum. He has also served on the faculties of Yale University and the Johns Hopkins School of Advanced International Studies. He has also served as a consultant to the World Bank, the Federal Reserve Bank of New York, the OECD, and UNCTAD. His books include *Single World, Divided Nations; Regionalism, Multilateralism, and Deeper Integration;* and *Can America Compete?*

ABOUT THE AUTHOR

Matthew J. Slaughter

Matthew J. Slaughter is Assistant Professor of Economics at Dartmouth College, a faculty research fellow at the National Bureau of Economic Research, a visiting fellow at the Institute for International Economics, and a term member at the Council of Foreign Relations. He served as a consultant to the World Bank, and was a visiting scholar at the International Monetary Fund and the Federal Reserve Bank of Minneapolis..

Editor's Queries

What are the major unresolved questions of international economics? What are likely to be the hot topics of the next decade?   In my own main research area, I think the major unresolved research question is how various aspects of globalization affect labor-market outcomes. A central part of answering this question is resolving the different ways trade and labor economists have gone about answering it. This area has seen a lot of work the past several years but, in some ways, many trade and labor participants seem farther apart now than before.

What advice do you have to offer graduate students in the field of international economics?   As someone not too long out of graduate school I feel unqualified to offer research advice to graduate students in international economics. In fact, this paper with Robert Lawrence was the first full research paper I ever wrote—it was chapter one of my dissertation. But I think there's one important thing I've learned about research at this point that I'd call advice-worthy. Don't take your work or yourself too seriously. As early as possible, get used to the idea that you almost surely will not win the Nobel Prize. Try to have fun in your work: Sometimes you'll make mistakes, but that's okay—everyone does, and it's part of the process.

In Search of Stolper-Samuelson Linkages between International Trade and Lower Wages (Excerpts)

EDWARD E. LEAMER

With the widening of the gap between wages of unskilled and skilled workers has come an intense effort by economists on both sides of the Atlantic to identify the cause. The top three suspects are education, technology, and international trade. Most casual observers hold the opinion that all three of these suspects are guilty. The public schools in the United States seem to be doing a poorer job preparing their graduates for the job market and have been adding to the supply of unskilled, ill-prepared workers. On the demand side, technological change is altering the nature of work. Many functions are being technologically transferred from unskilled to skilled workers (for example, typing this manuscript), while others are being downgraded to require the most minimal level of education (for example, clerking at McDonald's). Last of the three suspects is international trade.

Unlike the eyewitness accounts of the "damage" being done by a deteriorating educational system and the information revolution, the evidence against international trade is mostly circumstantial and largely captured in Figures 1 and 2. Figure 1 compares over the last several decades the levels of real wages in manufacturing (using both the Consumer Price Index [CPI] deflator and the Producer Price Index [PPI] deflator) and the U.S. trade dependence ratio, the ratio of exports plus imports divided by gross domestic product (GDP). Figure 2 illustrates the vast differences between wages earned by U.S. manufacturing workers and wages earned in much of the rest of the world.

Figure 1 reveals that the abrupt halt in the early 1970s to the previously steady rise in real wages came suspiciously at a time when the United States was experiencing a rapid increase in trade dependence. The reason why increasing trade dependence might hold

The work presented in this chapter was partially supported by NSF Grant SBR-9409011. The assistance of Christopher Thornberg, Robert Murdock, and Nadia Soboleva is gratefully acknowledged. I have benefited much from the comments of the discussants (Gene Grossman and Steve Davis) and the editor (Susan Collins), and from comments of participants at seminars at Dartmouth and Columbia, particularly Ronald Findlay.

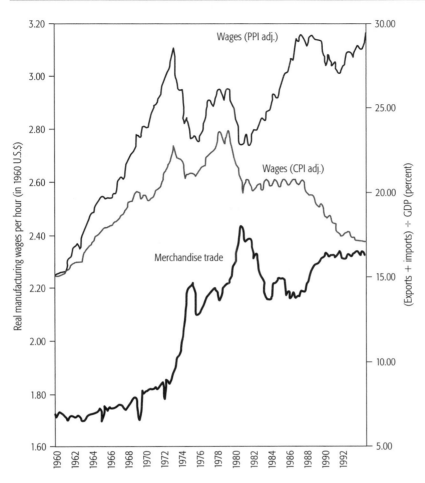

Figure 1

Gross Hourly Earnings of Manufacturing Production and Nonsupervisory Workers and Trade Dependence, 1960–92

Source: Citibase (Citibank Economic Database), New York: Citibank N.A.

down U.S. wages is suggested by Figure 2, in which each country is represented by a line segment with height equal to 1989 wages and width equal to population, and countries are sorted by wage levels. If this is the global labor pool, it is a strange one indeed, with the liquid deep at one end and barely there at the other. What could possibly be holding up the high end? Barriers is one answer. The arbitrage opportunities suggested by Figure 2 have not genuinely been present, because of the real and threatened interventions by governments that isolate workers in the high-wage countries from competition with workers in the low-wage third world. Now, according to this line of thinking, with the liberalizations that are sweeping the globe, U.S. workers are suddenly in direct

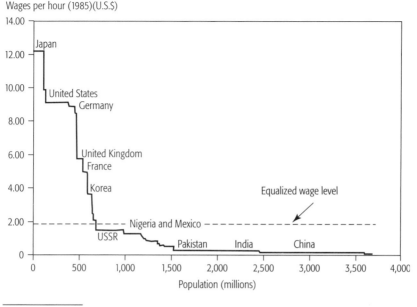

Figure 2

Industrial Wages and Population, 1989

Source: Song (1993).

competition with a huge mass of workers around the globe who are receiving wages that are a tiny fraction of U.S. ones. If the work forces in China and India and Mexico and South America are integrated through the exchange of products with the U.S. work force, how could the United States resist at least some decrease in wages of unskilled workers?

Although public opinion holds all three suspects guilty of wage suppression, the jury of academics seems to be rendering a quite different verdict. Education and globalization have been found innocent and technological change guilty. Labor economists have not found evidence of much change in the relative supply of unskilled workers as a result of educational failures. They also do not find evidence of much change in the demand for labor coming from international trade. Like Sherlock Holmes who counseled, "Eliminate the impossible, and all that is left is the truth," once these economists found education and globalization innocent, they have chosen to convict technology. Never mind that there is little organized evidence against this culprit.

My view is different. First of all, I object, Your Honor; the evidence that has been presented in support of the innocence of globalization is "incompetent, irrelevant, and immaterial." I move for a mistrial. ("Overruled; sit down, Mr. Scheck.")

Second, this is a crime that most likely could not have been committed by any one of the culprits, but requires that all three be working together. If, for example, the educational system had created a work force in the United States that had few unskilled workers, then economic integration of the goods markets with Mexico could benefit all U.S. workers, even the lowest skilled. Our fear of the North American Free Trade Agreement (NAFTA) speaks volumes regarding our confidence in our educational system.

Third, I would argue, the question is not: Which is the guilty force? The real question is: What are we going to do about it? If we find education and globalization innocent and technology guilty, we seem to me to be edging toward a passive response: There is nothing that we can do. The continuing and persistent belief that globalization is guilty (never mind the academic argument to the contrary) probably comes from the fact that globalization has an apparent remedy: economic isolation. A guilty verdict against education also points to a remedy. But educational investments have a long gestation period, and we cannot expect to have much fast impact on the income inequality trends by pulling the education lever.

Though free trade remains a target of political rhetoric, with both NAFTA and the World Trade Organization (WTO) now passed, the option of economic isolation may be gone. This leaves us with a question: What private educational investments and public investments in immobile knowledge or infrastructure assets are most appropriate for the twenty-first century—when products can be shipped around the globe with little risk of government intervention, when liquid pools of physical and knowledge capital can freely seek out workers with the lowest wages relative to productivity, and when computers are prepared to do many mundane tasks with great accuracy and efficiency?

This chapter will not move us much closer to an answer to this important question. It has the more modest goal of establishing the role that *one form* of globalization plays in the income inequality drama, namely relative price reductions for labor-intensive tradables. The view I offer is that at the end of World War II, countries sorted themselves into two different groups. Europe and Japan and the Asian newly industrialized countries (NICs) chose economic integration with the United States. But most of the rest of the world opted for inward-looking isolationist policies. Those that chose integration experienced a period of technological backwardness, but the technological lead that the United States enjoyed in the 1960s vis-à-vis the integrated economies dissipated rapidly in the 1970s, even as the gap increased vis-à-vis the isolated countries. Economic isolationism eventually collapsed as this technological gap became more and more intolerable. Now the global economy faces the wrenching task of integrating the enormous number of low-skilled workers living in countries that formerly chose isolation. This integration may or may not mean lower wages for unskilled workers in the advanced, high-wage countries.

One possibility is that high rates of investment in immobile assets, particularly human capital and infrastructure, will assure that these advanced countries will continue to attract more than their share of mobile physical and knowledge assets and will continue to have work forces that command comfortably high wages. Another possibility is that a combination of trade and capital flows will eliminate entirely the economic separation of workers at different points on the globe, and that wage levels will be determined only by skills and effort and not at all by geography. This would surely mean greatly reduced levels of wages of unskilled workers in the advanced, high-wage countries, because the liberalizations of the last two decades have added enormously to the supply of unskilled workers with no commensurate increase in human or physical capital.

Before I proceed I should emphasize that the forces that might be affecting income inequality in the United States are diverse and interactive. A list of possibilities is provided in the display below. Included are U.S. investment rates, U.S. labor supply changes, technological change, increased international factor mobility, and increased trade in goods and services. On this list are many forms of "globalization" including the increased international mobility of intangible knowledge assets, reduced market power for unions, delocalization of assembly operations, and so on. In this chapter only one globalization effect is considered: lower prices for labor-intensive tradables. The economic liberalizations that have increased the supply of labor-intensive tradables in the longer run will doubtless divert physical capital from the high-wage, developed countries to the low-wage, developing countries, which of course can work against labor in the high-wage countries. This and other forms of "globalization" are not considered here, not because they are unimportant or less important, but only because it is hard enough to try to get one piece of the puzzle to fit, let alone two or more! (Think about that metaphor.)

Forces Lowering Wages of Unskilled U.S. Workers

Inadequate investment
Education failures
Low savings rate

Labor-force changes
Female labor-force participation
Aging

Technological change
Factor-biased productivity
improvements in manufacturing
Sectoral-biased productivity
improvements in manufacturing
Productivity gains in services

International factor mobility
Immigration
Capital flows
Technology transfers

Globalization of the markets for goods and services
Lower prices for labor-intensive
tradables (for example, apparel)
Foreign demand for local services
from an external deficit
Reduced market power (for example,
autos and steel)
Delocalization (for example, assembly
in Mexico)
Internationalization of the service
sector (for example, computer
programming in India)

The first step in the argument is to get clear the circumstances in which price reductions for labor-intensive tradables will drive down wages in high-wage markets. The Heckscher-Ohlin (HO) model is a particularly rich conceptual setting for thinking about this issue. This is a model that ought to remind us that *prices are set on the margin*. It does not matter that trade in manufactures is a small proportion of GDP. It does not matter that employment in apparel is only 1 percent of the work force. What matters is whether or not the marginal unskilled worker is employed in the apparel sector, sewing the same garments as a Chinese worker whose wages are one-twentieth of the U.S. level. Then lower prices for apparel as a consequence of increased Chinese apparel supply causes lower wages for all unskilled workers in the same regional labor pool as the U.S. garment worker.

Wage determination in an HO model is described by the Stolper-Samuelson theorem, which links product prices with wages. This theorem reminds us that what matters is not the level of imports of apparel but rather their price. The quantity-oriented tradition of computing the labor embodied in trade and comparing it with the size of the U.S. labor force suffers from several defects that are more fully discussed by me elsewhere.[1] First and foremost is the fact that the factor contents are the *net* external factor supplies. The net external labor supply can change if the external price of labor changes, but it can also change if there are changes in either the internal labor demand or the internal labor supply. For example, technological change that lowers the internal demand for unskilled labor may offset the increase in imports of the services of unskilled workers that might otherwise have come from a fall in the external price. This can keep the imports of labor services low, even as the external marketplace is selecting a lower price for labor.

The first section is designed to present the HO model in as transparent a way as possible. An intellectual bridge between trade theory and labor economics is formed in this section by concentrating completely on the labor demand curve. What does the HO model imply about the labor demand curve? There are many surprising results. Indeed, the most important message of the HO model is that trade in commodities transforms a local labor demand curve into a global labor demand, even though there is not direct arbitrage through labor migration. Another important idea that comes from an HO framework is that the effects on wages of both globalization and technological change should be studied by cross-industry, not within-industry, comparisons. In this general equilibrium framework, with product prices held fixed and to a first order of approximation, it does not matter that the technological change reduces the inputs of unskilled workers in every sector; what matters is whether the technological improvement is concentrated in sectors that are intensive in unskilled workers, intensive in skilled workers, or intensive in capital. *Factor bias does not matter; sector bias does.*[2]

---

[1] Leamer (1995b).

[2] Factor bias can matter if the change is large enough to allow second-order effects, or if the factor-biased technological change precipitates sectoral-biased price adjustments, for example,

The second section is a discussion of various data displays suggested by the HO framework. From this section arises one important conclusion. The three decades under examination had quite different outcomes. The 1960s had relative price stability, growth in all sectors of the economy, and wage gains at every level of skill. The 1970s was the Stolper-Samuelson decade, with price, trade, and employment data consistent with the presence of Stolper-Samuelson effects on wage inequality. The 1980s on the other hand have no evidence of Stolper-Samuelson effects, but globalization nonetheless may be operative through, for example, declines in market power in metals and autos, or through the external deficit that makes the marginal demand for workers come from the local nontraded sector.

When the HO framework is only a loose guide for the examination of the data, it is impossible to infer how much effect relative price variability is having on wage rates. Therefore, in the final section of this chapter, I present a formal data analysis using a specific HO model that attempts to separate the technology effects and the Stolper-Samuelson effects on wage levels and wage inequality. Data on price changes, factor shares, and technological change are used to estimate the "mandated" wage changes required to maintain zero profits across sectors. In this exercise the separation of technology from globalization effects depends on how the observed product price variability is split between technological change and globalization. Ideally, one would have a global supply and demand model that could help to determine what impact technological change is having on product prices. Here a common "pass-through" rate is assumed for all sectors, meaning that a given percent of the technological improvement is passed on to consumers in the form of lower prices. The remaining variability in product prices is attributed to "globalization," thus acting as if product prices were completely determined by the external marketplace.

The analysis is done with the labor force sliced by wage levels and by the usual production/nonproduction distinction. Two conclusions emerge: the residual "globalization" effects on income inequality generally dominate the technological effects; and the 1970s was the Stolper-Samuelson decade with product price changes causing increases in inequality. Product price variability in the 1980s actually worked in the opposite direction. The numbers that emerge from this analysis are very large: 4 percent mandated reduction per year in wages of low-wage workers in the 1970s offset by 2 percent per year gains in the 1980s. Accumulated over the two decades, these numbers are big enough to account for most of the increase in income inequality in the United States.

The major shortcomings of the estimates of the relative impact of globalization and technological change reported in the third section of this chapter are the following:

---

reduction of prices of labor-intensive tradables as a consequence of labor-saving technological changes. However, if the demand for nontradables is highly elastic, the released factors can be absorbed in nontradables with little or no change in tradables prices.

—The estimates are based on one special HO model, which presumes first, that the demand for labor is infinitely elastic, and second, that the globalization "shock" is a product price change which stimulates a factor price response. In this framework, education cannot matter at all because changes in the supply of unskilled or skilled workers have no effect on wages.

—The separation of the observed changes of product prices into globalization and technological components is questionable. In particular, a constant pass-through rate is a doubtful assumption.

—The data on prices, factor shares, and total factor productivity (TFP) are all measured with error.

—There is no consideration whatsoever to the adjustment process by which the labor markets might absorb the news of product price changes. The mandated wage changes apply only over a time frame long enough to allow complete separation of worker and capital from the sectors in which they were originally deployed.

In other words, much is left to be done. We need to compute the "globalization" effects allowing for product-mix changes and/or allowing for the possibility that the marginal demand for labor comes internally from the non-traded-goods sector. We need to be more careful about the demand side to determine how technological change alters product prices. We need to link product price changes more clearly to globalization. We need to explore other ways of measuring the factor shares and TFP. We need to adjust econometrically for measurement errors including outlier problems. We need to consider empirically other forms of globalization including the effect of the external deficit on the demand for nontradables, the increased mobility of knowledge and physical assets, and reduced market power especially in metals and transportation equipment. Finally, we need to explore the implications of other conceptual frameworks, namely the Ricardo-Viner framework that has sector-specific, labor-related assets, as well as the Chamberlainian framework, with increasing returns to scale and imperfect competition.

Nonetheless, I believe that this chapter supports the view that increased competition from low-wage, developing countries during the 1970s had an important impact on the U.S. labor market either in that decade or subsequently. This was the Heckscher-Ohlin, Stolper-Samuelson decade during which there were substantial relative price declines for labor-intensive products made in the United States. The 1980s experienced no continuing price declines for labor-intensive goods, presumably because the U.S. economy had isolated itself from low-wage competition by product upgrading or by trade restrictions, particularly the Multi-Fiber Agreement (MFA). If it is the MFA, then we can expect another round of price reductions of labor-intensive products made in the United States as the MFA is phased out according to plan or as Mexico is able to access the U.S. marketplace relatively free of MFA restrictions. If it is product upgrading, then the United States may have positioned itself so that most categories of labor will benefit from cheaper imports coming from low-wage, developing countries. Research is under way to separate these two possibilities.

FORMAL DECOMPOSITION OF TECHNOLOGICAL AND STOLPER-SAMUELSON EFFECTS

This section reports a formal statistical analysis of a National Bureau of Economic Research (NBER) database on four-digit Standard Industrial Classification (SIC) products compiled by Bartelsman and Gray.[3] The goal is to estimate the impacts of both technological change and globalization on U.S. wages. This analysis uses the one-cone, HO model as a straitjacket. It is assumed that within each decade the mix of tradables produced is constant and sufficient to determine factor prices uniquely. The mix is allowed to vary from decade to decade. This data analysis is thus built on the (unlikely) assumption that the only way that globalization can affect the U.S. labor market is via relative price changes that induce Stolper-Samuelson wage responses. The external deficit is not a consideration, except as it may affect relative prices of tradables. Market power in autos and steel is also not considered.

A crucial step in this attempt to separate the effects of "globalization" from "technological change" is the division of the observed product price changes into components separately associated with these two forces. This calls for an elaborate consideration of both supply and demand sides of a general equilibrium model. Here we use a simple "pass-through" assumption that a selected proportion of the productivity increase is passed on to consumers in the form of lower prices. The residual price variability is attributed to "globalization" on the assumption that tradable-goods prices are determined in the international marketplace. Of course, in markets in which the United States is a major supplier or demander, these product price changes can come from events strictly internal to the United States. Thus we may be putting the "globalization" label onto something strictly internal to the United States. I would defend the analysis against this criticism in two ways. First, this is the methodological mirror image of the usual procedure, which extracts first the globalization effect and attributes everything else to technology.[4] It seems interesting, at least, to go in the opposite direction, first extracting the technological effect and then attributing everything else to globalization. Second and more important, even if the United States has market power, internal prices of tradables can be affected by tariffs and/or nontariff barriers (NTBs). Thus we are getting an answer to the policy question, whether or not the shock is internal or external. For example, when we conclude that relative price declines for apparel and textiles have led to increased income inequality, we are elliptically saying that things would have been different if the United States had used barriers aggressively to maintain relative prices. It does not matter whether the relative price decline came from internal or external events. To remind the reader of this point, the g—for general—replaces globalization in the narrative below.

---

[3] Bartelsman and Gray (1996).

[4] See Mishel and Bernstein (1994) for criticism of this procedure.

Methodology for Estimating the Separate Effects of Globalization and Technological Change on Factor Prices

The foundation of the Stolper-Samuelson theorem is the set of zero-profit conditions $p = A'w$, where p is the vector of product prices, w is the vector of factor costs and A is the matrix of input intensities, inputs per unit of output. Differentiating one of these zero-profit conditions produces

$$dp_i = \sum_k (A_{ik} dw_k + dA_{ik} w_k).$$

Using the usual notation $\hat{x} = dx/x$ this can be written as

$$\hat{p}_i = dp_i/p_i = \sum_k [(A_{ik} w_k/p_i)(dw_k/w_k) + dA_{ik} w_k/p_i] = \sum_k \theta_{ik} \hat{w}_k + \sum_k \theta_{ik} \hat{A}_{ik},$$

Then the input intensity $A_{ik} = v_{ik}/Q_i$, can be differentiated to obtain $\hat{A}_{ik} = \hat{v}_{ik} - \hat{Q}_i$.

Using this and the standard measurement in the growth of total factor productivity implies

$$\hat{TFP}_i = \hat{Q}_i - \sum_k \theta_{ik} \hat{v}_{ik} = -\sum_k \theta_{ik} \hat{A}_{ik},$$

from which we obtain the fundamental condition linking product price changes, factor costs changes, and technology changes

$$\hat{p}_i = \sum_k \theta_{ik} \hat{w}_k - \hat{TFP}_i = \theta_i \hat{w} - \hat{TFP}_i. \tag{1}$$

This is the equation that will serve as a foundation for separating the impacts of globalization and technology on factor prices. From data on a cross section of 450 four-digit SIC industries describing price changes $\hat{p}$, TFP growth $\hat{TFP}$, and beginning-period factor shares θ, we may estimate this equation and interpret the coefficients on the factor shares as the "mandated" changes in factor costs, $\hat{w}$.[5] These are the changes in factor costs that are needed to keep the zero-profits condition operative in the face of changes in technology and product prices. These mandated wage changes can then be compared with actual wage changes. If the two conform adequately, we will argue that we have provided an accurate explanation of the trends in wages. Incidentally, the mandated changes in factor costs may induce actual factor costs in a later decade. The model and the data analysis is entirely silent on issues of timing.

An important apparent implication of equation 1 is that the factor bias of technological change is entirely irrelevant. What matters is only the sectoral distribution of TFP

---

[5] See Leamer (1993, 1994) and Baldwin and Cain (1994) for regressions of this type, and Hilton (1984) for a related analysis.

growth, because only TFP growth by sector enters the equation. This conclusion applies only to small changes and only if the technological change does not induce sector-biased price changes.[6] For discrete changes, we need to include the second-order effects

$$dp_i = \sum_k (A_{ik} dw_k + dA_{ik} w_k + dw_k dA_{ik}).$$

Dividing this by the initial price level produces the equation

$$\hat{p}_i = dp_i/p_1 = \sum_k \theta_{ik} \hat{w}_k + \sum_k \theta_{ik} \hat{A}_{ik} + \sum_k [(A_{ik} w_k/p_i)(dA_{ik}/A_{ik})(dw_k/w_k)].$$

Thus, including the second-order effects, we have

$$\hat{p}_i = \theta_i \hat{w} - T\hat{F}P_i + \hat{A}_i diag(\theta_i) \hat{w}.$$

This does allow factor bias to matter in the general equilibrium through second-order effects involving the product of percentage changes in inputs and percentage changes in wages. This makes life even more complicated since a data analysis that properly deals with these second-order effects must allow for the endogeneity of the factor intensities A.

A second problem with equation 1 is that it is an equilibrium condition entirely silent on the relationship between price changes and TFP growth. Without knowledge of the price changes induced by TFP growth, it is impossible to disentangle the effects of technological change from the effects of globalization and other sources of product price variability. To make the underidentification problem clear, we can separate this equation into two, one part that is due to technology (t) and another that is due to other factors (g) (g standing for globalization but also encompassing demand shifts)

$$\hat{p}_i(t) + \hat{p}_i(g) = \theta_i \hat{w}(t) + \theta_i \hat{w}(g) - T\hat{F}P_i,$$

where

$$\hat{p}_i(t) = \theta_i \hat{w}(t) - T\hat{F}P_i$$
$$\hat{p}_i(g) = \theta_i \hat{w}(g)$$
$$\hat{p}_i = \hat{p}_i(t) + \hat{p}_i(g).$$

Obviously there are many values of the g-effect on wages that are compatible with this set of equations, given data on TFP growth and product price changes. To make any head-

---

[6]The startling conclusion that only sector bias matters was stated unequivocally in the original version of this chapter. A graph produced by Ronald Findlay and some words from Paul Krugman suggested otherwise. What follows is a mapping of the graph and the words into the algebra. In particular, Ronald Findlay's graph forced me to realize the potential importance of second-order effects; Paul Krugman's words made me realize the possibility that factor-biased technological change could induce sectoral-biased price changes.

way in disentangling the globalization effects from the technological effects, we need to get a handle on that portion of the product price change that is due to technological change. To do this in a completely convincing manner, we need to model worldwide demand and supply conditions. This would require a very large modeling effort. An *expedient* alternative is to assume that all sectors have the same "rate of technological pass-through" to product prices, namely $\hat{p}_i(t) = -\lambda T\hat{F}P_i$, where λ is the pass-through rate that is common across sectors.

A zero pass-through rate applies if technological change is specific to a small, open economy that takes product prices as given from the rest of the world. It may be that there are other conditions in which sectors would experience a common pass-through rate, but this would require a special kind of model. Generally, the effect of technological change on product prices is not even confined to the sector experiencing the change. For example, labor-saving technological change regardless of the sectors in which it occurs may induce product price reductions in labor-intensive tradables, thereby shifting demand to labor-intensive products and thus absorbing the workers released by the technological change. In other words, factor-biased technological change may induce sectoral-biased price changes. Then the factor bias of the technological change would matter. But the need for compensating sectoral-biased price changes is less, or possibly not present at all, if the demand for nontradables is highly elastic and if the nontradables sector can absorb the released factors without necessitating changes in the price of tradables.

Intermediate inputs raise yet another difficulty with the pass-through assumption. Including intermediate inputs in equation 1 is no great problem. We simply need to include in the equation the inner product of the materials inputs shares γ and the product prices

$$\textit{Zero-profit identity:} \quad \hat{p}_i = \theta_i\hat{w} + \gamma_i\hat{p} - T\hat{F}P_i. \tag{2}$$

The product prices on the right-hand side of this equation can be moved to the left to create a Stolper-Samuelson system of equations implicitly defining a mapping of "value-added prices" into factor prices

$$\hat{p}_i - \gamma_i\hat{p} = \theta_i\hat{w} - T\hat{F}P_i.$$

This looks good, because it is exactly as before, with value-added prices in place of final goods prices. But the next step is where the danger lurks, namely appropriately treating TFP effects on prices. The assumption that will be used in the calculations below is that TFP improvements affect only value-added prices

$$\textit{Pass-through assumption:} \quad \hat{p}_i(t) - \gamma_i\hat{p}(t) = -\lambda T\hat{F}P_i. \tag{3}$$

In fact, productivity improvements in one sector are likely to have both forward and backward linkages to other sectors. These affect the demand for inputs in the sector experiencing the improvement and also alter the prices of materials in sectors that use the product as an input. An alternative would be to apply the pass-through to final goods prices and to allow for the indirect effect of technological improvements on materials prices. If only the first-round effect on input prices is considered this produces the equation

$$\hat{p}_i(t) - \gamma_i'\{-\lambda T\hat{F}P_i\} = -\lambda T\hat{F}P_i,$$

which basically says that technologically induced price reductions are especially great in sectors that use as inputs the products experiencing technological improvements. Unfortunately, the data set we will be analyzing has materials inputs and materials input prices by sector but not the full set of input-output linkages. Anyway, if one went that route, allowing only for first-round effects would be uncomfortable.

Thus to do the job right, we really need a complete worldwide, general equilibrium, input-output model. We need this to deal with second-order effects, to select pass-through rates, and also to determine sectoral-biased price changes induced by factor-biased technological change. For now we can plow ahead, remembering that we are implicitly assuming that the second-order effects are small, that pass-through rates are similar and apply to value-added prices, and that the factor biases in technological change have not been enough to cause sectoral-biased price changes for tradable goods, possibly because of the absorptive capacity of the nontraded sectors.

Given the pass-through assumption 3, we can find the mandated changes in factor prices that accompany the technological change, namely factor prices satisfying

$$-\lambda T\hat{F}P_i = \theta_i\hat{w}(t) - T\hat{F}P_i, \text{ or equivalently}$$

Technological effect on wages: $\quad (1 - \lambda)T\hat{F}P_i = \theta_i\hat{w}(t).$ (4)

After allowing for some effect of technological change on product prices, what is left over is the globalization effect

$$\hat{p}_i(g) - \gamma_i\hat{p}(g) = (\hat{p}_i - \gamma_i\hat{p}) - [\hat{p}_i(t) - \gamma_i\hat{p}(t)] = \hat{p}_i - \gamma_i\hat{p} + \lambda T\hat{F}P_i.$$

Inserting this into 2 produces the equation linking g-price changes to mandated earnings.

Globalization effect on wages: $\quad \hat{p}_i + \lambda T\hat{F}P_i = \theta_i\hat{w}(g) + \gamma_i\hat{p}.$ (5)

The data analysis I discuss next thus involves two kinds of equations, both with factor shares as explanatory variables. In one set of equations, suggested by 4, the dependent variable is the sectoral growth in TFP. The estimated coefficients from this regression are multiplied by $(1 - \lambda)$ to find the technological effect on mandated earnings. In the other set of equations, suggested by equation 5, the dependent variable is the sectoral-inflation rate adjusted for TFP-induced changes. On the right hand side of equation 5 is the inner product of materials shares and product price changes. The data set does not contain detailed information on the material input shares, but it does contain the overall materials share and the corresponding price level, sector by sector. This is all that we need; we can replace the inner product of materials shares and price inflation rates with the overall materials share times the price inflation rate of materials inputs, sector by sector.

DESCRIPTIVE STATISTICS

Descriptive statistics of the Bartelsman and Gray NBER data on the *hourly earnings* of production workers and the average *annual earnings* of production and nonproduction workers are reported in Table 1.[7] The HO theory used here to explore quantitatively the impact of technological change and globalization on wages assumes that workers and other factors are mobile across sectors. At any point in time, the average wage in an industrial sector would then be determined exclusively by the skill mix in the sector, and not by historical sector-specific investments by workers in human or locational capital. With the additional assumption that skill proportions in each sector are (roughly) constant over time, changes in the distribution of wages across sectors would be driven by changes in wages at different levels of skills. Then the intersectoral dispersion of wages would be an indicator of income inequality. The first purpose of the displays in Table 1 is to support mildly this interpretation of the intersectoral distribution of earnings.

A way to measure wage inequality that does not rely on an assumption of fixed factor ratios would be to find subcategories of workers with skill levels that are fairly uniform within groups and substantially different across groups—perhaps scientists in one group and delivery workers in another. Then differences in the average wage levels of these categories could be used to measure income inequality. Unfortunately, data on employment and earnings for subcategories of workers are difficult to find. Data categorized into production and nonproduction workers are readily available and have been used by Lawrence and Slaughter to study the relationship between wages and globalization.[8] But some colleagues and I have argued that these categories are actually rather broad and suspiciously heterogeneous.[9] The second function of the displays in Table 1 is to cast a bit more doubt on the usefulness of the production/ nonproduction categorization for studying wage inequality across skill groups.

Table 1 has a variety of statistics concerning earnings and has several measures of income inequality highlighted in boldface. (These statistics are not weighted by sector size and can be influenced by relatively unimportant sectors.) Uncorrected for inflation, average hourly *earnings* of production workers rose from $2.27 to $11.11 per hour from 1961 to 1991. Over the same period, average *annual earnings* of production workers rose from $4,530 to $22,530 and nonproduction workers from $7,330 ($7,170) to $35,980.

---

[7] Defined as PRODW/PRODH, PRODW/PRODE, (PAY - PRODW)/(EMP-PRODE).

[8] Lawrence and Slaughter (1993).

[9] Leamer (1994); Mishel and Bernstein (1994).

TABLE 1

Earnings Data, 1961, 1971, 1981, and 1991[a]

	Hourly wages of production workers				Average annual earnings (thousands of U.S. $)								
					Production workers				Nonproduction workers				
	1961	1971	1981	1991	1961	1971	1981	1991	1961	1961[b]	1971	1981	1991
Mean	2.27	3.53	7.61	11.11	4.53	6.98	14.94	22.53	7.33	7.17	10.89	22.99	35.98
Median	2.28	3.55	7.46	10.82	4.63	7.05	14.60	21.87	7.33	7.29	10.99	22.95	35.55
Maximum	3.89	6.20	15.06	27.67	8.13	11.86	29.06	83.00	20.29	9.86	15.25	38.80	54.47
Minimum	1.19	2.00	3.42	4.00	2.20	3.66	5.88	4.00	2.87	2.87	4.93	12.25	17.50
Standard deviation	0.52	0.77	2.21	3.30	1.11	1.63	4.58	7.53	1.54	1.01	1.49	4.06	6.52
Coefficient of variation[c]	**0.23**	**0.22**	**0.29**	**0.30**	**0.24**	**0.23**	**0.31**	**0.33**	**0.21**	**0.14**	**0.14**	**0.18**	**0.18**
Range/median	**1.18**	**1.18**	**1.56**	**2.19**	**1.28**	**1.16**	**1.59**	**3.61**	**2.38**	**0.96**	**0.94**	**1.16**	**1.04**
Range/minimum	**2.28**	**2.10**	**3.40**	**5.92**	**2.69**	**2.24**	**3.94**	**19.75**	**6.07**	**2.44**	**2.09**	**2.17**	**2.11**
N	450	450	450	450	450	450	449	448	449	438	450	450	450

Ratio of nonproduction/production earnings

	1961	1961[b]	1971	1981	1991
Mean	**1.62**	**1.58**	**1.56**	**1.54**	**1.60**
Median	**1.58**	**1.57**	**1.56**	**1.57**	**1.63**

[a] Data not weighted by employment levels.
[b] Vetted sample.
[c] Income inequality measures in bold.
Source: Bartelsman and Gray (1996).

If one thought that the categories of production and nonproduction sorted workers by skill, then the ratio of nonproduction to production earnings would be the measure of income inequality. These ratios for the median earnings in the four periods were 1.58, 1.56, 1.57, and 1.63, thus suggesting that most of the increase in income inequality came after 1980, which is fairly similar with other measures of wage inequality.[10] However, there is a substantial amount of wage inequality across sectors *within* the production and nonproduction categories. In 1971, for example, there was a sector that had average production workers of $3,660 and another with $11,860. In the same period, average earnings of nonproduction workers varied across sectors from a low of $4,930 to a high of $15,250. The substantial overlap of the ranges of these earnings numbers casts doubt on the usefulness of the production/nonproduction categories.

Other measures of wage inequality of the economy are the coefficient of variation, the range relative to the median and the range relative to the minimum (*across sectors*), all of which are reported in Table 1. Most of these suggest an increase in inequality in 1971–81 and some further increase in 1981–91. The coefficient of variation of hourly wages of production workers remained almost unchanged from 1961 to 1971, but then grew by about one-third by 1981, with little change thereafter. The coefficient of variation of the average annual earnings of production workers is similar, as is the coefficient of variation of annual earnings of nonproduction workers, after vetting some extreme sectors in 1961.

Descriptive statistics for TFP growth are reported in Table 2. Note that the middle period, 1971–81, was a period of little TFP growth on average but a great deal of dispersion across sectors. The first decade, 1961–1971, had TFP growth of about 8

TABLE 2

TFP ANNUALIZED COMPOUND GROWTH RATE, 1961–91

	1961–71	1971–81	1981–91
Mean	0.78	0.00	0.33
Value-added weighted mean	0.79	0.17	0.46
Median	0.66	−0.08	0.36
Maximum	10.78	18.33	11.88
Minimum	−4.46	−10.56	−11.66
Standard deviation	1.72	2.18	11.78
Coefficient of variation	2.19	1,831.41	5.43
N	450	450	449

Sources: Bartelsman and Gray (1996); and author's calculations.

[10]For example, see Borjas and Ramey (1993).

percent annually. The third decade, 1981–91, had TFP growth of about 4 percent annually. Both had standard errors of about 1.7 percent. Incidentally, the increased dispersion of the TFP growth figures during the turbulent 1970s is a worrisome reminder that measurement errors may be important.

DISCUSSION OF ESTIMATES

Finally, we turn to estimates of equations 4 and 5 for pass-through rates equal to one and zero. Because the calculation of factor shares is somewhat suspect, it makes sense first just to look at the correlations between price inflation rates and various beginning-of-period sectoral indicators in Table 3. Notice in this table that the price changes are hardly correlated with any of the sectoral indicators in the first decade, 1961–71. In the second decade, 1971–81, price increases were especially high in capital intensive, high-production-wage sectors. In the third decade, 1981–91, price changes were negatively correlated with capital intensity and with material costs. Thus at a first glance, the three-decade story seems to apply. Relative price changes mattered little for determining relative wages in the 1960s; product price changes worked to lower wages in the 1970s, particularly for low-wage production workers; then in the 1980s it was capital that suffered with, possibly, all forms of labor gaining.

Although the simple correlations in Table 3 are highly suggestive, an implication of equations 4 and 5 is that simple correlations of price changes with arbitrarily scaled

TABLE 3

CROSS-SECTION CORRELATIONS OF PRICE INFLATION RATES WITH VARIOUS SERIES, 1961–91[a]

	Unweighted			Weighted by employment[b]		
	1961–71	**1971–81**	**1981–91**	**1961–71**	**1971–81**	**1981–91**
Capital per worker	−0.17	0.36	−0.33	−0.14	0.42	−0.24
Capital per earnings	−0.19	0.31	−0.34	−0.15	0.41	−0.23
Average wages	0.07	0.30	−0.13	0.06	0.16	−0.13
Nonproduction wages (average)	−0.03	0.14	−0.12	−0.06	0.09	−0.18
Production wages (average)	0.10	0.35	−0.12	0.09	0.37	−0.09
Ratio of nonproduction to production workers	0.07	0.01	0.08	0.08	−0.13	0.10
Materials costs as a share of value of shipments	−0.14	0.12	−0.38	−0.08	0.15	−0.27

[a] 450 four-digit SIC manufacturing sectors.
[b] Weighed correlations are estimated as the square root of the R^2 from the weighted OLS regressions where the dependent variable is the price inflation and the independent variable is the series of interest. Sign is determined by the sign of the corresponding coefficient. Weights are defined as the average employment for each sector over the 1961–91 period.
Sources: Bartelsman and Gray (1996); and author's calculations.

industry indicators cannot tell the story. Multiple regressions on factor shares are needed. The final set of tables report attempts to find regressions of this type that make sense. Table 4 reports data on earnings shares and the corresponding definitions of earnings in terms of the Bartlesman and Gray data series. These earnings shares have two important features that need to be mentioned. First, in the absence of direct data on capital rental costs, the capital earnings are simply set to 10 percent of book values of plants, equipment, and inventories. The best approach would be to multiply the sum of the real rate of interest plus depreciation times the capital current market value. The 10 percent real rate of interest is arbitrary but probably not very important, because it affects mostly the capital coefficients in the subsequent regressions and not much the labor coefficients. More important is the implicit assumption that depreciation rates do not vary across sectors. A second observation about the calculations reported in Table 4 is that the earnings of each factor are divided by total earnings, not the value of shipments. Included in the value of shipments are rents to sector-specific assets that come from unexpected price variability. These are explicitly excluded from consideration by the HO conceptual framework that we are using.

To determine earnings of "high-wage" and "low-wage" workers, the wage differences across sectors are interpreted as coming entirely from differences in the mixes of skilled and unskilled workers with the lowest wage sector having entirely low-wage workers and the highest wage sector having entirely high-wage workers. The proportion of high-wage and low-wage workers in other sectors is linearly extrapolated from the level of the wage. In the middle of Table 4 are the wage levels that are used to separate workers into high-wage and low-wage categories. At the bottom are sectors that have been excluded because of extreme values of the nonproduction wage. Note, by the way, that the high-wage production workers are paid considerably more than the low-wage nonproduction workers, thus the apparent overlapping of skills of the two groups.

According to the numbers reported in Table 4, materials constitute the largest share of total earnings, beginning at 61 percent and rising to 65 percent. This increase occurred exclusively in the 1971–81 decade. The capital share also grew, but only slightly, from 7 percent to 9 percent. The gain to materials and capital is almost exactly matched by a reduction in the share of production workers, which fell from 22 percent to 16 percent. This shift away from production workers is the focus of much of Lawrence and Slaughter's discussion.[11] The separation of workers into high-wage and low-wage subcategories has left a larger share of high-wage than low-wage workers. This means that in every case the mean wage level across sectors is lower than the median; the distributions are skewed to the right.

Table 5 contains estimates of equations 4 and 5 for three decades, 1961–71, 1971–81, and 1981–91, using only labor, capital, and materials as inputs. The dependent variables

---

[11]Lawrence and Slaughter (1993).

TABLE 4

AVERAGE FACTOR SHARES OF 450 SIC INDUSTRIES, 1961, 1971, 1981, AND 1991

	1961	1971	1981	1991	Formula for earnings[a]
Labor	0.32	0.32	0.27	0.26	PAY
Total					
High wage	0.25	0.21	0.17	0.17	wH × [PAY − (wL) × EMP] ÷ (wH − wL)
Low wage	0.07	0.11	0.09	0.09	wL × [− PAY + (wH) × EMP] ÷ (wH − wL)
Production	0.22	0.21	0.17	0.16	PRODW
High wage	0.14	0.13	0.12	0.13	wH × [PRODW − (wL) × PRODE] ÷ (wH − wL)
Low wage	0.08	0.08	0.05	0.03	wL × [− PRODW + (wH) × PRODE] ÷ (wH − wL)
Nonproduction	0.10	0.11	0.09	0.10	(PAY − PRODW) = NPRODW
High wage	0.07	0.09	0.06	0.07	wH × [NPRODW − (wL) × NPRODE] ÷ (wH − wL)
Low wage	0.03	0.02	0.03	0.03	wL × [− NPRODW + (wH) × NPRODE] ÷ (wH − wL)
Capital	0.07	0.08	0.08	0.09	0.1 × [(PLANT + EQUIP) × PIINV + INVENT]
Plant and equipment	0.05	0.06	0.06	0.07	0.1 × (PLANT + EQUIP) × PIINV
Plant	0.03	0.03	0.03	0.03	0.1 × (PLANT) × PIINV
Equipment	0.02	0.03	0.03	0.04	0.1 × EQUIP × PIINV
Inventories	0.02	0.02	0.02	0.02	0.1 × INVENT
Materials	0.61	0.60	0.65	0.65	MATCOST
Energy	0.02	0.02	0.04	0.03	ENERGY
Other	0.59	0.58	0.61	0.62	MATCOST − ENERGY
Production					
wH	8.13	11.86	29.06	83.00	Max(PRODW ÷ PRODE)
wL	2.20	3.66	5.88	4.00	Min(PRODW ÷ PRODE)
Nonproduction					
wH	14.93	15.25	38.80	54.47	Max[(PAY − PRODW) ÷ (EMP − PRODE)]
wL	2.87	4.93	12.25	17.50	Min[(PAY − PRODW) ÷ (EMP − PRODE)]
Total					
wH	9.00	13.39	36.13	46.81	Max(PAY ÷ EMP)
wL	1.92	4.03	7.32	12.01	Min(PAY ÷ EMP)

Excluded observations and their SIC codes[b]

	Nonproduction wage	SIC code	Code interpretation
1961	0.93	2519	Household furniture, not classified elsewhere
	20.28	3942	Dolls and stuffed toys
	20.25	2647	Paper products
	16.40	3519	Internal combustion engines, not classified elsewhere
1981	65.66	3339	Primary nonferrous metals, not classified elsewhere
1991	205	2384	Robes and dressing gowns
	2	2794	Printing

[a]Total earnings = PAY + 0.1 × [(PLANT + EQUIP) × PIINV + INVENT] + MATCOST. wH and wL refer to the highest and lowest earnings per worker across the 450 sectors in the given year. Labor shares have been calculated on vetted samples.

[b]Nonproduction wage estimates for 1961, 1981, and 1991 include observations that greatly deviate from the rest of the sample. These observations were excluded from the calculation of all labor shares for the corresponding year and subsequently are excluded from the later regressions (Tables 5–7). For total wages only one observation in 1991 (SIC 2794) was excluded.

Sources: Bartelsman and Gray (1996); and author's calculations.

TABLE 5

REGRESSIONS OF INFLATION AND TFP GROWTH ON BEGINNING-OF-PERIOD EARNINGS SHARES: CAPITAL AND LABOR, 1961–91[a]

	Annualized price inflation			Annualized price inflation plus annualized TFP growth			Annualized TFP growth		
	1961–71	1971–81	1981–91	1961–71	1971–81	1981–91	1961–71	1971–81	1981–91
Estimates									
Labor share	3.27	5.73	5.31	3.19	6.50	2.51	−0.07	0.78	−2.80
Capital share	−5.32	7.27	−4.07	7.93	9.24	9.30	13.25	1.98	13.37
Materials share	b	b	b	b	b	b	c	c	c
Standard errors									
Labor share	0.32	0.73	0.66	0.23	0.31	0.39	0.39	0.78	0.68
Capital share	1.49	2.88	2.34	1.05	1.24	1.38	1.80	3.08	2.39
Mean of dependent variable	1.91	8.01	2.38	2.74	8.18	2.70	0.83	0.17	0.32
S.D. of dependent variable	2.10	5.78	2.88	2.15	5.18	2.17	1.91	3.12	2.24
S.E. of regression	1.44	2.89	2.14	1.02	1.24	1.26	1.74	3.09	2.18

	0 Percent pass-through			100 Percent pass-through		
MAEG[d] due to price changes unrelated to technology[e]						
Labor	1.35	−2.29	2.93	1.28	−1.51	0.13
Capital	−7.24	−0.75	−6.45	6.02	1.23	6.92
MAREG[f] due to technological change						
Labor	−0.07	0.78	−2.80	0.83	0.17	0.32
Capital	13.25	1.98	13.37	0.83	0.17	0.32
Total MAEG						
Labor	1.28	−1.51	0.13	2.11	−1.34	0.45
Capital	6.02	1.23	6.92	6.85	1.40	7.25
Percent "share" due to "globalization"[g]						
Labor	95	75	51	61	90	29
Capital	35	27	33	88	88	96

[a] 450 four-digit SIC manufacturing sectors.
[b] The materials share coefficient is set equal to the sector-specific materials inflation rate.
[c] Materials input shares are excluded because the pass-through is assumed to apply to value-added prices.
[d] MAEG = mandated annualized earnings growth.
[e] Estimates minus inflation.
[f] MAREG = mandated annualized real earnings growth.
[g] Absolute effect ÷ sum of absolute effects.
Sources: Bartelsman and Gray (1996); and author's calculations.

are the compound annualized rate of increase in product prices over the decade and also the annualized growth of TFP. Explanatory variables are beginning-of-period factor shares θ for labor, capital, and materials. The top part of the table contains regressions of price inflation rates and TFP growth rates over three decades on the beginning-of-the-decade capital and labor shares. These regressions are used to form estimates of "mandated" earnings growth reported in the bottom part of the table. The set of regressions in the middle panel at the top of this table use the sum of inflation plus TFP growth as the dependent variable, implicitly assuming that technological change is passed on completely to consumers through lower prices. Notice that these numbers are just the sum of counterparts on the left and right. All these are weighted regression estimates with employment level averaged over the three initial periods as weights.[12]

The coefficients for the 1961–71 price-inflation equation reported in the first column of Table 5 suggest that a 3.27 percent rate of increase in wage rates and a − 5.32 percent rate of increase in capital rental rates would have been consistent with the least change in profits in the economy. With overall inflation equal to 1.91 percent, this means a net annualized real increase in earnings of these factors equal to 1.35 percent and − 7.24 percent, which are numbers reported under the heading "Mandated annualized earnings growth due to price changes unrelated to technology." Below those numbers are the effects of sectoral bias in technological change that are not accompanied by any price changes. These are just the regressions of TFP growth on factor shares. In this 1961–71 period, technological change worked slightly against labor and very much in favor of capital. The sum of these two sets of numbers are reported next in the same column. Thus the total mandated change in labor earnings is 1.28 percent per year, mostly due to the positive g-effect. Capital had a much higher mandated earnings growth of 6.02 percent per year, with a huge technological effect offsetting a large g-effect. If, on the other hand, the pass-through rate is 100 percent and any technological improvement also lowers prices by 100 percent of the TFP growth, then the TFP effect on earnings is neutral across factors and equal to the average TFP improvement in that decade of 0.83 percent. After adjusting for the TFP effect on prices, the mandated growth in wages due to the g-effect is reduced to 1.28 percent. Thus, although the choice of pass-through rate does not much affect the total mandated earnings in 1961–71, it does affect the separation into t-effects and g-effects.

The three-decades story is quite evident in this table.

THE 1960S. Capital-intensive sectors experienced rapid technological improvement but also relative price reductions. These offsetting effects left both labor and capital with improving conditions.

THE 1970S. Wage levels were under downward pressure in the 1970s, entirely because of product price changes that strongly worked against labor.

THE 1980S. Technological change worked strongly against labor. Whether the pass-through rate is low or high, the total mandated wage increases were modest; positive if high and negative if low.

---

[12] Weights are kept constant to avoid changes in the results coming from changing weights. Weights in econometric terms are the inverses of the variances (not standard errors). Employment weights and value-added weights give similar results. Unweighted regressions are entirely different.

TABLE 6

REGRESSIONS OF INFLATION AND TFP GROWTH ON BEGINNING-OF-PERIOD EARNINGS
SHARES: CAPITAL AND HIGH-WAGE AND LOW-WAGE LABOR, 1961–91[a]

	Annualized price inflation			Annualized price inflation plus annualized TFP growth			Annualized TFP growth		
	1961–71	1971–81	1981–91	1961–71	1971–81	1981–91	1961–71	1971–81	1981–91
Estimates									
Labor									
High wage	3.47	6.34	5.36	2.81	8.30	0.47	−0.65	1.96	−4.89
Low wage	2.58	4.79	5.26	4.38	3.75	5.13	1.80	−1.04	−0.14
Capital Share	−5.46	6.56	−4.14	8.30	7.17	11.54	13.75	0.61	15.68
Materials share	b	b	b	b	b	b	c	c	c
Standard errors									
Labor									
High wage	0.45	1.03	0.98	0.32	0.43	0.56	0.54	1.10	0.99
Low wage	1.08	1.34	1.13	0.76	0.55	0.65	1.30	1.43	1.15
Capital share	1.51	3.00	2.47	1.07	1.24	1.41	1.82	3.20	2.50
Mean of dependent variable	1.91	8.01	2.38	2.74	8.18	2.70	0.83	0.17	0.32
S.D. of dependent variable	2.10	5.78	2.88	2.15	5.18	2.17	1.91	3.12	2.24
S.E. of regression	1.44	2.89	2.14	1.01	1.20	1.22	1.73	3.09	2.16

	0 Percent pass-through			**100 Percent pass-through**		
MAEG[d] due to price changes unrelated to technology[e]						
Labor						
High wage	1.56	−1.67	2.98	0.90	0.29	1.91
Low wage	0.67	−3.23	2.89	2.46	−4.27	2.75
Capital	−7.37	−1.46	−6.52	6.39	−0.85	9.16
MAREG[f] due to technological change						
Labor						
High wage	−0.65	1.96	−4.89	0.83	0.17	0.32
Low wage	1.80	−1.04	−0.14	0.83	0.17	0.32
Capital	13.75	0.61	15.68	0.83	0.17	0.32
Total MAEG						
Labor						
High wage	0.90	0.29	−1.91	1.73	0.46	−1.59
Low wage	2.46	−4.27	2.75	3.29	−4.10	3.07
Capital	6.39	−0.85	9.16	7.21	−0.68	9.48
Percent "share" due to "globalization"[g]						
Labor						
High wage	70	46	38	52	63	86
Low wage	27	76	95	75	96	90
Capital	35	70	29	89	83	97

[a] 450 four-digit SIC manufacturing sectors.
[b] The materials share coefficient is set equal to the sector-specific materials inflation rate.
[c] Materials input shares are excluded because the pass-through is assumed to apply to value-added prices.
[d] MAEG = mandated annualized earnings growth.
[e] Estimates minus inflation.
[f] MAREG = mandated annualized real earnings growth.
[g] Absolute effect ÷ sum of absolute effects.
Sources: Bartelsman and Gray (1996); and author's calculations.

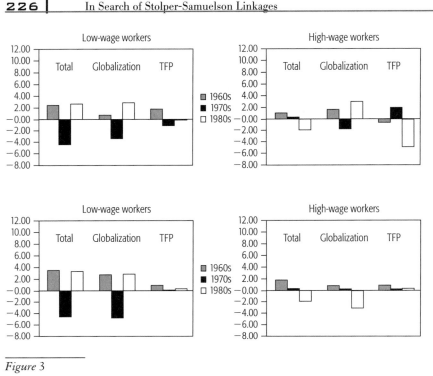

Figure 3

Mandated Wage Changes: Low-Wage and High-Wage Workers, 1960s–80s

Sources: Citibase (Citibank Economic Database), New York: Citibank N.A.; and author's calculations.

Table 6 has the same analysis, with labor categories divided into high-wage and low-wage subcategories. The mandated wage changes from this table are depicted in Figure 3. Here again the three-decades story emerges clearly. The decade of the 1970s is when the g-effect (non-TFP) worked strongly against low-wage workers. This was offset by favorable conditions in the 1980s. This conclusion is not at all affected by the pass-through rate. High-wage workers had smaller mandated wage changes with gains in the 1960s offset by losses in the 1980s. The division of the total losses in the 1980s depends critically on the pass-through rate, with the g-effect dominating for high pass-through rates and the t-effect dominating for low pass-through rates.

Finally, Table 7 and Figure 4 report the same analysis for production/nonproduction subcategories of labor. The conclusions suggested by this table are somewhat different. The pattern of the total effects for production workers is similar to the pattern for low-wage workers, but the nonproduction workers have positive mandated wage increases in all three decades, unlike high-wage workers, who had negative values for the 1980s. For the zero pass-through rate, much more of the action is on the technology side. In particular, the loss suffered by production workers in the 1970s is attributable to technology, not globalization. The reverse conclusion applies if the pass-through is 100 percent, where the action is all due to globalization. With zero pass-through,

TABLE 7

REGRESSIONS OF INFLATION AND TFP GROWTH ON BEGINNING-OF-PERIOD EARNINGS
SHARES: CAPITAL AND PRODUCTION AND NONPRODUCTION LABOR, 1961–91[a]

	Annualized price inflation			Annualized price inflation plus annualized TFP growth			Annualized TFP growth		
	1961–71	1971–81	1981–91	1961–71	1971–81	1981–91	1961–71	1971–81	1981–91
Estimates									
Labor									
Nonproduction	0.68	0.06	5.82	3.62	10.70	3.71	2.94	10.64	−2.11
Production	4.90	9.34	4.89	2.92	3.83	1.52	−1.98	−5.50	−3.37
Capital share	−5.95	6.71	−3.86	8.04	9.66	9.79	13.99	2.95	13.65
Materials share	b	b	b	b	b	b	c	c	c
Standard errors									
Labor									
Nonproduction	0.81	1.59	1.26	0.58	0.66	0.74	0.98	1.65	1.28
Production	0.57	1.15	1.10	0.41	0.48	0.64	0.69	1.20	1.12
Capital share	1.48	2.83	2.38	1.06	1.17	1.39	1.79	2.94	2.43
Mean of dependent variable	1.91	8.01	2.38	2.74	8.18	2.70	0.83	0.17	0.32
S.D. of dependent variable	2.10	5.78	2.88	2.15	5.18	2.17	1.91	3.12	2.24
S.E. of regression	1.42	2.84	2.14	1.02	1.18	1.25	1.72	2.95	2.18

	0 Percent pass-through			**100 Percent pass-through**		
MAEG[d] due to price changes unrelated to technology[e]						
Labor						
Nonproduction	−1.23	−7.95	3.45	1.71	2.68	1.33
Production	2.99	1.32	2.51	1.01	−4.18	−0.86
Capital	−7.87	−1.31	−6.24	6.12	1.65	7.41
MAREG[f] due to technological change						
Labor						
Nonproduction	2.94	10.64	−2.11	0.83	0.17	0.32
Production	−1.98	−5.50	−3.37	0.83	0.17	0.32
Capital	13.99	2.95	13.65	0.83	0.17	0.32
Total MAEG						
Labor						
Nonproduction	1.71	2.68	1.33	2.54	2.85	1.65
Production	1.01	−4.18	−0.86	1.83	−4.01	−0.54
Capital	6.12	1.65	7.41	6.95	1.82	7.73
Percent "share" due to "globalization"[g]						
Labor						
Nonproduction	29	43	62	67	94	81
Production	60	19	43	55	96	73
Capital	36	31	31	88	91	96

[a] 450 four-digit SIC manufacturing sectors.
[b] The materials share coefficient is set equal to the sector-specific materials inflation rate.
[c] Materials input shares are excluded because the pass-through is assumed to apply to value-added prices.
[d] MAEG = mandated annualized earnings growth.
[e] Estimates minus inflation.
[f] MAREG = mandated annualized real earnings growth.
[g] Absolute effect ÷ sum of absolute effects.
Sources: Bartelsman and Gray (1996); and author's calculations.

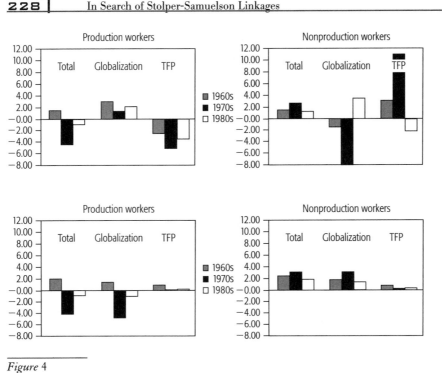

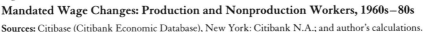

Figure 4

Mandated Wage Changes: Production and Nonproduction Workers, 1960s–80s

Sources: Citibase (Citibank Economic Database), New York: Citibank N.A.; and author's calculations.

technological change is working against production workers and in favor of nonproduction workers, except in the 1980s, when both kinds of labor suffered from sectoral bias in technological change. (Is that corporate downsizing?)

Thus the conclusions that *g*-effects dominate *t*-effects and that the 1970s was the Stolper-Samuelson decade, with product price changes causing increases in inequality, are found in three of the four cases—the exception being the estimates applicable to production/nonproduction workers using a zero pass-through. In that case it is the *t*-effects that dominate, the globalization effect worked to the advantage of production workers in the 1970s.

APPENDIX: DOCUMENTATION OF DATABASE USED IN THE SECTION ON PAGE 212

See documentation in Bartelsman and Gray (1996). This database contains annual information on 450 manufacturing industries from 1958 to 1991. The industries are those defined in the 1972 Standard Industrial Classification, and cover the entire manufacturing sector. Much of the data is taken from the Annual Surveys of Manufactures and Censuses of Manufactures, with the remainder created based on information from various government agencies.

Variable Descriptions and Comments

SIC, YEAR—identify each observation in the dataset (SIC ranges from 2011 to 3999 and YEAR ranges from 58 to 91)

EMP—number of employees (in thousands)—does not include employees in auxiliary (administrative) units

PAY—total payroll (millions of dollars)—does not include Social Security or other legally mandated payments, or employer payments for some fringe benefits

PRODE—number of production workers (in thousands)

PRODH—number of production worker hours (in millions of hours)

PRODW—production worker wages (millions of dollars)

VADD—value added by manufacture (millions of dollars; equals shipments − materials + inventory change)

MATCOST—cost of materials (millions of dollars)—includes energy spending, so to calculate spending on nonenergy materials one must use (MATCOST − ENERGY)

ENERGY—expenditures on purchased fuels and electrical energy (millions of dollars)

VSHIP—value of industry shipments (millions of dollars; not adjusted for inventory changes)

INVENT—end-of-year inventories (millions of dollars; pre-1982 based on any generally accepted accounting method; post-1982 based either at cost or at market, with LIFO users asked to report preadjustment values)

INVEST—new capital spending (millions of dollars; combines spending on structures and equipment)

CAP—real capital stock (millions of 1987 dollars, equals EQUIP + PLANT)

EQUIP—real equipment capital stock (millions of 1987 dollars)

PLANT—real structures capital stock (millions of 1987 dollars)

PISHIP—price deflator for value of shipments (equals 1 in 1987)

PIMAT—price deflator for materials (1 in 1987; all materials, not just nonenergy materials)

PIEN—price deflator for energy (1 in 1987)

PIINV—price deflator for new investment (1 in 1987; combines deflators for structures and equipment)

TFP—five-factor total factor productivity growth (calculated from other variables; expressed as annual growth rate)

REFERENCES

Baldwin, Robert E., and Glen G. Cain, 1994. "Trade and U.S. Relative Wages: Preliminary Results." University of Wisconsin, Department of Economics.

Bartlesman, Eric, and Wayne B. Gray, 1996. "The NBER Manufacturing Productivity Database." Working Paper 205. Cambridge, Mass.: National Bureau of Economic Research.

Bell, Linda A., and Richard B. Freeman, 1991. "The Causes of Increasing Inter-industry Wage Dispersion in the United States." *Industrial and Labor Relations Review* 44 (January):275–87.

Bhagwati, Jagdish, and Vivek H. Dehejia, 1994. "Freer Trade and Wages of the Unskilled—Is Marx Striking Again?" In *Trade and Wages: Leveling Wages Down?* edited by Jagdish Bhagwati and Marvin H. Kosters, 36–75. Washington: American Enterprise Institute.

Bhagwati, Jagdish, and Marvin H. Kosters, 1994. *Trade and Wages: Leveling Wages Down?* Washington: American Enterprise Institute.

Borjas, George J., and Valerie A. Ramey, 1993. "Foreign Competition, Market Power, and Wage Inequality: Theory and Evidence." Working Paper 4556. Cambridge, Mass.: National Bureau of Economic Research.

Davis, Steven J., and John C. Haltiwanger, 1991. "Wage Dispersion between and within U.S. Manufacturing Plants, 1963–86." *Brookings Papers on Economic Activity: Microeconomics*: 115–200.

———, 1995. "Employer Size and Wage Distribution in U.S. Manufacturing." Working Paper 5393. Cambridge, Mass.: National Bureau of Economic Research (December).

Deardorff, Alan V., and Dalia S. Hakura, 1994. "Trade and Wages: What Are the Questions?." In *Trade and Wages: Leveling Wages Down?* edited by Jadgish Bhagwati and Marvin H. Kosters, 76–107. Washington: American Enterprise Institute.

Hilton, R. Spence. 1984. "Commodity Trade and Relative Returns to Factors of Production." *Journal of International Economics* 16 (May):259–70.

Krugman, Paul R. 1995. "Technology, Trade, and Factor Prices." Working Paper 5355. Cambridge, Mass.: National Bureau of Economic Research (November).

Krugman, Paul, and Robert Z. Lawrence, 1993. "Trade, Jobs and Wages." Working Paper 4478. Cambridge, Mass.: National Bureau of Economic Research.

Lawrence, Robert Z., and Matthew J. Slaughter, 1993. "International Trade and American Wages in the 1980s: Giant Sucking Sound or Small Hiccup?" *Brookings Papers on Economic Activity 2: Microeconomics*: 161–226.

Leamer, Edward E. 1984. *Sources of International Comparative Advantage: Theory and Evidence.* MIT Press.

———. 1987. "Paths of Development in the Three-Factor *n*-Good General Equilibrium Model." *Journal of Political Economy* 95 (October):961–99.

———. 1993. "Wage Effects of a U.S.-Mexican Free Trade Agreement." In *The Mexico-U.S. Free Trade Agreement*, edited by Peter M. Garber, 57–125. MIT Press.

———. 1994. "Trade, Wages and Revolving Door Ideas." Working Paper 4716. Cambridge, Mass.: National Bureau of Economic Research (April).

———. 1995a. "The Heckscher-Ohlin Model in Theory and Practice." *Princeton Studies in International Finance* 77 (February).

———. 1995b. "What's the Use of Factor Contents?" Working Paper 5448. Cambridge, Mass.: National Bureau of Economic Research.

Mishel, Lawrence, and Jared Bernstein. 1994. "Is the Technology Black Box Empty? An Empirical Examination of the Impact of Technology on Wage Inequality and the Employment Structure." Washington: Economic Policy Institute.

Sachs, Jeffrey D., and Howard J. Shatz. 1994. "Trade and Jobs in U.S. Manufacturing." *Brookings Papers on Economic Activity 1*: 1–84.

Song, Ligang, 1993. "Sources of International Comparative Advantage: Further Evidence." Ph.D. dissertation, Australian National University.

ABOUT THE AUTHOR

Edward E. Leamer

Edward Leamer is the Chauncey J. Medberry Professor of Management, Professor of Economics, Professor of Statistics, and Director of the Business Forecast Project at the University of California at Los Angeles (UCLA). He received a B.A. in mathematics from Princeton, a Ph.D. in economics and an M.A. in mathematics from the University of Michigan. After serving as assistant and associate professor at Harvard University, he joined UCLA in 1975 as professor of economics and served as chair from 1983 to 1987. Professor Leamer is a fellow of the American Academy of Arts and Sciences, and a fellow of the Econometric Society.

Editor's Queries

What advice do you have to offer graduate students in the field of international economics? Find your passion and pursue it. The Epicureans tell us "pleasure, not truth, is the end and aim of life," to which I would add "truth is pleasure." If things go well, you will be asked to edit a volume of readings and you can stuff it full of your own work.

GRAVITY MODEL

Charles Engel and John H. Rogers

How Wide Is the Border?

CHARLES ENGEL AND JOHN H. ROGERS

We use CPI data for U.S. and Canadian cities for 14 categories of consumer prices to examine the nature of the deviations from the law of one price. The distance between cities explains a significant amount of the variation in the prices of similar goods in different cities. But the variation of the price is much higher for two cities located in different countries than for two equidistant cities in the same country. We explore some of the reasons for this finding. Sticky nominal prices appear to be one explanation but probably do not explain most of the border effect. (JEL F40, F41)

The failure of the law of one price in international trade has been widely documented (see Peter Isard [1977] for an early example). It should be no surprise that similar goods sold in different locations have different prices. Indeed, Gerard Debreu (1959 pp. 29–30) in *Theory of Value* defines goods to be different if they are not sold in the same place: "Finally wheat available in Minneapolis and wheat available in Chicago play also entirely different economic roles for a flour mill which is to use them. Again, a good at a certain location and the same good at a different location are *different* economic objects, and the specification of the location at which it will be available is essential." Only when costs are borne to transport wheat from Chicago to Minneapolis will the miller in Minneapolis consider the Chicago wheat equivalent to the Minneapolis wheat. But can the international failure of the law of one price be attributed entirely to this segmentation of markets by physical distance, or are there other factors, such as nominal price-stickiness, that help to explain the failure?

Engel: Department of Economics, University of Washington, Seattle, WA 98195-3330, and National Bureau of Economic Research; Rogers: Division of International Finance, Board of Governors of the Federal Reserve System, Washington, DC, 20551. We thank the participants in the workshops at the Federal Reserve Board, the Federal Reserve Banks of Kansas City and New York, the NBER Summer Institute, Columbia University, Indiana University, Michigan State University, Penn State University, Princeton University, the University of California-Santa Cruz, UCLA, and the University of Washington for very helpful comments. Some of the work on this project was done while Engel was a Visiting Scholar at the Federal Reserve Bank of Kansas City. The views expressed in this paper are those of the authors and do not necessarily reflect those of the Board of Governors or the Federal Reserve System. The National Science Foundation provided support for this project under grant number SBR-932078.

Recent evidence suggests that not only are failures of the law of one price significant, but they play a dominant role in the behavior of real exchange rates. Engel (1993, 1995) and Rogers and Michael Jenkins (1995) examine the time-series behavior of prices of goods across and within countries. They find that the movement of prices of similar goods across borders accounts for much of the motion in real exchange rates. The variation in these prices appears to be far more significant in explaining real exchange rates than are movements in relative prices of different goods within a country's borders (such as nontraded to traded goods prices).

We examine the importance of distance between locations where goods are sold and the presence of national borders separating locations in determining the degree of the failure of the law of one price. We employ consumer price data disaggregated into 14 categories of goods. We make use of data available for nine Canadian cities and 14 cities in the United States. The basic hypothesis is that the volatility of the price of similar goods between cities should be positively related to the distance between those cities; but holding distance constant, volatility should be higher between two cities separated by the national border.

Our basic empirical results show that both distance and the border are significant in explaining price dispersion across locations. We provide a measure of how important the border is relative to distance—the "width" of the border. While distance is an economically significant determinant of price dispersion, the effect of the border relative to distance is extremely large. We explore some of the possible reasons why the border is so important, such as nominal price stickiness, integration of labor markets and trade barriers. Nominal price stickiness appears to account for a large portion of the border effect, but most of the effect is left unexplained.

I. Price Dispersion among Locations

The failure of prices of similar goods to equalize between sites is a sign that the markets are not completely integrated. There are several notions of market integration in the literature. It is helpful to enunciate a simple general framework that highlights the roles of distance and the border in determining price variation between locations.

Consider all final goods sold to consumers to be nontraded. (Kalyan K. Sanyal and Ronald W. Jones [1982] analyze a competitive model with this assumption.) Even the prices of goods that are normally classified as tradable, such as nonperishable commodities, must reflect costs of marketing and distribution, which are nontraded services. On the other hand, all goods contain a tradable intermediate component. If the final product is sold by a profit-maximizing monopolist in each location j, the price of good i is determined by

$$p_j^i = \beta_j^i \alpha_j^i (w_j^i)^{\gamma_i} (q_j^i)^{1 - \gamma_i}. \tag{1}$$

With a Cobb-Douglas technology, γ_i is the share of the nontraded service in final output. The price of the nontraded service, w_j^i, and the price of the traded intermediate input, q_j^i, are determined in competitive markets. The total productivity of the final-goods sector is measured by α_j^i. The markup over costs, β_j^i, is inversely related to the elasticity of demand.[1]

Geographical separation of markets provides one reason that the price of similar goods might vary across locations. Recent work in international trade, spearheaded by Paul Krugman (1991) and including empirical work by Jeffrey Frankel et al. (1995) and John McCallum (1995),[2] suggests that much of the pattern of international trade can be explained by geographical considerations. Countries are more likely to trade with neighbors because transportation costs are lower. Transportation costs may also be an explanation for the failure of the law of one price (as in Bernard Dumas [1992]). In equation (1), q_j^i may vary across location if there are costs of transporting the tradable good. With the "iceberg" transportation costs of Krugman and others, price q_j^i is not necessarily equalized with the price in location k, q_k^i. The relative price could fluctuate in a range, $1/d_i \leq q_j^i/q_k^i \leq d_i$. The transportation cost, d_i, should depend positively on the distance between locations, so that the range of variation in q_j^i/q_k^i depends on that distance.[3]

It is also possible that places that are farther apart would have less similar cost structures, so that w_j^i/w_k^i and α_j^i/α_k^i might also vary more between more distant locations. From equation (1), these locations would have greater price dispersion.

However, we also entertain the possibility that price variation of similar goods over time might be higher if the cities lie across national borders, holding distance constant. The recent literature on pricing to market (e.g., Rudiger Dornbusch, 1987; Krugman, 1987; Avinash Dixit, 1989; Robert C. Feenstra, 1989; Kenneth A. Froot and Paul D. Klemperer, 1989; Michael N. Knetter, 1989, 1993; Kenneth Kasa, 1992) has examined markets that are segmented by borders.

There are a few reasons why the border might matter. Much of the pricing-to-market literature has emphasized that the markup, β_j^i, may be different across locations, and may vary with exchange rate changes. Alternatively, the markets for the nontraded marketing service might be more highly integrated on a national basis, so that w_j^i is more similar between two sites within a country than in two places separated by a border. These marketing services are likely to be highly labor-intensive. To the extent that the two national labor markets are more separated than are local labor markets within a country, there would be more variation in cross-border prices than in within-country prices. There might also be direct costs to crossing borders because of tariffs

---

[1] If ε is the elasticity, $\beta = \varepsilon/(\varepsilon - 1)$.

[2] The McCallum paper is complementary to this one, in that it uses data from the states in the United States and provinces in Canada to measure the effects on the volume of trade of distance and crossing the national border.

[3] In the iceberg model, a fraction $1 - (1/d_i)$ of the good melts.

and other trade restrictions. In addition, there may be more homogeneity to the relative productivity shocks, α_j^i/α_k^i, for city pairs within the same country than for cross-border city pairs, so that, from equation (1), cross-border pairs have more price volatility.

An important reason why the border matters is unrelated to equation (1): the price of a consumer good might be sticky in terms of the currency of the country in which the good is sold. Goods sold in the United States might have sticky prices in U.S. dollar terms, and goods sold in Canada might have sticky prices in Canadian dollar terms. The nominal exchange rate is, in fact, highly variable. In this case, the cross-border prices would fluctuate along with the exchange rate, but the within-country prices would be fairly stable. Price stickiness may be dependent upon market segmentation. It would be easier for a producer in one location to resist attempts to undercut his fixed nominal price if markets were separated.

The sticky-price explanation is a natural one that has been addressed in previous literature. Our test is in part inspired by Michael Mussa (1986), who noted that the variance of the real exchange rate based on all goods in the consumer price index is larger for Toronto versus Chicago, Vancouver versus Chicago, Toronto versus Los Angeles, and Vancouver versus Los Angeles than it is for Toronto versus Vancouver and Chicago versus Los Angeles when there are floating exchange rates between the United States and Canada. He attributes this pattern to sticky prices or, in his terms, nominal exchange-regime nonneutrality. Within the recent literature on pricing to market, Richard C. Marston (1990) and Alberto Giovannini (1988) specifically consider the role of nominal price stickiness.

II. Distance and the Border

A. The Regressions

We use consumer price data from 23 North American cities for 14 disaggregated consumer price indexes. The data cover the period from June 1978 to December 1994. Table 1 lists the goods and cities in our study. The Data Appendix provides more detail on the construction of the price data.

For our purposes, it is natural to choose the United States and Canada as the countries to study. First, the countries share a border. Were it not for the country borders, one would expect more trade to occur between Toronto and New York than between New York and Los Angeles. Indeed, there are no other examples of adjacent market economies that are as large in area (so that there can be significant distances between major cities within a country). Also, trade has been relatively free between the two countries. If the border matters, it is unlikely that it matters because of trade restrictions. The facts that both countries are mostly English-speaking and have similar cultural and political traditions suggest that there is likely to be more cross-border labor migration than between most countries.

TABLE 1

CATEGORIES OF GOODS IN DISAGGREGATED CONSUMER PRICE INDEXES AND CITIES USED

Good	United States	Canada
1	Food at home	Food purchased from stores
2	Food away from home	Food purchased — restaurants
3	Alcoholic beverages	Alcoholic beverages
4	Shelter	Shelter − 0.2135 (water, fuel, and electricity)
5	Fuel and other utilities	Water, fuel, and electricity
6	Household furnishings and operations	Housing excluding shelter
7	Men's and boys' apparel	0.8058 (Men's wear) + 0.1942 (boys' wear)
8	Women's and girls' apparel	0.8355 (Women's wear) + 0.1645 (girls' wear)
9	Footwear	Footwear
10	Private transportation	Private transportation
11	Public transportation	Public transportation
12	Medical care	Health care
13	Personal care	Personal care
14	Entertainment	0.8567 (Recreation) + 0.1433 (reading material)

Note: The cities included are: Baltimore, Boston, Chicago, Dallas, Detroit, Houston, Los Angeles, Miami, New York, Philadelphia, Pittsburgh, San Francisco, St. Louis, and Washington DC; Calgary, Edmonton, Montreal, Ottawa, Quebec, Regina, Toronto, Vancouver, and Winnipeg.

We hypothesize that the volatility of the prices of similar goods sold in different locations is related to the distance between the locations and other explanatory variables, including a dummy variable for whether the cities are in different countries.

Let $P^i_{j,k}$ be the log of the price of good i in location j relative to the price of good i in location k. (All prices are converted into U.S. dollars using a monthly average exchange rate before taking relative prices.) We take the difference in the log of the relative price between time t and $t - 2$ as our measure of $P^i_{j,k}$. We take the two-month difference because, for some of our U.S. cities, the price data are only reported every other month. We calculate its volatility as the standard deviation.[4]

We also consider a filtered measure of $P^i_{j,k}$. We regress the log of the relative price on 12 seasonal dummies and six monthly lags.[5] We then take the two-month-ahead in-sample

---

[4] We also performed all of our tests using the spread between the 10th and 90th percentiles as the measure of volatility. Our results were essentially identical to the results reported here.

[5] In the case of the data that are bimonthly, we regress the log of the relative price on three bimonthly lags and six seasonal dummies.

TABLE 2

AVERAGE PRICE VOLATILITY

Good	City pairs		
	U.S.–U.S.	Canada–Canada	U.S.–Canada
1	0.0139	0.0198	0.0247
2	0.0130	0.0100	0.0214
3	0.0185	0.0149	0.0271
4	0.0217	0.0085	0.0250
5	0.0486	0.0279	0.0498
6	0.0203	0.0097	0.0236
7	0.0483	0.0167	0.0461
8	0.0880	0.0178	0.0813
9	0.0618	0.0192	0.0505
10	0.0111	0.0186	0.0260
11	0.0443	0.0240	0.0628
12	0.0133	0.0190	0.0259
13	0.0258	0.0143	0.0271
14	0.0203	0.0083	0.0232
1–14	0.0321	0.0163	0.0367
Distance (miles):	1,024 (66 pairs)	1,124 (36 pairs)	1,346 (126 pairs)

Notes: Entries give the mean value of price volatility across all intercity combinations within the United States, within Canada, and across the U.S.–Canadian border, respectively. The measure of volatility is the standard deviation of the relative price series. Prices are measured as two-month differences. The average distance between cities is given in the final row. The sample period is September 1978–December 1994.

forecast error from this regression as our measure of $P^i_{j,k}$. The in-sample forecast errors cover the period from February 1979 to December 1994. Qualitatively, the results were very similar, irrespective of our measure of prices. We report regressions for the two-month difference of the logs because these numbers are easily reproducible.

For each good i, there are 228 city pairs for which we have observations.[6] For each city pair, we calculate our measure of volatility using the time series on relative prices. Then, we conduct our analysis based on the cross section of 228 volatility measures.

Table 2 reports selected summary statistics. For each of the 14 goods, we report the average standard deviation for pairs of cities that are (a) both in the United States, (b) both in

[6]We do not attempt to match the U.S. cities whose data is reported in odd-numbered months with the even-month cities.

Canada, and (c) one in each country. Table 2 also reports the average distance between those cities. The table reveals that the volatility of prices between U.S. city pairs is generally slightly higher than that between Canadian city pairs, but cross-border city pairs have much higher volatility. However, cross-border city pairs are farther apart, on average, as well.

These generalizations from Table 2 do not apply to goods 7, 8, and 9: men's and boys' apparel, women's and girls' apparel, and footwear. For these goods, the variance of prices across U.S. cities is substantial. In fact, on average, it is greater for the U.S. city pairs than for the cross-border city pairs, and far greater than for the Canadian city pairs. These are the only three goods that exhibit this pattern.

The apparel goods are different from the other goods in several respects: (i) This category of goods probably has some of the most product differentiation. (ii) The prices of these goods are very seasonal.[7] (iii) Compared to other goods, a large fraction of clothing is imported from outside of United States and Canada.

Our regressions attempt to explain $V(P^i_{j,k})$, the volatility of $P^i_{j,k}$. We estimate

$$V(P^i_{j,k}) = \beta^i_1 r_{j,k} + \beta^i_2 B_{j,k} + \sum_{m=1}^{n} \gamma^i_m D_m + u_{j,k} \qquad (2)$$

where $r_{j,k}$ is the log of the distance between locations. As in the gravity model of trade, we posit a concave relationship between relative-price volatility and distance. $B_{j,k}$ is a dummy variable for whether locations j and k are in different countries. For reasons we have explained, we expect the coefficient on this variable to be positive. The regression error is denoted as $u_{j,k}$. Note this is a cross-section regression.

We also include a dummy variable in equation (2) for each city in our sample, D_m. That is, for city pair (j, k) the dummy variables for city j and city k take on values of 1. There are a few reasons why we allow the level of the standard deviation to vary from city to city. First, there may be idiosyncratic measurement error or seasonalities in some cities that make their prices more volatile on average. Second, for the cities that report prices only bimonthly, there may be additional volatility that is introduced by measurement error from the less frequent observation of prices. Third, as Table 2 indicates, there seems to be somewhat higher average volatility for U.S. cities than for Canadian cities. This may be because the United States is a more heterogeneous country. Either labor markets or goods markets may be less integrated, so there can be greater discrepancies in prices between locations. Alternatively, there may be differences in methodologies for recording prices that lead to greater discrepancies in prices between locations in one country compared to the other.[8]

---

[7]However, we note that the apparel commodities show the same pattern of volatility when we use the filtered data, which presumably take out seasonals.

[8]We could impose the restriction that the coefficient on the dummy for all U.S. cities be equal, and that it be equal for all Canadian cities. In all of the regressions we report here, that restriction is strongly rejected.

Table 3 reports our regressions for each of the 14 goods. We find strong evidence that distance is helpful in explaining price dispersion across cities. The coefficient on the log of distance is positive for 13 of the 14 goods, and it is significant at the 5-percent level in ten of the regressions.[9] In the one case in which the sign is wrong, the coefficient is not significantly different from zero. In most of the cases, the t statistics are very large.

The coefficients on the dummy variable for the border are of the hypothesized sign and highly significant for all 14 of the goods. The interpretation of the coefficient on the border dummy in this regression is the difference between the average standard deviation of prices for city pairs that lie across the border less the average for pairs that lie within one of the two countries, taking into account the effect of distance.

We note that the model works well even for the apparel commodities. The excess volatility for U.S. apparel derives from a few cities, but with city dummy variables included, distance and the border still have significant explanatory power.

We test for the restrictions that the coefficients on distance are the same in all regressions and the coefficients on the border dummy are the same in all regressions. The test statistics (not reported) are large, and the restrictions are very strongly rejected. Nonetheless, we report the results for the regressions pooling the data across all goods. Because we allow a separate intercept term for each good and for all but one city, the coefficients reported for distance and the border dummy in the pooled regression are simply the average of the coefficients across the 14 goods. Thus, the pooled regression provides a useful summary of the relationship between price dispersion and the explanatory variables. The last row of Table 3 reports the pooled results for all goods. We find that the coefficients on distance and the border dummy are highly significant and of the hypothesized sign.

The results using the filtered measure for prices are recorded as specification 1 in Table 4 and are very similar to those for the two-month differences. Distance has a positive effect on price dispersion in all regressions and is significant for eight of the 14 goods. The coefficient on the border dummy is positive and significant in all cases. If we restrict our tests to just those cities for which we have monthly data, our results are virtually unchanged qualitatively. (These results are not reported.)

Regression results when the distance function is quadratic, rather than logarithmic, are reported as specification 2 in Table 4. This specification is interesting because it allows a test for our assumption of a concave distance relationship. In fact, we find that distance has a positive effect on price variability in 13 of the 14 regressions and is significant at the 5-percent level in 11 of those regressions. Furthermore, in all 13 regressions where distance has a positive effect, the square of distance has a negative effect. It is significantly

---

[9]We calculated bootstrapped distributions for the t statistics in the first line of Table 3. The inference from the bootstrapped distributions is approximately the same as from the t distribution. Details are in an econometric appendix available from the authors upon request.

TABLE 3

REGRESSIONS RELATING PRICE VOLATILITY TO
DISTANCE AND THE BORDER

Good	Log distance	Border	Adjusted R^2
1	4.95 (2.32)	7.50 (0.18)	0.94
2	1.84 (0.89)	9.71 (0.11)	0.97
3	3.50 (2.80)	9.98 (0.22)	0.93
4	8.37 (1.78)	9.42 (0.21)	0.93
5	35.7 (6.88)	10.5 (0.74)	0.81
6	1.11 (0.97)	8.26 (0.12)	0.97
7	10.5 (2.79)	12.9 (0.34)	0.96
8	28.1 (7.34)	26.4 (0.89)	0.93
9	7.74 (3.23)	9.20 (0.36)	0.97
10	9.80 (2.19)	10.8 (0.20)	0.95
11	32.9 (7.70)	27.3 (0.95)	0.87
12	−1.25 (2.23)	9.66 (0.23)	0.97
13	0.02 (1.67)	6.70 (0.18)	0.94
14	5.08 (1.13)	8.58 (0.14)	0.97
1–14	10.6 (3.25)	11.9 (0.42)	0.77

Notes: All regressions contain as explanatory variables dummies for each of the 23 individual cities, in addition to the variables listed in the cell. Heteroscedasticity-consistent standard errors (Halbert White, 1980) are reported in parentheses. Coefficients and standard errors on log distance are multiplied by 10^4, while those for "border" are multiplied by 10^3. The dependent variable is the standard deviation of the two-month difference in the relative price. Standard deviations are computed over the sample period from September 1978 to December 1994. There are 228 observations in each regression.

TABLE 4

ALTERNATIVE SPECIFICATIONS OF PRICE VOLATILITY REGRESSIONS

Good	Specification 1			Specification 2			
	Log distance	Border	Adjusted R^2	Distance	Distance squared	Border	Adjusted R^2
1	4.32 (1.92)	6.61 (0.17)	0.93	2.08 (0.92)	−6.53 (2.93)	7.53 (0.18)	0.93
2	2.26 (0.84)	9.81 (0.12)	0.97	1.00 (0.42)	−3.57 (1.69)	9.72 (0.11)	0.97
3	2.34 (2.79)	9.94 (0.21)	0.93	2.21 (1.04)	−7.88 (3.34)	10.0 (0.22)	0.93
4	7.00 (1.58)	9.96 (0.18)	0.95	3.56 (0.76)	−11.1 (2.78)	9.45 (0.20)	0.94
5	28.7 (5.29)	7.48 (0.59)	0.78	11.7 (3.62)	−33.8 (13.0)	10.7 (0.73)	0.78
6	1.21 (0.95)	8.90 (0.12)	0.97	0.48 (0.43)	−1.54 (1.60)	8.27 (0.12)	0.97
7	2.40 (2.40)	10.8 (0.32)	0.96	4.20 (1.07)	−13.1 (3.86)	13.0 (0.34)	0.96
8	12.2 (3.24)	17.0 (0.47)	0.97	8.76 (2.95)	−24.5 (10.6)	26.6 (0.88)	0.93
9	4.98 (3.04)	9.72 (0.33)	0.97	4.04 (1.30)	−12.9 (4.62)	9.19 (0.35)	0.97
10	9.04 (1.97)	11.0 (0.18)	0.96	4.17 (0.82)	−13.4 (2.71)	10.9 (0.20)	0.95
11	22.2 (4.91)	24.2 (0.65)	0.98	7.97 (2.91)	−13.6 (13.0)	27.2 (0.93)	0.88
12	0.25 (2.05)	8.51 (0.19)	0.98	20.42 (0.98)	0.75 (3.25)	9.68 (0.23)	0.97
13	1.31 (1.77)	7.02 (0.19)	0.93	0.78 (0.80)	−3.23 (2.76)	6.69 (0.18)	0.94
14	3.13 (0.94)	9.75 (0.11)	0.98	2.43 (0.39)	−7.69 (1.34)	8.58 (0.13)	0.97
1–14	7.24 (2.73)	10.8 (0.35)	0.77	3.79 (1.36)	−10.9 (4.68)	12.0 (0.42)	0.77

Notes: All regressions contain as explanatory variables a dummy for each of the 23 individual cities, in addition to the variables listed in the cell. Heteroscedasticity-consistent standard errors (White, 1980) are reported in parentheses. Coefficients and standard errors on log distance, border, distance, and distance squared are multiplied by 10^4, 10^3, 10^6, and 10^{10}, respectively. In specification 1, the dependent variable is the standard deviation of the two-month-ahead forecast error from the filtered relative price. In specification 2, the dependent variable is the standard deviation of the two-month difference in the relative price. Standard deviations are computed over the sample period from September 1978 to December 1994. There are 228 observations in each regression.

negative for the 11 goods that have a significantly positive distance effect. This is what we would expect if the distance relationship were concave. Once again, in this specification, the border dummy is positive and significant in all cases.

Although we report White's (1980) heteroscedasticity-consistent standard errors, we also specifically allow for the possibility that the variance of the error term might be greater for more distant cities. The first specification in Table 5 reports results when the left- and right-hand-side variables are all deflated by the log of distance, so that the standard deviation of the regression error is modeled as being proportional to the log of distance between cities. That is, we estimate

$$V(P_{j,k}^i)/r_{j,k} = \beta_1^i + \beta_2^i(B_{j,k}/r_{j,k}) + \sum_{m=1}^{n} \gamma_m^i(D_m/r_{j,k}) + \nu_{j,k}.$$

The constant terms and the coefficients on the deflated border dummy are positive, as predicted, and highly significant in the regressions for each of the 14 goods.

We try several extensions to test the robustness of our results. In order to conserve space, we do not report these results. One variation is to alter the period covered by the data. We eliminate the early 1980's from our sample, using only data starting in September 1985. Over this later period the U.S. dollar experienced large swings in its value. There was virtually no change in the results in these regressions from the ones using the entire sample.

We also split the sample at January 1990, when the Canadian–U.S. Free Trade Agreement went into effect. If trade barriers are an important reason why the border variable is economically significant in explaining price dispersion, one would expect that the magnitude of this variable would decline after 1989. In fact, we found a slight tendency in the opposite direction: the estimated border coefficients were usually larger in the post-1989 period.

In general, there was very little difference in our full-sample estimates and our post-September 1985 and post-January 1990 results. Distance and the border dummy had positive coefficients for the same goods in all three samples. Not surprisingly, the t-statistics were smaller in the shorter samples.

One other convex specification of the distance variable we tried is one in which we hypothesize that, after a certain critical distance (arbitrarily chosen to be 1,700 miles), additional distance does not contribute at all to volatility. In this model, there is a linear relation between volatility and distance for distances up to 1,700 miles, and then after 1,700 miles the derivative of volatility with respect to distance is zero. This model performs almost identically to the log-distance function in terms of the number of correct signs on coefficient estimates, the degree of significance, the adjusted R^2, and the magnitude of the coefficients on the border dummy.[10]

---

[10]We also included a dummy variable for pairs of cities in the same province or state. Inclusion of this dummy did not appreciably alter our results.

TABLE 5

ASSESSING THE ROLE OF DISTANCE

Good	Specification 1 Border			Specification 2		Specification 3	
	Constant	Log distance	Adjusted R^2	Log distance	Adjusted R^2	Log distance	Adjusted R^2
1	2.84 (0.22)	0.96 (0.05)	0.79	0.26 (0.12)	0.83	1.99 (0.53)	0.61
2	1.79 (0.14)	1.30 (0.03)	0.88	0.30 (0.11)	0.93	0.36 (0.11)	0.89
3	2.95 (0.30)	1.31 (0.06)	0.77	0.39 (0.21)	0.91	1.67 (0.72)	0.20
4	3.06 (0.28)	1.27 (0.05)	0.86	1.50 (0.36)	0.67	0.96 (0.27)	0.49
5	5.04 (0.33)	1.39 (0.13)	0.77	6.06 (1.00)	0.76	4.04 (0.84)	0.80
6	5.66 (0.40)	1.03 (0.05)	0.81	−0.05 (0.18)	0.87	50.2 (13.0)	0.58
7	10.2 (0.69)	1.59 (0.10)	0.87	0.38 (0.40)	0.85	1.91 (0.47)	0.55
8	19.1 (1.38)	3.41 (0.19)	0.89	2.29 (0.74)	0.85	1.57 (0.37)	0.90
9	10.2 (0.96)	0.95 (0.12)	0.87	−0.31 (0.72)	0.88	1.85 (0.49)	0.70
10	1.50 (0.17)	1.52 (0.05)	0.89	1.45 (0.24)	0.79	2.25 (0.40)	0.81
11	7.11 (0.63)	3.74 (0.15)	0.82	1.08 (0.51)	0.74	5.49 (0.78)	0.89
12	2.32 (0.25)	1.22 (0.07)	0.89	0.14 (0.16)	0.79	0.31 (0.31)	0.99
13	4.42 (0.50)	0.76 (0.06)	0.73	0.36 (0.26)	0.85	0.18 (0.13)	0.89
14	4.14 (0.31)	1.13 (0.04)	0.85	0.33 (0.17)	0.88	1.70 (0.09)	0.92
1–14	19.8 (1.19)	12.3 (0.41)	0.77	1.01 (0.32)	0.91	1.77 (0.26)	0.61

Notes: Heteroscedasticity-consistent standard errors (White, 1980) are reported in parenthesis. Specification 1 is the same as the specification in Table 3, with all variables deflated by the log of distance. In specification 2, the standard deviation of the two-month difference in the relative price for within-U.S. pairs is regressed on the log of distance and 14 individual U.S. city dummies. In specification 3, the standard deviation of the two-month difference in the relative price for within-Canada pairs is regressed on the log of distance and nine individual Canadian city dummies. All coefficients and standard errors have been multiplied by 1,000. Standard deviations are computed over the sample period from September 1978 to December 1994. There are 228 observations in each regression.

B. How Important Are Distance and the Border?

We have seen that physical distance plays a significant role in explaining the failure in the law of one price between two locations. But physical distance alone does not explain the variability in prices of similar goods if the two locations are in different countries—the border matters.

We would like to get an idea of the economic significance of the border relative to distance in determining price dispersion. One way to do this is by examining the average coefficients on log distance and the border dummy from the regression in Table 3, which equal the reported coefficients for the pooled regression. There, the coefficient on the border is 11.9×10^{-3}, and on the log of distance it is 10.6×10^{-4}. Thus, crossing the border adds 11.9×10^{-3} to the average standard deviation of prices between pairs of cities. In order to generate that much volatility by distance, the cities would have to be 75,000 miles apart.[11] This calculation indicates that crossing the border adds substantially to volatility. Actually, this statistic may overstate the economic importance of the border, given that the natural log function is concave, and given the imprecision of the estimate of the coefficient on log distance. The 95-percent confidence interval for the distance coefficient is $(5.3 \times 10^{-4}, 15.9 \times 10^{-4})$. If we were to use the upper end of the confidence interval as the measure of the impact of distance, then crossing the border is equivalent to 1,780 miles of distance between cities. The effect of distance may also be understated if the log-distance function is not the appropriate one.

This statistic may not be meaningful if distance does not contribute much to the dispersion of prices—but that is not the case. Consider the price dispersion for cross-border pairs of cities. From Table 2, the average standard deviation is 0.0367. The border, which adds 0.0119 to the standard deviation of cross-border pairs, accounts for 32.4 percent of this. The average log distance between cross-border pairs is 7.03, so on average distance adds 0.00745 to the standard deviation, which is 20.3 percent of the total.

Table 5 also reports the results of regressing the price dispersion on the log of distance (and city dummy variables) when we use only U.S. cities (second specification of Table 5) and only Canadian cities (third specification). We note that for U.S. cities distance has the hypothesized positive coefficient for 12 of the 14 cities and is significant at the 5-percent level for eight of the goods (and significant at the 6-percent level for two more). When all 14 goods are used jointly, the effect of distance is positive and highly significant. For the Canadian cities, distance has a positive effect for all 14 goods, and it is significant for 13 of those goods. Thus, if we do not consider the effect of the border at all, we find that distance has strong explanatory power for price dispersion.

---

[11]Calculated as $\exp[(11.9 \times 10^{-3})/(10.6 \times 10^{-4})]$ miles.

C. Why Does the Border Matter So Much?

Crossing the border adds significantly to price dispersion. In the Introduction, we proposed several reasons why the border would matter. Here we attempt to distinguish between a few of them.

We note that we have already tried a direct test for trade barriers and found that the size of the border coefficient was not diminished when the free-trade agreement between the United States and Canada went into effect. This, of course, does not rule out the possibility that informal trade barriers account for the price dispersion.

We suggested that labor markets might be more homogeneous within countries, so that w_j^i/w_k^i is less variable for city pairs (j, k) within a country than for cross-border pairs. We can investigate this hypothesis by seeing whether the explanatory power of the border dummy is affected by introducing relative wage volatility into the regression.

For each city, we construct a real wage as the average hourly wage for manufacturing employees (which is available for each city in the United States and by province in Canada) divided by the aggregate CPI for that city. We then calculate for each city pair the standard deviation of the two-month difference in the log of the relative real wages.

We add this wage-dispersion variable to our first regression, equation (2). These results are reported as the first specification in Table 6. As we expect, the wage dispersion coefficient is generally positive and significant. The coefficient is positive for 13 of the goods, and significant for ten.

However, the size of the border coefficient is not much affected by inclusion of the wage-dispersion variable. Apparently the border's importance does not arise because of the homogeneity of the labor markets within countries; but the distance coefficients are generally smaller and less significant. As we discuss in the Introduction, one of the reasons distance matters for intercity price dispersion is that more distant cities have less-integrated labor markets. The results from this regression bear out that hypothesis.

We investigate whether the sticky-price explanation for the importance of the border has power. In all of the regressions we have reported, if P_f is the U.S. dollar price of good f in a U.S. city, and P_f^* is the price in the Canadian city, the relative price is (the log of) P_f/SP_f^*, where S is the exchange rate. If P_f and P_f^* are sticky, then P_f/SP_f^* will fluctuate as S fluctuates. The border will be significant because it picks up the effect of the fluctuating exchange rate.

However, if we calculate the relative prices of good f between cities as relative real prices, then the nominal exchange rate will not appear in the calculation. That is, call P_f/P the real price of good f in the U.S. city, where P is an aggregate price index for that city, and P_f^*/P^* is the real price of good f in the Canadian city. Then the relative intercity price is $(P_f/P)/(P_f^*/P^*)$. If nominal price stickiness were the reason the border matters when we use P_f/SP_f^* as the measure of relative prices, then it should not be significant when we use $(P_f/P)/(P_f^*/P^*)$.

TABLE 6

ASSESSING WHY THE BORDER MATTERS

Good	Specification 1			Specification 2		Specification 3	
	Log distance	Border	SD of real wage	Log distance	Border	Log distance	Border
1	1.56 (1.15)	6.74 (0.23)	0.28 (0.08)	6.60 (1.87)	2.04 (0.14)	5.71 (2.08)	3.22 (0.16)
2	0.62 (1.02)	9.44 (0.13)	0.10 (0.03)	2.95 (0.93)	1.98 (0.11)	1.74 (0.60)	4.32 (0.09)
3	−0.84 (1.56)	9.01 (0.27)	0.36 (0.09)	5.44 (2.69)	3.46 (0.17)	4.47 (2.70)	4.28 (0.19)
4	5.72 (1.78)	8.83 (0.23)	0.22 (0.05)	4.99 (1.09)	2.66 (0.12)	6.69 (1.64)	6.15 (0.16)
5	31.5 (7.16)	9.53 (0.94)	0.35 (0.19)	28.6 (5.15)	3.47 (0.59)	28.6 (5.59)	4.19 (0.63)
6	−0.76 (1.01)	7.84 (0.15)	0.16 (0.03)	2.66 (0.87)	1.66 (0.10)	1.75 (0.85)	3.79 (0.11)
7	9.33 (2.97)	12.6 (0.46)	0.10 (0.11)	2.06 (2.42)	6.78 (0.32)	2.84 (2.38)	7.61 (0.31)
8	34.5 (7.97)	27.9 (1.12)	20.54 (0.23)	11.0 (3.46)	13.0 (0.49)	13.2 (3.06)	13.7 (0.46)
9	6.15 (3.14)	8.84 (0.45)	0.13 (0.11)	5.44 (2.86)	5.34 (0.31)	4.64 (3.02)	5.93 (0.32)
10	7.03 (1.75)	10.2 (0.23)	0.23 (0.08)	8.34 (1.53)	3.15 (0.15)	9.82 (1.92)	4.66 (0.16)
11	24.6 (6.82)	25.4 (1.11)	0.68 (0.22)	23.2 (4.98)	21.3 (0.66)	21.8 (5.18)	21.8 (0.67)
12	−4.60 (1.73)	8.91 (0.26)	0.28 (0.06)	3.17 (1.70)	1.99 (0.16)	1.36 (1.78)	3.89 (0.18)
13	−0.16 (1.80)	6.66 (0.23)	0.01 (0.06)	1.53 (1.39)	1.62 (0.16)	2.22 (1.48)	3.17 (0.17)
14	3.21 (1.08)	8.16 (0.14)	0.15 (0.03)	4.98 (0.99)	2.11 (0.12)	3.70 (0.93)	3.99 (0.12)
1–14	8.43 (3.22)	11.4 (0.52)	0.18 (0.11)	7.93 (2.68)	5.04 (0.35)	7.76 (2.76)	6.48 (0.36)

Notes: All regressions contain a dummy for each of the 23 individual cities, in addition to the variables listed in the cell. Heteroscedasticity-consistent standard errors (White, 1980) are reported in parentheses. Coefficients and standard errors on log distance (border) are multiplied by 10,000 (1,000). Specification 1 is the same as the specification in Table 3 but adds the standard deviation of the two-month difference in the intercity real wage. Specifications 2 and 3 use a measure of the real price of each good: in specification 2, the individual goods prices are deflated by the city's overall CPI, while in specification 3 the deflator is the national PPI. The measure of volatility in each case is the standard deviation of the two-month-ahead forecast error from the filtered relative price, over the sample period from September 1978 to December 1994. There are 228 observations in each regression. The adjusted R^2 estimates, not reported in order to save space, were never less than 0.77

When the log of $(P_f/P)/(P_f^*/P^*)$ is taken to be the relative price, the filtered measure of prices is a better measure than the two-month difference. The log of $(P_f/P)/(P_f^*/P^*)$ appears to be stationary for all of our goods, so the two-month difference would be an over-differenced series.

The second specification reported in Table 6 is for the regressions when prices for the individual goods in each city are taken relative to the CPI for all goods in that city. The standard deviation of the filtered prices is regressed on the log of distance, the border dummy, and individual city dummies, so the explanatory variables are the same as in equation (2). We find that the coefficients on distance are all positive, and generally significant. The coefficients on the border dummy are all positive and highly significant. Thus, even without the nominal exchange rate in the calculation of cross-border prices, the border matters.

How much does the border matter in this regression as compared to the regressions in which relative prices are calculated as the log of P_f/SP_f^*? From the first specification reported in Table 4, the coefficient on the border dummy using the filtered measure of the log of P_f/SP_f^* when all 14 goods are aggregated in a single regression is 10.8×10^{-3}. (Recall that the coefficients reported for the pooled regressions are the averages of the coefficients for the regressions for each of the 14 goods.) The average standard deviation for all cross-border city pairs using the filtered measure is 32.4×10^{-3}, so the border accounts for 33.3 percent of that standard deviation. When the log of $(P_f/P)/(P_f^*/P^*)$ is used as the measure of the relative price, the coefficient on the border dummy for the regression using all goods is 5.04×10^{-3} (last row of the second specification in Table 6). That compares to an average standard deviation of 26.6×10^{-3} for cross-border city pairs. Thus, the border accounts for only 18.9 percent of that standard deviation. Hence, when we drop the nominal exchange rate from our calculation of intercity prices, the percentage of the cross-border standard deviation accounted for by the border drops from 33.3 percent to 18.9 percent. We might conclude that the sticky-price story accounts for this difference; but we note that the border still accounts for a fairly large portion of the cross-border dispersion even after taking into account the role of sticky prices.

We also consider calculating the individual goods prices in each city relative to the national-level producer price index. The third row of Table 5 reports regressions using these prices, again taking the filtered measure of the log of $(P_f/P)/(P_f^*/P^*)$. We note that the results are qualitatively similar to the previous regression. Here, in the regression that uses all 14 goods, the coefficient on the border dummy is 6.48×10^{-3} (last row of the third specification in Table 6). The average standard deviation for cross-border city pairs with this measure of relative prices is 28.1×10^{-3}, so the border accounts for 23.1 percent of the total. This is still less than the 33.3 percent of the total when we use the log of P_f/SP_f^* as the measure of relative prices, but only about 30-percent less. Therefore, we can tentatively conclude that our sticky-nominal-prices story can explain about 30 percent of the border size.

We have not been able to explain fully why the border matters so much for intercity price dispersion. We have cast some doubt on the notion that formal trade barriers can explain it, while leaving open the possibility that informal barriers are significant. The hypothesis that wage costs are more homogeneous within countries does not seem to explain the border's importance. Sticky nominal prices do seem to account for a significant portion of the magnitude of the border effect, but apparently less than half. Other possibilities that we have not explored include differences in demand elasticities in the United States and Canada (which has received attention in the pricing-to-market literature) and homogeneity of productivity shocks within countries in the nontraded sectors (so that α_j^i / α_k^i from equation (1) has less dispersion within countries than between countries).

III. CONCLUSIONS

The major message of our empirical results is not just that the border matters for relative price variability; it is that both distance and the border matter. The literature on pricing to market has emphasized that, when markets are segmented, price discrimination can occur. The finding that distance is important in explaining price differences between locations lends support to this literature and the associated work on geography and trade. But our findings seem to suggest that there is more than standard price-discrimination behavior involved in cross-border price movements.

To the extent that our results indicate sticky nominal prices, they also shed some light on the price-setting process. We have found that the distance between markets influences prices, suggesting that price-setters take into account prices of nearby competitors. It is probably not too far-fetched to infer that firms would respond more to changes in prices of near substitutes, whether the nearness is in geographical space or product space. A reasonable model of price stickiness must take into account how isolated the market is for the product of the price setter. There appears to be potential for a marriage of the new-Keynesian literature on menu costs and the new trade literature emphasizing the role of geography.

Nominal price stickiness cannot account for all of the price dispersion between markets, however. The results of this paper confirm McCallum's (1995) finding that, despite the relative openness of the U.S.–Canadian border, the markets are still segmented.

DATA APPENDIX

Our data for the United States were obtained from the Bureau of Labor Statistics. The 14 goods from the United States are listed on the left-hand side of Table 1. All of the price and wage data (for both countries) are seasonally unadjusted.

We use comparable price and wage data for Canada that were obtained from Statistics Canada. There is not always an exact match between the price indexes available in Canada and those available in the United States. However, we were able to construct indexes for the 14 categories of goods in Canada, in some cases by using even more disaggregated Canadian indexes. For example, the U.S. data contain a series on men's and boys' apparel. There is no comparable series in Canada. However, we can obtain from Canada individual series on men's wear and on boys' wear. We then construct a men's and boys' apparel series for Canada by taking a weighted average of the men's wear series and the boys' wear series.[12] This type of construction was needed to arrive at five of the 14 Canadian price series. Table 1 indicates how these series were derived.

These categories of goods are mutually exclusive. Together they comprise 94.6 percent of purchases (using the weights in the U.S. consumer price index).

Monthly price data were used for nine Canadian cities: Calgary, Edmonton, Montreal, Ottawa, Quebec, Regina, Toronto, Vancouver, and Winnipeg. Monthly price data for the United States are available for four "core" cities: New York, Philadelphia, Chicago, and Los Angeles. In addition, for five cities, data are released in even-numbered months: Dallas, Detroit, Houston, Pittsburgh, and San Francisco. For five other cities, there are data available in odd-numbered months: Baltimore, Boston, Miami, St. Louis, and Washington.[13]

Consumer price data are closer to being monthly average data than point-in-time data. Typically to get the price of a single product, several outlets are sampled during the month. The outlets are not all sampled on the same day. The change in the price of the product from the previous month is calculated as the average change across the various outlets. For the cities that report data every second month, the prices are for the second month of the interval (rather than an average across both months).

In order to nullify a potential bias, we use a monthly average (U.S. dollar)/(Canadian dollar) exchange rate from the Citibase tape. Averaging tends to reduce the volatility of the series. Thus, if we were to use an exchange rate at a specific point in time, but use price data which is essentially averaged, we would introduce volatility into our measure of cross-border prices. That is compensated for by taking the monthly average exchange rate.

For each good, we calculated the intercity relative prices. Thus, when we are using only the Canadian cities and the core U.S. cities, for each good there are 78 intercity prices (13 cities $\times$ 12/2). Adding the five even-month U.S. cities adds another 75 prices, and adding the five odd-month U.S. cities adds another 75 prices.

We also use data on the distance between cities. We use two separate measures of distance, both obtained from the Automap (version 2) software. One measure is the great-circle distance, and the other is the quickest-driving-time distance. Our results were not affected by the choice of distance measure, so all results reported use the great-circle distance.

REFERENCES

Debreu, Gerard. *Theory of value*. New Haven, CT: Yale University Press, 1959.

Dixit, Avinash. "Hysteresis, Import Penetration, and Exchange Rate Pass-Through." *Quarterly Journal of Economics*, May 1989, *104*(2), pp. 205–28.

---

[12] The weights come from the current weights used in the U.S. consumer price index, which we obtained from the Bureau of Labor Statistics.

[13] Data for Cleveland are available every other month. However, the data switched from being odd-month to even-month in the middle of our sample. Also, at the beginning of the sample, Detroit data were monthly, but switched to even-month, while the reverse is true for San Francisco. We make use only of the even-month data for these two cities.

Dornbusch, Rudiger. "Exchange Rates and Prices." *American Economic Review*, March 1987, 77(1), pp. 93–106.

Dumas, Bernard. "Dynamic Equilibrium and the Real Exchange Rate in a Spatially Separated World." *Review of Financial Studies*, 1992, 5(2), pp. 153–180.

Engel, Charles. "Real Exchange Rates and Relative Prices: An Empirical Investigation." *Journal of Monetary Economics*, August 1993, 32(1), pp. 35–50.

———. "Accounting for U.S. Real Exchange Rate Changes." National Bureau of Economic Research (Cambridge, MA) Working Paper No. 5394, December 1995.

Feenstra, Robert C. "Symmetric Pass-Through of Tariffs and Exchange Rates under Imperfect Competition: An Empirical Test." *Journal of International Economics*, August 1989, 27(1/2), pp. 25–45.

Frankel, Jeffrey; Stein, Ernesto and Wei, Shang-Jin. "Trading Blocs and the Americas: The Natural, the Unnatural and the Super-natural." *Journal of Development Economics*, June 1995, 47(1), pp. 61–96.

Froot, Kenneth A. and Klemperer, Paul D. "Exchange Rate Pass-Through when Market Share Matters." *American Economic Review*, September 1989, 79(4), pp. 637–54.

Giovannini, Alberto. "Exchange Rates and Traded Goods Prices." *Journal of International Economics*, February 1988, 24(1/2), pp. 45–68.

Isard, Peter. "How Far Can We Push the Law of One Price?" *American Economic Review*, December 1977, 67(5), pp. 942–48.

Kasa, Kenneth. "Adjustment Costs and Pricing-to-Market: Theory and Evidence." *Journal of International Economics*, February 1992, 32(1/2), pp. 1–30.

Knetter, Michael N. "Price Discrimination by U.S. and German Exporters." *American Economic Review*, March 1989, 79(1), pp. 198–210.

———. "International Comparisons of Pricing-to-Market Behavior." *American Economic Review*, June 1993, 83(3), pp. 473–86.

Krugman, Paul. "Pricing to Market When the Exchange Rate Changes," in Sven W. Arndt and J. David Richardson, eds., *Real-financial linkages among open economies*. Cambridge, MA: MIT Press, 1987, pp. 49–70.

———. "Increasing Returns and Economic Geography." *Journal of Political Economy*, June 1991, 99(3), pp. 483–99.

Marston, Richard C. "Pricing to Market in Japanese Manufacturing." *Journal of International Economics*, November 1990, 29(3/4), pp. 217–36.

McCallum, John. "National Borders Matter: Regional Trade Patterns in North America." *American Economic Review*, June 1995, 85(3), pp. 615–23.

Mussa, Michael. "Nominal Exchange Rate Regimes and the Behavior of Real Exchange Rates: Evidence and Implications." *Carnegie-Rochester Conference Series on Public Policy*, Autumn 1986, 25, pp. 117–214.

Rogers, John H. and Jenkins, Michael. "Haircuts or Hysteresis? Sources of Movements in Real Exchange Rates." *Journal of International Economics*, May 1995, 38(3/4), pp. 339–60.

Sanyal, Kalyan K. and Jones, Ronald W. "The Theory of Trade in Middle Products." *American Economic Review*, March 1982, 72(1), pp. 16–31.

White, Halbert. "A Heteroskedasticity-Consistent Covariance Matrix Estimator and a Direct Test for Heteroskedasticity." *Econometrica*, May 1980, 48(4), pp. 817–38.

ABOUT THE AUTHORS

Charles Engel

Charles M. Engel is Professor of Economics at the University of Washington. He has also served on the faculty of the University of Virginia. He received his Ph.D. from the University of California at Berkeley.

Editor's Queries for both Engel and Rogers

What aspects of this paper would you do differently today, and why?   Ideally, we would like to use consumer price data that are more disaggregated, so that we could do a better job assessing the deviations from the law of one price. Also, we would like longer time series so that we could differentiate better between short-run and long-run price discrepancies. But we are limited by the availability of data.

How does this article fit into the literature?   The article really is in the spirit of the empirical literature on the gravity model of trade. That literature finds that the distance between two countries primarily determines their bilateral volume of trade. We were interested more generally in the question of what determines how integrated goods markets are. Our view is that price differentials give a more comprehensive view of integration. Two markets which are highly integrated may not trade much, but prices would be equalized between the regions.

Why did this article attract so much attention?   Clearly, one of the things that contributes to the interest in this paper is the clever way of stating the issue. The empirical work is simple and clean, and delivers very powerful conclusions.

What are the major unresolved questions of international economics?   We think we have a pretty poor understanding of the behavior of prices across countries. Prices are a pretty important variable in economics. This ought to be a hot topic of study.

John H. Rogers

John Rogers is a senior economist in the International Finance Division of the Board of Governors of the Federal Reserve. He has served on the faculty of Pennsylvania State University. He received his Ph.D. from the University of Virginia.

CHAMBERLINIAN MODEL
(ECONOMIES OF SCALE,
IMPERFECT COMPETITION, AND
STRATEGIC INTERACTIONS)

Paul R. Krugman

James Brander and Paul Krugman

Wilfred J. Ethier

Paul Krugman

Jonathan Eaton and Gene M. Grossman

David Hummels and James Levinsohn

Increasing Returns, Monopolistic Competition, and International Trade

PAUL R. KRUGMAN

Yale University, New Haven, CT 06520, USA

This paper develops a simple, general equilibrium model of noncomparative advantage trade. Trade is driven by economies of scale, which are internal to firms. Because of the scale economies, markets are imperfectly competitive. Nonetheless, one can show that trade, and gains from trade, will occur, even between countries with identical tastes, technology, and factor endowments.

1. INTRODUCTION

It has been widely recognized that economies of scale provide an alternative to differences in technology or factor endowments as an explanation of international specialization and trade. The role of economies of large scale production is a major sub-theme in the work of Ohlin (1933); while some authors, especially Balassa (1967) and Kravis (1971), have argued that scale economies play a crucial role in explaining the postwar growth in trade among the industrial countries. Nonetheless, increasing returns as a cause of trade has received relatively little attention from formal trade theory. The main reason for this neglect seems to be that it has appeared difficult to deal with the implications of increasing returns for market structure.

This paper develops a simple formal model in which trade is caused by economies of scale instead of differences in factor endowments or technology. The approach differs from that of most other formal treatments of trade under increasing returns, which assume that scale economies are external to firms, so that markets remain perfectly competitive.[1] Instead, scale economies are here assumed to be internal to firms, with the market structure that emerges being one of Chamberlinian monopolistic competition.[2]

---

[1] Authors who allow for increasing returns in trade by assuming that scale economies are external to firm include Chacoliades (1970). Melvin (1969), Kemp (1964), and Negishi (1969).

[2] A Chamberlinian approach to international trade is suggested by Gray (1973). Negishi (1972) develops a full general-equilibrium model of scale economies, monopolistic competition, and trade which is similar in spirit to this paper, though far more complex. Scale economies and product differentiation are also suggested as causes of trade by Barker (1977) and Grubel (1970).

Reprinted with permission from Paul R. Krugman "Increasing Returns, Monopolistic Competition and International Trade," *Journal of International Economics:* (1979), vol. 9, pp. 469–479. ©1979 by North-Holland Publishing Company.

The formal treatment of monopolistic competition is borrowed with slight modifications from recent work by Dixit and Stiglitz (1977). A Chamberlinian formulation of the problem turns out to have several advantages. First, it yields a very simple model; the analysis of increasing returns and trade is hardly more complicated than the two-good Ricardian model. Secondly, the model is free from the multiple equilibria which are the rule when scale economies are external to firms, and which can detract from the main point. Finally, the model's picture of trade in a large number of differentiated products fits in well with the empirical literature on 'intra-industry' trade [e.g. Grubel and Lloyd (1975)].

The paper is organized as follows. Section 2 develops the basic modified Dixit–Stiglitz model of monopolistic competition for a closed economy. Section 3 then examines the effects of opening trade as well as the essentially equivalent effects of population growth and factor mobility. Finally, Section 4 summarizes the results and suggests some conclusions.

2. MONOPOLISTIC COMPETITION IN A CLOSED ECONOMY

This section develops the basic model of monopolistic competition with which I will work in the next sections. The model is a simplified version of the model developed by Dixit and Stiglitz. Instead of trying to develop a general model, this paper will assume particular forms for utility and cost functions. The functional forms chosen give the model a simplified structure which makes the analysis easier.

Consider, then, an economy with only one scarce factor of production, labor. The economy is assumed able to produce any of a large number of goods, with the goods indexed by i. We order the goods so that those actually produced range from 1 to n, where n is also assumed to be a large number, although small relative to the number of potential products.

All residents are assumed to share the same utility function, into which all goods enter symmetrically,

$$U = \sum_{i=1}^{n} v(c_i), \qquad v' > 0, \quad v'' < 0, \tag{1}$$

where c_i is the consumption of the ith good.

It will be useful to define a variable, ε, where

$$\varepsilon_i = -\frac{v'}{v''c_i}, \tag{2}$$

and where we assume $\partial \varepsilon_i / \partial c_i < 0$. The variable ε_i will turn out to be the elasticity of demand facing an individual producer; the reasons for assuming that it is decreasing in c_i will become apparent later.

All goods are also assumed to be produced with the same cost function. The labor used in producing each good is a linear function of output,

$$l_i = \alpha + \beta x_i, \qquad \alpha, \beta > 0, \tag{3}$$

where l_i is labor used in producing good i, x_i is the output of good i, and α is a fixed cost. In other words, there are decreasing average costs and constant marginal costs.

Production of a good must equal the sum of individual consumptions of the good. If we identify individuals with workers, production must equal the consumption of a representative individual times the labor force:

$$x_i = Lc_i. \tag{4}$$

Finally, we assume full employment, so that the total labor force L must be exhausted by employment in production of individual goods:

$$L = \sum_{i=1}^{n} l_i = \sum_{i=1}^{n} [\alpha + \beta x_i]. \tag{5}$$

Now there are three variables we want to determine: the price of each good relative to wages, p_i/w; the output of each good, x_i; and the number of goods produced, n. The symmetry of the problem will ensure that all goods actually produced will be produced in the same quantity and at the same price, so that we can use the shorthand notation

$$\left. \begin{array}{l} p = p_i \\ x = x_i \end{array} \right\}, \quad \text{for all } i. \tag{6}$$

We can proceed in three stages. First, we analyze the demand curve facing an individual firm; then we derive the pricing policy of firms and relate profitability to output; finally, we use an analysis of profitability and entry to determine the number of firms.

To analyze the demand curve facing the firm producing some particular product, consider the behavior of a representative individual. He will maximize his utility (1) subject to a budget constraint. The first-order conditions from that maximization problem have the form

$$v'(c_i) = \lambda p_i, \qquad i = 1, ..., n, \tag{7}$$

where λ is the shadow price on the budget constraint, which can be interpreted as the marginal utility of income.

We can substitute the relationship between individual consumption and output into (7) to turn it into an expression for the demand facing an individual firm,

$$p_i = \lambda^{-1} v'(x_i/L). \tag{8}$$

If the number of goods produced is large, each firm's pricing policy will have a negligible effect on the marginal utility of income, so that it can take λ as fixed. In that case the elasticity of demand facing the ith firm will, as already noted, be $\varepsilon_i = -v'/v''c_i$.

Now let us consider profit-maximizing pricing behavior. Each individual firm, being small relative to the economy, can ignore the effects of its decisions on the decisions of other firms. Thus, the ith firm will choose its price to maximize its profits,

$$\Pi_i = p_i x_i - (\alpha + \beta x_i)w. \tag{9}$$

The profit-maximizing price will depend on marginal cost and on the elasticity of demand:

$$p_i = \frac{\varepsilon}{\varepsilon - 1} \beta w \tag{10}$$

or $p/w = \beta\varepsilon/(\varepsilon - 1)$.

Now this does not determine the price, since the elasticity of demand depends on output; thus, to find the profit-maximizing price we would have to derive profit-maximizing output as well. It will be easier, however, to determine output and prices by combining (10) with the condition that profits be zero in equilibrium.

Profits will be driven to zero by entry of new firms. The process is illustrated in Figure 1. The horizontal axis measures output of a representative firm; the vertical axis revenue and cost expressed in wage units. Total cost is shown by TC, while OR and OR^1

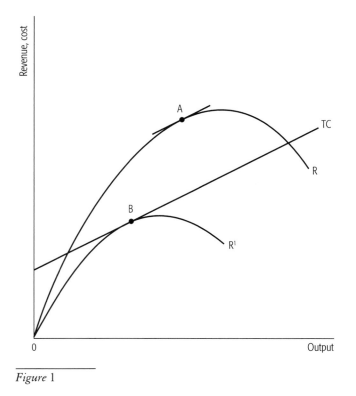

Figure 1

represent revenue functions. Suppose that given the initial number of firms, the revenue function facing each firm is given by OR. The firm will then choose its output so as to set marginal revenue equal to marginal cost, at A. At that point, since price (average revenue) exceeds average cost, firms will make profits. But this will lead entrepreneurs to start new firms. As they do so, the marginal utility of income will rise, and the revenue function will shrink in. Eventually equilibrium will be reached at a point such as B, where it is true both that marginal revenue equals marginal cost and that average revenue equals average cost. This is, of course, Chamberlin's famous tangency solution [Chamberlin (1962)].

To characterize this equilibrium more carefully, we need to show how the price and output of a representative firm can be derived from cost and utility functions. In Figure 2 the horizontal axis shows *per-capita* consumption of a representative good, while the vertical axis shows the price of a representative good in wage units. We have one relationship between c and p/w in the pricing condition (10), which is shown as the curve PP. Price lies everywhere above marginal cost, and increases with c because, by assumption, the elasticity of demand falls with c.

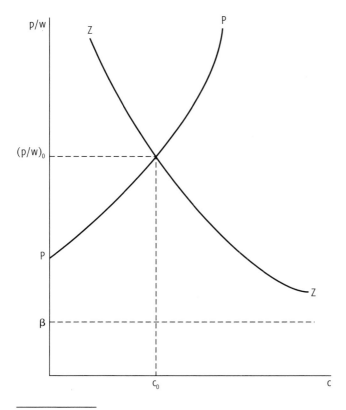

Figure 2

A second relationship between p/w and c can be derived from the condition of zero profits in equilibrium. From (9), we have

$$O = px - (\alpha + \beta x)w, \tag{11}$$

which can be rewritten

$$p/w = \beta + \alpha/x = \beta + \alpha/Lc. \tag{12}$$

This is a rectangular hyperbola above the line $p/w = \beta$, and is shown in Figure 2 as ZZ.

The intersection of the PP and ZZ schedules determines individual consumption of each good and the price of each good. From the consumption of each good we have output per firm, since $x = Lc$. And the assumption of full employment lets us determine the number of goods produced:

$$n = \frac{L}{\alpha + \beta x}. \tag{13}$$

We now have a complete description of equilibrium in the economy. It is indeterminate *which* n goods are produced, but it is also unimportant, since the goods enter into utility and cost symmetrically. We can now use the model to analyze the related questions of the effects of growth, trade, and factor mobility.

3. GROWTH, TRADE, AND FACTOR MOBILITY

The model developed in the last section was a one-factor model, but one in which there were economies of scale in the use of that factor, so that in a real sense the division of labor was limited by the extent of the market. In this section we consider three ways in which the extent of the market might increase: growth in the labor force, trade, and migration.

3.1. EFFECTS OF LABOR FORCE GROWTH

Suppose that an economy of the kind analyzed in the last section were to experience an increase in its labor force. What effect would this have? We can analyze some of the effects by examining Figure 3. The PP and ZZ schedules have the same definitions as in Figure 2; before the increase in the labor force equilibrium is at A. By referring back to eqs. (10) and (11) we can see that an increase in L has no effect on PP, but that it causes ZZ to shift left. The new equilibrium is at B: c falls, and so does p/w. We can show, however, that both the output of each good and the number of goods produced rise. By rearranging (12) we have

$$x = \alpha/(p/w - \beta), \tag{14}$$

which shows that output must rise, while since $n = L/(\alpha + \beta Lc)$, a rise in L and a fall in c imply a rise in n.

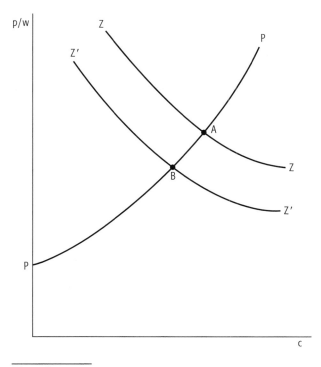

Figure 3

Notice that these results depend on the fact that the *PP* curve slopes upward, which in turn depends on the assumption that the elasticity of demand falls with c. This assumption, which might alternatively be stated as an assumption that the elasticity of demand rises when the price of a good is increased, seems plausible. In any case, it seems to be necessary if this model is to yield reasonable results, and I make the assumption without apology.

We can also consider the welfare implications of growth. Comparisons of overall welfare would be illegitimate, but we can look at the welfare of representative individuals. This rises for two reasons: there is a rise in the 'real wage' w/p, and there is also a gain from increased choice, as the number of available products increases.

I have considered the case of growth at some length, even though our principal concern is with trade, because the results of the analysis of growth will be useful next, when we turn to the analysis of trade.

3.2. Effects of Trade

Suppose there exist two economies of the kind analyzed in Section 2, and that they are initially unable to trade. To make the point most strongly, assume that the countries have identical tastes and technologies. (Since this is a one-factor model, we have already ruled out differences in factor endowments.) In a conventional model, there would be no reason for trade to occur between these economies, and no potential gains from trade. In this model, however, there will be both trade and gains from trade.

To see this, suppose that trade is opened between these two economies at zero transportation cost. Symmetry will ensure that wage rates in the two countries will be equal, and that the price of any good produced in either country will be the same. The effect will be the same as if *each* country had experienced an increase in its labor force. As in the case of growth in a closed economy, there will be an increase both in the scale of production and in the range of goods available for consumption. Welfare in both countries will increase, both because of higher w/p and because of increased choice.

The direction of trade—which country exports which goods—is indeterminate; all that we can say is that each good will be produced only in one country, because there is (in this model) no reason for firms to compete for markets. The *volume* of trade, however, is determinate. Each individual will be maximizing his utility function, which may be written

$$U = \sum_{i=1}^{n} v(c_i) + \sum_{i=n+1}^{n+n^*} v(c_i), \tag{15}$$

where goods 1, ..., n are produced in the home country and $n+1$, ..., $n+n^*$ in the foreign country. The number of goods produced in each country will be proportional to the labor forces:

$$n = \frac{L}{\alpha + \beta x},$$
$$n^* = \frac{L^*}{\alpha + \beta x}. \tag{16}$$

Since all goods will have the same price, expenditures on each country's goods will be proportional to the country's labor force. The share of imports in home country expenditures, for instance, will be $L^*/(L + L^*)$; the values of imports of each country will be national income times the import share, i.e.

$$M = wL \cdot L^*/(L + L^*)$$
$$= wLL^*/(L + L^*)$$
$$= M^*. \tag{17}$$

Trade is balanced, as it must be, since each individual agent's budget constraint is satisfied. The volume of trade as a fraction of world income is maximized when the economies are of equal size.

We might note that the result that the volume of trade is determinate but the direction of trade is not is very similar to the well-known argument of Linder (1961). This suggests an affinity between this model and Linder's views, although Linder does not explicitly mention economies of scale.

The important point to be gained from this analysis is that economies of scale can be shown to give rise to trade and to gains from trade even when there are no international differences in tastes, technology, or factor endowments.

3.3. Effects of Factor Mobility[3]

An interesting extension of the model results when we allow for movement of labor between countries or regions. There is a parallel here with Heckscher–Ohlin theory. Mundell (1957) has shown that in a Heckscher–Ohlin world trade and factor mobility would be substitutes for one another, and that factor movements would be induced by impediments to trade such as tariffs or transportation costs. The same kinds of results emerge from this model.

To see this, suppose that there are two regions of the kind we have been discussing, and that they have the same tastes and technologies. There is room for mutual gains from trade, because the combined market would allow both greater variety of goods and a greater scale of production. The same gains could be obtained without trade, however, if the population of one region were to migrate to the other. In this model, trade and growth in the labor force are essentially equivalent. If there are impediments to trade, there will be an incentive for workers to move to the region which already has the larger labor force. This is clearest if we consider the extreme case where no trade in goods is possible, but labor is perfectly mobile. Then the more populous region will offer both a greater real wage w/p and a greater variety of goods, inducing immigration. In equilibrium all workers will have concentrated in one region or the other. Which region ends up with the population depends on initial conditions; in the presence of increasing returns history matters.

Before proceeding further we should ask what aspect of reality, if any, is captured by the story we have just told. In the presence of increasing returns factor mobility appears to produce a process of agglomeration. If we had considered a many-region model the population would still have tended to accumulate in only one region, which we may as well label a city; for this analysis seems to make most sense as an account of the growth of metropolitan areas. The theory of urban growth suggested by this model is of the 'city lights' variety: people migrate to the city in part because of the greater variety of consumption goods it offers.

Let us return now to the two-region case to make a final point. We have seen that which region ends up with the population depends on the initial distribution of

---

[3] The results in this section bear some resemblance to some nontheoretical accounts of the emergence of backward regions. We might propose the following modification of the model: suppose that the population of each region is divided into a mobile group and an immobile group. Migration would then move all the mobile people to one region, leaving behind an immiserized 'Appalachia' of immobile people whose standard of living is depressed by the smallness of the market.

population. As long as labor productivity is the same in both regions, though, there is no difference in welfare between the two possible outcomes. If there is any difference in the conditions of production between the two regions, however, it does matter which gets the population—and the process of migration can lead to the wrong outcome.

Consider, for example, a case in which both fixed and variable labor costs are higher in one region. Then it is clearly desirable that all labor should move to the other region. But if the inferior region starts with a large enough share of the population, migration may move in the wrong direction.

To summarize: in the model of this paper, as in some more conventional trade models, factor mobility can substitute for trade. If there are impediments to trade, labor will concentrate in a single region; which region depends on the initial distribution of population. Finally, the process of agglomeration may lead population to concentrate in the wrong place.

4. SUMMARY AND CONCLUSIONS

This paper adapts a Chamberlinian approach to the analysis of trade under conditions of increasing returns to scale. It shows that trade need not be a result of international differences in technology or factor endowments. Instead, trade may simply be a way of extending the market and allowing exploitation of scale economies, with the effects of trade being similar to those of labor force growth and regional agglomeration. This is a view of trade which appears to be useful in understanding trade among the industrial countries.

What is surprising about this analysis is that it is extremely simple. While the role of economies of scale in causing trade has been known for some time, it has been underemphasized in formal trade theory (and in textbooks). This paper shows that a clear, rigorous, and one hopes persuasive model of trade under conditions of increasing returns can be constructed. Perhaps this will help give economies of scale a more prominent place in trade theory.

REFERENCES

Balassa, Bela, 1967, Trade liberalization among industrial countries (McGraw-Hill, New York).

Barker, Terry, 1977, International trade and economic growth: An alternative to the neoclassical approach, Cambridge Journal of Economics 1, no. 2, 153–172.

Chacoliades, Miltiades, 1970, Increasing returns and the theory of comparative advantage, Southern Economic Journal 37, no. 2, 157–162.

Chamberlin, Edward, 1962, The theory of monopolistic competition.

Dixit, Avinash and Joseph Stiglitz, 1977, Monopolistic competition and optimum product diversity, American Economic Review, June, 297–308.

Gray, Peter, 1973, Two-way international trade in manufactures: A theoretical underpinning, Weltwirtschaftliches Archiv 109, 19–39.

Grubel, Herbert, 1970, The theory of intra-industry trade, in: I.A. McDougall and R.H. Snape, eds., Studies in international economics (North-Holland, Amsterdam).

Grubel, Herbert and Peter Lloyd, 1975, Intra-industry trade (MacMillan, London).

Hufbauer, Gary and John Chilas, 1974, Specialization by industrial countries: Extent and consequences. in H. Giersch, ed., The international division of labour (Institut für Weltwirtschaft, Kiel).

Kemp, Murray, 1964, The pure theory of international trade (Prentice-Hall).

Kindleberger, Charles, 1973, International economics (Irwin).

Kravis, Irving, 1971, The current case for import limitations, in: Commission on International Trade and Investment Policy, United States Economic Policy in an Interdependent World (U.S. Government Printing Office, Washington).

Linder, Staffan Burenstam, 1961, An essay on trade and transformation (John Wiley and Sons).

Melvin, James, 1969, Increasing returns to scale as a determinant of trade, Canadian Journal of Economics and Political Science 2, no. 3, 389–402.

Mundell, Robert, 1957, International trade and factor mobility, American Economic Review 47, 321–335.

Negishi, Takashi, 1969, Marshallian external economies and gains from trade between similar countries, Review of Economic Studies 36, 131–135.

Negishi, Takashi, 1972, General equilibrium theory and international trade (North-Holland, Amsterdam).

Ohlin, Bertil, 1933, Interregional and international trade (Harvard University Press).

ABOUT THE AUTHOR

 *Paul R. Krugman*

Paul Krugman, Professor of Economics at Princeton University, is the winner of the 1991 John Bates Clark Medal. He received his B.A. fron Yale University and his doctorate from the Massachusetts Institute of Technology, and later served on the faculties of both. He was a Senior Economist at the Council of Economic Advisors in 1982–1983. He is highly regarded within the profession of economics for his creative work at the frontiers of economic knowledge. He is best known for his books on economics that present and develop difficult and abstract ideas in a manner understood and enjoyed by the general public.

A 'Reciprocal Dumping' Model of International Trade

James Brander

Queen's University, Kingston, Ontario K7L 3N6, Canada

Paul Krugman

Massachusetts Institute of Technology, Cambridge, MA 02139, USA

This paper develops a model in which the rivalry of oligopolistic firms serves as an independent cause of international trade. The model shows how such rivalry naturally gives rise to 'dumping' of output in foreign markets, and shows that such dumping can be 'reciprocal'—that is, there may be two-way trade in the same product. Reciprocal dumping is shown to be possible for a fairly general specification of firm behaviour. The welfare effects of this seemingly pointless trade are ambiguous. On the one hand, resources are wasted in the cross-handling of goods; on the other hand, increased competition reduces monopoly distortions. Surprisingly, in the case of free entry and Cournot behaviour reciprocal dumping is unambiguously beneficial.

1. Introduction

The phenomenon of 'dumping' in international trade can be explained by the standard theory of monopolistic price discrimination.[1] If a profit maximizing firm believes it faces a higher elasticity of demand abroad than at home, and it is able to discriminate between foreign and domestic markets, then it will charge a lower price abroad than at home. Such an explanation seems to rely on 'accidental' differences in country demands. In this paper, however, we show how dumping arises for systematic reasons associated with oligopolistic behaviour.

We would like to thank an anonymous referee for very helpful comments. J. Brander wishes to gratefully acknowledge financial support from a Social Sciences and Humanities Research Council of Canada post-doctoral fellowship.

---

[1] For an exposition of dumping as monopolistic price discrimination, see Caves and Jones (1977), pp. 152–154.

Reprinted with permission from James Brander and Paul Krugman, "A 'Reciprocal Dumping' Model of International Trade," *Journal of International Economics*: 1983, vol. 15, pp. 313–321.
© 1983 by Elsevier Science Publishers B.V. (North-Holland).

Brander (1981) develops a model in which the rivalry of oligopolistic firms serves as an independent cause of international trade and leads to two-way trade in identical products.[2] In this paper we build on Brander (1981) to argue that the oligopolistic rivalry between firms naturally gives rise to 'reciprocal dumping': each firm dumps into other firms' home markets.

We generalize Brander (1981) in that reciprocal dumping is shown to be robust to a fairly general specification of firms' behaviour and market demand. The crucial element is what Helpman (1982) refers to as a 'segmented markets' perception: each firm perceives each country as a separate market and makes distinct quantity decisions for each.

Reciprocal dumping is rather striking in that there is pure waste in the form of unnecessary transport costs.[3] Without free entry, welfare may improve as trade opens up and reciprocal dumping occurs, but it is also possible that welfare may decline. One wonders, therefore, if such a model might not provide a rationale for trade restriction. With free entry, the contrary seems to be true. We derive the fairly strong result that with free entry both before and after trade, the opening of trade (and the resultant reciprocal dumping) is definitely welfare improving for the Cournot case. The pro-competitive effect of having more firms and a larger overall market dominates the loss due to transport costs in this second best imperfectly competitive world.

Section 2 develops a simple model of Cournot duopoly and trade which shows how reciprocal dumping can occur, and presents the associated welfare analysis. Section 3 describes the free entry zero profit equilibrium and derives the result that trade is welfare-improving in this case. Section 4 contains concluding remarks.

2. THE BASIC MODEL

Assume there are two identical countries, one 'domestic' and one 'foreign', and that each country has one firm producing commodity Z. There are transport costs incurred in exporting goods from one country to the other. The main idea is that each firm regards each country as a separate market and therefore chooses the profit-maximizing quantity

---

[2] Two-way trade in similar (but not necessarily identical) products is often referred to as intra-industry trade. Standard references on the importance of intra-industry trade are Balassa (1966) and Grubel and Lloyd (1975). Alternative explanatory models include Krugman (1979) and Lancaster (1980).

[3] The 'basing point' pricing literature of the 1930s and 1940s was concerned largely with the waste due to cross-hauling in spatial markets. Of special interest is a paper by Smithies (1942) which contains a model of spatial imperfect competition in which cross-hauling arises. It is a short step to extend this model to an international setting. Smithies' model differs from ours in that he takes price as the strategy variable, but the basic insight that imperfect competition can cause cross-hauling is central to both.

for each country separately. Each firm has a Cournot perception: it assumes the other firm will hold output fixed in each country.

The domestic firm produces output x for domestic consumption and output x^* for foreign consumption. Marginal cost is a constant, c, and transport costs of the 'iceberg' type imply that the marginal cost of export is c/g, where $0 \leqq g \leqq 1$. Similarly, the foreign firm produces output y for export to the domestic country and output y^* for its own market, and faces a symmetric cost structure. Using p and p^* to denote domestic and foreign price, domestic and foreign profits can be written, respectively, as:

$$\pi = xp(Z) + x^*p^*(Z^*) - c(x + x^*/g) - F, \tag{1}$$

$$\pi^* = yp(Z) + y^*p^*(Z^*) - c(y/g + y^*) - F^*, \tag{2}$$

where asterisks generally denote variables associated with the foreign country and F denotes fixed costs. A little inspection reveals that the profit-maximizing choice of x is independent of x^* and similarly for y and y^*: each country can be considered separately.[4] By symmetry we need consider only the domestic country.

Each firm maximizes profit with respect to own output, which yields the first-order conditions:

$$\pi_x = xp' + p - c = 0, \tag{3}$$

$$\pi_y^* = yp' + p - c/g = 0, \tag{4}$$

where primes or subscripts denote derivatives. These are 'best-reply' functions in implicit form. Their solution is the trade equilibrium. Using the variable σ to denote y/Z, the foreign share in the domestic market, and letting $\varepsilon = -p/Zp'$, the elasticity of domestic demand, these implicit best-reply functions can be rewritten as:

$$p = c\varepsilon/(\varepsilon + \sigma - 1), \tag{3'}$$

$$p = c\varepsilon/g(\varepsilon - \sigma). \tag{4'}$$

Eqs. (3') and (4') are two equations that can be solved for p and σ. The solutions are:

$$p = c\varepsilon(1 + g)/g(2\varepsilon - 1), \tag{5}$$

$$\sigma = (\varepsilon(g - 1) + 1)/(1 + g). \tag{6}$$

These solutions are an equilibrium only if second-order conditions are satisfied:

$$\pi_{xx} = xp'' + 2p' < 0; \qquad \pi_{yy}^* = yp'' + 2p' < 0. \tag{7}$$

---

[4]This separation is a very convenient simplification that arises from the assumption of constant marginal cost. It is not essential to the results.

We also impose the following conditions:

$$\pi_{xy} = xp'' + p' < 0; \qquad \pi_{yx}^* = yp'' + p' < 0. \tag{8}$$

Conditions (8) mean that own marginal revenue declines when the other firm increases its output, which seems a very reasonable requirement. They are equivalent to reaction functions (or best-reply functions) being downward sloping. They imply stability and, if they hold globally, uniqueness of the equilibrium. It is not inconceivable that (8) might be violated by possible demand structures, but such cases would have to be considered unusual. In any case, pathological examples of noncooperative models are well understood [see, for example, Seade (1980) and Friedman (1977)] and we have nothing new to say about such problems here. Accordingly we assume (7) and (8) are satisfied.[5]

Positive solutions to (5) and (6) imply that two-way trade arises in this context. A positive solution will arise if $\varepsilon < 1/(1 - g)$ at the equilibrium since this implies that price exceeds the marginal cost of exports ($p > c/g$) and that $\sigma > 0$. Subject to this condition, and given (7) and (8), a unique stable two-way trade equilibrium holds for arbitrary demand. [Brander (1981) considered the case of linear demand only.] It can be easily shown[6] that, at equilibrium, each firm has a smaller market share of its export market than of its domestic market. Therefore, perceived marginal revenue is higher in the export market. The effective marginal cost of delivering an exported unit is higher than for a unit of domestic sales, because of transport costs, but this is consistent with the higher marginal revenue. Thus, perceived marginal revenue can equal marginal cost in both markets at positive output levels. This is true for firms in both countries, which thus gives rise to two-way trade. Moreover, each firm has a a smaller markup over cost in its export market than at home: the f.o.b. price for exports is below the domestic price, and therefore there is reciprocal dumping.

The case of constant elasticity demand, $p = AZ^{-1/\varepsilon}$, is a useful special case which is illustrated in fig. 1. For profit maximization by the domestic firm [condition (3)], p is decreasing in σ, while condition (4') for the foreign firm has price increasing in σ. The intercepts on the price axis are, respectively, $c\varepsilon/(\varepsilon - 1)$ and c/g. Thus, provided $c\varepsilon/(\varepsilon - 1) > c/g$ [or $\varepsilon < 1/(1 - g)$] the intersection must be at a positive foreign market share. This condition has a natural economic interpretation, since $c\varepsilon/(\varepsilon - 1)$ is the price which would prevail if there were no trade, while c/g is the marginal cost of exports. What the

---

[5]Conditions (7) and (8) taken together imply, if they hold globally, that $\pi_{xx}\pi_{yy}^* - \pi_{xy}\pi_{yx}^* > 0$ globally, which in turn implies that reaction functions cross only once and that they do so such that the equilibrium is stable. Allowing violation of (8) and the possibility of multiple equilibria clearly do not upset the result that a two-way trade equilibrium exists. It would, however, complicate welfare analysis in the usual way: one could not be sure which equilibrium would obtain so welfare comparisons of different regimes would usually be ambiguous.

[6]Expression (3) implies that $\varepsilon > (1 - \sigma)$, while (4) implies that $\varepsilon > \sigma$. Adding these it follows that $\varepsilon > 1/2$ at equilibrium. It is then clear from (6) that $\sigma < 1/2$ if $g < 1$. ($\sigma = 1/2$ if $g = 1$.)

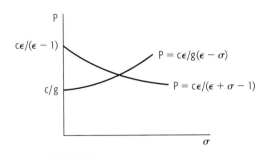

Figure 1

condition says is that reciprocal dumping will occur if monopoly markups in its absence were to exceed transport costs.

Clearly, the reciprocal dumping solution is not Pareto efficient. Some monopoly distortion persists even after trade, and there are socially pointless transportation costs incurred in cross-hauling. What is less clear is whether, given a second-best world of imperfect competition, free trade is superior to autarky. This is a question with an uncertain answer, because there are two effects. On the one hand, allowing trade in this model leads to waste in transport, tending to reduce welfare. On the other hand, international competition leads to lower prices, reducing the monopoly distortion.

If demand is assumed to arise from a utility function that can be approximated by the form $U = u(Z) + K$, where K represents consumption of a numeraire competitive good, then the welfare effects of trade can be measured by standard surplus measures.

Fig. 2 illustrates the point that there are conflicting effects on welfare. In the figure Z_0 is the pre-trade output of the monopolized good, p_0 is the pre-trade price, and c is marginal

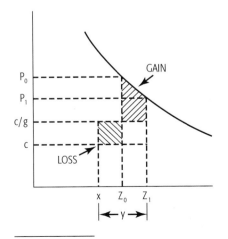

Figure 2

cost. After trade consumption rises to Z_1 and price falls to p_1. But output for domestic consumption falls to x, with imports y. As the figure shows, there is a gain from the 'consumption creation' $Z_1 - Z_0$, but a loss from the 'production diversion' $Z_0 - x$.

There are two special cases in which the welfare effect is clear. First, if transport costs are negligible, cross-hauling, though pointless, is also costless and the pro-competitive effect insures that there will be gains from trade.

At the other extreme, if transport costs are just at the prohibitive level, then decline slightly so that trade takes place, such trade is welfare reducing. This is easily shown as follows. Overall welfare is given by:

$$W = 2[u(Z) - cZ - ty] - F - F^*, \tag{9}$$

where we now use t to denote per unit transport costs instead of the iceberg notation. The 2 arises because there are two symmetric countries. A slight change in t alters welfare as indicated:

$$dW/dt = 2[(p - c)dZ/dt - t\,dy/dt - y]. \tag{10}$$

Starting at the prohibitive level, $p = c + t$ and $y = 0$; therefore since

$$dZ/dt = dx/dt + dy/dt,$$

eq. (10) reduces to:

$$dW/dt = 2(p - c)\,dx/dt = 2t\,dx/dt > 0. \tag{11}$$

A slight fall in transport costs tends to make x fall[7] (as imports y come in) implying that dW/dt is positive. Therefore, a slight fall in t from the prohibitive level would reduce welfare. The intuition runs along the following lines. A decrease in transport costs has three effects. First, costs fall for the current level of imports, which is a gain. Second, consumption rises; so, for each extra unit consumed, there is a net gain equal to price minus the marginal cost of imports. Finally, there is a loss due to the replacement of domestic production with high cost imports. For near prohibitive levels of transport costs the first two effects are negligible, leaving only the loss.

3. WELFARE EFFECTS UNDER FREE ENTRY

The Cournot duopoloy model of section 2 is quite specific. However, the existence result is robust to a wide variety of generalizations. One important generalization is to the free entry case. Moreover, this case has strong welfare properties. Maintaining the assump-

---

[7]The fact that x does fall is easily shown by totally differentiating (3) and (4), and using (7) and (8).

tions and notation of section 2, except that there will now be n firms in each country in equilibrium, the after-trade price and foreign market share ny/Z, are given by:

$$p = c\varepsilon n(1 + g)/g(2n\varepsilon - 1), \qquad (12)$$

$$\sigma = (n\varepsilon(g - 1) + 1)/(1 + g), \qquad (13)$$

where n is the number of firms that sets profits equal to zero for each firm i.

We now prove that, under free entry, trade improves welfare. Consider a pre-trade free entry equilibrium.[8] In the domestic industry each firm maximizes profit so that the following first-order condition is satisfied.

$$x_i p' + p - c = 0. \qquad (14)$$

Also, each firm earns zero profit:

$$\pi_i = x_i p - cx_i - F = 0. \qquad (15)$$

After trade opens price changes, and the direction of price movement determines whether consumer surplus rises or falls, and therefore determines the direction of welfare movement since profits remain at zero by free entry. If price falls, welfare rises. The main step in the argument, then, is that price must fall with the opening of trade.

This is most easily seen by contradiction. From (14), $x_i = -(p - c)/p'$, so:

$$dx_i/dp = (-p' + (p - c)p''dZ/dp)/(p')^2 \qquad (16)$$

$$= -(p' + x_i p'')/(p')^2, \qquad (17)$$

since $dZ/dp = 1/p'$ and $(p - c) = -p'x_i$. But (17) is strictly positive by (8), which means that x_i must rise if p rises. Also, x_i must stay constant if p remains constant, so as to satisfy (14). However, profits are now given by:

$$\pi_i = (p - c)x_i - F + (p^* - c/g)x_i^*. \qquad (18)$$

If price and quantity both rise or remain constant, then $(p - c)x_i - F$ is non-negative by (15), and $(p^* - c/g)x_i^*$ is strictly positive since $p^* > c/g$ if trade is to take place. Therefore, π_i must be strictly positive, which is a contradiction. Price must fall and welfare must rise.

The structural source of welfare improvement is that firms move down their average cost curves. Although x_i falls, $x_i + x_i^*$ must exceed the original production levels and average cost must fall. Profits remain at zero and consumer surplus rises.

---

[8] Demonstrating existence and uniqueness of free entry Cournot equilibrium is a general problem to which we have nothing to add. Clearly, there may be 'integer' problems in small-numbers cases. The interested reader might consult Friedman (1977) and the references cited there.

4. CONCLUDING REMARKS

This paper has shown that oligopolistic interaction between firms can cause trade in the absence of any of the usual motivations for trade; neither cost differences nor economies of scale are necessary. The model provides possible explanations for two phenomena not well explained by standard neoclassical trade theory: intra-industry trade and dumping. We refer to such trade as 'reciprocal dumping'. The welfare effects of such trade are interesting. If firms earn positive profits, the opening of trade will increase welfare if transport costs are low. On the other hand, if transport costs are high, opening trade may actually cause welfare to decline because the pro-competitive effect is dominated by the increased waste due to transport costs. However, in the free entry Cournot model, opening trade certainly increases welfare.

Reciprocal dumping is much more general than the Cournot model. One direction of generalization (either with or without free entry) is to a generalized conjectural variation model, of which the Cournot model is a special case. The essential element of the conjectural variation model is that each firm has a non-zero expectation concerning the response of other firms to its own output. Letting λ denote the expected change in industry output as own output changes, so that $\lambda = 1$ is the Cournot case, and letting foreign and domestic numbers of firms be n^* and n, respectively, yields $\sigma = (nn^*\varepsilon(g - 1) + n^*\lambda)/\lambda(n^* + ng)$ for the case of symmetric linear conjectural variations. This is positive for some range of transport costs. As long as $\lambda > 0$, so that firms believe that their behaviour can affect price, the possibility of reciprocal dumping arises.[9] In general, the conjectures need not be symmetric and, for that matter, they need not be linear. An easily developed special case is the Stackelberg leader-follower model in which each firm is, for example, a leader in its home market and a follower abroad.[10]

If price is the strategy variable, reciprocal dumping does not arise in the homogeneous product case. However, a slight amount of product differentiation will restore the reciprocal dumping result, in which case the intra-industry trade motives described here augment the usual product differentiation motives for intra-industry trade. The important element is just that firms have a segmented markets perception. Given this perception, the possibility of the kind of two-way trade described here is relatively robust.

---

[9] If $\lambda = 0$, the first-order conditions become $p = c$ for domestic firms and $p = c/g$ for foreigners. Clearly, these cannot both hold. There is a corner solution at $p = c$ and $\sigma = 0$ where the Kuhn–Tucker condition $y(p - c/g) = 0$ holds. Ignoring the lower bound at $y = 0$ leads to the nonsense result that foreign firms would want to produce negative output in the domestic market, which is why the expression for σ approaches $-\infty$ as λ approaches 0. σ should of course be bounded below at 0.

[10] Brander and Spencer (1981) examine the implications for tariff policy of a market structure in which the foreign firm is an entry-deterring or potentially Stackelberg leader in both markets.

Finally, we should briefly note another application of our basic analysis. Throughout this paper we have assumed that firms must produce in their home country. Given the assumed equality of production costs, however, firms clearly have an incentive to save transport costs by producing near the markets, if they can. But if we allow them to do this, each firm will produce in both countries—and we will have moved from a model of reciprocal dumping in trade to a model of two-way direct foreign investment.

REFERENCES

Balassa, Bela, 1966, Tariff reductions and trade in manufactures, American Economic Review 56, 466–473.

Brander, James A., 1981, Intra-industry trade in identical commodities, Journal of International Economics 11, 1–14.

Brander, James A. and Barbara J. Spencer, 1981, Tariffs and the extraction of foreign monopoly rents under potential entry, Canadian Journal of Economics 14, 371–389.

Caves, Richard and Ronald W. Jones, 1977, World trade and payments, 2nd edn. (Little, Brown and Company, Boston).

Ethier, Wilfred, 1982, Dumping, Journal of Political Economy 90, 487–506.

Friedman, James W., 1977, Oligopoly and the theory of games (North-Holland, Amsterdam).

Grubel, Herbert and Peter Lloyd, 1975, Intra-industry trade (Wiley, New York).

Helpman, Elhanan, 1982, Increasing returns, imperfect markets, and trade theory, Discussion Paper, Tel Aviv University.

Krugman, Paul, 1979, Increasing returns, monopolistic competition and international trade, Journal of International Economics 9, 469–479.

Lancaster, Kelvin, 1980, Intra-industry trade under perfect monopolistic competition, Journal of International Economics 10, 151–175.

Seade, Jesus, 1980, On the effects of entry, Econometrica 48, 479–489.

Smithies, Arthur, 1942, Aspects of the basing-point system, American Economic Review 32, 705–726.

ABOUT THE AUTHOR

James Brander

James Brander is a professor in the Faculty of Commerce at the University of British Columbia (UBC). He received an honors B.A. in economics from UBC and a Ph.D. from Stanford University. He is currently editor of the *Canadian Journal of Economics*, and has served on the faculty of Queen's University. He and his colleague (and wife) Barbara Spencer pioneered the area known as strategic trade policy. Professor Brander has also worked in the areas of financial economics and natural resource economics.

Editor's Queries

What accounts for the interest in this article? First, it was published at a time when international trade was becoming a much bigger part of the public policy debate in the United States and it was necessary to have models of international trade that could be used to discuss about the role of large firms. Second, the model is relatively simple and clear and provides a base from which many seemingly unrelated questions can be addressed. Finally, I would be disingenuous if I failed to note the exceptional abilities of my co-author, Paul Krugman, who has a way of getting to the essence of significant ideas and presenting them in ways that are appealing and accessible.

What are the major unresolved questions of international economics? What are the likely hot topics of the next decade? Knowing the right questions is more important than being skilled at working out answers, although the latter is also very important. I am not sure what issues will attract a lot of attention in the next decade. At present, one topic attracting considerable interest is the empirical effect of trade and trade liberalization on income distribution and on factor returns more broadly. At a theoretical level, it is not well understood how regional trade arrangements affect the distribution or magnitude of the gains from trade, although I suspect that this is an area where there is unlikely to be a dominant theoretical presumption, as outcome depends so heavily on the precise nature of the agreement, underlying market structures, and other factors. Another topic of continuing interest is the effect of trade and investment on economic growth, particularly in light of the recent downturn in East Asian economic growth and in the light of the difficulty many former Soviet bloc economies have had in taking advantage of integration in the world economy.

ABOUT THE AUTHOR

Paul Krugman

Paul Krugman, Professor of Economics at Princeton University, is the winner of the 1991 John Bates Clark Medal. He received his B.A. fron Yale University and his doctorate from the Massachusetts Institute of Technology, and later served on the faculties of both. He was a Senior Economist at the Council of Economic Advisors in 1982–1983. He is highly regarded within the profession of economics for his creative work at the frontiers of economic knowledge. He is best known for his books on economics that present and develop difficult and abstract ideas in a manner understood and enjoyed by the general public.

National and International Returns to Scale in the Modern Theory of International Trade

WILFRED J. ETHIER

University of Pennsylvania, Department of Economics

For over a quarter century, the Heckscher-Ohlin-Samuelson (H-O-S) trade model has thoroughly dominated work in the pure theory of international trade. Indeed this model is often identified as "the" modern theory of trade. But this dominance has always been rendered uneasy by a widespread suspicion that the salient facts of modern commerce are inconsistent with the theoretical structure. Two broad areas of suspicion may be identified.

The first, concerned with whether actual trade patterns and factor endowments are related as predicted by the theory, consists of the Leontief Paradox and the huge volume of work it stimulated. My interpretation of this literature is that the factor-endowments theory of trade fares reasonably well, but that its two-factor, two-commodity version is essentially an inadequate description of reality. I have on other occasions investigated the consequences of many goods and factors, and do not wish to do so now. This paper will accordingly confine itself to a factor-endowments model with two primary factors and two final goods.

The second (by no means unrelated) area of suspicion centers on the stylized fact that the largest and fastest growing component of world trade since World War II has been the exchange of manufactures between the industrialized economies. By contrast, the H-O-S model, and neoclassical theory generally, sees little basis for trade between similar economies. Two manifestations of this point may be found in the empirical literature. The first, of relevance to international monetary problems, concerns departures from purchasing-power parity among the industrial countries even for fairly disaggregated indices of traded goods (see Irving Kravis and Richard Lipsey). The second, a central concern of this paper, involves intraindustry trade.

Although two-way trade had long been observed, it first became of major concern when economists investigated the consequences of economic integration in Europe (see,

The research for this paper was supported by the National Science Foundation under grant no. SES-7925614. I have benefitted from seminars at the universities of Pennsylvania, Western Ontario, and Wisconsin, and Northwestern University. Richard Caves also supplied useful comments and suggestions.

for example, P. J. Verdoorn; Bela Balassa, 1966) and noted a tendency, not towards increased specialization, but rather for all countries to simultaneously increase exports of most categories of manufactures. Indeed in some cases specialization actually declined. Subsequent work divorced the phenomenon of intraindustry trade from economic integration, and exposed the pervasive expansion of such trade between all industrial countries and across most manufacturing sectors, irrespective of tariff barriers or their changes (Helmut Hesse; Herbert Grubel and Peter Lloyd, 1975; Emilio Pagoulatos and Robert Sorenson; and Richard Caves), furthermore this expansion does not appear to be a matter of transition between equilibria[1] (Caves).

The most natural explanations of intraindustry trade, advanced by Gottfried Haberler (p. 34) long ago, are product heterogeneity within aggregates and border trade (and its seasonal analog). But accumulated empirical work (for example, Hesse; Grubel and Lloyd, 1975; and Caves) strongly suggests that these explanations are inadequate.[2] Attention has accordingly shifted to product differentiation and economies of scale (in theory the two go together, as scale economies supply the limitation to the degree of differentiation).[3]

International trade theory does contain a sizable literature on increasing returns to scale (see, for example, R. C. O. Matthews; James Meade; and Murray Kemp, 1969), but this literature would not appear to offer much that is relevant to the phenomenon at issue. Indeed it has not on balance had great influence on trade theory generally. This is no doubt largely because increasing returns establish a strong presumption for complete specialization, multiple equilibria, and indeterminacy, conclusions that both vitiate the standard comparative statics methodology of trade theory and that also bear questionable relevance to the facts of contemporary trade. Furthermore, this theory has generally assumed that the economies of scale were external to the firm and appropriate at an aggregate level, assumptions that preclude much relevance to intraindustry trade. Empirical work has likewise encountered difficulty in coming to grips with scale economies, although many researchers have argued their importance (for example,

---

[1]See Gary Hufbauer and John Chilas for a contrasting argument that intra-industry trade is due to the GATT method of tariff reduction and to transitory responses with quasi-fixed factors of production. Joseph M. Finger also offers some contrasting evidence.

[2]Grubel and Lloyd (1975), for example, found significant Australian intraindustry trade even at the seven-digit level. I do not mean to suggest that such trade indicates a violation of commodity arbitrage and could not be made to disappear completely in the face of relentless disaggregation. Indeed the theory to follow will make use of product differentiation. Rather the point is that intraindustry trade appears significant even with sufficient disaggregation to remove relative cost differences between sectors as a likely determinant of such trade, so that the traditional theory, while not necessarily contradicted, fails to offer an explanation.

[3]Theoretical discussions of intraindustry trade can be found in Grubel; H. Peter Gray; Grubel and Lloyd (1975); and Robert Davies.

Balassa, 1961, 1967; Donald J. Daly et al., Nicholas Owen, and Caves), and some have found relevance to intraindustry trade.

Recently I pointed out (1979a) that scale economies resulting from an increased division of labor rather than from, say, an increased plant size, depended at an aggregate level upon the size of the world market rather than upon geographical concentration of the industry, as supposed in the traditional theory. Such "international" returns to scale were shown to be free of the presumption of indeterminancy and multiple equilibria[4] characteristic of "national" returns to scale, to imply a theory of intraindustry trade in intermediate goods, and generally to lead to conclusions much more in accord with the stylized facts of modern trade.

The purpose of this paper is to argue that, in the context of international returns, the factor-endowments theory is consistent with, and indeed helps to explain, the stylized facts discussed above. In order to do this I shall construct a simple but detailed model yielding international returns to scale, and employ this model to systematically explore the relations between such international returns, the traditional national returns to scale, and the modern (or factor endowments) theory of international trade. I have four broad messages. 1) International returns depend in an essential way on an interaction between the two types of scale economies, which is also an interaction of internal and external (to the firm) economies. 2) The basic theorems of the factor-endowments theory are essentially robust in the presence of such scale economies, in contrast to the conclusions of the traditional literature.[5] Nevertheless there are some important modifications. 3) Intraindustry trade, like interindustry trade, has a factor-endowments basis. However, such trade is basically *complementary* to international factor mobility. 4) Although the existence of internal-scale economies and product differentiation are essential to the theory, the degree of such phenomena need not be an essential determinant of the degree of intraindustry trade.

Recently Paul Krugman (1979, 1981); Avinash Dixit and Viktor Norman; Elhanen Helpman; and Colin Lawrence and Pablo Spiller have extended to an international context the Avinash Dixit-Joseph Stiglitz formalization of Chamberlinian monopolistic competition; and Kelvin Lancaster has also applied to international trade his product-characteristics approach to consumption theory. These authors are concerned with the same stylized facts that my earlier paper (1979a) had been, and they reach some broadly analogous conclusions, although from entirely different theoretical starting points. The present paper is not concerned with the differentiated consumer goods that are their

---

[4] International scale economies actually "bury" these problems rather than eliminate them, as will become clear below.

[5] In this respect the present paper complements recent work establishing the general validity of the basic H-O-S propositions. See Kemp (1976); Ronald Jones and José Scheinkman; my 1974, 1979b articles; Winston Chang, et al.

subject. However I do hope to treat the differentiated producer goods central to my own theory in such a way as to bring out the parallels between the approaches of these other authors and my earlier work on intraindustry trade (I cannot resist the temptation to point out that producers' goods are in fact much more prominent in trade than are consumers' goods).

I. NATIONAL AND INTERNATIONAL SCALE ECONOMIES

A. PRODUCTION

Capital and labor combine to produce wheat (W) and manufactures (M). Wheat is produced subject to constant returns to scale via a smooth production function of the familiar sort. Manufactures, on the other hand, are potentially subject to increasing returns to scale, and I suppose that the production function for M is separable in the sense that I can write $M = km$, where k is an index of scale economies and m an index of the scale of operations; m can be thought of as produced via a familiar smooth production function. Thus the endowment of capital and labor determines a transformation curve:

$$W = T(m).\tag{1}$$

The possibility of returns to scale in manufacturing arises, first, from exploitation of the division of labor, as in the hoary examples of Adam Smith's pin factory and the Swiss watch industry. Finished manufactures are costlessly assembled from intermediate manufactured components.[6] The number n of components that are actually produced will be endogenously determined, and, I assume, only a fraction of a large number of potentially producible intermediate goods.[7] I am not interested in issues which depend upon distinctions between potential intermediate goods, so I assume that they are all producible from capital and labor via identical production functions, and that all produced components contribute in totally symmetric fashion to the finished manufactures. Under these assumptions, all components which are actually produced will be produced in equal amounts, and I denote the output of each such component by x, so that the total number of produced components of all types is nx. Assume that the output of finished manufactures is given by

$$M = n^{\alpha - 1}(nx)\tag{2}$$

for some parameter $\alpha > 1$. It will be convenient to adopt the following specific form of the production function (2), where x_i denotes the quantity of the ith component and β is

---

[6]One could instead interpret the intermediate goods as successive stages. Austrian fashion, or alternatively, allow some of the components to be assembly services, so that assembly is not costless. Either interpretation would leave the balance of this paper unscathed.

[7]I ignore the difficulty of interpreting nonintegral values of n.

a parameter, $1 > \beta > 0$.

$$M = n^{\alpha} \left[\sum_{i=1}^{n} (x_i^{\beta}/n) \right]^{1/\beta}. \tag{2'}$$

With all the x_i equal to a common x, as will be the case in equilibrium, (2') reduces to (2). A higher value of β indicates that components can be more easily substituted for each other in the assembly of finished manufactures. Thus lower values of β correspond to greater "product differentiation" within the manufacturing sector. (Note the analogy to the ways in which Dixit-Stiglitz; Krugman, 1979, 1981; Dixit-Norman; and Helpman measure the utility obtained from a bundle of differentiated consumer goods.)

The gains from an increased division of labor would mandate the production of an infinitesimal amount of an infinite number of separate components if that were possible. I assume that indivisibilities in the production of components prevents this[8] (the division of labor is limited by the extent of the market). If the scale variable m is interpreted as an index of the number of bundles of factors devoted to manufacturing production, suppose that the number of such bundles required to produce x units of any component is $ax + b$, for some $a, b > 0$. Then

$$m = n(ax + b). \tag{3}$$

The technology of the model is formally summarized by equations (1), (2) (or (2')), and (3), with the usual H-O-S model behind the transformation curve $T(m)$.

Note that there are two distinct sources of increasing returns to scale. The individual component production functions, $ax + b$, display what Balassa (1967, ch. 5) refers to as "economies of scale in the traditional sense," and which I term "national" returns. These involve considerations of minimal plant size and the like, and they require total production x to be geographically concentrated. I assume that these economies are internalized by firms, and I shall examine equilibria in which the total output of each produced component is provided by a single firm in a single location. (I shall sometimes refer casually to b in equation (3) as "fixed costs," but I will not assume that b is variable in the long run.)

The finished-manufactures production function (2), or (2'), displays constant returns to scale for a given value of n. But an expansion of the manufacturing sector arising from an increased number of components (a rise in n with constant x) displays increasing returns, since M rises in greater proportion than nx. These economies reflect not an increased plant size but rather a greater division of labor; they are what Balassa (1967, ch. 5) refers to as "horizontal specialization" or "vertical specialization," and were the subject of my earlier paper (1979a), where they were called "international" returns to scale. Economies of this sort depend upon the size of the market for finished manufactures, and they do not

---

[8] This assumption was implicit in my earlier paper (1979a) and explicit in Dixit-Stiglitz and in Krugman (1979).

require that all manufacturing output be concentrated at a single place. I assume that these economies are external to the individual firm. Components are assembled into finished manufactures by many competitive firms, each of which takes n as a parameter and consequently views itself as subject to constant returns to scale.

B. Autarkic Equilibrium

Consider a closed economy with the above technology. An individual producer of finished manufactures uses components, subject to (2′), with n as a parameter. If q_0 and q denote the prices, in terms of wheat, of some pair of produced components with outputs x_0 and x, then cost minimization by producers of M, subject to (2′), requires

$$x_0 = x(q/q_0)^{1/(1-\beta)}. \tag{4}$$

If n is sufficiently large so that the producer of each component acts as though his behavior does not influence that of other component producers, condition (4) is the demand curve faced by the producer of x_0, for given q and x. This curve has an elasticity of $1/(1-\beta)$. The component-producer purchases the services of primary factors in competitive markets and therefore has a cost function given by $-T'(m)[ax_0 + b]$, where $T'(m)$ is exogenous to the individual firm. This firm will therefore equate marginal revenue and marginal cost, and maximize its profit, by charging the price

$$q_0 = -T'(m)a/\beta. \tag{5}$$

Because of the symmetry assumption, q_0 is the price of each component that is actually produced. The profit of each component-producing firm is $q_0x_0 + T'(m)[ax_0 + b]$. These profits will be driven to zero in equilibrium by the entry and exit of firms, that is, by variations in n, as each component is produced by only one firm. Thus, from equation (5),

$$x_0 = b\beta/a(1-\beta). \tag{6}$$

Finally, the number n of components is given by equation (3), for any given m and for $x = x_0$.

$$n = (1-\beta)m/b. \tag{7}$$

Equations (5), (6), and (7) now imply the value of k for $M = km$:

$$k = ([(1-\beta)/b]^{\alpha-1}\beta/\alpha)m^{\alpha-1}. \tag{8}$$

The relative supply price P_S of M in terms of wheat is given by $P_S M = q_0 nx$, or $P_S n^\alpha x = q_0 nx$, or $P_S = n^{1-\alpha}q_0$. Thus substitution yields the supply curve of M:

$$P_S = -T'(m)/k. \tag{9}$$

The supply curve is illustrated in Figure 1. The term M_0 denotes the value of M when $T = 0$, and the curve P_S shows for each value of M the minimum price at which that quantity would be supplied (i.e., expression (9)). Note from (6) that x is independent of m. Thus a reallocation of resources from W to M involves an expansion of M production

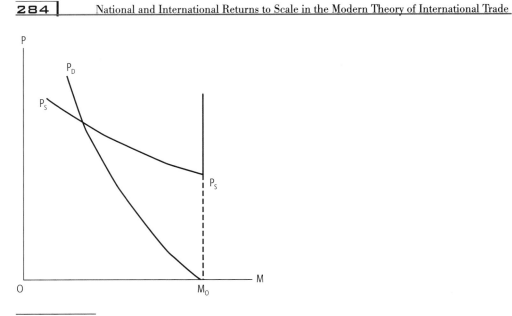

Figure 1

by an increase in n. The manufacturing sector thus displays increasing returns to scale, allowing a negatively sloped supply curve, as illustrated.

The picture of autarkic equilibrium is completed by a description of the demand for final goods. I assume that a constant fraction γ of income is always spent on manufactures. Each output combination M and W determines a demand price P_D that will clear commodity markets: $P_D M = \gamma[W + P_D M]$. Thus the demand curve can be written as

$$P_D = [\gamma/(1 - \gamma)]T(m)/km. \tag{10}$$

The demand curve has a negative slope, as illustrated in Figure 1, and it is easy to show that equations (9) and (10) imply that the demand curve intersects the supply curve from above. Thus in autarky the economy possesses a unique equilibrium which features production of both final goods.

C. INTERNATIONAL EQUILIBRIUM

Consider next free international trade between two economies—of the sort just described—identical in all respects other than factor endowments. Let m and m^* denote the scale of manufacturing operations at home and abroad (variables pertaining to the foreign country will be distinguished by an asterisk). In free-trade equilibrium the total output of each component will be concentrated in a single country. Thus, if m and m^* are both positive, the two countries produce distinct collections of components. Equation (4) continues to represent the demand curve faced by each component producer (in either country), and the same argument as before establishes that (6) gives the output of each component actually produced somewhere. Then, if n_H and n_F denote the number of components produced at home and abroad, respectively, it follows as before that $n_H = (1 - \beta)m/b$ and $n_F = (1 - \beta)m^*/b$ so that $n = n_H + n_F$ is given by

$$n = (1 - \beta)(m + m^*)/b, \tag{11}$$

and so, from (2), the world output of finished manufactures is

$$M + M^* = (\beta/\alpha)[(1 - \beta)/b]^{\alpha - 1}(m + m^*)^\alpha. \tag{12}$$

What determines m, m^* and the relative prices? To answer this question I use the allocation-curve technique[9] developed in my 1979a and forthcoming articles. For any m and m^*, the world demand price of finished manufactures in terms of wheat is given by

$$P_D = \frac{\gamma}{1 - \gamma} \frac{T(m) + S(m^*)}{M + M^*}$$

$$= \frac{\gamma}{1 - \gamma} \frac{a}{\beta} \left(\frac{b}{1 - \beta} \right)^{\alpha - 1} \frac{T(m) + S(m^*)}{(m + m^*)^\alpha} \tag{13}$$

where $S(m^*) = W^*$ denotes the foreign transformation curve. The home supply price P_S^H must be given by

$$P_S^H = -[(1 - \beta)(m + m^*)/b]^{1 - \alpha} T'(m)a/\beta. \tag{14}$$

Home-country equilibrium requires $P_D = P_S^H$, or, from equations (13) and (14),

$$\gamma[T(m) + S(m^*)] + (1 - \gamma)(m + m^*)T'(m) = 0. \tag{15}$$

Equation (15) defines the "home allocation curve": the collection of m and m^* for which the home country is in equilibrium in the international economy. This relation is depicted as the HH' curve in each panel of Figure 2. It is easily shown that the curve has a negative slope, that $P_D < P_S^H$ above the curve, and that $P_D > P_S^H$ below. In Figure 2, m_0 and m_0^* denote the manufacturing scales if the home and foreign economies, respectively, specialize to manufactures, so the world is confined to the rectangle $0m_0Em_0^*$ in each panel, and that part of the graph of (15) lying outside this rectangle is irrelevant (it is easy to see that the graph of (15) cannot be completely excluded from the rectangle). If the home economy specializes, equilibrium is consistent with an excess of the relative demand price of the produced good over its relative supply price. Thus the home allocation curve also contains any part of $0m_0^*$ that lies above the intersection of $H'H$ with the vertical axis, and also any part of m_0E below its intersection with $H'H$.

Similarly, the foreign allocation curve, showing the m and m^* for which $P_D = P_S^F$, the foreign relative supply price, is given by

$$\gamma[T(m) + S(m^*)] + (1 - \gamma)(m + m^*)S'(m^*) = 0. \tag{16}$$

---

[9]The remainder of this section is rather terse as it closely follows my 1979a article, to which the reader is referred for more detail.

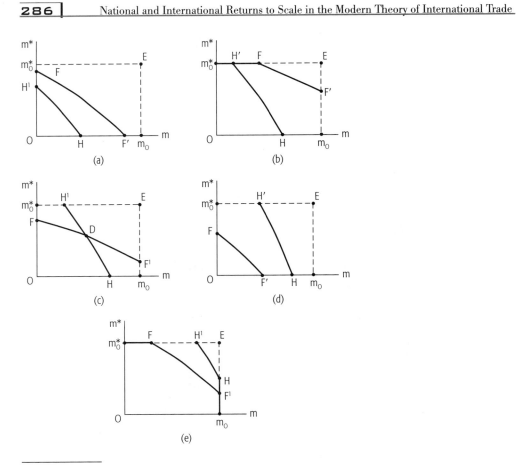

Figure 2

The graph of (16) is shown as FF' in each panel of Figure 2. As illustrated, FF' must decline less steeply than $H'H$, reflecting the fact that each country's supply price is relatively more sensitive than the world demand price to that country's allocation of resources compared to the foreign allocation. Any part of m_0^*E lying below FF' and any part of $0m_0$ above FF' also constitute part of the foreign allocation curve.

International equilibrium requires each country to be individually in equilibrium in the world economy and is therefore determined by the intersection of the two allocation curves. Figure 2 depicts the five qualitatively distinct possibilities; equilibrium is shown by points F, H', D, H, and F' in panels (a)–(e), respectively (in addition there are the two boundary cases, featuring complete specialization in both countries, between cases (a) and (b) and between (d) and (e)). Evidently each case yields a unique international equilibrium.

The equilibrium values of m and m^* determine the relative price of finished manufactures in terms of wheat from equation (13) (or (14)). Then n is given by (11) and

x by (6). The price of each component is as indicated by (5), or, if the home economy specializes to wheat, by the foreign analog.

Note that equation (12) can also be written $M + M^* = k(m + m^*)$ where $k = (\beta/a) \cdot [(1 - \beta)/b]^{\alpha-1}(m + m^*)^{\alpha-1}$, thereby emphasizing that the extent of external scale economies depends on the size of the world market alone. If M and M^* denote the quantities of finished manufactures to which the respective countries obtain effective title as a result of their manufacturing activity (i.e., the most finished manufactures each country could consume without offering any wheat in exchange), then,

$$M = km; \quad M^* = km^*. \tag{17}$$

Note that M and M^* need not equal the quantities of finished manufactures actually assembled in each country. With assembly costless it can be divided in any way between the two countries. (If one of the components were an assembly process, $M + M^*$ would be all assembled in the country where that process happened to be located.)

II. THE MODERN THEORY

Armed with a complete description of international equilibrium, this section inquires into the fate of the four central propositions supplied by the H-O-S model.[10] Henceforth manufacturing is assumed relatively capital intensive and wheat relatively labor intensive. Since inherent properties of the two factors do not figure in this paper, this pattern of factor intensities is in a formal sense only a definition. But the definition is not arbitrary: one intuitively associates a greater division of labor with significant use of capital. This could be introduced by letting manufacturing production explicitly take time, adding a positive interest rate, and allowing components to be producers' goods generally. It is straightforward to extend the main results of this paper to such a context by using the techniques in my article (1979b), provided attention is restricted to steady states.

A. FACTOR-PRICE EQUALIZATION

Suppose that both countries operate both sectors, so that equilibrium is as in Figure 2(c). Then equations (15) and (16) hold, implying that $T'(m) = S'(m^*)$. Likewise, T' and S' are necessarily unequal if one or both countries specializes completely.[11] Now, with the assumption of identical technology, equality of T' and S' implies that domestically produced components sell at the same price as all foreign-produced components, from (14) and its foreign counterpart. Since T and S are generated by conventional H-O-S technologies, the standard factor-price equalization argument can now be employed to yield

---

[10] For a discussion of the basic H-O-S propositions see, for example, Caves and Ronald Jones.

[11] Except, of course, for the borderline case of "incipient diversification" in one country.

PROPOSITION 1: Factor-Price Equalization. If both countries operate both sectors, and are not separated by a factor-intensity reversal, free trade implies factor-price equalization. A separating reversal, or (nonincipient) specialization in either country, precludes such equalization.

B. THE RYBCZYNSKI THEOREM

Note, first, that if domestic factor endowments are altered and $T'(m)$ is kept unchanged, the standard Rybczynski argument applies exactly: an increase in capital will cause a more than proportionate rise in m and a fall in W.

The next step is to relate the change in m to the production of individual components and finished manufactures. Expression (5) implies that constancy of $T'(m)$ is equivalent to constancy of the relative prices of components in terms of wheat. Then (6) implies that endowment changes cause *no* changes in the outputs of those components that are produced both before and after, while (7) reveals that the *number* of produced components varies in proportion to m. Thus:

PROPOSITION 2: Rybczynski. At constant relative component prices, an increase in the capital stock will absolutely reduce the production of wheat, have no effect on the outputs of all components initially produced, and increase the number of produced components in greater proportion than the rise in the capital stock itself.

Several features of this Rybczynski theorem deserve emphasis. First, despite the pervasive presence of economies of scale, the standard results are completely preserved at the interindustry level: changes in endowments produce magnified changes in the outputs of wheat and aggregate manufactures. Because all produced components sell at the same price and have equal outputs, aggregate component production can be measured by nx which changes proportionally to n since the adjustment of manufacturing output occurs through variations in the *number* of components rather than in the *outputs* of individual components.

Second, at a disaggregated level, endowment changes produce magnified changes in the outputs of wheat and of those components which change status (and thereby experience infinite proportional output changes). The (zero) proportional output changes of the other components will be weighted averages of proportional endowment changes if and only if the latter are in opposite directions.

Note, third, that the present version of the Rybczynski theorem places no restrictions on the relative price of finished manufactures. Nor does it make any claims about the effective output M of these final goods. This is because international economies of scale influence the production of final manufactures independently of the internal, national, economies associated with the production of individual components. The extent of the former depends upon patterns of production in both countries. Thus, in order to describe the effects of endowment changes in one country on that country's (effective) output of finished manufactures, the behavior of the rest of the world must be considered.

With relative component prices held fixed, m^* will be unchanged. Now equation (17) implies that the proportional changes in M equals that in m plus that in k. With m^* constant, the proportional change in k equals that in m multiplied by $[(\alpha - 1)m/(m + m^*)]$. This is straightforward: an increase in m takes the form of an increased number of components and thereby raises M both directly and indirectly through the scale economies made possible by the increased division of labor. The latter *scale effect* depends upon the rate $\alpha - 1$ at which scale economies are realized, plus the extent to which an increase in m constitutes an increase in world manufacturing $m + m^*$. In any event, M changes in the same direction as m and in even greater proportion, so that the effect of economies of scale is to simply accentuate the standard results.

With constant component prices, changes in the scale of manufacturing activity must change the relative price of finished manufactures. Equation (14) reveals that this price falls in the proportion $(\alpha - 1)[m/(m + m^*)]\hat{m}$ where I use a circumflex to denote proportional change. This is the same scale effect as above, entering in for the same reason. The relative price of finished manufactures falls in the proportion that k rises; thus the *value* of finished manufactures, in terms of either wheat or components, rises in the same proportion as aggregate component output. This is a reflection of the external character of the relevant scale economies.

PROPOSITION 3: *At constant relative component prices, an increase in capital increases the output of finished manufactures relative to that of components (and therefore to the capital stock), and also reduces the price of finished manufactures, so that the value of the output of finished manufactures rises in the same proportion as that of aggregate components.*

It is natural to wonder how the Rybczynski theorem is affected when the relative price of finished manufactures in terms of wheat is held constant. The exercise is not in fact very interesting because of the international interdependence. For example, equation (14) reveals that any increase in m brought about by endowment changes must be accompanied by an increase in T' sufficient to leave $(m + m^*)^{1-\alpha}T'$ unchanged. Thus the relative price of components in terms of wheat rises, and the factor prices and techniques must change as well. Furthermore, if the rest of the world is not specialized to wheat, the equilibrium condition of equal component prices requires foreign changes in factor prices and techniques.

C. THE STOLPER-SAMUELSON THEOREM

Expression (5) implies that the wheat price of components is linked to factor prices in essentially the same way as are commodity prices in the standard H-O-S model. Then the usual argument establishes the following:

$$\hat{P}_C = \theta_{km}\hat{r} + \theta_{Lm}\hat{w}; \tag{18}$$

$$\hat{P}_W = \theta_{kW}\hat{r} + \theta_{LW}\hat{w}. \tag{19}$$

In these equations P_C, P_W, r, and w denote the nominal prices of industrial components, wheat, capital and labor, respectively (so that $q = P_C/P_W$). The θ_{kW} and θ_{LW} denote capital's and labor's distributive shares in the wheat industry and analogously for θ_{km} and θ_{Lm} in the components industry. The following is immediate from (18) and (19).

PROPOSITION 4: *An increase in the price of wheat relative to the price of all components will raise the wage relative to the prices of both wheat and components and will reduce the rent relative to the prices of both wheat and components.*

Industrial components are intermediate goods, and only wheat and finished manufactures are consumed. Thus Proposition 4 says nothing about real factor rewards and so fails to come to grips with the essence of the Stolper-Samuelson Theorem. The price P_M of finished manufactures is related to that of components by $P_M = n^{1-\alpha}P_c$, so that

$$\hat{P}_M = \hat{P}_C - (\alpha - 1)\hat{n}. \tag{20}$$

Now $\hat{n} = \hat{m}[m/(m + m^*)]$, and $\hat{m}$ can be related to $\hat{P}_M - \hat{P}_W$ by differentiation of (14) to obtain

$$(\hat{P}_m - \hat{P}_W) = \left[m \frac{T''}{T'} - (\alpha - 1)\frac{m}{m + m^*} \right]\hat{m}. \tag{21}$$

Substitution into (20) gives

$$(\hat{P}_M - \hat{P}_C) = Z(\hat{P}_M - \hat{P}_W) \tag{22}$$

where the elasticity of the *intraindustry* price structure P_M/P_C with respect to the *interindustry* price structure P_M/P_W is $Z = 1/(1 - [mT''/T']/[(\alpha - 1)m/(m + m^*)])$.

Note first that, although Z may be of either sign, it can never fall between zero and unity. Thus variations in the intraindustry price structure are never damped versions of variations in the interindustry structure. This reflects the role of scale economies. A change in relative prices involves a reallocation of resources. If resources move into manufacturing, that is, if $\hat{m} > 0$, this will be associated with an increase in P_C/P_W to a degree dependent upon the curvature of the transformation curve. Since the cost of components contributes towards the cost of manufactures, this will also tend to be associated with a rise in P_M/P_W. This effect is simply the familiar H-O-S phenomenon, and I accordingly call it the *intersectoral price effect* of $\hat{m}$; it is reflected in the first term in the brackets in (21).

The variation in m will involve a variation in n rather than x, so individual firms will not experience internal scale economies. But the expansion of world manufacturing will induce external scale economies, and this *scale effect* will tend to reduce the cost of finished manufactures and will therefore work against the intersectoral effect. This scale effect, reflected in the second term in brackets in (21), is the same elasticity of k with respect to m encountered above. If the intersectoral effect dominates, P_M/P_W will therefore change in the same direction as, but to a lessor extent than, P_C/P_W, whereas a dominant scale effect[12] means that a rise in P_C/P_W actually reduces P_M/P_W.

PROPOSITION 5: *If the scale effect dominates the intersectoral effect ($Z > 0$), changes in the intrasectoral price structure P_M/P_C are magnifications of changes in the intersectoral structure P_M/P_W. If the intersectoral effect dominates the scale effect ($Z < 0$), the two relative prices always change in opposite directions.*

We are now in a position to relate factor rewards to final-goods prices. Substituting equation (22) into (18) and (19) gives

$$\hat{P}_M = \theta_{kW}\left[\frac{(\theta_{km}/\theta_{kW}) - Z}{1 - Z}\right]\hat{r} + \theta_{LW}\left[\frac{(\theta_{Lm}/\theta_{LW}) - Z}{1 - Z}\right]\hat{w} \qquad (23)$$

$$\hat{P}_W = \theta_{kW}\,\hat{r} + \theta_{LW}\,\hat{w}. \qquad (19)$$

Note first that (19) is not affected, so that the proportional change in the price of wheat is still a weighted average of those in the two factor rewards. Second, the coefficients of $\hat{w}$ and $\hat{r}$ in (23) sum to unity, as in (18). With labor designated intensive to wheat, $\theta_{Lm} < \theta_{LW}$, so that the exclusion of Z from between zero and unity renders the coefficients of $\hat{w}$ in (23) positive. Thus that of $\hat{r}$ is less than unity. This is all that can be said without restrictions on technology.

If $Z < 0$, the coefficient of $\hat{r}$ in (23) is positive, so that $\hat{P}_M$ is a weighted average of $\hat{r}$ and $\hat{w}$. Furthermore, the coefficient of $\hat{r}$ in (23) exceeds that of $\hat{r}$ in (19), and the usual Stolper-Samuelson argument follows. If, on the other hand, $Z > 0$, then in fact $Z > 1$, so the coefficient of $\hat{r}$ in (23) is less than that in (19) and the standard results cannot possibly hold.

PROPOSITION 6: *Stolper-Samuelson. An increase in the price of manufactures relative to wheat raises the rent and lowers the wage relative to both final-goods prices, if and only if the intersectoral effect dominates the scale effect.*

The reason for this result is straightforward. A dominant intersectoral effect ensures that a change in P_M/P_W produces a larger change, in the same direction, in P_C/P_W, to which Proposition 4 can be applied to yield the standard result. A dominant scale effect precludes this result by causing P_C/P_W to change in the opposite direction. Note that Propositions 5 and 6 together give a very simple test for the validity of the Stolper-Samuelson theorem: The intrasectoral price structure P_M/P_C and the intersectoral structure P_M/P_W should always change in opposite directions.

If Z exceeds unity it may or may not also exceed θ_{km}/θ_{kW}. If the scale effect is sufficiently dominant so that Z does exceed this latter term, the coefficient of $\hat{r}$ in

---

[12]These conclusions can perhaps be made clearer by rewriting equation (22) as
$(\hat{P}_C - \hat{P}_W) = (1 - Z)(\hat{P}_M - \hat{P}_W)$ and noting that Z cannot fall between zero and unity.

equation (23) is again positive and $\hat{P}_M$ is a weighted average of $\hat{w}$ and $\hat{r}$. But the coefficient of $\hat{r}$ in (23) is less than that of $\hat{r}$ in (19). Thus the standard Stolper-Samuelson argument applies, but with the role of the factor-intensity pattern reversed, so that an "anti-Stolper-Samuelson" result follows.

PROPOSITION 7: *An increase in the price of manufactures relative to wheat raises the wage and reduces the rent relative to both final-good prices, if and only if the scale effect dominates the intersectoral effect sufficiently so that $Z > \theta_{km}/\theta_{kW}$.*

Finally, if Z lies between unity and θ_{km}/θ_{kW}, the coefficient of $\hat{r}$ in (23) is negative, and that of $\hat{w}$ in (23) exceeds that of $\hat{w}$ in (19). Thus any change in P_M/P_W causes w to rise relative to one final-good price and fall relative to the other, but the rental still behaves as above.

PROPOSITION 8: *The relative price of manufactures and the real income of capital vary in the same or opposite directions according as the intersectoral and intrasectoral price structures vary in identical or opposite directions.*

Note that a large scale effect tends to destroy the duality between the Stolper-Samuelson and Rybczynski theorems, since it works to reverse the former while leaving the latter unscathed.[13]

D. THE HECKSCHER-OHLIN THEOREM

Suppose that both countries produce both goods in international equilibrium, as in Figure 2(c). Then $T'(m) = S'(m^*)$, and Proposition 3 implies that the output ratio M/W is higher in the country endowed with the higher capital-labor ratio. Since the two countries consume the two final goods in equal proportions, each country is a net exporter of the sector intensive to its relatively abundant factor.

Next suppose that at least one country specializes completely. As illustrated in Figure 2, the home allocation curve is steeper than the foreign and, in this case, must lie either wholly outside or wholly inside the foreign. In the former case (Figure 2, panels (d) and (e)) the home country is a wheat importer and in the latter case (Figure 2, panels (a) and (b)) a wheat exporter. What distinguishes the two cases?

At point F', m and m^* satisfy equation (16). In the home country, from equations (13) and (14),

$$P_D - P_S^H = \frac{a}{\beta}\left(\frac{b}{1-\beta}\right)^{\alpha-1}(m + m^*)^{1-\alpha}\left[\frac{\gamma}{1-\gamma}\frac{T+S}{m+m^*} + T'\right].$$

---

[13] See Krugman (1981) for an interesting alternative treatment of income distribution in a model featuring relative factor-endowment differences and intraindustry trade in differentiated consumer goods.

Substitution of (16) into this expression reveals that, at F', $P_D - P_S^H$ has the same sign as $[T'(m) - S'(m^*)]$. Now, if F' falls in the interval $0m_0$, $m^* = 0$ and $0 < m \leq m_0$, whereas $0 \leq m^* < m_0^*$ and $m = 0$ if F' lies in the interval m_0E. In either case, $T' - S'$ is necessarily negative if the foreign country is relatively capital abundant, provided that the two countries are not separated by a factor-intensity reversal. Then $P_D < P_S^H$ at F, which implies that F' lies above the home allocation curve. A similar argument applied to F reveals that the home allocation curve necessarily lies above the foreign when the home country is relatively capital abundant. Panels (a) and (b) of Figure 2 accordingly illustrate home relative labor abundance, and panels (d) and (e) illustrate home capital abundance.

PROPOSITION 9: *Heckscher-Ohlin. In international equilibrium, each country necessarily exports the good intensive in its relatively abundant factor, if the two countries are not separated by a factor-intensity reversal.*

The quantity version of the Heckscher-Ohlin theorem remains intact. Clearly the price version cannot similarly escape unscathed: the scale effect can alter the relation between commodity and factor prices. Also, Section I showed that relative autarkic commodity prices depend upon national size as well as relative endowments. Since only the latter determine trade patterns, these patterns need not reflect autarkic price differences.

But in spite of all this, the price version does have a role to play, a role that depends on a distinction between intraindustry trade and interindustry trade. Basically, the pattern of free *interindustry* trade (the net exchange of manufactures for wheat) will correspond to what the pattern of relative factor prices in the two countries would be in the absence of such trade but with free *intraindustry* trade (the exchange of components). The latter in effect isolates the influence of internationally decreasing costs.

To see this, consider a *quasi-autarkic equilibrium* in which the two countries freely exchange industrial components, but in which there is no trade in wheat. That is, the home economy consumes $W = T(m)$ and $M = km$, where $k = \beta[(m + m^*)(1 - \beta)/b]^{\alpha-1}/a$, and analogously abroad. Such an equilibrium is as described in Section I.B. for each country, except that the two economies are linked by a common value of k dependent upon $m + m^*$. The equilibrium values of m and m^* are the solution to

$$\gamma T(m) - (1 - \gamma)T'(m)(m + m^*) = 0$$

$$\gamma S(m^*) + (1 - \gamma)S'(m^*)(m + m^*) = 0.$$

In such an equilibrium, the home relative demand and supply prices are given by equations (10) and (9), and analogously abroad. If relative demand prices happen to be equal in the two countries, (10) implies $T(m)/m = S(m^*)/m^*$, since in quasi-autarkic equilibrium the countries share common values of k and n. Thus $T'(m)/m$ exceeds or falls short of $S'(m^*)/m^*$ according as the home country is relatively capital or labor abundant (in a physical sense). Or, in view of (9), the home relative supply price is less or greater than the foreign according as the home economy is relatively capital abundant or not. For demand price to equal supply price in each country, it is consequently necessary that the quasi-autarkic equilibrium relative price of manufactures be less in the relatively capital-abundant country. Proposition 9 then implies that the free-trade exchange of wheat for manufactures is accurately predicted by comparative quasi-autarkic relative commodity prices.

Since in quasi autarky the two countries have distinct relative prices but common values of n and k, the logic of Proposition 6 can be employed to compare the two national equilibria in the absence of a scale effect. This gives the present form of the price version of the Heckscher-Ohlin Theorem.

PROPOSITION 10: *Quasi-Autarky Theorem. In the absence of a separating factor-intensity reversal, each country in free trade is a net exporter of the sector relatively intensive in that factor with the lower relative quasi-autarkic price in that country.*

Note that the quasi-autarky theorem applies to a world such as that envisioned by Gary Hufbauer and John Chilas, who stress that trade between industrial countries is largely intraindustry and involves much less interindustry specialization than does interregional trade within the United States. They see this as due in large part to the pattern of tariff reductions made since the war.

III. THE FACTOR-ENDOWMENTS BASIS OF INTRAINDUSTRY TRADE

The previous sections have established the continued relevance to *interindustry* trade of the basic Heckscher-Ohlin idea that trade is a substitute for international factor mobility. The present environment, for example, does no violence to the factor-price-equalization theorem.

The purpose of this section is to establish that *intraindustry* trade likewise has a factor-endowments basis, but that such trade is *complementary* to international factor mobility. Thus a similarity of factor endowments between nations tends to promote such trade as it limits the scope for interindustrial exchange. This property is emerging as a central feature of models with intraindustry trade. The result was first deduced in my article (1979a) and subsequently appeared in the quite distinct work based on differentiated consumer goods.

A. THE COMPLEMENTARITY THEOREM

Recall the assumption that finished manufactures are costlessly assembled from bundles of all components. The above analysis established that if both countries produce manufactures, they specialize to distinct collections of components.

It will prove convenient, and consistent with both the balance of this paper and most empirical work, to measure intraindustry trade as what it would be if finished manufactures were assumed to be costlessly assembled where consumed, and if no component entered trade more than once, so that international trade in manufactures therefore consisted entirely of the shipment of components from their country of manufacture to where they are combined with other components and consumed. Then the home country's import M_C and export X_C of manufactures (components) must be

$$M_C = n_F x g, \qquad X_C = n_H x(1 - g);$$

where g equals domestic national income as a fraction of world income (i.e., $(PM + W)/[P(M + M^*) + W + W^*]$). I shall use the relative index[14] employed by Hesse, Grubel and Lloyd, Caves and others: $\rho = 1 - |X_C - M_C|/(X_C + M_C)$. Then substitution yields

$$\rho = 2g n_F/[(1 - g)n_H + g n_F] \qquad \text{if } n_H \geq gn,$$

$$2(1 - g)n_H/[(1 - g)n_H + g n_F] \qquad \text{if } n_H \leq gn. \qquad (24)$$

Higher values of ρ indicate relatively more intraindustry trade; $\rho = 1$ if all manufacturing trade is intraindustry and $\rho = 0$ if it is all interindustry.

The complementarity between intraindustry trade and factor movements should now be apparent. Let h and h^* denote the capital-labor endowment ratios at home and abroad, and designate the home country as the capital abundant one, so that $h > h^*$. Suppose that the two countries freely trade, with neither country specialized and with factor prices equalized. Suppose now that the factors are slightly "traded" between the two countries so as to reduce $h - h^*$ while leaving each country's income unchanged at the unchanged factor prices and commodity prices. Then n_H falls, n_F rises by the same amount, and g is unchanged. Now, since the home economy is relatively capital abundant, its share of the world output of components (n_H/n) must exceed its share of world income, g. Thus ρ equals the top expression in (24), which directly reveals that a relative-endowment-equalizing trade of factors must raise ρ.

PROPOSITION 11: *Complementarity Theorem. If both countries initially produce both goods, and if there are no separating factor-intensity reversals, a small relative-endowment-equalizing trade of primary factors will increase ρ.*

The basic complementarity property becomes most apparent upon the comparison of extreme cases. If the two countries' endowments differ sufficiently so that one country specializes to wheat there is no intraindustry trade and all trade is interindustrial. If, on the other hand, $K = K^*$ and $L = L^*$, there is no basis at all for interindustry trade (each country will be self-sufficient in wheat), but intraindustry trade will be maximized since the two countries will produce distinct collections of an equal number of components.

B. TECHNOLOGICAL STRUCTURE AND INTRAINDUSTRY TRADE

While the Complementarity Theorem establishes that intraindustry trade is sensitive to factor endowments, it is nonetheless clear that the existence of such trade is due to the assumptions about the technology of manufacturing production. Attention thus naturally focuses on the sensitivity of my measure of intraindustry trade to the technological parameters: a, b, and β.

---

[14] Alternative measures are discussed in Grubel and Lloyd (1971).

Note, first, that these parameters do not influence the basic allocation of resources which, by Proposition 9, is determined as described by the modern theory of international trade. The intersection of the allocation curves determines m and m^*, and these curves are invariant with respect to all three parameters. Attention therefore focuses on equations (6) and (7).

Consider the relative measure ρ. Changes in the technological parameters will not change g, because they produce offsetting changes on the volume and the relative price of finished manufactures, from (12) and (14). Substitution of (7) into the top line of (24) gives $\rho = 2gm^*/[(1 - g)m + gm^*]$. This immediately yields

PROPOSITION 12: *The relative index of intraindustry trade is invariant with respect to the degree of product differentiation and the levels of fixed and marginal costs.*

An increase in marginal costs, by reducing x with n_H and n_F constant, lowers both types of trade in proportion. An increase in product differention also reduces interindustry trade *pari-passu* with intraindustry trade. This is surprising: with the existence of intraindustry trade dependent upon product differentiation, one might expect more differention to increase such trade. But the explanation is simple. From (7) the number of components does rise, but (6) reveals that the output of each falls in even greater proportion, because of fixed costs.

In sum, the technological parameters play a knife-edge role: their existence is crucial for the present theory, but changes in their values have few effects, or sometimes counterintuitive effects, upon intraindustry trade. Empirical investigations have so far produced mixed results (see Pagoulatos and Sorenson; Caves; and references cited therein).

C. MULTILATERAL TRADE

A brief consideration of this paper's implications for multilateral trade further illustrates the above discussion and also brings out some features that cannot arise at all in the two-country framework, but that reflect the stylized facts of modern trade.

The model used thus far is retained, except that many countries of the sort described above are allowed. Suppose that no factor-intensity reversal is displayed by the common technology. Let h_m and h_w denote the capital-labor ratios in the two sectors in countries which diversify production at the existing prices. Denote by h' the capital labor ratio having the property that any country with an endowment $h > h'$ necessarily imports wheat, and any country with an endowment $h < h'$ necessarily exports wheat.[15] Assume $h_m > h' > h_w$. The various possibilities an individual country could experience are indicated in Table 1.

The concerns of the Complementarity Theorem are best brought out in Cases II, III, and IV where similarities of endowments (to each other and to the world as a whole) foster

---

[15] If all countries diversify in production, h' equals the world capital-labor ratio.

TABLE 1

POSSIBILITIES IN MULTILATERAL TRADE

Case	Endowment	Production	Intraindustry Trade	Interindustry Trade
I	$h \geq h_m$	specialized to m	with all other I, II, III, IV countries	imports W from IV and V
II	$h_m > h \geq h'$	diversified	with all other I, II, III, IV countries	imports some W from IV and V
III	$h = h'$	diversified	with all other I, II, III, IV countries	none
IV	$h' > h > h_W$	diversified	with all other I, II, III, IV countries	exports some W to I and II
V	$h_W \geq h$	specialized to W	none	exports W to I and II

intraindustry trade while limiting interindustry trade. Cases I and V, on the other hand, illustrate behavior that cannot arise in a two-country context. Countries in Case I engage in extensive intraindustry trade with the rest of the world (including other Case I countries), by virtue of their specialization to manufacturing, despite the fact that their endowments are quite different from that of the rest of the world as a whole. Countries in Case V, because they specialize to wheat, engage in no intraindustry trade at all with each other (or with anyone else), no matter how closely the factor endowments of these countries resemble each other. The relevance of all this to the stylized facts of contemporary trade should be clear.

IV. CONCLUSION

This paper has developed a simple model of the interaction of national scale economies—internal to individual firms—with international returns to scale—external to firms—and with the modern, factor-endowments, theory of international trade. The result furnishes a detailed microeconomic backdrop to my earlier paper (1979a). In addition two conclusions emerge.

First, as formalized in the Complementarity Theorem, intraindustry trade in manufactures is complementary to international factor movements. Although the existence of such trade depends upon product differentiation and scale economies, these features play a knife-edge role and thereby leave the determination of the level of intraindustry trade largely to relative factor endowments. Second, the basic propositions of the modern theory of international trade remain, on the whole, essentially valid in the presence of scale economies, although some significant modifications do arise.

The second conclusion contrasts rather strongly with the traditional increasing-returns literature—thoroughly preoccupied with national returns to scale. The present treatment also gives national returns a prominent place. The indeterminancy and multiple equilibria characteristic of the standard analysis are still present (because national returns are still present), in terms of the location of production of individual components. But the sharp difference in my conclusions follows from the fact that, when national and international economies are allowed to interact, disturbances to equilibrium typically take the form of changes in the number of production units rather than in their size, so that the concerns of the traditional theory do not arise. Of course it is possible to chip away at this conclusion by relaxing some of my assumptions, especially those that components are symmetric and that internal scale economies arise solely from fixed costs. These assumptions reflect in simple form my views of what is relatively important, but they cannot be literally accurate.

My earlier paper (1979a) argued that international increasing returns to scale are significant in the modern world economy. The present paper suggests that the conclusions of the earlier need not be altered even if national scale economies are also widespread and important. The resulting theory appears empirically relevant, with respect to both the stylized facts cited at the beginning of this article and also to recent studies—see Caves, and Rudolf Loertscher and Frank Wolter.

REFERENCES

Balassa, Bela, *The Theory of Economic Integration*, Homewood: Irwin, 1961.

———, "Tariff Reduction and Trade in Manufactures among the Industrial Countries," *American Economic Review*, June 1966, *56*, 466–73.

———, *Trade Liberalization among Industrial Countries*, New York: McGraw-Hill, 1967.

Caves, Richard, "Intra-Industry Trade and Market Structure in the Industrial Countries," *Oxford Economic Papers*, March 1981, *33*, 203–33.

——— and Jones, Ronald W., *World Trade and Payments*, 2nd ed., Boston: Little Brown, 1977.

Chang, Winston, Ethier, Wilfred J., and Kemp, Murray C., "The Theorems of International Trade with Joint Production," *Journal of International Economics*, August 1980, *10*, 377–94.

Daly, Donald J., Key, B. A., and Spence, E. J., *Scale and Specialization in Canadian Manufacturing*, Staff Study No. 21, Economic Council of Canada, 1968.

Davies, Robert, "Two-Way International Trade: A Comment," *Weltwirtschaftliches Archiv*, 1977, No. 1, *113*, 179–81.

Dixit, Avinash K. and Norman, Viktor, *Theory of International Trade*, Cambridge: Cambridge University Press, 1980.

——— and Stiglitz, Joseph, "Monopolistic Competition and Optimum Product Diversity," *American Economic Review*, June 1977, *67*, 297–308.

Ethier, Wilfred J., "Some of the Theorems of International Trade With Many Goods and Factors," *Journal of International Economics*, May 1974, *4*, 199–206.

———, (1979a) "Internationally Decreasing Costs and World Trade," *Journal of International Economics*, February 1979, *9*, 1–24.

———, (1979b) "The Theorems of International Trade in Time-Phased Economies," *Journal of International Economics*, May 1979, *9*, 225–38.

———, "Decreasing Costs in International Trade and Frank Graham's Argument for Protection," *Econometrica*, forthcoming.

Finger, Joseph M., "Trade Overlap and Intra-Industry Trade," *Economic Inquiry*, December 1975, *13*, 581–89.

Gray, H. Peter, "Two-Way International Trade in Manufactures: A Theoretical Underpinning," *Weltwirtschaftliches Archiv*, 1973, No. 1, *109*, 19–29.

Grubel, Herbert G., "The Theory of Intra-Industry Trade," in I. A. McDougall and R. H. Snape, eds., *Studies in International Economics*, Amsterdam: North-Holland, 1970.

———— and Lloyd, Peter J., "The Empirical Measurement of Intra-Industry Trade," *Economic Record*, December 1971, *47*, 494–517.

———— and ————, *Intra-Industry Trade: The Theory and Measurement of International Trade in Differentiated Products*, London: Macmillan, 1975.

Haberler, Gottfried, *The Theory of International Trade, with its Applications to Commercial Policy*, London: W. Hodge, 1936.

Helpman, Elhanen, "International Trade in the Presence of Product Differentiation, Economies of Scale and Monopolistic Competition," *Journal of International Economics*, August 1981, *11*, 305–40.

Hesse, Helmut, "Hypotheses for the Explanation of Trade Between Industrial Countries, 1953–1970," in H. Giersch ed., *The International Division of Labour: Problems and Perspectives*, Tubingen: J. C. B. Mohr, 1974.

Hufbauer, Gary C. and Chilas, John C., "Specialization by Industrial Countries: Extent and Consequences," in H. Giersch, ed., *The International Division of Labour: Problems and Perspectives*, Tubingen: J. C. B. Mohr, 1974.

Jones, Ronald and Scheinkman, José A., "The Relevance of the Two-Sector Production Model in Trade," *Journal of Political Economy*, October 1977, *85*, 909–36.

Kemp, Murray C., *The Pure Theory of International Trade and Investment*, Englewood Cliffs: Prentice-Hall, 1969.

————, *Three Topics in the Theory of International Trade*, Amsterdam: North-Holland, 1976.

Kravis, Irving B. and Lipsey, Richard E., "Price Behavior in the Light of Balance of Payments Theories," *Journal of International Economics*, May 1978, *8*, 193–246.

Krugman, Paul, "Increasing Returns, Monopolistic Competition, and International Trade," *Journal of International Economics*, November 1979, *9*, 469–80.

————, "Intraindustry Specialization and the Gains from Trade," *Journal of Political Economy*, October 1981, *89*, 959–73.

Lancaster, Kelvin, "Intra-Industry Trade under Perfect Monopolistic Competition," *Journal of International Economies*, May 1980, *10*, 151–76.

Lawrence, Colin and Spiller, Pablo, "Product Diversity, Economies of Scale and International Trade," mimeo., 1980.

Loertscher, Rudolf and Wolter, Frank, "Determinants of Intra-Industry Trade," *Weltwirtschaftliches Archiv*, 1980, *116*, 280–93.

Matthews, R. C. O., "Reciprocal Demand and Increasing Returns," *Review of Economic Studies*, 1950, No. 2, *17*, 149–58.

Meade, James E., *A Geometry of International Trade*, London: George Allen and Unwin, 1952.

Owen, Nicholas, "Scale Economies in the EEC," *European Economic Review*, February 1976, 7, 143–63.

Pagoulatos, Emilio and Sorenson, Robert, "Two-Way International Trade: An Econometric Analysis," *Weltwirtschaftliches Archiv*, 1975, No. 3, *111*, 454–65.

Verdoorn, P. J., "The Intra-Block Trade of Benelux," in E. A. G. Robinson, ed., *Economic Consequences of the Size of Nations*, London: Macmillan, 1960.

ABOUT THE AUTHOR

Wilfred J. Ethier

Wilfred J. Ethier received his B.A., as well as his Ph.D., from the University of Rochester. He has been a faculty member of the economics department of the University of Pennsylvania since 1969, is a former editor of the *International Economic Review,* and is a Fellow of the Econometric Society.

Increasing Returns and Economic Geography

PAUL KRUGMAN

Massachusetts Institute of Technology

This paper develops a simple model that shows how a country can endogenously become differentiated into an industrialized "core" and an agricultural "periphery." In order to realize scale economies while minimizing transport costs, manufacturing firms tend to locate in the region with larger demand, but the location of demand itself depends on the distribution of manufacturing. Emergence of a core-periphery pattern depends on transportation costs, economies of scale, and the share of manufacturing in national income.

The study of economic geography—of the location of factors of production in space—occupies a relatively small part of standard economic analysis. International trade theory, in particular, conventionally treats nations as dimensionless points (and frequently assumes zero transportation costs between countries as well). Admittedly, models descended from von Thünen (1826) play an important role in urban studies, while Hotelling-type models of locational competition get a reasonable degree of attention in industrial organization. On the whole, however, it seems fair to say that the study of economic geography plays at best a marginal role in economic theory.

On the face of it, this neglect is surprising. The facts of economic geography are surely among the most striking features of real-world economies, at least to laymen. For example, one of the most remarkable things about the United States is that in a generally sparsely populated country, much of whose land is fertile, the bulk of the population resides in a few clusters of metropolitan areas; a quarter of the inhabitants are crowded into a not especially inviting section of the East Coast. It has often been noted that nighttime satellite photos of Europe reveal little of political boundaries but clearly suggest a center-periphery pattern whose hub is somewhere in or near Belgium. A layman might have expected that these facts would play a key role in economic modeling. Yet the study of economic geography, at least within the economics profession, has lain largely dormant for the past generation (with a few notable exceptions, particularly Arthur [1989, 1990] and David [in press]).

The purpose of this paper is to suggest that application of models and techniques derived from theoretical industrial organization now allows a reconsideration of

Reprinted with permission from Paul Krugman, "Increasing Returns and Economic Geography," *The Journal of Political Economy*: (1991), vol. 99, no. 3, pp. 483–499. © 1991 by the University of Chicago.

economic geography, that it is now time to attempt to incorporate the insights of the long but informal tradition in this area into formal models. In order to make the point, the paper develops a simple illustrative model designed to shed light on one of the key questions of location: Why and when does manufacturing become concentrated in a few regions, leaving others relatively undeveloped?

What we shall see is that it is possible to develop a very simple model of geographical concentration of manufacturing based on the interaction of economies of scale with transportation costs. This is perhaps not too surprising, given the kinds of results that have been emerging in recent literature (with Murphy, Shleifer, and Vishny [1989a, 1989b] perhaps the closest parallel). More interesting is the fact that this concentration of manufacturing in one location need not always happen and that whether it does depends in an interesting way on a few key parameters.

The paper is divided into four sections. Section I sets the stage with an informal discussion of the problem. Section II then sets out the analytical model. In Section III, I analyze the determination of short-run equilibrium and dynamics. Section IV analyzes the conditions under which concentration of manufacturing production does and does not occur.

I. BASES FOR REGIONAL DIVERGENCE

There has been fairly extensive discussion over time of the nature of the externalities that lead to localization of particular industries. Indeed, Alfred Marshall's original exposition of the concept of external economies was illustrated with the example of industry localization. Most of the literature in this area follows Marshall in identifying three reasons for localization. First, the concentration of several firms in a single location offers a pooled market for workers with industry-specific skills, ensuring both a lower probability of unemployment and a lower probability of labor shortage. Second, localized industries can support the production of nontradable specialized inputs. Third, informational spillovers can give clustered firms a better production function than isolated producers. (Hoover [1948] gives a particularly clear discussion of agglomeration economies.)

These accounts of industry localization surely have considerable validity. In this paper, however, I shall offer a somewhat different approach aimed at answering a somewhat different question. Instead of asking why a particular industry is concentrated in a particular area—for example, carpets in Dalton, Georgia—I shall ask why manufacturing in general might end up concentrated in one or a few regions of a country, with the remaining regions playing the "peripheral" role of agricultural suppliers to the manufacturing "core." The proposed explanation correspondingly focuses on generalized external economies rather than those specific to a particular industry.

I shall also adopt the working assumption that the externalities that sometimes lead to emergence of a core-periphery pattern are *pecuniary* externalities associated with either demand or supply linkages rather than purely technological spillovers. In competitive general equilibrium, of course, pecuniary externalities have no welfare significance and could not lead to the kind of interesting dynamics we shall derive later. Over the past decade, however, it has become a familiar point that in the presence of imperfect competition and increasing returns, pecuniary externalities matter; for example, if one firm's actions affect the demand for the product of another firm whose price exceeds marginal cost, this is as much a "real" externality as if one firm's research and development spills over into the general knowledge pool. At the same time, by focusing on pecuniary externalities, we are able to make the analysis much more concrete than if we allowed external economies to arise in some invisible form. (This is particularly true when location is at issue: how far does a technological spillover spill?)

To understand the nature of the postulated pecuniary externalities, imagine a country in which there are two kinds of production, agriculture and manufacturing. Agricultural production is characterized both by constant returns to scale and by intensive use of immobile land. The geographical distribution of this production will therefore be determined largely by the exogenous distribution of suitable land. Manufactures, on the other hand, we may suppose to be characterized by increasing returns to scale and modest use of land.

Where will manufactures production take place? Because of economies of scale, production of each manufactured good will take place at only a limited number of sites. Other things equal, the preferred sites will be those with relatively large nearby demand, since producing near one's main market minimizes transportation costs. Other locations will then be served from these centrally located sites.

But where will demand be large? Some of the demand for manufactured goods will come from the agricultural sector; if that were the whole story, the distribution of manufacturing production would essentially form a lattice whose form was dictated by the distribution of agricultural land, as in the classic schemes of Christaller (1933) and Lösch (1940). But it is not the whole story: some of the demand for manufactures will come not from the agricultural sector but from the manufacturing sector itself.

This creates an obvious possibility for what Myrdal (1957) called "circular causation" and Arthur (1990) has called "positive feedback": manufactures production will tend to concentrate where there is a large market, but the market will be large where manufactures production is concentrated.

The circularity created by this Hirschman (1958)–type "backward linkage" may be reinforced by a "forward linkage": other things equal, it will be more desirable to live and produce near a concentration of manufacturing production because it will then be less expensive to buy the goods this central place provides.

This is not an original story; indeed, a story along roughly these lines has long been familiar to economic geographers, who emphasize the role of circular processes in the emergence of the U.S. manufacturing belt in the second half of the nineteenth century (see in particular Pred [1966] and Meyer [1983]). The main goal of this paper is to show that this story can be embodied in a simple yet rigorous model. However, before we move on to this model, it may be worth pursuing the intuitive story a little further to ask two questions: How far will the tendency toward geographical concentration proceed, and where will manufacturing production actually end up?

The answer to the first question is that it depends on the underlying parameters of the economy. The circularity that can generate manufacturing concentration will not matter too much if manufacturing employs only a small fraction of the population and hence generates only a small fraction of demand, or if a combination of weak economies of scale and high transportation costs induces suppliers of goods and services to the agricultural sector to locate very close to their markets. These criteria would have been satisfied in a prerailroad, preindustrial society, such as that of early nineteenth-century America. In such a society the bulk of the population would have been engaged in agriculture, the small manufacturing and commercial sector would not have been marked by very substantial economies of scale, and the costs of transportation would have ensured that most of the needs that could not be satisfied by rural production would be satisfied by small towns serving local market areas.

But now let the society spend a higher fraction of income on nonagricultural goods and services; let the factory system and eventually mass production emerge, and with them economies of large-scale production; and let canals, railroads, and finally automobiles lower transportation costs. Then the tie of production to the distribution of land will be broken. A region with a relatively large nonrural population will be an attractive place to produce both because of the large local market and because of the availability of the goods and services produced there. This will attract still more population, at the expense of regions with smaller initial production, and the process will feed on itself until the whole of the nonrural population is concentrated in a few regions.

This not entirely imaginary history suggests that small changes in the parameters of the economy may have large effects on its qualitative behavior. That is, when some index that takes into account transportation costs, economies of scale, and the share of nonagricultural goods in expenditure crosses a critical threshold, population will start to concentrate and regions to diverge; once started, this process will feed on itself.

The story also suggests that the details of the geography that emerges—which regions end up with the population—depend sensitively on initial conditions. If one region has slightly more population than another when, say, transportation costs fall below some critical level, that region ends up gaining population at the other's expense; had the distribution of population at that critical moment been only slightly different, the roles of the regions might have been reversed.

This is about as far as an informal story can take us. The next step is to develop as simple a formal model as possible to see whether the story just told can be given a more rigorous formulation.

II. A Two-Region Model

We consider a model of two regions. In this model there are assumed to be two kinds of production: agriculture, which is a constant-returns sector tied to the land, and manufactures, an increasing-returns sector that can be located in either region.

The model, like many of the models in both the new trade and the new growth literature, is a variant on the monopolistic competition framework initially proposed by Dixit and Stiglitz (1977). This framework, while admittedly special, is remarkably powerful in its ability to yield simple intuition-building treatments of seemingly intractable issues.

All individuals in this economy, then, are assumed to share a utility function of the form

$$U = C_M^{\mu} C_A^{1-\mu}, \tag{1}$$

where C_A is consumption of the agricultural good and C_M is consumption of a manufactures aggregate. Given equation (1), of course, manufactures will always receive a share μ of expenditure; this share is one of the key parameters that will determine whether regions converge or diverge.

The manufactures aggregate C_M is defined by

$$C_M = \left[\sum_{i=1}^{N} c_i^{(\sigma-1)/\sigma} \right]^{\sigma/(\sigma-1)}, \tag{2}$$

where N is the large number of potential products and $\sigma > 1$ is the elasticity of substitution among the products. The elasticity σ is the second parameter determining the character of equilibrium in the model.

There are two regions in the economy and two factors of production in each region. Following the simplification suggested in Krugman (1981), each factor is assumed specific to one sector. Peasants produce agricultural goods; without loss of generality we suppose that the unit labor requirement is one. The peasant population is assumed completely immobile between regions, with a given peasant supply $(1 - \mu)/2$ in each region. Workers may move between the regions; we let L_1 and L_2 be the worker supply in regions 1 and 2, respectively, and require only that the total add up to the overall number of workers μ:[1]

$$L_1 + L_2 = \mu. \tag{3}$$

The production of an individual manufactured good i involves a fixed cost and a constant marginal cost, giving rise to economies of scale:

$$L_{Mi} = \alpha + \beta x_i, \tag{4}$$

where L_{Mi} is the labor used in producing i and x_i is the good's output.

---

[1] This choice of units ensures that the wage rate of workers equals that of peasants in long-run equilibrium.

We turn next to the structure of transportation costs between the two regions. Two strong assumptions will be made for tractability. First, *transportation of agricultural output will be assumed to be costless.*[2] The effect of this assumption is to ensure that the price of agricultural output and, hence, the earnings of each peasant are the same in both regions. We shall use this common agricultural price/wage rate as numeraire. Second, transportation costs for manufactured goods will be assumed to take Samuelson's "iceberg" form, in which transport costs are incurred in the good transported. Specifically, of each unit of manufactures shipped from one region to the other, only a fraction $\tau < 1$ arrives. This fraction τ, which is an inverse index of transportation costs, is the final parameter determining whether regions converge or diverge.

We can now turn to the behavior of firms. Suppose that there are a large number of manufacturing firms, each producing a single product. Then given the definition of the manufacturing aggregate (2) and the assumption of iceberg transport costs, the elasticity of demand facing any individual firm is σ (see Krugman 1980). The profit-maximizing pricing behavior of a representative firm in region 1 is therefore to set a price equal to

$$p_1 = \left(\frac{\sigma}{\sigma - 1}\right)\beta w_1, \tag{5}$$

where w_1 is the wage rate of workers in region 1; a similar equation applies in region 2. Comparing the prices of representative products, we have

$$\frac{p_1}{p_2} = \frac{w_1}{w_2}. \tag{6}$$

If there is free entry of firms into manufacturing, profits must be driven to zero. Thus it must be true that

$$(p_1 - \beta w_1)x_1 = \alpha w_1, \tag{7}$$

which implies

$$x_1 = x_2 = \frac{\alpha(\sigma - 1)}{\beta}. \tag{8}$$

That is, output per firm is the same in each region, irrespective of wage rates, relative demand, and so forth. This has the useful implication that the number of manufactured

---

[2] The reason for this assumption is that since agricultural products are assumed to be homogeneous, each region is either exporting or importing them, never both. But if agricultural goods are costly to transport, this would introduce a "cliff" at the point at which the two regions have equal numbers of workers and thus at which neither had to import food. This is evidently an artifact of the two-region case: if peasants were spread uniformly across a featureless plain, there would be no discontinuity.

goods produced in each region is proportional to the number of workers, so that

$$\frac{n_1}{n_2} = \frac{L_1}{L_2}. \tag{9}$$

It should be noted that in zero-profit equilibrium, $\sigma/(\sigma - 1)$ is the ratio of the marginal product of labor to its average product, that is, the degree of economies of scale. Thus although σ is a parameter of tastes rather than technology, it can be interpreted as an inverse index of equilibrium economies of scale.

I have now laid out the basic structure of the model. The next step is to turn to the determination of equilibrium.

III. Short-Run and Long-Run Equilibrium

This model lacks any explicit dynamics. However, it is useful to have a concept of short-run equilibrium before we turn to full equilibrium. Short-run equilibrium will be defined in a Marshallian way, as an equilibrium in which the allocation of workers between regions may be taken as given. We then suppose that workers move toward the region that offers them higher real wages, leading to either convergence between regions as they move toward equality of worker/peasant ratios or divergence as the workers all congregate in one region.

To analyze short-run equilibrium, we begin by looking at the demand within each region for products of the two regions. Let c_{11} be the consumption in region 1 of a representative region 1 product, and c_{12} be the consumption in region 1 of a representative region 2 product. The price of a local product is simply its free on board price p_1; the price of a product from the other region, however, is its transport cost—inclusive price p_2/τ. Thus the relative demand for representative products is

$$\frac{c_{11}}{c_{12}} = \left(\frac{p_1 \tau}{p_2}\right)^{-\sigma} = \left(\frac{w_1 \tau}{w_2}\right)^{-\sigma}. \tag{10}$$

Define z_{11} as the ratio of region 1 *expenditure* on local manufactures to that on manufactures from the other region. Two points should be noted about z. First, a 1 percent rise in the relative price of region 1 goods, while reducing the relative *quantity* sold by σ percent, will reduce the *value* by only $\sigma - 1$ percent because of the valuation effect. Second, the more goods produced in region 1, the higher their share of expenditure for any given relative price. Thus

$$z_{11} = \left(\frac{n_1}{n_2}\right)\left(\frac{p_1 \tau}{p_2}\right)\left(\frac{c_{11}}{c_{12}}\right) = \left(\frac{L_1}{L_2}\right)\left(\frac{w_1 \tau}{w_2}\right)^{-(\sigma - 1)}. \tag{11}$$

Similarly, the ratio of region 2 spending on region 1 products to spending on local products is

$$z_{12} = \left(\frac{L_1}{L_2}\right)\left(\frac{w_1}{w_2 \tau}\right)^{-(\sigma - 1)}. \tag{12}$$

The total income of region 1 workers is equal to the total spending on these products in both regions. (Transportation costs are included because they are assumed to be incurred in the goods themselves.) Let Y_1 and Y_2 be the regional incomes (including the wages of peasants). Then the income of region 1 workers is

$$w_1 L_1 = \mu \left[\left(\frac{z_{11}}{1 + z_{11}} \right) Y_1 + \left(\frac{z_{12}}{1 + z_{12}} \right) Y_2 \right], \tag{13}$$

and the income of region 2 workers is

$$w_2 L_2 = \mu \left[\left(\frac{1}{1 + z_{11}} \right) Y_1 + \left(\frac{1}{1 + z_{12}} \right) Y_2 \right]. \tag{14}$$

The incomes of the two regions, however, depend on the distribution of workers and their wages. Recalling that the wage rate of peasants is the numeraire, we have

$$Y_1 = \frac{1 - \mu}{2} + w_1 L_1 \tag{15}$$

and

$$Y_2 = \frac{1 - \mu}{2} + w_2 L_2. \tag{16}$$

The set of equations (11)–(16) may be regarded as a system that determines w_1 and w_2 (as well as four other variables) given the distribution of labor between regions 1 and 2. By inspection, one can see that if $L_1 = L_2$, $w_1 = w_2$. If labor is then shifted to region 1, however, the relative wage rate w_1/w_2 can move either way. The reason is that there are two opposing effects. On one side, there is the "home market effect": other things equal, the wage rate will tend to be higher in the larger market (see Krugman 1980). On the other side, there is the extent of competition: workers in the region with the smaller manufacturing labor force will face less competition for the local peasant market than those in the more populous region. In other words, there is a trade-off between proximity to the larger market and lack of competition for the local market.

As we move from short-run to long-run equilibrium, however, a third consideration enters the picture. Workers are interested not in nominal wages but in real wages, and workers in the region with the larger population will face a lower price for manufactured goods. Let $f = L_1/\mu$, the share of the manufacturing labor force in region 1. Then the true price index of manufactured goods for consumers residing in region 1 is

$$P_1 = \left[f w_1^{-(\sigma - 1)} + (1 - f) \left(\frac{w_2}{\tau} \right)^{-(\sigma - 1)} \right]^{-1/(\sigma - 1)}; \tag{17}$$

that for consumers residing in region 2 is

$$P_2 = \left[f \left(\frac{w_1}{\tau} \right)^{-(\sigma - 1)} + (1 - f) w_2^{-(\sigma - 1)} \right]^{-1/(\sigma - 1)}. \tag{18}$$

The real wages of workers in each region are

$$\omega_1 = w_1 P_1^{-\mu} \tag{19}$$

and

$$\omega_2 = w_2 P_2^{-\mu}. \tag{20}$$

From (17) and (18), it is apparent that if wage rates in the two regions are equal, a shift of workers from region 2 to region 1 will lower the price index in region 1 and raise it in region 2 and, thus, raise real wages in region 1 relative to those in region 2. This therefore adds an additional reason for divergence.

We may now ask the crucial question: How does ω_1/ω_2 vary with f? We know by symmetry that when $f = \frac{1}{2}$, that is, when the two regions have equal numbers of workers, they offer equal real wage rates. But is this a stable equilibrium? It will be if ω_1/ω_2 decreases with f, for in that case whenever one region has a larger work force than the other, workers will tend to migrate out of that region. In this case we shall get regional convergence. On the other hand, if ω_1/ω_2 *increases* with f, workers will tend to migrate *into* the region that already has more workers, and we shall get regional divergence.[3] As we have seen, there are two forces working toward divergence—the home market effect and the price index effect—and one working toward convergence, the degree of competition for the local peasant market. The question is which forces dominate.

In principle, it is possible simply to solve our model for real wages as a function of f. This is, however, difficult to do analytically. In the next section an alternative approach is used to characterize the model's behavior. For now, however, let us simply note that there are only three parameters in this model that cannot be eliminated by choice of units: the share of expenditure on manufactured goods, μ; the elasticity of substitution among products, σ; and the fraction of a good shipped that arrives, τ. The model can be quite easily solved numerically for a variety of parameters. Thus it is straightforward to show that depending on the parameter values we may have either regional convergence or regional divergence.

Figure 1 makes the point. It shows computed values of ω_1/ω_2 as a function of f in two different cases. In both cases we assume $\sigma = 4$ and $\mu = .3$. In one case, however, $\tau = .5$

---

[3] This description of dynamics actually oversimplifies in two ways. First, it implicitly assumes that ω_1/ω_2 is a monotonic function of f, or at least that it crosses one only once. In principle, this need not be the case, and there could be several stable equilibria in which both regions have nonzero manufacturing production. I have not been able to rule this out analytically, although it turns out not to be true for the numerical example considered below. The analytical discussion in the next section simply bypasses the question. Second, a dynamic story should take expectations into account. It is possible that workers may migrate into the region that initially has fewer workers because they expect other workers to do the same. This kind of self-fulfilling prophency can occur, however, only if adjustment is rapid and discount rates are not too high. See Krugman (1991) for an analysis.

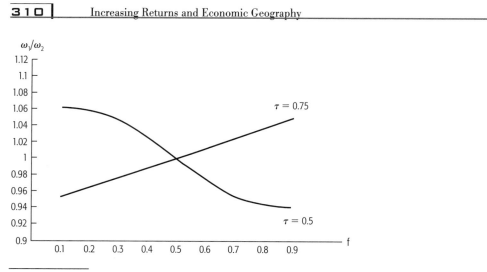

Figure 1

(high transportation costs); in the other, $\tau = .75$ (low transportation costs). In the high-transport-cost case, the relative real wage declines as f rises. Thus in this case we would expect to see regional convergence, with the geographical distribution of the manufacturing following that of agriculture. In the low-transport-cost case, however, the slope is reversed; thus we would expect to see regional divergence.

It is possible to proceed entirely numerically from this point. If we take a somewhat different approach, however, it is possible to characterize the properties of the model analytically.

IV. NECESSARY CONDITIONS FOR MANUFACTURING CONCENTRATION

Instead of asking whether an equilibrium in which workers are distributed equally between the regions is stable, this section asks whether a situation in which all workers are concentrated in one region is an equilibrium. This is not exactly the same question: as noted above, it is possible both that regional divergence might not lead to complete concentration and that there may exist stable interior equilibria even if concentration is also an equilibrium. The questions are, however, closely related, and this one is easier to answer.

Consider a situation in which all workers are concentrated in region 1 (the choice of region of course is arbitrary). Region 1 will then constitute a larger market than region 2. Since a share of total income μ is spent on manufactures and all this income goes to region 1, we have

$$\frac{Y_2}{Y_1} = \frac{1 - \mu}{1 + \mu}. \tag{21}$$

Let n be the total number of manufacturing firms; then each firm will have a *value* of sales equal to

$$V_1 = \left(\frac{\mu}{n}\right)(Y_1 + Y_2), \tag{22}$$

which is just enough to allow each firm to make zero profits.

Now we ask: Is it possible for an individual firm to commence production profitably in region 2? (I shall refer to such a hypothetical firms as a "defecting" firm.) If not, then concentration of production in region 1 is an equilibrium; if so, it is not.

In order to produce in region 2, a firm must be able to attract workers. To do so, it must compensate them for the fact that all manufactures (except its own infinitesimal contribution) must be imported; thus we must have

$$\frac{w_2}{w_1} = \left(\frac{1}{\tau}\right)^{\mu}. \tag{23}$$

Given this higher wage, the firm will charge a profit-maximizing price that is higher than that of other firms in the same proportion. We can use this fact to derive the value of the firm's sales. In region 1, the defecting firm's value of sales will be the value of sales of a representative firm times $(w_2/w_1\tau)^{-(\sigma-1)}$. In region 2, its value of sales will be that of a representative firm times $(w_2\tau/w_1)^{-(\sigma-1)}$, so the total value of the defecting firm's sales will be

$$V_2 = \left(\frac{\mu}{n}\right)\left[\left(\frac{w_2}{w_1\tau}\right)^{-(\sigma-1)}Y_1 + \left(\frac{w_2\tau}{w_1}\right)^{-(\sigma-1)}Y_2\right]. \tag{24}$$

Notice that transportation costs work to the firm's disadvantage in its sales to region 1 consumers but work to its advantage in sales to region 2 consumers (because other firms must pay them but it does not).

From (22), (23), and (24) we can (after some manipulation) derive the ratio of the value of sales by this defecting firm to the sales of firms in region 1:

$$\frac{V_2}{V_1} = \tfrac{1}{2}\tau^{\mu(\sigma-1)}[(1 + \mu)\tau^{\sigma-1} + (1 - \mu)\tau^{-(\sigma-1)}]. \tag{25}$$

One might think that it is profitable for a firm to defect as long as $V_2/V_1 > 1$, since firms will collect a constant fraction of any sales as a markup over marginal costs. This is not quite right, however, because fixed costs are also higher in region 2 because of the higher wage rate. So we must have $V_2/V_1 > w_2/w_1 = \tau^{-\mu}$. We must therefore define a new variable,

$$\nu = \tfrac{1}{2}\tau^{\mu\sigma}[(1 + \mu)\tau^{\sigma-1} + (1 - \mu)\tau^{-(\sigma-1)}]. \tag{26}$$

When $\nu < 1$, it is unprofitable for a firm to begin production in region 2 if all other manufacturing production is concentrated in region 1. Thus in this case concentration of manufactures production in one region is an equilibrium; if $\nu > 1$, it is not.

Equation (26) at first appears to be a fairly unpromising subject for analytical results. However, it yields to careful analysis.

First note what we want to do with (26). It defines a *boundary*: a set of critical parameter values that mark the division between concentration and nonconcentration. So we need to evaluate it only in the vicinity of $\nu = 1$, asking how each of the three parameters must change in order to offset a change in either of the others.

Let us begin, then, with the most straightforward of the parameters, μ. We find that

$$\frac{\partial \nu}{\partial \mu} = \nu\sigma(\ln \tau) + \frac{1}{2}\tau^{\sigma\mu}[\tau^{\sigma-1} - \tau^{-(\sigma-1)}] < 0. \tag{27}$$

That is, the larger the share of income spent on manufactured goods, the lower the relative sales of the defecting firm. This takes place for two reasons. First, workers demand a larger wage premium in order to move to the second region; this "forward linkage" effect is reflected in the first term. Second, the larger the share of expenditure on manufactures, the larger the relative size of the region 1 market and hence the stronger the home market effect. This "backward linkage" is reflected in the second term in (27).

Next we turn to transportation costs. From inspection of (26), we first note that when $\tau = 1$, $\nu = 1$; that is, when transport costs are zero, location is irrelevant (no surprise!). Second, we note that when τ is small, ν approaches $(1 - \mu)\tau^{1-\sigma(1-\mu)}$. Unless σ is very small or μ very large, this must exceed one for sufficiently small τ (the economics of the alternative case will be apparent shortly). Finally, we evaluate $\partial\nu/\partial\tau$:

$$\frac{\partial \nu}{\partial \tau} = \frac{\mu\sigma\nu}{\tau} + \frac{\tau^{\mu\sigma}(\sigma - 1)[(1 + \mu)\tau^{\sigma-1} - (1 - \mu)\tau^{-(\sigma-1)}]}{2\tau}. \tag{28}$$

For τ close to one, the second term in (28) approaches $\mu(\sigma - 1) > 0$; since the first term is always positive, $\partial\nu/\partial\tau$ for τ near one.

Taken together, these observations indicate a shape for ν as a function of τ that looks like Figure 2 (which represents an actual calculation for $\mu = .3$, $\sigma = 4$): at low levels of τ (i.e., high transportation costs), ν exceeds one and it is profitable to defect. At some critical value of τ, ν falls below one and concentrated manufacturing is an equilibrium, and the relative value of sales then approaches one from below.

The important point from this picture is that at the critical value of τ that corresponds to the boundary between concentration and nonconcentration, $\partial\nu/\partial\tau$ is negative. That is, higher transportation costs militate against regional divergence.

We can also now interpret the case in which $\sigma(1 - \mu) < 1$, so that $\nu < 1$ even at arbitrarily low τ. This is a case in which economies of scale are so large (small σ) or the share of manufacturing in expenditure is so high (high μ) that it is unprofitable to start a firm in region 2 no matter how high transport costs are.

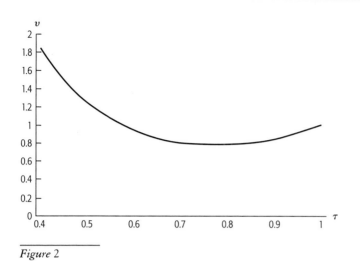

Figure 2

Finally, we calculate $\partial v/\partial\sigma$:

$$\frac{\partial v}{\partial\sigma} = \ln(\tau)\{\mu v + \tfrac{1}{2}\tau^{\mu\sigma}[(1 + \mu)\tau^{\sigma-1} - (1 - \mu)\tau^{-(\sigma-1)}]\}$$

$$= \ln(\tau)\left(\frac{\tau}{\sigma}\right)\left(\frac{\partial v}{\partial\tau}\right). \tag{29}$$

Since we have just seen that $\partial v/\partial\tau$ is negative at the relevant point, this implies that $\partial v/\partial\sigma$ is positive. That is, a higher elasticity of substitution (which also implies smaller economies of scale in equilibrium) works against regional divergence.

The implications of these results can be seen diagrammatically. Holding σ constant, we can draw a boundary in μ, τ space. This boundary marks parameter values at which firms are just indifferent between staying in a region 1 concentration and defecting. An economy that lies inside this boundary will not develop concentrations of industry in one or the other region; an economy that lies outside the boundary will. The slope of the boundary is

$$\frac{\partial\tau}{\partial\mu} = -\frac{\partial v/\partial\mu}{\partial v/\partial\tau} < 0.$$

If we instead hold μ constant and consider changing σ, we find

$$\frac{\partial\tau}{\partial\sigma} = -\frac{\partial v/\partial\sigma}{\partial v/\partial\tau} > 0.$$

Thus an increase in σ will shift the boundary in μ, τ space outward.

Figure 3 shows calculated boundaries in μ, τ space for two values of σ, 4 and 10. The figure tells a simple story that is precisely the intuitive story given in Section I. In an economy characterized by high transportation costs, a small share of footloose

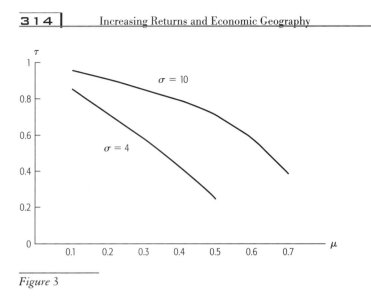

Figure 3

manufacturing, or weak economies of scale, the distribution of manufacturing production will be determined by the distribution of the "primary stratum" of peasants. With lower transportation costs, a higher manufacturing share, or stronger economies of scale, circular causation sets in, and manufacturing will concentrate in whichever region gets a head start.

What is particularly nice about this result is that it requires no appeal to elusive concepts such as pure technological externalities: the external economies are pecuniary, arising from the desirability of selling to and buying from a region in which other producers are concentrated. It also involves no arbitrary assumptions about the geographical extent of external economies: distance enters naturally via transportation costs, and in no other way. The behavior of the model depends on "observable" features of the tastes of individuals and the technology of firms; the interesting dynamics arise from interaction effects.

Obviously this is a vastly oversimplified model even of the core-periphery issue, and it says nothing about the localization of particular industries. The model does illustrate, however, how tools drawn from industrial organization theory can help to formalize and sharpen the insights of a much-neglected field. Thus I hope that this paper will be a stimulus to a revival of research into regional economics and economic geography.

REFERENCES

Arthur, W. Brian. "Competing Technologies, Increasing Returns, and Lock-in by Historical Events." *Econ. J.* 99 (March 1989): 116–31.

———. "Positive Feedbacks in the Economy." *Scientific American* 262 (February 1990): 92–99.

Christaller, Walter. *Central Places in Southern Germany*. Jena: Fischer, 1933. English translation by Carlisle W. Baskin. London: Prentice-Hall, 1966.

David, Paul. "The Marshallian Dynamics of Industralization: Chicago, 1850–1890." *J. Urban Econ.* (in press).

Dixit, Avinash K., and Stiglitz, Joseph E. "Monopolistic Competition and Optimum Product Diversity." *A.E.R.* 67 (June 1977): 297–308.

Hirschman, Albert O. *The Strategy of Economic Development.* New Haven, Conn.: Yale Univ. Press, 1958.

Hoover, Edgar M. *The Location of Economic Activity.* New York: McGraw-Hill, 1948.

Krugman, Paul. "Scale Economies, Product Differentiation, and the Pattern of Trade." *A.E.R.* 70 (December 1980): 950–59.

———. "Intraindustry Specialization and the Gains from Trade." *J.P.E* 89 (October 1981): 959–73.

———. "History versus Expectations." *Q.J.E.* 106 (May 1991).

Lösch, August. *The Economics of Location.* Jena: Fischer, 1940. English translation. New Haven, Conn.: Yale Univ. Press, 1954.

Murphy, Kevin M.; Shleifer, Andrei; and Vishny, Robert W. "Income Distribution, Market Size, and Industrialization." *Q.J.E.* 104 (August 1989): 537–64. (*a*)

———. "Industrialization and the Big Push." *J.P.E* 97 (October 1989): 1003–26. (*b*)

Meyer, David R. "Emergence of the American Manufacturing Belt: An Interpretation." *J. Hist. Geography* 9, no. 2 (1983): 145–74.

Myrdal, Gunnar. *Economic Theory and Under-developed Regions.* London: Duckworth, 1957.

Pred, Allan R. *The Spatial Dynamics of U.S. Urban-Industrial Growth, 1800–1914: Interpretive and Theoretical Essays.* Cambridge, Mass.: MIT Press, 1966.

von Thünen, Johann Heinrich. *The Isolated State.* Hamburg: Perthes, 1826. English translation. Oxford: Pergamon, 1966.

ABOUT THE AUTHOR

Paul Krugman

Paul Krugman, Professor of Economics at Princeton University, is the winner of the 1991 John Bates Clark Medal. He received his B.A. from Yale University and his doctorate from the Massachusetts Institute of Technology, and later served on the faculties of both. He was a Senior Economist at the Council of Economic Advisors in 1982–1983. He is highly regarded within the profession of economics for his creative work at the frontiers of economic knowledge. He is best known for his books on economics that present and develop difficult and abstract ideas in a manner understood and enjoyed by the general public.

Optimal Trade and Industrial Policy under Oligopoly*

JONATHAN EATON

University of Virginia and N.B.E.R.

GENE M. GROSSMAN

Princeton University and N.B.E.R.

We analyze the welfare effects of trade and industrial policy under oligopoly, and characterize optimal intervention under a variety of assumptions about market structure and conduct. When all output is exported, optimal policy with a single home firm depends on the difference between foreign firms' actual responses to the home firm's actions and the responses that the home firm conjectures. A subsidy often is indicated for Cournot behavior, but a tax generally is optimal if firms engage in Bertrand competition. If conjectures are "consistent," free trade is optimal. With domestic consumption, intervention can raise national welfare by reducing the deviation of price from marginal cost.

I. INTRODUCTION

Implicit in many arguments for interventionist trade or industrial policy that have been advanced recently in popular debate appears to be an assumption that international markets are oligopolistic. It can be argued that international competition among firms in many industries is in fact imperfectly competitive, either because the number of firms is few, because products are differentiated, or because governments themselves have cartelized the national firms engaged in competition. They may do so implicitly through tax policy, or explicitly through marketing arrangements.

Government policies that affect the competitiveness of their firms in international markets, as well as the welfare of their consumers, involve not only traditional trade policy (trade taxes and subsidies) but policies that affect other aspects of firms' costs, such as output taxes and subsidies. We refer to intervention of this sort as industrial policy.

*Financial support for this research was provided by the National Science Foundation under grants SES 8207643 and PRA 8211940 and by the International Labor Affairs Bureau, U.S. Department of Labor, under contract J9K 30006. We are grateful to Jim Brander, Avinash Dixit, James Mirrlees, Barbara Spencer, and Larry Summers for helpful discussions and comments.

Until recently, the theory of commercial policy has considered the implications of intervention only under conditions of perfect competition or, more rarely, pure monopoly. As a consequence, this literature cannot respond to many of the arguments that have been advanced recently in favor of activist government policies. Our purpose in this paper is to extend the theory of nationally optimal policy to situations in which individual firms exercise market power in world markets.

The primary implications of oligopoly for the design of trade policy are (i) that economic profits are not driven to zero, and (ii) that a price equal to marginal cost does not generally obtain. The first of these means that government policies that shift the industry equilibrium to the advantage of domestic firms may be socially beneficial from a national perspective. The second feature of oligopolistic competition suggests that trade policy may be a substitute for antitrust policy if policies can be devised that shrink the wedge between opportunity cost in production and marginal valuation to consumers.

A number of recent papers have focused on the profit-shifting motive for trade policy under oligopoly. Brander and Spencer [1985] develop a model in which one home firm and one foreign firm produce perfectly substitutable goods and compete in a third-country market. They consider a Cournot-Nash equilibrium, and find that if the home country's government can credibly precommit itself to pursue a particular trade policy before firms make production decisions (and if demand is not very convex), then an export subsidy is optimal.[1] Dixit [1984] has extended the Brander-Spencer result to cases with more than two firms, and established that an export subsidy in a Cournot oligopoly equilibrium is optimal so long as the number of domestic firms is not too large. Finally, Krugman [1984] shows that under increasing returns to scale, protection of a local firm in one market (e.g., by an import tariff) can shift the equilibrium to the firm's advantage in other markets by lowering its marginal cost of production.

These papers all provide examples in which interventionist trade policy can raise national welfare in imperfectly competitive environments. Yet each makes special assumptions about the form of oligopolistic competition, the substitutability of the goods produced, and the markets in which the goods are sold. It is difficult to extract general principles for trade policy from this analysis. Our purpose here is to provide an integrative treatment of the welfare effects of trade and industrial policy under oligopoly, and to characterize the form that optimal intervention takes under a variety of assumptions about the number of firms, their assumptions about rivals' responses to their actions, the substitutability of their products, and the countries where their products are sold.

---

[1] Spencer and Brander [1983] study a two-stage game in which a capacity or R&D investment is made at a stage prior to production. In such a setting, export subsidies and R&D subsidies are each welfare improving if implemented separately, but an optimal policy package involves an export subsidy and an R&D tax. Brander and Spencer [1984] extend the basic argument for intervention to situations in which duopolistic competition takes place in the home market. In such cases an import tariff often is beneficial.

The paper is organized as follows. In the next section we consider a general conjectural variations model of a duopoly in which a single home firm competes with a foreign firm either in the foreign firm's local market or in a third-country market. We find that the sign of the optimal trade or industrial policy (i.e., whether a tax or subsidy is optimal) depends on the relationship between the home firm's conjectural variation and the actual equilibrium reactions of the foreign firm. We note the form that optimal policy takes in Cournot and Bertrand equilibria and in what Bresnahan [1981] and Perry [1982] have called a "consistent" conjectures equilibrium.

We extend these results to incorporate the interaction between the policies of the home government and an activist foreign government in Section III. Here we consider optimal intervention in a two-stage game in which governments achieve a Nash equilibrium in policies prior to the time that firms engage in product-market competition. In Section IV we further extend the analysis by allowing for oligopoly with arbitrary numbers of firms in each country.

The analysis in Sections II, III, and IV assumes a constant, exogenous number of firms. In Section V we discuss briefly how our results would be modified if firms can enter or exit in response to government policies. Finally, in Section VI we return to the duopoly case and introduce domestic consumption for the first time. This allows us to consider the potential role for trade policy as a (partial) substitute for antitrust policy.

The main findings of the paper are summarized in a concluding section.

II. OPTIMAL TRADE POLICY AND THE ROLE OF CONJECTURAL VARIATIONS: THE CASE OF DUOPOLY

In this and subsequent sections we characterize optimal government policy in the presence of oligopolistic competition among domestic and foreign firms in international markets. Each firm produces a single product that may be a perfect or imperfect substitute for the output of its rivals. We specify competition among firms in terms of output quantities with arbitrary conjectural variations.[2] The domestic government can tax (or

---

[2]We recognize the serious limitation of the conjectural variations framework in its attempt to collapse the outcome of what is actually a dynamic process into a static formulation. While there exist extensive-form representations of Cournot and Bertrand competition, such is not the case for other conjectural assumptions, including that of "consistent conjectures" introduced below. Nevertheless, characterizing the equilibrium in terms of conjectural variations does provide a parsimonious representation of alternative assumptions of firm interaction that includes Cournot and Bertrand equilibria as special cases. In addition, this approach highlights the source of the potential benefit from policy intervention, namely, the deviation between conjectured and actual responses.

Ideally, oligopolistic behavior would be modeled as a truly dynamic, multistage game. Since the development of such models remains, as of now, at a fairly nascent stage, and since existing work on optimal trade policy under oligopoly has been formulated in terms of static models, we choose to pursue the simpler conjectural variations approach.

(footnote continues)

subsidize) the output of domestic firms, tax (or subsidize) the exports of these firms, and tax (or subsidize) the imports from the foreign rivals of domestic firms. Its objective is to maximize national welfare.

The government acts as a Stackelberg leader vis-à-vis both domestic and foreign firms in setting tax (subsidy) rates.[3] Thus, firms set outputs taking tax and subsidy rates as given. In other words, the government can precommit itself to a specific policy intervention that will not be altered even if it is suboptimal ex post, once firms' outputs are determined. At first we assume the absence of government policy in other countries. We also treat the number of firms as given. The implications of relaxing these assumptions are discussed below.

In this section we consider optimal government policy when oligopolistic competition takes its simplest possible form: a single domestic firm competes with a single foreign firm in a foreign market. In the absence of domestic consumption, government trade policy (export taxes and subsidies) is equivalent to government industrial policy (output taxes and subsidies). We assume that the government places equal weight on the home-firm's profit and government tax revenue in evaluating social welfare. Its objective is therefore one of maximizing national product.

Denote the output (and exports) of the home firm by x and let $c(x)$ be its total production cost, $c'(x) > 0$. Uppercase letters denote corresponding magnitudes for the foreign firm, with $C'(X) > 0$. Pretax revenue of the home and foreign firms are given by the functions $r(x, X)$ and $R(x, X)$, respectively. These satisfy the conditions that

$$r_2(x, X) \equiv \frac{\partial r(x, X)}{\partial X} \leq 0$$

$$R_1(x, X) \equiv \frac{\partial R(x, X)}{\partial x} \leq 0,$$

i.e., that an increase in the output of the competing product lowers the total revenue of each firm. They are implied by the assumption that the products are substitutes in consumption.[4] Total after-tax profits of the home and foreign firms are given by

$$\pi = (1 - t)r(x, X) - c(x)$$

Note that, within the class of static, conjectural variations models, restricting attention to those involving output rivalry entails no loss of generality. Kamien and Schwartz [1983] demonstrate that any conjectural variations equilibrium (CVE) in quantities has a corresponding CVE in prices.

[3] Analysis of government policy in international markets typically is based on this assumption. See, e.g., Spencer and Brander [1983]. It may be justified by specifying the political process of establishing policy as time-consuming and costly or by endowing the government with a reputation for adhering to announced policy.

[4] The case of complementary goods can be analyzed similarly. When the two goods are complements ($r_2 > 0$), some of the results reported here (e.g., Theorem 1) are reversed.

and

$$\Pi = R(x, X) - C(X),$$

respectively. Here t denotes the ad valorem output (or export) tax.[5] The domestic firm's conjecture about the foreign firm's output response to changes in its own output is given by the parameter γ. The foreign firm's corresponding conjectural variation is Γ.

The Nash equilibrium quantities, given the level of home country policy intervention, are determined by the first-order conditions:

$$(1 - t)[r_1(x, X) + \gamma r_2(x, X)] - c'(x) = 0; \tag{1}$$

$$R_2(x, X) + \Gamma R_1(x, X) - C'(X) = 0. \tag{2}$$

We assume that the second-order conditions for profit maximization and the conditions for stability of the industry equilibrium are satisfied. We now demonstrate

THEOREM 1: *A positive (negative) output or export tax can yield higher national welfare than laissez-faire ($t = 0$) if the home firm conjectures a foreign change in output in response to an increase in its own output that is smaller (larger) than the actual response.*

Proof: National product generated by the home firm is given by w, where

$$w = (1 - t)r(x, X) - c(x) + tr(x, X)$$
$$= r(x, X) - c(x). \tag{3}$$

The change in welfare resulting from a small change in the tax (or subsidy) rate t is

$$\frac{dw}{dt} = [r_1(x, X) - c'(x)]\frac{dx}{dt} + r_2(x, X)\frac{dX}{dt}. \tag{4}$$

Substituting the first-order condition (1) into (4), we obtain[6]

$$\frac{dw}{dt} = \left[-\gamma r_2 - \frac{tc'}{1 - t}\right]\left(\frac{dx}{dt}\right) + r_2\left(\frac{dX}{dt}\right). \tag{5}$$

Expression (2) implicitly defines the output of the foreign firm X as a function of domestic output x. Denote this function $\Psi(x)$. The tax rate t does not appear directly as an argument of this function, since t does not appear in expression (2). Therefore, $dX/dt = \Psi'(x)(dx/dt)$. Define $g = (dX/dt)/(dx/dt) = \Psi'(x)$. The term g measures the slope of the foreign firm's

---

[5]For concreteness, we consider the case of ad valorem taxes and subsidies. Our results would not be affected by the introduction of *specific* taxes and subsidies, as the reader may verify.

[6]We henceforth drop the arguments of the revenue and cost functions and their partial derivatives whenever no confusion is created by doing so. The revenue functions and their partial derivatives are understood to be evaluated at the equilibrium value of (x, X), while the cost functions and their derivatives are evaluated at x or X, whichever is appropriate.

reaction curve, i.e., its *actual* reaction to exogenous changes in x. A first-order condition for maximizing national welfare obtains when $dw/dt = 0$,[7] or, incorporating the definition of g into equation (5),

$$-r_2(g - \gamma) = tc'/(1 - t). \tag{6}$$

Since $r_2 < 0$, the left-hand and right-hand sides of expression (6) are of the same sign if $1 > t > 0$ and $g > \gamma$, or $t < 0$ and $g < \gamma$. The term $g - \gamma$ is the difference between the actual response of X to a change in x (i.e., $\Psi'(x)$) and the home firm's conjectural variation. When $g > \gamma$, a tax can yield more income than laissez-faire, conversely when $g < \gamma$.

Q.E.D.

An intuitive explanation of this result is as follows. Government policy is implemented before the two firms choose their outputs, which they do simultaneously. Intervention consequently allows the domestic firm to achieve the outcome that would obtain if it were able to act as a Stackelberg leader with respect to its competitor. If $g > \gamma$, then the equilibrium output absent policy involves more domestic output than at the Stackelberg point because the home firm cannot or does not fully account for the foreign firm's reaction to an increase in its own quantity in choosing its output level. Conversely, if $g < \gamma$, the home firm's output more than fully reflects the extent of actual reaction by the rival. The sign of the optimal policy is determined accordingly.

We now turn to some specific conjectural variations that are commonly assumed in models of oligopolistic competition.

A. Cournot Conjectures

Under Cournot behavior, each firm conjectures that when it changes its output the other firm will hold its output fixed. Thus, $\gamma = \Gamma = 0$ in this case, and (6) becomes

$$-gr_2 = tc'/(1 - t). \tag{7}$$

Totally differentiating the equilibrium conditions (1) and (2) to solve for g, we may write this expression as

$$r_2 R_{21}/(R_{22} - C'') = tc'/(1 - t). \tag{8}$$

The second-order condition for the foreign firm's profit maximization ensures that the left-hand side of this expression has the sign of R_{21}. Letting t^* denote the optimal export tax (or subsidy, if negative), we have established:

PROPOSITION 1: *In a Cournot duopoly with no home consumption,* $\operatorname{sgn} t^* = \operatorname{sgn} R_{21}$.

---

[7] The second-order condition for a maximum is satisfied locally as long as (i) the home firm's first- and second-order conditions for profit maximization are satisfied and (ii) the foreign firm's actual response to a change in x does not differ substantially from the response conjectured by the home firm.

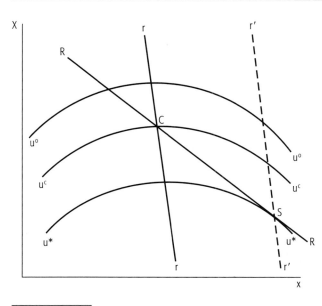

Figure 1
Optimal Policy with Cournot Competition

Proposition 1 restates the Brander-Spencer [1985] argument for an export subsidy: this policy raises domestic welfare in a Cournot equilibrium by transferring industry profit to the domestic firm. This point is illustrated in Figure 1. In the figure, representative isoprofit loci for the home firm are depicted in output space by u^o, u^c and u^*. Lower curves correspond to higher levels of profit. The Cournot reaction function for the home firm rr connects the maxima of the isoprofit loci. The direction of its slope is given by the sign of r_{12}. The foreign firm's reaction curve RR is found similarly, and its slope is determined by the sign of R_{21}. Linear demand necessarily implies that $r_{12} < 0$ and $R_{21} < 0$, and many, but not all, specifications of demand imply this sign as well.

The Cournot equilibrium is at point C, where the home firm earns a profit corresponding to u^c. Note that among the points along RR, u^c does not provide the highest level of profit to the home firm and therefore does not yield the highest possible level of home country welfare. Rather, maximum profit corresponds to u^*, which would be the equilibrium if the home firm could credibly precommit its output level and thus act as a Stackelberg leader. Lacking this ability, the home country could nonetheless achieve the outcome at u^* in a Nash equilibrium if the home government were to implement a trade policy that shifted the home firm's reaction locus to intersect RR at S. This is the optimal profit-shifting trade policy; it involves an export subsidy under the Cournot assumptions provided that RR is downward sloping (i.e., $R_{21} < 0$). A downward (upward) sloping foreign reaction curve implies a level of output in the Cournot equilibrium that is less (greater) than that at the point of Stackelberg leadership: thus, the sign of the optimal trade policy in this case.[8]

Note that the optimal export subsidy with Cournot competition benefits the home firm (and country) at the expense of the foreign firm. Indeed, the equilibrium with one country pursuing its optimal policy involves smaller (net-of-subsidy) profits for the two firms together than in the laissez-faire equilibrium. Consumers of the product benefit from lower prices when the subsidy is in place, and the net effect on world welfare is positive, since policy pushes prices toward their competitive levels.

B. BERTRAND CONJECTURES

In a Bertrand equilibrium each firm conjectures that its rival will hold its price fixed in response to any changes in its own price. Define the *direct* demand functions for the output of the home and foreign firms as $d(p, P)$ and $D(p, P)$, respectively. The total profits of the two firms are

$$\pi(p, P) = (1 - t)pd(p, P) - c(d(p, P))$$

and

$$\Pi(p, P) = PD(p, P) - C(D(p, P)).$$

Each firm sets its price to maximize its profit, taking the other firm's price as constant. First-order conditions for a maximum imply that

$$\pi_1 = (1 - t)(d + pd_1) - c'd_1 = 0, \tag{9a}$$
$$\Pi_2 = D + (P - C')D_2 = 0. \tag{9b}$$

The actual and conjectured price responses can be translated into quantity responses by totally differentiating the demand functions to obtain

$$\begin{bmatrix} dx \\ dX \end{bmatrix} = \begin{bmatrix} d_1 & d_2 \\ D_1 & D_2 \end{bmatrix} \cdot \begin{bmatrix} dp \\ dP \end{bmatrix}.$$

The Bertrand conjecture on the part of the home firm implies a conjectured quantity response given by

$$\gamma = \left(\frac{dX}{dp} \Big/ \frac{dx}{dp} \right)\Big|_{dP=0} = \frac{D_1}{d_1}. \tag{10}$$

---

[8]If products are complements ($r_2 > 0$), the presumption is also in favor of an export subsidy, since in this case most specifications of demand, including the linear, imply that $R_{21} > 0$: the rival expands output when the domestic firm does, to the benefit of the home firm. The home firm consequently produces less, in Cournot competition, than it would as a Stackelberg leader.

The actual response is

$$g = \frac{dX}{dp} \bigg| \frac{dx}{dp} = \frac{D_1 - D_2\Pi_{21}/\Pi_{22}}{d_1 - d_2\Pi_{21}/\Pi_{22}}. \tag{11}$$

It is straightforward to show, using the conditions for stability of the industry equilibrium, that the term $g - \gamma$ is positive if and only if $\Pi_{21} > 0$ (the foreign firm responds to a price cut by cutting its price). Applying Theorem 1, we conclude.

PROPOSITION 2: *In a Bertrand duopoly with no home consumption,* $\operatorname{sgn} t^* = \operatorname{sgn}\Pi_{21}$.

If the two products are substitutes (i.e., $d_2 > 0$ and $D_1 > 0$) and returns to scale are nonincreasing ($c'' \geq 0$, $C'' \geq 0$), then $\Pi_{21} > 0$ *unless* an increase in its rival's price has a significantly negative effect on the *slope* of the demand curve facing the home firm. In the special cases of either perfect substitutes or linear demands, this sign necessarily obtains. Presumption regarding the sign of the optimal trade intervention when duopolistic behavior is Bertrand is consequently the opposite of that in the Cournot case; that is, an export *tax* is generally required.

Figure 2 illustrates this result. Representative isoprofit loci of the home firm (in price space) are shown as u^o, u^b, and u^*. Higher curves now correspond to higher profit. The Bertrand reaction curves are depicted by rr for the home firm and RR for the foreign firm, and the directions of their slopes correspond to the signs of π_{12} and Π_{21}, respectively.

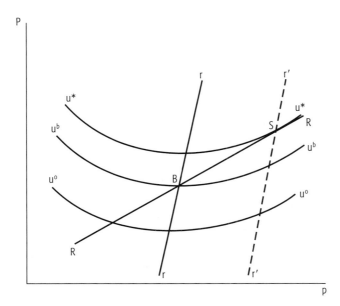

Figure 2
Optimal Policy with Bertrand Competition

The Bertrand equilibrium absent policy intervention is the intersection of the two curves, at point B. Here the home firm earns a profit corresponding to u^b. Given RR, a higher profit could be attained at point S, where the home firm charges a higher price than at B. However, unless the home firm can precommit to the higher price or act as a Stackelberg leader, point S is not achievable under laissez-faire. An appropriate output or export tax shifts the home reaction curve to $r'r'$, whence the Nash equilibrium in the resulting product-market competition yields the superior welfare outcome.[9] Notice that the Bertrand equilibrium for the case in which the foreign reaction curve is upward sloping in price space involves a lower domestic price and therefore a higher domestic output than at the Stackelberg leadership point. This is in contrast to the Cournot outcome, and accounts for the qualitative difference in the policy conclusions.[10]

Another contrast with the Cournot outcome is that implementation of the optimal policy by the home government raises profits of the foreign firm. It does so by alleviating oligopolistic rivalry. Of course, the tax affects consumers adversely, and world welfare falls as the equilibrium becomes less competitive.

C. CONSISTENT CONJECTURES

The final special case we consider is one in which the home firm's conjecture about its rival's response is "consistent," as is the case if the home firm is a Stackelberg leader vis-à-vis its foreign rival or in a "consistent conjectures equilibrium." This second concept, as defined and analyzed by Bresnahan [1981] and Perry [1982] among others, is an equilibrium in which each firm's conjectural variation is equal to the actual equilibrium responses of its rivals that would result if that firm actually were to change its output by a small amount at the equilibrium point.

---

[9]When products are complements, $D_2 < 0$. The presumption then is that $\Pi_{21} < 0$: a price increase by the home firm engenders a price cut by its competitor. So, in this case as well, an export tax is optimal. Such a tax causes the foreign firm to lower its price, increasing the home firm's revenue.

[10]Our findings for the cases of Cournot and Bertrand competition can be stated concisely using the phraseology suggested by Bulow, Geanokoplos, and Klemperer [1985]. They introduce the terms "strategic substitutes" and "strategic complements" to denote situations where "more aggressive" behavior on the part of one firm, respectively, lowers and raises the "marginal profitability" of similar moves by its rival. The classification of goods as strategic substitutes or complements can be made only after the designation of a specific strategy variable, which then gives meaning to the term "more aggressive." For Cournot and Bertrand competition, in which quantity and price are the strategy variables, respectively, their classification hinges on the slope of the reaction curves in the relevant strategy spaces. Accordingly, our Propositions 1 and 2 could be rephrased as follows: *for Cournot and Bertrand competition among (ordinary) substitutes, optimal policy involves subsidizing exports if the goods are strategic substitutes and taxing exports otherwise*. If the goods instead are (ordinary) complements, then the opposite correspondence between strategic substitutes and complements and optimal policy obtains.

The slope of the foreign reaction curve in our model is given by g. Thus, the home firm's conjectures about its rival's response are consistent in the sense of Bresnahan and Perry if $\gamma = g$. The following proposition follows immediately from expression (6):[11]

PROPOSITION 3: *In a duopoly with consistent conjectures on the part of the home firm and no home consumption, $t^* = 0$.*

The optimality of free trade with consistent conjectures on the part of the home firm emerges because there exists no shift of the home firm's reaction curve that can transfer industry profit to that firm, given the response of its rival.

* * *

The duopoly example with no home consumption highlights the profit-shifting motive for trade policy intervention in an imperfectly competitive industry. Under optimal intervention the government uses its first-mover advantage to shift its national firm's reaction function so that it intersects the foreign firm's curve at a point of tangency between the latter curve and a (laissez-faire) isoprofit locus of the home firm. The direction of this shift, and thus the qualitative nature of the optimal policy, depends in general on the sign of the deviation of the home firm's conjectural variation from the slope of the foreign firm's reaction curve.

We now extend the basic result to allow for a foreign policy response, multifirm oligopoly, endogenous market structure, and domestic consumption.

III. FOREIGN POLICY RESPONSE

In the analysis up to this point, we have assumed that the foreign rival's government pursues a laissez-faire policy. Imagine now a two-stage game with both governments active in which the governments first arrive at a Nash equilibrium in policy parameters and then duopolistic competition between the firms takes place. For simplicity, we assume no consumption in the rival's country as well. All consumption is elsewhere.

Denoting the foreign ad valorem output or export tax rate as T, the foreign firm's first-order condition for profit maximization, equation (2), becomes

$$(1 - T)[R_2(x, X) - \Gamma R_1(x, X)] - C'(X) = 0. \qquad (2')$$

A Nash equilibrium in policies is a pair of tax-subsidy rates (t, T) such that t maximizes w, given T, and T maximizes $W = R(x, X) - C'(X)$, given t, where equations (1) and (2') determine x and X.

For $T < 1$, the presence of a foreign tax does not affect the *qualitative* results of the previous section. Theorem 1 is unaffected. For Cournot competition equation (8) is

---

[11] The second-order condition for a social optimum is satisfied at the free-trade equilibrium if the product-market equilibrium is stable.

replaced by

$$\frac{r_2(1 - T)R_{21}}{(1 - T)R_{22} - C''} = \frac{tc'}{1 - t'} \tag{8'}$$

so that the sign of t^* remains that of R_{21}. For Bertrand competition the profit of the foreign firm may be written as

$$\Pi(p, P) = (1 - T)PD(p, P) - C(D(p, P)).$$

Appropriate substitution into the previous analysis implies that Proposition 2 is unaffected as well. Similarly, Proposition 3 remains. Consequently, the *direction* of the optimal policy is unaffected by the possible presence of a foreign export tax or subsidy.

A parallel analysis determines the level of T that maximizes W given t. The following results are immediate.

Under Cournot competition between substitutes with $r_{12} < 0$ and $R_{21} < 0$, the perfect Nash equilibrium is for both governments to subsidize exports. Government interventions together move the product-market equilibrium away from the joint-profit-maximizing outcome toward the competitive equilibrium. Graphically, in terms of Figure 1, both reaction loci shift outward. Both countries will typically benefit from a mutual agreement to desist from attempts to shift profit homeward via export subsidization. The effect on consumers and on world welfare of such an agreement is, of course, the opposite.

Under Bertrand competition with $\pi_{12} > 0$ and $\Pi_{21} > 0$, the perfect Nash equilibrium is for both governments to tax exports. Intervention moves the equilibrium toward the joint-profit-maximizing point away from the competitive equilibrium. In terms of Figure 2 both reaction curves shift out. The exporters gain, consumers lose, and world welfare declines.

Finally, if both firms' conjectures are consistent, the perfect Nash equilibrium is laissez-faire.

IV. OPTIMAL TRADE POLICY: THE CASE OF MULTIFIRM OLIGOPOLY AND CONSISTENT CONJECTURES

In this section we extend our analysis to situations of oligopoly, by allowing for the presence of n home firms and m foreign firms in the industry. For analytical convenience we confine our attention to configurations that are *symmetric*, in the sense that (i) each firm, home or foreign, has the same cost function, (ii) the revenue functions of any two firms i and j (home or foreign) are identical, except that the arguments x^i and x^j are interchanged, and (iii) any two firms producing at the same output level hold the same conjectures about the effect of changes in their own outputs on those of each of their rivals (including each other).

We assume that the conjectures held by all home firms are consistent. We take this as our benchmark case in order that we may isolate the new implications for trade policy that are introduced when the market structure is oligopolistic rather than duopolistic. When conjectures are other than consistent, the optimal trade policy will incorporate an element of the profit-shifting motive, as discussed in Section II, in addition to the terms-of-trade motive that is the focus of our attention in the present section. We also continue to assume that there is no home consumption of the outputs of the oligopolistic industry. This assumption, too, is dictated by our desire to isolate and discuss a single motive for trade policy at a time. Our basic result is stated in

PROPOSITION 4: *In a symmetric, oligopolistic equilibrium with n home firms and m foreign firms and no home consumption, if the domestic firms' conjectures are consistent, then the optimal production or export tax is zero if n = 1 and positive if n > 1.*

Proof: See Appendix A.   Q.E.D.

The result can be understood intuitively by noting that when home firms' conjectures about the responses of foreign firms are consistent, the profit-shifting motive for government intervention is not present. What remains is the standard terms-of-trade argument for export policy. Whenever there is more than a single home country firm and these firms do not collude perfectly, each home firm imposes a pecuniary externality on other domestic firms when it raises its output. Private incentives lead to socially excessive outputs, since home income includes all home firm profits. The government can enforce the cooperative equilibrium in which the home firms act as a group to maximize the home country's total profit by taxing exports or sales. The externality does not arise when there is only one home firm; consequently, free trade is optimal in that case.

Once we depart from the assumption of consistent conjectures, the profit-shifting and the terms-of-trade motives for trade policy intervention can be present simultaneously. Thus, Dixit [1984] finds that for a linear, Cournot, homogeneous-product oligopoly an export subsidy is optimal if the number of domestic firms is not "too large." In this case, the two motives for intervention identified here work in opposition. The two can also be reinforcing, as would generally occur when each of several domestic firms holds Bertrand conjectures.

V. ENDOGENOUS ENTRY AND EXIT

The analysis up to this point has assumed a fixed, exogenous number of firms. This assumption is reasonable if entry costs are large relative to the effect of policies on total profit or if other government policies determined the number of firms. Otherwise, trade and industrial policy is likely to affect the total number of firms in an industry, both domestically and abroad. A thorough treatment of optimal policies with endogenous market structure lies beyond the scope of this paper. Instead, we discuss how endogenous entry and exit would modify some of our previous results.[12]

The first point to make is that allowing for free entry and exit does not necessarily eliminate the profit-shifting motive for trade or industrial policy. All firms may earn positive profits in a free-entry equilibrium if fixed costs are relatively large compared with market size. Then, despite positive returns to firms present in the market, an additional firm could not enter profitably. Alternatively, heterogeneity among firms could imply zero profit for the marginal entrant but positive profits for inframarginal participants. In either of these cases an incentive remains for governments to use policy to shift profits toward domestic participants in the industry. Only if firms are homogeneous and the market can accommodate a large number of them, so that profits of all firms are identically zero, does the profit-shifting motive for trade or industrial policy vanish.

Two new issues are relevant for the formulation of optimal trade and industrial policy when market structure is endogenous. The first arises because policy alters the total number of firms active in an industry in equilibrium. If governments set their policy parameters before firms choose whether or not to incur their fixed costs of entry, or if firms anticipate policies that will be invoked after entry costs are borne, then export or production subsidies will encourage more firms to be active. This entry can raise industry average cost and cause the addition to national product deriving from profit-shifting to be (more than) dissipated in increased entry fees (see Horstmann and Markusen [1984]). Then, a tax on exports or production that discourages entry may be called for even when a subsidy would be optimal given an exogenous market structure.

Second, trade and industrial policy alters the relative numbers of domestic and foreign firms. A subsidy to exports or production in the home country causes foreign firms to exit as domestic firms enter. When residual profits exist, the replacement of foreign firms by domestic ones raises national product. Dixit and Kyle [1985] analyze the potential role for trade policy in deterring foreign entry or encouraging domestic entry.[13] In their analysis, a subsidy can be optimal even if it entails no profit shifting among a *given* set of firms.

---

[12]Horstmann and Markusen [1984] and Venables [1985] analyze the effects of trade policy with free entry for the case of Cournot competition. The first authors assume, as we do in Section VI below, that world markets are integrated. The second assumes segmented national markets. Both assume large numbers of homogeneous firms, so that all firms' profits are zero.

[13]In Venables [1985] the simultaneous exit of foreign firms and entry of an equal number of domestic firms is beneficial because national markets are segmented and transport costs are present. For a given total number of firms, consumer prices at home are lower the greater is the relative number of domestic participants.

VI. TRADE AND INDUSTRIAL POLICY WHEN GOODS ARE CONSUMED DOMESTICALLY

Thus far we have ruled out domestic consumption of the outputs of the oligopolistic industry under consideration. This has allowed us to focus on the profit-shifting and terms-of-trade motives for trade policy. However, by making this assumption, we have neglected a third way in which interventionist trade or industrial policy might yield welfare gains when markets are imperfectly competitive. Since oligopolistic markets are generally characterized by a difference between the price and the marginal cost of a product, there is a potential second-best role for trade and industrial policy (in the absence of first-best antitrust policy) to reduce this distortion.

When domestic consumption is positive, production taxes or subsidies and export taxes or subsidies are no longer identical. In this section we shall consider the welfare effects of both types of policies in the duopoly model of Section II, recognizing that if we were to allow for the existence of more than one domestic firm, the national-market-power motive for taxation of output or exports would also be present. In addition, in order to focus on the considerations for trade and industrial policy introduced by the presence of domestic consumption, we shall continue to use the consistent-conjectures duopoly model as our benchmark case.

To make our point as simply as possible, we assume that the duopolistic competitors produce a single, homogeneous good. We also assume perfect arbitrage with zero transport costs, so that under a production tax or subsidy consumers at home and abroad face the same price for the product. Thus, we consider the case of an integrated world market, where the potential second-best role for trade policy as a substitute for domestic antitrust policy is greatest.[14]

A. PRODUCTION TAX OR SUBSIDY

Let $p(x + X)$ be the inverse world demand function, and let home country direct demand be $h(p)$. The corresponding foreign demand is $H(p)$. If a production tax at rate t is imposed, the profit of the domestic firm is $\pi = (1 - t)p(x + X)x - c(x)$. Consumer surplus at home is $\int_p^\infty h(q)\, dq$.[15] Domestic tax revenue is tpx. Summing these gives total home country welfare from producing, consuming, and taxing the product:

$$w = px - c + \int_p^\infty h(q)\, dq.$$

---

[14] If world markets are segmented, as has been assumed in a number of the previous studies of trade policy under conditions of oligopoly (e.g., Dixit [1984] and Krugman [1984]), then trade policy can act as a second-best substitute for domestic antitrust policy only to the extent that marginal cost is not constant, so that the quantities supplied by an oligopolist to the various markets are interdependent.

[15] We assume that this integral is bounded.

The change in home welfare resulting from a small change in the output tax is

$$\frac{dw}{dt} = (p + xp' - c')\frac{dx}{dt} + xp'\frac{dX}{dt} - h\frac{dp}{dt}.$$

Upon substitution of the first-order condition for the home firm's profit maximization, this becomes

$$\frac{dw}{dt} = \{xp'(g - \gamma) + t[p + xp'(1 + \gamma)]\}\frac{dx}{dt} - h\frac{dp}{dt}. \tag{12}$$

Evaluating (12) at $t = 0$, and imposing the condition that conjectures are consistent ($g = \gamma$), we find that $dw/dt = -h\,dp/dt$. The choice between a production tax and a production subsidy hinges on which policy lowers the price faced by domestic consumers, thereby reducing the consumption distortion associated with imperfect competition.

It is easy to calculate $dp/dt = p'(x + X)(dx + dX)/dt$. Applying Cramer's rule to the total differentials of the two firms' first-order conditions, we have

$$\frac{d(x + X)}{dt} = \frac{c'}{\Delta}[(C' - p)X - C''], \tag{13}$$

where Δ is the determinant of the 2×2 Jacobian matrix, and is assumed to be positive for stability. If foreign marginal cost is increasing ($C'' > 0$), then $p > C'$, and the right-hand side of (13) is unambiguously negative. A production subsidy raises world output, and hence lowers world price. Alternatively, if marginal costs at home and abroad are constant ($c'' = 0$ and $C'' = 0$), then the consistent conjectures equilibrium is the Bertrand equilibrium (see Bresnahan [1981]), so that $p = C'$ and $d(x + X)/dt = 0$. In this case the optimal industrial policy is laissez-faire.

PROPOSITION 5: *In a homogeneous product duopoly with consistent conjectures and nonzero domestic consumption,*
(i) *if $c'' = 0$ and $C'' = 0$, then $t^* = 0$,*
(ii) *if $C'' > 0$, then $t^* < 0$.*

B. TRADE TAX OR SUBSIDY

Finally, we consider the welfare effects of a small export tax or import subsidy at rate τ.[16] Under this policy domestic consumers pay a price $p(1 - \tau)$ for the good, and home

---

[16]One consequence of our assumption that world markets are integrated is that at most one firm will export. Two-way trade of the sort discussed by Brander [1981] will not emerge as an equilibrium outcome. Thus, our trade policy tool τ, which combines a production tax and a consumption subsidy at equal rates, corresponds to an export tax or an import subsidy, depending on the direction of net industry trade.

government revenue is $p\tau(x - h)$. The world inverse demand function is now written as $p(x + X, \tau)$, where $p_1 = 1/\{H'(p) + (1 - \tau)h'[p(1 - \tau)]\}$ and $p_2 = ph'[p(1 - \tau)]p_1$. Proceeding as before, we find that

$$\left.\frac{dw}{d\tau}\right|_{\tau=0} = hp_1\frac{d(x + X)}{d\tau} + p_2(x - h).$$

In this case, however, it is no longer possible to sign unambiguously the effect of a small trade tax or subsidy on total world output. In addition, there is a second term that now enters the expression for $dw/d\tau$, which at $\tau = 0$ is unambiguously positive or negative depending upon whether the home country is a net exporter or importer of the product. Given total output, an export tax raises the world price of an export good, while an import tariff lowers the world price of an import good. This standard terms-of-trade effect provides a further motive for an export tax or import tariff, just as it does when the market is competitive.

To recapitulate the arguments of this subsection, a trade policy of either sign may raise domestic welfare in a duopolistic market with domestic consumption. When conjectures are consistent, any profit-shifting motive for policy intervention is absent. What remains is a standard terms-of-trade motive on the consumption side, and what might be termed a "consumption-distortion motive," arising from the gap between price and marginal cost. The former always indicates an export tax or import tariff, while the latter may favor either a tax or a subsidy, depending on the precise forms of the demand and cost functions.

V. CONCLUSIONS

We have analyzed the welfare effects of trade policy and industrial policy (production taxes and subsidies) for a range of specifications of an oligopolistic industry. A number of general propositions for optimal policy emerge. First, either trade policy or industrial policy may raise domestic welfare if oligopolistic profits can be shifted to home country firms. Policies that achieve this profit shifting can work only if the government is able to set its policy in advance of firms' production decisions, and if government policy commitments are credible. Furthermore, in the duopoly case, profits can be shifted only if firms' conjectural variations differ from the true equilibrium responses that would result if they were to alter their output levels. The choice between a tax and a subsidy in this case depends on whether home firm's output in the laissez-faire equilibrium exceeds or falls short of the level that would emerge under "consistent" or Stackelberg conjectures.

Second, whenever there is more than one domestic firm, competition among them is detrimental to home-country social welfare. In other words, there exists a pecuniary externality when each domestic firm does not take into account the effect of its own actions on the profits of other domestic competitors. A production or export tax will lead domestic firms to restrict their outputs, shifting them closer to the level that would result with collusion. In this familiar way a production or export tax enables the home country to exploit its monopoly power in trade fully.

These propositions are unaffected by extension of the analysis to cases in which optimal interventions are set simultaneously by two policy-active governments. But allowing for endogenous entry and exit introduces two new considerations. First, policy-induced entry (exit) could raise (lower) the average cost of production. When subsidies engender profit shifting, the gain in national income can be dissipated in additional entry fees. Second, policy alters the relative numbers of domestic and foreign firms in an oligopolistic industry. In the presence of residual profits there is a potential role for trade or industrial policy that serves to deter foreign entry or promote domestic entry.

Finally, when there is domestic consumption of the output of the oligopolistic industry, there are two further motives for policy intervention. First, consumers' marginal valuation of the product will generally differ from domestic marginal cost of production due to the collective exertion of monopoly power by firms in the industry. A welfare-improving policy for this reason should increase domestic consumption. When industrial policy is used, a production subsidy will achieve this result, whereas the appropriate trade policy instrument may be either an export (or import) tax or an export (or import) subsidy. Second, there is the usual externality caused by the multiplicity of small domestic consumers, who do not take into account the effect of their demands on world prices. Industrial policy cannot be used to overcome this externality, but if the country is a net exporter (importer), an export (import) tax will have a favorable impact on the country's terms of trade. The formulation of optimal trade or industrial policy in general requires the weighting of these various influences.

APPENDIX A

Proof of Proposition 4

The profit of the representative home firm i is

$$\pi^i = (1 - t)r_i(x^1, ..., x^n, X^{n+1}, ..., X^{n+m}) - c(x^i),$$

where the t denotes the output or export tax imposed on domestic firms. A typical foreign earns

$$\Pi^j = R_j(x^1, ..., x^n, X^{n+1}, ..., X^{n+m}) - C(X^j).$$

(A foreign policy may be allowed for by defining R^j to be after-tax revenue.) The first-order conditions for profit maximization are

$$(1 - t)r_i^i - c^{i\prime} + (1 - t)\sum_{\substack{j=1 \\ j \neq i}}^{n+m} r_j^i \gamma^{ij} = 0, \qquad i = 1, ..., n; \tag{A1a}$$

$$R_i^i - C^{i\prime} + \sum_{\substack{j=1 \\ j \neq i}}^{n+m} R_j^i \Gamma^{ij} = 0, \qquad i = n + 1, ..., n + m, \tag{A1b}$$

where γ^{ij} (Γ^{ij}) is the conjecture by the home (foreign) firm i about the output response by firm j, for $j \neq i$, $j = 1, ..., n + m$.

Home-country national product deriving from this industry is

$$w = \sum_{i=1}^{n} (r^i - c^i). \tag{A2}$$

Differentiating (A2) with respect to t at $t = 0$, and imposing the condition of symmetry of the initial (free trade) equilibrium gives

$$\left. \frac{dw}{dt} \right|_{t=0} = nr_2^1 \left[(n - 1)(1 - \gamma) \frac{dx^i}{dt} + m \frac{dX^j}{dt} - m\gamma \frac{dx^i}{dt} \right], \tag{A3}$$

where $\gamma = \gamma^{ij}$ for all $j \neq i, i = 1, ..., n + m$.

Next we differentiate the first-order conditions (A1a) and (A1b) and again impose symmetry (i.e., $dx^i = dx^k$, for $i, k = 1, ..., n$ and $dX^j = dX^l$, for $j,l = n + 1, ..., n + m$) to derive

$$\begin{bmatrix} \alpha + (n - 1)\beta & m\beta \\ n\beta & \alpha + (m - 1)\beta \end{bmatrix} \begin{bmatrix} dx^i \\ dX^j \end{bmatrix} = \begin{bmatrix} \lambda \, dt \\ 0 \end{bmatrix}, \tag{A4}$$

where

$$\alpha \equiv r_{ii}^i - c^{i\prime} + (n + m - 1)r_{ij}^i\gamma$$

$$\beta \equiv r_{ij}^i + r_{jj}^i\gamma + (n + m - 2)r_{jk}^i\gamma$$

$$\gamma \equiv r_i^i + (n + m - 1)r_j^i\gamma.$$

Note that the free trade equilibrium has symmetry not only among home firms, but also between home and foreign firms, so that about this point $r_i^i = R_j^i$ and similarly for other derivatives. Using this fact and solving (A4) gives

$$\frac{dx^i}{dt} = \frac{[\alpha + (m - 1)\beta]\lambda}{(\alpha - \beta)[\alpha + (n + m - 1)\beta]} \tag{A5a}$$

and

$$\frac{dX^j}{dt} = \frac{-n\beta\lambda}{(\alpha - \beta)[\alpha + (n + m - 1)\beta]}. \tag{A5b}$$

The value of γ determined by imposing the condition that conjectures be consistent is found by perturbing the equilibrium in (A1a) and (A1b) by an exogenous shift in the output of one firm, e.g., x^1, and solving for the full equilibrium response dx^i/dx^1, $i \neq 1$ (see the discussion in Perry [1982], especially footnote 7). Doing so, we find that

$$\gamma = -\beta/[\alpha + (n + m - 1)\beta]. \tag{A6}$$

Finally, we substitute (A5a), (A5b), and (A6) into (A3), and perform some straightforward algebraic manipulations, which yield

$$\left. \frac{dw}{dt} \right|_{t=0} = \frac{n(n - 1)r_2^1\lambda}{\alpha + (n + m - 2)\beta}. \tag{A7}$$

The denominator of (A7) must be negative for stability of the industry equilibrium [Seade, 1980]. From the first-order condition (A1a), $\lambda = c^{i\prime}/(1 - t) > 0$. The sign of expression (A7) is consequently opposite to that of r_2^1 if $n > 1$ i.e., positive for goods that are substitutes. For $n = 1$, the expression is zero.

                                                                                            Q.E.D.

REFERENCES

Brander, J. A., "Intra-Industry Trade in Identical Commodities," *Journal of International Economics*, XI (1981), 1–14.

———, and B. J. Spencer, "Tariff Protection and Imperfect Competition," in H. Kierzkowski, ed., *Monopolistic Competition in International Trade* (Oxford: Oxford University Press, 1984), pp. 194–206.

———, and ———, "Export Subsidies and International Market Share Rivalry," *Journal of International Economics*, XVIII (1985), 83–100.

Bresnahan, T. F., "Duopoly Models with Consistent Conjectures," *American Economic Review*, LXXI (1981), 934–45.

Bulow, J.I., J. D. Geanakoplos, and P. D. Klemperer, "Multimarket Oligopoly: Strategic Substitutes and Complements," *Journal of Political Economy*, XCIII (1985), 488–511.

Dixit, A. K., "International Trade Policy for Oligopolistic Industries," *Economic Journal Conference Papers*, XCIV (1984), 1–16.

———, and A. S. Kyle, "The Use of Protection and Subsidies for Entry Promotion and Deterrence," LXXV (1985), 139–52.

Horstmann, I., and J. R. Markusen, "Up Your Average Cost Curve: Inefficient Entry and the New Protectionism," mimeographed, November 1984.

Kamien, M. I., and N. L. Schwartz, "Conjectural Variations," *Canadian Journal of Economics*, XVI (1983), 191–211.

Krugman, P. R., "Import Protection as Export Promotion: International Competition in the Presence of Oligopoly and Economies of Scale," in H. Kierzkowski, ed., *Monopolistic Competition in International Trade* (Oxford: Oxford University Press, 1984), pp. 180–93.

Perry, M. K., "Oligopoly and Consistent Conjectural Variations," *Bell Journal of Economics*, XIII (1982), 197–205.

Seade, J. K., "On the Effects of Entry," *Econometrica*, XLVIII (1980), 479–89.

Spencer, B. J., and J. A. Brander, "International R&D Rivalry and Industrial Strategy," *Review of Economic Studies*, L (1983), 702–22.

Venables, A. J., "Trade and Trade Policy with Imperfect Competition: The Case of Identical Products and Free Entry," *Journal of International Economics*, XIX (1985), 1–20.

ABOUT THE AUTHOR

Kal Zabarsky/Boston University Photo Services

Jonathan Eaton

John Eaton is Department Chair and Professor of Economics at Boston University and a Research Associate at the National Bureau of Economic Research. He received his Ph.D. from Yale University. He was a National Fellow at Stanford's Hoover Institution. He has also served on the faculties of the University of Geneva, the Australian National University, and Tel Aviv University, among others.

Editor's Queries

What aspect of this paper would you do differently today, and why?   I would now look at the problem in a framework that takes the timing of moves more seriously. Writing this paper made me aware of the importance of timing in competition, which let me to write "Intertemporal Price Competition" with Maxim Engers. That paper appeared in *Econometrica* in 1990.

How does this article fit into the literature? Do you think it will continue to attract attention?   Our paper was a response to a series of influential and provocative papers on R&D and export subsidies by Jim Brander and Barbara Spencer, primarily ``Export Subsidies and and International Market Share Rivalry," *Journal of International Economics,* 1985, and "International R&D Rivalry and Industry Strategy," *Review of Economic Studies,* 1983. One reason that I think the paper generates interest is that it shows quite generally how what Krishna and Thursby subsequently called strategic externalities interact with trade policy. As for the future, I have had no success in forecasting the tastes of the profession.

What are the major unresolved questions of international economics? What are likely to be the hot topics of the next decade?   Why isn't there more trade? Why are transactions so limited by space? How much do borders, rather than distance matter, and why?

What advice do you have to offer graduate students in the field of international economics?   Do a better job than we have at never straying too far from either theory or data.

ABOUT THE AUTHOR

Gene Grossman

Gene Grossman is the Jacob Viner Professor of International Economics, Professor of Economics and International Affairs, and Director, International Economics Section at Princeton University.

Editor's Queries

What has been the reaction to this article? One thing that surprised me at the time was the controversy the paper stirred. To me, it seemed only natural to investigate how different assumptions implied different conclusions about optimal trade policy. But some established trade economists criticized my co-author and me for lending legitimacy to a new potential argument for protection. Others saw us instead as a force for good, inasmuch as we had shown that the pro-protection findings of Brander and Spencer were not robust. My message to young researchers: do research to promote understanding; don't worry about how your findings might be used (or abused) by those with policy interests.

How would you write the paper differently today? If I have one regret about the paper, it is that we chose to employ conjectural variations to characterize alternative modes of conduct. I no longer feel that this is a useful tool for describing different forms of oligopolistic competition. The conjectural variations model is an attempt to capture a dynamic concept in a static setting, a worthy goal but one without firm game-theoretic foundations. More to the point, our use of conjectural variations, and especially our mention of "consistent conjectures" opened a can of worms that distracted from the main point we wanted to make. Now, when I teach strategic trade policy, I only describe the Cournot, Bertrand, and Stackelberg cases, showing how the optimal policy changes from subsidy to tax to free trade as the strategic environment changes.

Monopolistic Competition and International Trade: Reconsidering the Evidence (Excerpts)

DAVID HUMMELS AND JAMES LEVINSOHN

We test some propositions about international trade flows that are derived from models of monopolistic competition developed by Elhanan Helpman and Paul Krugman. We investigate whether the volume of trade between OECD countries is consistent with the predictions of a model in which all trade is intraindustry trade in differentiated products. We then repeat the test with non-OECD countries. We also investigate whether the share of intraindustry trade is consistent with a more general theoretical model in which some, but not all, trade is intraindustry trade. Our results lead us to question the apparent empirical success of these models.

I. INTRODUCTION

This paper is about testing a relatively new theory of international trade. The life cycle of trade theories seems to progress in the following three steps. In an effort to explain observed trade flows, theorists arrive at a rigorous and logically consistent theory. Next, the theory is subjected to an initial barrage of empirical tests. Frequently, these tests yield conflicting evidence and seldom is the theory unconditionally accepted or rejected.[1] The third step involves sorting out the puzzles and paradoxes to arrive at a set of facts that international economists consider part of their received wisdom. In the case of traditional endowments-based international trade, Heckscher and Ohlin [1991 translation] exemplify the first step, Leontief [1953] the second step, and Leamer [1984, 1987 with Bowen and Sveikauskas] the third.

If those are the three steps in the life cycle of international trade theories, this paper is part of the second stage. This time around the theory tested is that of monopolistic competition and international trade. In this paper, we point out some puzzles and paradoxes. We do not provide many answers. At best, we pave the way for the third stage of the theory's life cycle. At worst, we leave matters confused and unsettled.

We are grateful to James Brander, Ronald Cronovich, Alan Deardorff, Jonathan Eaton, Martin Feldstein, Gene Grossman, Elhanan Helpman, Anne Krueger, Paul Krugman, Edward Leamer, and the editors for helpful comments, suggestions, and skepticism.

[1] For a recent survey of these tests, see Leamer and Levinsohn [1994].

Reprinted with permission from David Hummels and James Levinsohn, "Monopolistic Competition and International Trade: Reconsidering the Evidence," *The Quarterly Journal of Economics,* 110:3 (August, 1995), pp. 799–836. © 1995 by the President and Fellows of Harvard College and the Massachusetts Institute of Technology.

There is a long and distinguished literature examining the *theory* of international trade and monopolistic competition. The first papers were by Krugman [1979, 1981] and Lancaster [1980]. This work was further developed and expanded in Helpman [1981], and it is nicely summarized in Helpman and Krugman [1985]. This line of work was in part motivated by the observation that much international trade appears to be in goods that are quite similar. While traditional factor endowments-based explanations of international trade did not explain this empirically relevant component of international trade, Helpman and Krugman showed that a model of monopolistic competition could.[2] There are many models of monopolistic competition and international trade, each with different sets of assumptions. In general, though, these are models in which firms produce differentiated products with an increasing-returns-to-scale technology, while on the consumption side, consumers have utility functions that reward product diversity.

There is also a lengthy literature examining the empirical side of this topic. These studies typically construct an index of intraindustry trade and investigate correlates of that index.[3] While these studies are certainly interesting, their relationship to the theory of monopolistic competition and international trade is often tenuous. An important exception to this is a paper by Helpman [1987] in which he developed some simple models of monopolistic competition and tested some hypotheses which were directly motivated by the theory.

Of the many papers that empirically investigate intraindustry trade, the Helpman paper is especially noteworthy. It constructs two very straightforward theoretical models designed to yield empirically testable hypotheses. Taking the theory on its own terms, Helpman then asks whether the data are consistent with two predictions that come out of the theory. Helpman's first hypothesis concerns the volume of trade in a model in which *all* trade is in differentiated products. He next asks whether the share of intraindustry trade in total trade is consistent with a model joining factor endowment stories for trade with monopolistic competition. Using graphical methods and some simple regressions, Helpman finds that the data appear to be consistent with the models tested.

In this paper, we revisit Helpman's tests and reconsider the evidence. We do not substantively amend Helpman's theoretical models. Rather, we apply a combination of different data and different econometric methods and ask whether the data still support the theory's specific predictions. In the course of our investigation, we successfully replicate Helpman's results, pose several new puzzles and, in the end, find less than overwhelming empirical support for the theory.

---

[2] Recent work by Donald Davis [1992] shows that if intraindustry trade is defined as trade in goods embodying similar factors, traditional (Ricardian) trade theory can indeed explain intraindustry trade.

[3] See Loertscher and Wolter [1980] for an early example and Greenaway and Milner [1987] for a nice overview of these studies.

The remainder of the paper is organized as follows. In Section II a model in which all trade is motivated by monopolistic competition is presented. This model generates predictions about the volume of trade. We retest the model's predictions using Helpman's data and an alternative data set. In Section III a more general model involving both intraindustry and interindustry (Heckscher-Ohlin) trade is described. We then test the model's predictions concerning the intraindustry trade share. Section IV concludes by summarizing the puzzles generated by the two tests of the theory.

II. MONOPOLISTIC COMPETITION AND THE VOLUME OF TRADE

We begin with the simplest model.[4] Here, all trade between countries is assumed to be intraindustry trade. Firms each produce a different variety of a differentiated product with an increasing returns to scale technology and monopolistic competition prevails. An important and testable result generated by this theoretical setup is that relative country size determines the volume of trade between countries. This is in contrast to the traditional factor-endowments based explanations for trade in which "differences in relative country size ... have no particular effect (on the volume of trade)."[5]

Helpman shows that if countries have identical and homothetic preferences and trade is balanced, then

$$\frac{V^A}{GDP^A} = e_A \left[1 - \sum_{j \in A} (e_A^j)^2 \right], \tag{1}$$

where

V^A is the volume of trade between countries in group A,

GDP^A is the GDP of the group of countries comprising group A,

e_A is the share of group A's GDP in relation to world GDP, and

e_A^j is the share of country j's GDP in relation to group A's GDP.[6]

The right-hand side of (1) is a measure of size dispersion that increases as countries become more similar in size. The theory dictates exactly *how* relative country size ought to matter. Equation (1) is a structural equation from a model of monopolistic competition and international trade; it is not a reduced-form equation.[7]

---

[4]See Appendix 1 of original paper for a full description of this model.

[5]From Helpman, 1987, p. 64.

[6]The derivation of (1) is provided in Appendix 1, original paper.

[7]Helpman amends (1) to account for trade imbalances and finds this makes little difference to his empirical results. We also find this to be true and so report only the balanced trade model for expositional simplicity.

Helpman noted that as countries become more similar in size, the volume of trade as a proportion of group GDP should increase. To investigate this hypothesis, he selected a subset of the OECD countries. This seems a judicious choice, for if any group of countries can support the predictions of a model in which all trade is intraindustry, the OECD countries are likely candidates. Using this group of countries, he computed the left-hand-side of (1) (the volume of intra-OECD trade relative to OECD GDP) and the right-hand-side index for every year from 1956 to 1981. This yielded 26 points which, when graphed, showed a clear positive correlation between the ratio of intragroup volume of trade to group GDP and the index of size dispersion. That is, as country size became more similar, intragroup trade volume rose.

It is important to note that Helpman (and Krugman) were not the first to suggest a relationship between the volume of trade and some combined measure of trading partners' incomes, nor is their model of monopolistic competition the only way to generate equation (1). Indeed, (1) fits the general form of the "gravity equation" given by $VT_{ij} = f(Y_i, Y_j, Z)$, where VT_{ij} is the volume of trade between countries i and j, Y_i is a measure of income from country i and Z may include various measures of trade resistance. It is well known that such an equation fits the data remarkably well, but for years this has been an empirical regularity in search of a theoretical foundation.[8] The contribution of monopolistic competition models is not so much the observation that trade volumes are related to GDPs (we already knew that!), but rather in presenting a coherent theory of *why* product differentiation occurs. That is, the role of monopolistic competition in these models is to insure that all goods are produced in only one country.

Having each good produced in only one country is crucial to deriving (1), and monopolistic competition is one way of generating this outcome. There are other ways. If consumers view goods as differentiated by country of origin (the Armington assumption), trade will be given by (1).

With this background in mind, are Helpman's results surprising? On the one hand, yes. The theory that generated the estimating equation seems quite restrictive: every good is produced in only one country and all countries have identical homothetic preferences. Whether this structure is the outcome of monopolistic competition or of an Armington assumption does not alter our surprise. We do not view either of these sets of underlying assumptions as particularly plausible. Nonetheless, the data appear consistent with the theories. On the other hand, since the theory's prediction closely mimics that of gravity equations (which we know work well empirically), the results are not surprising.

What can one hope to learn by further testing of such a model if one already knows that it will perform well empirically? First, gravity equation estimation is almost invariably performed in a cross section, while Helpman's study uses a time-series

---

[8] See Anderson [1979] and Bergstrand [1985] for careful theoretical work.

approach. Using variation over time allows him to better address deeper questions. For example, is the rising trade-to-income ratio observed in postwar data due to increasing size similarity? Second, further testing can help put the relevance of monopolistic competition into a more reasonable perspective. Many studies motivate the use of the gravity model by appealing to the underlying framework of monopolistic competition as if it were a foregone conclusion that monopolistic competition is the true source of their results. One of our purposes here is to see if gravity results pertain even in cases where we think the monopolistic competition framework is inappropriate.

We revisit Helpman's first test and apply more standard econometric methods. Helpman's original graph of 26 points, while a prudent methodology given the small sample size, did not allow him to conduct standard hypothesis tests. The theory holds for country groups of any size. Rather than aggregating over the entire OECD sample, we opt to treat each country-pair in each year as an observation. This yields 91 country-pair observations for each of the 22 years for which we have OECD data (1962–1983). This gives a total of 2002 observations.

There are several reasons why, even if the underlying theoretical model is correct, the model might not fit the data exactly in every year for every country-pair. For example, border trade, seasonal trade, trade restrictions that vary across country-pairs, language, and cultural ties may encourage or discourage international trade. Because these factors are country-pair specific, they can be accurately modeled as a country-pair fixed effect. There are also idiosyncratic reasons why the model might not fit exactly even if the underlying theory is correct. Prominent among these is measurement error in the volume of trade. Indexing country-pairs by i and years by t and taking logs of (1), rearranging yields

$$\ln(V_{it}) = \alpha_1 \ln[GDP_{it} (1 - (e_{it}^1)^2 - (e_{it}^2)^2)] + \mu_i + \varepsilon_{it}, \qquad (2)$$

where

e_{it}^1 is the first country's share of country-pair i's GDP,

e_{it}^2 is the second country's share of country-pair i's GDP,

$v_i = \mu_i + \ln(e_i)$ is the country-pair fixed effect,[9]

and ε_{it} is the idiosyncratic component of the disturbance term.

Prior to estimating (2), we first plot the right-hand-side variable against the left-hand-side variable. This is our analog to Helpman's graphical test of the hypothesis. The plot, using mean-differenced data to capture the fixed effects, is given in Figure 1. This plot of over 2000 country-pair-years shows a clear positive correlation between a measure of trade volume and country size.

---

[9] e_i is considered to be a constant because we assume, like Helpman, that group GDP as a fraction of world GDP, is constant over time.

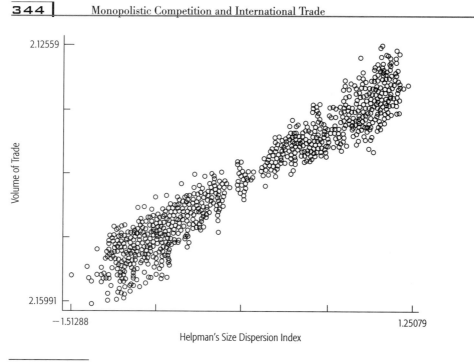

Figure 1

We next estimate (2).[10] Our base-case estimates are for the fixed-effects estimator. The results are given in the first column of Table 1. The results confirm the simple plot of the data as well as Helpman's initial findings. With a *t*-statistic of 110.8, there is little doubt that the particular measure of country size dispersion dictated by the theory is quite important in explaining trade volumes. Indeed, inclusive of the fixed effects, the model explains about 98 percent of the variation in trade volumes.

There are, though, several reasons why the fixed-effects estimate of (2) might be misspecified. First, the disturbance term ε_{it} may be correlated with the included regressor. That is, if exports receive a positive shock, trade volume rises, but by an accounting identity, so does GDP. Since a function of GDP appears as a regressor, we have an endogeneity problem. The standard solution to this is to employ an instrumental variables estimator. Following Harrigan [1992], we use countries' factor endowments as instruments.[11] Factor endowments are excellent instruments (variation in factor endowments explains a very large share of the variation in GDP) and are likely to be orthogonal to idiosyncratic trade shocks. The results with the fixed effects instrumental

---

[10]See Appendix 2, original paper.

[11]The factors used as instruments are labor, divided into two skill levels, and capital stock.

TABLE 1

EQUATION (2) ESTIMATES OECD DATA (1962–1983)

	Fixed effects	Random effects	Fixed effects (instrumental variables)	Fixed effects (detrended data)	OLS (detrended data)
α_1	1.405	1.403	1.268	1.094	1.170
t-statistic	110.8	110.8	47.7	33.7	44.8
R_2	.865	.860	—	.373	.501
(w/dummies)	.981			.980	
No. of obs.	2002	2002	2002	2002	2002

variables estimator are given in column three of Table 1, and differ little from OLS estimates.

Additional robustness checks included in Table 1 include use of random (rather than fixed) effects, and the use of detrended data. The message of this table is that even controlling for trends and country-pair fixed effects, our regressions strongly support Helpman's original finding.[12]

We began with a simple model in which all trade is trade in differentiated products, and everyone has identical and homothetic tastes. This model implied a very specific estimating equation in which a very particular index of size dispersion was predicted to explain trade volume. And it all worked! Is the world really so simple?

To address this question, the model is reestimated using a data set which we believe, ex ante, is grossly inappropriate for a model of monopolistic competition and international trade. Instead of using the OECD countries, we create a data set comprised of Brazil, Cameroon, Columbia, Congo, Greece, Ivory Coast, South Korea, Nigeria, Norway, Pakistan, Paraguay, Peru, Phillipines, and Thailand. This group of countries is referred to as the NOECD countries.

---

[12] We also estimated the equations reported in Tables 1 and 2 using slightly different specifications in order to test the robustness of the relationship between the volume of trade and a measure of size dispersion. We estimated two alternative specifications based on (1). These are: (i) estimating $\ln(V_{it}) = \alpha_1 \ln(Total\ GDP)_{it} + \alpha_2 Size_{it}$ to investigate whether it is the total GDP variable or the size dispersion index that is driving the correlation; and (ii) estimating $\ln(VT/Total\ GDP)_{it} + \alpha_1 Size_{it}$. For the OECD data set, including total GDP separately, as in (i), yields $\ln(V_{it}) = 1.290 \ln(Total\ GDP)_{it} + .976 Size_{it}$, with a t-statistic on the size variable of 28 and of 50 on the GDP variable. Estimating (ii) gave a coefficient of .813 with a t-statistic of 25. Estimates with the NOECD data set are quite similar. We interpret all this to mean that, while total GDP is important (rather sensibly, the trade volume between two big countries is greater than the trade volume between two small countries), the size dispersion index is also very important in these regressions.

TABLE 2

EQUATION (2) ESTIMATES NOECD DATA (1962–1977)

	Fixed effects	Random effects	Fixed effects (instrumental variables)	Fixed effects (detrended data)	OLS (detrended data)
α_1	1.57E–3	1.52E–3	1.54E–3	1.62E–3	1.18E–3
t-statistic	24.40	24.93	22.03	19.40	21.60
R^2	.304	.299	—	.215	.242
(w/dummies)	.671			.654	
No. of obs.	1456	1456	1456	1456	1456

All estimates are in levels.

Equation (2) is reestimated in levels from 1963–1977 (several countries stopped reporting trade data in 1978, and levels are used as many observations on trade volumes are zero or close to it).[13] Column 1 of Table 2 reports the fixed-effects estimates. Even for this sample of countries, the particular measure of size dispersion suggested by the theory matters, and it matters in a precisely measured way. The t-statistic drops to 24, but by any conventional standard, this is remarkably significant. Furthermore, the result is robust. When (2) is estimated with NOECD data using random effects, fixed-effects instrumental variables, and detrended data (fixed effects and OLS), the results do not vary much. While using the NOECD data set does not explain as much of the variation in the volume of trade as was the case with OECD data (the R^2 falls from .98 to .67 in one specification), the results of Table 2 still provide strong support for the theory. Put another way, if Table 2 had been presented prior to Table 1, most would agree that the model fit the data well.

We set out to see if a monopolistic competition model's predictions about the volume of trade provided insights into the theoretical source of the gravity equation. We find that while the model explains trade volumes well, it may actually explain them too well. The predictions hold for a set of countries that we feel fit the assumptions of the monopolistic competition model—goods are differentiated, demands are identical and homothetic—reasonably well. But the predictions also hold for a set of countries that we feel is not appropriately characterized by differentiated goods trade or by identical homothetic demands. The estimated equation works extremely well in both cases, and this causes us to question whether monopolistic competition is the right theoretical justification for it.

This leaves several possible explanations unaddressed. First, it is possible that our ex ante beliefs about the nature of production in the NOECD country set are wrong. That is, perhaps

---

[13] If the NOECD data set is applied to (2) in logs rather than levels, the magnitudes of the coefficients are similar to those reported for the OECD data set. In particular, $\ln(V_{it}) = 2.08 * Size$ with a t-statistic if 20.8 and an R^2 of .792.

it really is appropriate to think of goods from these countries as also being differentiated. Or perhaps the Armington assumption really is correct. Second, perhaps our understanding of the role of country size in a traditional Heckscher-Ohlin model is incomplete. It remains an intriguing topic for future research to determine if one can generate gravity-like results without the assumption of complete specialization in production.

III. A More General Approach

In Section II we used a model of monopolistic competition to show how the presence of intraindustry trade results in a specific and testable, but not unique, hypothesis about the bilateral volume of trade. One of the underlying assumptions of that section was that all trade was intraindustry. In this section, we relax that assumption and assume that some trade is intraindustry and some interindustry. We then examine how the fraction of trade that is intraindustry varies between countries and over time. In particular, we employ the model in Helpman [1987], which shows that the bilateral share of intraindustry trade increases as two countries become more similar in factor composition.[14]

The intuition is as follows. In a model with homogeneous and differentiated goods, some interindustry trade will be motivated by relative factor abundance, and some intraindustry trade will be motivated by the exchange of varieties of differentiated goods. A standard measure of intraindustry trade is the Grubel-Lloyd [1975] index. The share of intraindustry trade between countries j and k in industry i is given by

$$IIT_{ijk} = \frac{2\min(X_{ijk}, X_{ikj})}{(X_{ijk} + X_{ikj})},$$

where X_{ijk} are exports of industry i from country j to country k. The share of intraindustry trade between country j and k, over all industries, is given by

$$IIT_{jk} = \frac{2\Sigma_i \min(X_{ijk}, X_{ikj})}{\Sigma_i(X_{ijk} + X_{ikj})}.$$

The numerator captures two-way trade within industries, and the denominator is the total volume of trade. More transparently, we can think of this index as

$$IIT_{jk} = \frac{INTRA}{INTRA + INTER}.$$

In a two-country, two-factor model with one homogeneous goods sector and one differentiated goods sector, allow both countries to have identical capital-to-labor ratios. Then no trade is motivated by relative factor abundance. That is, $INTER = 0$, and the intraindustry trade index (IIT_{jk}) equals one. Now, perturb the capital-to-labor ratios, *holding*

---

[14]See Appendix 1 of original paper for a formal statement of the $2 \times 2 \times 2$ case. It is important to note that this result may not hold in a model with many countries, many goods, or many factors.

relative size constant.[15] *INTER* increases as some trade is now motivated by factor differences. *INTRA* will decrease,[16] and the above index will decrease as well.

To test the relationship between factor differences and the share of intraindustry trade, Helpman estimated equation (3) on a cross section of 91 country-pairs, using separate regressions for each year from 1970–1981:

$$IIT_{jk} = \alpha_0 + \alpha_1 \log \left| \frac{GDP^j}{N^j} - \frac{GDP^k}{N^k} \right| + \alpha_2 \min(\log GDP^j, \log GDP^k)$$
$$+ \alpha_3 \max(\log GDP^j, \log GDP^k) + \varepsilon_{jk}, \tag{3}$$

where IIT_{jk} is the Grubel-Lloyd [1975] index for the bilateral trade of a country-pair consisting of countries j and k, N^j is the population of country j, and an industry is defined as a four-digit SITC group. Per capita GDP is used to proxy factor composition. *MINGDP* and *MAXGDP* are included to control for relative size effects. The model predicts $\alpha_1 < 0$, $\alpha_2 > 0$, and $\alpha_3 < 0$.

Helpman found that the data supported these predictions. In particular, he found a negative and significant correlation between factor differences and the IIT_{jk} index, although it weakened toward the end of his sample.[17] Helpman does not exploit the panel nature of his data. Moreover, he uses per capita income as a proxy for factor composition. This is problematic for two reasons.

First, per capita income is an appropriate proxy if there are only two factors of production and all goods are traded. Second, this approach runs afoul of a long-standing debate on whether per capita income is proxying factor endowments or consumer tastes. Linder [1961] hypothesized that products must first be developed for home markets before they can be exported successfully. If per capita income is a good gauge of demand, then countries with similar per capita income will have similar demand, and will produce and export similar goods.[18] To address these potential problems with the proxy variable, we employ per capita income and actual factor data to measure differences in factor composition.

---

[15]We know from Section II that relative size can have an important effect on the volume of trade in differentiated products. A reallocation of capital and labor that widened factor differences and also changed relative size (for example, making the two countries more equal), may actually increase intraindustry trade.

[16]See Appendix 1 of original paper.

[17]Specifically, the coefficient on his factor differences variable is negative and significant in the first seven years, but becomes insignificant thereafter. Also, the R^2 in the regression drops steadily from .266 in 1970 to .039 by 1981.

[18]Krugman [1980] and Bergstrand [1990] have subsequently demonstrated the importance of taste differences in more rigorous models of monopolistic competition with nonhomothetic demand. The empirical literature has generally interpreted differences in per capita income as a demand side phenomenon, and found good support for a negative relationship between per capita income and intraindustry trade.

We begin by estimating equations similar to (3) for our OECD sample separately for each year from 1962 to 1983.[19] In the first estimation, we use per-worker GDP.[20] In the second, we use actual capital-to-labor and land-to-labor ratios. The estimating equations, then, are given by

$$IIT_{jk} = \alpha_0 + \alpha_1 \log \left| \frac{GDP^j}{L^j} - \frac{GDP^k}{L^k} \right| + \alpha_2 \min(\log GDP^j, \log GDP^k)$$

$$+ \alpha_3 \max(\log GDP^j, \log GDP^k) + \varepsilon_{jk}, \tag{4}$$

$$IIT_{jk} = \alpha_0 + \alpha_1 \log \left| \frac{K^j}{L^j} - \frac{K^k}{L^k} \right| + \alpha_2 \log \left| \frac{T^j}{L^j} - \frac{T^k}{L^k} \right|$$

$$+ \alpha_3 \min(\log GDP^j, \log GDP^k) + \alpha_4 \max(\log GDP^j, \log GDP^k) + \varepsilon_{jk}, \tag{5}$$

where L^j is the working population of country j, T^j is j's land endowment, and K^j is j's capital stock. We label $\log |(GDP^j/L^j - GDP^k/L^k)|$, which gives differences in income per worker, YDIF. Analogously, KLDIF will refer to the differences in capital per worker, and TLDIF will refer to differences in land per worker [as in (5)].

GDP, K (constructed capital stock), and L (labor force) come directly from, or are constructed from, Penn World Tables, Mark V data. GDP and K are measured in constant 1985 international prices. T (land) is constructed from land estimates contained in Leamer [1984].

Equations (4) and (5) are estimated with ordinary least squares (OLS). IIT_{jk} is an index varying between zero and one. We apply a logistic transformation to IIT so that OLS using the transformed variable is appropriate. The results are reported in Tables 3 and 4.

Table 3 reports the results of estimating (4). The results are quite similar to Helpman's. The coefficient on YDIF is negative in each sample year, but is only significant through roughly half of the sample. The coefficients on MINGDP and MAXGDP are consistent with theory, but only MINGDP is significant. Finally, like Helpman, the explanatory power of the regression drops steadily over time.

Just as in Helpman's study, the relationship between the share of intraindustry trade and differences in factor composition is strongly negative in early years of the sample, but breaks down in later years. Having replicated Helpman's results, we turn to the estimation of equation (5), where per worker income as a proxy for factor composition is replaced with actual factor data.

---

[19]Unlike the test in Section II, we do not replicate this test using NOECD data. This is because the NOECD set, by construction, contains virtually no intraindustry trade and would therefore be of little use in studying cross-country variation in an IIT index.

[20]We use per worker GDP instead of per capita GDP, since the former seems more consistent with the underlying theory.

TABLE 3

EQUATION (3) ESTIMATES WITH GDP PER WORKER INSTEAD OF
GDP PER CAPITA (1962-1983)

Year	YDIF	MINGDP	MAXGDP	R^2
1962	− 0.275**	0.389**	− 0.012	.209
1963	− 0.316**	0.377**	− 0.009	.239
1964	− 0.227**	0.371**	− 0.013	.216
1965	− 0.255**	0.366**	0.022	.239
1966	− 0.290**	0.334**	0.011	.242
1967	− 0.217**	0.349**	0.023	.230
1968	− 0.234**	0.309**	0.007	.213
1969	− 0.206**	0.332**	− 0.009	.214
1970	− 0.156*	0.355**	− 0.062	.171
1971	− 0.196*	0.335**	− 0.085	.176
1972	− 0.222**	0.336**	− 0.040	.188
1973	− 0.233*	0.253**	− 0.031	.147
1974	− 0.109	0.235**	− 0.058	.074
1975	− 0.189	0.226*	− 0.045	.089
1976	− 0.159	0.181*	− 0.050	.056
1977	− 0.260**	0.152	− 0.043	.095
1978	− 0.214*	0.111	0.004	.067
1979	− 0.126	0.130	− 0.057	.028
1980	− 0.074	0.127	− 0.090	.008
1981	− 0.078	0.116	− 0.106	.011
1982	− 0.064	0.103	− 0.105	.011
1983	− 0.091	0.054	− 0.064	.003

The estimated regression is

$$IIT_{jk,t} = \alpha_0 + \alpha_1 \log \left| \frac{GDP_t^j}{L_t^j} - \frac{GDP_t^k}{L_t^k} \right| + \alpha_2 \min(\log GDP_t^j, \log GDP_t^k)$$
$$+ \alpha_3 \max(\log GDP_t^j, \log GDP_t^k) + \varepsilon_{jk,t}$$

*indicates statistical significance at the 95% level.
**indicates statistical significance at the 99% level.

In Table 4, we see that TLDIF is negative and highly significant in all sample years. KLDIF is negative and significant initially, but in later years becomes positive and significant. Also, the explanatory power of the estimates in Table 4 are roughly double that of the estimates in Table 3. These results would seem to support the hypothesis that factor differences, especially the difference in land-to-labor ratios, are important in

TABLE 4

EQUATION (3) OLS ESTIMATES WITH CAPITAL-TO-LABOR AND LAND-TO-LABOR RATIOS (1962–1983)

Year	KLDIF	TLDIF	MINGDP	MAXGDP	R^2
1962	−0.289**	−0.184**	0.392**	−0.058	.357
1963	−0.261**	−0.190**	0.395**	−0.074	.390
1964	−0.201*	−0.201**	0.359**	−0.042	.392
1965	−0.139*	−0.203**	0.350**	−0.010	.385
1966	−0.196*	−0.209**	0.319**	−0.041	.416
1967	−0.183*	−0.208**	0.324**	−0.011	.426
1968	−0.157*	−0.223**	0.291**	−0.049	.442
1969	−0.130	−0.217**	0.318**	−0.048	.435
1970	−0.112	−0.231**	0.316**	−0.073	.442
1971	−0.071	−0.231**	0.293**	−0.093	.421
1972	−0.051	−0.224**	0.300**	−0.056	.393
1973	−0.033	−0.209**	0.238**	−0.058	.354
1974	−0.015	−0.228**	0.194**	−0.045	.395
1975	−0.016	−0.208**	0.204**	−0.047	.313
1976	0.048	−0.202**	0.169*	−0.051	.277
1977	0.037	−0.207**	0.160	−0.066	.260
1978	0.052	−0.190**	0.116	−0.016	.225
1979	0.069	−0.172**	0.130	−0.056	.203
1980	0.095	−0.170**	0.126	−0.073	.197
1981	0.123*	−0.168**	0.120	−0.089	.209
1982	0.166*	−0.148**	0.122	−0.091	.216
1983	0.221**	−0.159**	0.078	−0.049	.237

The estimated regression is

$$IIT_{jk,t} = \alpha_0 + \alpha_1 \log \left| \frac{K_t^j}{L_t^j} - \frac{K_t^k}{L_t^k} \right| + \alpha_2 \log \left| \frac{T_t^j}{L_t^j} - \frac{T_t^k}{L_t^k} \right| + \alpha_3 \min(\log GDP_t^j, \log GDP_t^k)$$
$$+ \alpha_4 \max(\log GDP_t^j, \log GDP_t^k) + \varepsilon_{jk,t}$$

* indicates statistical significance at the 95% level.
** indicates statistical significance at the 99% level.

explaining the share of intraindustry trade. Using actual factor data instead of the proxy yields results more consistent with the theory's predictions.

A second way to improve upon Helpman's approach is to take advantage of the panel nature of the data. For reasons outside of the model (e.g., geography, culture and language ties, trade barriers) and resulting specification, intraindustry trade between Japan and the United Kingdom might always be quite low relative to the sample as a whole. This suggests examining the relationship between intraindustry trade and factor differences as they change over time for a given country-pair.

We pool our 22 years into a single panel. We first estimate a panel data version of (5) in order to pick up both cross-sectional and time series variation in $IIT_{jk,t}$. The estimating equation becomes

$$IIT_{jk,t} = \alpha_0 + \alpha_1 \log \left| \frac{K_t^j}{L_t^j} - \frac{K_t^k}{L_t^k} \right| + \alpha_2 \min(\log GDP_t^j, \log GDP_t^k)$$
$$+ \alpha_3 \max(\log GDP_t^j, \log GDP_t^k) + \varepsilon_{jk,t}, \tag{6}$$

where jk indexes a country-pair as before and t now indexes time. Because land endowments show little variation over time for a given country pair, they are highly collinear with the fixed effects and so are omitted from this specification. However, an ANOVA for the remaining variables shows that there is significant variation over time within the country pairs to yield meaningful panel results.

We also estimate a variant of (6) which includes a vector of country-pair-specific fixed effects, v_{jk}, thereby sweeping out all of the cross-sectional variation. Hence we have

$$IIT_{jk,t} = \alpha_0 + \alpha_1 \log \left| \frac{K_t^j}{L_t^j} - \frac{K_t^k}{L_t^k} \right| + \alpha_2 \min(\log GDP_t^j, \log GDP_t^k)$$
$$+ \alpha_3 \max(\log GDP_t^j, \log GDP_t^k) + v_{jk} + \varepsilon_{jk,t}, \tag{7}$$

The OLS results using either income per worker or capital per worker as a regressor are reported in the first two columns of Table 5. The results differ considerably depending on which regressor is included. The income per worker variable is negative and highly significant, while the capital per worker variable is not significantly different from zero. These results are generally consistent with those reported in Tables 3 and 4.[21] For both OLS regressions, the coefficient on *MINGDP* is consistent with theory and precisely estimated, while the coefficient on *MAXGDP* is not precisely estimated in the regressions using income differences.

Country-pair fixed-effects estimators are presented in the third and fourth columns of Table 5. The coefficient on the income differences variable, *YDIF*, is now positive and quite significant, whereas before it was negative and very significant. In the regression using capital per worker, the factor difference variable, *KLDIF*, is both positive and significant. For both regressions, *MINGDP* and *MAXGDP* are as before, and the

---

[21] That is, the coefficient on *YDIF* is negative and significant throughout, while the coefficient on *KLDIF* goes from negative to positive in later years, resulting in an ambiguous effect over the whole sample.

TABLE 5

EQUATION (7) ESTIMATES (1962–1983)

Variable	No fixed effects		Fixed effects		Random effects	
YDIF	−0.194		0.038		0.027	
	(−10.900)		(3.609)		(2.432)	
KLDIF		−0.007		0.029		0.027
		(−.402)		(3.235)		(2.786)
MINGDP	0.281	0.312	1.315	1.327	0.897	0.938
	(14.038)	(15.297)	(18.483)	(18.666)	(18.794)	(18.817)
MAXGDP	−0.009	−0.051	−0.005	−0.013	0.195	0.190
	(−0.488)	(−2.690)	(−0.079)	(−0.197)	(4.529)	(4.231)
R^2	.164	.115	.524	.523	.433	.447
(w/dummies)			.965	.966		

The estimated regression is

$$IIT_{jk,t} = \alpha_0 + \alpha_1 \log \left| \frac{K_t^j}{L_t^j} - \frac{K_t^k}{K_t^k} \right| + \alpha_2 \log \left| \frac{T_t^j}{L_t^j} - \frac{T_t^k}{L_t^k} \right| + \alpha_3 \min(\log GDP_t^j, \log GDP_t^k)$$

$$+ \alpha_4 \max(\log GDP_t^j, \log GDP_t^k) + \nu_{jk} + \varepsilon_{jk,t}$$

t-statistics are in parentheses. The reported R^2 in the fixed effects model is that for the regression using mean-differenced data.

explanatory power of the regressions increases substantially. Country-pair dummies seem to explain a tremendous proportion of the variation in our intraindustry trade index (when country dummies are employed in the regressions, the R^2 jumps to around .96).[22] Accounting for fixed effects yields precisely estimated results exactly counter to those implied by the theory. Employing a random effects estimator yields a similar message — country-pair effects drastically change the empirical role of factor differences.[23]

Why is this? One explanation borrows from the aggregation critique of intraindustry trade. (See Finger, 1975.) SITC categories sometimes group goods with similar consumption uses, but different factor inputs. Trade within this "industry" would be measured as intraindustry, when in fact it is motivated by relative factor abundance. When SITC classifications fail to capture appropriate industry definitions, the sign on the

---

[22] One interpretation of this result is simply that the fixed effects are picking up differences in land endowments. We return to this issue below.

[23] These results are robust to the use of a levels specification, the omission of *MINGDP* and *MAXGDP*, and quadratic terms on the variables. See Table VI in original paper.

factor differences variable becomes ambiguous. The difficulty with this explanation is that there is no necessary reason why factor differences and intraindustry trade should be negatively correlated in cross section, and positively correlated in time series. Indeed, this offers another plausible reason for preferring a fixed effects estimator. If the bias in the data due to inappropriate aggregation is constant over time, it will be swept out when we mean-difference the data.

A second explanation emphasizes the role of geography. There are several ways in which geography might play a significant role in intraindustry trade. Countries sharing a long border may see two-way trade in homogeneous goods in order to minimize shipping costs. Transport costs (captured by distance) may also reduce intraindustry trade more quickly than interindustry trade. An analysis of the fixed effects from estimates of equation (7) indicates a strong geographic component to intraindustry trade shares.[24]

If proximate countries also have similar per capita (or per worker) income, we may see a spurious correlation between factor differences and the IIT_{jk} index in cross section. By estimating country pair dummies in (7), we sweep out the constant effect of geography on intraindustry trade. Only the correlation between intraindustry trade and factor differences, independent of geography, remains, and it is no longer negative as predicted by theory.

To address this issue, we include a distance variable in our estimation of equation (5). We report the results in Table 6, and compare them to Table 4.[25] We see that the coefficient on *DISTANCE* is negative and highly significant. *TLDIF* (differences in land-to-labor ratios) is negative as in Table 4, but the significance of the estimates is reduced, especially in the later years. The explanatory power of the estimates that include *DISTANCE* is much higher than that of the estimates that do not. As noted earlier, there are a large number of combinations of factor difference variables we might include in estimating equation (5), and that only *TLDIF* and *TKDIF* had previously been negative and significant. After including *DISTANCE* in the estimation, only *TLDIF* retains any significance, and even that is much reduced. These results all suggest that the distance between trading partners is quite important in understanding intraindustry trade both in cross section and time series.

In this section we tested the relationship between the share of intraindustry trade and factor differences. Existing studies utilize cross-sectional analysis and find a negative correlation between intraindustry trade and factor differences. We investigate the behavior of intraindustry trade over time, and find either no relationship or a positive correlation. The difference appears to lie in geographic effects that explain intraindustry trade well, but are omitted in cross-sectional studies.

---

[24]See Tables VII, VIII and IX in the original paper.

[25]Table VI is identical to Table IX in the original paper.

TABLE 6

EQUATION (7) OLS ESTIMATES WITH DISTANCE, CAPITAL-TO-LABOR, AND LAND-TO-LABOR RATIOS (1962–1983)

Year	KLDIF	TLDIF	MINGDP	MAXGDP	DIST	R^2
1962	− 0.086	− 0.056	0.464**	0.160*	− 0.601**	.647
1963	− 0.124	− 0.073*	0.456**	0.124	− 0.527**	.630
1964	− 0.097	− 0.103**	0.412**	0.123	− 0.427**	.558
1965	− 0.059	− 0.095**	0.408**	0.165*	− 0.461**	.593
1966	− 0.086	− 0.104**	0.372**	0.140*	− 0.447**	.624
1967	− 0.071	− 0.100**	0.373**	0.178**	− 0.443**	.631
1968	− 0.072	− 0.115**	0.337**	0.137*	− 0.428**	.650
1969	− 0.059	− 0.110**	0.358**	0.141*	− 0.418**	.633
1970	− 0.040	− 0.118**	0.354**	0.126*	− 0.428**	.642
1971	− 0.030	− 0.111**	0.334**	0.118*	− 0.458**	.668
1972	− 0.028	− 0.102**	0.341**	0.154*	− 0.463**	.641
1973	0.011	− 0.080**	0.279**	0.167**	− 0.478**	.66
1974	0.037	− 0.108**	0.232**	0.166**	− 0.441**	.669
1975	0.029	− 0.075*	0.245**	0.197**	− 0.509**	.654
1976	0.071	− 0.061*	0.211**	0.206**	− 0.546**	.668
1977	0.057	− 0.065*	0.200**	0.199**	− 0.558**	.652
1978	0.064	− 0.067*	0.151*	0.213**	− 0.489**	.559
1979	0.078	− 0.036	0.169**	0.200**	− 0.544**	.642
1980	0.094*	− 0.035	0.161**	0.190**	− 0.546**	.644
1981	0.116**	− 0.030	0.152**	0.190**	− 0.570**	.697
1982	0.127**	− 0.021	0.146**	0.175**	− 0.541**	.709
1983	0.116**	− 0.043	0.094	0.203**	− 0.515**	.653

The estimated regression is

$$IIT_{jk,t} = \alpha_0 + \alpha_1 \log \left| \frac{K_t^j}{L_t^j} - \frac{K_t^k}{L_t^k} \right| + \alpha_2 \log \left| \frac{T_t^j}{L_t^j} - \frac{T_t^k}{L_t^k} \right| + \alpha_3 \min(\log GDP_t^j, \log GDP_t^k)$$

$$+ \alpha_4 \max(\log GDP_t^j, \log GDP_t^k) + \alpha_5 DISTANCE + \varepsilon_{jk,t}$$

* indicates statistical significance at the 95% level.
** indicates statistical significance at the 99% level.

IV. INCONCLUSIONS

From the outset, our goal has been to test some hypotheses generated from a formal model of monopolistic competition and international trade. Previous tests had been encouraging. Studies that were not especially informed by the theory of monopolistic competition and international trade still found reasonable correlates of indexes of intraindustry trade. A study that was directly guided by the theory also found encouraging support for the theory. After reconsidering the evidence, we are not so sure.

The first test presented in this paper seems based on very unrealistic assumptions, but the theory passes with flying colors. We found that the volume of trade is well explained by a theoretically well-motivated index of the size similarity of trading partners. When confronted with data for which the theory is probably quite inappropriate, it still passes with high marks. Adding country-pair fixed or random effects, allowing for linear trends in the data, and accounting for issues of econometric endogeneity of regressors does not alter this conclusion. The relative unanimity of our results suggests that something other than monopolistic competition may be responsible for the empirical success of the gravity model. The second test we conducted allows a more reasonable underlying theoretical structure, but we find, at best, very mixed empirical support for the theory. Instead of factor differences explaining the share of intraindustry trade, much intraindustry trade appears to be specific to country pairs. Further investigation suggests that distance is especially important to this relationship.

The results of the first test leave us genuinely puzzled. The results of the second test leave us, on one hand, pessimistic. If much intraindustry trade is specific to country-pairs, we can only be skeptical about the prospects for developing any general theory to explain it. On the other hand, these results suggest ways in which one might refine the theory to better fit the data. Distance, and possibly tax policy towards multinationals, are empirically important variables that are not well accounted for in the simple models we tested.[26]

The theory of monopolistic competition and international trade is elegant and seems to address important aspects of reality. We hope our results motivate others to also investigate the empirical relevance of the theory, for, as promised in the introduction, we provide few answers.

REFERENCES

Anderson, James, "A Theoretical Foundation of the Gravity Equation," *American Economic Review*, LXIX (1979), 106–16.

Bergstrand, Jeffrey, "The Heckscher-Ohlin-Samuelson Model, the Linder Hypothesis, and the Determinants of Bilateral Intra-industry Trade," *Economic Journal*, C (1990), 1216–29.

Bowen, Harry, Edward Leamer, and Leo Sveikauskas, "Multicountry, Multifactor Tests of the Factor Abundance Theory," *American Economic Review*, LXXVII (1987), 791–809.

Brainard, S. Lael, "An Empirical Assessment of the Proximity/Concentration Tradeoff Between Multinational Sales and Trade," mimeo, MIT, 1995.

---

[26] An admirable move in this direction is Brainard [1995].

Davis, Donald, "Intraindustry Trade: A Heckscher-Ohlin-Ricardo Approach," mimeo, Harvard University, 1992.

Finger, Michael, "Trade Overlap and Intra-industry Trade," *Economic Inquiry*, XIII (1975), 581–89.

Greenaway, David, and Chris Milner, "Intra-industry Trade: Current Perspectives and Unresolved Issues," *Weltwirtschaftliches Archiv*, CXXIII (1987), 39–48.

Grubel, Harry, and Peter Lloyd, *Intra-industry Trade: The Theory and Measurement of International Trade in Differentiated Products* (London: Macmillan, 1975).

Harrigan, James, "Openness to Trade in Manufactures in the OECD," mimeo, University of Pittsburgh, 1992.

Heckscher, Eli, and Bertil Ohlin, *Heckscher-Ohlin Trade Theory*, Harry Flam and June Flanders, eds. (Cambridge: MIT Press, 1991).

Helpman, Elhanan, "International Trade in the Presence of Product Differentiation, Economies of Scale and Monopolistic Competition: A Chamberlin-Heckscher-Ohlin Approach," *Journal of International Economics*, XI (1981), 305–40.

Helpman, Elhanan, "Imperfect Competition and International Trade: Evidence from Fourteen Industrial Countries," *Journal of the Japanese and International Economies*, I (1987), 62–81.

Helpman, Elhanan, and Paul Krugman, *Market Structure and Foreign Trade: Increasing Returns, Imperfect Competition and the International Economy* (Cambridge: MIT Press, 1985).

Hummels, David, and James Levinsohn, "Product Differentiation as a Source of Comparative Advantage?" *American Economic Review, Papers and Proceedings*, LXXXIII (1993), 445–49.

Krugman, Paul, "Increasing Returns to Scale, Monopolistic Competition and International Trade, *Journal of International Economics*, IX (1979), 469–79.

——, "Intra-industry Specialization and the Gains from Trade," *Journal of Political Economy*, LXXXIX (1981), 959–73.

Lancaster, Kelvin, "Intra-Industry Trade under Perfect Monopolistic Competition," *Journal of International Economics*, X (1980), 151–75.

Leamer, Edward, *Sources of International Comparative Advantage* (Cambridge: MIT Press, 1984).

——, "Testing Trade Theory," mimeo, University of California, Los Angeles, 1993.

Leamer, Edward, and James Levinsohn, "International Trade Theory: The Evidence," mimeo, University of Michigan, 1994.

Leontief, Wassily, "Domestic Production and Foreign Trade: The American Capital Position, Re-Examined," *Proceedings of the American Philosophical Society*, XCVII (1953), 332–49.

Linder, Stefan, *An Essay on Trade and Transformation* (New York: Wiley, 1961).

Loertscher, R., and F. Wolter, "Determinants of Intra-industry Trade: among Countries and across Industries," *Weltwirtschaftliches Archiv*, VIII (1980), 280–93.

ABOUT THE AUTHOR

David Hummels

David Hummels is an assistant professor of economics at Purdue University. He is a member of the editorial council for the *Review of International Economics*. He has served on the faculty of the University of Chicago's School of Business.

ABOUT THE AUTHOR

James Levinsohn

James Levinsohn is a professor of economics at the University of Michigan. He received his Ph.D. from Princeton University. His research focuses on empirical microeconomics. He has published articles in the fields of international trade, industrial organization, econometrics, public economies, and development economics. Some of these articles have appeared recently in the *American Economic Review*, *Econometrica*, the *Review of Economic Studies*, the *Economic Journal*, and the *Journal of International Economics*, of which he was co-editor. He is on the editorial board of the *Journal of Economic Literature*.

International
Economics

International
International Economics
Economics

NONTRADITIONAL
PRODUCTION FUNCTIONS

James R. Markusen

Michael Kremer

International Economics

International
Economics

Multinationals, Multi-Plant Economies, and the Gains from Trade

JAMES R. MARKUSEN

University of Western Ontario, London, Ontario N6A 5C2, Canada

A general equilibrium model of a multinational enterprise based on economies of multi-plant operation is developed. These economies are modelled as arising from the existence of a joint input whose productivity in each production facility is independent of the number of facilities maintained by a firm. The multinational thus offers the world increased technical efficiency by eliminating the duplication of the joint input that would occur with independent national firms. Since this technical efficiency may come at the expense of increased market power, the full determinants of home country, host country, and world welfare are considered.

INTRODUCTION

For many years there has existed a debate as to the allocative and distributive effects of multinational corporations. There is little general agreement as to these effects and, indeed, formal trade theory has largely failed to provide a rationale as to why these corporations exist at all. The empirical evidence sheds some light on this very basic question insofar as it suggests that the level of multinational activity in a particular industry is related to the importance of 'intangibles' in that industry's overall operation [Caves (1980)]. These 'intangibles' involve activities not directly related to the physical production of goods such as R & D, advertising, marketing, and distribution.[1]

Ideas contained in this paper were first presented at the Workshop on 'Production and Trade in a World with Internationally Mobile Factors of Production' financed by the Bank of Sweden Tercentenary Foundation, and held at the Institute for International Economic Studies, University of Stockholm, 4–15 August, 1980. The author would like to thank participants in the workshop for helpful comments and suggestions, and thank the Social Sciences and Humanities Research Council of Canada for financial support.

[1] A few of the relevant works include McManus (1972), Buckley and Casson (1976), Dunning (1977), Kindleberger (1969, 1970), Caves (1971, 1974), Vernon (1971), Horst (1976), Hymer (1976), Gorecke (1976), and Parry (1980).

Reprinted with permission from James R. Markusen, "Multinationals, Multi-Plant Economies, and the Gains from Trade," *Journal of International Economies*: (1984), vol. 16, pp. 205–226.
© 1984 by Elsevier Science Publishers B.V. (North-Holland).

Intangibles in turn seem to be closely related to the concept of economies of multi-plant operation [Scherer et al. (1975), Scherer (1980)]. By 'economies of multi-plant operation' we will mean technical or pecuniary advantages possessed by a single owner of two or more production facilities over an industry in which there are independent (even if joint-profit maximizing) owners of the same production facilities. The great body of research on Canada in particular seems to repeatedly emphasize economies of multi-plant operating in explaining the incidence across industries of United States multinationals operating in Canada [Eastman and Stykolt (1967), Caves et al. (1980)].

These stylized facts suggest two alternative avenues for developing a satisfactory theory of the multinational enterprise (MNE). One is based on strategic considerations such as using R & D, marketing investments, and foreign branch plants to pre-empt foreign competition. This is the approach taken by Magee (1977) and Horstmann and Markusen (1983). The second approach is to examine aspects of technology which by themselves (i.e. quite apart from strategic behaviour) imply the superior efficiency of multi-plant production. This second approach is used in this paper to develop a technology-based theory of MNE. The model is then used to address issues relating to market power, technical efficiency, the pattern of trade, and world income distribution.

In attempting to meet these objectives, a satisfactory model should meet five conditions. (a) The model should provide a rationale as to why a firm wishes to engage in direct rather than in portfolio investment. (b) The model should not rely on factor movements or factor price differences insofar as the MNE literature stresses that the MNE often provides for much of its needs from local factor markets. Both requirements imply that the general-equilibrium literature on factor movements is of little use and that a theory of the firm approach may be more useful.[2] (c) The model should explain why multi-plant operation is superior to price collusion among independent producers. (d) The model must justify the fact that the MNE, by definition, chooses to carry on at least one type of activity in each of several countries rather than supply all countries from a single production facility. (e) The model should allow for positive economic profits since alternative distributions of profits may have important implications for the gains from trade. This suggests that a monopoly/duopoly model in which firms produce a single

---

[2]Recent analyses of general-equilibrium theory of factor movements can be found, for example, in Jones (1967), Kemp (1969), Brecher and Alejandro (1977), Bhagwati and Brecher (1980) and Markusen and Melvin (1979). These articles are not entirely satisfactory for the study of direct foreign investment since they provide no motivation as to why foreign investment might be concentrated in certain sectors, much less why it might direct rather than portfolio investment. Batra and Ramachandran (1980) have recently formalized the ideas of Caves (1971), who notes that international investment is often sector specific. Yet Batra and Ramachandran still do not come to grips with the issue of direct versus portfolio investment insofar as their model provides no motivation as to why a firm wishes to control a foreign subsidiary versus simply making a portfolio investment in the foreign industry. Like earlier works, the Batra and Ramachandran model continues to rely on perfect competition, constant returns, and physical factor flows generated by ex ante factor price differences.

homogeneous good may provide a richer treatment than the more recent monopolistic competition models [Krugman (1979), Helpman (1981)].

It seems that these requirements simply cannot be met by any model that relies on the assumptions of either constant returns in production or increasing returns of the usual neoclassical variety. In the former case, there is no role for the individual enterprise and hence direct foreign investment cannot be distinguished from portfolio investment. In the latter case, there will be a tendency for the firm to centralize rather than to geographically diversify production. Similarly, superior technical knowledge combined with an incentive to jump a tariff barrier is not an entirely satisfying basis for a theory. While differences in know-how may imply strategic considerations [Magee (1977), Horstmann and Markusen (1983)], there is no purely technical reason why branch-plant production is superior to simply selling or licensing the superior technology.

The notion of multi-plant economies is thus appealing from a theoretical as well as an empirical point of view. The problem is that to the best of my knowledge, no one has precisely specified this notion in formal algebraic notation. To do so will be the first task of this paper.

2. ECONOMIES OF MULTI-PLANT OPERATION

Sources of multi-plant economies are often found in firm-specific as opposed to plant-specific activities. These firm-specific activities include things like R & D, advertising, marketing, distribution, and management services, as noted above [Scherer et al. (1975), Scherer (1980)]. One characteristic of these activities that I wish to capture here is that they often involve a 'public goods' or 'jointness' aspect with respect to the firm's various production facilities. R & D expenditures on designing better products and/or production processes provide an interesting example. Once an innovation is made, it can be incorporated into any number of additional plants without reducing the marginal product of that innovation in existing plants.[3] The efficiency advantage of the multi-plant firm as modelled below lies in its ability to avoid the duplication in R & D and other activities which is necessarily involved in single-plant operation.[4]

---

[3] Technological assumptions presented below ensure that there will be only a single plant in each country. Also, I should point out that the type of MNE modelled here would probably be termed a 'horizontal' MNE in that production facilities in the two countries are concerned with producing only one good. On the other hand, countries will be partially specialized as to the activities they perform in the production of this good, and thus there is something of a 'vertical' (or 'hierarchical') dimension to this MNE as well. Caves (1980) notes that 'a number of studies have established that the importance of intangible assets to an industry is an excellent predictor of horizontal direct investment'.

[4] We will assume throughout the paper that economies of multi-plant operation are such that independent firms have at best an imperfect ability to transfer 'intangibles' among themselves. The idea is that to share fully in these economies, two independent firms would have to be fully integrated in everything but name (e.g. the two firms' engineers and managers would have to work together). Throughout the paper, the term joint-profit maximization will refer only to price collusion.

We should also note that the MNE often tends to centralize these firm-specific activities (corporate headquarters); that is, R & D, marketing, finance, etc. are often centralized in a particular location while production activities are geographically dispersed. It is easy to think of reasons as to why this might be the case. The total output of two scientists working independently may, for example, be less than their output working cooperatively in the same location. Similarly, communication among different managerial and technical departments is more efficient in a centralized location. The model presented below will attempt to capture this 'centralization' aspect as well as the 'public-goods' or 'jointness' aspect mentioned above.

The model consists of two goods (X and Y) and two countries (m and h). Superscripts m and h will denote countries throughout the model, with m denoting the MNE's home country and h denoting the host country in the MNE version of the problem. Other features of the model are as follows.

(a) X and Y are each produced from labour and sector-specific capital. Total endowments of all factors are fixed.

(b) Countries m and h have identical factor endowments, identical technology, and identical, homothetic community utility functions.

(c) Y is produced with constant returns to scale by a competitive industry.

(d) The output of X is the product of the outputs of two activities: activity C (for corporate or control) and activity F (for factory). C and F may be geographically separated in the production of X.

(e) Capital which is sector specific to X is used in F but not in C, which uses only labour. F is characterized by constant returns (eliminating the possibility of many domestic plants) and thus $X = C \cdot F$ is characterized by increasing returns.

(f) Increasing returns in X are assumed to be weak relative to factor intensity effects such that the production set of each country is strictly convex. This ensures that a monopolist will maintain plants in both countries (i.e. become a MNE) rather than attempt to supply both countries from a single plant.[5]

(g) For the multi-plant firm, the C activity has a 'public goods' or 'jointness' aspect in that additional geographic locations of F activities may be added to the firm without reducing the marginal product of C in existing F activities.

(h) For the multi-plant firm, the C activity is also characterized by a 'centralization' aspect in that for a fixed total allocation of labour to C activities, the output of C is maximized by undertaking C at a single location.

---

[5] See Herberg and Kemp (1969) for an analysis of some local properties of the production frontier with increasing returns to scale. By assuming CES production functions, Markusen and Melvin (1981) are able to derive some global properties. Herberg and Kemp note that the production set must be non-convex in a small neighbourhood about $X = 0$, given Heckscher-Ohlin technology. This result does not necessarily hold for the specific-factors technology and we shall simply assume convexity of the production set over the relevant range of the production frontier.

(i) Equity ownership may cross international borders, but factors of production are immobile. There are no barriers to trade.

The C activity in producing X is intended to represent the R & D, marketing and managerial factors referred to above. F is intended to represent the physical transformation of inputs into outputs. Assumption (b) is made in order to neutralize the usual Heckscher–Ohlin, Ricardian, and demand bases for trade. The reason for this is that I wish to show clearly how multi-plant economies of scale can affect the pattern of trade and production. If we were to assume differences in factor endowments as well as the existence of scale economies, we would in general not be able to obtain any clear results or be able to tie results to one effect or the other. For the same reasons that we do not normally mix differences in technology (Ricardian trade models) with differences in factor endowments (Heckscher–Ohlin trade models) we will restrict the present analysis to a single basis for trade (scale economies).

The jointness and centralization aspects of C have been briefly discussed above. Only the results having to do with the volume and direction of trade depend on the centralization property as will be discussed from time to time. Gains from trade and welfare results will depend only on the jointness aspect.

Given the specification (a)–(i) production functions for the single-plant and two-plant enterprises are given as follows:

$$X^i = C(L_c^i)F(L_f^i), \qquad i = m, h, \tag{1}$$

$$X^m + X^h = C(L_c^m, L_c^h)[F(L_f^m) + F(L_f^h)]. \tag{2}$$

Given the sector-specific nature of capital, we can simply omit the capital arguments in the F functions which as a result are assumed to be characterized by $F'' < 0$.[6] The jointness aspect of the C activity is captured in (2) by $[F^m + F^h]$: changes in physical production (F) in one location do not affect the marginal product of C in the other location. F^m and F^h are also assumed to be independent in that there are no externality effects between geographically separated production facilities.

The centralization property of C is modelled by allowing the C isoquants to be concave to the origin in L^m amd L^h space. While this is not in general sufficient to ensure that the MNE will centralize C (L_c^m or L_c^h equal to zero) due to the concavity of Y and F, it will be sufficient if $C(L_c^m, L_c^h) = \max (L_c^m, L_c^h)$; that is, running independent C activities is so inefficient that it is completely redundant. In what follows we will simply assume C is centralized at the MNE equilibrium. It must be emphasized that this assumption plays no role in the welfare analysis and simply serves to make the positive analysis of trade more interesting by introducing an asymmetry into the MNE equilibrium.[7]

---

[6]See Jones (1971) and Neary (1978) for a discussion of sector-specific factors models.

[7]Centralization of C could also be achieved by differences in factor endowments between countries m and h and differences in factor intensities between C and F activities. While such factor proportions effects may be empirically quite important, they are well understood from the existing literature. More to the point, one purpose of this paper is to suggest an entirely different basis for trade, as noted above.

In order to facilitate comparisons of eqs. (1) and (2), we will assume the following:

$$C(\overline{L}_c^m, 0) = C(0, \overline{L}_c^h) = C(\overline{L}_c^i), \quad \text{for} \quad \overline{L}_c^h = \overline{L}_c^m = \overline{L}_c^i. \tag{3}$$

Eq. (3) states that if C is carried on in only one location by the MNE, the output of C activities is the same as the output from a single-plant operation given equal levels of L_c in the two cases. Eq. (3) states, in other words, that the number of plants is irrelevant to the production function for C activities. In what follows, $C(L_c^m)$ will be used as shorthand for $C(L_c^m, 0)$ since we have assumed that centralization is optimal for the MNE and will arbitrarily assume that C is centralized in the home country.

3. THE NATIONAL ENTERPRISE EQUILIBRIA

In this section we will derive reference solutions by assuming that there exists an independent monopoly (or duopoly) producer of X in each country. This formulation will be referred to as the national enterprise (NE) case. The list of NE equilibria is not comprehensive but rather is chosen to illustrate the possible trade-off between technical efficiency and market power when a MNE replaces two domestic firms.

It is assumed, as noted above, that all consumers including the monopolist have identical, homothetic utility functions and that the monopolist (or rather duopolist) in each country maximizes profits. With distributional and income effects thus removed, demand prices are simply a function of the relative outputs of X and Y (X/Y). If production takes place along the efficient production frontier of each country, the demand price ratio can be specified even more simply as just a function of X, since Y is uniquely related to X along the production frontier [Markusen (1981), Melvin and Warne (1973)]. Production must take place on the efficient production frontier even if the duopolists exercise monopsony power since there is only one factor mobile between sectors in this model. We will assume throughout the paper, however, that producers of X view factor prices as parametric.[8] This is of some help in simplifying the graphical comparison of the MNE and NE equilibria, as noted below. The formal analysis of section 5 will not rely on this assumption.

Let p denote the price of X in terms of Y. The autarky equilibrium conditions in which there is a single monopoly producer of X in each country are given very simply as follows [Melvin and Warne (1973), Markusen (1981)]:

$$p^i(1 - 1/\eta_x^i) = MRT^i; \quad \eta_x^i = -\frac{p}{X}\frac{dX}{dp} > 0, \quad i = m, h, \tag{4}$$

---

[8] The assumption that firms have no monopsony power may seem strained in a two-good model. However, none of the results to follow relies on the fact that there are only two goods. All results continue to hold if there are many competitive sectors such that we could more reasonably assume that the X sector is a small employer of labour. Recent general-equilibrium models of monopsony include Feenstra (1980), McCulloch and Yellen (1980), and Markusen and Robson (1980).

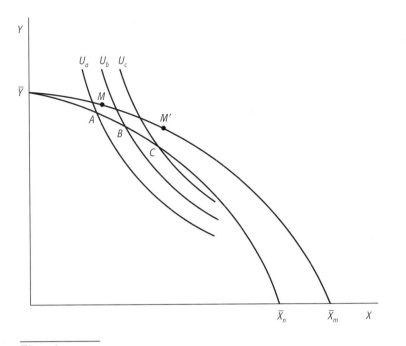

Figure 1

where MRT^i is the marginal rate of transformation along country i's production frontier and η^i_x is the elasticity of demand for X in country i. Second-order conditions for (4) will be satisfied if η^i_x is less than one and is a decreasing function of X (or, more correctly, of X/Y). Melvin and Warne (1973) and Markusen (1981) show that these conditions will be satisfied for example by any CES utility function with an elasticity of substitution greater than one.

Given our assumptions of identical tastes, technology, and factor endowments, it should be apparent that the solutions to (4) must be identical for the two countries. Autarky outputs, commodity prices, elasticities of demand, and factor prices will be the same in the two countries. With p^i, η^i_x and MRT^i the same in each country, it must also be true that production takes place on the efficient world production frontier.

The equilibrium given by (4) is shown in Figure 1 by point A. The production frontier $\overline{YX}_n$ can represent either the domestic or world production frontiers, with the latter being simply a radial blow-up of the former. Similarly, U_a can represent either the world or the national community indifference curve given the symmetry in the solution. Factor prices are also equalized in the autarky equilibria.[9]

----

[9] The commodity price and factor price equalization property of the autarky equilibrium breaks down if countries are of different size. With increasing returns to scale in X, the production frontier of the larger country will be flatter along any ray from the origin. This implies a lower autarky price ratio in the large country, and a world production bundle which is interior to the world production frontier [see Markusen and Melvin (1981) and Markusen (1981)].

When trade is possible, the symmetry in the model implies that any type of symmetric behaviour on the part of the two duopolists results in: (a) production on the world production frontier; and (b) no trade by virtue of the fact that outputs, commodity prices, etc. are equalized without trade. Interestingly enough, if the two duopolists engage in price collusion to maximize joint profits or engage in a market-shares rivalry, exactly the same equilibrium will be reached as occurred with autarky production. There are no gains to be realized here from price collusion since the equilibrium condition is simply (4) with p^i and η_x^i equalized between countries.[10] But the two equations in (4) are already equalized at the autarky equilibrium. It is in turn fairly well known that a market-shares rivalry results in an outcome identical to price collusion in this type of model.

Cournot–Nash behaviour on the part of the duopolists does on the other hand produce a distinct equilibrium [Markusen (1981)]. Suppose the duopolist in country m now views X^h as parametric. Revenue and marginal revenue as viewed by the duopolist in m are now given by:

$$R^m = p(X^m + \overline{X}^h)X^m; \qquad MR^m = p + X^m \frac{dp}{dX}$$

$$MR^m = p + (X^m + X^h)\frac{dp}{dX}\left(\frac{X^m}{X^m + X^h}\right) = p\left(1 - \frac{\sigma^m}{\eta_x}\right), \qquad \sigma^i = \frac{X^i}{X^m + X^h},$$

$$(5)$$

where σ^m represents m's market share and η_x continues to represent the world elasticity of demand for X. The Cournot–Nash equilibrium is thus given by:

$$p(1 - \sigma^i/\eta_x) = MRT^i, \qquad i = m, h. \tag{6}$$

As in the previous three cases, the solutions to (6) must be symmetric for m and h. Each country must have the same outputs, market share, consumption levels, factor prices, and so forth. Note, however, that there are gains from (potential) trade in the sense that welfare levels will be higher than in autarky. The symmetric equilibria in (6) must imply a market share of one-half for each duopolist. Thus, at the autarky equilibrium (point A in Figure 1), each duopolist will now find that perceived marginal revenue exceeds marginal costs. The national or world equilibrium must now be at a point like B in Figure 1 which, given our demand assumptions, constitutes an unambiguous improvement in welfare relative to A.[11] Further increases in production and welfare could be realized if the firms engaged in average-cost pricing to prevent entry (point C in Figure 1).

---

[10] This result will generally not hold if there are strongly increasing returns in X such that the production frontiers of m and h are convex (i.e. the production sets are non-convex). In that case, the joint maximum will involve a non-symmetric equilibrium in which countries specialize [see Melvin (1969), Kemp (1969), or Markusen and Melvin (1981)].

[11] I should be a bit careful in talking about 'social welfare', since there are, of course, distributional differences between A and B in Figure 1 (e.g. the monopolists are worse off at B). From either a revealed preference or a compensation principle approach, however, B is superior to A.

We could of course also examine some non-symmetric NE equilibria such as Stackelberg leader–follower behaviour. But the point here is simply to establish that competitive forms of duopoly behaviour (Cournot–Nash, average-cost pricing) create a situation in which it is unclear whether or not replacing an inefficient duopoly with an efficient monopoly will increase welfare. Since the properties of a Stackelberg equilibrium require a rather lengthy analysis, we do not therefore present this case here.

4. THE MULTINATIONAL ENTERPRISE EQUILIBRIUM

Since it is not obvious that the MNE will produce efficiently, perhaps we should solve for the conditions that characterize the efficient world production frontier and compare them to the MNE's equilibrium conditions. It now makes little sense to talk about national production frontiers since the position of country h's production frontier will, for example, be determined by the level of C activities carried on in country m. A similar problem confronted Ethier (1979) in dealing with international externalities.

Assuming that it is optimal to centralize the C activity in country m, the conditions characterizing the efficient production frontier can be found by maximizing the output of X for a given level of Y production:

$$\max C(L_c^m)[F(L_f^m) + F(L_f^h)]$$

s.t.

$$\overline{Y} = G(\overline{L} - L_c^m - L_f^m) + G(\overline{L} - L_f^h), \qquad (7)$$

$$\frac{G^{m'}}{C^{m'}(F^m + F^h)} = \frac{G^{m'}}{C^m F^{m'}} = \frac{G^{h'}}{C^m F^{h'}} = MRT, \qquad (8)$$

where $\overline{L}$ denotes each economy's endowment of labour and $Y = G(L_y)$.

Let w^i denote the wage of labour in terms of Y. $w^i = G^{i'}$ follows from the assumption that factor markets and the Y industry are competitive ($G^{i'}$ equals the marginal product of labour in the production of Y). The MNE's programming problem and first-order conditions are given as follows:

$$\max pC(L_c^m)[F(L_f^m) + F(L_f^h)] - w^m(L_c^m + L_f^m) - w^h L_f^h, \qquad p = p(X), \qquad (9)$$

$$p\left(1 - \frac{1}{\eta_x}\right) = \frac{G^{m'}}{C^{m'}(F^m + F^h)} = \frac{G^{m'}}{C^m F^{m'}} = \frac{G^{h'}}{C^m F^{h'}}, \quad \text{since} \quad w^i = G^{i'}. \quad (10)$$

Eq. (10) satisfies the conditions given in (8) for the efficient use of inputs. Thus, the MNE equilibrium lies on the efficient MNE world production frontier. As shown in the next section, this MNE frontier will lie everywhere outside the NE frontier except at the Y axis ($\overline{YX}_m$ and $\overline{YX}_n$ in Figure 1, respectively).

In the centralized equilibrium (10), the intra-country labour allocations cannot be the same. Suppose, for example, that $L_y^m = L_y^h$, then it must be the case that $L_f^m < L_f^h$, since some of L^m must be used in C. Such an allocation cannot satisfy (10) since $L_f^m < L_f^h$

implies $F^{m'} > F^{h'}$. A similar argument implies that L_f^m cannot equal L_f^h. In short, we must have the following:

$$\frac{G^{m'}}{C^m F^{m'}} = \frac{G^{h'}}{C^m F^{h'}},$$

if and only if $L_y^m < L_y^h, L_f^m < L_f^h$, given $L_c^m > L_c^h = 0$ \hfill (11)

The centralized equilibrium must imply that country m has less resources in both Y and F such that both $G^{m'}$ and $F^{m'}$ exceed $G^{h'}$ and $F^{h'}$. Country m has more total resources in X ($L_y^m < L_y^h$) but the distribution of these resources between C and F differs from that in country h. Since $G^{m'} > G^{h'}$, the wage rate must be higher in country m in terms of Y but also in terms of X since commodity prices are equalized. Conversely, both forms of capital must earn a lower return in country m. Each country has a relatively high price for the factors used intensively in its predominant activity (C for country m and G and F for country h).

The relationship between outputs in the two countries is not however so simple. Whether or not country m's production ratio (X/Y) differs from country h's ratio depends on the global properties of G and F. The fact that $(G^{m'}/F^{m'}) = (G^{h'}/F^{h'})$ from (10) does not imply that $(X^m/Y^m) = (X^h/Y^h)$ or alternatively that $(G^m/F^m) = (G^h/F^h)$.

The implication of this dependence on the properties of G and F is that the direction and volume of trade cannot be fully predicted in the model. If the solution of (10) by pure chance involves $(X^m/Y^m) = (X^h/Y^h)$ as just noted, then trade will consist simply of a one-way profit repatriation of both commodities in the same production ratio. If the solution involves different production ratios, then identical, homothetic demand may imply two-way trade with m exporting Y, for example, if $(X^m/Y^m) < (X^h/Y^h)$.

These findings suggest that MNE activity as modelled above does affect the intersectoral allocation of economic activity in a country (i.e. $L_y^m < L_y^h$) and does therefore provide a basis for trade. It does not however offer a simple prediction as to the direction of trade. Nevertheless, there will always exist some trade (profit repatriation at a minimum) in the MNE equilibrium as opposed to the symmetric no-trade NE equilibria.

5. COMPARING THE MNE AND NE EQUILIBRIA

Consider a fixed allocation of resources between the X and Y sectors for the NE version of the model. First-order conditions imply an optimal allocation of labour in X between the C and F activities. Denoting these labour allocations as $\bar{L}_j^i$, the maximum value of world X production given the fixed level of Y production is given by:

$$\bar{X} = C(\bar{L}_c^m)F(\bar{L}_f^m) + C(\bar{L}_c^h)F(\bar{L}_f^h),$$ \hfill (12)

where $\bar{L}_i^m = \bar{L}_i^h$ by virtue of the symmetry of all of the NE equilibria.

The efficiency advantage of the MNE can easily be demonstrated by considering a simple (although not optimal) production plan. Specifically, the two-plant MNE enterprise could if it wished produce $\overline{X}$ from $\overline{L}_c^m$, $\overline{L}_f^m$, and $\overline{L}_f^h$ and still have $\overline{L}_c^h$ left over:

$$\overline{X} = C(\overline{L}_c^m)[F(\overline{L}_f^m) + F(\overline{L}_f^h)]. \tag{13}$$

Indeed, the MNE can do even better by optimally reallocating labour among the four X-sector activities so as to satisfy the MNE first-order conditions given in (10). Thus, producing $\overline{X}$ with $\overline{L}_c^h$ left over is the *minimum* improvement in productive efficiency that the MNE can realize.

In a sense, production by the MNE thus represents a technical improvement in the world production function for X. The efficient MNE world production frontier must lie everywhere outside the efficient NE world production frontier (except at $X = 0$). This is shown in Figure 1, where $\overline{YX}_m$ represents the world MNE production frontier and $\overline{YX}_n$ represents the world *NE* production frontier.

An analysis of total world gains or losses from the MNE is straightforward. The process begins by noting that with a convex world production set, the value of the MNE equilibrium production bundle evaluated at a 'price ratio' tangent to the production frontier at the MNE production point must exceed the value of any other feasible production bundle evaluated at the same price ratio [Kemp (1969), Markusen (1981)]. In our case, this 'price ratio' is given by the *MRT* at the MNE equilibrium and therefore by $p_m(1 - 1/\eta_x)$, where subscript m denotes the MNE equilibrium value. The principle is illustrated in Figure 1: at M, for example, the value of production evaluated at $(MRT)_m$ exceeds the value at that price ratio of all other feasible production bundles. Using subscript i to denote any arbitrary NE equilibrium allocation, this value relationship becomes:

$$(Y_m^m + Y_m^h) + p_m(1 - 1/\eta_x)(X_m^m + X_m^h)$$
$$\geqq (Y_i^m + Y_i^h) + p_m(1 - 1/\eta_x)(X_i^m + X_i^h). \tag{14}$$

Let C_{ij} denote the consumption of good j in allocation i. Aggregate market clearing requires that:

$$(Y_i^m + Y_i^h) = (C_{iy}^m + C_{iy}^h), \qquad (X_i^m + X_i^h) = (C_{ix}^m + C_{ix}^h). \tag{15}$$

Substituting (15) into (14) and rearranging, we have:

$$[(C_{my}^m + C_{my}^h) + p_m(C_{mx}^m + C_{mx}^h)] \geqq [(C_{iy}^m + C_{iy}^h) + p_m(C_{ix}^m + C_{ix}^h)]$$
$$+ (p_m/\eta_x)(X_m^m + X_m^h - X_i^m - X_i^h). \tag{16}$$

Eq. (16) states, for example, that the value of MNE consumption will exceed the value of NE consumption (i.e. the MNE bundle will be revealed preferred) if the total output of X is higher in the MNE equilibrium relative to the NE equilibrium $(X_m^m + X_m^h > X_i^m + X_i^h)$.

It is easy to show that the MNE production of X exceeds the combined autarky totals, implying from (16) that welfare is higher in the MNE equilibrium. If the NE autarky equilibrium is at point A in Figure 1, then the MNE equilibrium must be at a point like M or M' in that diagram. M or M' must be 'downhill' of the point on $\overline{YX}_m$ which lies on the same ray from the origin as point A. On such a ray, the MNE would face the same marginal revenue as the NE firms at A (since X/Y is the same) but a lower MRT (at equal X/Y, the MRT on $\overline{YX}_m$ is less than the MRT of $\overline{YX}_n$). Total X production at M or M' in Figure 1 must exceed total production at A.

The relation between the MNE and Cournot–Nash equilibria (point B in Figure 1) is ambiguous. Along the same ray from the origin as that through B, the MRT on $\overline{YX}_m$ is less than on $\overline{YX}_n$ but marginal revenue for the MNE is also less than the perceived marginal revenue of the Cournot–Nash duopolies. Thus, the MNE may continue to achieve a gain in welfare over the NE equilibrium as shown by points M' and B in Figure 1. On the other hand, the MNE and Cournot–Nash equilibria could be at points M and B, respectively, in Figure 1, indicating a deterioration in welfare. Relative to the Cournot–Nash equilibrium, the MNE equilibrium enjoys greater productive efficiency at the expense of a higher degree of exercised market power. A more complete welfare analysis requires that we exploit profit and entry restrictions at the level of the individual countries, a subject to which we now turn.

Consider first the situation in the MNE's home country. A sufficient condition for country m to be better off with the MNE is that

$$C^m_{my} + p_m C^m_{mx} \geqq C^m_{iy} + p_m C^m_{ix}, \tag{17}$$

where subscript i again denotes some arbitrary NE equilibrium. The balance of payments constraint for country m is given by

$$C^m_{my} + p_m C^m_{mx} = Y^m_m + p_m X^m_m + \pi^*, \tag{18}$$

where π^* is profits repatriated from country h. Assuming that we are comparing the MNE equilibrium with a symmetric NE equilibrium with no trade, we will have $C^m_{ij} = X^m_{ij}$. Substituting this relationship and (18) into (17) gives us the sufficient condition for home country gains:

$$Y^m_m + p_m X^m_m + \pi^* \geqq Y^m_i + p_m X^m_i. \tag{19}$$

Now subtract from each side of (19) the value of the economy's factor endowment evaluated at the MNE equilibrium factor prices. This is given by:

$$w_m \overline{L} + r_{my} \overline{K}_y + r_{mx} \overline{K}_x = w_m L^m_{jy} + w_m L^m_{jx} + r_{my} \overline{K}_y + r_{mx} \overline{K}_x, \tag{20}$$

where $\overline{K}_y$ and $\overline{K}_x$ are the endowments of sector-specific capital in Y and X and r_y and r_x their respective rental rates. L and w are the total endowment of labour and the wage rate, respectively. Subtracting (20) from (19), the latter becomes:

$$[Y^m_m - w_m L^m_{my} - r_{my} \overline{K}_y] + [p_m X^m_m - w_m L^m_{mx} - r_{mx} \overline{K}_x] + \pi^*$$
$$\geqq Y^m_i - w_m L^m_{iy} - r_{my} \overline{K}_y] + [p_m X^m_i - w_m L^m_{ix} - r_{mx} \overline{K}_x]. \tag{21}$$

Eq. (21) expresses the gains from trade inequality in terms of industry profits evaluated at the MNE equilibrium. Sufficient conditions for (21) to hold and therefore for gains from trade to occur are that

$$\{Y_m^m - w_m L_{my}^m - r_{my}\overline{K}_y] \geqq [Y_i^m - w_m L_{iy}^m - r_{my}\overline{K}_y] \tag{22}$$

and

$$[p_m X_m^m - w_m L_{mx}^m - r_{mx}\overline{K}_x] + \pi^* \geqq [p_m X_i^m - w_m L_{ix}^m - r_{mx}\overline{K}_x]. \tag{23}$$

Eq. (22) can be rewritten as:

$$[1 - w_m a_{lm} - r_{my} a_{km}]Y_m^m \geqq [1 - w_m a_{li} - r_{my} a_{ki}]Y_i^m, \tag{24}$$

where a_{lm} and a_{li} are, for example, the unit labour requirements at the MNE and NE equilibria, respectively, for good Y. The left-hand side of (24) is thus unit revenue ($p_y = 1$) minus unit cost at the MNE equilibrium. This is zero due to the assumption of constant returns and perfect competition in Y. The right-hand side of (24) is unit revenue minus unit costs evaluated at the MNE prices but using the NE input coefficients. Since (a_{lm}, a_{km}) are the profit-maximizing input coefficients at prices (w_m, r_{my}), costs must be greater using unit inputs (a_{li}, a_{ki}) and thus the right-hand side of (24) is negative. Thus, the inequality shown in (24) and (22) does indeed hold.

The inequality in (24) is illustrated in Figure 2, where $Y_m = Y_i = 1$ is the unit isoquant for Y. M and N are the efficient input combinations at the MNE and NE factor prices, respectively. Unit costs at the MNE equilibrium are just tangent to $Y = 1$, as shown. Unit costs using the NE inputs (point N) but MNE factor prices are greater than one as shown in Figure 2. The left-hand side of (24) thus equals zero, while the right-hand side is negative.

To demonstrate that (19) and (17) hold such that country m gains from the MNE now only requires us to show that (23) holds. The left-hand side of (23) is the MNE's total profits (domestic plus foreign repatriation), while the right-hand side is the profits from the NE output evaluated at the MNE prices. This inequality has a revealed preference interpretation similar to the one used above; that is, if (23) holds the MNE's profits are revealed preferred to its alternative NE profits. If this inequality did not hold, then the MNE would find it advantageous to drop one plant or alternatively to not have become a MNE in the first place. Thus, profit maximization plus freedom of entry or exit from MNE operation assures us that (23) does hold and thus (17) holds. If the MNE exists, the home country must gain.

Equations equivalent to (17)–(24) can be derived for the host country, the only difference being that π^* enters with a minus sign in (18), (19), (21) and (23). The analysis of (24) and Figure 2 remains valid for the Y industry, and thus the host country equivalent of (22) holds. Gains from trade will therefore be realized if the host country equivalent of (23) holds. This is written as:

$$[p_m X_m^h - w_m L_{mx}^h - r_{mx}\overline{K}_x] - \pi^* \geqq [p_m X_i^h - w_m L_{ix}^h - r_{mx}\overline{K}_x]. \tag{25}$$

The left-hand side of (25) is the profits earned by the MNE minus the profits repatriated and is assumed to be greater than or equal to zero. The right-hand side is the profits that

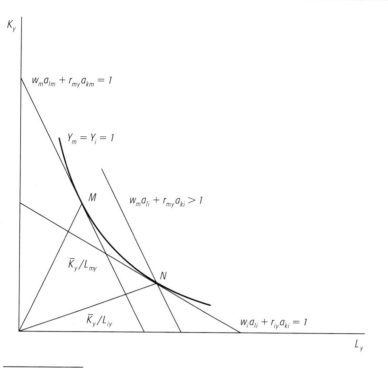

Figure 2

would be earned by producing the NE output at the MNE prices. This is not necessarily negative, as will be discussed below. Thus, even though the MNE produces with greater technical efficiency, the fact that it repatriates profits which might otherwise have gone to host country entrepreneurs means that gains are not assured for the host country.

The possible trade-offs between efficiency and market power are shown in Figures 3 and 4, where $\overline{Y}^h\overline{X}_h^h$ represents the NE transformation frontier for country h. $\overline{Y}^h\overline{X}_m^h$ gives the MNE frontier under the assumption that activity C is centralized in m and thus resources are freed for production in h. M denotes the MNE equilibrium and N the NE equilibrium in each diagram. The value of gross output measured in terms of Y is given by point G.

Since F is characterized by constant returns (as is Y), the marginal costs of producing X and Y equal average costs. Payments to domestic factor owners which equal total domestic income at the MNE equilibrium are therefore given in terms of Y by point F in each diagram (the slope of $\overline{Y}^h\overline{X}_m^h$ at M is the ratio of marginal costs). The budget line of domestic factor owners is constructed by drawing a line with slope p_m through point F. The distance between the price lines through G and F gives the MNE profits.

Using the revealed preference criteria employed above, the host country is assured of gains if the price line through F passes above N which gives national income (factor income plus profits of the domestic firm) at the NE equilibrium. (The dotted line in each diagram gives

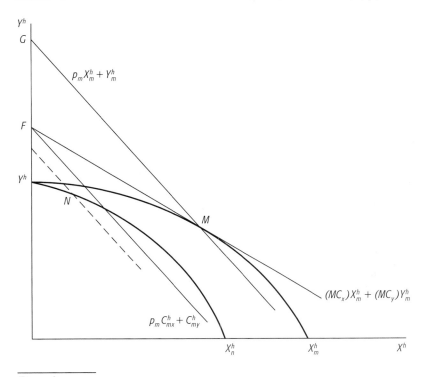

Figure 3

NE income at MNE prices.) As constructed, this does occur in Figure 3 but not in Figure 4. In the latter case, domestic gross income increases with the MNE, but repatriation leaves the host country worse off. The question now is whether or not the possibility illustrated in Figure 4 can be ruled out by further considerations such as limit pricing.

Suppose that the entrants in the host country behave in a 'Bertrand' fashion, viewing the MNE's prices as parametric in making their entry decision. Assume further that the MNE prices to prevent entry by these Bertrand firms; that is, the MNE must produce an output sufficiently large that at the resulting commodity and factor prices there is no profitable output that a single-plant entrant could produce. The right-hand side of (25) gives the profits that an entrant could earn at MNE prices by producing the NE output. If there is no profitable output that could be produced by a single-plant entrant at these prices, then this expression must be negative. This type of pricing to prevent entry by Bertrand firms thus implies that the inequality in (25) holds and that the host country is assured of gains.

Bertrand behaviour by entrants is not, of course, the only or the most reasonable form of entry behaviour. Unfortunately, it is also true that other forms of behaviour do not ensure that the right-hand side of (25) is non-positive. Suppose, for example, that entrants behave in a Cournot fashion, viewing the output of the MNE as fixed. The entrant then knows that if he enters, the price of X will fall as world production increases.

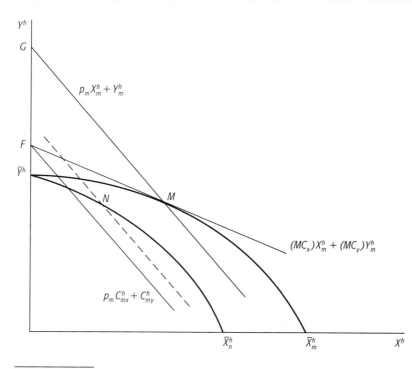

Figure 4

With increasing returns to scale, he may therefore not find it profitable to enter even if the right-hand side of (25) is positive (e.g. if X_i^h is actually produced, price changes will lead to negative profits).

We can, however, offer one alternative sufficient condition for gains which looks at the problem from a somewhat different perspective. Suppose that country h taxes repatriated profits (in a non-distortionary manner) such that the left-hand side of (25) is positive. If the tax is set such that the revenue (country h's share of profits) is at least equal to the profits that would be earned by a domestic entrepreneur producing the NE output at MNE prices, then (25) holds and gains are assured.

6. Extensions

The purpose of this section is to very briefly discuss the implications of relaxing some of the assumptions used throughout the paper.

6.1. Non-Centralization

As noted above, the assumption that the MNE finds it optimal to centralize C plays no role at all in the welfare analysis and the results thereof. Centralization of C is only assumed in order to generate an asymmetric equilibrium in which the two identical countries engage in a positive amount of trade. Assuming that the C isoquants in (2) are convex to the origin would simply imply that the MNE equilibrium is symmetric, with $L_c^m = L_c^h > 0$.

6.2. Monopsony

With only one factor mobile between sectors, allowing firms to exercise monopsony power makes no difference to the qualitative analysis of the NE. Monopsony does not pull the countries off their efficient production frontiers, but rather simply shifts each equilibrium shown in Figure 1 toward the Y axis.[12] With centralization and asymmetric production in the two countries, the MNE exercising monopsony power may produce at different MRT in the two countries and thus may not produce on the efficient world production frontier. The sufficient conditions for gains from trade are however unaffected by this complication.

6.3. Tariffs

I noted above that multi-plant economies form a basis for direct foreign investment irrespective of the existence of tariffs. The addition of tariffs to the model would create an additional incentive for multi-plant production, but otherwise leaves the analysis pretty much unchanged. The complication is that domestic prices will appear in (17) while world prices appear in (18). Eq. (19) will consequently have an additional positive term on the right-hand side which will equal tariff revenue. The sufficient conditions for gains from trade will still be valid if there was no trade at the NE equilibrium or if tariff revenue at the MNE equilibrium exceeded revenue at the NE equilibrium.

6.4. Two MNEs

In this model, two MNEs (one in each country) will produce an equilibrium identical to the NE equilibrium with the same form of duopoly behaviour. Each firm would simply capture a symmetric share of its rival's market with its foreign plant. There are no gains from MNE activity since the gains noted above arise from avoiding the duplication of C activities that exists when there are two independent firms.

6.5. Non-Symmetric NE Equilibria

Non-symmetric NE equilibria such as Stackelberg leader-follower behaviour could be analyzed, but note again that the sufficient conditions for gains from trade do not depend on symmetry assumptions. Certain positive aspects of the NE equilibrium would change (e.g. the volume of trade), but not the welfare aspects of the MNE-NE comparison.

---

[12]This result generally does not hold if there is more than one factor mobile between sectors [Feenstra (1980), McCulloch and Yellen (1980), Markusen and Robson (1980)].

7. SUMMARY AND CONCLUSIONS

(1) The purpose of this paper was to develop a general-equilibrium model which explains the allocative and distributive effects of multinational corporations. In doing so, it was noted that an adequate model should meet five pre-conditions: (a) it should provide rationale for direct versus portfolio investment; (b) it should preferably not rely on international factor movements, factor price differences, or barriers to international trade; (c) it should explain why monopoly production is superior to collusion among independent producers; (d) it should explain why a multinational corporation might wish to diversify geographically, yet possibly carry on different activities in otherwise identical countries; and (e) it should allow for positive economic profits insofar as profits may play an important role in the gains from trade. I argued that these conditions could be met by a model based on the industrial-organization concept of economies of multi-plant operation.

(2) These economies are modelled algebraically by an activity which enters the firm's production function as a joint input across production facilities. The technical (as opposed to economic) efficiency advantage of the MNE then lies in its ability to avoid the duplication of this joint input that would occur with independent national enterprises.

(3) Two versions of the basic model were developed and compared. In one version, world production of a good was monopolized by a multinational enterprise (MNE) while in the other version there was a single independent national enterprise (NE) producing the good in each of two countries. In certain cases (e.g. the NEs behave in a Cournot–Nash fashion), the MNE produces with greater technical efficiency at the possible expense of higher exercised market power. In these cases it is not clear that the MNE will increase world welfare or the welfare of either country. It was shown that a sufficient condition for the MNE to increase world real income relative to the NE equilibrium was simply that the MNE increased the output of the good in question.

(4) Sufficient conditions for the home country to gain from the MNE were that the MNE's profits are 'revealed preferred' to the profits it could earn as a single plant firm at an alternative NE equilibrium. Since this condition presumably must hold if the firm is rational, the home country is guaranteed of gains in this model.

(5) The situation for the host country is more uncertain due to the fact that the MNE and the home country capture monopoly rents that would accrue to host country entrepreneurs at the NE equilibrium. Nevertheless, we were able to derive two alternative sufficient conditions which ensured gains for the host country. First, if the MNE must price to prevent entry by Bertrand firms in the host country, then that country is assured of gains. Second, if the host country can retain a share of the MNE's profits (via some tax) which is at least equal to the profits that would be earned by producing the NE output at MNE prices, then the host country gains.

(6) When the MNE finds it efficient to concentrate certain activities in the home country, the equilibrium involves the identical countries specializing in different activities

and producing different bundles of goods. Thus, the MNE can lead to trade creation and to an 'international division of labour' [Hymer (1976)]. MNE activity can, per se, form a basis for trade. Alternatively, this finding notes that direct investment, unlike portfolio capital movements, can act as a complement rather than as a substitute to commodity trade [Markusen (1983)].

(7) The MNE equilibrium involves unequal factor prices between countries, whereas the symmetric NE equilibria all involve factor price equalization. At the MNE equilibrium each country has a relatively high price for the factors used intensively in its predominant activities (C for country m and G and F for country h). Note that if factors are then permitted to move internationally, factors will flow in a manner that increases the degree of international specialization and the volume of commodity trade. Similar to the previous point, this implies that direct investment, unlike portfolio capital movements, can make countries more unequal in certain respects. These results are in fact quite consistent with the findings in related papers by Melvin (1969), Krugman (1979), Markusen and Melvin (1981), and Markusen (1981, 1983) who note that with imperfect competition and/or increasing returns, trading equilibria may involve specialization by two identical economies and a complementarity between trade in factors and trade in goods.

REFERENCES

Batra, R.N. and R. Ramachandran, 1980, Multinational firms, and the theory of international trade and investment, American Economic Review 70, 278–290.

Bhagwati, Jagdish and Richard A. Brecher, 1980, National welfare in an open economy in the presence of foreign owned factors of production, Journal of International Economics 10, 103–115.

Brecher, Richard A. and Carlos Diaz Alejandro, 1977, Tariffs, foreign-capital and immiserizing growth, Journal of International Economics 7, 317–322.

Buckley, P.J. and M. Casson, 1976, The future of the multinational enterprise (Macmillan, London).

Caves, Richard E., 1971, International corporations: The industrial economics of foreign investment, Economica 38, 1–27.

Caves, Richard E., 1974, Causes of direct investment: Foreign firms' shares in Canadian and U.K. manufacturing industries, Review of Economics and Statistics 56, 279–293.

Caves, Richard E., 1980, Investment and location policies of multinational companies, Harvard University Working Paper.

Caves, R.E., M.E. Porter and M. Spence, 1980, Competition in the open economy: A model applied to Canada (Harvard University Press, Cambridge, Mass).

Dunning, J.H., 1977, The determinants of international production, Oxford Economic Papers 25, 289–330.

Eastman, H.C. and S. Stykolt, 1967, The tariff and competition in Canada (Macmillan, Toronto).

Ethier, Wilfred, 1979, Internationally decreasing costs and world trade, Journal of International Economics 9, 1–24.

Feenstra, R.C., 1980, Monopsony distortions in the open economy: A theoretical analysis, Journal of International Economics 10, 213–236.

Gorecke, Paul K., 1976, The determinants of entry by domestic and foreign enterprises in Canadian manufacturing, Review of Economics and Statistics 58, 485–488.

Helpman, Elhanan, 1981, International trade in the presence of product differentiation, economies of scale, and monopolistic competition, Journal of International Economics 11, 305–340.

Herberg, Horst and Murray C. Kemp, 1969, Some implications of variable returns to scale, Canadian Journal of Economics 2, 403–415.

Horst, Thomas, 1976, American multinationals and the U.S. economy, American Economic Review 66, 149–154.

Horstmann, Ignatius and James R. Markusen, 1983, Strategic investments, firm specific capital, and the development of multinationals, University of Western Ontario Working Paper.

Hymer, Stephen H., 1976, The international operation of national firms: A study of direct foreign investment (MIT Press, Cambridge, Mass.).

Jones, Ronald W., 1967, International capital movements and the theory of tariffs, Quarterly Journal of Economics 81, 1–38.

Jones, Ronald W., 1971, A three-factor model in theory, trade and history, in: Jagdish N. Bhagwati et al., eds., Trade, balance of payments and growth: Papers in honor of Charles P. Kindleberger (North-Holland, Amsterdam) 3–21.

Kemp, Murray C., 1969, The pure theory of international trade and investment (Prentice-Hall, New York).

Kindleberger, Charles P., 1969, American business abroad (Yale University Press, New Haven).

Kindleberger, Charles P., 1970, ed., The international corporation (MIT Press, Cambridge, Mass.).

Krugman, Paul, 1979, Increasing returns, monopolistic competition and international trade, Journal of International Economics 9, 395–410.

Magee, Stephen P., 1977, Application of the dynamic limit pricing model to the price of technology and international technology transfer, in: K. Brunner and A. Meltzer, eds., Optimal policies, control theory and technology exports (North-Holland, Amsterdam) 203–224.

McCulloch, R. and J.L. Yellen, 1980, Factor market monopsony and the allocation of resources, Journal of International Economics 10, 237–248.

McManus, J.C., 1972, The theory of the international firm, in: G. Paquet, ed., The multinational firm and the nation state (Collier–Macmillan, Don Mills, Ontario) 66–93.

Markusen, James R., 1981, Trade and the gains from trade with imperfect competition, Journal of International Economics 11, 531–551.

Markusen, James R., 1983, Factor movements and commodity trade as complements, Journal of International Economics 13, 341–356.

Markusen, James R. and James R. Melvin, 1979, Tariffs, capital mobility and foreign ownership, Journal of International Economics 9, 395–410.

Markusen, James R. and James R. Melvin, 1981, Trade, factor prices and the gain from trade with increasing return to scale, Canadian Journal of Economics 14, 450–469.

Markusen, James R. and Arthur Robson, 1980, Simple general equilibrium with a monopsonized sector, Canadian Journal of Economics 13, 668–682.

Melvin, James R., 1969, Increasing returns to scale as a determinant of trade, Canadian Journal of Economics 2, 389–402.

Melvin, James R. and Robert Warne, 1973, Monopoly and the theory of international trade, Journal of International Economics 3, 117–134.

Neary, J. Peter, 1978, Short-run capital specificity and the pure theory of international trade, Economic Journal 88, 488–510.

Parry, Thomas G., 1980, The multinational enterprise: International investment and host-country impacts (Jai Press, Greenwich, Connecticut).

Scherer, F.M., 1980, Industrial market structure and economic performance, 2nd edn. (Rand McNally, Chicago).

Scherer, F.M., et al., 1975, The economics of multi-plant operation: An international comparisons study (Harvard University Press, Cambridge, Mass.).

Vernon, Raymond, 1971, Sovereignty at bay: The multinational spread of U.S. enterprises (Basic Books, New York and London).

ABOUT THE AUTHOR

James R. Markusen

James Markusen is a professor of economics at the University of Colorado. A native of Canada, he has examined trade firsthand through visiting appointments in eight other countries. Much of his research has centered on the industrial-organization approach to trade, particularly the positive theory. Many of his articles focus on endogenizing multinational firms into general-equilibrium trade models.

Editor's Queries

Which article not reprinted here would you most highly recommend to graduate students in international economics? Within the industrial-organization-approach subfield, I rank Ethier's 1982 AER article as a "must read." I think that we have spent way too much time on differentiated final goods, and neglected trade in intermediates and the productivity-enhancing effects that such trade can have. Ethier's article, in some sense, is the foundation for the trade and endogenous-growth literature that appeared years later. Ethier's intermediate-inputs approach seems empirically very relevant, and formal econometric work would be very welcome.

What advice do you have to offer graduate students in the field of international economics? I didn't take any advice on what to work on when I was a graduate student. I can give advice, but no one should take it seriously. Primarily, I would urge you to follow your interests. You will do much better work if you attack an area that interests you, even if it is not currently in fashion. A few years ago I gave a paper at MIT and had lunch with a group of graduate students. They told me that a VIP who had been there a few weeks earlier told them that "you have to have a chapter on political economy in your thesis." I was absolutely astonished by this. I asked a couple of them what they were interested in working on, and got some really good answers. But they were clearly and inappropriately nervous because there was no political economy included. So if you are insistent on getting my advice, forget specific advice on topic areas and pursue your instincts and interests.

The O-Ring Theory of Economic Development

MICHAEL KREMER

Massachusetts Institute of Technology

This paper proposes a production function describing processes subject to mistakes in any of several tasks. It shows that high-skill workers—those who make few mistakes—will be matched together in equilibrium, and that wages and output will rise steeply in skill. The model is consistent with large income differences between countries, the predominance of small firms in poor countries, and the positive correlation between the wages of workers in different occupations within enterprises. Imperfect observability of skill leads to imperfect matching and thus to spillovers, strategic complementarity, and multiple equilibria in education.

Many production processes consist of a series of tasks, mistakes in any of which can dramatically reduce the product's value. The space shuttle *Challenger* had thousands of components: it exploded because it was launched at a temperature that caused one of those components, the O-rings, to malfunction. "Irregular" garments with slight imperfections sell at half price. Companies can fail due to bad marketing, even if the product design, manufacturing, and accounting are excellent. This paper argues that the analysis of such processes can help explain several stylized facts in development and labor economics.

The first section of the paper proposes a production function in which production consists of many tasks, all of which must be successfully completed for the product to have full value. I assume that it is not possible to substitute several low-skill workers for one high-skill worker, where skill refers to the probability a worker will successfully complete a task. Subsection I.1 solves for equilibrium wages as a function of worker skill under this production function, and shows that firms will match together workers of similar skill. Subsection I.2 argues that this production function is consistent with a series of stylized facts in development and labor economics, including the enormity of wage and productivity differences between rich and poor countries and the positive correlation between wages of workers in different occupations within firms. A variant of the model in which tasks are performed sequentially implies that the share of agriculture in GNP will

I am grateful to Roland Benabou, Kala Krishna, Eric Maskin, Paul Romer, Sherwin Rosen, Xavier Sala-i-Martin, Philippe Weil, many former classmates at Harvard, and especially Robert Barro for comments and suggestions. The National Science Foundation provided financial support during the period this paper was written.

fall with development. Subsection I.3 shows that higher skill workers will use more complex technologies that incorporate more tasks. This may help explain why household production and small firms are the dominant form of industrial organization in developing countries and why there is a positive correlation between wages and firm size within countries. Although each of these stylized facts may be due to a variety of factors, taken together, they suggest that this type of production function is empirically relevant.

Section II endogenizes worker skill as the product of investment in human capital. If workers are matched together perfectly, investment in human capital will be Pareto optimal. However, if worker skill cannot be perfectly observed, so matching is imperfect, there will be underinvestment in human capital, so education subsidies will be optimal. Moreover, there will be strategic complementarity in this investment, so these subsidies will have multiplier effects, and small differences between countries in exogenous factors will cause large differences in worker skill. If strategic complementarity is strong enough, there will be multiple equilibria.

Section III generalizes the argument to production functions with arbitrary returns to scale, and discusses extensions to production functions which induce firms to match together workers of dissimilar skill and to production functions in which different tasks enter the production function asymmetrically. A conclusion summarizes the results.

The model builds on Rosen's [1981] analysis of superstars and on Rosen [1982], Miller [1983], and Lucas [1978], which build models of organizational hierarchy in which managerial skill enters the production function multiplicatively, and unskilled labor enters with standard diminishing returns. In these models, agents with skill below some cutoff level become workers, and agents with skill above the cutoff level become managers. Higher skill managers supervise more employees. This paper differs in examining skill interaction among workers at the same level of hierarchy. In this model, rather than supervising more employees, high-skill agents are matched with high-skill coworkers.[1] This paper thus combines Rosen's analysis of multiplicative quality effects with Becker's [1981] analysis of matching in marriage markets. It is also related to the work of Sah and Stiglitz [1985, 1986] and Sobel [1992] in applying the literature on reliability to organizations.

I. THE O-RING PRODUCTION FUNCTION AND APPLICATIONS

I.1. THE O-RING PRODUCTION FUNCTION

Consider a firm using a production process consisting of n tasks. For example, in an automobile factory one task might be installing the brakes, and in a restaurant one task might be waiting on tables. For simplicity of exposition, I assume that each task

---

[1] An appendix available from the author works out an example in which higher quality workers have both more subordinates and higher skill coworkers.

requires a single worker, but this need not be true in general, and n should be taken as referring to the number of tasks, not the number of workers. For now I shall assume that n is technologically fixed. Firms can replicate the production process an arbitrary number of times. A worker's skill (or quality) at a task, q, is defined by the expected percentage of maximum value the product retains if the worker performs the task. Thus, a q of 0.95 could refer to a worker who has a 95 percent chance of performing the task perfectly and a 5 percent chance of performing it so badly the product is worthless, to a worker who always performs a task in such a way that the product retains 95 percent of its value, or to a worker who has an 50 percent chance of performing the task perfectly and a 50 percent chance of making a mistake that reduces the value of the product to 90 percent of its maximum possible value. The probability of mistakes by different workers is independent. Capital k enters the production function in conventional Cobb-Douglas form and is not differentiated by quality. Define B as output per worker with a single unit of capital if all tasks are performed perfectly. Expected production is thus

$$E(y) = k^\alpha (\Pi_{i=1}^n q_i)\, nB. \tag{1}$$

Firms are risk-neutral, so the remainder of the paper drops the distinction between production and expected production. There is a fixed supply of capital, k^*, and a continuum of workers following some exogenous distribution of quality, $\phi(q)$. Workers face no labor-leisure choice and supply labor inelastically.

This O-ring production function differs from the standard efficiency units formulation of labor skill, in that it does not allow quantity to be substituted for quality within a single production chain. For example, it assumes that it is impossible to substitute two mediocre advertising copywriters, chefs, or quarterbacks for one good one.[2] The particular functional form set forth in this section exhibits increasing returns to the skill of the workforce taken as a whole, but as Section III discusses, much of the analysis generalizes to symmetric production functions with a positive cross derivative in worker skill.

It is possible to solve for a competitive equilibrium—defined as an assignment of workers to firms, a set of wage rates, $w(q)$, and a rental rate r, such that firms maximize profits and the market clears for capital and for workers of all skill levels.

Firms facing a wage schedule, $w(q)$, and a rental rate, r, choose a level of capital, k, and the skill of each worker, q_i, to maximize revenue minus cost:

$$\max_{k, \{q_i\}} k^\alpha (\Pi_{i=1}^n q_i)\, nB - \sum_{i=1}^n w(q_i) - rk. \tag{2}$$

---

[2] This production function is similar to that in Stinchcombe and Harris [1969].

The first-order condition associated with each of the q_i is

$$\frac{dw(q_i)}{dq_i} = \frac{dy}{dq_i} = (\Pi_{j \neq i} q_j) \, nBk^\alpha. \tag{3}$$

Thus, the increase in output a firm obtains by replacing one worker with a slightly higher skill worker while leaving the skill of its other workers unchanged must equal the increase in its wage bill necessary to pay the higher skill worker. The marginal product of skill, dy/dq_i, must equal the marginal cost of skill, $dw(q_i)/dq_i$, or else the firm would prefer to employ either lower or higher skill workers.

The search for equilibria can be restricted to those allocations of workers to firms in which all workers employed by any single firm have the same q. This is because the derivative of the marginal product of skill for the ith worker with respect to the skill of the other workers is positive:

$$\frac{d^2y}{dq_i d(\Pi_{j \neq i} q_j)} = nBk^\alpha > 0. \tag{4}$$

This positive cross derivative means that firms with high q workers in the first $n - 1$ tasks place the highest value on having high-skill workers in the nth task, so they bid the most for these workers. Thus, in equilibrium, workers of the same skill are matched together in firms, just as marriage partners of similar quality are matched together in Becker's [1981] marriage model.[3] For now I assume perfect matching; Section II examines imperfect matching.

Given that workers of the same skill are matched together, $q_j = q_i$ for all j and the first-order condition on q can be rewritten as

$$\frac{dw}{dq} = q^{n-1} nBk^\alpha. \tag{5}$$

The first-order condition on capital, $\alpha k^{\alpha-1} q^n nB = r$, implies that

$$k = \left(\frac{\alpha q^n nB}{r} \right)^{1/(1-\alpha)}. \tag{6}$$

It is straightforward to show that payments to capital are αy. The equilibrium rental rate on k, r, will be that which equates the supply of capital, k^*, with the demand, which is given by summing up the capital demanded by the firms hiring all the different skill levels of workers, from zero to one. Since the density of firms hiring workers of a particular

---

[3] Becker [1981, p. 72] reproduces a formal proof by William Brock which shows that a positive cross derivative implies positive assortative matching. See also Sattinger [1975].

skill is $1/n$ times the density of workers of that skill level, this implies that

$$\int_0^1 \left(\frac{\alpha q^n nB}{r} \right)^{1/(1-\alpha)} \frac{1}{n} \, \partial \phi(q) = k^*. \tag{7}$$

Thus, $r = \alpha Bn^\alpha [\int_0^1 q^{n/(1-\alpha)} \partial \phi(q)/R^*]^{1-\alpha}$.

(Alternatively, in an open economy, r would be fixed, and k^* would be the equilibrium level of capital.) The first-order condition on q, (5), can be rewritten by substituting in the value of k from equation (6):

$$\frac{dw}{dq} = nq^{n-1} B \left(\frac{\alpha q^n nB}{r} \right)^{\alpha/(1-\alpha)}. \tag{8}$$

Integrating generates the set of wage schedules that allows firms hiring workers of any single level of skill to satisfy this first-order condition:

$$w(q) = (1 - \alpha)(q^n B)^{1/(1-\alpha)} \left(\frac{\alpha n}{r} \right)^{\alpha/(1-\alpha)} + c, \tag{9}$$

or equivalently,

$$w(q) = (1 - \alpha)q^n Bk^\alpha + c. \tag{10}$$

The constant of integration, c, represents the wage of a worker of skill zero, who never performs a task successfully. Multiplying the wage schedule by n, the number of workers, shows that the total wage bill is $(1 - \alpha)Y + nc$. Since payments to capital are αY, the zero profit condition implies that the constant of integration must equal zero.

Since profits are zero for all firms given the wage schedule $w(q)$, firms are indifferent as to the skill level of their workers as long as their labor force is of homogenous skill. Equilibrium holds when firms demand the number of workers of each skill available in the population. Since this is a well-behaved problem, this competitive equilibrium is optimal and unique up to reassignments of workers of equal skill.

I.2. APPLICATIONS TO DEVELOPMENT AND TO LABOR MARKETS

O-ring production functions are consistent with a series of stylized facts in development and labor economics. While each of these stylized facts may be due to a variety of different factors, taken together, they suggest that O-ring production functions are empirically relevant.

1. Wage and productivity differentials between rich and poor countries are enormous.

According to the World Bank [1990], United States GDP per capita is twenty times that of Bangladesh using purchasing-power-parity adjusted figures, and more than 100 times that of Bangladesh using exchange rate valuations, which presumably indicate ability to produce tradable goods. Either way, the disparity is enormous. Differences in physical capital have been used to explain international income differences, but as Lucas [1990] argues, physical capital should be mobile given large enough incentives. Lucas calculates that if the income difference between the United States and India were due to differences in physical capital alone, the marginal product of capital in India would be 58 times that of the United States.

Worker quality could be another potential source of differences in income levels. Barro [1991] and Mankiw, Romer, and Weil [1992] find that human capital is an important factor in economic growth. Moreover, microeconomic studies find astonishingly large differences between countries in worker productivity: Clark [1987] examines early twentieth century textile mills and finds that "... one New England cotton textile operative performed as much work as 1.5 British, 2.3 German, and nearly 6 Greek, Japanese, Indian, or Chinese workers." Noting that the same equipment was used worldwide, Clark rules out differences in technology and capital intensity as causes of these productivity differences, and points to differences in "personal efficiency" between workers in different countries. However, even if some national differences in worker skill were plausible, it would be difficult to understand what could cause differences of these magnitudes.

An O-ring production function provides a mechanism through which small differences in worker skill create large differences in productivity and wages. As is clear from equation (9), under this production function, equilibrium wages are homogenous of degree $n/(1-\alpha)$ in q, so small differences in worker skill create large differences in output and wages. Moreover, in equilibrium more physical capital is used with higher skill workers, thus helping answer Lucas' question about why capital does not flow from rich to poor countries. Intuitively, higher skill workers are less likely to make mistakes that waste the rental value of capital, and it is therefore optimal for them to use more capital.

2. Firms hire workers of different skill and produce different quality products.

In many industries different firms hire different qualities of workers. Restaurants, for example, come in a range of quality levels. McDonald's does not hire famous chefs, and Maxim's does not hire teenage waiters. Charlie Parker and Dizzy Gillespie work together, and so do Donny and Marie Osmond. For tradable goods this division is often international, creating implications for both development and labor markets. Italy, Taiwan, and China all export bicycles. Perhaps part of what allows Italian companies to compete with cheaper Chinese labor is substitution of cheaper Italian capital. But an argument similar to Lucas' indicates that tremendous differences in the cost of capital would be needed to equalize production costs between Italy and China. Systematic differences in product quality, associated with differences in the skill of the employees, are a more plausible explanation of why Italian bicycle manufacturers can compete with their Chinese counterparts.

3. There is a positive correlation among the wages of workers in different occupations within enterprises.

Secretaries working for investment banks or major law firms earn more than secretaries working in retail banks or local law offices.[4] Pressures for intrafirm equity and industry rents have been suggested as explanations; but O-ring production functions provide another explanation, since they imply that the highest q secretaries will work with the highest q lawyers and bankers.

4. Firms only offer jobs to some workers rather than paying all workers their estimated marginal product.

Under a conventional production function, a construction firm, for example, could hire bricklayers of any skill and pay according to estimated future output. Under an O-ring production function, the firm needs bricklayers whose skill matches that of its carpenters, electricians, and plumbers. The firm will therefore be willing to expend resources interviewing a number of employees for a single position to find a bricklayer of the right skill. Although the firm could offer to hire a bricklayer of inappropriate skill, this would be pointless since the wage would be far from what the worker could earn elsewhere, and might even be negative. O-ring production functions thus help provide a rationale for job search theories of unemployment, such as Jovanovic [1979], in which workers have different productivity at different firms.

5. Income distribution is skewed to the right.

The model fits the distribution of income, at least to the extent that one believes fundamental parameters are distributed symmetrically. Under the model, if q is distributed symmetrically, y will be skewed to the right, and log y will be symmetric.[5] In fact, the distribution of income is skewed to the right, both within and between countries. The log of income is distributed approximately symmetrically.

I.3. SEQUENTIAL PRODUCTION

So far, I have assumed that all tasks are performed simultaneously. In fact, some production processes consist of several stages, undertaken with a technology that allows workers to detect mistakes and avoid wasting further work on defective items. For example, one of Rembrandt's assistants would prepare the canvas, another would paint in most of a figure, and finally, if that were acceptable, Rembrandt would paint the face and hands. As Sobel [1992] has demonstrated in a similar framework, in such processes the highest q workers are allocated to the later stages of production in equilibrium since mistakes there destroy higher valued inputs than in earlier stages. This is similar to hierarchy models, in that one higher stage worker works with more than one lower stage worker.

---

[4]See Katz and Summers [1989, Table III] for evidence that janitors and secretaries earn more in industries where the average wage is higher.

[5]I am grateful to Sherwin Rosen for pointing this out to me.

To see this more formally, assume that several stages of production are needed to transform some free, unproduced primary good into a final good. Each stage requires one unit of labor and one unit of output from the previous stage of production. All stages of production could be conducted within a single firm, or each stage could be conducted in a separate firm. To simplify, I shall henceforth assume that $\alpha = 0$, so capital does not enter the production function. A worker of skill q successfully transforms a unit of the $i-1$st stage good into the ith stage good with probability q and makes a mistake that destroys the product with probability $1 - q$.[6] Let p_i denote the price of the good at the ith stage of production. Expected profits for a firm in the ith stage of production employing one worker of skill q_i and using one unit of the $i-1$st good as an input are $q_i p_i - p_{i-1} - w(q_i)$. In equilibrium firms earn zero profits, and therefore $q_i p_i - p_{i-1} - w(q_i) = 0$. This implies that $w(q_i) = q_i p_i - p_{i-1}$, and since $p_i > p_j$ for $i > j$ the equilibrium wage schedule is steeper in q at later stages of production.

Suppose that there were an equilibrium allocation of workers to tasks in which $q_i < q_j$ for $i > j$, that is, in which a higher stage of production had a lower skill worker. Since $i > j$, $p_i > p_j$. Given the wage schedule derived earlier, if the two workers switched jobs, their total income would change by $(p_i - p_j)(q_j - q_i)$. Since both these terms are positive, total income increases if the workers switch jobs, and hence the allocation of workers to tasks is not an equilibrium. Hence in equilibrium, higher q workers must be allocated to later stages of production.

This variant of the production function is consistent with the following two stylized facts.

6. Poor countries have higher shares of primary production in GNP.

7. Workers are paid more in industries with high value inputs.

Under sequential production, countries with high-skill workers specialize in products that require expensive intermediate goods, and countries with low-skill workers specialize in primary production. In fact, poor countries have a consistently high share of agriculture and primary production in GNP, even when their land endowments are small. El Salvador, for example, has only one-twelfth of Canada's endowment of arable land per capita, yet its share of agriculture in GDP is 19 percent, compared with 3 percent in Canada. Since Salvadorans are poorer, it is not surprising that they have a larger share of food in consumption, but given the possibility of trade, it is not clear why they have a larger share of agriculture in production. Although other explanations, such as low human capital intensity in agriculture, have been posited, the sequential production model may provide part of the explanation of why poor countries concentrate on primary production. Kwon [1992] finds that productivity in the former Soviet Union lagged the most relative to the United States in final and intermediate goods industries

---

[6] Unlike the rest of the paper, this variant of the production function assumes that workers perform their task either perfectly or so badly that the product is worthless and cannot be used in further stages of production.

and was closest to United States levels in primary goods industries. (Agriculture was an exception, but this may have been due to worker monitoring problems that make agriculture highly unsuited to state ownership.) Within countries, sequential production helps explain why automobile workers, diamond cutters, and others who work with high value inputs are highly paid.

In addition to fitting the stylized facts above, O-ring production functions increase the quantitative importance of efficiency wages, bottlenecks, and trade restrictions. O-ring production functions strengthen efficiency wage effects because they magnify the loss from shirking. They increase the impact of bottlenecks not only directly, but also indirectly, through their impact on incentives to invest in skill. To see this, assume, for example, that n tasks are required to produce a good, and, taking q as task-specific, consider the effect of halving the q of all the economy's workers in two tasks, say machine maintenance and accounting. Assignments of workers to firms do not change, because the highest q people in the last two tasks are still matched with the highest q people in the first $n - 2$ tasks. Production, however, falls by 75 percent. Moreover, the marginal product of quality, dw/dq_i, falls by 75 percent in the other $n - 2$ sectors and hence so does the incentive to invest in q (through education, for example). As workers in these sectors reduce their investment in skill, they further reduce the level of q in the economy, and thus the incentive to accumulate skill.

Although bottlenecks generate high returns to the missing skills, the market may not remove bottlenecks caused by low quality inputs of public goods such as police protection, electricity and water, or communication and transportation infrastructure. More generally, low domestic capacity in sectors where trade is costly or impossible can create bottlenecks. As Clague [1991a, 1991b] points out, enterprises may become vertically integrated to avoid using unreliable inputs from other parts of the economy. Thus, Chinese factories provide schools and housing for their workers, and western multinationals working in developing countries import some requirements and set up enclave economies to provide others. For example, in Russia, McDonald's could not buy the quality of beef it needed domestically, was not allowed to import it, and therefore arranged its own beef production. However, in becoming vertically integrated, firms are prone to a breakdown anywhere along a longer production chain.

The current view in development economics is that trade restrictions cause large welfare losses, rather than the proverbial small Harberger triangles. O-Ring production functions provide support for this view, since they indicate that trade restrictions, especially quantitative restrictions, can paralyze production by preventing bottleneck sectors from being bypassed.

1.4. Equilibrium Choice of Technology

So far, I have taken n, the number of tasks, as technologically fixed, but the analysis can be generalized to allow firms to choose among technologies with different n. A VCR manufacturer could build anything from a simple $150 VCR player to an $800 machine with timer, remote control, and automatic commercial cutting. A farmer could scatter seeds and wait for them to grow or could build terraces, dig irrigation ditches, grow seedlings in a nursery, apply fertilizer to his fields, and hedge risks on the futures market. More fundamentally, firms can choose whether to produce complex products such as aircraft, or simpler products, such as textiles. To simplify, I assume that all tasks require the same amount of labor and define $B(n)$ as the value of output per task if all tasks are performed perfectly. I assume that if all tasks are performed correctly there are benefits to using more complex techology, at least over some range, but that these benefits diminish as technology becomes more complex, so that $B'(0) > 0$ and $B''(n) < 0$.[7]

By increasing n, I do not mean subdividing existing tasks through Smithian division of labor: there is no reason to assume that the chance of a mistake increases if one worker puts on the bolt and another puts on the nut. Rather, increasing n means switching to different production techniques or products in which there are more potential areas for mistakes that affect the value of the product as a whole. Thus, making a car involves more tasks than making a bicycle, because there are more things that can go wrong. It is more difficult to make cardinal statements about the number of tasks. For example, a waiter can be thought of as performing a single task with a q of 0.97, or three tasks—taking—the order, serving the food, and collecting the check—each with a q of approximately 0.99.

In choosing the technology, firms face the problem:

$$\max_{n, \{q_i\}} (\Pi_{i=1}^{n} q_i)\, nB(n) - \sum_{i=1}^{n} w(q_i). \tag{11}$$

In equilibrium each firm must satisfy a first-order condition for optimal choice of n and each of the q_i. Since the first-order condition on choice of the q_i is the same as in subsection I.1, the search for equilibria can again be restricted to allocations of workers to firms in which workers of the same skill are matched together, and the firm's problem can be written as

$$\max_{n, q} q^n nB(n) - nw(q). \tag{12}$$

The first-order condition on choice of n is therefore

$$q^n B(n) - w(q) + n[\log(q)q^n B(n) + B'(n)q^n] = 0. \tag{13}$$

The first-order condition on q implies that $w(q) = q^n B(n)$, as in subsection I.1. Substituting for $w(q)$ and simplifying,

$$-\log(q) = B'(n)/B(n). \tag{14}$$

---

[7] It is possible to replicate the argument below with n restricted to integers, using integer analogues of the assumptions that $B'(0) > 0$ and $B''(n) < 0$.

The left-hand side declines monotonically in q. Since $B'(0) > 0$ and $B''(n) < 0$, the right-hand side declines monotonically in n as long as $B'(n) > 0$. Therefore, n is an implicit function of q with $n'(q) > 0$. Hence, firms producing products or using technologies requiring high n will employ high q workers. Intuitively, mistakes are more costly to firms with high n, so they place higher value on skilled workers, and are allocated these workers in equilibrium.

In a more general model in which the products of technologies with different n were imperfect substitutes, the assignment of a worker to a technology would depend not only on his own q, but also on the distribution of q in the economy. For example, if the highest q workers were assigned to the aircraft industry and a particular country had a large supply of high q workers, it might have a higher cutoff level of q above which people worked in the aircraft industry.

The relationship between n and q fits the next stylized fact.

8. Rich countries specialize in complicated products.

The prediction that countries with high q will use technologies requiring more tasks fits the pattern of international specialization in which rich countries specialize in complicated products, such as aircraft, and poor countries produce simpler products such as textiles. One measure of product complexity is the number of different inputs, and Clague [1991a, 1991b] finds that poor countries are relatively less efficient in industries with a large number of input sectors and a high dispersion of input shares, as measured by the U.S. input-output table.

Strictly speaking, n refers to the number of tasks rather than the number of workers. In the absence of a fully worked out theory of the firm, it is difficult to make strong statements about the relationship between a firm and a production process. Nonetheless, if workers improve their efficiency by specializing in particular tasks and if there are a span of control problems in replicating a production process indefinitely and transaction cost problems in dividing it up arbitrarily, then there is likely to be a positive correlation between the number of tasks and the number of workers. Given such a positive correlation, the model is consistent with the following stylized facts.

9. Firms are larger in rich countries.

10. Firm size and wages are positively correlated.

The model predicts that firms in poorer countries will choose lower n technologies, and if there is a correlation between n and firm size, this implies that firms will be smaller in poorer countries. In fact, firms consisting of a single household predominate in most poor countries. This reflects not only the higher share of agriculture in developing countries, but also the structure of firms within sectors. In food retailing, for example, firms in developing countries typically consist of a single person or household, whereas rich countries have giant supermarket chains with specialized cashiers, stockers, truckers, and advertising copywriters. Clague [1991a, 1991b] finds that rich countries have higher relative efficiency in industries with more employees per firm. Within countries, the model's implication that higher n firms will employ higher q workers matches the empirical correlations between firm size and observable indicators of worker quality, and between firms size and wages, documented by Brown and Medoff [1989], among others.

II. Endogenizing Skill under Imperfect Information

Section I took q as exogenous and argued that small differences in q can have important effects. This section endogenizes skill as the product of investment in education or effort, e, in order to model possible sources of skill differences. If workers can match perfectly—that is, if workers can be matched with others of similar skill no matter what their choice of skill—they will face the wage schedule derived in Section I, and will therefore choose skill optimally.[8] As mentioned above, workers in different countries might choose different q due to differences in education systems, tax policies, or nontradable bottleneck sectors that affect incentives to invest in education. Under O-ring production functions output is a convex function of q, so the accumulation problems faced by workers may be nonconvex even if q is a concave function of education. As others have shown, if capital markets are imperfect, nonconvex accumulation problems can lead to multiple equilibria in levels of human capital [Dechert and Nishimura, 1983], and to Kuznets curves [Galor and Zeira, 1989]. While interesting dynamics can thus arise even under perfect matching, this paper focuses on incentives for accumulation of human capital when workers are imperfectly matched, and hence do not face the wage schedule of Section I, and need not choose the socially optimal e. It first shows that imperfect matching due to limited availability of workers of certain skill levels can lead to the formulation of specialized cities that will be especially attractive to people with high human capital. It

---

[8]With a continuum of workers and perfectly observable skill, the wage schedule derived in Section I is the unique competitive equilibrium, and it will induce optimal investment in education. However, there could, hypothetically, be additional, suboptimal, Nash equilibria and strategic complementarity in selection among these equilibria. The additional equilibria arise because if all workers chose the same level of skill there would be missing markets for other skill levels. Workers considering choosing skill levels other than the one chosen by all other agents would therefore face lower than competitive equilibrium wages, and hence the economy could coordinate on a suboptimal level of skill (zero, for example). However, I believe that it is unrealistic to focus on these additional equilibria. Doing so is analogous to claiming that there could be an equilibrium in which neither of two complementary goods is produced due to the absence of the other good. These equilibria are fragile because a small number of people could form a self-enforcing agreement to choose the optimal level of education. Moreover, if there were a small error term creating heterogeneity in skill, workers over a range of skill levels would find identical partners and therefore receive the competitive equilibrium wage schedule. Assuming that the net payoff to education was concave under the competitive equilibrium wage schedule, workers would always receive a higher payoff by choosing a level of education slightly closer to the competitive equilibrium than that chosen by other agents, and this would eliminate any suboptimal equilibria.

then shows that imperfect matching due to imperfect observability of skill leads to underinvestment in skill, strategic complementarity in that investment, and the possibility of multiple equilibria.

In a finite population, in which skill is determined by education and a random error term with a continuous distribution, workers will not be able to match perfectly. Instead they will match in rank order of skill, with the division of a firm's output among its heterogeneous workers determined by a complex bargaining problem. Since skill is often industry- and task-specific, large populations may be needed for people to find close matches in their field. Fred Astaire was born in Omaha, Nebraska; Ginger Rogers, in Independence, Missouri. They had to go to New York to meet each other. Matching thus creates incentives for people to cluster in cities. If there are congestion costs, it may be efficient for tradable sectors to concentrate in different cities: autos in Detroit, fashion in Milan, country music in Nashville.

Under imperfect matching, the marginal product of skill, $dw/dq_i = E(\Pi_{j \neq i} q_j)$, increases with population. With a larger population the coworkers' skills are likely to be closer together, and thus the expectation of this product will be greater.[9] Thus, technological advances that allow matching between different regions or political or cultural changes that allow matching between different groups will increase not only production, but also incentives to invest in human capital. The greater return to q in areas with high population may help explain why educated people are more likely to migrate from rural areas to cities.

One problem with using differences in worker skill as an explanation of international income differences is that income differences between countries are large relative to those within countries, and it is unclear why skill differences between countries would be large relative to differences within countries. Imperfect matching provides a partial explanation, since it reduces variation in income within countries relative to variation in average income between countries. To see this, assume that q is a function of education and that choice of education depends both on individual-specific factors, such as tastes for education, and country-specific factors, such as taxes on labor income. Further, assume that the distribution of q within each country due to individual-specific factors is thicker in the center than in the tails. Agents then have an incentive to choose a level of investment in education that puts them nearer the center of the distribution, where closer matches are available. This process is self-reinforcing, because as agents choose levels of education that put them near the center of the distribution the tails become even thinner.

Imperfect information about skill is another, probably more important, cause of imperfect matching. Below, I argue that imperfect information leads to underinvestment in skill and to strategic complementarity in this investment. Intuitively, it is more

---

[9]This assumes that each worker has more than one coworker, or equivalently, that firms consist of three or more workers.

valuable to be a high-skill worker if one has high-skill coworkers, and under imperfect matching, the expected skill of one's coworkers increases in the level of education chosen by the rest of the population. Hence each worker has more incentive to choose a high level of education if other workers choose a high level of education. This creates multiplier effects: for example, a small education subsidy can create large differences in q and production. Sufficiently strong strategic complementarity creates multiple equilibria in investment in skill. To see these effects more formally, suppose that the production technology is

$$Y = n\Pi^n_{i=1}q_i, \tag{15}$$

where n is fixed, and there is a stochastic education technology such that skill q depends on e, education or effort,

$$\log(q) = \log[g(e)] + \epsilon \qquad \epsilon \sim N(0, \sigma^2_\epsilon), \tag{16}$$

where

$$g' > 0 \qquad g'' < 0 \qquad g'(0) = \infty \qquad g(e) > 0 \qquad g(\infty) = 1. \tag{17}$$

Skill is observed (even by the worker himself) only through a test score, t, which is a stochastic function of true skill.

$$\log t = \log q + \mu \qquad \mu \sim N(0, \sigma^2_\mu) \qquad \text{cov}(\mu, \epsilon) = 0. \tag{18}$$

The logarithmic form for the errors is chosen so that q takes on only positive values.[10] The error terms ϵ and μ correspond to random variation in workers' ability to absorb education and to translate their skill into test scores, respectively.

There are two periods. In the first, risk-neutral workers choose a level of education and obtain realizations of q, their true skill, and t, their test score. In the second, risk-neutral firms match together workers with the same test score, and pay them according to their expected productivity given their test score. Normalizing the cost of a unit of education to one, the worker's payoff V is his wage minus his education.

The analysis below follows Bulow, Geanakoplos, and Klemperer [1985] and Cooper and John [1988]. I examine only pure strategy symmetric Nash equilibria (SNE), in which all agents choose a level of education, e, which makes it optimal for each agent to choose e as his level of education. Thus, at an SNE $V_1(e, e) = 0$, where V is the payoff, the first argument is the agent's level of education, and the second argument is the level of education chosen by the other agents, who are potential coworkers.

The optimal e depends on the wage schedule, which in turn depends on the level of education chosen by all other workers in the economy, $\bar{e}$. Deriving the wage schedule

---

[10]This formulation allows for $q > 1$ if people receive a favorable realization of ϵ. This departs from the interpretation of q as reflecting the percentage of maximum value retained, but does not otherwise affect the analysis.

requires solving a signal extraction problem to find the conditional expectation of a worker's skill given his test score and the test scores of other agents in the economy.

In equilibrium, all agents choose the effort level $\bar{e}$ and hence the expectation of $\log(q)$ and $\log(t)$ for all agents is $\log(\bar{q})$, where $\bar{q}$ is defined as $q(\bar{e})$. Firms can deduce $\bar{e}$ and thus $\bar{q}$ by observing the distribution of all agents' test scores. Since $\log(q) = \log(\bar{q}) + \epsilon$ and $\log(t) = \log(\bar{q}) + \epsilon + \mu$, and ϵ and μ are independent normals, the conditional distribution of $\log q$ for an agent with test score t given $\bar{q}$ is

$$\log q \,|\, t, \bar{q} \sim N\left(\theta \log t + (1 - \theta) \log \bar{q}, \frac{\sigma_\epsilon^2 \sigma_\mu^2}{\sigma_\epsilon^2 + \sigma_\mu^2} \right), \tag{19}$$

where θ is the share of the variance in the test score due to variance in true ability,

$$\theta \equiv \sigma_\epsilon^2 / (\sigma_\epsilon^2 + \sigma_\mu^2). \tag{20}$$

Thus, if there is no testing error ($\sigma_\mu^2 = 0$), the expected skill equals the test score, whereas if there is no variation in ability to absorb education ($\sigma_\epsilon^2 = 0$), the expected skill is the average level of skill, $\bar{q}$.

Given the conditional distribution of $\log(q)$ for a single worker with test score t, a firm hiring workers of test score t has a conditional distribution of log output of

$$\log(n\Pi_{i=1}^n q_i) \,|\, t, \bar{q} \sim N\left[\log n + n(\theta \log t + (1 - \theta)\log \bar{q}), n \frac{\sigma_\epsilon^2 \sigma_\mu^2}{\sigma_\epsilon^2 + \sigma_\mu^2} \right]. \tag{21}$$

The conditional expectation of output is therefore

$$E(n\Pi_{i=1}^n q_i) \,|\, t, \bar{q} = n \exp[n(\theta \log t + (1 - \theta)\log \bar{q} + \log A)]. \tag{22}$$

where A is the constant

$$A \equiv \exp\left[\frac{1}{2} \frac{\sigma_\epsilon^2 \sigma_\mu^2}{\sigma_\epsilon^2 + \sigma_\mu^2} \right]. \tag{23}$$

This simplifies to

$$E(n\Pi_{i=1}^n q_i) \,|\, t, \bar{q} = nt^n \bar{q}^{n\theta(1-\theta)} A^n. \tag{24}$$

By the zero profit condition, the wage is $1/n$ times the expected product:

$$w(t, \bar{q}) = t^{n\theta} \bar{q}^{n(1-\theta)} A^n. \tag{25}$$

For $0 < \theta < 1$, each agent's wage is increasing not only in his own test score but also in $\bar{q}$, the skill level chosen by other agents. (Note that in the special case of no measurement error, both θ and A equal one, and the formula for the wage is the same as that derived in Section I under perfect matching.)

The marginal product of education increases with the education of other agents. The payoff V is the wage minus the cost of education:

$$V(e, \bar{e}) = [g(e) \exp(\epsilon + \mu)]^{n\theta} g(\bar{e})^{n(1-\theta)} A^n - e. \tag{26}$$

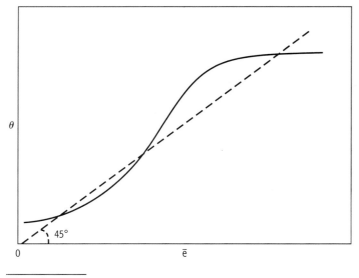

Figure 1
Optimal e as $f(\bar{e})$

Thus, for any realizations of ϵ and μ, the cross derivative of the payoff with respect to own education and others' education will be positive:

$$V_{12} = n\theta[g(e)]^{n\theta-1}g'(e)[\exp(\epsilon + \mu)]^{n\theta}n(1 - \theta)g(\bar{e})^{n(1-\theta)-1}g'(\bar{e})A^n > 0; \qquad (27)$$

and hence there is strategic complementarity. Agents increase their education in response to increases in education by other agents.[11]

Figure 1 shows the optimal e as a function of the level of $\bar{e}$ chosen by the other agents. Since $g(e) > 0$ and $g'(0) = \infty$, zero education can never be optimal and since $g(e)$ is bounded, the optimal e is bounded. SNE occur where the reaction function crosses the 45 degree line. Cooper and John show that a necessary condition for multiple equilibria is that the slope of the reaction function, ρ, be greater than one at some point, and a sufficient condition is that ρ be greater than one at an SNE. ρ is given by

$$\rho = -\frac{V_{12}(e, e)}{V_{11}(e, e)} = -\frac{g(e)g'(e)n(1 - \theta)g'(\bar{e})}{[(n\theta - 1)g'(e)^2 + gb(e)g''(e)]g(\bar{e})}. \qquad (28)$$

---

[11]Cooper and John [1988] assume that $V_{11} < 0$. Although this game is not necessarily globally concave in own education, their analysis still applies, since the optimal choice of e must lie in a region where $V_{11} < 0$.

At an SNE, $e = \bar{e}$, so a sufficient condition for multiple equilibria is that at an SNE,

$$\rho \equiv \frac{g'(e)^2 n(1 - \theta)}{(1 - n\theta)g'(e)^2 - gb(e)g''(e)} > 1. \qquad (29)$$

For this to hold, the denominator must be positive and smaller in absolute value than the numerator. This implies that

$$\theta < \frac{g'(e)^2 - g(e)g''(e)}{ng'(e)^2} < 1. \qquad (30)$$

These inequalities are equivalent to the conditions under which $V_{11} < 0$, but $V_{11} > 0$ under perfect matching. Examination of Figure 1 shows that ρ must be greater than one at some SNE if there are multiple equilibria, and hence multiple equilibria are impossible if output is a globally concave function of education under perfect matching. Note also that multiple equilibria are more likely the lesser θ, the variation in true ability relative to the variation in test scores.

Since the game has positive spillovers, all SNE will be inefficient, and there will exist some level of education subsidy that improves welfare. Since there is strategic complementarity, these education subsidies will have multiplier effects. They will directly lead people to choose higher e, and this will indirectly lead people to further increase their e. Thus, small differences between countries in exogenous multiplier variables, such as tax rates, the quality of the education system, or bottlenecks, can cause large differences in q between countries. If there are multiple equilibria, variance in q between countries could be entirely endogenous. Multiple equilibria may also help explain income differences between ethnic groups within countries. If employers think an ethnic group is in a low equilibrium, they will pay a lower wage for any test score and a lower increment in the wage for any increment in the test score. Hence workers in the group will choose a lower e, validating the employers' expectations. This model of self-fulfilling statistical discrimination among microeconomically identical agents is similar to Arrow [1973] and Coate and Loury [1991], but unlike those models, which impose non-convexity on the problem by restricting agents to one of two skill levels, qualified or unqualified, this model allows workers to take a continuum of different skill levels.

While it is not clear that this model explains a significant portion of racial discrimination in the United States, it is worth noting that historically white workers have had a higher return to education than black workers [Card and Krueger, 1992], as would be the case in the model if whites were in a higher equilibrium. Although the match with the model is far from precise, one might think that years of education completed might serve as an observable signal of how much one has learned in school, similar to the test score in the model. (Years of education would not correspond to e in the model, since e cannot be directly observed.) Under the model, legal requirements to pay black and white workers with similar observable test scores the same amount would switch both groups into the same equilibria, at least if the legal requirements were viewed as a permanent change. In fact, there is evidence that returns to education for blacks have increased since the civil rights laws of the 1960s and that blacks' education has increased accordingly [Card and Krueger, 1992]. Although Card and Krueger attribute much of the increase in returns to education for blacks to improvements in the quality of segregated black schools in the South, these improvements do not fully explain the increase, and Donahue and Heckman [1991] argue that federal policy played an important role in the 1960s. They note that this occurred despite relatively low expenditure on enforcement, as would be consistent with the existence of multiple equilibria.

III. GENERALIZATIONS AND EXTENSIONS

The matching analysis of Section I generalizes to symmetric production functions in worker skill as long as the cross derivative of output in the skill of different workers is positive. Positive cross derivatives could arise for many reasons. For example, doctors, lawyers, and academics often match with similar skill coworkers in hospitals, law firms, and universities. This may be due to learning spillovers within the firm in which high quality workers are better able to teach and learn from their coworkers.

The matching analysis and its implications thus apply to production functions that are homogeneous of degree less than one, such as

$$Y = (\Pi_{i=1}^{n} q_i)^{\psi} \qquad 0 < \psi < \frac{1}{n}. \tag{31}$$

The principal differences under production functions with decreasing returns to the skill of the workforce taken as a whole are that given differences in q create smaller rather than larger differences in output and wages; a symmetric distribution of skill leads to a distribution of income that is skewed to the left rather than to the right; and the human capital accumulation problem faced by workers is globally concave. Although strategic complementarity still arises with a decreasing returns production function under imperfect information, multiple equilibria cannot arise, since ρ can never be greater than one at an SNE if the wage is concave in e under perfect matching. This paper has concentrated on the increasing returns case, but whether decreasing or increasing returns is a more appropriate assumption is an empirical question, which presumably has different answers in different industries.

Kremer and Maskin [1993] extend the analysis to production functions with negative cross derivatives and to asymmetric production functions. Negative cross derivatives could arise, for example, if two workers were assigned to a critical task, like flying an airplane, with one serving as a backup in case the other failed to perform the task. In this case, it is optimal to match the highest and lowest skill workers together. The techniques used in Section I can be adapted to solve for equilibrium wages. Since agents match with others of different skill, each agent's wage depends on the distribution of q in the population, rather than simply on his own q. Current research focuses on endogenizing the number of workers assigned to a task, which may help bridge the gap between the efficiency units treatment of labor skill, in which quantity can simply be substituted for quality, and the O-ring approach, in which there are a fixed number of workers per task in a given production line.

A previous version of this paper (available from the author) solves for equilibrium wage schedules and assignment of workers to tasks under an asymmetric production function in which there are two types of tasks: managerial and professional tasks which are subject to multiplicative quality interaction, and unskilled tasks in which worker skill is not important. In equilibrium, agents become workers below some cutoff level of skill and managers above it. The more highly skilled managers are matched with higher quality management teams and, as in Rosen [1981] and Lucas [1978], supervise more unskilled workers. Kremer and Maskin [1993] examine a more general asymmetric production function, in which output is sensitive to the skill of all types of workers, but in different degrees. For example, the output of an orchestra might be more sensitive to the skill of the violinist than of the cellist. If workers choose their occupation before their skill is determined, the techniques of Section I can be used to solve for equilibrium wage schedules and assignment of workers to firms. The general equilibrium problem of simultaneously assigning agents to occupations and firms given their skill is more difficult. Depending on the distribution of skill, it may be optimal either for agents of similar skill to match together in firms or for agents of similar skill to take the same occupation in different firms. For example, the second highest skill musician will in some cases become a cellist with the best orchestra and in others a violinist with the second best orchestra.

In summary, the framework used in this paper readily generalizes to symmetric production functions in which quantity cannot be substituted for quality and there is a positive cross derivative in worker skill. Kremer and Maskin [1993] extend the approach to production functions with negative cross derivatives in worker skill and to asymmetric production functions.

IV. Conclusion

People in business talk about quality all the time. "Quality is Job One," "America just doesn't produce quality products anymore," "Quality Control"—all these are phrases associated with businesspeople, not economists. This paper makes a stab at modeling quality.

The paper proposes an O-ring production function in which quantity cannot be substituted for quality, shows that under this production function workers of similar skill will be matched together, and derives an equilibrium schedule of wages as a function of worker skill. Under this production function, small differences in worker skill lead to large differences in wages and output, so wage and productivity differentials between countries with different skill levels are enormous. The production function implies that workers will be sorted by quality so there will be a positive correlation among the wages of workers in different occupations within the same firm, and that firms will offer jobs to only some workers rather than paying all workers their estimated marginal product.

If tasks are performed sequentially, high-skill workers will be allocated to later stages of production. Poor countries will therefore have higher shares of primary production in GNP, and workers will be paid more in industries with high value inputs. If firms can choose among technologies with different numbers of tasks, the highest skill workers will use the highest n technology. This is consistent with the tendency of rich countries to specialize in complicated products, and, given a correlation between n and firm size, with the larger average firm size in rich countries and the positive correlation between firm size and wages within countries. These predictions of the model match stylized facts about the world, and although each of these facts may be due to a variety of causes, together they suggest that O-ring production functions are empirically relevant.

Imperfect matching of workers due to imperfect information about worker skill leads to positive spillovers and strategic complementarity in investment in human capital. Thus, subsidies to investment in human capital may be Pareto optimal. Small differences between countries in such subsidies or in exogenous factors such as geography or the quality of the educational system lead to multiplier effects that create large differences in worker skill. If strategic complementarity is sufficiently strong, microeconomically identical nations or groups within nations could settle into equilibria with different levels of human capital.

The matching results and their implications apply to a general symmetric production function in which quantity cannot be substituted for quality, as long as there is a positive cross derivative in worker skill. Current research focuses on adapting these techniques to solve for equilibrium wages and assignment of workers to firms under production functions with negative cross derivatives and under asymmetric production functions.

REFERENCES

Arrow, K., "The Theory of Discrimination," in O. Ashenfelter and A. Rees, eds., *Discrimination in Labor Markets* (Princeton, NJ: Princeton University Press, 1973).

Barro, Robert, "Economic Growth in a Cross Section of Countries," *Quarterly Journal of Economics*, CVI (May 1991), 407–43.

Becker, Gary, *Treatise on the Family* (Cambridge: Harvard University Press, 1981).

Brown, Charles, and James Medoff, "The Employer Size-Wage Effect," *Journal of Political Economy*, XCVII (1989), 1027–59.

Bulow, Jeremy I., John D. Geanakoplos, and Paul D. Klemperer, "Multimarket Oligopoly: Strategic Substitutes and Complements," *Journal of Political Economy*, XCIII (1985), 488–511.

Card, David, and Alan Krueger, "School Quality and Black-White Relative Earnings: A Direct Assessment," *Quarterly Journal of Economics*, CVII (1992), 151–200.

Clague, Christopher, "Relative Efficiency, Self-Containment, and Comparative Costs of Less-Developed Countries," *Economic Development and Cultural Change* XXXIX (1991a), 507–530.

———, "Factor Proportions, Relative Efficiency and Developing Countries Trade," *Journal of Development Economics*, XXXV (1991b), 357–80.

Clark, Gregory, "Why Isn't the Whole World Developed? Lessons from the Cotton Mills," *Journal of Economic History*, XLVII (March 1987), 141–73.

Coate, Stephen, and Glenn Loury, "Affirmative Action as a Remedy for Statistical Discrimination," mimeo, Harvard University, 1991.

Cooper, Russell, and Andrew John, "Coordinating Coordination Failures in Keynesian Models," *Quarterly Journal of Economics*, CIII (August 1988), 441–64.

Dechert, W. Davis, and Kazuo Nishimura, "A Complete Characterization of Optimal Growth Paths in an Aggregated Model with a Non-Concave Production Function," *Journal of Economic Theory*, XXXI (1983), 332–54.

Donahue, John, and James Heckman, "Continuous Versus Episodic Change: The Impact of Affirmative Action and Civil Rights Policy on the Economic Status of Blacks," *Journal of Economic Literature*, XXIX (1991), 1603–43.

Galor, Oded, and Joseph Zeira, "Income Distribution and Macroeconomics," Working Paper No. 89–25, 1989.

Jovanovic, Boyan, "Job Matching and the Theory of Turnover," *Journal of Political Economy*, LXXXVII (1979), 972–90.

Katz, Lawrence, and Lawrence Summers, "Industry Rents: Evidence and Implications," *Brookings Papers on Economic Activity: Microeconomics* (1989), 209–75.

Kremer, Michael, and Eric Maskin, "Matching Heterogeneous Workers to Firms and Occupations: Preliminary Notes," 1993.

Kwon, Goohoon, "A Comparison of Sectoral Productivity Levels of the USSR and USA," mimeo, 1992.

Lucas, Robert, "On the Size Distribution of Business Firms," *Bell Journal cf Economics*, IX (1978), 508–23.

———, "Why Doesn't Capital Flow from Rich to Poor Countries?" *American Economic Review*, LXXX (May 1990), 92–96.

Mankiw, N. Gregory, David Romer, and David N. Weil, "A Contribution to the Empirics of Economic Growth," *Quarterly Journal of Economics*, CVII (May 1992), 407–38.

Miller, Frederick, "The Distribution of Ability and Earnings Once Again," mimeograph, Johns Hopkins, 1983.

Murphy, Kevin, Andrei Shleifer, and Robert Vishny, "The Allocation of Talent: Implications for Growth," *Quarterly Journal of Economics*, CVI (1991), 503–30.

Rosen, Sherwin, "The Economics of Superstars," *American Economic Review*, LXXI (1981), 845–58.

———, "Authority, Control, and the Distribution of Earnings," *Bell Journal of Economics*, XIII (Autumn 1982), 311–23.

Sah, Raaj, and Joseph Stiglitz, "Human Fallibility and Economic Organization," *American Economic Review*, LXXV (May 1985), 292–97.

Sah, Raaj, and Joseph Stiglitz, "The Architecture of Economic Systems: Hierarchies and Polyarchies," *American Economic Review*, LXXVI (September 1986), 716–27.

Sattinger, Michael, "Comparative Advantage and the Distributions of Earnings and Abilities," *Econometrica*, XLIII (1975), 455–68.

Sobel, Joel, "How to Count to One Thousand," *Economic Journal*, CII (January 1992), 1–8.

World Bank, *World Development Report 1990* (New York: Oxford University Press, 1990).

ABOUT THE AUTHOR

Michael Kremer

Michael Kremer is Professor of Economics at Harvard University and Senior Fellow at the Brookings Institution. He received his A.B., as well as his Ph.D., from Harvard University. He is a recipient of a MacArthur fellowship, and in 1996 received a Presidential Early Career Award for Scientists and Engineers. Kremer's research spans a wide range of topics, including incentives for research and development, the economics of education in developing countries, the epidemiology of AIDS, the economics of elephant poaching, payroll taxation and youth unemployment, and income distribution dynamics.

International
Economics

International
Economics

International
Economics

POLITICAL ECONOMY
OF PROTECTION

Gene M. Grossman and Elhanan Helpman

International
Economics

INTERNATIONAL ECONOMICS

Protection for Sale

GENE M. GROSSMAN AND ELHANAN HELPMAN

We develop a model in which special-interest groups make political contributions in order to influence an incumbent government's choice of trade policy. The interest groups bid for protection with their campaign support. Politicians maximize their own welfare, which depends on total contributions collected and on the welfare of voters. We study the structure of protection that emerges in the political equilibrium and the contributions by different lobbies that support the policy outcome. We also discuss why the lobbies may in some cases prefer to have the government use trade policy to transfer income, rather than more efficient means. (JEL F13, D72)

When asked why free trade is so often preached and so rarely practiced, most international economists blame "politics." In representative democracies, governments shape trade policy in response not only to the concerns of the general electorate, but also to the pressures applied by special interests. Interest groups participate in the political process in order to influence policy outcomes. Politicians respond to the incentives they face, trading off the financial and other support that comes from heeding the interest groups' demands against the alienation of voters that may result from the implementation of socially costly policies.

Research on the political economy of trade policy seeks to explain the equilibrium outcome of this political process. Two different approaches are prominent in the literature (which is nicely surveyed by Arye Hillman [1989]). One approach stresses *political competition* between opposing candidates. In the work of Stephen Magee et al. (1989) and Hillman and Heinrich Ursprung (1988), competing parties announce trade policies that they are committed to implement, if elected. Organized lobby groups evaluate their members' prospects under the alternative policy proposals and contribute resources to the party that promises them the highest level of welfare. The parties use the

Grossman: Woodrow Wilson School, Princeton University, Princeton, NJ 08544; Helpman: Department of Economics, Tel Aviv University, Tel Aviv 69978, Israel, and the Canadian Institute for Advanced Research. We are grateful to Robert Baldwin, Avinash Dixit, Joanne Gowa, Arye Hillman, Paul Krugman, Tom Romer, Henry Ursprung, and two anonymous referees for helpful suggestions and the National Science Foundation and the U.S.-Israel Binational Science Foundation for financial support.

resources to sway voters, who are presumed to be imperfectly informed about candidates' positions. In making their giving decisions, the lobbies weigh the benefit of an increased probability of their favorite party being elected against the direct cost of the donation. Clearly, the motivation for political contributions in this setting is to influence the election outcome.

The second approach, pioneered by George Stigler (1971) and first used to study endogenous protection by Hillman (1982), sees economic policies as being set by an incumbent government seeking to maximize its *political support*. The "political-support function" has as arguments the welfare that designated interest groups derive from the chosen policies and the deadweight loss that the policies impose on society at large. In this formulation, campaign contributions do not enter directly into the analysis (although they may be implicit in the notion of "support" by special interests), and the political competition of the next election is kept in the background. While the incumbent government maximizes support with the apparent goal of being reelected, the election itself is not explicitly considered, nor are the positions of potential rivals.

Both of these approaches contribute to our understanding of the political optimization underlying the endogenous determination of trade policy. Political competition seems most important for explaining the broader contours of trade policy: Will it be liberal or interventionist? Benefit capital or labor? Benefit the rich or the poor? At this level of generality, competing parties can articulate opposing positions and can inform (at least some) voters of the differences among them. For the finer details of policy—such as the extent to which different industries will be favored, or the designation of what sorts of instruments will be used—the political-support approach seems more appropriate. Often incumbent governments find themselves in a position to make the detailed policy choices unencumbered by immediate competition from political rivals. Of course, if the choices made by the government turn out to be ill-advised, the incumbent officeholders may be held accountable in subsequent elections.

This paper seeks to explain the equilibrium *structure of trade protection*. We are interested in understanding which special interest groups will be especially successful in capturing private benefits from the political process. We are also interested in understanding why lobbies may hold preferences over the types of policies that are used to redistribute income and why they may support institutional constraints on the set of instruments available to the government. For these purposes we adopt the perspective of the political-support approach; we model incumbent politicians who make policy choices while being aware that their decisions may affect their chances for reelection.

In developing our model of political support we take what we feel are significant steps beyond the existing literature. Previous authors have specified a reduced form for the politicians' objective function, assuming that the government places different fixed weights on the welfare levels of different groups in society. Here we derive the government's objective from more primitive preferences defined over campaign contributions and voter well-being. While it might be argued that these preferences too have more fundamental determinants in the details of the political process, our formulation does offer a distinct advantage over more reduced-form approaches for some types of questions. One can easily imagine changes in the international rules of the game that would affect government's willingness and ability to protect particular sectoral interests but would not affect politicians' weighting of campaign contributions relative to general voter dissatisfaction. We believe that our approach could be used (in future research) to investigate how such institutional changes would affect equilibrium policies *by endogenously changing the shape of the political-support function.*

Not only do we derive the weights that the government places on different groups endogenously, but we also make explicit the process by which the government comes to pay special attention to the concerns of particular interests. Organized interest groups are able to offer political contributions, which politicians value for their potential use in the coming election (and perhaps otherwise). It is this ability to contribute (as well as the ability to deliver blocks of votes, a channel of influence that we neglect in the current paper) that gives special interests their favored position in the eyes of the government.

In our model, lobbies represent industry interests. The lobbies make (implicit) offers that relate prospective contributions to the trade policies chosen by the incumbent government. The government then sets policy—a vector of import and export taxes and subsidies—to maximize a weighted sum of aggregate social welfare and total contributions. In this process the various interest groups vie for the government's favor. The lobbies' equilibrium bids are each optimal, given the contributions promised by the others. Here, in contrast to the literature on political competition, an individual interest group does not see a link between its own (relatively small) contribution and the election outcome; rather, the groups are motivated to make contributions by the prospect of *influencing policy.* In other words, politicians' penchant for campaign gifts makes "protection for sale."[1]

We proceed to show that equilibrium trade policies obey a modified Ramsey rule: all else equal, industries with higher import demand or export supply elasticities will have smaller deviations from free trade; but the rates of protection also reflect the relative political strengths of the various interest groups and parameters describing the nation's political economy. The paper goes on to discuss the determinants of the relative sizes of the political contributions that the various interest groups must make to support the equilibrium policy choices. Finally, we examine the reasons why lobbies may prefer in some circumstances to constrain the set of policy instruments that governments can use to redistribute income.

---

[1] We recognize, of course, that influence-peddling is illegal in most political systems. The policy-contingent contribution offers that we have in mind need not be explicit. Special-interest groups can readily make it known, as indeed most do, that they intend to support more generously those politicians who take positions that benefit their cause.

I. OVERVIEW

We begin with an overview of our analytical approach, postponing the formal development of our model until the next section. We consider a small, competitive economy that faces exogenously given world prices. Free trade is efficient for such an economy, so any policy interventions can be ascribed to the political process. The economy produces a numeraire good, with labor alone, and each of n additional products using labor and an input that is specific to the particular sector. We assume that there is a high degree of concentration in the ownership of many of the n specific inputs and that the various owners of some of these inputs have banded together to form lobby groups. We do not at this point have a theory of lobby formation; rather we take it as given that some factor owners overcome the free-rider problem to conduct joint lobbying activities, while others do not.

The lobby groups may offer political contributions to the incumbent officeholders, who are in a position to set the current trade policy. The lobbies do not contribute to any challenger candidates, nor do they take into account any effect of their contribution on the likelihood that the incumbents will be reelected. Although we recognize the absence of explicit political competition as a potential shortcoming of our approach, we believe that the available evidence for the United States supports our assumptions as a reasonable first approximation. In particular, political action committees (PAC's) gave more than three-quarters of their total contributions in the 1988 Congressional campaigns to incumbent candidates. If elections for open seats are excluded, incumbents received 6.3 times as much in contributions from PAC's as did their challengers (David Magelby and Candice Nelson, 1990 p. 86). Moreover, 62 percent of the campaign contributions by PAC's in the 1987–1988 campaign occurred in the first 18 months of the election cycle, often before a challenger to the incumbent had even been identified (Magelby and Nelson, 1990 p. 67). Many of these incumbents would not be involved in close races when the elections came. Also, few single contributions were large relative to total spending by any candidate. In short, PAC contributions can best be seen as attempts to curry favor.[2]

While the lobby groups ignore the effects of their individual contributions on the election probabilities, the incumbent politicians may see a relationship between *total* collections (which can be used to finance campaign spending) and their reelection prospects.[3] At the

---

[2] Magelby and Nelson (1990 p. 55) report that, of the 255 incumbent Congress members who received the greatest portion of their funding from PAC's, only 19 took part in races where the challenger received 45 percent or more of the vote. They conclude from their review of the evidence that "PAC money is interested money" with "more than an electoral objective in mind."

[3] Gary C. Jacobson (1978, 1987) has argued that an incumbent's campaign spending level has little quantifiable effect on his or her chance of winning reelection. However, Donald Philip Green and Jonathan S. Krasno (1988) challenge this view, pointing out that Jacobson has either failed to control for the correlation between spending and the quality of the opponent or has used inappropriate instruments. They find a much larger influence of incumbent spending on election outcomes once challenger quality is taken into account.

same time, they may believe that their odds of survival depend on the utility level achieved by the average voter. With these considerations in mind, we suppose that the incumbent politicians' objective is to maximize a weighted sum of total political contributions and aggregate social welfare. Such an objective function seems plausible for a government that is concerned about the next election, but broader interpretations also are possible. For example, aggregate welfare might enter the government's objective if some representatives are civil-minded. In addition, politicians may value contributions not only for financing future campaigns, but also for retiring debts from previous elections (which many times are owed to the politician's personal estate), for deterring competition from quality challengers,[4] and for showing the candidates' abilities as fundraisers and thereby establishing their credibility as potential candidates for higher political or party office. In any event, politicians have, over the years, revealed their considerable taste for amassing such contributions.

We model the lobbying process as follows. Each organized interest group representing one of the sector-specific factors confronts the government with a *contribution schedule*. The schedule maps every policy vector that the government might choose (where policies are import and export taxes and subsidies on the *n* nonnumeraire goods) into a campaign contribution level. Of course, some policies may evoke a contribution of zero from some lobbies. The government then sets a policy vector and collects from each lobby the contribution associated with its policy choice. An equilibrium is a set of contribution schedules such that each lobby's schedule maximizes the aggregate utility of the lobby's members, taking as given the schedules of the other lobby groups. In calculating their optimal schedules, the lobbies recognize that the politicians ultimately will set policy to maximize their own welfare. The Nash-equilibrium contribution schedules implement an equilibrium trade-policy choice.

Our model has the structure of a *common agency problem*, that is, a situation that arises when several principals attempt to induce a single agent to take an action that may be costly for the agent to perform. The government here serves as an agent for the various (and conflicting) special interest groups, while bearing a cost for implementing an inefficient policy that stems from its accountability to the general electorate. B. Douglas Bernheim and Michael D. Whinston (1986) have coined the term *menu auction* to describe a situation of complete information where bidders announce a "menu" of offers for various possible actions open to an "auctioneer" and then pay the bids associated with the action selected. They have analyzed a class of such auctions and derived several results that will prove useful below for characterizing the political equilibrium in our economy.

---

[4]In their study of campaign spending in the 1978 Congressional election, Edie N. Goldenberg et al. (1986) suggest that incumbents stockpiled contributions and made early campaign expenditures in order to dissuade strong challengers from entering the race. However, Krasno and Green (1988) find little evidence of such strategic spending in their regression analysis of challenger quality.

II. FORMAL FRAMEWORK

A small economy is populated by individuals with identical preferences but different factor endowments. Each individual maximizes utility given by

$$u = x_0 + \sum_{i=1}^{n} u_i(x_i) \tag{1}$$

where x_0 is consumption of good 0 and x_i is consumption of good i, $i = 1, 2, ..., n$. The sub-utility functions $u_i(\cdot)$ are differentiable, increasing, and strictly concave. Good 0 serves as numeraire, with a world and domestic price equal to 1. We denote by p_i^* the exogenous world price of good i, while p_i represents its domestic price. With these preferences, an individual spending an amount E consumes $x_i = d_i(p_i)$ of good i, $i = 1, 2, ...,$ n [where the demand function $d_i(\cdot)$ is the inverse of $u_i'(x_i)$] and $x_0 = E - \Sigma_i p_i d_i(p_i)$ of the numeraire good. Indirect utility takes the form

$$V(\mathbf{p}, E) = E + s(\mathbf{p}) \tag{2}$$

where $\mathbf{p} = (p_1, p_2, ..., p_n)$ is the vector of domestic prices of the nonnumeraire goods and $s(\mathbf{p}) \equiv \Sigma_i u_i[d_i(p_i)] - \Sigma_i p_i d_i(p_i)$ is the consumer surplus derived from these goods.

Good 0 is manufactured from labor alone with constant returns to scale and an input-output coefficient equal to 1. We assume that the aggregate supply of labor is large enough to ensure a positive supply of this good. Then the wage rate equals 1 in a competitive equilibrium. Production of each nonnumeraire good requires labor and a sector-specific input. The technologies for these goods exhibit constant returns to scale, and the various specific inputs are available in inelastic supply. With the wage rate fixed at 1, the aggregate reward to the specific factor used in producing good i depends only on the domestic price of that good. We denote this reward by $\pi_i(p_i)$.

In this paper, we restrict the set of policy instruments available to politicians. For now, we allow the government to implement only trade taxes and subsidies. These policies drive a wedge between domestic and world prices. A domestic price in excess of the world price implies an import tariff for a good that is imported and an export subsidy for one that is exported. Domestic prices below world prices correspond to import subsidies and export taxes. The net revenue from all taxes and subsidies, expressed on a per capita basis, is given by

$$r(\mathbf{p}) = \sum_i (p_i - p_i^*)\left[d_i(p_i) - \frac{1}{N}y_i(p_i)\right] \tag{3}$$

where N measures the total (voting) population and $y_i(p_i) = \pi_i'(p_i)$ is domestic output of good i. We assume that the government redistributes revenue uniformly to all of the country's voters. Then $r(\mathbf{p})$ gives the net government transfer to each individual.

A typical individual derives income from wages and government transfers, and possibly from the ownership of some sector-specific input. We assume that claims to the specific inputs are indivisible and nontradable (e.g., claims to sector-specific human capital) and that individuals own at most one type. Clearly, those who own some of the specific input used in producing good i will see their income tied to the domestic price of that good. These individuals will have a direct stake in the tax or subsidy applicable to trade in good i that goes beyond their general interest as consumers in trade policies that affect any domestic prices.

The various owners of the specific factor used in industry i, with their common interest in protection (or export subsidies) for their sector, may choose to join forces for political activity. Mancur Olson (1965) has discussed "the logic of collective action," but also the difficulties associated with overcoming free-rider problems. We have nothing to add to his discussion here, so we simply assume that in some exogenous set of sectors, denoted L, the specific-factor owners have been able to organize themselves into lobby groups. The lobbies serve to coordinate campaign giving decisions and to communicate the political "offers" to the government. In the remaining sectors (if any), the individual owners of the specific factors remain unorganized. Any individual perceives himself or herself as too small to communicate political demands effectively or to influence policy. Therefore, the unorganized factor owners, as well as all individuals who own no claims to a specific input, refrain from making political contributions.

The lobby representing an organized sector i makes its political contribution contingent on the trade-policy vector implemented by the government. Since the country is small, it can equivalently relate the gift to the realized vector of domestic prices. We denote by $C_i(\mathbf{p})$ the contribution schedule tendered by lobby i. The lobby tailors this schedule to maximize the total welfare (income plus consumer surplus less contributions) of its members. It then collects the necessary donations from its members in such a way as to allow all to share in the gains from political coordination.

It will prove convenient in what follows to express the joint welfare of the members of lobby group i as $V_i = W_i - C_i$, where W_i is their gross-of-contributions joint welfare. We note that

$$W_i(\mathbf{p}) \equiv \ell_i + \pi_i(p_i) + \alpha_i N[r(\mathbf{p}) + s(\mathbf{p})] \tag{4}$$

where ℓ_i is the total labor supply (and also the labor income) of owners of the specific input used in industry i and α_i is the fraction of the voting population that owns some of this factor.

The incumbent government cares about the total level of political contributions and about aggregate well-being. The government values contributions, because they can be used to finance campaign spending, and as noted above, they may provide other direct benefits to the officeholders. Social welfare will be of concern to the incumbent government if voters are more likely to reelect a government that has delivered a high standard of living. We choose a linear form for the government's objective function, namely,

$$G = \sum_{i \in L} C_i(\mathbf{p}) + aW(\mathbf{p}) \qquad a \geq 0 \tag{5}$$

where W represents aggregate, gross-of-contributions welfare.[5] Aggregate gross welfare equals aggregate income plus trade tax revenues plus total consumer surplus; that is,

$$W(\mathbf{p}) = \ell + \sum_{i=1}^{n} \pi_i(p_i) + N[r(\mathbf{p}) + s(\mathbf{p})]. \tag{6}$$

We are interested in the political equilibrium of a two-stage noncooperative game in which the lobbies simultaneously choose their political contribution schedules in the first stage and the government sets policy in the second. An equilibrium is a set of contribution functions $\{C_i^o(\mathbf{p})\}$, one for each organized lobby group, such that each one maximizes the joint welfare of the group's members given the schedules set by the other groups and the anticipated political optimization by the government; and a domestic price vector $\mathbf{p}^o$ that maximizes the government's objective taking the contribution schedules as given. We characterize the equilibrium structure of protection in the next section and the political contributions that underlie the government's policy choice in the section that follows.

III. THE STRUCTURE OF PROTECTION

As we noted near the end of Section II, the interaction between the various lobbies and the government in this economy has the structure of a menu-auction problem. Bernheim and Whinston (1986) have characterized the equilibrium for a class of such problems. Although they limited their analysis to situations where players bid for a finite set of objects, it is clear that their main results apply also when, as here, the auctioneer can choose from a continuum of possible actions. Accordingly, we allow the government's choice set (of domestic price vectors) to be continuous.

Let $\mathcal{P}$ denote the set of domestic price vectors from which the government may choose. We bound $\mathcal{P}$ so that each domestic price p_i must lie between some minimum $\underline{p}_i$ and some maximum $\bar{p}_i$. For the most part, we restrict attention to equilibria that lie in the interior of $\mathcal{P}$. Lemma 2 of Bernheim and Whinston (1986) implies that an equilibrium to the trade-policy game can be characterized as follows:

PROPOSITION 1 (B-W): $(\{C_i^o\}_{i\in L}, \mathbf{p}^o)$ is a subgame-perfect Nash equilibrium of the trade-policy game if and only if:
(a) C_i^o is feasible for all $i \in L$;
(b) $\mathbf{p}^o$ maximizes $\sum_{i\in L} C_i^o(\mathbf{p}) + aW(\mathbf{p})$ on $\mathcal{P}$;

---

[5] We could equally well write the government's welfare function as $\tilde{G} = a_1 \Sigma_{i\in L} C_i + a_2(W_i - \Sigma_{i\in L} C_i)$, where a_1 is the weight the government attaches to campaign contributions and a_2 is the weight it attaches to *net* aggregate welfare. Maximizing $\tilde{G}$ is equivalent to maximizing G in (5) with $a = a_2/(a_1 - a_2)$ provided that $a_1 > a_2$. We assume that this is so (i.e., that politicans value a dollar in their campaign coffers more highly than a dollar in the hands of the public). This assumption implies no restriction on the size of the parameter a.

(c) $\mathbf{p}^o$ *maximizes*

$$W_j(\mathbf{p}) - C^o_j(\mathbf{p}) + \sum_{i \in L} C^o_i(\mathbf{p}) + aW(\mathbf{p})$$

on $\mathcal{P}$ for every $j \in L$;

(d) *for every $j \in L$ there exists a $\mathbf{p}^j \in \mathcal{P}$ that maximizes $\sum_{i \in L} C^o_i(\mathbf{p}) + aW(\mathbf{p})$ on $\mathcal{P}$ such that $C^o_j(\mathbf{p}^j) = 0$.*

Condition (a) restricts each lobby's contribution schedule to be among those that are feasible (i.e., contributions must be nonnegative and no greater than the aggregate income available to the lobby's members). Condition (b) states that, given the contribution schedules offered by the lobbies, the government sets trade policy to maximize its own welfare. The last two conditions allow us to characterize the equilibrium structure of protection and the equilibrium pattern of political contributions, respectively. We derive and apply condition (c) here, while postponing discussion of condition (d) until the next section.

Condition (c) stipulates that, for every lobby j, the equilibrium price vector must maximize the joint welfare of that lobby and the government, given the contribution schedules offered by the other lobbies. If this were not the case, then lobby j could reformulate its policy bids to induce the government to choose the jointly optimal price vector and could appropriate some (in fact, nearly all) of the surplus from the switch in policy. Suppose, for example, that the government contemplated choosing the price vector $\tilde{\mathbf{p}}$, whereas $\hat{\mathbf{p}}$ is jointly optimal for lobby j and the government. All lobby j need do is design a new contribution schedule that pays the government for any price vector $\mathbf{p}$ the difference between its welfare at $\tilde{\mathbf{p}}$ and its welfare at $\mathbf{p}$, plus a little bit more for choosing $\mathbf{p}$. The "little bit more" would vary with $\mathbf{p}$ and would be maximal for $\mathbf{p} = \hat{\mathbf{p}}$. Then the government would gain by choosing $\hat{\mathbf{p}}$ in place of $\tilde{\mathbf{p}}$, and would prefer $\hat{\mathbf{p}}$ to any other policy choice. The government's gain would be small, however, and the lobby would capture nearly all of the surplus.[6] In equilibrium, no such unexploited profit opportunities can exist for any lobby.

Let us assume now that the lobbies set political-contribution functions that are differentiable, at least around the equilibrium point $\mathbf{p}^o$. In a moment we will argue that there are some compelling reasons for focusing on contribution schedules that have this property. With contribution functions that are differentiable, the fact that $\mathbf{p}^o$ maximizes

---

[6] More formally, let $\tilde{C}_i(\mathbf{p})$ be the contemplated bid schedules for the lobbies $i \in L$. Suppose they induce the government to choose $\tilde{\mathbf{p}}$, but $\hat{\mathbf{p}} \neq \tilde{\mathbf{p}}$ maximizes $V_j + G$, given $\{\tilde{C}_i(\mathbf{p})\}$ for $i \neq j$. Now let lobby j reformulate its contribution schedule as $\hat{C}_j(\mathbf{p}) \equiv \sum_{i \in L} \tilde{C}_i(\tilde{\mathbf{p}}) + aW(\tilde{\mathbf{p}}) - \sum_{i \in L, i \neq j} \tilde{C}_i(\mathbf{p}) - aW(\mathbf{p}) + \varepsilon h(\mathbf{p})$, where $h(\cdot)$ is any nonnegative function that reaches a unique maximum at $\mathbf{p} = \hat{\mathbf{p}}$. Faced with this new schedule in place of $\tilde{C}_j(\mathbf{p})$, the government maximizes G by choosing the policy vector $\hat{\mathbf{p}}$ as long as $\varepsilon > 0$. Lobby j's welfare becomes $W_j(\hat{\mathbf{p}}) - \hat{C}_j(\hat{\mathbf{p}}) = W_j(\tilde{\mathbf{p}}) - \tilde{C}_j(\tilde{\mathbf{p}}) + \Delta - \varepsilon h(\hat{\mathbf{p}})$, where $\Delta > 0$ represents the gain in joint welfare $V_j + G$ that results from replacing $\tilde{\mathbf{p}}$ with $\hat{\mathbf{p}}$. For ε small enough, we have $\Delta > \varepsilon h(\hat{\mathbf{p}})$, which implies $W_j(\hat{\mathbf{p}}) - \hat{C}_j(\hat{\mathbf{p}}) > W_j(\tilde{\mathbf{p}}) - \tilde{C}_j(\tilde{\mathbf{p}})$ (i.e., the lobby gains from this change in its contribution schedule).

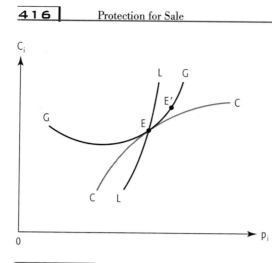

Figure 1
Local Truthfulness

$V_j + G$ implies that a first-order condition is satisfied at $\mathbf{p}^o$, namely,

$$\nabla W_j^o(\mathbf{p}^o) - \nabla C_j^o(\mathbf{p}^o) + \sum_{i \in L} \nabla C_i^o(\mathbf{p}^o) + a\nabla W(\mathbf{p}^o) = 0 \qquad \text{for all } j \in L. \qquad (7)$$

However, the government's maximization of G requires the first-order condition

$$\sum_{i \in L} \nabla C_i^o(\mathbf{p}^o) + a\nabla W(\mathbf{p}^o) = 0. \qquad (8)$$

Taken together, (7) and (8) imply

$$\nabla C_i^o(\mathbf{p}^o) = \nabla W_i(\mathbf{p}^o) \qquad \text{for all } i \in L. \qquad (9)$$

Equation (9) establishes that the contribution schedules all are *locally truthful* around $\mathbf{p}^o$; that is, each lobby sets its contribution schedule so that the marginal change in the contribution for a small change in policy matches the effect of the policy change on the lobby's gross welfare. In other words, the shapes of the schedules reveal the lobbies' true preferences in the neighborhood of the equilibrium. The intuition for this result can be seen in Figure 1, where we plot the contribution C_i made by lobby i along the vertical axis and the domestic price p_i along the horizontal axis. The curve labeled GG is an indifference curve for the government. It shows the contributions from lobby i that would compensate the government for altering the price of good i, in view of the change in aggregate welfare *and* the change in contributions from all other lobbies that would result from the price change. The curve labeled LL depicts an indifference curve for lobby i. These curves must be upward-sloping in the neighborhood of the equilibrium, although this fact is not needed for the present argument. Now suppose that the lobby offers the contribution schedule CC, inducing the government to maximize its welfare at point E. Since CC is not tangent to LL at E, there exists a point E' along GG that yields greater welfare to lobby i than point E. The lobby could induce the government to choose E' instead of E by offering a contribution schedule that coincides with CC until a point somewhere below point E, falls below CC at that point and then rises to be tangent with GG at E'. It will always be possible for the lobby to reconfigure its contribution schedule like this so as to raise its net welfare, unless CC and LL are tangent to one another (and to GG) at the equilibrium point.

We can extend this notion of "truthfulness" to define (as Bernheim and Whinston [1986] do) a *truthful contribution schedule*. This is a contribution schedule that *everywhere* reflects the true preferences of the lobby. It pays to the government for any policy **p** the excess (if any) of lobby *j*'s gross welfare at **p** relative to some base level of welfare. Formally, a truthful contribution function takes the form

$$C_j^T(\mathbf{p}, B_j) = \max[0, W_j(\mathbf{p}) - B_j] \tag{10}$$

for some B_j. Notice that truthful schedules are differentiable, except possibly where the contribution becomes nil, because the gross benefit functions are differentiable. Bernheim and Whinston (1986) have shown that players bear essentially no cost from playing truthful strategies, because the set of best responses to *any* strategies played by one's opponents includes a strategy that is truthful. They have also shown that all equilibria supported by truthful strategies, and only these equilibria, are stable to nonbinding communication among the players (i.e., they are "coalition-proof"). For these reasons they argue that *truthful Nash equilibria* (those equilibria supported by truthful bid functions) may be focal among the set of Nash equilibria.

Truthful Nash equilibria (TNE) have an interesting property. The equilibrium price vector of any TNE satisfies[7]

$$\mathbf{p}^o = \underset{\mathbf{p} \in \mathcal{P}}{\arg\max} \left[\sum_{j \in L} W_j(\mathbf{p}) + aW(\mathbf{p}) \right]. \tag{11}$$

Equation (11) says that, in equilibrium, truthful contribution schedules induce the government to behave as if it were maximizing a social-welfare function that weights different members of society differently, with individuals represented by a lobby group receiving a weight of $1 + a$ and those not so represented receiving the smaller weight of a. Our model thus provides microanalytic foundations for the reduced-form political-support function used by, for example, Ngo Van Long and Neil Vousden (1991).

---

[7]To see this, note that condition (b) of Proposition 1 implies that $\sum_{j \in L} C_j^o(\mathbf{p}^o) + aW(\mathbf{p}^o) \geq \sum_{j \in L} C_j^o(\mathbf{p}) + aW(\mathbf{p})$ for all $\mathbf{p} \in \mathcal{P}$. If the contribution functions are truthful, then from the definition (10), $C_j^o(\mathbf{p}^o) = W_j(\mathbf{p}^o) - B_j^o$ (where B_j^o is the equilibrium net benefit to lobby *j*) and $C_j^o(\mathbf{p}) \geq W_j(\mathbf{p}) - B_j^o$ for all $j \in L$ and all $\mathbf{p} \in \mathcal{P}$. Therefore $\sum_{j \in L} W_j(\mathbf{p}^o) + aW(\mathbf{p}^o) \geq \sum_{j \in L} W_j(\mathbf{p}) + aW(\mathbf{p})$ for all $\mathbf{p} \in \mathcal{P}$.

We return now to the characterization of equilibrium trade policies that can be supported by differentiable—although not necessarily globally truthful—contribution schedules.[8] We sum (9) over i and substitute the result into (8) to derive

$$\sum_{i \in L} \nabla W_i(\mathbf{p}^\circ) + a\nabla W(\mathbf{p}^\circ) = 0. \tag{12}$$

This equation characterizes the equilibrium domestic prices supported by differentiable contribution functions. Notice that this is just the first-order condition that is necessary for the maximization in (11), although we see that it must hold more generally (i.e., for all differentiable contribution schedules, not just those that are everywhere truthful).

Our next step is to calculate how marginal policy changes affect the welfare of the various groups in society. Looking first at the members of some lobby i we find from (3) and (4) that

$$\frac{\partial W_i}{\partial p_j} = (\delta_{ij} - \alpha_i)y_j(p_j) + \alpha_i(p_j - p_j^*)m_j'(p_j) \tag{13}$$

where $m_j(p_j) \equiv Nd_j(p_j) - y_j(p_j)$ denotes the net import demand function and δ_{ij} is an indicator variable that equals 1 if $i = j$ and 0 otherwise. Equation (13) states that lobby i gains from an increase in the domestic price of good i above its free-trade level and gains from a decrease in the price of any other good (because $m_j' < 0$). The specific-factor owners benefit more from an increase in the price of their industry's output the larger is the free-trade supply of the good. The benefit to lobby i that results from a decline in the price of another good j falls as the share of the members of lobby i in the total population shrinks, and it vanishes completely in the limit when $\alpha_i = 0$. When the members of lobby i are a negligible fraction of the total population, they receive only a negligible share of the transfers generated by taxes on good j, and they enjoy only a negligible share of the surplus that derives from consumption of good j. In this case, they are unaffected by changes in the domestic price of that good.

Since all organized interest groups submit locally truthful contribution schedules, we need to know how a policy change impinges on the gross welfare of the entire group of individuals who are actively trying to influence policy. Accordingly, we sum the expressions in (13) for all $i \in L$ to derive

$$\sum_{i \in L} \frac{\partial W_i}{\partial p_j} = (I_j - \alpha_L)y_j(p_j) + \alpha_L(p_j - p_j^*)m_j'(p_j) \tag{14}$$

---

[8]Even if one does not accept the Bernheim-Whinston argument for TNE, one might want to require that contribution schedules be differentiable, because these schedules will be robust to small mistakes in calculation on the part of the lobbies, whereas a lobby might suffer a large penalty for a small miscalculation if it used a nondifferentiable payment schedule.

where $I_j \equiv \Sigma_{i \in L} \delta_{ij}$ is an indicator variable that equals 1 if industry j is organized and 0 otherwise, while $\alpha_L \equiv \Sigma_{i \in L} \alpha_i$ denotes the fraction of the total population of voters who are represented by a lobby. Equation (14) reveals that, starting from free-trade prices, lobby members as a whole benefit from a small increase in the domestic price of any good that is produced by an organized industry and (provided $\alpha_L > 0$) from a small decline in the price of any good that is produced by an unorganized industry.

Finally, we compute the effect of a marginal price change on aggregate welfare. Using the definition of W in (6), we find

$$\frac{\partial W}{\partial p_j} = (p_j - p_j^*)m_j'(p_j) \tag{15}$$

which reveals, of course, that marginal deadweight loss grows as the economy deviates further and further from free trade. Substituting (14) and (15) into (12) allows us to solve for the domestic prices in political equilibrium, assuming that these prices lie in the interior of $\mathcal{P}$.[9] We express the result in terms of the equilibrium ad valorem trade taxes and subsidies, which are defined by $t_i^o \equiv (p_i^o - p_i^*)/p_i^*$.

PROPOSITION 2 (EQUILIBRIUM POLICIES): *If the lobbies use contribution schedules that are differentiable around the equilibrium point, and if the equilibrium lies in the interior of $\mathcal{P}$, then the government chooses trade taxes and subsidies that satisfy*

$$\frac{t_i^o}{1 + t_i^o} = \frac{I_i - \alpha_L}{a + \alpha_L}\left(\frac{z_i^o}{e_i^o}\right) \qquad for\ i = 1, 2, ..., n$$

where $z_i^o = y_i(p_i^o)/m_i(p_i^o)$ is the equilibrium ratio of domestic output to imports (negative for exports) and $e_i^o = -m_i'(p_i^o)p_i^o/m_i(p_i^o)$ is the elasticity of import demand or of export supply (the former defined to be positive, the latter negative).

Proposition 2 describes a modified Ramsey rule. All else equal, industries that have high import demand or export supply elasticities (in absolute value) will have smaller ad valorem deviations from free trade. This is true for two reasons. First, the government may bear a political cost from creating deadweight loss (if $a > 0$). To the extent that this is so, all else equal, it will prefer to raise contributions from sectors where the cost is small. Second, even if $a = 0$, if $\alpha_L > 0$ the members of lobbies as a group will share in any

---

[9]The domestic price of good i may be driven to the boundary of $\mathcal{P}$ if one of several constraints becomes binding. First, the owners of the specific factor used in industry i may not have sufficient resources to "protect themselves" from other lobbies (i.e., the political contributions needed to keep p_i above $\underline{p}_i$ may exceed their aggregate income). Second, some lobby group j may bid for such a large export subsidy that the income of some individuals will not be sufficient to cover the per capita levy needed to finance the subsidy. Then p_j will be driven to $\bar{p}_j$. These extreme outcomes, which are made possible by the linearity in our specification, are not an especially interesting feature of the model. Thus, we do not pursue the equilibria with corner solutions any further.

deadweight loss that results from trade policy. The owners of specific inputs in industries other than i will bid more to avoid protection in sector i the greater is the social cost of that protection.

Considerations of deadweight loss are modified by political variables in the determination of the equilibrium structure of protection. First, note that *all* sectors that are represented by lobbies are protected by import tariffs or export subsidies in the political equilibrium.[10] In contrast, import subsidies and export taxes are applied to all sectors that have no organized representation. In other words, the organized interest groups collectively manage to raise the domestic prices of goods from which they derive profit income and to lower the prices of goods that they only consume. The political power of a particular organized sector is reflected by the ratio of domestic output to imports. In sectors with a large domestic output, the specific-factor owners have much to gain from an increase in the domestic price, while (for a given import demand elasticity) the economy has relatively little to lose from protection when the volume of imports is low.[11]

The smaller is the weight that the government places on a dollar of aggregate welfare compared with a dollar of campaign financing, the larger in absolute value are all trade taxes and subsidies. An interior solution remains possible, however, even if the government cares only about contributions ($a = 0$). This is because the interest groups themselves do not want the distortions to grow too large. As the share of voters who are members of one interest group or another increases, equilibrium rates of protection for the organized industries decline. At the extreme, when all voters belong to an interest group ($\alpha_L = 1$) and all sectors are represented ($I_i = 1$ for all i), then free trade prevails in all markets. In this case, the various interest groups neutralize one another, so that an industry's demand for protection is matched in equilibrium by the opposing interest groups' bids for a low domestic price. On the other hand, if interest-group members comprise a negligible fraction of the voting population ($\alpha_L = 0$), then no trade taxes or subsidies will be applied to goods not represented by a lobby (for which $I_i = 0$). When

---

[10] The formula for the equilibrium trade tax can be expressed as

$$t_i^o = \frac{I_i - \alpha_L}{a + \alpha_L}\left(\frac{y_i(p_i^o)}{[-p_i^* m_i'(p_i^o)]}\right).$$

If this equation has a solution for a case where $I_i = 1$, then it must involve $t_i^o > 0$. If the equation has no solution, then $p_i^o = \bar{p}_i$, and again $t_i^o > 0$.

[11] Our formula suggests that only two variables (the elasticity of import demand and the ratio of domestic output to imports) should explain the cross-industry variation in protection levels. Empirical studies of the structure of protection are reviewed by Robert E. Baldwin (1984) and Kym Anderson and Baldwin (1987). However, the existing studies fail to control for import demand elasticities, while including many variables that are not indicated by our model (but which may be correlated with the omitted variable), thus rendering the regression results impossible to interpret in the light of our theory.

the potential political contributors are few in number, they stand little to gain from trade interventions in sectors other than their own.

IV. POLITICAL CONTRIBUTIONS

We have characterized the structure of protection that emerges from the political process whenever the interest groups use contribution schedules that are locally differentiable. This restriction on the contribution functions leaves latitude for schedules with many different shapes (away from equilibrium), and in fact the set of contribution schedules that supports the equilibrium policy vector is not unique. Different sets of equilibrium contribution schedules give rise to different equilibrium donations by the various lobby groups and thus to different net payoffs for the groups' members. If we are to say something more about which lobbies contribute the most to influence policy, we must introduce additional assumptions that allow us to select among the set of Nash equilibria.

We focus henceforth on truthful Nash equilibria; recall that these are equilibria that arise when lobbies announce truthful contribution schedules. With this restriction on the nature of the policy bids the competition between the lobbies involves only a choice of the scalars $\{B_i\}$. Given these "anchors" for the contribution functions, the truthfulness requirement dictates the shapes of the schedules [see the definition in (10)].

What incentive does a lobby i face with regard to its choice of B_i? From the definition of a truthful contribution schedule, we see that the net welfare to lobby i will be B_i whenever the lobby makes a positive contribution to the government in equilibrium. The lobby therefore wishes to make B_i as large as possible (and the contribution as small as possible), but without going so far as to induce the government to deviate from $\mathbf{p}^o$ to some alternative policy that might be damaging to its interests.

This point can be made clear with an example. Suppose for the moment that there are exactly two lobbies and that the government cares only about campaign financing ($a = 0$). Let the lobbies contemplate setting the anchors $\hat{B}_1$ and $\hat{B}_2$ for their truthful contribution schedules. With these anchors the lobbies' contributions will be $C_1^T(\mathbf{p}, \hat{B}_1)$ and $C_2^T(\mathbf{p}, \hat{B}_2)$, which depend of course on the policy action taken by the government. In Figure 2, the shaded area represents the set of contribution pairs (C_1, C_2) that the government might collect for all of the various policy choices open to it. Given this shaded opportunity set, a government that cares only about maximizing total contributions will opt for point Q, where the outer frontier is tangent to a line with a slope of -1. Underlying this point is some policy vector. If the figure is to represent an equilibrium situation, it must be the policy identified in Proposition 2.

Now we examine whether lobby 1 might wish to raise B_1 slightly above $\hat{B}_1$. By doing so, it would reduce all of its contributions *by the same amount*. The shaded area would shift uniformly to the left, to the location indicated by the dotted lines. The government would then be faced with a new set of possibilities and would choose the point Q', a leftward displacement of point Q. But the policy underlying point Q' must be the same

C_2

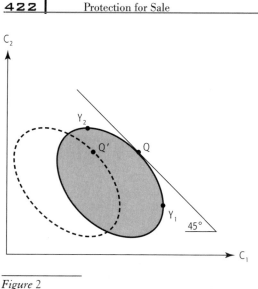

Figure 2
Excessive Contributions

as that for point Q, since the relative desirability of different policies has not changed from the government's (political) perspective. Evidently, lobby 1 must benefit from this increase in B_1. Of course, the situation illustrated in the figure affords lobby 2 the same opportunity to improve its net welfare; so Figure 2 cannot represent an equilibrium situation.

The lobbies will continue to see an incentive to raise their B_i's at least as long as the contributions associated with the entire set of feasible policies remain positive. But eventually, when B_i gets sufficiently large, some policies will elicit a contribution of zero from lobby i [again see (10)]. Subsequent increases in B_i no longer affect the government's choices uniformly; the positive reward associated with a policy that is favorable to lobby i is reduced by an increase in B_i, but the nil contribution corresponding to a policy that is unfavorable to lobby i does not change. Lobby i must be careful not to raise B_i so far that the government decides to adopt one of these disadvantageous policies.

Figure 3 depicts an equilibrium configuration. Here both lobbies have increased their B_i's (relative to the situation depicted in Figure 2), so that some policy choices available to the government generate a contribution of zero from one or the other of the lobbies. Consider, for example, the point Y_1, which corresponds to the similarly labeled point in Figure 2. This point is not feasible now, because lobby 2 cannot offer a negative contribution as implied. Rather, if the government were to choose the policy underlying this point (which, incidentally, is the policy most preferred by lobby 1) it would receive the pair of contributions at Z_1: a large donation from a thankful lobby 1 and a nil contribution from lobby 2. In Figure 3, the government collects the same total donations for choosing any one of Q, Z_1, and Z_2. No other point offers contributions as great as

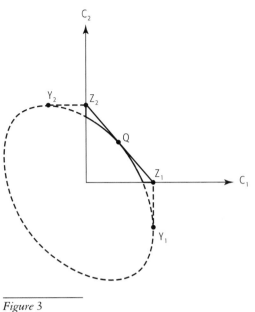

Figure 3
Equilibrium Contributions

these, so the policies that underlie these three points comprise the set of welfare-maximizing choices for the government. The government willingly chooses point Q; and neither lobby wishes to raise its B_i any further, for fear that the government then would select the policy most preferred by its rival.

Notice that our equilibrium conforms to condition (d) of Proposition 1. That condition requires that for every i there must exist a policy that elicits a contribution of zero from lobby i which the government finds equally attractive as the equilibrium policy $\mathbf{p}^o$. In the figure, these policies are, for lobbies 1 and 2, the ones that underlie points Z_2 and Z_1, respectively.

In our 1992a working paper we present a formal procedure for calculating the equilibrium contributions and net welfare levels when an arbitrary number of lobbies set truthful contribution schedules and the government has the more general objective function described in (5). Here we will present the procedure informally, relying on the intuition developed for the special case just discussed. Then we will calculate the contributions for several examples, showing in the process how the political environment determines the division of surplus between the interest groups and the politicians.

Our special case suggests that each lobby must worry about what policy would be chosen if it were to raise its B_i to a level where the government would opt to neglect its interests entirely. We define $\mathbf{p}^{-i}$ as the policy that would emerge from political maximization by the government, if the contribution offered by lobby i were zero; that is,

$$\mathbf{p}^{-i} = \underset{\mathbf{p} \in \mathcal{P}}{\arg\max} \sum_{\substack{j \in L \\ j \neq i}} C_j^T(\mathbf{p}, B_j^o) + aW(\mathbf{p}) \qquad \text{for } i \in L. \tag{16}$$

We have seen in the example that lobby i will raise its B_i to the point where the government is just indifferent between choosing the policy $\mathbf{p}^{-i}$ and choosing the equilibrium policy $\mathbf{p}^o$. The following equation expresses this indifference:

$$\sum_{\substack{j \in L \\ j \neq i}} C_j^T(\mathbf{p}^{-i}, B_j^o) + aW(\mathbf{p}^{-i}) = \sum_{j \in L} C_j^T(\mathbf{p}^o, B_j^o) + aW(\mathbf{p}^o) \qquad \text{for all } i \in L. \tag{17}$$

These two sets of equations allow us to solve for the net welfare levels of the various lobbies in a truthful Nash equilibrium (TNE) with positive contributions by all lobbies. As a consistency check, we must make sure that at B_i^o, lobby i would make no contribution were the policy $\mathbf{p}^{-i}$ to be chosen by the government. This requires $W_i(\mathbf{p}^{-i}) \leq B_i^o$ for all $i \in L$. If this inequality fails for some i, then that lobby benefits from raising its B_i (reducing its equilibrium contributions) until the constraint that payments must be nonnegative becomes binding. Such a lobby would contribute nothing in the political equilibrium, and the equilibrium policy would be the same as if the factor owners represented by this lobby were politically unorganized.

We now examine three special cases, to see how the equilibrium contributions are determined in different situations.

Example 1: A Single Organized Lobby. — Suppose that there is only one politically active lobby group, which represents the interests of the specific-factor owners in some industry i. The equilibrium policy vector in this case provides protection for sector i ($p_i^o > p_i^*$), and so long as $\alpha_i > 0$, it calls for import subsidies and export taxes on all other goods ($p_j^o < p_j^*$ for $j \neq i$). We know that the government would opt for free trade in the absence of any contributions from the one and only special-interest group; thus (16) gives $\mathbf{p}^{-i} = \mathbf{p}^*$. Using (17), we find the equilibrium campaign contribution of lobby i, $C_i^T(\mathbf{p}^o, B_i^o) = aW(\mathbf{p}^*) - aW(\mathbf{p}^o)$. We see that the lobby contributes an amount that is proportional to the excess burden that the equilibrium trade policies impose on society. The factor of proportionality is the weight that the government attaches to aggregate gross welfare (relative to campaign contributions) in its own objective function. In this political equilibrium, the politicians derive exactly the same utility as they would have achieved by allowing free trade in a world without influence payments. In other words, *a lobby that faces no opposition from competing interests captures all of the surplus from its political relationship with the government.*

Example 2: All Voters Represented as Special Interests. — The next example is one in which all of the voters are represented in the political process by one lobby group or another. We have seen that the political competition in this case results in free trade ($\mathbf{p}^o = \mathbf{p}^*$). Nonetheless, each lobby must make a positive campaign contribution in order to induce the government to choose this outcome rather than one that would be still worse from its perspective. Take for example the case where there are only two nonnumeraire goods and two lobbies. Using (17), we have

$$C_i^T(\mathbf{p}^o, B_i^o) = [C_j^T(\mathbf{p}^{-i}, B_j^o) + aW(\mathbf{p}^{-i})]$$
$$- [C_j^T(\mathbf{p}^o, B_j^o) + aW(\mathbf{p}^o)] \qquad \text{for } i = 1, 2; j \neq i. \qquad (18)$$

By the definition of $\mathbf{p}^{-i}$ and the fact that $\mathbf{p}^{-i} \neq \mathbf{p}^* = \mathbf{p}^o$, we know that the right-hand side of (18) is positive for $i = 1, 2$. Thus, both lobbies must actively contribute to the incumbent government in order to support the free-trade outcome. *When all voters are active in the process of buying influence, the rivalry among competing interests is most intense, and the government captures all of the surplus from the political relationships.*

Which of the two lobbies makes the larger contribution? To answer this question, we rewrite equation (18) as[12]

$$C_i^T(\mathbf{p}^o, B_i^o) = [W_j(\mathbf{p}^{-i}) + aW(\mathbf{p}^{-i})]$$
$$- [W_j(\mathbf{p}^*) + aW(\mathbf{p}^*)] \qquad \text{for } i = 1, 2; j \neq i. \qquad (19)$$

This equation says that each lobby i must contribute to the politicians an amount equal to the difference between what its rival and the government could jointly achieve were lobby i not itself active in the political process and what the two actually attain in the full political equilibrium. Thus, *each lobby pays according to the political strength of its rival.* Take for example the case in which the industries are symmetric except that they have different, perfectly inelastic supply functions $y_i(\mathbf{p}) = \bar{y}_i$. Then the interest group representing factor owners with the smaller endowment makes the *larger* political contribution.

Example 3: Represented Special Interests Are Highly Concentrated. — The final example is one where the ownership of the specific factors is so highly concentrated that interest-group members account for a negligible fraction of the total voting population. The political equilibrium in this case has positive protection for all organized sectors. But since $\alpha_i = 0$ for all i, the members of each interest group receive only a negligible share of government transfer payments and derive only a negligible share of the surplus from consuming nonnumeraire products. Thus, no lobby is willing to contribute toward trade intervention in any sector other than its own. The policy $\mathbf{p}^{-i}$ that the government would choose if lobby i failed to contribute allows free trade in good i (since this policy is socially efficient and no other lobby bids for any intervention) but has the same

---

[12]In order to do so, we need $C_j^T(\mathbf{p}^{-i}, B_j^o) - C_j^T(\mathbf{p}^*, B_j^o) = W_j(\mathbf{p}^{-i}) - W_j(\mathbf{p}^*)$ Given that the contribution schedules are truthful, this will be the case if both $C_j^T(\mathbf{p}^{-i}, B_j^o)$ and $C_j^T(\mathbf{p}^*, B_j^o)$ are positive. We have already seen that the latter is true. Since the right-hand side of (18) is positive and $W(\mathbf{p}^{-i}) < W(\mathbf{p}^*)$, we have $C_j^T(\mathbf{p}^{-i}, B_j^o) > C_j^T(\mathbf{p}^*, B_j^o)$. Thus, the former must be true as well.

protection on all other goods as in the full equilibrium (since the presence or absence of lobby i has no bearing on the political interaction between the government and those with interests in these other sectors). The common agency problem here is the same as for a set of separate principal–agent arrangements between each industry lobby and the government. As in Example 1, each lobby i must compensate the government for the political cost of providing protection (it pays a times the deadweight loss imposed by the industry policy p_i^0). *But with no political rivalry between the special interests, each industry group captures all of the surplus from its own political relationship with the government.*[13]

V. WHY LOBBIES MAY PREFER TRADE POLICIES

In deriving the political-economic equilibrium, we have limited the government's choice of policy instruments to trade taxes and subsidies. It may seem that the interest groups would prefer to have the government use more efficient means to transfer income. Our model implies that this is not necessarily the case. In fact, the lobby groups may support institutions that constrain the government to transfer income as inefficiently as possible. Accordingly, a regime that allows only voluntary export restraints (with quota rents transferred to foreigners) may be even more desirable to the lobbies than one that allows for import tariffs. We will discuss now why this is so.[14]

Suppose that the government could use output subsidies instead of (or in addition to) trade policies to transfer income to groups that bid for special treatment. It is well known that such subsidies generate less deadweight loss than tariffs and export subsidies, for an equivalent amount of income transfer. But would the interest groups share in these efficiency gains?

Consider first the case where factor ownership is highly concentrated, so that the members of the lobby groups account for a negligible fraction of the total population. In this case the interests of the industry lobbies are not directly opposed. As we have seen, no lobby would bid against policies that favored other interest groups under these circumstances. The equilibrium output subsidies would be the ones that maximized the joint welfare of each lobby and the government. Of course, joint welfare is higher in a regime that allows output subsidies than in one that does not, because the output subsidies generate less deadweight loss than the trade policies. Moreover, each lobby compensates the government only for the political cost associated with its special treatment (an amount a times the deadweight loss). Therefore, the lobbies capture *all* of the surplus from the use of the more efficient policy instrument.

---

[13] The interested reader can refer to our 1992a working paper for further details.

[14] Our point is related to, but not the same as, one made by Dani Rodrik (1986) and John D. Wilson (1990). These two have argued that a policy regime with tariffs only may be socially preferred to one with output subsidies, because the distortions that endogenously emerge in the former regime may be smaller than those in the latter. Our arguments concern the institutional preferences of special-interest groups, not those of an external observer.

However, consider now the case where all voters are represented by an organized lobby group. In this situation, as we have seen, the political competition among the groups is quite intense. We know that the equilibrium policy in any TNE maximizes a weighted sum of the utilities of represented and unrepresented voters, and that when all voters are represented in the bidding process the equilibrium policy maximizes aggregate welfare. So the equilibrium entails laissez-faire, just as free trade emerged as the political equilibrium when the government could invoke only trade policies. However, the lobbies must make larger political contributions to induce the laissez-faire outcome in the equilibrium with output subsidies than they must make to support a free-trade outcome in the regime that allows only trade interventions. This is because each lobby must contribute in equilibrium the difference between what rival lobbies and the government could jointly achieve in the absence of its own participation in the political process and what they in fact achieve in the political equilibrium. The equilibrium entails the same joint welfare under either regime; but the rival lobbies and the government can jointly attain greater welfare in a policy regime that allows output subsidies (or other, more efficient policies) than in one that does not. It follows that the lobbies' contributions will be higher and net welfare lower if the political regime allows output subsidies.

These examples suggest that the extent of competition between rival interest groups determines their preferences among alternative policy regimes. When competition between interest groups is intense (because their interests are in direct opposition), the availability of an efficient income-transfer tool makes credible an implicit government threat to join forces with the opposing lobbies. Individual interest groups have little political power under these conditions, and they prefer to tie the hands of the government. However, when the interests of the lobbies are orthogonal to one another, the groups do not compete for favors, but instead seek to extract gains at the expense of the underrepresented masses. Then each lobby prefers to grant politicians access to the most efficient means possible for transferring income.

VI. SUMMARY AND EXTENSIONS

We have developed a new approach to analyzing the formation of trade policy in a representative democracy. Like many previous authors we view politicians as maximizing agents who pursue their own selfish interests rather than as benevolent agents seeking to maximize aggregate welfare. Our modeling focuses on the political interactions between a government that is concerned both with campaign contributions and with the welfare of the average voter and a set of organized special-interest groups that care only about the welfare of their members. What is distinctive in our approach is the role that we ascribe to political contributions: we see the gifts made by interest groups not so much as investments in the outcomes of elections, but more as a means to influence government policy. In our view, the manner of campaign and party finance in many democratic nations creates powerful incentives for politicians to peddle their policy influence. Then the structure of trade protection is bound to reflect the outcome of a competition for political favors; this is the central theme in our story.

In our model, lobbies make implicit offers of political contributions as functions of the vector of trade policies (import and export taxes and subsidies) adopted by the government. Taking account of these offers, the government sets policy to further its own objectives, which include (perhaps among other things) a concern for reelection. In the political equilibrium neither the government nor any lobby has an incentive to alter its behavior; no lobby can revise its contribution schedule so as to induce the government to choose a policy that would yield its members higher net welfare, nor can the government realize political gains by changing policy given the contribution offers it faces.

We have derived an explicit formula for the structure of protection that emerges in such a setting. Our formula relates an industry's equilibrium protection to the state of its political organization, the ratio of domestic output in the industry to net trade, and the elasticity of import demand or export supply. Also, the protection provided to all politically organized industries increases with the relative weight the government attaches to campaign contributions vis-à-vis voter welfare and falls with the fraction of voters that belong to an organized lobby group. We have discussed in some detail the determinants of the size of the equilibrium contributions made by different interest groups, the relative political power of these groups, and the division of political surplus between the government and the lobbies.

The questions we have addressed in this paper are of considerable independent interest. Beyond this, the tools that we have developed for studying the relationship between special interest groups and policymakers may be applicable to many additional problems. For example, our approach could be used to study the endogenous design of social transfer schemes, environmental regulations, or government spending programs. We conclude the paper with a brief discussion of two possible extensions, still within the area of trade policy, that show the flexibility and potential usefulness of our approach.

The first extension allows for more political competition among the special-interest groups. In our model such competition is highly circumscribed, because the various industry groups oppose one another only to the extent that owners of specific factors also protect their interests as ordinary *consumers*. In reality, the most serious political opposition to protection arises when higher prices stand to harm other *producer* interests downstream. The users of intermediate inputs often are as politically active against import barriers as are the domestic manufacturers who favor such protection.

The model can readily be extended to allow for imported intermediate inputs. Suppose, for example, that there is one such good, producible at home with labor and a sector-specific input. Suppose further that the intermediate good is used in some or all of the sectors producing nonnumeraire goods, but not in the sector that produces good 0. Then the aggregate reward to the owners of the specific factor used in the production of final good i becomes $\pi_i(p_i, q)$, where q is the domestic price of the intermediate good. The reward to the owners of the specific factor used in domestic production of the intermediate good depends only on q. We can proceed as before to derive the equilibrium trade policies and campaign contributions.

Two notable results emerge from such an exercise. First, imports of the intermediate good may be subsidized in the political equilibrium, even if the interests of the owners of the specific factor used in producing that good are represented in the political process. This contrasts with the situation for politically organized final-good producers, all of whom succeed in securing at least some (effective) trade protection. Producers of intermediates are more vulnerable politically, because the representatives of the final-goods producers bid vigorously against tariffs on intermediates, whereas opposition to protection on consumer goods is much less intense. Second, the formula for the equilibrium import tariff or export subsidy applicable to trade in any final good can be decomposed into two terms, one with the same form as in Proposition 2, the other being an increasing function of the equilibrium tariff applicable to intermediate inputs. Both of these results suggest that the political process tends to favor the interests of final-good producers relative to those of intermediate-good producers.

The second extension incorporates policy interdependence among large trading economies. The literature on tariff wars, starting with the classic paper by Harry Johnson (1953), examines noncooperative policy games between governments that single-mindedly serve the public interest. Similarly, studies of negotiated tariff agreements (see e.g., Wolfgang Mayer, 1981) generally begin with the assumption that the state enters international negotiations with the aim of maximizing aggregate welfare. Greater insight could be gained into international economic relations, we believe, by considering governments that are guided in their external dealings by domestic political pressures. Our 1992b working paper takes a first step in this direction, applying our approach to domestic politics in an analysis of international trade wars and trade talks. A next step might be to assess the relative desirability of alternative international "rules of the game." Such rules limit the policy choices open to national governments and change the nature of the strategic interactions between elected officials and their constituents. Our framework could be used to generate predictions about what domestic policies will emerge from the political process in different institutional settings, and therefore to evaluate which rules give rise to preferred policy outcomes.

REFERENCES

Anderson, Kyan and Baldwin, Robert E. "The Political Market for Protection in Industrial Countries," in A. M. El-Agraa, ed., *Protection, cooperation, integration and development: Essays in honour of Professor Hiroshi Kitamura*. London: Macmillan, 1987, pp. 20–36.

Baldwin, Robert E. "Trade Policies in Developed Countries," in R. W. Jones and P. B. Kenen, eds., *Handbook of international economics*, Vol. 1. Amsterdam: North-Holland, 1984, pp. 571–611.

Bernheim, B. Douglas and Whinston, Michael D. "Menu Auctions, Resource Allocation, and Economic Influence." *Quarterly Journal of Economics*, February 1986, *101*(1), pp. 1–31.

Goldenberg, Edie N.; Traugott, Michael W. and Baumgartner, Frank R. "Preemptive and Reactive Spending in U.S. House Races." *Political Behavior*, 1986, *8*(1), pp. 3–20.

Green, Donald Philip and Krasno, Johnathan S. "Salvation for the Spendthrift Incumbent: Reestimating the Effects of Campaign Spending in House Elections." *American Journal of Political Science*, November 1988, *32*(4), pp. 884–907.

Grossman, Gene M. and Helpman, Elhanan. "Protection for Sale," National Bureau of Economic Research (Cambridge, MA) Working Paper No. 4149, 1992a.

———. "Trade Wars and Trade Talks." Discussion Paper in Economics No. 163, Woodrow Wilson School of Public and International Affairs, Princeton University, 1992b.

Hillman, Arye L. "Declining Industries and Political-Support Protectionist Motives." *American Economic Review*, December 1982, *72*(5), pp. 1180–87.

———. *The political economy of protection*. Chur: Harwood, 1989.

Hillman, Arye and Ursprung, Heinrich W. "Domestic Politics, Foreign Interests, and International Trade Policy." *American Economic Review*, September 1988, *78*(4), pp. 729–45.

Jacobson, Gary C. "The Effects of Campaign Spending in Congressional Elections." *American Political Science Review*, June 1978, *72*(2), pp. 769–83.

———. *The politics of Congressional elections*, 2nd Ed. Boston: Little, Brown, 1987.

Johnson, Harry G. "Optimal Tariffs and Retaliation." *Review of Economic Studies*, 1953, *21*(2), pp. 142–53.

Krasno, Jonathan S. and Green, Donald Philip. "Preempting Quality Challengers in House Elections." *Journal of Politics*, November 1988, *50*(4), pp. 920–36.

Long, Ngo Van and Vousden, Neil. "Protectionist Responses and Declining Industries." *Journal of International Economics*, February 1991, *30*(1–2), pp. 87–103.

Magee, Stephen P.; Brock, William A. and Young, Leslie. *Black hole tariffs and endogenous policy theory: Political economy in general equilibrium*. Cambridge: Cambridge University Press, 1989.

Magelby, David B. and Nelson, Candice J. *The money chase: Congressional campaign finance reform*. Washington, DC: Brookings Institution, 1990.

Mayer, Wolfgang. "Theoretical Considerations on Negotiated Tariff Adjustments." *Oxford Economic Papers*, March 1981, *33*(1), pp. 135–53.

Olsen, Mancur. *The logic of collective action*. Cambridge, MA: Harvard University Press, 1965.

Rodrik, Dani. "Tariffs, Subsidies, and Welfare with Endogenous Policy." *Journal of International Economics*, November 1986, *21*(3/4), pp. 285–96.

Stigler, George J. "The Theory of Economic Regulation." *Bell Journal of Economics*, Spring 1971, *2*(1), pp. 359–65.

Wilson, John D. "Are Efficiency Improvements in Government Transfer Policies Self-Defeating in Political Equilibrium?" *Economics and Politics*, November 1990, *2*(3), pp. 241–58.

ABOUT THE AUTHOR

Gene Grossman

Gene Grossman is the Jacob Viner Professor of International Economics, Professor of Economics and International Affairs, and Director, International Economics Section at Princeton University.

Editor's Queries

What has been the reaction to this article? One thing that surprised me at the time was the controversy the paper stirred. To me, it seemed only natural to investigate how different assumptions implied different conclusions about optimal trade policy. But some established trade economists criticized my co-author and me for lending legitimacy to a new potential argument for protection. Others saw us instead as a force for good, inasmuch as we had shown that the pro-protection findings of Brander and Spencer were not robust. My message to young researchers: do research to promote understanding; don't worry about how your findings might be used (or abused) by those with policy interests.

How would you write the paper differently today? If I have one regret about the paper, it is that we chose to employ conjectural variations to characterize alternative modes of conduct. I no longer feel that this is a useful tool for describing different forms of oligopolistic competition. The conjectural variations model is an attempt to capture a dynamic concept in a static setting, a worthy goal but one without firm game-theoretic foundations. More to the point, our use of conjectural variations, and especially our mention of "consistent conjectures" opened a can of worms that distracted from the main point we wanted to make. Now, when I teach strategic trade policy, I describe only the Cournot, Bertrand, and Stackelberg cases, showing how the optimal policy changes from subsidy to tax to free trade as the strategic environment changes.